THE MERCANTILE LAW OF SCOTLAND

THE
Mercantile Law of Scotland

SIXTH EDITION

BY

J. A. LILLIE, Q.C., LL.B.

ADVOCATE, AND OF THE MIDDLE TEMPLE, BARRISTER-AT-LAW,
SHERIFF OF FIFE AND KINROSS

BEING THE SUCCESSOR TO THE WORK OF

THE LATE ALLAN M'NEIL, M.A., S.S.C.

AND

J. A. LILLIE, Q.C., LL.B.

EDINBURGH

W. GREEN & SON, LTD.

PUBLISHERS

1965

First Published	.	.	.	.	1923
Second Edition	.	.	.	.	1929
Third Edition .	.	.	.	.	1937
Reprinted	.	.	.	.	1947
Fourth Edition	.	.	.	.	1949
Fifth Edition .	.	.	.	.	1956
Sixth Edition .	.	.	.	.	1965

Printed in Great Britain
by
The Eastern Press Ltd.
London and Reading
for
W. Green & Son, Ltd.

PREFACE TO SIXTH EDITION

THIS new edition is called for mainly because of new enactments affecting the subjects expounded in the book. These include, in particular, the Cheques Act, 1956, the Floating Charges (Scotland) Act, 1961, the Transport Act, 1962, the Betting, Gaming and Lotteries Act, 1963, the Hire-Purchase Act, 1964, and others. The citation of cases has been brought up to date. I must make acknowledgment of a great deal of help from Mr. David Maxwell, Q.C., Lecturer on Mercantile Law in the University of Edinburgh, towards expediting the publication of this edition, and from Mr. W. A. Wilson of the Faculty of Law in that University in connection with hire-purchase.

J. A. L.

EDINBURGH
March, 1965

PREFACE TO FIRST EDITION

THE aim of this volume is to supply an acknowledged deficiency, and to provide students preparing for the many examinations where Mercantile Law is now a compulsory subject with a comprehensive and systematic exposition of this branch of law divested as far as possible of technicalities of expression. To the student a comprehension of the systematic or scientific scheme of the law is of the utmost importance if his study of it is not to amount to little more than the memorising of a mass of undigested details. On the other hand, a real advance will have been made by the student who has appreciated the uniformity which the law seeks to achieve by the application of suitable principles to the diversity of circumstance. In treating of the application of these principles in detail, selection has had, necessarily, to be resorted to, and has been dictated by a regard to those matters which best illustrate the working out of principle and are most common in practice.

The citation of authority is not full, and has been more or less confined to the noting of leading cases and the latest decisions. The citation is intended not merely for the purpose of vouching the statements in the text, but also for the use of those who desire further examples or to improve their study by an examination of the reasoning which underlies the decisions.

It is believed that the book, as containing a concise statement of principles and a collection of leading cases, may be of use to practitioners for preliminary reference before consulting detailed treatises on particular branches of the subject.

Each chapter is the separate work of either Mr. M'Neil or Mr. Lillie, and the work of each has been revised by the other.

Acknowledgment is due to Mr. C. de B. Murray, Advocate, for assistance in checking references to authorities.

EDINBURGH
16th March, 1923

CONTENTS

TABLE OF CASES

CHAPTER 1

THE LAW OF CONTRACT

1. WHAT IS A CONTRACT?

A CONTRACT has been defined as an agreement which creates, or is intended to create, a legal obligation between the parties to it.[1]

A contract accordingly is a particular kind of agreement. It necessarily involves at least two parties to it. Whether in the first place there is in any particular case an agreement is a question of the interpretation of, or inference from, the words or acts of the parties to it whereby each conveys to the other the expression of his intention.[2] When the minds of the parties meet in agreement there is said to be *consensus in idem*.[3]

Whether in the second place an agreement is one which creates, or is intended to create, a legal obligation between the parties to it depends in the first place on whether the parties so intended. Their intention may be indicated by the words they use [4] or by the nature of the agreement itself. For instance, an agreement to dine with a friend plainly is not intended to create any legal obligation to do so. In the second place, the creation of a legal obligation depends on whether the court will treat the agreement as binding the parties and will enforce it by compelling either party to observe it. Thus, for instance, a bet or wager is not a contract because the relations involved are held, in the law of Scotland, not to be among those subjects for which courts of justice were instituted.[5] The same applies to a social engagement, such as the agreement to dine instanced above.[6] Some patrimonial interest, *i.e.*, some material gain or loss, must be involved.[7] To sum up, to constitute a binding contract the parties must have intended and agreed to bind each other,[8] and the agreement must be one of a nature which the courts will enforce.

---

[1] Jenks, *Digest of English Civil Law,* bk. ii, tit. i.
[2] *e.g., Mathieson Gee (Ayrshire) Ltd.* v. *Quigley,* 1952 S.C.(H.L.) 38.
[3] All the essentials have to be settled: what are the essentials may vary according to the particular contract under consideration—Lord Dunedin in *May & Butcher Ltd.* v. *The King* [1934] 2 K. B. 17, 21, applied in *R. & J. Dempster Ltd.* v. *Motherwell Bridge & Engineering Co. Ltd.* 1964 S.L.T. 113.
[4] *Gloag on Contract,* 2nd ed., p. 11; *Rose and Frank Co.* v. *J. R. Crompton & Bros. Ltd.* [1925] A.C. 445. The courts will not enforce a mere "gentlemen's agreement."
[5] Gloag, *op. cit.,* p. 8.
[6] And *vide* Illegal and Immoral Contracts, *infra,* p. 25.
[7] *Anderson* v. *Manson,* 1909 S.C. 838.
[8] This may be so, though part remains to be determined, *e.g.,* the price in a sale of goods—see Sale of Goods Act, 1893, s. 8 (1), *infra,* p. 97.

1

2. HOW CONTRACT CONSTITUTED—FORMATION

To create a legal obligation there is required the expression by the party undertaking the obligation of willingness to be bound. In all cases the obligation requires for its constitution expression in words or acts. Whatever may have been the real intention of a party the court, in a question of legal obligation, gathers his intention to bind himself from such expression.[9] Such an expression may consist of a promise made by one party only, a unilateral obligation. To amount to a contract binding on both parties, it must be followed by an acceptance. No one can be forced to accept a gift. But it is irrevocable unless refused, and can be enforced if fulfilment be demanded within a reasonable time, acceptance being sufficiently indicated by a demand for fulfilment.[10] If both parties undertake obligations to each other, the legal obligations are created by offer by the one party and acceptance by the other. The offer is not binding, however, unless and until clinched by words or acts indicating acceptance. An undertaking to keep an offer open for a time is an example of an offer combined with a promise.

Offer.—What constitutes an offer? A mere expression of intention may not have obligatory force. Thus where a shareholder of a company said he was willing to take up an issue of new shares and did not apply for them, he was held not bound to take up shares allotted to him.[11] A request for tenders, unless providing that the lowest will be accepted, is not binding as an offer. Again, a mere proposal to do business may or may not, according to circumstances, amount to an offer. Thus where a merchant who dealt in a particular commodity wrote to other merchants dealing in the same commodity quoting prices he was held bound by an acceptance, an example of an " order in trade."[12] Again, a common carrier, who is bound to exercise his vocation on demand, is bound by the list of fares he publishes as an offer to carry for these fares. An offer of reward for lost property is binding if the property is restored by a person in knowledge of the offer.[13] A general offer to the public, if accepted by a particular person, is good. For example, an advertisement of goods for sale, on the inducement that they will produce certain results, is an offer, as where the Carbolic Smoke Ball Co. offered a reward to users of their smoke ball if they took influenza.[14]

---

[9] Lord President Dunedin in *Muirhead & Turnbull* v. *Dickson* (1905) 7 F. 686, 694.
[10] *Wallace* v. *Gibson* (1895) 22 R.(H.L.) 56.
[11] *Mason* v. *Benhar Coal Co.* (1882) 9 R. 883.
[12] *Philp* v. *Knoblauch*, 1907 S.C. 994.   [13] *Petrie* v. *Earl of Airlie* (1834) 13 S. 68.
[14] *Carlill* v. *Carbolic Smoke Ball Co.* [1893] 1 Q.B. 256; *cf. Hunter* v. *General Accident, etc., Corporation*, 1909 S.C. 344; affd. 1909 S.C.(H.L.) 30. As to the effect of the display of goods in a shop window, see Gloag, *op. cit.*, p. 22; see also *Pharmaceutical Society of Great Britain* v. *Boots Cash Chemists (Southern) Ltd.* [1953] 1 All E.R. 482.

Acceptance.—What constitutes a valid acceptance? (1) Acceptance may be made by words or acts, and in either case must be communicated to the offerer.[15] Thus if goods ordered are supplied, the act of supplying them constitutes an acceptance. Failure to refuse an offer may amount to acceptance, as in orders in trade, or where there is a previous course of dealing between the parties, or by custom of trade or when acceptance is waived by the offerer. (2) An acceptance, to bind the offerer, must be unqualified. Where the parties negotiate in a correspondence, each conditional acceptance amounts to a new offer or counter-offer.[16] (3) The acceptance must meet the offer. But it need not recapitulate it.[17] Slight variations may not matter, and if acted on cannot be afterwards repudiated.

When is a contract completed by acceptance?—Acceptance by post.—A very usual method of forming a contract is by letter through the post or telegram. The contract is completed when the acceptance is dispatched, *i.e.*, posted or telegraphed.[18] Unless otherwise stipulated or shown to be intended it is presumed the offerer intended reply to be by post or telegram. The post office is supposed to be the agent of the offerer, hence delivery of the letter to the post office is delivery to the offerer. If the offer gives a definite time for acceptance it is accepted if the acceptance is dispatched though not received within the time.[19] It is undecided what the effect is if the acceptance though dispatched never arrives.[20] In England posting is held sufficient to complete the contract.[21] If the offerer is made aware of the fact of acceptance that is of course enough.[22]

Timeous acceptance.—As a general rule an offer remains open until accepted or recalled. When no time for acceptance is fixed it must be made within a reasonable time. An undertaking to keep an offer open for a certain time or until the happening of a certain event is binding. Also, as a general rule, an acceptance posted in the ordinary course of

---

[15] A custom of trade or a waiver of acceptance by the offerer or a prior obligation to make an offer will have the same effect, *e.g.*, *W. Beardmore & Co. Ltd.* v. *Park's Exrs.*, 1928 S.L.T. 143.

[16] For meaning of " accepted subject to formal contract," see opinion of Lord President Cooper in *Stobo Ltd.* v. *Morrisons (Gowns) Ltd.*, 1949 S.C. 184.

[17] *Philp* v. *Knoblauch, supra.*

[18] Where, however, a contract is made by instantaneous communication, e.g. by telephone, the contract is completed only when the acceptance is received by the offerer—*Entores Ltd.*, v. *Miles Far East Corporation* [1955] 2 Q.B. 327.

[19] *Jacobsen* v. *Underwood* (1894) 21 R. 654.

[20] *Mason* v. *Benhar Coal Co.* (1882) 9 R. 883, *per* Lord Shand at p. 890; *Higgins* v. *Dunlop, Wilson & Co.* (1847) 9 D. 1407, *per* Lord Fullerton at p. 1414; affd. (1848) 6 Bell's App. 195.

[21] *Household Fire Insurance Co.* v. *Grant* (1879) 4 Ex.D. 216; *Eccles* v. *Bryant* [1947] 2 All E.R. 63.

[22] *Chapman* v. *Sulphite Paper Pulp Co.* (1892) 19 R. 837.

business is timeous, even though there be delay in delivery.[23] If the offerer indicates a particular method of dispatch, the risk of loss or delay in transmission falls on the acceptor if he does not follow the method indicated, and the offerer is not otherwise made aware of the fact of acceptance.

Recall of offer.—An offer may be recalled at any time before it has been validly accepted. There is said to be *locus poenitentiae*. In addition, it falls by the death of either party, by the insanity of the offerer,[24] or his bankruptcy before acceptance, by refusal of the offer or by failure to accept within the time stated or a reasonable time when no time for acceptance is fixed.[25] What is a reasonable time depends on the circumstances. Thus in mercantile offers to sell or buy particular goods acceptance should be by return of post, otherwise it may be ignored.[26]

Recall of acceptance.—Whether an acceptance once dispatched can be recalled by bringing the recall to the notice of the offerer before, or together with, receipt of the acceptance, has not been definitely decided in Scotland, but probably it can.[27]

3. Proof of the Constitution of Contracts

The method of proof of the constitution of a contract depends to a large extent on the way in which it has been or may be constituted.[28] Broadly speaking, a contract may be constituted by writing or without; and the method of proof may further depend on whether the contract is mutual, *i.e.*, with obligations by both parties, or is unilateral.

(a) Contracts not requiring constitution in writing.—In the absence of any writing the ordinary rule is that verbal agreement is sufficient to bind the parties,[29] and this may be proved by parole evidence, *i.e.*, the oral evidence of witnesses. Some contracts, however, while they may be constituted verbally, may not be proved by parole evidence but only by the writ or the oath of the party. In this case writing is not necessary to the formation of the contract, and is required merely as evidence—*in modum probationis*, as it is called. The writ or the oath of the party denying the contract is required here in the absence of admission of an agreement. Contrast this case with that about to be

---

23 *Higgins* v. *Dunlop, Wilson & Co.* (1847) 9 D. 1407; affd. (1848) 6 Bell's App. 195.
24 *Loudon* v. *Elder's Trs.*, 1923 S.L.T. 226.
25 *Thomson* v. *James* (1855) 18 D. 1.
26 *Wylie & Lochhead* v. *McElroy* (1873) 1 R. 41, *per* Lord President Inglis.
27 *Vide Countess of Dunmore* v. *Alexander* (1830) 9 S. 190; *Thomson* v. *James* (1855) 18 D. 1; *Curtice* v. *London City and Midland Bank* [1908] 1 K.B. 293; *Gloag on Contract*, 2nd ed., p. 38.
28 Lord Benholme in *Edmonston* v. *Edmonston* (1861) 23 D. 995, 1002.
29 Stair Instit., iv, 434; Erskine Instit., iii, 2, 1.

mentioned where writing is a solemnity—that is, essential to the formation of the contract. Where the solemnity is wanting an admission of agreement would not bind a party, as without the solemnity there is no completed contract.[30]

The following contracts require proof, though not constitution, by writ [31] or oath, *viz.*—gratuitous obligations [32]; loan,[33] but not a loan not exceeding £100 Scots (£8 6s. 8d.); trust [34]; express obligations of relief [35]; innominate and unusual contracts, *i.e.*, a contract not one of those usually known by a distinctive name, for example a contract expressed in sale notes and intended as a contract of agency [36]; and a prescribed debt.[37]

(b) Written contracts.—Some contracts, however, at common law or by statute require to be entered into in writing, and mere verbal agreement is not sufficient to bind the parties. Such obligations are known as *obligationes literis*. Here writing is, as it is called, a solemnity and necessary to the constitution, not merely to the proof, of the contract. This requirement ensures deliberation on the part of those who enter into certain contracts of importance. These contracts are: (1) Contracts for the sale of heritage and for the lease of heritage for not less than a year; (2) contracts for service for more than a year [38]; (3) contracts for the assignation of incorporeal rights; (4) contracts of insurance; (5) cautionary obligations; (6) certain contracts of mandate.[39]

It must, however, be kept in mind that, where writing has been resorted to though not necessary to constitute or prove the contract, it is incompetent to introduce parole evidence to contradict the writing. This rule is subject to certain reservations to be afterwards noticed.[40]

It should also be noted that, there being a contract in form validly constituted, where the question is raised whether there ever was that *consensus in idem* which is necessary to its validity, such a question may be the subject of parole or other proof. Thus it is competent by parole evidence to prove that one party never gave any assent or that his

---

[30] His admission on oath of a verbal agreement, if followed by *rei interventus*, would bind him. *Gowan's Trs.* v. *Carstairs* (1862) 24 D. 1382. *Vide Rei Interventus, infra*, p. 11.

[31] The writ need not be probative—*Paterson* v. *Paterson* (1897) 25 R. 144 (loan).

[32] *Dickson on Evidence*, § 598; Walker and Walker, *Law of Evidence*, p. 134.

[33] *Ibid.* § 594. Walker and Walker, *op. cit.*, p. 114. *M'Kie* v. *Wilson*, 1951 S.C. 15. Proof is not thus limited in the case of a series of transactions in account current—Lord President Dunedin in *Smith's Tr.* v. *Smith*, 1911 S.C. 653, 659.

[34] Act 1696, c. 25 (Blank Bonds and Trusts Act, 1696).

[35] But see *Gloag on Contract*, 2nd ed., p. 195.

[36] *Müller & Co.* v. *Weber & Schaer* (1901) 3 F. 401; *Cook* v. *Grubb*, 1963 S.C. 1. An innominate contract which is not of an unusual, anomalous or peculiar kind may be proved by parole evidence—Gloag, *op. cit.*, p. 196; *Smith* v. *Reekie*, 1920 S.C. 188.

[37] *Vide* Prescription, *infra*, p. 50 *et seq.*

[38] *e.g.*, *Nisbet* v. *Percy*, 1951 S.C. 350.

[39] As to the cases where the writ must be probative, see Gloag, *op. cit.*, Chap. 10.

[40] *Vide* Interpretation of Contracts, *infra*, p. 32.

assent was obtained by misrepresentation, fraud, or other improper means,[41] or that the contract was entered into in circumstances or with objects which would make it void or reducible as a *pactum illicitum* or illegal agreement.[42]

(c) **Unilateral contracts.**—Here the obligations are by one party only, and accepted by the other. As already noticed, a gratuitous obligation, if not constituted in writing, can be proved only by the writ or oath of the obligant.[43]

Delivery.—When a mutual contract, that is one involving obligations on both sides, is reduced to writing, it is complete and becomes binding on both parties when duly executed, and it is immaterial in whose custody the actual document may be. The obligations on both sides are created by the signatures, and there is no necessity for delivery.[44] Where, on the other hand, the deed or writing is unilateral, *i.e.*, involving obligations on the granter only, its delivery by the granter to the grantee, or some equivalent for delivery, is necessary to bind the granter. Until delivery the deed is merely deliberative, not obligatory. There are, however, exceptions, namely, where the granter of a unilateral deed was under a prior obligation to execute it, for then the grantee is entitled to it, and where a creditor is granter of an assignation of a debt due him, followed by intimation to the debtor. That is enough without delivery to complete the transfer.

The question whether a deed has been delivered is always one of fact. That question is whether the granter has consented to place the deed absolutely beyond his own control.[45] There are certain presumptions. Thus a deed in the hands of the granter is presumably not delivered. And a deed in the hands of the grantee presumably is. But where the deed is in the hands of a third party it depends on the capacity in which he holds the deed which way the presumption lies. The law agent of either party is presumed to hold for his client. A neutral depository is presumed to hold for the granter if the deed is gratuitous, but for the grantee if it is granted for onerous considerations.[46] Again, in certain circumstances there may be a strong presumption that a deed undelivered was intended by the granter to be binding, as where it has been recorded by him in the Books of Council and Session for preservation or preservation and execution[47]: and

[41] *Duran* v. *Duran* (1904) 7 F. 87; *Bell Bros.* (*H.P.*) *Ltd.* v. *Aitken,* 1939 S.C. 577.
[42] *Vide* Validity of Contracts, *infra,* p. 25 *et seq.*
[43] Gloag, *op. cit.,* pp. 4, 50; *Gray* v. *Johnston,* 1928 S.C. 659. *Vide* Reference to Oath, *infra,* p. 54.
[44] *Robertson's Trs.* v. *Lindsay* (1873) 1 R. 323, *per* Lord President Inglis.
[45] *Cameron's Trs.* v. *Cameron,* 1907 S.C. 407.
[46] Erskine Instit., iii, 2, 43.
[47] *Obers* v. *Paton's Trs.* (1897) 24 R. 719; *Carmichael* v. *Carmichael's Exrx.,* 1920 S.C. (H.L.) 195, *per* Lord Dunedin at p. 201.

registration of a disposition of land in the Register of Sasines may be equivalent to delivery.[48]

Sometimes a deed contains a clause dispensing with delivery. That does not give it any contractual effect so long as it is undelivered and the granter is alive and so able to revoke it. If he dies without revoking the effect is testamentary, not contractual.

A deed is presumed to be delivered from its date if it be in the hands of the grantee or of someone holding for him.[49]

(d) Formalities of written contracts.—The sufficiency of various kinds of writings to constitute or to prove the constitution of various kinds of contracts may now be shortly considered.

Writings for this purpose may be conveniently classified, according to the considerations which govern their value as proof, as probative, i.e., tested or holograph, writings *in re mercatoria* and other " privileged " writings, and improbative or informal writings.

(i) *Probative writings*

A probative document is one which, in consequence of its being tested or holograph, does not require to be proved genuine by extrinsic evidence. That is to say, the formality of attestation or the fact of its being written by the granter himself is taken as proof of its genuineness. Such a document may be set aside if it can be proved to have been granted because of fraud or essential error,[50] but these are different questions, and do not touch the question of the genuineness of the document as being truly the document of the person by whom it bears to have been granted.

All deeds relating to heritable title and obligations of importance, i.e., with regard to sums over £100 Scots (£8 6s. 8d.), except writings *in re mercatoria* and several others of a non-mercantile character,[51] must in order to be probative be either holograph or tested.[52]

Formalities of attestation.—An attested writing to be probative should be signed by the granter on each page and by the granter and two witnesses on the last page. But the memorandum of association and the articles of association of a company registered under the Companies Acts and a bill of sale of a ship require the signature of one witness only. A witness must be at least fourteen years of age. The designation of the witnesses should be appended to their signatures or set forth in a testing clause at the end of the deed. These designations when appended to their signatures may be added at any time

---

[48] *Carmichael* v. *Carmichael's Exrx., supra, per* Lord Dunedin, at p. 202.
[49] Bell's Prin., § 23.   [50] *Vide* Validity of Contracts, *infra*, p. 17 *et seq.*
[51] *Vide infra*, pp. 9, 10.
[52] Documents may also be probative if they comply with the provisions of a particular statute, *e.g.*, Emergency Powers (Defence) Act, 1939, s. 8, now repealed.

before the deed is recorded in any register for preservation or founded on in any court, and need not be written by the witnesses themselves.[53] Witnesses must either see the party sign or hear him acknowledge his signature and have credible information as to the party's identity.[54] A witness who sees the granter sign or hears him acknowledge his signature should also sign there and then. The signing of the granter and then the witnesses should be a continuous transaction.[55] The date of signing, though not essential, being in most cases very important should be stated in the testing clause.

After the deed is executed, the testing clause is added at the end above the signatures. It sets forth the details regarding the execution in the following manner: " In witness whereof these presents are subscribed by me at Glasgow on the 1st day of June 1965, before these witnesses, John Smith [*designation*] and Alexander Anderson [*designation*]." All alterations in the body of the document should be authenticated by the initials of the granter, and declared in the testing clause. No deed, subscribed by the granter and bearing to be attested by two witnesses subscribing, is, however, to be deemed invalid or denied effect according to its legal import because of any informality of execution, but the burden of proving that such deed so attested was subscribed by the granter and by the witnesses by whom such deed bears to be attested lies upon the party using or upholding the same.[56] If, however, the execution was *ex facie* correct, the burden of proving the want of a solemnity, such as that the witness did not see the granter sign or hear him acknowledge his signature, would be on the party challenging the validity of the execution.[57]

If the granter of a deed is, from any cause permanent or temporary, blind or unable to write, a law agent, notary public or justice of the peace may sign the document for him.[58] The deed must first be read over to the granter in the presence of two witnesses, who must hear or see authority given to sign the deed. The law agent, notary or justice must sign the deed in the presence of the granter and the witnesses. A docquet is then written on the deed by the law agent, notary or justice in his own hand and subscribed by him and the witnesses.[59] The following is the statutory docquet[60]:

---

[53] Conveyancing Act, 1874, s. 38.
[54] *Brock* v. *Brock,* 1908 S.C. 964.
[55] *Walker* v. *Whitwell,* 1916 S.C.(H.L.) 75.
[56] Conveyancing Act, 1874, s. 39; *Walker* v. *Whitwell,* 1916 S.C.(H.L.) 75; *e.g., Elliot's Exrs.—Petrs.,* 1939 S.L.T. 69; Conveyancing (Scotland) Act, 1924, s. 18 (2) extends s. 39 to deeds executed notarially.
[57] *Walker* v. *Whitwell, supra.*
[58] The person so signing must be independent—if he will benefit from the signature of the deed, his signature may be a nullity: *Gorrie's Tr.* v. *Stiven's Exrx.,* 1952 S.C. 1; *Finlay* v. *Finlay's Trs.,* 1948 S.C. 16; *Ferrie* v. *Ferrie's Trs.* (1863) 1 M. 291.
[59] Conveyancing Act, 1924, s. 18, and Sched. I.   [60] *Ibid.* Sched. I.

" Read over to and signed by me for and by authority of the above-named A. B. [*without designation*], who declares that he is blind (*or* is unable to write), all in his presence and in the presence of the witnesses hereto subscribing.

C. D., Law Agent (*or* Notary Public), Edinburgh (*or as the case may be*),

or E. F., Justice of the Peace for the County of

M. N., *witness*.

P. Q., *witness*.

Any deed to which a company is a party is validly executed in Scotland on behalf of the company if it is sealed with the common seal of the company and subscribed on behalf of the company by two of the directors or by a director and the secretary, whether such subscription is attested by witnesses or not.[61] A contract requiring to be in writing may be made on behalf of the company in writing signed by any person acting under its authority, express or implied.[62] It is usual in Scotland for a company to execute deeds by sealing, and with witnesses. When with witnesses, the benefits of the Conveyancing (Scotland) Act, 1874, s. 39, whereby informalities in execution are not to invalidate a deed " bearing to be attested by two witnesses," would appear to be available.[63]

Holograph writings.—Holograph deeds are probative when they declare that they have been wholly, or at least in their essential parts, written by the granter.[64] Such are presumed to be genuine. The fact that the deed is holograph, if not stated but disputed,[65] must be proved by extrinsic evidence. Alterations should be initialled by the granter, but holograph additions need not be signed. In some cases the document need not be signed if it bears the granter's name *in gremio, i.e.,* in the body of the document, or if it be of a kind not usually signed, as an entry in an account book or a postscript to a letter. A letter signed by one of several partners on behalf of a firm is holograph of the firm.[66]

(ii) *Writings in re mercatoria*

The international character of trade relations and the necessity for rapid dispatch in business furnish the ground for dispensing, in the

---

[61] Companies Act, 1948, s. 32 (4).   [62] *Ibid.*

[63] *e.g., Shiell, Petr.,* 1936 S.L.T. 317. The Stock Transfer Act, 1963 (*q.v.*) permits transfers of stock of a company by the signature to the transfer of the transferor above and without witnesses.

[64] The declaration is not evidence that the signature is genuine: *Harper* v. *Green,* 1938 S.C. 198.

[65] *McIntyre* v. *National Bank of Scotland,* 1910 S.C. 150 (bill).

[66] *Nisbet* v. *Neil's Tr.* (1869) 7 M. 1097. As to typewritten documents, see *Chisholm* v. *Chisholm,* 1949 S.C. 434; *M'Beath's Trs.* v. *M'Beath,* 1935 S.C. 471; *McGinn* v. *Shearer,* 1947 S.C. 334.

case of mercantile writings, with the ordinary rules as to authentication and date.[67] Such writings and some others are therefore called " privileged " writings. For, while not probative in the sense of being tested or holograph, they are accorded a probative quality out of consideration for the practical convenience of trade so long as their authenticity is not challenged. Accordingly, such documents are valid to prove the constitution of the contract they embody if merely subscribed. If their authenticity is challenged it may be proved by parole evidence. Subscription may be by initials or by cross or mark, but in these cases the subscription must be proved to be genuine, and to be the form ordinarily employed by the subscriber.[68] It is proper but not essential it be adhibited before witnesses.

Under this privilege are held to be comprehended bills, notes and cheques on bankers; orders for goods, mandates and procurations; guarantees (but it is a question whether it extends to a guarantee granted to a bank for future advances),[69] offers and acceptances to sell or to buy wares or merchandise or to transport them from place to place, and, in general, all the variety of engagements, or mandates, or acknowledgments which the infinite occasions of trade may require.[70]

A writ *in re mercatoria* proves its own date only in a question which relates to the ordinary mercantile purposes for which such a document is granted.[71]

Other privileged writings.—The most important writings of a non-mercantile character to which are extended the same privileges as writings *in re mercatoria* are discharges for rent, feu-duties, wages, and, on the ground of mercantile usage, other termly payments, such as interest and premiums of insurance, also awards of judicial referees or of counsel to whom parties have agreed to submit their case.[72] Accounts relating to business transactions, though not *in re mercatoria*, if docqueted by the debtor admitting them to be correct, are also privileged.

(iii) *Improbative writings*

Where the law does not require the constitution of a contract to be in probative writing, the proof of it is as a rule unlimited, and therefore an informal writing may be of value along with other evidence to that end.

---

[67] 1 Bell's Comm. 325.
[68] *Ibid.*
[69] *National Bank of Scotland* v. *Campbell* (1892) 19 R. 885, *per* Lord Kyllachy and Lord M'Laren.
[70] 1 Bell's Comm. 325; *U.K. Advertising Co.* v. *Glasgow Bagwash Laundry*, 1926 S.C. 303.
[71] *Dickson on Evidence*, § 794; *Walker and Walker on Evidence*, p. 102; *Maxwell Witham* v. *Teenan's Tr.* (1884) 11 R. 776.
[72] *Fraser* v. *Lovat* (1850) 7 Bell's App. 171.

Where, on the other hand, probative writing is essential to the constitution of a contract, if the writing be improbative it is not necessarily null. Thus, where a deed is signed by the granter and two witnesses but is lacking in some other formality it may be enforced on proof that the signatures are genuine.[73] Where the want of formality is more deep-seated the improbative document, even if admittedly genuine, is inept, unless (1) it has been followed by *rei interventus*, that is, actings by one party known to the other on the faith of the informal contract so that he would be prejudiced if the other were allowed to repudiate the contract on the ground of the informality of the writing, or (2) validated by homologation, that is, by the act of the granter himself in treating it as if valid. Where *rei interventus* or homologation is alleged the informal writ is admissible in evidence and, if impugned, may be proved by parole evidence, as may also the *rei interventus*. These exceptions, *rei interventus* and homologation, are applications of the doctrine of personal bar. A party to an incomplete contract has *locus poenitentiae*, *i.e.*, right to withdraw up to the time the contract is complete. In the case of a contract incomplete for the want of a fully probative writing the granter of the improbative writing is personally barred from exercising his right to resile if he has permitted *rei interventus* to take place or has himself homologated the document.[74]

Rei interventus.—*Rei interventus* is " inferred from any proceedings not unimportant on the part of the obligee, known to and permitted by the obligor to take place on the faith of the contract as if it were perfect, and productive of alteration of circumstances, loss, or inconvenience, though not irretrievable." [75] Thus where the tenant of an hotel maintained a formally incomplete contract of lease until it was too late for the landlord to apply for a licence, he was held barred from founding upon the incompleteness to get rid of the lease.[76]

The averment of *rei interventus* must be specific. It is not enough to aver generally that the parties acted on the faith of the agreement.[77]

The actings relied on as setting up *rei interventus* must have been known to and permitted by the granter of the obligation. Actual knowledge is not necessary if the actings were those which would normally and almost necessarily take place if he relied on the improbative agreement. Thus an improbative guarantee was held established

---

[73] Conveyancing (Scotland) Act, 1874, s. 39, and *vide supra*, p. 9.
[74] *Consensus in idem* is assumed: *Mitchell* v. *Stornoway Trs.*, 1936 S.C.(H.L.) 56, *per* Lord Macmillan at p. 66; *East Kilbride Development Corporation* v. *Pollok*, 1953 S.L.T. 211.
[75] Bell's Prin., § 26.
[76] *Station Hotel, Nairn* v. *Macpherson* (1905) 13 S.L.T. 456; *e.g.*, also *Boyd* v. *Shaw*, 1927 S.C. 414.
[77] *Van Laun* v. *Neilson, Reid & Co.* (1904) 6 F. 644, *per* Lord Kinnear at p. 653.

by advances made to the principal debtor although it was not proved
the guarantor was aware the advances were made.[78]

The acts constituting *rei interventus* must be unequivocally referable
to the contract. Acts done before it are necessarily excluded.[79] Thus
where a tenant negotiated for the purchase of his farm, but certain
conditions had not been finally arranged, and he proceeded to make
considerable alterations on the subjects, acquiesced in by the seller,
these actings were held to be ascribable to purchase, not to contract
of lease.[80]

The personal bar affects not only the party who has allowed the
other to act on it, but also the party who so acts.[81]

Homologation.—Homologation is present where the granter of a
deed, unenforceable because improbative, himself supplies by his
actings the defect.[82] Rules of authentication being for the benefit of
the granter of a deed cannot deprive him of the power of remedying
the defects himself. He may recognise the binding character of the
writ by treating it as binding upon him, *e.g.*, by paying interest on an
improbative bond. There is not apparently any rule that the homo-
logator of an improbative deed must have known of its improbative
character at the time he homologated it.

Adoption.—Where the contract is itself void, as where the granter
being under age is incapable of contracting, there is no room for
homologation. But the writ may afterwards be adopted by the granter
should he acquire the power to contract. Adoption as a general rule
makes the contract binding only as from the date of the adoption
unless the person adopting by his words or acts otherwise undertakes.

(e) Stamping of documents.—In connection with the subject of
proof the question may arise whether a fact can be proved by means
of an unstamped document which the law requires to be stamped and
declares null if unstamped. If the document is probative it cannot
receive effect as a probative document. Unstamped documents have,
however, been admitted when supported by other evidence, in proof of
obligations which by themselves they are not admissible to prove.[83]
A judge or arbiter must take notice of any omission or insufficiency of
the stamp on a document.[84]

---

[78] *Johnston* v. *Grant* (1844) 6 D. 875; *National Bank of Scotland* v. *Campbell* (1892)
19 R. 885.
[79] *e.g., Pollok* v. *Whiteford,* 1936 S.L.T. 255.
[80] *Colquhoun* v. *Wilson's Trs.* (1860) 22 D. 1035; *cf. Mitchell* v. *The Stornoway Trs.,*
1935 S.C. 558, and in the House of Lords, 1936 S.L.T. 509.
[81] Different in England—*Caton* v. *Caton* (1866) L.R. 1 Ch. 137.
[82] *Mitchell* v. *The Stornoway Trs., supra.*
[83] *Bannatyne* v. *Wilson* (1855) 18 D. 230; *Matheson* v. *Ross* (1849) 6 Bell's App. 374;
Fraser v. *Bruce* (1857) 20 D. 115.   [84] Stamp Act, 1891, s. 14 (1).

The law requiring stamping is entirely statutory. The principal Act is the Stamp Act, 1891, the First Schedule to which prescribes most of the rates of duty presently exigible. Stamps may be adhesive, where permitted, but not over 2s. 6d.,[85] or impressed. Where the stamp is adhesive, the instrument is not deemed duly stamped unless (a) the person required by law to cancel it does so by writing on or across the stamp his name or initials together with the date of so doing, or otherwise effectively cancels the stamp and renders it incapable of being used for any other instrument or for postal purposes; or (b) it is otherwise proved that the stamp appearing on the instrument was affixed thereto at the proper time.[86] In some cases special adhesive stamps are required to be used, called " appropriated stamps." These are required on contract notes. Adhesive or impressed stamps may be used in the case of agreements liable to the fixed duty of 6d., bills of exchange including cheques, promissory notes, policies of insurance other than life insurance, and others.[87]

An unstamped or insufficiently stamped instrument may, as a rule, be stamped after the execution thereof on payment of the unpaid duty and a penalty of £10, or, if the duty is over £10, with in addition interest on the duty from the time when first executed.[88]

4. MATTERS AFFECTING THE VALIDITY OF CONTRACTS

There are some contracts which confer no rights or are at least unenforceable by one or both of the parties even though they are formally complete. This may be due to the incapacity of the parties to bind themselves, or the contract may have been entered into in error or obtained by improper means such as misrepresentation, fraud, force, or undue influence, or be prohibited by law. A contract which is open to any of these objections may be void and null, may be voidable and reducible, or may be merely unenforceable. The difference in effect between a void and a voidable contract is that in the former case no third party can acquire rights under the contract whatever, whereas in the latter a third party can do so before it is challenged and reduced.[89]

(a) **Capacity to contract.**—Incapacity to contract on the part of one or both parties to the contract has the same effect as if no contract had been entered into, *i.e.*, the contract is void from the beginning,

---

[85] *Ibid.* s. 7.
[86] *Ibid.* s. 8 (1).
[87] See *Sergeant on Stamp Duties,* 4th ed., pp. 28-29.
[88] Stamp Act, 1891, s. 15 (1).
[89] In both cases equitable considerations may affect the consequences if the contract has been acted on. See Gloag, *op. cit.,* 531.

because there can have been no true consent to be bound. Parties wholly or partly incapable of contracting are pupils, minors and persons labouring under mental derangement or intoxicated.

Pupils.—Pupils are persons under the age of puberty, which is twelve in the case of girls, fourteen in the case of boys. A contract by a pupil alone is void if challenged by him, or in his interest, at any time within the twenty years of the negative prescription.[90] But if it is for his advantage and he acts on it the other party is bound to perform it. Indirectly a pupil by contracting may incur obligations. Thus where necessaries, *i.e.*, such as food and clothing, are bought by a pupil he must pay a reasonable price for them,[91] and where money is lent to a pupil and spent on his estate he will be liable in so far as he has been thereby enriched.[92]

Pupils' contracts are properly made on their behalf by their guardians or tutors, and these are good subject to certain limitations. The natural guardian or tutor of a pupil child is his or her father. On the father's death the mother, if surviving, may be tutor or guardian either alone or jointly with anyone appointed tutor by the father.[93] Tutors may be appointed by will of the father or mother and by the court.[94]

Contracts made on behalf of a pupil by his tutor or guardian are not void from the beginning, but may be reduced by the pupil after he or she attains majority and during four years thereafter (the *quadriennium utile*) on proof of lesion, *i.e.*, loss and injury, provided the loss is considerable, and the contract was not proper and reasonable at the time it was made. When the contract is so reduced it is set aside as from the beginning, and so far as possible there must be mutual restitution.[95]

The Betting and Loans (Infants) Act, 1892, the Moneylenders Act, 1900, and the Moneylenders Act, 1927, contain special provisions for the protection of pupils and minors against moneylenders. The main provision is to the effect that where any minor or pupil who has contracted a loan which is void in law agrees after he comes of age to repay it, such agreement is absolutely void.[96]

Minors.—Minors are persons above the age of pupilarity and under the age of twenty-one. They have capacity to contract, but subject

---

90 *Vide infra*, p. 50.
91 Sale of Goods Act, 1893, s. 2.
92 *Scott's Tr.* v. *Scott* (1887) 14 R. 1043.
93 Guardianship of Infants Act, 1925, s. 4, as amended by Children Act, 1948, s. 50, and Children and Young Persons Act, 1963, s. 50.
94 *Ibid.*
95 Bell's Comm., 7th ed., 1, 128, 131.
96 Betting and Loans (Infants) Act, 1892, s. 5.

to certain qualifications. If the minor has a guardian or curator, contracts by him, as a rule, require the consent of such guardian or curator and are null if made by him alone. He may, in certain circumstances, validly contract alone. Thus (1) if a minor enters into a profession, trade or business, the contracts made by him in the ordinary course thereof are fully binding on him.[97] There is a presumption that bonds, bills of exchange and other such documents granted by a minor engaged in business are granted by him for the purposes of his business. This would not hold of a cautionary obligation, a gamble on the stock exchange or a bill to a moneylender. (2) If a minor holds himself out as of full age so as actually to deceive parties with whom he contracts, the contract is binding on him. (3) Contracts by a minor for necessaries are valid and he must pay a reasonable price for them as in the case of pupils. In the case of a minor contracting with consent of his guardian or, where he has none, by himself alone, the contract may be reduced during the *quadriennium utile* as in the case of pupils.

These principles are well illustrated by the case of partnership. Thus a minor who is partner in a firm cannot plead minority and lesion in a question with creditors, but can in questions with his co-partners.

The law as to moneylending transactions by pupils applies also to minors.

Insane persons.—As a general rule a person while insane is incapable of entering into a contract for he is incapable of giving the necessary consent.[98] His contract is void. Whether a person was or was not at the time of his undertaking a legal obligation of any kind so insane as to be incapable of entering into a contract is a question of fact and degree. A person may be sane at one time and not at another, sane on one subject and insane on another, sufficiently sane to enter into a simple contract but not a complex one. Until proved insane his sanity is presumed. When a person has been legally declared insane he is as regards capacity to contract in the same position as a pupil, and his tutor-at-law alone can contract for him. When he has not been legally declared insane the court will, on petition, and on being satisfied that he is unable to manage his own affairs, appoint a *curator bonis* to do so. Insanity supervening during the currency of a continuing contract entered into during sanity may not end the contract, *e.g.*, if it be between agent and client,[99] or a contract of partnership.[1] The court may, however, dissolve a partnership on this ground.[2]

---

[97] *McFeetridge* v. *Stewarts & Lloyds*, 1913 S.C. 773.
[98] Stair, i, 10, 13; Erskine, i, 7, 51; Bell's Prin., §§ 10, 2105 *et seq.*
[99] *Wink* v. *Mortimer* (1849) 11 D. 995; *Pollok* v. *Paterson*, Dec. 10, 1811, F.C.
[1] Partnership Act, 1890, s. 35.
[2] *Ibid.*

Intoxicated persons.—Intoxication may produce temporary incapacity to give the consent requisite to make a contract.[3] The contract, however, is not void from the beginning.[4] The intoxicated person must, to undo it, as soon as he recovers and realises what he has done, repudiate it.[5] It is a question of fact to be ascertained by proof whether a person was so intoxicated as to be unable to make a particular contract.[6]

Married women.—By the Married Women's Property Act, 1920, the law as to the capacity of a married woman effectually to contract on her own behalf has undergone a radical change. Prior thereto the general rule was that without the consent and concurrence of her husband in his capacity as her curator and administrator-in-law she could not effectually contract. In some cases even his consent was not sufficient to render the contract effectual against her separate estate. Her personal obligation was a nullity. Thus she could not effectually sign a bill as guarantor or undertake a personal obligation.[7] By that Act [8] the husband's right of administration over his wife's estate has been " wholly abolished." If she is of full age she can without her husband's consent, or even against his wish, dispose of her estate. She can contract, sue and be sued as if unmarried, and her husband is not liable on any contract she makes on her own behalf.[9] It is an apparent, but not a real exception that, where she is judicially separated from him, if he fails to pay aliment decreed upon the separation, he is liable for necessaries supplied for her use.[10] Though not judicially separated from him, but justifiably living apart from him, he is liable for necessaries under his obligation to maintain her.[11] Should she be in minority the husband, if of full age, is her curator, and consequently the rules applicable to minors who have curators apply to her case. If her husband be a minor, her father or other guardian is her curator.[12]

The consequence of the above change is that the wife is alone and personally liable in all her contracts. When, of course, she is acting not for herself, but as her husband's agent as *praeposita negotiis domesticis,* he is liable, as under the former law, but this is not a question of her capacity to contract as principal.[13]

---

3 Stair, i, 10, 13; Erskine, iii, 1, 18.
4 *Wilson & Fraser* v. *Nisbet* (1736) Mor. 1509.
5 *Pollok* v. *Burns* (1875) 2 R. 497.
6 *Taylor* v. *Provan* (1864) 2 M. 1226.
7 *Galbraith* v. *Provident Bank* (1900) 2 F. 1148.
8 Married Women's Property (Scotland) Act, 1920, s. 1.
9 *Ibid.* s. 3.
10 Conjugal Rights (Scotland) Amendment Act, 1861, s. 6; Married Women's Property (Scotland) Act, 1920, s. 3. (2).
11 See *Walton on Husband and Wife,* 3rd ed., 204, 205.
12 Married Women's Property (Scotland) Act, 1920, s. 2.   13 *Vide infra,* p. 70.

(b) Error or mistake, misrepresentation and fraud.[14]—A contract otherwise completely constituted may in the next place be reduced as invalid on the ground that there was no genuine consent to be bound owing to error or mistake, or misrepresentation or fraud at the time it was constituted.

(i) *Error or mistake*

A contract may be affected by error in two cases: first, an error in expression where by some slip or blunder the contract is concluded or recorded in terms other than those to which the parties to it consented; second, an error of intention, that is where, though the contract accurately represents the immediate intention of the parties, that intention was formed by one or both of them owing to a misapprehension as to some matter regarded as material in determining whether they should enter into the contract.[15]

Error of expression.—The court has a wide equitable power to rectify a mistake in the execution of an obligatory document so as to give effect to the real intention of the parties. If the mistake is admitted, or is obvious on inspection of the document, there is no difficulty. Where a mistake is not admitted by one party nor obvious it can only be established by extrinsic proof.[16] And where a clerical error is not discovered until the interests of third parties have become involved rectification is still competent. The court will not, however, supply the want of statutory formalities necessary to the validity of an instrument as a probative deed.

An offer containing an error in expression, even though accepted, may not be binding on the offerer. It will not be binding if the acceptor knew that a mistake had been made.[17] If the acceptor has no knowledge of the mistake and accepts *in bona fide*, there is some conflict of authority whether the offerer is bound or not.[18] Where an offer is incorrectly transmitted, as by mistake of a telegraph operator, and the offer is read by the recipient in terms materially different from those in which it was made, his acceptance does not conclude a contract.[19]

Error of intention.—One party may be in error, or both. The case

---

[14] See Prof. T. B. Smith, " Error in the Scottish Law of Contract " (1955) 71 L.Q.R. 507.

[15] *Gloag on Contract*, 2nd ed., p. 345.

[16] *Krupp* v. *Menzies*, 1907 S.C. 903, commented on in *Anderson* v. *Lambie*, 1954 S.C.(H.L.) 43; *Shipley U.D.C.* v. *Bradford Corporation* [1936] 1 Ch. 375.

[17] *Webster* v. *Cecil* (1861) 30 Beav. 62; *Steuart's Trs.* v. *Hart* (1875) 3 R. 192; *Hartog* v. *Colin and Shields* [1939] 3 All E.R. 566.

[18] *Sword* v. *Sinclair* (1771) Mor. 14241; *Seaton Brick & Tile Co.* v. *Mitchell* (1900) 2 F. 550; *Wilkie* v. *Hamilton Lodging House Co.* (1902) 4 F. 951.

[19] *Verdin Bros.* v. *Robertson* (1871) 10 M. 35; *cf. Falck* v. *Williams* [1900] A.C. 176.

of error by one party induced by the misrepresentation of the other is dealt with later.[20]

Error of one party.—There is error of intention when it can be shown that one of the parties would not have entered into the contract, or would not have assented to its particular terms, if he had been aware of the true state of the facts. The general rule is that mere error of one party has no legal effect.[21] If a man buys too dear or sells too cheap he is not by reason of his mistake protected from loss.[22] Such error of one party is not enough in itself to nullify a contract. " It must further be proved that the error was mutual, *i.e.*, common to both parties, or that it was induced by misrepresentations, either innocent or fraudulent, made by the other party to the contract or that it was induced by fraudulent concealment." [23] It is immaterial that the error was due to a man's own fault or that of a third party, and he has no remedy unless he can charge the other party with misrepresentation.[24] It is also clear that where the error alleged is as to some circumstance external to the contract itself that will not release the person in error, as where a party leased a theatre and afterwards discovered that the plays he meant to produce were illegal.[25] The rule applies where the contract is onerous, but not when it is gratuitous, or in substance so.[26]

The above general rule does not, however, apply where the error is so fundamental or substantial as to exclude any agreement, that is, where there is really no contract to enforce. That is, error in substantials (*error in substantialibus*) may invalidate consent, whereas error in regard to collateral matters (*error concomitans*) leaves the parties as they are.

Where there is error in the substantials of a contract it is void, and even third parties can acquire no rights. The cases of error in substantials avoiding a contract are exceptions to the general rule that the intentions of parties are to be derived from the words in which they express themselves. Errors in substantials may be (1) as to the party contracted with, (2) as to the contract entered into, (3) as to the subject-matter of the contract, (4) as to the price or consideration.[27] Examples may be given.

(1) ERROR AS TO PARTY.—The identity of the other party must be material. In a case in England one Blenkarn ordered goods from a

---

[20] *Vide* p. 20.   [21] *Bell* v. *Lever Brothers, Ltd.* [1932] A.C. 161.
[22] Bell's Prin., § 11.
[23] Lord Skerrington in *A. B.* v. *C. B.*, 1914 2 S.L.T. 107, 110.
[24] *Wallace's Factor* v. *McKissock* (1898) 25 R. 642.
[25] *Cloup* v. *Alexander* (1831) 9 S. 448.   [26] *Macandrew* v. *Gilhooley*, 1911 S.C. 448.
[27] Bell's Prin., § 11 Price may not be an essential. *R. & J. Dempster Ltd.* v. *Motherwell Bridge & Engineering Co. Ltd.*, 1964 S.L.T. 113.

manufacturer. They were supplied in the belief the order came from Blenkiron, a well-known dealer who had premises in the street from which Blenkarn wrote and whose credit the manufacturer knew to be good. Having got the goods Blenkarn resold them. Blenkarn failing to pay for the goods the manufacturer sought to recover the goods from the purchasers to whom Blenkarn sold them, and it was held, owing to the manufacturer's mistake as to Blenkarn's identity, there was no contract and Blenkarn could not give a title to the purchasers from him.[28]

(2) ERROR AS TO CONTRACT.—The usual case is where a person signs an obligatory document thinking he is signing as a witness or a different document. So where a person signs a bill of exchange thinking he is signing as a witness the bill cannot be enforced by a holder in due course.[29]

(3) ERROR AS TO SUBJECT-MATTER.—This covers both the case where the parties are at variance as to the particular thing about which they contract, and the case where they differ materially about the qualities the thing is supposed to possess. Thus, in the former case, there were two ships both called the *Peerless* and both sailing with cotton on board from Bombay, though at different dates. Where a party bought the cotton on board the *Peerless* thinking of the one ship, and the seller thinking of the other, it was held there was no contract.[30] In the latter case there is no contract if the difference in quality amounts to a difference in kind, but not otherwise.[31] Thus a purchaser of new oats, thinking they were old, failed to reduce the contract.[32]

(4) ERROR AS TO PRICE OR CONSIDERATION.—Where in a verbal sale of cattle one party thought the price had been fixed and the other thought it was to be settled after, there was held to be no completed contract.[33]

The above examples are all errors of fact. Where there is error by one party as to the legal effect of a contract, such error does not as a rule affect his liability.[34] But this does not apply where the

[28] *Cundy* v. *Lindsay* (1878) 3 App.Cas. 459; *cf. Morrisson* v. *Robertson*, 1908 S.C. 332; *Lake* v. *Simmons* [1927] A.C. 487; *Said* v. *Butt* [1920] 3 K.B. 497; *Dennant* v. *Skinner & Collom* [1948] 2 K.B. 164.
[29] *Foster* v. *Mackinnon* (1869) L.R. 4 C.P. 704; *Buchanan* v. *Duke of Hamilton* (1878) 5 R.(H.L.) 69; *Ellis* v. *Lochgelly Iron & Coal Co.*, 1909 S.C. 1278, *per* Lord Dunedin at p. 1282; *Muskham Finance Ltd.* v. *Howard* [1963] 1 Q.B. 904.
[30] *Raffles* v. *Wichelhaus* (1864) 2 H. & C. 906; *cf. Wallis* v. *Pratt* [1911] A.C. 394.
[31] Bell's Comm. 1, 314.
[32] *Smith* v. *Hughes* (1871) L.R. 6 Q.B. 597. *Vide Bell* v. *Lever Bros. Ltd.* [1932] A.C. 161, *per* Lord Atkin at p. 218.
[33] *Wilson* v. *Marquis of Breadalbane* (1859) 21 D. 957. If matters are not entire, the buyer may have to pay a reasonable price—*Stuart & Co.* v. *Kennedy* (1885) 13 R. 221.
[34] *Muirhead & Turnbull* v. *Dickson* (1905) 7 F. 686, *per* Lord M'Laren. Money paid under an erroneous interpretation of a public statute is not recoverable; *Glasgow Corporation* v. *Lord Advocate*, 1959 S.C. 203.

parties stand in a fiduciary relation to one another, as, for example, between partners, nor in gratuitous obligations, nor where money has been paid unnecessarily, as in the case of over-payments.[35]

Mutual error.—Where both parties have contracted on the mistaken assumption of the existence of a certain state of facts the contract may be void or at least voidable.[36] Thus, under the Sale of Goods Act, 1893, s. 6, " where there is a contract for the sale of specific goods, and the goods without the knowledge of the seller have perished at the time when the contract is made, the contract is void "; or where one purchases a thing which already belongs to him, neither party being aware of the fact.[37] The only remedy is reduction.[38] Mutual error will not, on the other hand, avoid a contract where the error is one of opinion,[39] or as to the value of a thing which is the subject-matter of a sale.[40] Mutual error as to the construction of a private contract and not affecting third parties renders money paid recoverable.[41]

(ii) *Misrepresentation*

Error due to misrepresentation by one party inducing the other to contract may be either innocent or fraudulent. In both cases, where the misrepresentation touches the substantials of the contract, the contract is void: otherwise it is merely voidable.

A distinction should be noted, that between a representation and a warranty, for they are not always easily distinguished and have different legal effects. A representation is a statement which induces a party to contract but is not part of the contract. A misrepresentation is not, therefore, a breach of contract; but it may give rise to a right to rescind it.[42] A warranty, however, is something which a party has undertaken to fulfil as part of the contract, and breach of it is, therefore, a breach of the contract, and the legal remedy is damages for breach of the contract, not rescission. Thus, statements as to the description of goods sold are not representations but warranties.[43] It is generally a question of the intention of the parties whether a statement is a

---

35 *Henderson & Co.* v. *Turnbull & Co.*, 1909 S.C. 510.
36 *Hamilton* v. *The Western Bank* (1861) 23 D. 1033.
37 *Magistrates of Inverness* v. *Highland Ry.* (1893) 20 R. 551.
38 *Pender-Small* v. *Kinloch's Trs.* 1917 S.C. 307.
39 *British Homophone* v. *Kunz, etc., Co.* (1935) 152 L.T. 589—mutual error as to parties' legal obligation to enter into a contract.
40 *Bell* v. *Lever Brothers, Ltd.* [1932] A.C. 161. Or in the special case of sale under a well-known trade description; *Harrison & Jones Ltd.* v. *Bunten & Lancaster Ltd.* [1953] 2 W.L.R. 840.
41 *British Hydro-carbon Chemicals Ltd.* v. *British Transport Commission*, 1961 S.L.T. 280.
42 *Bell Bros. (H.P.) Ltd.* v. *Aitken*, 1939 S.C. 577.
43 Sale of Goods Act, 1893, s. 13; *Hyslop* v. *Shirlaw* (1905) 7 F. 875, *per* Lord Kyllachy at p. 881.

representation or a warranty, and much will depend on the nature of the contract. In determining whether a statement is of the one character or the other, if it refers not to the subject-matter, but to something collateral, it is usually merely a representation.

Innocent misrepresentation and concealment.—A misrepresentation may consist in failure to disclose a material fact or in an actual statement or in an act. The legal effect of misrepresentation without fraudulent intent is to render the contract voidable unless touching the substantials, when it is void. It seems to be settled that an innocent misrepresentation can render a contract voidable.[44] It undoubtedly does so where the contract is one *uberrimae fidei, i.e.*, one where there is a duty on the parties, owing to the nature of the contract, to disclose all material facts with accuracy, for example, contracts of insurance or partnership agreements [45] or agreements to take shares founded on a prospectus.[46]

To render a contract voidable, misrepresentation must be material [47] and essential, *i.e.*, such as would, if known, have deterred the party deceived from entering into the contract,[48] and must have, in fact, either by itself or along with other representations, induced the contract. Therefore it has no effect if the other party knew the facts.[49] If the statement is ambiguous, proof that it was understood in the misleading sense must be led. Unless there was a duty to enquire, the fact that by enquiry the party deceived might have discovered the truth does not deprive him of his remedy.[50]

Failure to disclose.—The general rule is that each party relies on his own means of knowledge. They are " at arm's length." [51] Thus a party need not inform the other that he has doubts of his own solvency and consequent ability to fulfil obligations undertaken. Again, he need not disclose his reasons for making an offer, even though he knew these, if disclosed, would prevent acceptance. In contracts *uberrimae fidei*, however, *e.g.*, insurance, there is a duty to disclose all material facts known.

---

[44] *Stewart* v. *Kennedy* (1890) 17 R.(H.L.) 25. See also *Mair* v. *Rio Grande Rubber Estates Ltd.*, 1913 S.C.(H.L.) 74; *Westville Shipping Co.* v. *Abram Steamship Co.*, 1922 S.C. 571; 1923 S.C.(H.L.) 68; *Gloag on Contract*, 2nd ed., p. 471.

[45] *Ferguson* v. *Wilson* (1904) 6 F. 779.

[46] *Blakiston* v. *London & Scottish Banking Corporation* (1894) 21 R. 417.

[47] See *Smith* v. *Chadwick* (1884) 9 App.Cas. 187; *City of Edinburgh Brewery Co.* v. *Gibson's Tr.* (1869) 7 M. 886.

[48] *Menzies* v. *Menzies* (1893) 20 R.(H.L.) 108, *per* Lord Watson at p. 142. This use of the word " essential " has been questioned—Prof. T. B. Smith, " Error in the Scottish Law of Contract " (1955) 71 L.Q.R. 507.

[49] *Cruickshank* v. *Northern Accident Insurance Co.* (1895) 23 R. 147.

[50] *Scottish Widows' Fund* v. *Buist* (1876) 3 R. 1078, *per* Lord President Inglis at p. 1083.

[51] *Young* v. *Clydesdale Bank* (1889) 17 R. 231; *Royal Bank* v. *Greenshields*, 1914 S.C. 259 (cautionary obligations).

On the other hand, conduct amounting to active concealment is a misrepresentation, and is often equivalent to fraud, e.g., to conceal the fact that an article is a sham antique.[52] A half truth may be a misrepresentation.[53] Again, if change of circumstances renders a statement untrue which was true when made, or if believed to be true when made and later discovered by the maker to be untrue, the fact must be communicated if it was such as would affect the judgment of a reasonable man.[54]

Misrepresentation by actual statements.—When these turn out to be incorrect it depends on the character of the statement whether it amounts to a misrepresentation. An honest expression of mere opinion is not a misrepresentation.[55] A statement as to the law, if general, is mere opinion; if as to the legal effect of a particular document, it is a statement of fact and may amount to a misrepresentation.[56] An exaggerated or unduly laudatory statement by a seller in praise of his goods is not necessarily a misrepresentation. The law allows a certain latitude to statements of an advertising nature. Statements must be taken in their reasonable meaning. They must not be given a strained though possible construction.[57]

A misrepresentation of an agent is treated as a misrepresentation of a principal. No principal can take advantage of his agent's mis-statements,[58] unless the principal has explicitly and in advance disclaimed responsibility for the agent's statements.

(iii) *Fraudulent misrepresentation and fraud*

Fraud has been defined as a false representation of fact made with a knowledge of its falseness, or in reckless disregard if it be true or false, with the intention it should be acted upon, and actually inducing the other party to the contract to act upon it.[59] It may consist in a statement of what is false or a concealment of what is true. It must, of course, be material. Also it may consist of an act, as where the seller at a sale by auction bid though he made no representation that he meant to do so.[60] If a statement be honestly made, even though

52 *Patterson* v. *Landsberg* (1905) 7 F. 675; *Edgar* v. *Hector*, 1912 S.C. 348; *Gibson* v. *National Cash Register Co.*, 1925 S.C. 500.
53 *Crossan* v. *Caledon Shipbuilding Co.* (1906) 14 S.L.T.(H.L.) 33; *Royal Bank* v. *Greenshields, supra.*
54 *Gowans* v. *Dundee Steam Navigation Co.* (1904) 12 S.L.T. 137; *Shankland* v. *Robinson*, 1919 S.C. 715; revd. 1920 S.C.(H.L.) 103; *With* v. *O'Flanagan* (1936) 154 L.T. 634.
55 *Bile Beans Co.* v. *Davidson* (1906) 8 F. 1181; *Plotzer* v. *Isaacs* (1907) 15 S.L.T. 186; *Long* v. *Lloyd* [1958] 2 All E.R. 402.
56 *Romanes* v. *Garman*, 1912 2 S.L.T. 104.
57 *Brownlie* v. *Miller* (1878) 5 R. 1076; affd. (1880) 7 R.(H.L.) 66.
58 *Mair* v. *Rio Grande Rubber Estates Ltd.*, 1913 S.C.(H.L.) 74.
59 Lord Herschell in *Derry* v. *Peek* (1889) 14 App.Cas. 337 at p. 374.
60 Sale of Goods Act, 1893, s. 58.

negligently, it cannot be fraudulent.[61] The fraud must have been successful, and the party deceived must have sustained damage thereby. The features distinguishing a fraudulent from an innocent misrepresentation are the knowledge of its falseness and the intention it should be acted upon.

The distinction in effect between innocent and fraudulent misrepresentation is that in the former case the party deceived has only the remedy of reduction, in the latter he has also the remedy of damages. The reduction is based upon the misrepresentation, the claim of damages upon the civil wrong of fraud.[62]

The effect of fraud upon a contract is to render it voidable at the instance of the party deceived. The whole contract must be reduced.[63] The action can only be at the instance of a party to the contract, not of a third party on the ground of fraudulent statements not made to him.[64] The sole exception appears to be where a man, from the nature of the case, is bound to contemplate that his statements will be acted upon by others than the person to whom he makes them.[65] A fraudulent misrepresentation made to the public will give a right of action to anyone who is misled by it and suffers loss.[66] Where a fraudulent misrepresentation of a third party has caused a person to make a contract, he can sue the third party for damages, but cannot insist that he take over the contract from him.[67]

(c) Facility and circumvention, undue influence, force and fear and extortion.—*Facility and circumvention.*—A contract is voidable and may be reduced on the above grounds. In facility and circumvention there is presupposed a weakness or facility of mind in the one contracting party, due for instance to old age or severe illness, taken advantage of by the other in order to obtain or impetrate from him a deed or contract. It is distinguishable from insanity in respect that the facile party has capacity to contract, and from fraud in that the end is the more easily attained owing to the state of mind of the defrauded party. There must have been also the motive to mislead, which is involved in

---

[61] *Boyd & Forrest* v. *Glasgow & South-Western Ry.*, 1912 S.C.(H.L.) 93 at p. 98; *Derry* v. *Peek, supra; Manners* v. *Whitehead* (1898) 1 F. 171.

[62] The leading case is *Derry* v. *Peek, supra.* A claim of damages is competent though the person defrauded does not seek reduction—*Smith* v. *Sim*, 1954 S.C. 357.

[63] *Spence* v. *Crawford*, 1939 S.C.(H.L.) 52.

[64] *Re Discoverers Finance Corporation* (1909) 26 T.L.R. 98; *Edinburgh United Breweries* v. *Molleson* (1893) 20 R. 581; affd. (1894) 21 R.(H.L.) 10; *Macfarlane Strang & Co.* v. *Bank of Scotland* (1903) 40 S.L.R. 746.

[65] *Langridge* v. *Levy* (1837) 2 M. & W. 519; *Robinson* v. *National Bank*, 1916 S.C.(H.L.) 154; see also *Fortune* v. *Young*, 1918 S.C. 1.

[66] *Lees* v. *Tod* (1882) 9 R. 807 (prospectus and annual reports); *Peek* v. *Gurney* (1873) L.R. 6 H.L. 377 (only original shareholders).

[67] *Thin & Sinclair* v. *Arrol & Sons* (1896) 24 R. 198; *Brown* v. *Stewart* (1898) 1 F. 316, *per* Lord Kinnear at p. 323.

the idea of circumvention. Consent must therefore have been improperly obtained.[68]

Undue influence.—Where there is not facility, acts of circumvention falling short of fraud do not warrant reduction except in the special case where a party acquiring a benefit has abused a position of trust and influence. To this form of circumvention is given the specific name of "undue influence." The factors going to make a case of undue influence have been summarised as the existence of a relation creating a dominant or ascendant influence by the one over the other, a confidence and trust arising out of such relation, a material and gratuitous benefit given to the prejudice of that other and the absence of independent advice. Undue influence may occur in contracts between near relations, *e.g.*, parent and child [69]; between a clergyman and a person over whom he exercises spiritual influence [70]; between a doctor and his patient.[71] Such contracts are reducible for want of true consent.

Force and fear and extortion.—Bell [72] says: " Force and fear annul engagement, when not vain or foolish fear, but such as to overcome a mind of ordinary firmness." The contract is void, not merely voidable. The threats must have been the active inducing cause of the contract and must have been such as would have affected the mind of a reasonable person. The threat, *e.g.*, of imprisonment, must not have been justified. The threat must have been a threat to the contracting, not to a third party. Where a wife signed deeds at her husband's request on being informed by him that he was in danger of imprisonment and would flee the country if she declined she was held not entitled to reduce.[73]

Closely resembling the case of contracts reduced on the ground of extortion by force or fear are certain moneylending transactions which the court annuls as manifestly and grossly extortionate. Under the Moneylenders Acts, 1900 and 1927, the courts have power to reopen a moneylending transaction should they, looking to all the circumstances, in particular to the risk undertaken by the moneylender, consider it harsh and unconscionable, and to fix the debtor's liability at what may be adjudged to be reasonable.[74] The more general rule, however, is that persons of full contractual capacity dealing at arm's

---

[68] *Liston* v. *Cowan* (1865) 3 M. 1041.
[69] *Smith Cuninghame* v. *Anstruther's Trs.* (1872) 10 M.(H.L.) 39.
[70] *Munro* v. *Strain* (1874) 1 R. 522.
[71] *Dent* v. *Bennett* (1839) 1 My. & Cr. 269.
[72] *Princ.*, § 12.
[73] *Priestnell* v. *Hutcheson* (1857) 19 D. 495.
[74] Act of 1900, s. 1, as extended by the Act of 1927, ss. 10, 13 (2); *Young* v. *Gordon* (1896) 23 R. 419; *Gordon* v. *Stephen* (1902) 9 S.L.T. 397.

length with each other are bound by their contracts whether fair or not.[75]

(d) Contracts prohibited by law.—Illegal and immoral contracts.— The validity of a contract may be challenged by either of the parties on the grounds already noticed. Illegal contracts, however—known as *pacta illicita*—are all invalid to this effect, that they cannot be enforced by action, irrespective of whether the plea of illegality is taken by a party, because it is the duty of the court at its own hand to take cognisance of the illegality.

Illegal contracts include those which are forbidden by statute and those which are illegal at common law. A particular contract may be open to objection that it is both illegal at common law and forbidden or penalised by statute.

(i) *Illegality by statute*

Under this head are considered contracts which are unobjectionable at common law, though prohibited or penalised by statute. In such cases the statute may either declare an act or agreement of a particular kind illegal or void, or may merely impose a penalty, or may merely declare the contract unenforceable. Illegality is a matter of degree and in each case it is a question of construction of the statute. But in general the law is as follows.

Where a statute prohibits as illegal what is covered by a contract the doing of it cannot found a claim under the contract.[76]

Where a contract, unobjectionable at common law, is declared void, or penalised by statute, while it cannot be enforced or damages recovered under it, the parties to it will not be deprived of any right enforceable by law. The court will take cognisance of rights incidentally arising, as where the contract is in part implemented, and intervene to prevent one party obtaining an advantage over the other. There is a maxim, *in turpi causa melior est conditio possidentis*, which, if applicable, would prevent the court giving any such assistance, but a statutory provision avoiding a contract would not fall within this rule. Thus where a contract for the sale of potatoes by the Scots acre was void under the Weights and Measures Acts, the seller was held entitled to recover the market value of the potatoes as at the date of delivery.[77]

Where a statute, without declaring the contract void, imposes a penalty upon a particular contract, or upon a contract entered into without the observance of statutory conditions or the payment of a statutory duty, there is a general presumption that the imposition of a

---

[75] *A.B.* v. *Joel* (1849) 12 D. 188; *Caledonian Ry.* v. *North British Ry.* (1881) 8 R.(H.L.) 23 at p. 31.
[76] *e.g., Jamieson* v. *Watt's Tr.,* 1950 S.C. 265.
[77] *Cuthbertson* v. *Lowes* (1870) 8 M. 1073. See also Trading Stamps Act, 1964, s. 3.

penalty implies illegality. But in exceptional cases it may be held that the imposition of a penalty is the sole effect of the statute, either because its object is merely the collection of revenue or because the circumstances are such as to make the avoidance of contracts a penalty greater than the legislature can be supposed to have intended to inflict. Thus it was held that the effect of the Companies Clauses Consolidation (Scotland) Act, 1845, s. 89, whereby, if a director of a company should be either directly or indirectly concerned in a contract with the company, his office should become vacant, was that the office became vacant but the contract was not affected. And under the provisions of the Moneylenders Act, 1900, which imposes a penalty on infringement of its provisions, it has been held on the one hand that where a moneylender entered into a contract without having registered at all the name under which he carried on business, as required by the statute, the contract was void.[78] On the other hand, where the moneylender had registered, but not under the name which was his usual trade name, he was subject to the penalty for contracting under his unregistered trade name, but not to avoidance of his contracts, as being too severe a penalty in the absence of express enactment covering such a case.[79] Again, where a statute imposes a stamp duty on a particular contract, with a penalty on the party failing to affix the stamp, it has been held the provision is merely intended for revenue purposes and does not avoid the contract.

Where a statute, without declaring a contract illegal, or imposing any penalty, declares it unenforceable, there seems to be no general rule.[80] Examples are to be found in the Trade Union Act, 1871, and the Tippling Act, 1750. Under the latter Act no action is maintainable to recover any debt on account of any spirituous liquors unless bona fide contracted at one time to the amount of twenty shillings and upwards. It has been held that the Act does not merely cut off the right of action but renders such furnishings illegal, to the effect, for example, of reading out of a tradesman's account items for such furnishings occurring at the end in a question whether the triennial prescription applied to it.[81]

(ii) *Illegality at common law*

A contract may be illegal at common law because its object is the furtherance of a criminal, fraudulent, or immoral act or of an act contrary to public policy. Gaming contracts in Scots law require separate consideration.[82]

---

[78] *Sagar* v. *McAdam*, 1914, 1 S.L.T. 93.
[79] *Whiteman* v. *Sadler* [1910] A.C. 514.
[80] *Gloag on Contract*, 2nd ed., p. 553. *e.g., A. V. Pound & Co. Ltd.* v. *M. W. Hardy & Co.* [1956] A.C. 588.
[81] *Macpherson* v. *Jamieson* (1901) 4 F. 218.   [82] *Infra*, p. 29.

A contract to commit an act indictable as a crime is *pactum illicitum*, and the court will not only not enforce it but will take no cognisance of the rights of parties under it.[83]

An agreement to defraud a third party is an unlawful contract on which no action can be based.[84] So also is an agreement tending to induce breach of trust, or a collusive agreement in bankruptcy to defeat the equal rights of creditors in distribution of a bankrupt estate.[85]

A contract having for its object the furtherance of illicit sexual intercourse, as where a woman sought to enforce a bond granted to reward her for having submitted to intercourse, is an immoral and unlawful contract.[86] Certain contracts interfering with the liberty of marriage or marital relations are illegal, such as marriage brocage contracts, in which obligations are granted in consideration of bringing about a marriage.[87] So also are contracts interfering with the relation of parent and child. Further, contracts in themselves innocent may be treated as *pacta illicita* if entered into for the purpose of promoting an illegal or immoral purpose, as, for example, where money is lent for the purpose of playing an illegal game, or where a house is let which to the knowledge of the landlord is to be used by the tenant in order to keep a mistress.[88] In such cases it must be shown that the party suing was aware of the purpose.[89]

Contracts void because contrary to public policy have been classified as those conflicting with national foreign policy, with the administration of the law, with individual liberty or with freedom of trade.[90] Thus contracts entered into with any person residing in and making contracts from an enemy State are illegal as conflicting with national foreign policy. And where war is declared its effect is to suspend the operation of contracts between the subjects of the belligerent States until peace is restored. A contract to interfere with the free and responsible right to vote at an election, or one to obstruct the course of justice, such as to bribe a judge, or one to evade the revenue laws, as by smuggling, is void as conflicting with the administration of the law.[91]

Contracts in restraint of trade.—Contracts in restraint of trade merit special mention. Restrictive covenants are usually imposed as

[83] *Macdougall* v. *Bremner* (1907) 15 S.L.T. 193.
[84] *Henderson* v. *Caldwell* (1890) 28 S.L.R. 16.
[85] *Macfarlane* v. *Nicoll* (1864) 3 M. 237; *Farmer's Mart, Ltd.* v. *Milne*, 1914 S.C.(H.L.) 84. See also *Munro* v. *Rothfield*, 1920 2 S.L.T. 172 and Bankruptcy (Scotland) Act, 1913, s. 150.   [86] *Thomas* v. *Waddell* (1869) 7 M. 558.
[87] *Hermann* v. *Charlesworth* [1905] 2 K.B. 123.
[88] *Upfill* v. *Wright* [1911] 1 K.B. 506.
[89] *Smith's Advertising Agency* v. *Leeds Laboratory Co.* (1910) 26 T.L.R. 335.
[90] *Gloag on Contract*, 2nd. ed., p. 565.
[91] *Cf. Trevalion* v. *Blanche*, 1919 S.C. 617; *Eisen* v. *McCabe*, 1920 S.C. (H.L.) 146.

a condition in contracts of service or apprenticeship, contracts for the sale of a business, and in analogous cases.[92] An agreement not to exercise a particular trade or profession may be *pactum illicitum* if it imposes a restriction wider than is reasonably necessary to safeguard the interests of the persons it is designed to protect. Such is void if the circumstances of the individual case do not justify the restriction of individual liberty. What is reasonable depends on the circumstances of both parties.[93] An employer may legitimately protect his business connection and his trade and professional secrets, but otherwise may not protect himself from the competition of his former employees; on the other hand, the purchaser of a business may within limits protect himself from the competition of the seller.[94] Both the interests of the individual and of the public are to be taken into account.[95] The restriction must refer to a particular business or profession.[96] There should be some limit to the restriction in point either of area or time. If the restriction is too wide, it falls.[97] The restriction must not be capricious,[98] and the interest to restrict must exist at the time when it is proposed to enforce it.[99] Where a question of construction of contract arises the court will prefer a construction which makes the contract enforceable.[1]

Some examples may be given. An obligation by a doctor to discontinue practice in a particular district, involving an obligation to resign the post of medical officer to local authorities, has been held reasonable.[2] An agreement by a commercial traveller, limited to twelve months after leaving his employment, not to sell or travel in any of the towns or districts traded in by his employer has been held unenforceable on the ground that the restriction was wider than was reasonably necessary.[3] Restrictions on a servant taking up business

---

[92] *e.g., Trego* v. *Hunt* [1896] A.C. 7; *Stewart* v. *Stewart* (1899) 1 F. 1158; *Wyatt* v. *Kreglinger* [1933] 1 K.B. 793; *Scottish Farmer's Dairy Co. (Glasgow) Ltd* v. *McGhee*, 1933 S.L.T. 142.

[93] *Meikle* v. *Meikle* (1895) 33 S.L.R 362 (painter); *Mulvein* v. *Murray*, 1908 S.C. 528 (traveller); *Dumbarton Steamboat Co.* v. *Macfarlane* (1899) 1 F. 993 (carriers); *Mason* v. *Provident Clothing, etc., Co.* [1913] A.C. 724 (canvasser); *Palmolive Co.* v. *Freedman* [1928] 1 Ch. 264 (retailers); *Routh* v. *Jones* [1947] 1 All E.R. 758 (doctor).

[94] *Fitch* v. *Dewes* [1920] 2 Ch. 156; [1921] A.C. 158; *Morris* v. *Saxelby* [1916] A.C. 688; *Mason* v. *Provident Clothing, etc., Co.* [1913] A.C. 724; *Jenkins* v. *Reid* [1948] 1 All E.R. 471 (medical practice).

[95] *Nordenfeldt* v. *Maxim-Nordenfelt Gun, etc., Co.* [1894] A.C. 535; *M'Ellistrim* v. *Ballymacelligott Co-operative, etc., Society Ltd.* [1919] A.C. 548.

[96] *Mulvein* v. *Murray*, 1908 S.C. 528.

[97] *Dumbarton Steamboat Co.* v. *Macfarlane, supra; Mulvein* v. *Murray, supra.*

[98] *Hepworth Manufacturing Co.* v. *Ryott* [1920] 1 Ch. 1.

[99] *Berlitz School of Languages* v. *Duchene* (1903) 6 F. 181; *Rodger* v. *Herbertson*, 1909 S.C. 256; *General Billposting Co.* v. *Atkinson* [1909] A.C. 118.

[1] *Watson* v. *Neuffert* (1863) 1 M. 1110, *per* Lord Cowan.

[2] *Ballachulish Slate Quarries Co., Ltd.* v. *Grant* (1903) 5 F. 1105; *Whitehill & Others* v. *Bradford* [1952] 1 T.L.R. 66. [3] *Mulvein* v. *Murray, supra.*

on the cessation of his employment within a certain time or distance from his place of employment are not binding on a servant who is unwarrantably dismissed.[4] A worldwide restriction, though sustained when granted in favour of a maker of cannon,[5] is unreasonable when designed to protect a local business.[6] Restrictions imposed by an association on its members intended to promote the business of the members have been held legal.[7] Price maintenance agreements are not necessarily illegal, e.g., tied houses,[8] or where a purchaser undertakes not to resell under a certain price.[9] But collective resale price maintenance agreements [10] and individual resale price maintenance agreements [11] are now prohibited by statute, subject to exemption by the Restrictive Practices Court. In the case of patented articles, power to adjust restrictive conditions is limited by statute.[12]

(iii) Gaming contracts

Under statute.—There is no general prohibition of an action founded on a gaming or wagering contract in Scotland, differing from England,[13] and such contracts are not regarded as *pacta illicita*.[14] There are, however, Acts which affect the enforceability of such contracts. (1) The Act 9 Anne, c. 14, provides that all notes, bills, bonds, securities, or other conveyances where the whole or any part of the consideration is for money lost in playing at any game or betting on the result of a game, or is for repayment of money advanced or lent for such betting or gaming, are absolutely void. The Act is now repealed.[15] But the Gaming Act, 1835, provides that every note, bill or mortgage which would under the former Act have been absolutely void is to be deemed and taken to have been made, drawn, accepted, given, or executed for an illegal consideration.[16] The effect of this, applying the Bills of Exchange Act, 1882, s. 30 (2), is that an indorsee of such a bill may sue upon it if he proves he gave value for the bill without notice of its origin.[17] A bond or other security or conveyance granted for a gaming

---

4 *General Billposting Co.* v. *Atkinson, supra,* note 95.
5 *Nordenfeldt* v. *Maxim-Nordenfeldt Gun, etc., Co., supra.*
6 *Dumbarton Steamboat Co.* v. *Macfarlane* (1899) 1 F. 993; *cf. Connors Brothers Ltd. & Ors.* v. *Bernard Connors* (1940) 57 T.L.R. 76.
7 *e.g., British Motor Trade Association* v. *Gray,* 1951 S.C. 586 (covenant by purchasers of new motor vehicles not to resell within specified period).
8 *Noakes & Co.* v. *Rice* [1902] A.C. 24.
9 *Elliman Sons & Co.* v. *Carrington* [1901] 2 Ch. 275; *Morton* v. *Muir Brothers,* 1907 S.C. 1211; *Palmolive Co.* v. *Freedman* [1928] 1 Ch. 264.
10 Restrictive Trade Practices Act, 1956.
11 Resale Prices Act, 1964
12 Patents Act, 1949, s. 57.
13 *Levy* v. *Jackson* (1903) 5 F. 1170.
14 *Clayton* v. *Clayton,* 1937 S.C. 619.
15 Gaming Act, 1845, s. 15; *Rayner* v. *Kent & Stansfield,* 1922 S.L.T. 331.
16 *William Hill (Park Lane) Ltd.* v. *Hofman* (1950) 66 T.L.R. (Pt. 1) 915.
17 *Woolf* v. *Hamilton* [1898] 2 Q.B. 337

debt, and therefore for an illegal consideration, could not be enforced
by an assignee against the granter, but the assignee could probably
recover the consideration for the assignation from the cedent.[18] (2)
Under the Betting, Gaming and Lotteries Act, 1963, betting and
gaming, if conducted in accordance with certain statutory conditions,
are lawful, but lotteries, with statutory exceptions in favour of, *inter
alia*, art unions under certain conditions,[19] small lotteries incidental
to certain entertainments,[20] private lotteries as regulated by the Act,[21]
and certain small lotteries conducted for charitable, sporting or other
purposes[22] are unlawful.[22a] The purchase of a ticket in a foreign
lottery is not, however, illegal.[23] (3) The Life Assurance Act, 1774,
declares void any contract of insurance in which the insured has no
insurable interest or made by way of gaming or wagering.[24]

At common law.—Sponsiones ludicrae.—The courts will not decide
who is the winner of a competition. They pay no regard to *sponsiones
ludicrae,*[25] or to contracts subsequently entered into merely for the
purpose of giving time to implement *sponsiones ludicrae.* These not
being, however, regarded as *pacta illicita*, the fact that the relations of
parties is due to a *sponsio ludicra* will not debar the court from interfering to protect the rights of parties once the winner is decided.[26]
Thus a broker or agent employed to bet may recover his commission
and expenditure from the principal,[27] and the principal may recover
from the agent winnings actually received.[28]

Gaming or wagering contracts.—If the court is satisfied that the
contract sought to be enforced is one of gaming or wagering, it will
not deal with the case at all. But there may be gambling without
gaming. It is a question of the intention of both the parties. Thus
a mere speculator in stocks and shares, or even commodities, is not
necessarily barred from maintaining an action.[29] Again, while the
speculator may not mean to take up the shares or commodities, and is
merely gambling on differences, and so gaming, it may not be a gaming
transaction so far as his relations with the broker with whom he deals

---

[18] *Ferrier* v. *Graham's Trs.* (1828) 6 S. 818; see *Gloag on Contract,* 2nd ed., p. 580.
[19] Art Unions Act, 1846; *Christison* v. *McBride* (1881) 9 R. 34.
[20] Betting, Gaming & Lottery Act, 1963, § 43.
[21] *Ibid.,* § 44.
[22] *Ibid.,* § 45.
[22a] *Ibid.,* § 41.
[23] *Clayton* v. *Clayton*, 1937 S.C. 619
[24] See Insurance, *infra.*
[25] *Kelly* v. *Murphy,* 1940 S.C. 96; *cf. Robertson* v. *Balfour*, 1938 S.C. 207.
[26] *Calder* v. *Stevens* (1871) 9 M. 1074.
[27] *Levy* v. *Jackson* (1903) 5 F. 1170; *Foulds* v. *Thomson* (1857) 19 D. 803; *Knight & Co.*
v. *Stott* (1892) 19 R. 959.
[28] *Bridges* v. *Savage* (1885) 15 Q.B.D. 363.
[29] *Mollison* v. *Noltie* (1889) 16 R. 350.

are concerned. To constitute a gaming or wagering transaction both parties must intend the transaction to be fictitious, and one must lose, neither being bound to accept delivery of the stocks, shares or goods.[30]

(iv) *Effect of illegality in contracts*

Where a contract involves an element of illegality, as distinguished from the case where it is merely declared void by statute, the effect is to debar the parties from recourse to the courts. The principle is expressed in two legal maxims, *viz.*, *ex turpi causa non oritur actio*, that is, the parties are debarred from maintaining an action, and *in turpi causa melior est conditio possidentis*, that is, one wrongdoer may with impunity take any advantage of the other which the circumstances admit of. Thus, where a scheme by several parties to defraud a third party has proved successful, the conspirator who has obtained the profit cannot be legally compelled to share it with the others.[31] So also if an illegal transaction results in a loss, the party who has sustained the loss will not be allowed to plead the illegality in order to get relief from the other party.[32] The general test of whether an action is excluded is whether the pursuer can establish his case without exposing that he has been guilty of illegality.

There are certain exceptions to the rule that a party to an illegal contract is debarred from suing on it. Thus, where the illegal purpose involves a mere temporary right, as where property is let or hired for an improper object, while the rent or hire cannot be recovered,[33] the owner of the property might sue to recover it when the temporary purpose was over.[34] Again, where the parties are not *in pari delicto, i.e.*, equally blameworthy, the less blameworthy may found upon the illegality. This applies where one party has been in a position to compel the other in an illegal act, as where a creditor has obtained a secret preference from the debtor as the price of his concurrence in a composition. Again, where the illegality arises under a statute which has been passed to protect a particular class, in contrast to the public interest,[35] a member of that class may sue to recover what he has paid under the illegal contract.[36] In England it has been held that if money is paid for an illegal object it may be recovered if demanded before the illegal object has been carried out, as in the case of money paid to a matrimonial agency when no marriage followed.[37] And if

---

[30] *Foulds* v. *Thomson* (1857) 19 D. 803; *Universal Stock Exchange Co.* v. *Howat* (1891) 19 R. 128. For full definition of a wager as distinct from a speculative contract, see *Carlill* v. *Carbolic Smoke Ball Co.* [1892] 2 Q.B. 484, *per* Hawkins J. at p. 490.

[31] *Laughland* v. *Millar, Laughland & Co.* (1904) 6 F. 413.

[32] *Anderson* v. *Torrie* (1857) 19 D. 356.   [33] *Upfill* v. *Wright* [1911] 1 K.B. 506.

[34] *Gloag on Contract*, 2nd ed., p. 586.   [35] *Re Mahmoud and Ispahani* [1921] 2 K.B. 716.

[36] *Phillips* v. *Blackhurst*, 1912, 2 S.L.T. 254.

[37] *Hermann* v. *Charlesworth* [1905] 2 K.B. 123 at p. 129; *cf. Harry Parker Ltd.* v. *Mason* [1940] 2 K.B. 590.

the contract is only partly illegal and is divisible the part not tainted with the illegality may be enforced, as in contracts not to carry on a particular trade where there are two restrictions, one permissible, the other not.[38]

Where rights under a contract tainted with illegality are assigned to a third party the general rule is that the third party takes no better title than his cedent. This does not apply to bills of exchange, promissory notes, and cheques if subsequent to the illegality the indorsee has in good faith and without notice of the illegality given value for the bill, when he may enforce payment against all parties liable on the bill.[39]

5. CONSTRUCTION AND INTERPRETATION OF CONTRACTS

There has already been considered under formation of contracts the manner in which their constitution requires to be proved before they can be effectively founded on. Assuming, then, the formation of a valid contract capable of being proved as to its constitution, there now fall to be considered questions which may arise out of or in relation to the terms in which the contract is expressed. This matter may be considered under the following heads: (a) the construction of contracts generally; (b) the interpretation of particular terms; (c) proof in matters of construction and interpretation.

(a) The construction of contracts generally.—Where a contract is constituted and proved verbally it is mainly a question of the credibility of the witnesses as to the meaning which they respectively put on the terms used. Where the contract is in writing, while the question is what was the intention of the parties, that question is to be determined, not from what they respectively say they intended by a particular expression, but by the sense in which an expression used by the one party would be reasonably understood by the other.[40] Or, as the matter has been otherwise put, the court is to endeavour to place itself in the position of a reasonable and disinterested third party, duly instructed, if necessary, as to the law.[41] And in arriving at a construction the general rule is that the whole contract must be looked at.[42]

---

[38] *Mulvien* v. *Murray*, 1908 S.C. 528; *Malcolm Muir Ltd.* v. *Jamieson*, 1947 S.C. 314.

[39] Bills of Exchange Act, 1882, ss. 30, 38.

[40] *Fowkes* v. *Manchester & London Assurance Association* (1863) 3 B. & S. 917, *per* Lord Blackburn at p. 929; *Muirhead & Turnbull* v. *Dickson* (1905) 7 F. 686, *per* Lord President Dunedin at p. 694.

[41] *Gloag on Contract*, 2nd ed., p. 398. *Cf. Upton R.D.C.* v. *Powell* [1942] 1 All E R. 220.

[42] *e.g., James B. Fraser & Co.* v. *Denny, Mott & Dickson*, 1944 S.C.(H.L.) 35; *Dryburgh* v. *Macpherson*, 1944 S.L.T. 116; *George Shaw Ltd.* v. *Duffy*, 1943 S.C. 350; *Scottish Milk Marketing Board* v. *Cardowan Creameries Ltd.*, 1940 S.C. 1; *Norval* v. *Abbey* 1939 S.C. 724; *Young* v. *M'Kellar Ltd.*, 1909 S.C. 1340, *per* Lord Low at p. 1346; *Fraser* v. *Cox*, 1938 S.C. 506.

Mutuality of contracts.—Where a contract is mutual or *hinc inde*, as it is called, that is, contains obligations by both parties, and not merely a series of independent obligations, the general rule is that both parties must be bound or neither. This has been called the principle of mutuality. The principle may apply both when the obligations are express and when merely implied. Thus, where a school teacher was appointed without any express arrangement as to the duration of his employment or notice of dismissal, and claimed damages for dismissal without reasonable notice, it was held that as a school teacher could not be supposed to be entitled to leave without notice there was a correlative obligation on the school board to give him corresponding notice.[43] Again, the principle will be applied where the incidence of contractual obligation is altered by statute. Thus the Sale of Goods Act, 1893, s. 58, provides that a sale by auction is complete when the auctioneer announces its completion by the fall of the hammer. It has been held on this principle that before the fall of the hammer an exposer may withdraw the article from sale.[44]

Conditions in contracts.—A contractual obligation is termed pure when it can be enforced at once and is not subject to any condition; future, or to a day, when it will become a pure obligation at a fixed date or on the occurrence of an event which is certain to happen; conditional or contingent when its enforceability is dependent on an event which may not happen.[45] A debt instantly and unconditionally payable is a pure obligation. A debt which, though not presently exigible, is dependent on no other condition than the arrival of the day of payment or the occurrence of an event which is certain to happen, *e.g.*, the death of a particular person, is a future debt. Where the event, on the occurrence of which the enforceability of an obligation to pay depends, may or may not happen, it is a contingent or conditional debt.

A contingent obligation may be of two kinds. When the obligation does not become exigible until the occurrence of an uncertain event, the condition is suspensive, otherwise called a condition precedent, as in sale where there is an agreement to sell but the sale is suspended until the price is paid. Where, on the other hand, the obligation though presently exigible may cease to be so on the occurrence of an uncertain event before it is exacted, it is resolutive.[46] In each case it is a question of the construction of the particular contract which it is.

Another classification of conditions is that of potestative, casual, and mixed. A condition is potestative where its purifying depends on

[43] *Morrison* v. *Abernethy School Board* (1876) 3 R. 945.
[44] *Fenwick* v. *Macdonald, Fraser & Co.* (1904) 6 F. 850.
[45] Bell's Prin., § 53.   [46] *Hardy* v. *Sime*, 1938 S.L.T. 18.

the action of one party to the contract. If that party is the debtor in the obligation there is an implied obligation on him not to oppose any obstacle to its being purified, and if he does it will be held to be purified. In some cases he may be even bound to promote fulfilment,[47] but not usually. A casual condition is one the fulfilment of which depends on chance or on the action of a third party. A mixed condition is one which depends on the combined action of one of the parties and an external agency.

Implied conditions.—Conditions may be expressed or implied. Where a contract is of a well-known and usual nature the courts will read into it as implied therein the conditions or obligations recognised by law as incident thereto, and conditions may be supplied by custom or previous similar contracts between the parties.[48] Such implied conditions may be negatived by express conditions. But where the contract is constituted by performance of the act called for or acceptance is in general terms the acceptor is not bound by special terms or conditions unless he knew or had reasonable means of knowing them. Thus, where a ticket is issued by a railway company for left luggage containing conditions limiting its liability at common law, it must give adequate notice of the special conditions, as by a reference on the face of the ticket to conditions which are on the back.[49] The court may read an implied term into a written contract if its nature is such that it must necessarily be implied to give the contract business efficacy.[50]

Joint and several obligations.—There may be several debtors in an obligation and there may be several creditors. In such cases each debtor may be liable only *pro rata, i.e.,* in a share of the obligation, and each creditor may have only the right to exact a share. Where each debtor may be made to fulfil the whole obligation each is said to be liable *in solidum*, and debtors bound " conjunctly and severally " are said to be liable *singuli in solidum*. Likewise where each creditor can exact the whole from the debtor his right is *in solidum*. Unless otherwise provided in the contract the general rule is that the rights and liabilities are *pro rata*.

In certain contracts liability *in solidum* is implied. Thus, co-acceptors in a bill of exchange and all other parties liable as drawers or indorsers are liable conjunctly and severally to a holder.[51] Each

---

[47] *e.g., Re Anglo-Russian Merchant Traders* [1917] 2 K.B. 679.
[48] Sale of Goods Act, 1893, s. 8 (as to price).
[49] *Lyons* v. *Caledonian Ry.*, 1909 S.C. 1185; *Henderson* v. *Stevenson* (1873) 1 R. 215; affd. (1875) 2 R. (H.L.) 71; *Taylor* v. *Glasgow Corporation*, 1952 S.C. 440; *McCutcheon* v. *David MacBrayne Ltd.*, 1964 S.L.T. 66.
[50] *M'Whirter* v. *Longmuir*, 1948 S.C. 577: *Martin Baker Aircraft Co. Ltd.* v. *Canadian Flight Equipment Ltd.* [1955] 2 Q.B. 556 (duration).
[51] Bell's Prin., § 61.

partner of a firm is jointly and severally liable for all the obligations of the firm incurred while he is partner.[52]   Several persons who join in contracting for a common object are presumed to be conjunctly and severally bound in any resulting liability, as where several proprietors employed a tradesman to build a bridge.[53]   And where the obligation is *ad factum praestandum, i.e.,* to do something, as distinct from paying money, there is an implication of joint and several liability to perform or to pay damages.[54]

Where there are joint creditors a discharge by one is good against the rest, and probably a decree of absolvitor against one creditor, where the question at issue was the validity of the claim, would be *res judicata* against the rest.[55]   Co-obligants have, as a rule, a right of relief against each other for the other's share of a debt paid, and, accordingly, if a creditor frees one of the co-obligants from his liability, the other obligants if primarily or equally liable are freed also, unless, when freeing a co-obligant, the creditor expressly reserves his right against the others and thereby their right of relief against the obligant freed.[56]

(b) Interpretation of particular terms of contracts.—In construing a contract the object is to ascertain the intention of the parties.   Where the contract is in writing that intention is to be ascertained from the terms used, looking to the whole contract.[57]   As a rule it is not competent to go outside the writing for extrinsic evidence of what the parties intended.[58]   In certain circumstances that may be permitted.[59]

In construing the terms of a contract the general rule is that ordinary words are to be taken as used in their ordinary meaning if there is nothing in the context or the rest of the contract to imply the contrary.[60]   Conversely, technical terms are to be given their technical sense, with the aid, if necessary, of extrinsic evidence thereasto.

Where an ambiguous expression is used it is construed *contra proferentem,* that is, against the interest of the party who used it, as where a contract is dictated in detail by one party and accepted in general terms by the other, *e.g.,* in insurance policies the construction favourable to the insured is taken,[61] and similarly in a prospectus in a

---

[52] Partnership Act, 1890, s. 9.   [53] *French* v. *Earl of Galloway* (1730) M. 14706.
[54] The enforcement of decrees *ad factum praestandum* is now regulated by the Law Reform (Miscellaneous Provisions) (Scotland) Act, 1940, s. 1.
[55] *Gloag on Contract,* 2nd ed., p. 104; *Allen* v. *McCombie's Trs.,* 1909 S.C. 710.
[56] *Morton's Trs.* v. *Robertson's Judicial Factor* (1892) 20 R. 72.
[57] See p. 38, *supra,* note 42, and cases there cited.
[58] *Norval* v. *Abbey,* 1939 S.C. 724.   [59] See Proof, *infra,* p. 36.
[60] See Lord Wensleydale in *Grey* v. *Pearson* (1857) 6 H.L.C. 61 at p. 106; *J. L. Kier & Co. Ltd.* v. *Whitehead Iron & Steel Co. Ltd.* (1938) 54 T.L.R. 452.
[61] *Hunter* v. *General Accident, etc., Assurance Corporation,* 1909 S.C. 344; affd. 1909 S.C. (H.L.) 30; *Izzard* v. *Universal Insurance Co. Ltd.* [1937] A.C. 773.

question with the promoters of a company,[62] or of a guarantee contained in a printed form of agreement supplied by the creditor,[63] or of a private Act of Parliament,[64] or in a " leonine " bargain,[65] or to prevent a person gaining from his own default or wrong.[66] The principle has been held not to extend to informal guarantees *in re mercatoria.*

Another principle is that of two possible constructions the court will generally prefer that which makes a contract as against one which will deprive it of operative effect.[67] If the language is very vague the court may decide that the contract cannot be enforced.[68]

An important rule of construction is that of *ejusdem generis,* that is, where a list of things is followed by general words such as " or any other " the general words are limited in meaning to things of the same class as those in the preceding list.[69] But the things enumerated must all be of the same *genus* or description.[70] The general words may be so general as to exclude the principle, such as " all whatever." [71]

Where particular cases are provided for by a contract without any general or inclusive words there is a presumption that similar cases not expressly provided for are excluded, on the principle *expressio unius est exclusio alterius.*

(c) **Proof in questions of construction.**—The general rule is that the language used is alone to be looked to, but in certain circumstances it gives way and extrinsic evidence is allowed to explain or contradict the terms of the written contract.

Where a formal deed has been executed, not merely parole evidence of the intention of the parties, but of all prior communings between the parties, is excluded.[72] The general rule excluding extrinsic evidence applies to all conditions which the law would imply in the absence of express stipulation by the parties. Further, it is incompetent to prove a verbal agreement to add to the terms of a written contract, though not contradictory of its terms express or implied. But in some cases

---

[62] *Gluckstein* v. *Barnes* [1900] A.C. 240.
[63] *Aitken's Trs.* v. *Bank of Scotland,* 1944 S.C. 270; 1945 S.L.T. 84.
[64] *Colquhoun* v. *Glasgow Procurators' Widows' Fund,* 1908 S.C.(H.L.) 10.
[65] *e.g., Harrower, Welsh & Co.* v. *McWilliam,* 1928 S.C. 326—payment for goods according to the amount stated in the bill of lading whether that amount was actually shipped or not.
[66] *Robinson* v. *Baker* [1929] K.B. 513.
[67] *Hillas & Co. Ltd.* v. *Arcos Ltd.* (1932) 147 L.T. 503.
[68] *Bishop & Baxter* v. *Anglo-Eastern Trading Co.* [1943] 2 All E.R. 598; *cf. Leavey & Co.* v. *Hirst & Co.* [1943] 2 All E.R. 581.
[69] Ersk., iii, 4, 9.
[70] *United Towns Electric Co. Ltd.* v. *Att.-Gen.* (1938) 55 T.L.R. 382; *Minister of Pensions* v. *Ballantyne,* 1948 S.C. 176.
[71] But see *Turner* v. *Wilson,* 1954 S.C. 296.
[72] *Inglis* v. *Buttery & Co.* (1878) 5 R.(H.L.) 87.

such evidence has been allowed, as where the writing was merely a document *in re mercatoria*, or an I O U.[73]

Where an ambiguous term is used extrinsic evidence is not admissible to explain it, if patent, *i.e.*, obviously ambiguous from the context. The document must be construed as best can be. But where the ambiguity is latent, *i.e.*, only disclosed by the surrounding circumstances, such evidence is admissible, for example, as to the identity of the parties or the subject-matter of the contract.[74]

It is always competent to lead evidence as to the circumstances surrounding the parties at the time the contract was made,[75] but not, as a rule, as to their actings during the operation of the contract as evidence of their intention unless in contracts of ancient date.[76] And where something depends on the extent of the knowledge of parties at the time of entering into the contract, evidence is admissible.[77]

Extrinsic evidence is necessarily admitted where a reference to the oath of the defender or a proof by his writ subsequent to the contract [78] is permissible, for these if successful amount to an admission by defender of pursuer's case. The court can then take evidence as to what the real bargain was.

Again, extrinsic evidence is allowed where the question of the intention of the parties is with or between third parties who have an interest to prove what the real intention was, as, for instance, to prove that a transaction in the form of a sale was really by way of security.[79]

Another and important exception to the rule excluding extrinsic evidence is where a custom of trade is allowed to be proved where circumstances arise for which the parties have made no express provision, or to add an unexpressed condition or to give words a meaning they do not naturally bear. This would apply to the effect of varying the incidents which the law ordinarily applies to the contract.[80] The custom of trade must, however, be lawful and not contrary to the general law of the country. It must be known to the parties, or at least notorious, and it must be reasonably fair. A custom of trade cannot be used to contradict the express and unambiguous terms of a contract.[81]

---

[73] *Black* v. *Gibb*, 1940 S.C. 24.
[74] *Robertson's Tr.* v. *Riddell*, 1911 S.C. 14; *Macdonald* v. *Newall* (1898) 1 F. 68.
[75] *Bank of Scotland* v. *Stewart* (1891) 18 R. 957, *per* Lord President Inglis at p. 960.
[76] *Heriot's Hospital* v. *Macdonald* (1830) 4 W. & S. 98; *North British Ry.* v. *Mags. of Edinburgh*, 1920 S.C. 409.
[77] *Jacobs* v. *Scott & Co.* (1899) 2 F. (H.L.) 70; *Taylor* v. *Lewis*, 1927 S.C. 891.
[78] *Stewart* v. *Clark* (1871) 9 M. 616.
[79] Sale of Goods Act, 1893, s. 61 (4); *Rennet* v. *Mathieson* (1903) 5 F. 591; *Gavin's Tr.* v. *Fraser*, 1920 S.C. 674.
[80] Bell's Comm., i, 457; Sale of Goods Act, 1893, s. 55.
[81] *Duthie & Co.* v. *Merson & Gerry*, 1947 S.C. 43; *Tancred, Arrol & Co.* v. *Steel Co. of Scotland* (1890) 17 R.(H.L.) 31.

Lastly, parole evidence is allowed by statute in the case of bills of exchange, promissory notes and cheques relevant to any question of liability thereon [82] other than payment [83] and in the case of proof of trust proof may be by writ or oath of the defender.[84]

Proof of the alteration of a written contract by subsequent verbal agreement cannot be by parole evidence, unless of actings following upon it amounting to *rei interventus* and clearly inconsistent with the written contract,[85] but may be by writ or oath of the opponent.

6. ASSIGNATION OF CONTRACTS

(a) **Definition.**—The assignation of an obligation means the transfer of the rights of a creditor in the obligation to a third party. The granter of an assignation is called the cedent, the grantee the assignee or cessionary. When the assignee transfers the right to a third party the deed is termed a translation, and when the assignee reassigns to the cedent the deed is termed a retrocession. Assignations include translations and retrocessions.[86] An assignation in some cases requires to be in the form of a deed, in others not.

(b) **Form of deed.**—The Transmission of Moveable Property Act, 1862, introduced a form of assignation which may be used by any person in right of a bond or of a conveyance of moveable estate, and a form which may be written on the bond or conveyance itself. Bonds in this connection include personal bonds of every kind, decrees of court, policies of assurance, protests of bills or promissory notes and assignations. Moveable estate includes all personal debts and obligations and moveable or personal property or effects of every kind. The form simply states the consideration and assigns the bond or other deed described.

(c) **How transfer completed.**—*By assignation in writing and intimation.*—Intimation of the assignment to the holder of the property transferred or the debtor in the obligation is necessary to complete the transfer of the property or rights from cedent to assignee. Such intimation has the effect both of divesting the old creditor of his right and of putting the debtor under the duty of paying to the new creditor in place of the old.

The most formal method of intimation is proper notarial intimation attested by notarial instruments. Formal intimation may be made [87]

---

[82] Bills of Exchange Act, 1882, s. 100; *Pert* v. *Bruce,* 1937 S.L.T. 475.
[83] *Robertson* v. *Thomson* (1900) 3 F. 5, approved in *Nicol's Trs.* v. *Sutherland,* 1951 S.C.(H.L.) 21.
[84] Trusts (Scotland) Act, 1696 (Blank Bonds and Trusts Act, 1696).
[85] *Lavan* v. *Gavin Aird & Co.,* 1919 S.C. 345.
[86] The Transmission of Moveable Property (Scotland) Act, 1862.   [87] *Ibid.*

(1) by a notary delivering a certified copy of the deed to the debtor in presence of two witnesses, the evidence of which is a certificate to that effect in statutory form; and (2) by the holder of the assignation, or anyone authorised by him, transmitting a copy by post, certified as correct, a written acknowledgment of the receipt of the copy being evidence of intimation. Anything, however, which brings home to the debtor a distinct knowledge of the assignation is equivalent. Thus, a charge upon a bond at the instance of the assignee, or his citation of the debtor in an action for payment, is equivalent. So also any act of the debtor undertaking to pay or acknowledging the debt to the assignee, or paying interest to the assignee. But mere private knowledge, though it may put the debtor in bad faith in a question with the assignee, is not equivalent to intimation in competition with other properly completed assignations, legal or voluntary—that is, in a question between assignees. And there is a class of assignations, namely, legal and judicial, which, being themselves public, require no intimation in order to give them priority over other assignations of the same right, *e.g.*, the act and warrant of the trustee in a sequestration. In this class of assignation intimation is still necessary to prevent the debtor paying to the former creditor.

By delivery.—Writing is not in all cases required for a valid assignation. Thus, in the case of corporeal moveables and certain classes of debts the right to which runs with the voucher, as bank-notes, bills payable to bearer or bills blank indorsed, transfer, whether by way of sale or security, is complete by mere delivery. It is otherwise, and writing and intimation are required, if corporeal moveables are in the hands of a third party, and in some cases where statute-law requires a written transfer, as in the case of ships and patent rights.

By indorsation and delivery.—In certain cases the law merchant, for the convenience of traders, recognises indorsation as an equivalent to the deed of assignation. This is so in the case of a bill of exchange payable to order, a promissory note, a cheque and a bill of lading, these being negotiable documents. Where the obligation therein contained is transferred by mere indorsation and delivery, intimation is not required.

By transfer of document of title.—A " document of title " is defined by the Factors Acts and Sale of Goods Act to include any bill of lading, dock warrant, warehouse-keeper's certificate, and warrant or order for delivery of goods, and any other document used in the ordinary course of business as proof of the possession or control of goods, or authorising or purporting to authorise, either by indorsement or delivery, the possessor of the document to transfer or receive goods thereby represented.[88]

Where goods are represented by a document of title the transfer of the document coupled with intimation completes the assignation. Transfer without intimation is, however, enough in the case of a bill of lading. The transfer may be by indorsement, or where the document is by custom or by its express terms transferable by delivery, or makes the goods deliverable to bearer, then by delivery.[89] Intimation is necessary, except, as above noted, in the case of a bill of lading, in order to complete the right of the transferee.[90]

(d) What contracts are assignable.—Not all contracts are assignable· It is settled that a claim for payment of money is assignable. Contracts involving mutual obligations, other than payment for goods or services rendered, are generally unassignable.[91] But where a contract involves obligations other than payment of money the question of assignability depends generally upon whether the obligations involve an element of *delectus personae*—that is, when the personality of the contracting party may be of importance.[92] Thus, while a partner in a firm may assign his rights in the firm he cannot make the assignee a partner.[93]

The question of whether there is *delectus personae* arises sharply in the case of executorial contracts, *i.e.*, contracts containing obligations to do or not to do something, as distinct from obligations which are immediately performed, as in a sale over the counter. Thus, there is *delectus personae*, and therefore no assignability, where the contract is for personal services involving literary, artistic or professional skill.[94] A servant cannot be transferred, without his consent, to the employment of a party he has not agreed to serve.[95] On the other hand, a contract for the execution of work to be done through the instrumentality of ordinary labourers involves no element of *delectus personae*, and the contractor may validly assign the performance of the contract to another, but will not, therefore, free himself from liability if the

---

[88] Factors Acts, 1889, s. 1 (4), 1890, s. 1; Sale of Goods Act, 1893, s. 62. Not the registration-book of a motor-car—*Pearson* v. *Rose & Young Ltd.* (1950) 66 T.L.R. (Pt. 2) 886; *Joblin* v. *Watkins* (1948) 64 T.L.R. 464.

[89] The Factors Act, 1889, s. 11; the Factors (Scotland) Act, 1890, s. 1.

[90] *Connal & Co.* v. *Loder & Ors.* (1868) 6 M. 1095, *per* Lord Justice-Clerk Inglis at p. 1110. Intimation to the custodier is probably not necessary in the case of pledge of documents of title to goods by a mercantile agent—Factors Act, 1889, s. 3; Factors Act, 1890, s. 1; *Inglis* v. *Robertson & Baxter* (1898) 25 R.(H.L.) 70.

[91] *Kemp* v. *Baerselman* [1906] 2 K.B. 604; *Grierson, Oldham & Co. Ltd.* v. *Forbes, Maxwell & Co.* (1895) 22 R. 812; *International Fibre Syndicate* v. *Dawson* (1901) 3 F.(H.L.) 32.

[92] *Boulton* v. *Jones* (1857) 2 H. & N. 564; *Cole* v. *Handasyde & Co.*, 1910 S.C. 68 at p. 70.

[93] Partnership Act, 1890, s. 31.

[94] *Cole* v. *Handasyde & Co.*, *supra*, *per* Lord President Dunedin at p. 73.

[95] *Berlitz School of Languages* v. *Duchene* (1903) 6 F. 181; *Nokes* v. *Doncaster Amalgamated Collieries Ltd.* [1940] A.C. 1014.

contract is not performed.[96] It is a question of the intention of the parties whether both rights and liabilities may pass to an assignee. Where no *delectus personae* is present, a contracting party may undoubtedly get others to perform the services contracted for without assigning the contract.[97] And where the death of a party to an obligation takes place, his personal representatives, while liable on his contracts to the extent of the deceased's estate, are not liable for personal services undertaken by him. Where the assignation is by operation of law, as in bankruptcy, the trustee cannot carry out contracts in which the personal qualities of the bankrupt were relied on.[98]

(e) **Effect of assignation.**—Where a contract involving a personal obligation is validly assigned, the general rule is expressed in the legal maxim *assignatus utitur jure auctoris*—an assignee exercises the right of his cedent. The assignee has all the rights of action which the cedent had under the contract, and the debtor may plead against the assignee any defence which was available against the cedent at the time the assignation was intimated.[99] Thus, if the cedent was in breach of a material condition of the contract, and so could not enforce the obligation which he assigns, the assignee has no higher right. If the debtor had a good plea of compensation against the cedent at the time of intimation of the assignation it would remain open to him against the assignee. And if the contract were reducible in a question with the cedent on the ground of misrepresentation, fraud, etc., it remains so reducible in the hands of the assignee. Thus an insurance company may reduce the policy on the ground of misstatement by the assured in his declaration, though the policy has been sold to a bona fide purchaser.[1]

The debtor may, however, be barred from pleading against the assignee a defence open to him against the cedent, as where the terms of intimation of the assignee show that the assignee relies on the apparent right and the debtor takes no exception,[2] or the debtor, knowing he has a defence, makes payments to the assignee.

Again, where the obligation is contained in a negotiable instrument the maxim does not apply, for a bona fide holder for value of such an instrument holds it free from any defects in title of a prior party to the

---

[96] *Cf. Shank's Exrs.* v. *Aberdeen Ry.* (1850) 12 D. 781; *Stewart* v. *Reavell's Garage* [1952] 1 T.L.R. 1266.

[97] *Stevenson & Sons* v. *Maule & Son,* 1920 S.C. 335.

[98] *Anderson* v. *Hamilton & Co.* (1875) 2 R. 355, *per* Lord Neaves; *Caldwell* v. *Hamilton,* 1919 S.C.(H.L.) 100.

[99] Bell's Prin., § 1468.

[1] *Scottish Equitable etc., Co.* v. *Buist* (1877) 4 R. 1076; affd. (1878) 5 R. (H.L.) 64.

[2] *Mangles* v. *Dixon* (1852) 3 H.L.C. 702, *per* Lord St. Leonards L.C.

bill.[3] This element of negotiability may be present not only in the case of bills of exchange, promissory notes and cheques during their currency, but also in transferable bonds and debentures.[4]

7. Extinction of Contractual Obligations

A contractual obligation may be extinguished by (1) performance, or payment and discharge or by certain equivalents, namely, (2) novation, (3) delegation, (4) confusion, (5) compensation; and by (6) prescription; (7) impossibility of performance, and (8) breach of the contract.

(1) Performance, payment and discharge.—Performance.—When a contractual obligation has been fully performed it is, of course, at an end.

Payment and discharge.—The obligation of a debtor to pay a debt which has become due is extinguished when he has made or tendered payment to the creditor in the appropriate manner and at the proper place.   When payment is so tendered it is the duty of the creditor to accept payment.

Where the debtor is released from his obligation by the creditor without payment this is termed acceptilation.

(a) *Duty of debtor to tender payment*

When a debt is actually due and exigible it is the duty of the debtor to tender payment.   Accordingly a party who has sold and delivered goods would be entitled, unless a period of credit is provided either expressly or by the custom of the particular trade, to raise an immediate action for the price.   This he would be entitled to do without even sending in an account or making a demand for payment, although such a course is not usually to be recommended.   On the other hand he may not.   If, for instance, a bill of exchange for the amount of a debt has been accepted by the debtor, while there is an implied obligation on him to make payment on the day when the bill is payable, it is not dishonoured and cannot be sued upon until presented for payment.[5]

Method of payment.[6]—A debtor is not discharged of his obligation to pay unless he tenders payment in the appropriate manner.   Thus, if a debtor disregards a stipulation by a creditor for a particular method of payment or if he adopts some method of payment not in the ordinary

---

[3] Bills of Exchange Act, 1882, s. 29 (1) (*b*).
[4] It may be present in a bill of lading, but as against stoppage *in transitu* only—*Fuentes* v. *Montis* (1868) L.R. 3 C.P. at 276; *Leduc* v. *Ward* (1888) 20 Q.B.D. 475; *Scrutton on Charterparties, etc.*, 17th ed., pp. 169–170.
[5] Bills of Exchange Act, 1882, ss. 46, 47.
[6] As to the modern development of payment by confirmed credit, see Gow, *The Mercantile and Industrial Law of Scotland* at 182 and 1959 S.L.T.(News) 45.

course of business and affording facilities for fraud, *e.g.*, a cheque to bearer,[7] or a cheque sent by post, he takes the risk of his remittance being lost or stolen.[8] If there is no express provision to the contrary a creditor is within his rights in refusing to accept an offer of payment in any form other than legal tender, that is, gold coin of the realm and notes of denominations of less than five pounds of the Bank of England up to any amount, silver and cupro-nickel up to forty shillings and bronze up to one shilling.[9] Notes of the Scottish banks are not legal tender anywhere.[10] If a cheque is sent, the creditor, if he does not mean to accept it, must return it at once, otherwise he will be held to have accepted payment.[11] When payment by cheque is accepted, however, it operates merely conditional payment, the condition being that the cheque is honoured. The condition is resolutive and the debt is extinguished, but it revives if the cheque is not honoured.[12] But if the creditor who has accepted a cheque fails to present it for payment within a reasonable time with resulting loss to the debtor the debt is held to be discharged to the extent of such loss,[13] as, for instance, should the bank fail in the interval.

Place of payment.—The legal implication is that the debtor is bound and entitled to tender payment to the creditor at his residence or place of business.[14] In the absence of arrangement to the contrary any expenses resulting from payment elsewhere than at the creditor's residence fall upon the debtor, *e.g.*, a difference in exchange.[15]

(b) *Obligation of Creditor to accept payment*

It is the duty of a creditor to accept payment when offered. But, while he may agree to accept payment by instalments, he is not bound to accept partial payment.[16] Further, he is under no obligation to receive payment before it is due. And a creditor who is taking no active steps to enforce his debt is under no obligation to accept an offer of payment made by anyone but the debtor or someone having his authority.[17] But if he is taking measures to enforce payment or to realise securities, he is bound to accept payment by, and to grant an assignation to, anyone who can show an interest to intervene, such

---

[7] *Robb* v. *Gow Bros. & Gemmell* (1905) 8 F. 90.
[8] *Pennington* v. *Crossley & Sons Ltd.* (1897) 13 T.L.R. 513.
[9] *Glasgow Pavilion Ltd.* v. *Motherwell* (1903) 6 F. 116, *per* Lord Young. Coinage Act, 1870, s. 4; Coinage Act, 1946, s. 1; Currency and Bank Notes Act, 1954, s. 1.
[10] In time of national emergency these notes and postal orders may temporarily be made legal tender, *e.g.* Currency (Defence) Act, 1939, s. 2.
[11] *Pollock* v. *Goodwin's Trs.* (1898) 25 R. 1051.
[12] *Leggatt Bros.* v. *Gray*, 1908 S.C. 67.
[13] Bills of Exchange Act, 1882, s. 74; *Hopkins* v. *Ware* (1869) L.R. 4 Ex. 268.
[14] *Haughhead Coal Co.* v. *Gallocher* (1903) 11 S.L.T. 156.
[15] *Shrewsbury* v. *Shrewsbury* (1907) 23 T.L.R. 277.
[16] *Wilson's Trs.* v. *Watson & Co.* (1900) 2 F. 761, *per* Lord Moncreiff at p. 770.
[17] *Smith* v. *Gentle* (1844) 6 D. 1164, *per* Lord Mackenzie.

as a friend of the debtor.[18] And a co-obligant who has paid the debt, or more than his proportionate share, is entitled to claim from the creditor an assignation of the debt, any securities held for it and any diligence that may have been done on it, to enable him to work out his relief against his co-obligants.[19] This only applies, however, where he has paid the debt to the creditor in full.[20]

(c) *Appropriation of payments.—Ascription by debtor*

When a debtor owes more than one debt to the same creditor he is entitled on making a payment to ascribe it to any one or more of the debts which may suit him, and a creditor who has received a payment ascribed by instructions of the debtor to a particular debt has no right to apply the payment to meet some other liability of the debtor to him.[21] A creditor may, however, decline to accept payment of principal when interest is due and unpaid. Thus, if there is only one debt, with arrears of interest, and the debtor, in making a remittance, ascribes it to part payment of the principal, this is not a proposal to which the creditor is bound to accede, but if he keeps the money he must apply it in accordance with the debtor's instructions.[22] Where money is sent by someone on behalf of the debtor as a compromise in settlement of the whole debt the creditor has no right to take it as part payment, and, if he keeps the money, the inference will be that he has agreed to the proposed compromise and that the debt is discharged.[23]

Unappropriated payments.—Rights of creditor.—If a debtor makes a payment without any direction or previous agreement as to the debt to which it is to be ascribed, he impliedly leaves it to the creditor to ascribe it as he pleases.[24] Accordingly the intention of the creditor, express, implied or presumed, governs the application of the money.[25] Thus he may ascribe it to an unsecured debt, leaving unpaid a debt for which he holds security. This he may do in a question not merely with the debtor himself but, for instance, with a cautioner for the debtor.[26] He may ascribe it to interest, leaving principal unpaid.[27] Again the creditor may ascribe indefinite payments to a debt which does not bear interest, rather than to a debt which does.[28] But

---

18 *Ibid.*
19 *Fleming* v. *Burgess* (1867) 5 M. 856.
20 *Ewart* v. *Latta* (1865) 3 M.(H.L.) 36.
21 Bell's Prin., § 563; *Brenes & Co.* v. *Downe,* 1914 S.C. 97.
22 *Wilson's Trs.* v. *Watson & Co.* (1900) 2 F. 761, *per* Lord Moncreiff.
23 *Punamchand* v. *Temple* [1911] 2 K.B. 330.
24 *Jackson* v. *Nicoll* (1870) 8 M. 408.
25 *Long Bros.* v. *Owners of the Mecca* [1897] A.C. 286; *Deeley* v. *Lloyds Bank Ltd.* [1912] A.C. 756.
26 *Anderson* v. *North of Scotland and Town and County Bank,* 1909 2 S.L.T. 262.
27 *Watt* v. *Burnett's Trs.* (1839) 2 D. 132.
28 *Bremner* v. *Mabon* (1837) 16 S. 213.

indefinite payments cannot be ascribed by the creditor to a debt in which the party who made them is merely a cautioner in preference to one in which he is principal debtor,[29] to a debt which is known to be disputed,[30] to a debt of which the debtor was unaware,[31] to a deb which, under statutory provisions, cannot be enforced,[32] nor contrary to general understanding between the parties.[33] The creditor may render an account containing separate items of debt without making any appropriation without barring himself from appropriation afterwards.[34]

Where there is an account current on which payments are made without any appropriation by the debtor the general rule, at least between banker and customer, is that payments on the credit side of the account are held to extinguish the items on the debit side in the order of their date. This is known as the rule in *Clayton's Case*.[35] The rule probably only applies to accounts between banker and customer or where the account substantially involves the relation of banker and customer between the parties.[36] It does not apply to separate accounts kept at a bank.[37] It does not apply to a tradesman's account where partial payments have been made but the element of advances made by the creditor is absent.[38] It is of importance chiefly where there is a cautioner.

(d) *Proof of payment*

Where no receipt or discharge can be produced to prove the extinction of a debt the general rule, to which, however, there are numerous exceptions, is that the extinction of the claim must be effected in the same way as it was constituted. A debt may be one which is constituted or proved by a document, or it may be one which, without being so constituted, is sued for as the result of a contract between the parties, or it may have been constituted verbally.

Where the creditor founds on a document of debt, *e.g.*, a bond, bill, or I O U, proof of payment is limited to the writ, such as a discharge or receipt, or to the oath of the creditor.[39] But proof by

---

[29] *Dickson* v. *Moncrieff* (1853) 16 D. 24.
[30] *Dougall* v. *Lornie* (1899) 1 F. 1187.
[31] *Couper* v. *Young* (1849) 12 D. 190
[32] *Maitland* v. *Rattray* (1848) 11 D. 71.
[33] *Scott* v. *Sandeman* (1852) 1 Macq. 293.
[34] *Hay & Co.* v. *Torbet*, 1908 S.C. 781.
[35] *Devaynes* v. *Noble*, 3 Ross Leading Cases, 643 at p. 654; (1816) 1 Mer. 529; *cf. Royal Bank* v. *Christie* (1838) 1 D. 745; affd. (1841) 2 Rob. 118; *Deeley* v. *Lloyds Bank Ltd.* [1912] A.C. 756.
[36] *McLaren* v. *Bradley* (1874) 2 R. 185. It has now been held in England to apply only to banking accounts—*Re Diplock* [1948] Ch. 465 at 555.
[37] *Bradford Old Bank* v. *Sutcliffe* [1918] 2 K.B. 833.
[38] *Hay & Co.* v. *Tarbet, supra*.
[39] *Bishop* v. *Bryce*, 1910 S.C. 426; *Keanie* v. *Keanie*, 1940 S.C. 549; *vide* Reference to Oath, *infra*, p. 54.

parole evidence may be allowed of grounds for holding the debt to be extinguished in other ways than by actual payment, and that the creditor has no proper right to have the document of debt with him [40]; for example, evidence of some transaction or settlement between the creditor and the debtor subsequent to contraction of the debt which necessarily leads to the conclusion that the debt was discharged,[41] such as a settlement of accounts followed by a discharge in general terms.[42]

Where the money debt arose under a contract *ad factum praestandum, e.g.,* to supply goods or render services, if the contract was in writing proof of the payment of money becoming due under it must be by writ or oath of the creditor.[43]

If the debt has arisen under a verbal contract, the method of proof of payment depends on the nature of the contract. Thus parole evidence is admissible to prove payment of a loan which is not vouched by any writing,[44] and of wages due under a verbal contract of service, at least if under £100 Scots (£8 6s. 8d.).[45] But where there has been a substantial interval between the delivery of goods and the alleged payment, or if the sale was on credit, proof is limited to the writ or oath of the seller, even although the sale was purely verbal.[46]

Proof of payment by writ of the creditor.—Where a debtor proposes to prove payment by the writ of the creditor the writ produced need not be probative.[47] A receipted account, however, only lays the onus of proof of non-payment on the creditor, and such proof may be by parole evidence.[48] But where an acknowledgment of the receipt of money has been made in a formal and probative deed, such as acknowledgment of the receipt of the price in a disposition of lands, the creditor is limited in proof of non-payment to the writ or oath of the party founding on it, *i.e.,* the debtor. Where, however, a creditor avers that his acknowledgment has been obtained by fraud he may prove the averments by parole evidence.[49]

The meaning of a discharge must be arrived at by a consideration of its terms, and parole evidence of the intention of the party who granted it is incompetent.[50] Fitted accounts, *i.e.,* accounts between

---

[40] *Bishop* v. *Bryce, supra.*
[41] *Chrystal* v. *Chrystal* (1900) 2 F. 373.
[42] *Neilson's Trs.* v. *Neilson's Trs.* (1883) 11 R. 119.
[43] *Foggo* v. *Hill* (1840) 2 D. 1322, *per* Lord Fullerton at p. 1334.
[44] *Newlands* v. *M'Kinlay* (1885) 13 R. 353.
[45] *Brown* v. *Mason* (1856) 19 D. 137.
[46] *Young* v. *Thomson*, 1909 S.C. 529; *Hope Bros.* v. *Morrison*, 1960 S.C. 1.
[47] *Paterson* v. *Paterson* (1897) 25 R. 144.
[48] *Henry* v. *Miller* (1884) 11 R. 713.
[49] *Grant's Trs.* v. *Morison* (1875) 2 R. 377, *per* Lord President Inglis at p. 380. See also Cheques Act, 1957, s. 3.
[50] *M'Taggart* v. *Jeffrey* (1830) 4 W. & S. 361, *per* Lord Wynford at p. 367.

parties who have had business transactions, rendered by one party and docqueted as correct by the other without any express discharge, raise a presumption, which the party who avers an outstanding account must overcome, that all claims were settled.[51] But a general discharge is not binding if granted on a specific payment when both parties were unaware that any further claim was maintainable. A bank passbook made up and initialled by the officers of the bank as correct does not preclude parole evidence that a particular entry has been made by mistake.[52]

Presumption of payment.—Certain debts are presumed to be paid, so as to put the onus of proof of non-payment on the creditor, *e.g.*, tavern bills, after the guest has left.[53] The production of receipts for three consecutive instalments of a termly payment, such as feu-duty, rent, or interest, raises a presumption (*apocha trium annorum*) that all prior instalments have been paid. The presumption of payment is mainly inferred from the reiteration of discharges without reservation of the creditor's claim to prior unpaid instalments, which no prudent man is presumed to do, not from a single discharge for the amount due for several terms.[54]

If a document of debt is in the hands of the debtor, although *ex facie* undischarged, the debt is presumed to be paid, as expressed in the legal maxim *chirographum apud debitorem repertum praesumitur solutum*. But the creditor may prove by parole evidence that the document got into the hands of the debtor by mistake, or by some method which gives him no right to retain it, and that the debt has not in fact been paid.[55]

The proof of payment may also be affected by the operation of one or other of the shorter prescriptions.[56]

(2) Novation.—A debt, though not expressly discharged, may be extinguished by novation when a new obligation by the same debtor is substituted for it. If a debt for which a new debt is substituted is regularly discharged no claim can be founded upon it, in the absence of any grounds for impeaching the validity of the discharge.[57] The general presumption, however, is that if there is no discharge, but a new obligation is undertaken, the original obligation is not extinguished, and the new one is to be regarded as a security for it, or as the addition of a more convenient way of enforcing payment.[58] Thus where one

---

[51] *Laing* v. *Laing* (1862) 24 D. 1362; *Struthers* v. *Smith*, 1913 S.C. 1116.
[52] *Commercial Bank of Scotland* v. *Rhind* (1857) 19 D. 519; revd. 3 Macq. 643.
[53] *Barnet* v. *Colvil & Henderson* (1840) 2 D. 337.
[54] Dickson, *Evidence*, s. 177; Walker & Walker, *The Law of Evidence*, 58.
[55] *Henry* v. *Miller* (1884) 11 R. 713.   [56] *Vide* Prescription, *infra*, p. 50 *et seq.*
[57] *Gloag on Contract*, 2nd ed., p. 725; *Jackson* v. *MacDiarmid* (1892) 19 R. 528.
[58] Gloag, *op cit.*, p. 724; *Anderson* v. *M'Dowal* (1865) 3 M. 727.

document of debt is given in place of another, as where a bill is renewed, or a new promissory note given for one in danger of prescribing, but the original document is not given up or cancelled, the presumption is that any rights depending upon it are still preserved. So where several parties are liable on a bill, and a new bill for the same debt is granted by one or more of them, but the old bill is retained by the creditor, those who are parties to the old bill may be made liable on it in the event of the new bill not being met, and if the granters of the new bill have paid it the others are liable in relief to them.[59] It is probably competent to prove by parole evidence that the arrangement was that the original debt, with all claims depending upon it, was given up.[60] But where a bill or note is given up, on a new one being granted, it will be inferred that the creditor has elected to trust to the new security, and on its failure he has no right to recover the original bill and found upon it.[61] This does not raise any presumption that a claim for interest arising *ex lege* on the original document is abandoned.[62] And when a document of an obligatory character, such as a bill or cheque, is given for a debt resting upon open account, as distinguished from one where the balance between the parties has been agreed upon, the presumption is strongly against novation. Hence a bill or cheque, unless paid at maturity, does not extinguish the debt for which it is taken.[63] The principle of novation applies to other obligations besides payment of a money debt, but is best illustrated by the latter.

(3) **Delegation of debt.**—A debt, though not expressly discharged, may be extinguished by delegation when the obligation of a new party is substituted for that of the original debtor. Delegation is a form of novation. There is a strong presumption against delegation.[64] It is not as a general rule in the option of a debtor to substitute the obligation of another party, who may be a person of no means, for his own.[65] The consent of the creditor must in some way be obtained. It may be given at the time when the obligation is constituted, or a custom of trade may create an implied condition that delegation is permitted.[66] When consent is not given at the time when the obligation is constituted, the debtor must prove that the creditor assented to his discharge. The consent is not to be inferred merely from the fact that the creditor

---

59 *Stevenson* v. *Campbell* (1806) Hume 247.
60 *Hope Johnstone* v. *Cornwall* (1895) 22 R. 314.
61 Gloag, *op. cit.*, p. 724.
62 *Hope Johnstone* v. *Cornwall, cit. sup.*
63 *Leggatt Brothers* v. *Gray*, 1908 S.C. 67.
64 *M'Intosh & Son* v. *Ainslie* (1872) 10 M. 304, *per* Lord President Inglis at p. 309.
65 *University of Glasgow* v. *Yuill's Trs.* (1882) 9 R. 643.
66 *North* v. *Basset* [1892] 1 Q.B. 333.

accepts a new obligant. Prima facie he is accepted as a further security. Thus when a partner in a firm retires, and the business is carried on by the remaining partners without the introduction of a new one, it will not be presumed that a creditor of the original firm has voluntarily given up the liability of a retiring partner for a debt due by the firm at the time he retired and accepted the liability of the firm as newly constituted in substitution for his original claim. But where a creditor who is in possession of a document of debt gives it up, at the same time obtaining the obligation of a new debtor, there is a presumption that the real agreement between the parties is that the liability under the original document of debt is discharged.[67]

(4) Confusion.—Confusion arises where the same person comes to be both debtor and creditor under the obligation. Thus where the right of a creditor in a debt is assigned to the debtor, or the creditor undertakes liability on the debt, the debt is said to be extinguished *confusione*, for no person can be creditor or debtor to himself.[68] The fusion of creditor and debtor may also arise where the debtor succeeds to his creditor. Confusion only operates, however, where a party becomes both debtor and creditor in the same capacity. If, for example, the debtor becomes the executor of his creditor on the latter's death, the debt is not extinguished. If the debtor is not the primary obligant, but is, for example, merely a cautioner and becomes the creditor, the debt is not necessarily extinguished by confusion. It may be enforced against the principal debtor.[69]

(5) Compensation.—Compensation is the term used in Scotland for the right to set one claim off against another, with the result that if equal in amount both are extinguished; if not equal, that the larger claim is extinguished *pro tanto*.

The law of compensation is founded on the Compensation Act, 1592, which in effect provides that compensation operates only by way of exception. That is to say, compensation does not *ipso facto* extinguish a debt. To have that effect it must be pleaded in an action. Accordingly, a debt which might have been extinguished earlier by the fact that the debtor had a claim against the creditor, and on which compensation, if pleaded, would have been sustained, cannot in any subsequent question be regarded as having been extinguished.[70] If, therefore, a creditor will not admit a claim by the debtor to set off a debt due by the creditor to him, the only course for the debtor is to refuse payment, and so compel the creditor to bring an action for the debt, in which compensation can be pleaded.

---

[67] *Stevenson* v. *Lord Duncan* (1805) Hume 245.
[68] Ersk., iii, 4, 23.
[69] *Ibid.* iii, 4, 24.   [70] Bell's Prin., § 575.

Requisites of compensation.—(a) The debtor must plead compensation before a decree against him for the debt. Otherwise he will have to sue for it in a special action. (b) In a pure question of compensation arising between parties who are both solvent, the debts in respect of which compensation is pleaded must be both liquid, that is, actually due and the amount ascertained.[71] Thus a debt not yet payable by the pursuer, or on which his liability is only contingent,[72] or a claim of damages arising from a separate contract or other relations between the debtor and creditor, or a claim which is disputed, unless instantly verifiable, cannot relevantly be pleaded in defence to an action for payment. (c) There must be *concursus debiti et crediti, i.e.,* the parties must be debtor and creditor in the same legal capacity and at the same time. Thus a party sued for a private debt could not set off a debt due to him as an executor.[73] On the other hand, the death of a party and the confirmation of his executor do not affect rights of compensation.[74] The *concursus* must have existed before bankruptcy of either party, and the plea must not be inconsistent with the good faith of the contract under which the claim arose. When compensation is pleaded and sustained it dates back to the period when the concourse of debtor and creditor took place, with the result that no interest is due *ex lege* from that date, even though the debt was not originally liquid and therefore not pleadable during part of the period of concourse. In short, both compensation and liquidation draw back to the date of concourse.

(6) Prescription.—Contractual obligations may, under the rules of prescription, be extinguished by lapse of time. On the other hand, the effect of these rules may be merely to alter the onus and method of proof. In so far as the rules of prescription relate to mercantile contracts, obligations are extinguished by the negative prescription, but the shorter prescriptions, or, more properly, limitations—the triennial, the quinquennial, the sexennial, and the vicennial [75]—merely alter the onus or the mode of proof. The general rule in the construction of the shorter prescriptions is that they introduce no presumptions, but enact certain specific and imperative rules on the subject of probation. Only indirectly therefore can they be said to extinguish obligations.

The Negative prescription.—Obligations prescribe, *i.e.,* cease to be enforceable, after the expiry of twenty (formerly forty) years—a rule

---

[71] Bell's Comm., ii, 122; *e.g., Fulton Clyde Ltd.* v. *J. F. McCallum & Co. Ltd.,* 1960 S.L.T. 253.   [72] *Paul & Thain* v. *Royal Bank* (1869) 7 M. 361.
[73] *Stuart* v. *Stuart* (1869) 7 M. 366.
[74] *Globe Insurance Co.* v. *Scott's Trs.* (1849) 11 D. 618; affd. 7 Bell's App. 296; *Mitchell* v. *Mackersy* (1905) 8 F. 198, overruling *Gray's Trs.* v. *Royal Bank* (1895) 23 R. 199.   [75] For Septennial Prescription of Cautionary Obligations, see Chap. 11.

referred to as the negative prescription.[76] It applies generally to all contractual rights and obligations except such as amount to a real right of property in lands. Thus the lapse of twenty years excludes the enforcement of a right contracted for, such as a debt due by a bank on current account not operated on for twenty years,[77] or an obligation to restore moveable property lent or given in security, or to pay a principal sum due under a bond of corroboration,[78] and is a bar to the reduction of a contract even on the ground of fraud or any other extrinsic ground,[79] or to a claim of repetition of money paid by mistake.[80] On the other hand, the negative prescription does not bar the challenge of a right which can only be defended by founding on a nullity, such as a forged deed,[81] or a deed entirely unauthenticated,[82] or possession traceable to theft,[83] or on a sale of property which is *extra commercium* and so could not have been lawfully acquired.[84] In the case of annuities, where there is no direct claim to the capital sum, the negative prescription only applies to the claim for each term's payment, in contrast to ordinary bonds where it extinguishes the principal sum, and, with it, any further claim for interest. Again, where the right is one which the creditor may exact or not at pleasure (*res merae facultatis*), the negative prescription is excluded, *e.g.*, a contractual right such as the right to alter a common stair.

The prescriptive period starts from the day when it first became possible for the creditor to enforce his right by action.[85] Thus a bond prescribes from the date of payment, not from the date of granting.[86] Where the party who has for the time being the right to enforce the claim is in minority, or is under some legal disability which prevents him from asserting his right, the years during which the minority or legal disability lasts are not to be deducted in reckoning the twenty years.[87]

If the running of the twenty years is interrupted before it has expired the period prior to the interruption ceases to count, as where a debtor makes a written acknowledgment of the existence of the

---

[76] The Prescription Acts, 1469, 1474 and 1617; Conveyancing (Scotland) Act, 1924, s. 17, as amended by Conveyancing Amendment (Scotland) Act, 1938, s. 4.
[77] *Macdonald* v. *North of Scotland Bank,* 1942 S.C. 369.
[78] *Yuill's Trs.* v. *Maclachlan's Trs.,* 1939 S.C.(H.L.) 40.
[79] *Cubbison* v. *Hyslop* (1837) 16 S. 112, *per* Lord Corehouse at p. 119.
[80] *Magistrates of Edinburgh* v. *Heriot's Trust* (1900) 7 S.L.T. 371.
[81] *Graham* v. *Watt* (1843) 5 D. 1368; affd. (1846) 5 Bell's App. 172.
[82] *Kinloch* v. *Bell* (1867) 5 M. 360.
[83] Stair, ii, 12, 10.
[84] *Magistrates of Dumbarton* v. *Edinburgh University,* 1909, 1 S.L.T. 51.
[85] *Simpson* v. *Melville* (1899) 6 S.L.T. 355.
[86] Ersk., iii, 7, 36.
[87] Conveyancing (Scotland) Act 1924, s. 17, as amended by the Conveyancing Amendment (Scotland) Act, 1938, s. 4. The Acts have altered the law as to deduction.

claim,[88] or makes payment of part of the principal sum or interest,[89] or where there is judicial interruption, such as an action against the debtor, or diligence if regularly effected,[90] or a petition by the creditor for the debtor's sequestration,[91] or liquidation.[92]

The short prescriptions.—The triennial prescription.—By the Prescription Act, 1579, all actions of debt for house mails, *i.e.*, the rent of a house, men's ordinaries, *i.e.*, for example, accounts for board and lodging, servants' fees, *i.e.*, wages, merchants' accounts, and other the like debts that are not founded upon written obligations, must be pursued within three years, otherwise the creditor shall have no action, except by proof by the writ or oath of the debtor. The terms of the Act have been held to cover, *inter alia*, the accounts of a law agent, architect, engineer, stockbroker and surgeon, but not cases of mercantile agency,[93] nor the accounts of insurance brokers for disbursements in respect of policies.[94] " Merchants " means shopkeepers, or other persons engaged in trade analogous to that of a shopkeeper, such as builders or contractors. It does not apply generally to mercantile transactions. The general principle is that it applies to accounts between trader and consumer, not to accounts between manufacturer or producer and retailer, or between a merchant and his correspondent. There is some doubt as to whether it applies to an account for the supply of a single article.[95]

Where payments should have been made termly each separate term runs a separate course of prescription, *e.g.*, servants' wages.[96] In other cases prescription runs from the close of the account between the parties,[97] when it is calculated from the date of the last item which is enforceable, even where the items vary in character.[98] Prescription begins to run on the account as soon as it is definitely closed, though a new one be opened between the same parties.[99]

The triennial prescription does not extinguish the debt. But whereas within the three years the onus is on the debtor to prove payment, after the three years the creditor must prove not only that the debt was incurred but that it is still resting owing, and he is limited

---

[88] *Marr's Exrx.* v. *Marr's Trs.,* 1936 S.C. 64.
[89] *Briggs* v. *Swan's Trs.* (1854) 16 D. 385.
[90] Bell's Prin., § 621.
[91] Bankruptcy (Scotland) Act, 1913, s. 105.
[92] Companies Act, 1948, s. 318.
[93] *Brown* v. *Brown* (1891) 18 R. 889; see Mercantile Agents, Chap. 2.
[94] *Lamont, Nisbet & Co.* v. *Hamilton* (1904) 12 S.L.T. 624.
[95] *Millar on Prescription,* p. 128; *Gobbi* v. *Lazaroni* (1859) 21 D. 801.
[96] *Douglas* v. *Duke of Argyll* (1736) Mor. 11102.
[97] Bell's Prin., § 631.
[98] *Ross* v. *Cowie's Exrx.* (1888) 16 R. 224.
[99] *Christison* v. *Knowles* (1901) 3 F. 480

to proof by the writ or oath of the debtor.[1] But constitution and resting owing being established the burden of proof of subsequent payment reverts to the debtor. The principle of interruption is not properly applicable to cases of triennial prescription. But the assertion of the debt in a legal process, even though not that in which prescription has been pleaded, excludes the prescription, *e.g.*, where the plea was one of compensation.[2] Time during which the creditor is in minority is not deducted.

The writ of the debtor relied on to redargue the effect of the triennial prescription need not be probative,[3] or addressed to the creditor.[4] Thus an entry in the debtor's books amounting to an explicit statement of the debt is proof by his writ.[5] The writ of the debtor if adduced as proof either of constitution or of resting owing may be dated within the three years.[6] The amount of the debt may, after proof of constitution and of resting owing, be proved by parole evidence.[7]

The quinquennial prescription.—The quinquennial prescription, introduced by the Prescription Act, 1669, applies to rents after the tenant has left and bargains concerning moveables provable by witnesses, *i.e.*, verbal bargains not requiring writing for their constitution. In the case of rents it applies only after the tenant has removed, and is excluded by action or diligence within the five years.[8] In the case of bargains concerning moveables, the Act applies to all sales, locations and other consensual contracts concerning moveables to the constitution of which writing is not necessary.[9] It applies to the sale of a single article.[10] In the case of the quinquennial prescription the years during which the creditor is in minority are to be deducted. After the five years, proof of constitution and resting owing are limited to writ or oath of the debtor.

The sexennial prescription.—The sexennial prescription applies to bills of exchange, and was introduced by the Bills of Exchange (Scotland) Act, 1772. By the Act diligence or action upon a bill of exchange, or inland bill or promissory note is excluded unless diligence be raised and executed or action commenced thereon within six years after the term at which the sum in the bill or note became exigible.

1 *Borland* v. *Macdonald Ltd.*, 1940 S.C. 124; 1940 S.L.T. 194.
2 *Sloan* v. *Birtwhistle* (1827) 5 S. 742; Bankruptcy (Scotland) Act, 1913, s. 105; *Millar on Prescription*, p. 117.
3 Dickson, *Evidence*, § 512; Walker & Walker, *Law of Evidence*, 137–138, 146.
4 *Wilson* v. *Scott* (1908) 15 S.L.T. 948.
5 *Neilson* v. *Magistrates of Falkirk* (1899) 2 F. 118.
6 *Johnson* v. *Tillie, Whyte & Co.*, 1917 S.C. 211.
7 *Fife* v. *Innes* (1860) 23 D. 30.
8 *M'Donald* v. *Jackson* (1826) 5 S. 28.
9 Ersk. Inst., iii, 7, 20.
10 *Kennard & Sons* v. *Wright* (1865) 3 M. 946.

The bill or note then ceases to exist as an enforceable document of debt and proves nothing, although it may be used along with other evidence to set up the debt. But proof of the constitution of the debt contained in the bill or note, and of the resting owing, by writ or oath of the debtor, thereafter is permitted. If the creditor can vouch the debt in some other way he may prove the constitution in the manner applicable to the particular debt, notwithstanding that he has taken a bill or note which has prescribed. The prescription is interrupted by the years of minority of the creditor. Bank notes are excluded from the operation of the Act, but cheques have been held to be included.[11]

When proof by writ of resting owing is attempted the general rules as to the character of the writ required are the same as those applicable in the case of the triennial prescription.

The vicennial prescription.—The Prescription Act, 1669, provides " that holograph letters and holograph bonds and subscriptions in compt books without witnesses not being pursued for within twenty years shall prescribe in all time thereafter, except the pursuer offer to prove by the defender's oath the verity of the said holograph bonds and letters and subscriptions in the compt books." The Act has been held to extend to all holograph writings on which an obligation can be founded,[12] except probably bills and notes.[13] After the expiry of twenty years the creditor has to establish the genuineness of the writing, not merely of the signature, by the debtor's oath. Once he has done so he need not establish the resting owing. The only admissible exception to the operation of the Act is action or diligence by the creditor within the twenty years. Hence mere payment of interest by the debtor will not exclude the operation of the Act.[14] The years of the creditor's minority fall to be deducted.

In addition to the above prescriptions and limitations various statutes limit the period within which certain contracts may be enforced.[15]

Reference to oath.—When liability is sought to be set up by a reference to the oath of the debtor he is not entitled to resort to a general denial, but must answer all relevant questions. If a defender denying liability in his oath qualifies the denial the qualification, if it negative liability, is said to be intrinsic of the oath, but if it does not necessarily negative liability it is said to be extrinsic and liability may

---

[11] *M'Craw* v. *M'Craw's Trs.* (1906) 13 S.L.T. 757.
[12] *Mowat* v. *Banks* (1856) 18 D. 1093; *Macadam* v. *Findlay,* 1911 S.C. 1366; *Baird* v. *Baird's Trs.,* 1954 S.L.T. 68.
[13] *Drummond* v. *Lees* (1880) 7 R. 452. As regards I O U s there are conflicting decisions in the Outer House (*Dick* v. *Thomson's Trs.,* 1929 S.L.T. 637).
[14] *Macadam* v. *Findlay,* 1911 S.C. 1366.
[15] *e.g.,* the Moneylenders Act, 1927, s. 13 (1).

be inferred. Thus if the defender in his oath qualifies his denial of liability by saying that the debt was compensated or the goods supplied were not according to contract the qualification is extrinsic, and the oath amounts to an admission of the debt. When, however, the qualification is, for example, that money which is sued for in repayment of a loan was received by the debtor in payment for services rendered, that is an intrinsic qualification and is therefore negative of the receipt of a loan.[16] The court may refuse to allow a reference if it considers that such allowance would be inequitable.[17]

(7) **Impossibility of performance.**—Where it is impossible for an obligant to perform a contractual obligation the contract may or may not be terminated in consequence. The result may be, on the one hand, to put an end to all rights and duties, present and future, between the contracting parties, or, on the other hand, merely to relieve a contracting party from being compelled to perform in terms of his obligation, but leave him liable in damages to the other for failure so to perform. These alternative results may follow either in the case where it never was possible to perform the obligation, or in the case where it has become impossible to perform it owing to the occurrence of some event.

Impossibility personal to the obligant.—Where the impossibility is personal to the obligant the obligation continues. Thus it is no defence that performance is " commercially impossible," *e.g.,* the obligant has not enough money or that a loss will result to him,[18] or that it cannot be done within the time stipulated,[19] or that performance depends on some third party over whom the obligant has no control, as where a person becomes cautioner or gives a guarantee for the payment of a debt or fulfilment of a contract.[20]

Impossibility at date of contract.—Where an obligation at the time the contract was made was impossible of performance either then or in the future, the contract is void. This is so where the impossibility of performance is due to the mutual error or mistake of the parties, the parties having contracted on the assumption of the existence of a certain thing or state of things.[21] There is then no real consent between the parties. This is so also, and there is held to be no real consent, where, though the element of mutual mistake is not present,

---

[16] *M'Kie* v. *Wilson,* 1951 S.C. 15.
[17] *Hamilton* v. *Hamilton's Exrx.,* 1950 S.C. 39.
[18] *Hong-Kong and Whampoa Dock Co.* v. *Netherton Shipping Co.,* 1909 S.C. 34; *Tsakiroglou & Co. Ltd.* v. *Noblee Thorl* [1962] A.C. 93 (Closing of Suez Canal).
[19] *Steel* v. *Bell* (1900) 3 F. 319; *cf. Milligan* v. *Ayr Harbour Trs.,* 1915 S.C. 937.
[20] *Stevenson* v. *Wilson,* 1907 S.C. 445, *per* Lord Dunedin at p. 455.
[21] *Vide* Error or Mistake, *supra* p. 17 *et seq.*

the thing intended to be done is known by all reasonable men to be physically or legally impossible. The rule also extends to cases where both deem performance possible but its impossibility is part of the stock of knowledge of the average man, *e.g.*, an agreement to discover treasure by magic.[22] On the other hand, an obligation impossible of performance at the time of contracting, but expected to have become possible at the date fixed for performance, *e.g.*, by an advance in scientific knowledge or a change in the law, may be binding.[23] In such cases, performance not being manifestly impossible, the party who undertook the obligation takes the risk of its impossibility. Where there is legal impossibility, as in a case of something *extra commercium* and therefore not saleable, such as a seat in a parish church, there is no contract. Such contracts are to be distinguished from contracts which can be performed but only by the commission of an illegal act.[24]

Supervening impossibility.[25]—Where, on the other hand, an obligation possible at the time of contracting becomes impossible by an alteration in circumstances before the date of performance, the legal effect may be affected by the nature of the circumstances from which the impossibility results. These circumstances may be (1) a change in the law, (2) a change in circumstances material to the contract, and (3) a change in the condition of the obligant.

(1) If, before the time fixed for performance, a change in the law has made the act prestable under the contract either impossible or illegal,[26] performance is excused. The validity of a contract is, however, not affected by a change in the law which merely alters the nature of the rights conferred or the burden of the obligation imposed. Accordingly, an obligation may be enforceable although subsequent legislation has made it more difficult or expensive to perform. Thus a party who has undertaken to supply goods must do so although the imposition of a duty may have made his contract unprofitable.[27] Where the contract is of extended or indeterminate duration and the supervening illegality is of a temporary nature, as where the contract is affected by a declaration of war, the effect seems to depend on the probability or otherwise of the illegality ceasing during

---

22 Indian Contract Act, 1877, s. 56.
23 *Clifford* v. *Watts* (1870) L.R. 5 C.P. 577, *per* Willes J. at p. 585.
24 *Vide* Illegal Contracts, *supra*, p. 25 *et seq.*
25 See Lord Cooper's *Selected Cases*, 124.
26 *Shipton Anderson & Co.* v. *Harrison* [1915] 3 K.B. 676; *Metropolitan Water Board* v. *Dick Kerr & Co.* [1918] A.C. 119; *Marshall* v. *Glanvill* [1917] 2 K.B. 87; *Leith School Board* v. *Rattray's Trs.*, 1918 S.C. 94; *British Movietonews Ltd.* v. *London & District Cinemas Ltd.* [1951] 2 T.L.R. 571.
27 *McLellan* v. *Adam* (1795) Mor. 14247; *Trinidad Shipping Co.* v. *Alston* [1920] A.C. 888.

the currency of the contract.[28] The effect at common law of a
declaration of a state of war on contracts between subjects of
the King and his enemies is to abrogate any subsisting right to
further performance, but not accrued rights such as the right to
payment of a debt. Enforcement of such accrued rights is,
however, suspended.[29]

(2) Where a contract involves anything to be done in the future,
and something occurs to render fulfilment by one party impossible, the contract may be terminated and both parties freed
from their obligations by the terms, express or implied, of the
contract or implied by the court. In Scotland, where by the
nature of the contract its performance depends on the existence
of a particular thing or state of things, the failure or destruction
of that thing or state of things without default on either side
liberates both parties.[30] A common case for which there is not
usually an express provision in a contract is the accidental
destruction of some particular thing to which the contract
relates and without which it cannot be performed. As a general
rule, if a thing essential to a contract perishes without fault of
either party the party whose obligation is thereby rendered
impossible is excused from performance or payment of damages.[31] This is known as *rei interitus*. Whether the contract
is ended or not thus depends on whether the continued existence
of the thing was an express or to be implied condition. Another
case is where, though there may be no physical impossibility
involved, emerging circumstances have effected a radical change
in the nature of the obligations undertaken by one or both of
the parties. The contract may be terminated on the theory that
its basis is gone. This is known as " frustration of the adventure." [32] For example, there may have been non-occurrence of
an expected event, as in the cases known as the " *Coronation
Cases*," arising out of the postponement of the Coronation of

---

[28] *Leiston Gas Co.* v. *Leiston Urban Council* [1916] 2 K.B. 428; *Tamplin Steamship Co.*
v. *Anglo-Mexican, etc., Co.* [1916] 2 A.C. 397; *Modern Transport Co.* v. *Duneric
Steamship Co.* [1917] 1 K.B. 370; *Bank Line Co.* v. *Capel* [1919] A.C. 435; *Trevalion*
v. *Blanche,* 1919 S.C. 617; *James B. Fraser & Co. Ltd.* v. *Denny, Mott & Dickson Ltd.,*
1944 S.C.(H.L.) 35; 1945 S.L.T. 2. As to effect of change in foreign law, see *Aurdal*
v. *Estrella,* 1916 S.C. 882; *Kursell* v. *Timber Operators* [1927] 1 K.B. 298.

[29] *Ertel Bieber & Co.* v. *Rio Tinto Co. Ltd.* [1918] A.C. 260. For a discussion of the
legal effect on contractual rights of residence in enemy or enemy-occupied territory,
see *Re Anglo-International Bank Ltd.* [1943] Ch. 233, and cases there cited.

[30] Bell's Prin., 10th ed., § 29.

[31] *Taylor* v. *Caldwell* (1863) 3 B. & S. 826; *London Shipping Co.* v. *The Admiralty,* 1920
S.C. 309. There may be " constructive " total destruction, *e.g., Mackeson* v. *Boyd,*
1942 S.C. 56 (house requisitioned by military).

[32] *Tamplin Steamship Co.* v. *Anglo-Mexican, etc., Co.* [1916] 2 A.C. 397; *Bank Line* v.
Arthur Capel & Co. [1919] A.C. 435, *per* Lord Finlay L.C. at 442.

King Edward VII.[33] An occurrence may, on the one hand, have been foreseen and expressly provided against in the contract. The contract may nevertheless be at an end. For example, where the contract provides against non-fulfilment due to delay from specified and excepted causes, the party so protected by the contract may not be entitled to insist on the other party performing his part, and so the contract may be at an end. It is a condition implied by the court that if performance after delay would in a business sense be a different thing from performance at the proper time, delay, though due to an excepted cause, will entitle the other party to rescind the contract. For example, if a ship is chartered to convey goods, but is prevented from proceeding to the port of loading by perils of the sea excepted in the contract of affreightment, the charterer may be entitled to declare the contract at an end in respect that, taking into consideration the object for which the ship was required, the offer of the ship came too late for the implement of the original contract.[34] An occurrence may, on the other hand, not have been expressly provided against, and the rights of the parties will then depend on the nature of the occurrence. When frustrating circumstances supervene there is no longer any obligation as to future performance though up to that moment obligations which have accrued remain in force.[35] It may be added that mere changes in economic conditions, however deeply they affect the contract, do not amount to frustration so as to avoid it.[36]

(3) Lastly, performance of an obligation may be rendered impossible by a change in the condition of an obligant, such as his

---

[33] e.g., *Krell* v. *Henry* [1903] 2 K.B. 740; *Chandler* v. *Webster* [1904] 1 K.B. 493; but see *Maritime National Fish Ltd.* v. *Ocean Trawlers Ltd.* [1935] A.C. 524. In so far as these cases decided that, by English law, money paid in advance cannot be recovered if the fulfilment of the consideration for which it was paid becomes impossible, these cases are not now authoritative. Such moneys can be recovered in Scotland under the doctrine of restitution—the *condictio causa data causa non secuta* of the civil law; *Cantiere San Rocco* v. *Clyde Shipbuilding Co.*, 1923 S.C.(H.L.) 105. The adjustment of the rights and liabilities of parties to a contract governed by English law in such cases is now regulated by the Law Reform (Frustrated Contracts) Act, 1943; see also *Fibrosa Spolka Akcyjna* v. *Fairbairn Lawson Combe Barbour Ltd.* [1943] A.C. 32, overruling, on this point, *Chandler* v. *Webster, cit. sup.*

[34] *Jackson* v. *Union Marine Insurance Co. Ltd.* (1874) L.R. 10 C.P. 125; *cf. The Penelope* [1928] P. 180; *Court Line Ltd.* v. *Dant and Russell Inc.* (1939) 161 L.T. 35 (ship detained in river by boom erected by belligerents).

[35] e.g., *Bank Line* v. *Arthur Capel & Co.* [1919] A.C. 435; *Hirji Mulji* v. *Cheong Yue SS. Co.* [1926] A.C. 497; *James B. Fraser & Co. Ltd.* v. *Denny, Mott and Dickson Ltd.*, 1944 S.C.(H.L.) 35; 1945 S.L.T. 2; see *per* Lord Wright at 42–44 as to theory of frustration.

[36] See *Gloag on Contract*, 2nd ed., 354; *Davis Contractors Ltd.* v. *Fareham Urban District Council* [1956] A.C. 696.

death, insanity, serious illness and, in certain cases, his bankruptcy. Thus, if a man has been chosen for a contract in reliance on his personal qualities, his continuance in life is an implied condition of the contract and his death annuls it, as in the case of contracts of service, partnerships, agency and cautionary obligations. If the contract is for personal service of a kind which can only be rendered by the sane, the insanity of the obligant must determine it.[37] If a musician is engaged for a particular occasion and is too ill to perform, neither party is under any liability.[38] The bankruptcy of a partner dissolves the partnership, subject to any agreement to the contrary.[39]

8. BREACH OF CONTRACT

(1) Rights of party not in breach.—General.—The primary right of a creditor in a contractual obligation is to performance of the obligation. He may accordingly invoke the aid of the court to compel it by action for specific implement or interdict, as the case may be. He may seek compensation in damages if such remedy is appropriate.[40] Also the breach of a contract by one party may, if the breach be material, entitle the other party to rescind and so put an end to the contract. These are positive remedies. But in some cases the law also confers on the creditor in an obligation the right to adopt, if he choose, defensive measures to enable him to minimise loss which the default of the debtor threatens to entail. Thus the creditor may have the right of withholding performance of obligations incumbent on him until those in which he is creditor are performed or secured. Retention and lien are such measures. The competency of such defensive measures is based on the principle of mutuality, that is, that obligations in a contract are as a rule interdependent and conditional on each other. The kind of remedy open depends in general on the terms of the contract and the nature of the breach.

Anticipatory breach.—The contract entitles the parties not merely to performance when due, but to the expectation of performance when it shall fall due. Hence, if one party intimates by word or act a definite and distinct refusal to implement his obligation before the time for performance has arrived and there has therefore been no actual breach, the other is entitled to treat this as a repudiation of the

---

[37] *Liddell* v. *Easton's Trs.*, 1907 S.C. 154.
[38] *Robinson* v. *Davison* (1871) L.R. 6 Ex. 269.
[39] Partnership Act, 1890, ss. 33, 47.
[40] *McArthur* v. *Lawson* (1877) 4 R. 1134 (partnership); *McLellan* v. *Dallas's Ltd.*, 1928 S.C. 503.

contract and avail himself at once of the remedies that may be open.[41] The possible remedies in such cases are rescission and damages. It should be noted that repudiation by the debtor does not by itself amount to rescission, for one party to a contract cannot by his own act rescind it, but, as it has been said, it puts it in the power of the other party to agree to a rescission subject to his claim of damages.[42] The party entitled to rescind may, on the other hand, refuse to rescind and, when the date of performance arrives, sue for damages calculated on the loss inflicted on him as at that date.[43] If, however, he does not rescind on repudiation, a defence which arises subsequently, e.g., impossibility of performance,[44] will then be available to the party refusing to perform. Two contrasting situations may determine whether an act is one of repudiation or not. If, on the one hand, performance is due on demand or on the occurrence of an event which may happen at any time, an act by which a party voluntarily puts it out of his power to perform may be treated as equivalent to a refusal to perform,[45] e.g., A sells to C an article which A has agreed to sell to B on demand. If, on the other hand, the date for performance is a fixed future date, the act will amount to repudiation only if the act be irremediable,[46] e.g., if A could buy back from B before the date for delivery to C, the sale by A would not be irremediable in this sense.

(2) When the various remedies are available.—Positive remedies.— These are specific implement or interdict, rescission and damages.

Specific implement.—The right to demand specific implement is in the law of Scotland the general rule, with exceptions where that remedy is unsuitable.[47] The court may be applied to for a decree *ad factum praestandum* or for interdict against doing an act of repudiation, according to the circumstances.[48] If such a decree be disregarded it is contempt of court and makes the defender liable to imprisonment.[49]

---

[41] *Hegarty & Kelly* v. *Cosmopolitan Insurance Corporation Ltd.,* 1913 S.C. 377, *per* Lord MacKenzie; *Forslind* v. *Bechely-Crundall,* 1922 S.C.(H.L.) 173. Contrast *Cory (William) & Son Ltd.* v. *London Corporation* [1951] 1 K.B. 8 (causing frustration, not anticipatory breach by repudiation).

[42] *White & Carter (Councils) Ltd.* v. *McGregor,* 1962 S.L.T. 9.

[43] *Dingwall* v. *Burnett,* 1912 S.C. 1097.

[44] *Avery* v. *Bowden* (1856) 6 E. & B. 953 (outbreak of war).

[45] *North British Ry.* v. *Benhar Coal Co.* (1886) 14 R. 141; *Omnium d'Entreprises* v. *Sutherland* [1919] 1 K.B. 618.

[46] *Harvey* v. *Smith* (1904) 6 F. 511, *per* Lord Kinnear.

[47] The English law is different. Part implement and damages Scots law rejects as a new bargain. *Stewart* v. *Kennedy* (1890) 17 R.(H.L.) 1, *per* Lord Watson at 9.

[48] See *Burn Murdoch on Interdict,* 168–171; *Waddell* v. *Campbell* (1898) 25 R. 456; *Kelso School Board* v. *Hunter* (1874) 2 R. 228.

[49] By the Law Reform (Scotland) Act, 1940. There is no automatic order to imprison on breach of a decree of specific implement in most cases, if the respondent can show he is not wilfully refusing to comply with the decree.

In certain cases the court will not grant decree for specific implement. There appear to be five such cases.[50] These are:

(1) Where the obligation is to pay money. As a rule the sole remedy of a creditor for payment of money is to enforce payment by diligence, that is, taking the debtor's property under judicial authority and using it to pay the debt.[51]

(2) Where forced compliance would be worse than none, e.g., of a contract of service or partnership.[52]

(3) If compliance is impossible.

(4) Where the court could not enforce a decree of specific implement, e.g., where the defender is a foreigner who cannot be imprisoned, or a corporate body whose whole members could not be imprisoned.[53]

(5) Where there is no *pretium affectionis*, that is, where not a specific article but a kind is contracted for, e.g., in the case of general sales of a commodity which can be obtained in open market, such as so many bushels of wheat, not a particular lot of wheat. The purchaser's remedy is to supply himself at the expense of the seller and sue him for any loss.[54]

Rescission.[55]—*Materiality of breach.*—In breach of contract a party entitled to rescind may, as a general rule, if he prefer, claim damages instead of rescission. Or he may have both remedies. But rescission is not always open. To justify rescission a breach of contract must be material. A minor breach may give rise only to a claim of damages or a right to withhold performance of counter-obligations.[56] What is material is a pure question of the intention of the parties, that is, the construction of the contract which may be express on the point or not. If not express, the court must decide as to the materiality of the breach. In relation to materiality a breach may be of four kinds. First, there may be a total failure of performance or refusal to perform by one party. The other is entitled to treat it as repudiation and may rescind. Secondly, where there is a failure or refusal to perform one of several stipulations, the question of its materiality arises, e.g., where a comedian

---

[50] The grant or refusal of the remedy of specific implement depends on the nature of the obligation to be implemented, e.g., *Rollo's Trs.* v. *Rollo,* 1940 S.C. 578.

[51] A contract to take up and pay for debentures in a company is an exception—Companies Act, 1948, s. 92. In other cases, there may be an order to consign the money in court, that is, *ad factum praestandum, e.g., Mackenzie* v. *Balerno Paper Mill Co.* (1883) 10 R. 1147.

[52] *M'Arthur* v. *Lawson* (1877) 4 R. 1134; *Pert* v. *Bruce,* 1937 S.L.T. 475 (partnership).

[53] *Gall* v. *Loyal Glenbogie Lodge* (1900) 2 F. 1187; contrast *Collins* v. *Barrowfield Oddfellows,* 1915 S.C. 190.

[54] *Union Electric Co. Ltd.* v. *Holman & Co.,* 1913 S.C. 954.

[55] See also Irritancies, *infra.*

[56] *Wade* v. *Waldon,* 1909 S.C. 571.

engaged to perform in a theatre in the following year and undertook to give the theatre fourteen days' notice of his readiness to fulfil, accompanied by bill matter, before the date he was to appear. Though ready to fulfil his engagement, he failed to give notice and supply the bill matter, and the theatre manager cancelled his engagement. The comedian was held entitled to damages in respect that his own breach was not so material as to justify the other party in rescinding.[57] Thirdly, where a contractual obligation has been performed but the performance is defective, materiality of the breach depends on the degree of failure. Thus, if the contract provides for the supply of goods of a certain kind or quality or for work to be done of a certain character or quality, failure in quality is generally material. And in the Sale of Goods Act, 1893,[58] it is provided that the delivery by seller to buyer of a smaller quantity than ordered, or of a larger quantity, or of the goods ordered mixed with goods of a different description, are all failures sufficiently material to justify rejection of the goods by the buyer. On the other hand, in the case of a sale of machinery, a remediable defect probably does not justify rejection. The buyer's remedy is to have the defect cured at the expense of the seller.[59] Fourthly, where the failure is in respect of time of performance, in general its materiality depends on the nature and terms of the contract. Thus stiuplations as to the time of payment for goods sold are not treated as material conditions so as to justify rescission unless so intended.[60] Apart from payment of money, in mercantile contracts there is a presumption that time is of the essence of the contract. Thus in contracts for the sale or supply of goods which vary in price in the market from day to day stipulations as to the time of giving or taking delivery are prima facie of the essence of the contract. But it is not an absolute rule that a short delay will justify rescission. It may then be justifiable if the market for the goods is subject to sudden fluctuations in prices, or if the conduct of the party in delay was such as to cause a reasonable apprehension that he had no intention of performing. Otherwise, a party must wait for a time reasonable in the circumstances before taking the extreme step of declaring the contract rescinded.[61] In each case it is a question of degree and much depends on the particular circumstances and the reasonableness or otherwise of the conduct of the parties.

If then a breach is not so material as to justify rescission only damages are due as a positive remedy.

[57] *Wade* v. *Waldon,* 1909 S.C. 571; contrast *Shaw* v. *McDonnell* (1786) Mor. 9185.
[58] s. 30.
[59] *Morrison & Mason Ltd.* v. *Clarkson Bros.* (1898) 25 R. 427, *per* Lord McLaren at 437.
[60] Sale of Goods Act, 1893, s. 10 (1).
[61] *Carsewell* v. *Collard* (1892) 19 R. 987, *per* Lord McLaren; affd. 20 R.(H.L.) 47.

Defensive measures.—*Retention and lien.*—These remedies are always open, but are used mainly where rescission would confer no advantage, *e.g.*, where the contract is already partly performed, or where the breach is not sufficiently material to justify it. Retention is the right to refuse to pay a debt when due. Lien is the right to refuse to deliver a particular thing. The word retention is sometimes used to include lien. Retention is to some extent an exception to the rule that there may not be refusal to pay a debt admittedly due unless compensation may be pleaded. It is in a sense an extension of compensation. On the principle of compensation only debts which are liquid and presently payable may be pleaded by way of set-off against each other and be extinguished. Retention is permissible not only where compensaton can be pleaded, but also in two other cases where compensation could not be pleaded, namely, where both claims arise under the same contract,[62] and where the creditor in a liquid claim is bankrupt. Thus the creditor in an unliquidated claim of damages for breach of a contract may withhold payment of a debt due by him under the contract until the amount due to him as damages is established. Thus a carrier's claim for freight may be met by a claim of damages for injury to the goods carried caused by the carrier's negligence.[63] Or again, a purchaser of goods may retain the price against his claim for loss due to the seller's failure to deliver the goods within a specified or reasonable time.[64] And a debtor to a bankrupt who has an illiquid claim against the bankrupt is entitled to withhold payment until the amount of the illiquid claim is ascertained and then to compensate the one against the other, and that even though the two claims do not arise out of the same contract.[65]

An example of lien is the right of a party employed to do work, and who has thereby been placed in possession of property of his employer, to retain the property until his claim for work is satisfied, *e.g.*, a bookbinder. This is known as special lien.[66] It is really a right in security and is considered under Rights in Security.

(3) Damages for breach of contract

(a) **General.**—The contract may itself provide for the consequences of a breach, or it may not. Where there is no provision, or where a conventional provision is found to be unenforceable, the party aggrieved is in almost all cases legally entitled to damages. The principal exception is where the breach consists in failure to pay money at

---

[62] *e.g., Fulton Clyde Ltd.* v. *J. F. McCallum & Co. Ltd.,* 1960 S.L.T. 253.
[63] *Taylor* v. *Forbes* (1830) 9 S. 113.
[64] *British Motor Body Co. Ltd.* v. *Thomas Shaw (Dundee) Ltd.,* 1914 S.C. 922.
[65] Bell's Comm., ii, 122.
[66] *Paton's Trs.* v. *Finlayson,* 1923 S.C. 872.

the appointed date. Then, though interest may be due, no general damages can be demanded.

(b) Measure of damages.—The claim may be for general damages or for special damages, or for both.

(1) MEASURE OF GENERAL DAMAGES.—THE PRINCIPLE AND ITS CONSEQUENCES.—When damages are claimed for breach of contract it is the aim of the law to ensure that a person whose contract has been broken by the other party shall be placed as nearly as possible in the same position as if it had not.[67] They are, that is, intended as compensation for loss. They are not punishment of the party in breach; and it is irrelevant as a rule to consider what profit was made by the party in breach by breaking his contract.[68] It is also irrelevant to consider the ability of the defender to meet the damages, or on the other hand any injury to the pursuer's feelings or credit or reputation,[69] as in a wrongful dismissal from service.[70]

A further, and important, consequence of the principle of compensation for loss is that a party claiming such compensation is bound to take all reasonable means to minimise his resulting loss. He can recover as damages only the amount which the adoption of such means would have failed to avert.[71] Thus, when a buyer delays to purchase goods in place of those with which he ought to have been supplied by the seller and the price in the market continuously rises, he cannot demand more than the loss he would have sustained if he had bought in the market at once.[72] Conversely, if a buyer has refused to take delivery of and pay for the goods bought, his seller must resell, no matter what the state of the market, if he is to claim the difference between the contract price and the market price from the buyer. These are reasonable means to minimise loss. But it would be unreasonable to require a purchaser to supply himself with goods obtainable only with difficulty and in remote markets.[73]

(2) LIMITATIONS ON THE CLAIM FOR DAMAGES.[74]—Even where a party aggrieved by a breach of contract has taken all reasonable means

---

67 *Chaplin* v. *Hicks* [1911] 2 K.B. 786, *per* Fletcher Moulton L.J. at 794; *Bell Brothers (H.P.) Ltd.* v. *Aitken*, 1939 S.C. 577; *Pomphrey* v. *James A. Cuthbertson, Ltd.*, 1951 S.C. 147. This may involve consideration of the element of tax—*Spencer* v. *Macmillan's Trs.*, 1958 S.C. 300; 1959 S.L.T. 41.
68 *Teacher* v. *Calder* (1898) 25 R. 661; affd. (1899) 1 F.(H.L.) 39; *cf. Watson Laidlaw & Co.* v. *Pott, Cassels & Williamson*, 1913 S.C. 762.
69 Unless the maintenance of the pursuer's credit and reputation was made a term of the contract—*Wilson* v. *United Counties Bank Ltd.* [1920] A.C. 102.
70 These however may found a claim of damages for delict or wrong.
71 *Ross* v. *Macfarlane* (1894) 21 R. 396.
72 *Ireland & Son* v. *Merryton Coal Co.* (1894) 21 R. 989; *Clippens Oil Co.* v. *Edinburgh Water Trs.*, 1907 S.C.(H.L.) 9; Sale of Goods Act, 1893, ss. 50, 51.
73 *Gunter & Co.* v. *Lauritzen* (1894) 31 S.L.R. 359; *Clippens Oil Co.* v. *Edinburgh Water Trs.*, 1907 S.C.(H.L.) 9. 74 See *Gloag on Contract*, 2nd ed., p. 660 *et seq.*

to minimise the consequences of the breach it does not follow that he will necessarily be entitled to recover his loss or the whole of it. The general rule as to the items of damage for which a party in breach may be held responsible has been authoritatively laid down in *Hadley* v. *Baxendale*.[75] The damages which the party not in breach ought to receive should be either (1) such as may fairly and reasonably be considered as arising naturally, that is according to the usual course of things, from such breach of contract itself, known as general damages, or (2) such as may reasonably be supposed to have been in the contemplation of both parties at the time they made the contract as the probable result of the breach of it, known as special damages. The claim may accordingly be limited on two grounds, the one that the loss claimed, though real, is too remote a consequence of the breach of contract; the other, that though the loss is the direct, *i.e.*, not a remote, result of the breach, yet it arises from some exceptional circumstances of which the party in breach was not aware, and the effect of which in causing loss he could not be expected to foresee.[76]

Remoteness of damage.—Remoteness is always a question of circumstances. For example, it has been held that a seller who fails to supply goods will be liable in damages found due, or for loss of profit, on a subcontract by which the buyer may have resold them, provided neither damages nor loss were altogether exceptional.[77] Again, expenses reasonably incurred in consequence of a breach of contract may also be recovered as damages, and possibly the expenses of litigation with a third party, if the ordinary and natural result of the breach.[78] Again, an allowance for the inconvenience and dislocation of business involved in the breach of any mercantile contract is permissible even where no actual pecuniary loss can be established.[79] Again, where the breach consists of failure to do a particular act the cost of having it done may be recovered.[80]

Special or consequential damages.—A claim on this ground may arise, for example, where a party gives an undertaking to do or supply something by a particular date and fails to fulfil it, with the result that the delay has caused the loss of opportunity of using the goods or disposing of them to exceptional advantage, or where the delay has caused loss due to the fact that the particular thing was necessary for

[75] (1854) 9 Ex. 341.
[76] A recent example of the application of these principles is *Collins* v. *Howard* (1949) 65 T.L.R. 598 (damages refused on both branches of the rule).
[77] *Ströms Bruks Aktie Bolag* v. *Hutchison* (1904) 6 F. 486, revd. (1905) 7 F.(H.L.) 131.
[78] *Le Blanche* v. *London and North Western Ry.* (1876) 1 C.P.D. 286.
[79] *Webster* v. *Cramond Iron Co.* (1875) 2 R. 752.
[80] *Duke of Portland* v. *Wood's Trs.*, 1926 S.C. 460; affd. 1927 S.C.(H.L.) 1.

some larger enterprise.[81] There is a claim for such loss only if the party in breach had knowledge of these special facts, and could reasonably have foreseen that a breach was likely to result in such loss.[82]

(3) INTEREST ON DAMAGES.—Where a court decrees for payment of a sum of money as damages, it may include decree for interest thereon.[83]

(4) DAMAGES FOR DELAY IN PAYMENT OF MONEY.—This is a special case. It is a general rule that no damages are due for the consequences of delay in the payment of money.[84] An exception is the breach of contract involved in the failure of a banker to honour his customer's cheque. The customer may recover damages for the resulting injury to his credit.[85] In certain cases, however, while damages are not due, interest may be demanded.

When interest due.—The question whether interest is due *ex lege*, that is, by implication of law, where there is no provision for it, express or implied, in the contract, depends on the nature of the contract out of which the debt arises.[86] There is no clear dividing line of principle. It may be accepted however that interest is due only by usage of trade or by virtue of a principal sum of money having been wrongfully withheld and not paid on the day when it ought to have been paid.[87] But not always then. Thus, it is due *ex lege* or by implication as liquidated damages on a dishonoured bill of exchange, or promissory note [88]; on a loan [89]; on a balance due to or by a mercantile agent [90]; and when a party was deprived of an interest-bearing security, or profit producing corporeal moveable.[91] Interest has been held not to be due on arrears of feuduty [92] or probably of rent,[93] or on an I O U until demand made for repayment,[94] or on open account unless and until action has been raised for payment, when it runs from the date

---

[81] *Gloag on Contract*, 2nd ed., 701.
[82] *Victoria Laundry (Windsor) Ltd.* v. *Newman Industries Ltd.* [1949] 2 K.B. 528; *Pilkington* v. *Wood* [1953] Ch. 770.
[83] Interest on Damages (Scotland) Act, 1958.
[84] *Stephen* v. *Swayne* (1861) 24 D. 158, *per* Lord President McNeill at 163.
[85] *King* v. *British Linen Co.* (1899) 1 F. 928; but see *Gloag on Contract*, 2nd ed., p. 680. Compare Bills of Exchange Act, 1882, ss. 57, 73, which allow interest but provide no damages for loss of credit. In *Gibbons* v. *Westminster Bank* [1939] 2 K.B. 882, it was held that if the customer is not a trader he may be entitled only to nominal damages.
[86] *Haddon's Exrx.* v. *Scottish Milk Marketing Board*, 1938 S.L.T. 230 is a case of implied contract for interest.
[87] *Carmichael* v. *Caledonian Ry.* (1870) 8 M.(H.L.) 119, *per* Lord Westbury at 131.
[88] Bills of Exchange Act, 1882, ss. 57, 89.
[89] *Hope Johnstone* v. *Cornwall* (1895) 22 R. 314.
[90] *Findlay & Co.* v. *Donaldson* (1864) 2 M.(H.L.) 86.
[91] *Kolbin & Son* v. *Kinnear & Co.*, 1931 S.C.(H.L.) 128 at 137.
[92] *Maxwell's Trs.* v. *Bothwell School Board* (1893) 20 R. 958.
[93] *Blair's Trs.* v. *Payne* (1884) 12 R. 104, *per* Lord Fraser at 110.
[94] *Winestone* v. *Wolifson*, 1954 S.C. 77.

of citation of the defender, or intimation has been given that interest will be claimed in the event of non-payment, when it runs from the date in the intimation.[95] In the case of a claim of damages arising out of a breach of contract it runs from the date of decree, that is, the date of constitution of the claim,[96] or earlier if allowed by the Court.[97]

Compound interest, that is, interest on interest, is a demand which can be maintained only in commercial dealings such as an overdrawn bank account,[98] or in breach of trust. It has been refused in arrears of interest on a bond.[99]

(5) CONVENTIONAL DAMAGES.—This is a matter in which absolute freedom of contract is not allowed. A provision in a contract for the incurrence of a penalty, in the event of a breach, will be enforced according to its terms only if it admits of being construed as a fair estimate of damages. The law will not let people punish each other.[1] If it is sustained as a fair estimate it is regarded as liquidated or ascertained damages. Proof of actual damage sustained is then unnecessary,[2] and proof of larger damage is inadmissible.[3] If on the other hand the provision is regarded as a penalty, it is inoperative. There must then be proof of actual loss and the amount recoverable is not limited to the amount of the penalty.[4] It may be noticed that in a sale a provision that the purchaser must deposit in advance a portion of the price, to be forfeited if he fails to carry out his contract, is in substance a penalty, but is not so regarded. And a provision for agreed damages is not a licence to a party to the contract to break it on payment of the penalty[5]; penalties are " by and attour performance."

(6) IRRITANCIES.—A conventional remedy for breach of contract analogous in nature to conventional damage is the conventional irritancy. Remedies for breach of contract may be supplemented by a provision for an irritancy, that is, a right to put an end to the contractual relation on failure to implement it. Such a provision can be

---

[95] *Somervell's Tr.* v. *Edinburgh Life Assurance Co.*, 1911 S.C. 1069 at 1071–1072.
[96] *Roger* v. *J. & P. Cochrane & Co.*, 1910 S.C. 1; *F. W. Green & Co. Ltd.* v. *Brown & Gracie Ltd.*, 1960 S.L.T. (Notes) 43.
[97] Interest on Damages (Scotland) Act, 1958: *R. & J. Dempster Ltd.* v. *Motherwell Bridge & Engineering Co.*, 1964 S.L.T. 113.
[98] *Reddie* v. *Williamson* (1863) 1 M. 228.
[99] *McNeill* v. *McNeill* (1830) 4 W. & S. 455.
[1] *Per* Lord Young in *Robertson* v. *Driver's Trs.* (1881) 8 R. 555.
[2] *Clydebank Engineering Co.* v. *Castaneda* (1904) 7 F.(H.L.) 77.
[3] *Drestal* v. *Stevenson* [1906] 2 K.B. 345.
[4] *Dingwall* v. *Burnett*, 1912 S.C. 1097. In *Cellulose Acetate Silk Co. Ltd.* v. *Widnes Foundry (1925) Ltd.* [1933] A.C. 20, Lord Atkin (and the court) expressly left open the question whether, where a penalty is plainly less in amount that the prospective damages, there is any legal objection to suing upon it or, in a suitable case, ignoring it and suing for damages. [5] *Roberts & Cooper* v. *Salvesen & Co.*, 1918 S.C. 794.

enforced, of course, only by the party aggrieved by the breach.[6]   In such cases the breach cannot as a rule be " purged," that is, wiped out by doing the act or repairing the omission which constituted the breach.   Considerations of hardship in enforcing the irritancy have been held to be out of place where the provision is unambiguous.[7] But this again is a matter in which absolute freedom of contract is not allowed.   It has been laid down that the court has an equitable jurisdiction to allow an irritancy to be purged where its enforcement can be shown to be oppressive, e.g., where the irritancy was sought to be enforced without giving adequate notice that a debt was due.[8] And if what is in terms an irritancy in substance amounts to a penalty it cannot be enforced.   So where in a contract of sale at a price payable in instalments a provision is made for the irritancy of the contract and forfeiture of all that has been paid, this is in substance a penalty and will not be enforced.[9]   An apparent exception is a hire-purchase agreement, but there the instalments include not only part payment of the price, but also payment for the hire of the article and interest on what is unpaid.

---

[6] Bekonlac v. Sinclair's Trs. (1889) 17 R. 144; New Zealand Shipping Co. v. Société des Ateliers, etc. [1919] A.C. 1.
[7] Chalmers' Trustee v. Dick's Trustee, 1909 S.C. 761.
[8] Stewart v. Notson (1864) 2 M. 1414.
[9] Steedman v. Drinkle [1916] 1 A.C. 275.

CHAPTER 2

THE LAW OF AGENCY

1. DEFINITION

AGENCY is a contract, express or implied, whereby one person, the principal, authorises another, the agent, to act on his behalf in a legal relationship between the principal and a third party.

2. CAPACITY.—WHO MAY APPOINT AND BE APPOINTED AS AGENT

The capacity of a principal to contract or otherwise act through an agent is co-extensive with the principal's own capacity to act for himself. Thus a person under full age, *e.g.*, a minor, when acting through an agent can bind or be bound by a third party only to the same extent that a minor can himself bind, or be bound by, one with whom he contracts. On the other hand, a person with limited or no capacity can be appointed by, and act as, agent of another person to the fullest extent. But such an agent has no personal liability or rights beyond what a person of his limited capacity ordinarily has.[1]

3. HOW AGENCY CONSTITUTED

The relationship of principal and agent exists by virtue of the express or implied assent of both principal and agent, and, it may be added, in certain cases arises out of necessity. There is no special form for the constitution of agency. It may be constituted by express appointment by the principal, by implication of law from the actings of the parties, or by subsequent ratification by the principal of acts done on his behalf by the person acting as agent.

(a) Express appointment of agent.—Where an appointment is express it may be oral [2] or in writing. The writing may be formal or informal. When, however, the contract is written the writing is the measure of the authority conferred, and it will not be extended to anything which the terms of the writing do not expressly or impliedly warrant. The formal writing usually takes the form of a power of attorney, frequently granted for the management of affairs abroad, or by a person abroad for the management of his affairs at home; or it may take the form of a factory and commission, a deed generally granted by a landed proprietor leaving Scotland and committing the charge of his estate to a friend or his law agent. Less formal writings may take the form, for example, of letters of mandate or powers of procuration.

---

[1] *Vide* Capacity to Contract, *supra*.   [2] *Pickin* v. *Hawkes* (1878) 5 R. 676.

(b) Implied appointment as agent.—Again, an authority to act as agent may be constituted by implication, as where a man is put into a shop as manager or shopkeeper or permitted to take charge of an office or business and remains in charge with possession of the goods or documents. That will be enough to signify to the public that the man is held out as agent and all the usual powers follow.

Holding out.—The principle of holding out applies chiefly in connection with the dealings of merchants and commission agents. The principle is this, that when one permits another to act for him in a certain course of business repeatedly he is barred *personali exceptione* from denying a grant of authority in a question with a third party with whom the alleged agent has transacted within the scope of such business.[3] Thus where a buyer paid for goods by cash to the seller's agent without challenge and in good faith in a series of transactions and the agent embezzled the money, it was held, in an action for payment at the instance of the sellers against the buyer, that the payments made to the agent were valid in respect that the buyer had no reason to believe that the agent was not entitled to receive the payments in that form.[4] In Scotland a wife has a presumed mandate, while she remains in family with her husband, to provide things proper and necessary for the family, for the price of which the husband is liable. The husband may expressly withdraw her authority so to bind him by advertising that he will not be responsible for her debts or (as now only accepted by the press for advertisement) unless contracted by himself,[5] or by warning individual tradesmen not to look to him for payment.[6] Again, a person may so act as to be precluded from denying the agent's authority, no matter what instructions he gave the agent. Thus, in *Pickering* v. *Busk*,[7] a broker was employed by a merchant to buy hemp. The broker did so, and at the request of the buyer the hemp was left at the broker's wharf. The broker sold the goods. The sale was held good on the principle that if the owner of goods permits a person whose ordinary course of business it is to sell that class of goods to have possession of the goods or of the documents of title to the goods, and the goods are sold to a person who buys them in the belief that the holder has authority to sell, the owner is bound by the sale.[8]

---

[3] *Barnetson* v. *Petersen Bros.* (1902) 5 F. 86.

[4] *International Sponge Importers Ltd.* v. *Watt & Sons* 1911 S.C.(H.L.) 57.

[5] Such advertisement must be proved to have been brought to the notice of a tradesman subsequently claiming from the husband payment of an account incurred by the wife: *Walton on Husband and Wife*, 3rd ed., 207.

[6] See, as to wife's capacity to bind the husband for necessaries supplied to her when living apart from him, *ante*, p. 16.   [7] (1812) 15 East 38.

[8] This is now statutory under s. 2 (1) of the Factors Act, 1889, applied to Scotland by the Factors (Scotland) Act, 1890. *Vide* Mercantile Agents, *infra*, p. 83.

Procuration to sign bills of exchange.[9]—Procuration, which signifies appointment to act for or instead of another and under his authority, is deserving of special attention, where it is procuratory to draw, accept or indorse bills of exchange. The power of procuratory may be granted in so many words: " I, A. B., constitute you, C. D., my procurator, to draw, accept or indorse bills for me in the course of my business." Or it may be implied. It may, for example, arise out of the position in which a man is placed—for example, his being at the head of a business where the power is absolutely necessary for conducting the business.[10] A mere mandate to act as managing clerk and pay and discharge debts does not amount to a procuration to sign bills. Again, procuration by implication will be inferred where there is a course of dealing by the principal recognising the acts of his agent relative to bills, *i.e.*, where the agent has no express power, but has for some time been in the habit of drawing, accepting and indorsing his principal's bills, and the principal has paid or passed the bills in his accounts. Another case where the implication would arise would be where one man has signed the name of another on a bill at his request, and a succession of bills so signed have been presented in the course of business and been paid by the man whose name they bear.

It should be observed that a bill drawn, accepted or indorsed " per pro " is a warning to everybody taking it that it is drawn or indorsed by a person having limited power for special purposes, and a warning to them to see that the bill is being used for the special purposes to which the procurator had a right to apply it.[11] Thus, in *Union Bank* v. *Makin & Sons*,[12] an English firm gave their manager in Scotland a procuratory to sign bills limited to those " necessary to the conducting of business." The manager got discounted at the bank bills indorsed by him " per pro Makin & Sons," the drawers, the acceptances of various firms with which he or his firm were in the habit of dealing having been forged by him on the bills. The bank discounted the bills in ordinary course and in good faith. The manager absconded with the money. It was held, however, that the bank was entitled to recover the money from Makin & Sons as the principals, but only because the bank had exercised all reasonable care, and had no warning that the money was not for the purposes of the business of Makin & Sons.

(c) Ratification of agency.—Agency may further be constituted by subsequent ratification where authority to act has not been created expressly or impliedly, or the agent has exceeded his authority. Such ratification may be express or implied.

---

[9] And *vide* Bills of Exchange, *infra*.
[10] *Edmonds* v. *Bushell & Jones* (1865) L.R. 1 Q.B. 97.
[11] Bills of Exchange Act, 1882, s. 25.   [12] (1873) 11 M. 499.

The effect is as if at the date of the contract between the agent and the third party the authority had existed, except that the rights of third parties acquired before ratification cannot be prejudicially affected by the ratification. There can be no ratification, however, if the act was in its inception void, nor if the contract was not made as on behalf of the principal who seeks to ratify it,[13] nor if the principal was not in existence at the date of the contract,[14] as where the promoters of a company enter into a contract on behalf of a company before its incorporation. The company, after formation, would require to enter into a new contract on the same terms as the old. Again, ratification of an act may be impossible after a certain time if time is essential to the validity of an act and has expired[15] and third parties would be prejudiced, e.g., ratification of an unauthorised stoppage in transitu after the transit was at an end.[16] Otherwise ratification may be at any time.

(d) **Agency of necessity.**—Lastly, agency may arise out of necessity though not otherwise implied. Thus, a common carrier may be agent of necessity for the care of goods sent under his charge if there is no one to receive the goods at their destination.[17] And a shipmaster, when he cannot communicate with the owners, may if necessary make them liable in cases to which his ordinary powers as agent would not extend.[18] The class of agents of necessity will not readily be extended.[19]

4. THE AGENT'S POWERS OR AUTHORITY

(a) **Extent as regards Third Parties.—General and Special Agency.**— The extent of the authority of an agent varies in different circumstances. Thus, an agent's authority may be general; he may act for the principal in all his affairs in any particular business, e.g., the master of a ship or a solicitor. On the other hand, the authority may be special, in which case he is employed to act in regard to a particular matter only. With regard to special and general agents, it is of importance to observe the different rules as to the care which third parties transacting with them must take as to the power which these agents respectively have. In the case of a man employed to act in a particular piece of business, he will not bind the principal if he oversteps the special powers with which he is invested.[20] In dealing with him,

---

13 *Keighley, Maxsted & Co.* v. *Durant* [1901] A.C. 240.
14 *Tinnevelly Sugar Co. Ltd.* v. *Mirrlees Watson & Varyan Co. Ltd.* (1894) 21 R. 1009.
15 *Goodall* v. *Bilsland* 1909 S.C. 1152 at p. 1182.
16 *Bird* v. *Brown* (1850) 4 Ex. 786.
17 *G.N. Ry.* v. *Swaffield* (1874) 43 L.J.Ex. 89.
18 *Vide* Merchant Shipping, *infra; Atlantic Mutual Insurance Co.* v. *Huth* (1879) 16 Ch.D. 474.
19 *Sachs* v. *Miklos* [1948] 2 K.B. 23, followed in *Munro* v. *Willmott* [1949] 1 K.B. 295.
20 *Bell Bros. (H.P.) Ltd.* v. *Reynolds*, 1945 S.C. 213, at 222.

accordingly, care should be taken to ascertain precisely the terms of his commission. On the other hand, in the case of a general agent it is safe to trust him in all matters within his functions according to the usage of his particular trade. To that extent he has an ostensible authority and may bind his principal. For example, a stockbroker is entitled to act in accordance with the rules and customs of the Stock Exchange, and accordingly will bind his principal in any contract he makes for him in accordance with the rules. And an auctioneer, as he may not sell on credit, will not bind his principal if he does so. The general agent has full powers according to his ostensible authority. As a general rule, however, a general agent has no implied power to borrow, though a partner may borrow when necessary to meet an emergency in the business of his firm.[21]

Delegation of authority of agent.—The relation of agency is of a personal character. The personal nature of the relationship is expressed in the maxim *delegatus non potest delegare.* In other words, a person with delegated authority cannot delegate that authority to anyone else. He must do what he was commissioned to do himself, unless expressly or impliedly authorised to delegate it. Where the principal may reasonably be held to have relied on the personal skill or discretion of the agent selected by him delegation is excluded, *e.g.,* in the case of a law agent. But authority to delegate may be implied from the usage of the particular trade, or the nature of the employment may be such as to render the employment of a sub-agent necessary. Thus, an architect has been held entitled to employ a surveyor, to whom the principal is liable,[22] for when delegation proper takes place the contract is then between the principal and the sub-agent.[23]

(b) Extent as between principal and agent.—As between principal and agent the actual authority must be followed to the letter, and deviation from it may involve the agent in damages.[24] If the terms of the authority are ambiguous, and are capable of two constructions, an agent acting honestly on one construction is deemed to have been duly authorised.[25]

5. THE DUTIES AND LIABILITIES OF AGENT TO PRINCIPAL

(a) Duties.—The relationship of agency is of a fiduciary character. It is a relation of personal confidence. The agent must give his best

---

[21] *Sinclair Moorhead & Co.* v. *Wallace & Co.* (1880) 7 R. 874.
[22] *Black* v. *Cornelius* (1879) 6 R. 581.
[23] *De Bussche* v. *Alt* (1878) 8 Ch.D. 286, *per* Thesiger L.J.
[24] *Bank of Scotland* v. *Dominion Bank* (1891) 18 R.(H.L.) 21.
[25] *Ireland* v. *Livingston* (1872) L.R. 5 H.L. 395, applied in *Finn* v. *Shelton Iron, Steel and Coal Co.* (1924) 131 L.T. 213.

exertions in his principal's interest. And he must not seek his own profit at all, beyond the commission or salary that has been stipulated.

To carry out instructions.—The agent's first duty is to carry out the principal's instructions, whether express, or implied by the usage of trade or a previous course of dealing between the parties. Only necessity will excuse non-compliance with express or implied instructions. Thus, if he was instructed to insure goods and does not do so he will be responsible for any loss.[26] In the absence of instructions or special usage the agent must act to the best of his judgment in the interests of the employer. The standard of care required is such care and diligence as would be shown by a man of ordinary prudence in the same line of employment.[27] Even a person who acts gratuitously may be liable in damages if he fails to exercise reasonable care.[28] When an agency is undertaken requiring special skill for its performance the standard is the ordinary skill of a person in the particular profession or trade. Failure to use the skill or care required renders the agent liable in damages to the principal. Thus, if a law agent, from want of proper care or skill, passes a bad title, and a security which he takes over the property is in consequence lost, he will be liable to the principal for the amount of the bond. As a general rule the law agent is responsible for a good title, but not for sufficient value in the security. The agent is liable in damages even though the loss would have occurred independently of his failure of duty, for it is a matter of contract between him and his principal.

To keep accounts.—The agent is bound to keep accounts and to account punctually.

To act solely in interests of principal.—It is an agent's duty to make an effectual contract and to give his principal the full benefit of the contract he has made. This arises out of the fiduciary character of the relationship. The principle extends beyond agency.[29] He is not entitled to any benefit over and above the commission or salary stipulated for.[30] If he pays accounts he must account for any discount. It is illegal for him to take a secret profit or commission, as, for example, when purchasing on behalf of his principal to get something off the order from the seller for bringing it to him.[31] If employed

---

[26] *Smith* v. *Lascelles* (1788) 2 T.R. 187.
[27] Bell's Prin., § 221; *e.g., Gokal Chand-Jagan Nath* v. *Nand Ram Das-Atma Ram* [1939] A.C. 106.
[28] *Stiven* v. *Watson* (1874) 1 R. 412.
[29] *e.g., Reading* v. *Att.-Gen.* [1951] A.C. 507. Contrast *Nordisk Insulinlaboratorium* v. *Gorgate Products Ltd.* [1953] Ch. 430.
[30] *e.g., Solloway* v. *M'Laughlin* [1938] A.C. 247.
[31] *Pender* v. *Henderson & Co.* (1864) 2 M. 1428; *Gray's Trs.* v. *Drummond & Reid* (1881) 8 R. 956.

to sell goods for his principal he may not buy them himself without permission from the principal. The principal would be entitled to take back the goods, or, if the agent had resold at a profit, to debit the agent with the profit on the resale.[32] So also an agent may not buy for his principal, he being himself the seller, without the principal's knowledge and consent. The principal can refuse to take the goods or may debit the agent with the profit he has made. Again, a law agent may not take a gift from a client without neutral advice and assistance for the client, nor can he draw a client's will in his own favour, unless he proves it was made deliberately and without undue influence on his part.[33] The law agent's account must be according to the fixed scale for law agent's business as taxed by the auditor of the court.[34] It is an implied term of the contract of agency that the agent will not, without his principal's consent, make use, to his principal's detriment, of any information or materials which he has acquired in the course of his agency.[35]

An agent is further liable to criminal prosecution if he corruptly accepts or obtains, or agrees to accept or obtain from any person, for himself or for any other person, any gift or consideration as an induce-ment or reward for doing or forbearing to do any act in relation to his principal's affairs or business. A person who corruptly endeavours to induce an agent to do so is also liable to prosecution. Further, if an agent knowingly uses, with intent to deceive his principal, any receipt, account or other document in respect of which the principal is interes-ted, and which contains any statement which is false or erroneous or defective in any material particular and intended to mislead the princi-pal, he is liable to prosecution.[36]

(b) **Liabilities.**—As a general rule an agent incurs no personal liability to his principal in respect of a contract entered into by him on his principal's behalf. The exceptions are *del credere* agents and insurance brokers. A *del credere* agent is one who by arrangement with his principal guarantees that the other party to the contract will fulfil it, *e.g.*, when selling for his principal guarantees that the buyer is solvent, and undertakes to pay the principal in the event of his in-solvency. An insurance broker is an agent who is employed to negotiate a policy of marine insurance. He is agent for both parties. But he is liable to the underwriter for payment of the premium, and has a lien over the policy of insurance against the assured for the premiums.

---

[32] *De Bussche* v. *Alt* (1878) 8 Ch.D. 286.
[33] *Weir* v. *Grace* (1898) 1 F. 253.
[34] *Anstruther* v. *Wilkie* (1856) 18 D. 405.
[35] *Liverpool Victoria Legal Friendly Society* v. *Houston* (1900) 3 F. 42.
[36] Prevention of Corruption Acts, 1906 and 1916.

In accounting or paying money the agent must follow the instruction of his principal. If he remits money in some other fashion he takes the risk.[37] If he has no directions he should remit through a bank of good repute or a chartered bank, or according to the usage of the trade.[38]

6. RIGHTS OF AGENT AGAINST PRINCIPAL

The rights of an agent against his principal are (a) remuneration for the services rendered, either as commission, brokerage, salary, or *quantum meruit;* (b) reimbursement of necessary expenses incurred in furtherance of the principal's business; (c) indemnity from all responsibilities and liabilities come under towards third parties; (d) a right of retention or lien over goods in his hands belonging to the principal in order to make good his claims.

(a) **Remuneration.**—In the case of commission or brokerage the rate is settled by stipulation or usage. Where the remuneration is settled by contract or stipulation, custom or usage cannot come in to modify the agreed rate, but may be invoked to explain any ambiguity in the terms of the contract. Remuneration is presumed to be due in the case of a mercantile agent,[39] and also where the agent makes such duties as he has undertaken to perform the trade or profession by which he earns his livelihood. Where a person is not, for instance, a professional broker, but does broker's work so as to entitle him to remuneration, his commission is a *quantum meruit* depending upon the circumstances.[40]

Commission is generally due only where the agent's duty has been completely fulfilled; and if fulfilment is prevented by some cause for which the principal is not responsible no claim for commission emerges.[41] Where there is an agreement under which commission is payable, the question whether commission has been earned depends upon the construction of the agreement.[42] If the agent can show that the transaction in respect of which the commission is claimed is the result of his introduction although the business may be concluded by others, commission is due.

---

[37] *Warwicke* v. *Noakes* (1790) 3 R.R. 653.
[38] *Mackenzie's Trs.* v. *Jones* (1822) 2 S. 75.
[39] See Mercantile Agents, *infra.*
[40] *Kennedy* v. *Glass* (1890) 17 R. 1085; see *Way* v. *Latilla* [1937] 3 All E.R. 759, where the House of Lords indicates the proper practice of the court in fixing a *quantum meruit.*
[41] *e.g., Boots* v. *E. Christopher & Co.* [1952] 1 K.B. 89.
[42] The right to commission may depend on an implied term of the agreement. See *Dudley Bros. & Co.* v. *Barnet,* 1937 S.C. 632; *Luxor (Eastbourne) Ltd.* v. *Cooper* [1941] A.C. 108.

A broker, who is an agent to sign for both buyer and seller, and whose business it is to introduce the principals to each other, is entitled to a commission if a contract follows. The commission is usually paid by the principal who first employs the agent. He may be a mercantile agent within the meaning of the Factors Acts, and commission is therefore presumed to be due. By custom recognised by law shipbrokers and house agents are entitled to a commission for the mere introduction of buyer and seller.[43]

(b) Reimbursement of expenses.—The agent, being entitled to be reimbursed his expenses as far as properly incurred, may set these off against what comes into his hands on behalf of his principal.

(c) Indemnity against third parties.—The principal must take the burden of all liabilities and obligations necessarily assumed by the agent in order to discharge his duties towards the principal.[44] Thus, where a principal refused to implement a contract entered into by an agent on his behalf, thereby rendering the agent liable to a claim of damages, the principal was held bound to relieve him,[45] But where an agent incurred expenses in successfully defending a criminal charge against him for doing something as agent which would not have been within his duty as agent to do, he was held not entitled to indemnification by the principal.[46]

(d) Right of retention or lien.—Where property of the principal is in the hands of the agent the latter has a right of retention or lien over it, whether goods, documents of debt, or moneys coming into his hands in the course of the agency, to the effect of securing payment of his commission and indemnity from any obligations undertaken by him on behalf of the principal.[47] The lien is termed in law a " possessory " one, and is lost when the goods are parted with. Lien may be special or general. Special lien is a security to the agent for the fulfilment by the principal of his part of the obligation connected with the goods retained. General lien, however, is a security for a general balance due by the principal. It may arise either from custom or contract. Thus a banker has a lien over all unappropriated moneys and documents of debt of his customer in his hands for the general balance of the customer's account, although not over bills sent to him to be discounted which he has refused to discount.[48] Again, a mercantile factor has a lien over the goods in his possession for a general balance due him by the principal.[49] And a law agent has such a lien over the writs and

---

[43] e.g., *Walker, Donald & Co.* v. *Birrell, Stenhouse & Co.* (1883) 11 R. 369.
[44] *Erskine, Oxenford & Co.* v. *Sachs* [1901] 2 K.B. 504.
[45] *Stevenson & Sons* v. *Duncan and Ors.* (1842) 5 D. 167.
[46] *Tomlinson* v. *Liqrs. of Scottish Amalgamated Silks Ltd.,* 1935 S.C.(H.L.) 1.
[47] *Glendinning* v. *Hope,* 1911 S.C.(H.L.) 73, *per* Lord Kinnear at p. 78.
[48] *Lang* v. *Brown* (1859) 22 D. 113.　　[49] *Gairdner* v. *Milne & Co.* (1858) 20 D. 565.

titles of his client for payment of his business account, though not for cash advances, salary or commission.[50] A stockbroker also has a general lien.[51]

7. RELATIONS BETWEEN AGENT AND THIRD PARTIES

An agent is liable to third parties for his own negligence, misrepresentation, or fraud, whether his principal is bound or not, and whether the wrongful act was authorised by his principal or not. Apart from such cases it is, generally speaking, a question of the intention of the parties and the authority of the agent what are the rights and liabilities between an agent and third parties with whom he contracts. On the other hand, the rights of a third party may depend not so much on what was the actual as on what was the apparent authority of the agent. Three classes of case may occur: (a) The agent may be acting for a disclosed principal; (b) he may be acting for an undisclosed principal; (c) the supposed principal may be non-existent.

(a) **Where principal disclosed.**—Where the agent has contracted expressly as agent on behalf and on account of a named principal the agent is not liable on the contract, for the contract is then between the principal and the third party.[52] The agent may, of course, when contracting as agent, agree to be made liable on the contract,[53] or a custom of trade may make him liable; and a factor or a mercantile agent who has contracted for a named principal has by virtue of his possession of the goods and his lien for his commission and charges an interest and a title to enforce the contract against the third party with whom he has made it.[54] Such cases apart, he cannot competently sue or be sued on the contract; but as, when he contracts as agent, he warrants his authority, should he exceed his powers he is liable in damages to the third party for any loss caused by a breach of the implied warranty of authority [55] and he does not, as a rule, bind his principal.[56] He has failed to perform the duty he undertook to perform, namely, to make an effectual contract, and the measure of damages in such a case is the loss sustained by the third party as a natural and probable result of the agent's failure.[57]

While an agent may in general agree to be made liable on a contract,

[50] *Drummond* v. *Muirhead & Guthrie Smith* (1900) 2 F. 585.
[51] *Glendinning* v. *Hope, supra.*
[52] *Stone & Rolfe* v. *Kimber Coal Co.,* 1926 S.C.(H.L.) 45.
[53] *e.g., Lindsay* v. *Craig,* 1919 S.C. 139.
[54] *Mackenzie* v. *Cormack,* 1950 S.C. 183; see also p. 84, *infra.*
[55] *Anderson* v. *Croall & Sons, Ltd.* (1904) 6 F. 153.
[56] *Wylie & Lochhead Ltd.* v. *Hornsby* (1889) 16 R. 907.
[57] *Firbank's Exrs.* v. *Humphreys* (1886) 18 Q.B.D. 54; *Meek* v. *Wendt* (1888) 21 Q.B.D. 126.

or be so by custom of trade, there are certain classes of agents who are bound to contract only in the name of their principal. These are brokers, such as shipbrokers, marine commission agents, stockbrokers,[58] and others. They are mere middlemen or negotiators whose business is to bring the contracting parties together.

Foreign principal.—In one case an agent may be liable on the contract even where he truly contracts on behalf of a disclosed principal, namely, when the principal is resident abroad. It is not in ordinary course for a foreign principal to give an agent in this country authority to pledge his credit to those with whom he contracts.[59] The foreign principal is bound if the agent has in fact express authority to bind the principal and the third party is made aware of the authority. Further, if it can be shown that the third party knew the agent to be the established agent of the foreign principal in the country, and not merely a commission agent acting on special orders, the third party is bound to the foreign principal and the agent free.[60]

(b) Where principal undisclosed.—Here the agent contracts in his own name. He may contract as principal, or expressly for a principal whose name he does not disclose. In either case he cannot at his own hand by disclosing the principal escape liability under the contract, and similarly he can himself sue as a principal on the contract.[61] On the other hand, as in fact he is an agent, the third party, if he discovers there is a principal behind the agent, can go against the concealed principal. The only condition is that no prejudice shall thereby be suffered by the principal. If, for example, the third party, whether in knowledge of the concealed principal or not, has continued dealing with the agent and on his credit, and the principal has in the meantime altered the state of accounts between himself and the agent, as for instance by paying to the agent the price due to the third party for goods bought from him, so that it is to the principal's prejudice to have to pay again to the third party, the third party may not be able to go against the principal.[62] The decisions have varied. In some cases the courts have held that the third party is not barred from going against the principal unless the third party has himself produced the prejudice to the principal by keeping only to the agent's credit.[63] Accordingly, it would

---

[58] Stockbrokers are in a special position, and by the rules of the Stock Exchange act as principals *inter se.*
[59] *Armstrong* v. *Stokes* (1872) L.R. 7 Q.B.D. 598; *Hutton* v. *Bulloch* (1874) L.R. 9 Q.B.D. 572; *Millar* v. *Mitchell* (1860) 22 D. 833.
[60] *Bennett* v. *Inveresk Paper Co.* (1891) 18 R. 975; *Girvan, Roper & Co.* v. *Monteith* (1895) 23 R. 129.
[61] *Hersom* v. *Bernett* [1954] 3 W.L.R. 737.
[62] *Armstrong* v. *Stokes, supra.*
[63] *Irvine* v. *Watson* (1880) 5 Q.B.D. 414.

appear that, in order to preserve recourse against the principal, the third party must, as soon as he discovers there is a principal, find out who he is and claim recourse against him.[64] It follows that the undisclosed principal may sue the third party on the contract,[65] and in that case the third party, having been in ignorance that there was a principal behind the agent, is entitled to plead against the principal compensation on the state of accounts between him and the agent, but not if the third party knew there was an undisclosed principal.[66]

When a third party discovers who is the undisclosed principal he is entitled to elect whether he will hold the agent or the principal liable. He cannot be compelled to elect immediately, but when his election is made the other party is exempt from liability.[67] What constitutes election is a question of fact.[68] In particular markets there may be a custom that brokers are liable as principals in addition to the alternative liability of the principal.[69]

(c) **Where principal non-existent.**—Where an agent contracts ostensibly for a disclosed principal who does not exist or is unable to contract, he is personally liable on the contract. Thus, where A, B and C signed a promissory note in the name and on behalf of a particular congregation, it was held that, as a congregation could not be bound by a promissory note, A, B and C were liable as contracting parties.[70] The same rule applies in the case of a contract made on behalf of a club [71] or a company not yet incorporated.[72]

8. Relations Between Principal and Third Parties

Where a contract has been made by an agent for a disclosed principal the principal alone has in general a title to sue on the contract.[73]

Every act done by an agent professedly on behalf of his principal and within the scope of his authority is binding upon the principal, whether the authority be express, or implied from his acting on behalf of the principal in the course of his employment and within the apparent scope of his authority, as where the agent is a general agent or is held out by the principal as having authority. But if the agent is acting

---

64 *McIntosh* v. *Ainslie* (1872) 10 M. 304.
65 *Bennett* v. *Inveresk Paper Co.* (1891) 18 R. 975.
66 *Matthews* v. *Auld & Guild* (1874) 1 R. 1224; *Wester Moffat Colliery Co.* v. *Jeffrey*, 1911 S.C. 346.
67 *Morel* v. *Earl of Westmorland* [1904] A.C. 11.
68 *Lamont, Nisbet & Co.* v. *Hamilton*, 1907 S.C. 628.
69 *Thornton* v. *Fehr & Co.* (1935) 51 Ll.L.R. 330.
70 *M'Meekin* v. *Easton* (1889) 16 R. 363.
71 *Thomson* v. *Victoria Eighty Club* (1905) 43 S.L.R. 628.
72 *Kelner* v. *Baxter* (1866) L.R. 2 C.P. 174. Contrast *Newborne* v. *Sensolid (Great Britain) Ltd.* [1952] 2 T.L.R. 763.
73 See *Gloag on Contract,* 2nd ed., p. 133.

in excess of his actual authority, whether apparent or not, and the person dealing with him has notice or has reason to believe that in doing such act he is exceeding his authority, the principal is not bound.[74]

When an agent becomes bankrupt with the money or goods of the principal in his possession the principal is entitled to recover them if distinguishable from the agent's private funds or goods. The principal has a higher right than any third party creditor of the agent.[75]

A principal is liable for the wrongful acts of his agent in carrying out the transaction entrusted to him or committed within the scope of his employment. Where the principal has taken benefit from his agent's wrong, there is no doubt that this is so,[76] unless he is not only himself innocent of the fraud but also has acquired its results for a valuable consideration.[77] The principal is also liable in respect of the negligence of his agent in carrying out the transaction entrusted to him or in the ordinary course of his employment.[78] If, on the other hand, the principal employs an independent agent or contractor to do a lawful thing from which, if properly done, no injurious consequences would follow, the employer is not liable for his negligence or dishonesty in carrying out the contract. It would be different if the contractor were merely a servant of the principal, or if, for example, without special stipulation a railway company contracts to carry goods from one place to another, and employs another company as sub-agents to perform part of the contract. The contracting company would then be liable for any loss due to the negligence of the sub-agents.[79]

9. TERMINATION OF THE CONTRACT OF AGENCY

The contract of agency may be determined either by the act of the parties or by operation of law.

(a) By act of the parties.—(i) *By mutual agreement.*—The parties may terminate the agency by mutual agreement.

(ii) *By act of principal.*—Agency may be terminated by the principal by express recall or by appointment of a new agent to do the same act.[80] The principal may terminate the contract of agency at any time in most kinds of mercantile agency.

Relations with agent.—He must then pay the agent any remuneration to which he is entitled. The agent will further be entitled to relief

---

74 *Walker* v. *Smith* (1906) 8 F. 619; *Forman* v. *The Ship " Liddesdale "* [1900] A.C. 190.
75 *Macadam* v. *Martin's Tr.* (1872) 11 M. 33.
76 *Clydesdale Bank* v. *Paul* (1877) 4 R. 626; *Briess* v. *Woolley* [1954] 2 W.L.R. 832.
77 *Gibbs* v. *British Linen Co.* (1875) 4 R. 630.
78 *Citizens' Life Assurance Co.* v. *Brown* [1904] A.C. 423.
79 *Metzenburg* v. *Highland Ry.* (1869) 7 M. 919.
80 *Patten* v. *Carruthers* (1770) 2 Paton 238.

from the principal of obligations incurred, even though exigible only after the termination of the agency.

The principal is not entitled to revoke at such time as to prejudice the agent. Accordingly the agent is entitled to go on and complete any transaction in which he is engaged, and where the agent's authority is " coupled with an interest " it cannot be revoked by the principal at pleasure. Thus, when brokers agreed to take, and took, shares in a ship on condition of being appointed sole chartering brokers, their agency was held not terminable by the principal at will, but only on showing reasonable cause.[81] If a time was fixed in the contract for the duration of the agency, the principal may not dismiss the agent before such time, and he will be liable in damages for terminating it without just cause. And where the principal expressly or by implication agrees to continue to carry on business during the term for which the relation of agency subsists, he is liable as for breach of contract if he fails. On the other hand, where an agent is employed for a definite term, say five years, there is no necessary breach of the agreement if, say, after one year, the principal finds it impossible to carry on the business.[82] Where, however, the principal undertakes to employ the agent for a certain term independently of change of circumstances, failure to do so infers a breach of contract.[83]

Relations with third parties.—When a principal recalls an agency, if he wishes to keep himself safe from the further actings of his agent he is bound to give notice to the customers with whom the agent has dealt, and when the authority of the agent is derived from " holding out " on the part of the principal, he must intimate that the agent's ostensible authority is at an end [84] by notice to customers and by advertisement in the *Gazette* and newspapers to the public.

(iii) *By act of agent.*—The agent may renounce his agency at any time, but not in the middle of a transaction.

(b) **By operation of law.**—Agency is terminated where the special object for which it is created is accomplished, or, as in any other contract by impossibility of performance,[85] as by destruction of the subject-matter, *e.g.*, if an article which an agent is employed to sell is destroyed, or by death, bankruptcy or insanity.

---

[81] *Galbraith & Moorhead* v. *"Arethusa" Ship Co. Ltd.* (1896) 23 R. 1011; *Rhodes* v. *Forwood* (1876) 1 App.Cas. 256; *Turner* v. *Goldsmith* [1891] 1 Q.B. 544.

[82] *Patmore & Co.* v. *B. Cannon & Co. Ltd.* (1892) 19 R. 1004.

[83] *Turner* v. *Goldsmith, supra*; *Shirlaw* v. *Southern Foundries (1926) Ltd.* [1939] 2 K.B. 206 (managing director of company).

[84] *Ferguson & Lillie* v. *Stephen* (1864) 2 M. 804.

[85] *e.g., Marshall* v. *Glanvill* [1917] 2 K.B. 87 (agent called up for military service).

By death.—The death of the principal terminates the agency,[86] but so long as the agent continues to act in bona fide in ignorance of the death of the principal his acts are good against his principal's estate.[87] And the agent, as in the case of revocation by the principal, may complete any transaction in which he is engaged. The death of the agent also, necessarily, terminates the agency.

By bankruptcy.—Bankruptcy of the principal terminates the agency to the same effect as in the case of death. That is, the agent may complete a transaction and he will bind the principal's estate if he continues to act in ignorance of the bankruptcy. The bankruptcy of the agent does not necessarily terminate the agency.

Death and bankruptcy are public facts, and no notice of the death or bankruptcy of the principal is required, so that, after a reasonable time, the knowledge will be supposed to have reached the customers.

By insanity.—Insanity of the agent terminates the agency. Insanity of the principal, if of a temporary character, does not of itself interrupt the agent's power to act.[88] If of a permanent character, the agency seems to subsist until the third party contracting is put in bad faith by having knowledge of the principal's insanity.[89]

10. CLASSES OF AGENTS

The best-known classes of agents in mercantile affairs are auctioneers, bankers, factors, and brokers, and in addition may be mentioned the agencies of partners and shipmasters. With the exception of bankers, factors, and brokers, these are all dealt with elsewhere in this work.

(a) Bankers.—The relationship of banker and customer is substantially that of debtor and creditor, or lender and borrower, respectively, but the banker is the agent of the customer to pay sums of money as ordered. At common law he has a general lien over all unappropriated negotiable instruments belonging to and deposited with him as banker by a customer for the amount of a general balance due by such customer on banking transactions, but not, apart from express contract, for debts due to the banker in any other capacity. The owner can sell the subjects over which the lien extends without the consent of the bank, but the purchaser is not entitled to enforce delivery unless and until the debt due to the bank is paid.

(b) Mercantile agents, factors and brokers.—Factors and brokers are mercantile agents. A factor has been defined as an agent employed to sell for a compensation goods or merchandise consigned or delivered

[86] *Life Association of Scotland* v. *Douglas* (1886) 13 R. 910.
[87] *Campbell* v. *Anderson* (1829) 3 W. & Sh. 384.
[88] *Wink* v. *Mortimer* (1849) 11 D. 995.
[89] Bell's Prin., § 228; *Pollok* v. *Paterson*, Dec. 10, 1811, F.C.

to him by or for his principal. A broker has been defined as an agent employed to make bargains and contracts in matters of trade, commerce or navigation between other parties for a compensation, usually called brokerage. The chief points of difference between a factor and a broker are that, whereas a factor has possession of the principal's goods, a broker has not, and that a factor may sell in his own name, whereas a broker may not. Brokers on the Stock Exchange, however, usually transact among themselves with personal liability according to the rules of the Exchange. The broker is a mere middleman, who, for a commission, introduces the two principals to each other. Thus, when a man wishes to buy or have built a ship, but does not know to which shipbuilder to go, he goes to a shipbroker who knows which shipbuilder is likely to suit him. The broker charges a percentage commission to the shipbuilder for the introduction. The shipbuilder adds the commission to the price payable by the purchaser, and with it pays the broker.

The factor may pledge the goods of the principal in his possession, and has a lien on any goods that have come to him *qua* factor, and on the proceeds of such goods, for the general balance of his charges.[90]

The position of a mercantile agent having in the customary course of his business as such agent authority either to sell goods, or to consign goods for the purposes of sale, or to buy goods, or to raise money on the security of goods, has been defined by the Factors Act, 1889, and the Factors (Scotland) Act, 1890, in his relation with third parties. These Acts lay down that where such an agent is, with the consent of the owner, in possession of goods or of the documents of title to goods, any sale, pledge, or other disposition of the goods made by him, when acting in the ordinary course of his business [91] as a mercantile agent, shall be as valid as if he were expressly authorised by the owner to make the same: provided that the person taking under the disposition acts in good faith, and has not at the time of the disposition notice that the person making the disposition has not authority to make the same.[92] These provisions do not apply to a broker, as he has not possession of the goods. They are an application of the doctrine of holding out or ostensible authority. While a third party acting in good faith and without notice of the agent's want of authority gets a good title to the goods, the rights of the true owner as against the agent are preserved. The main exception to the statutory rule is that the pledge of the goods shall not be for an antecedent debt of the

---

[90] *Mackenzie* v. *Cormack*, 1950 S.C. 183.
[91] *Pearson* v. *Rose & Young Ltd.* (1950) 66 T.L.R.(Pt. 2) 886.
[92] Factors Act, 1889, s. 2 (1); *Lloyds Bank Ltd.* v. *Bank of America National Trust and Savings Association* [1938] 2 K.B. 147; *Stadium Finance Ltd.* v. *Robbins* [1962] 2 Q.B. 664.

agent.   That is to say, if a mercantile agent pledges goods or documents of title to goods belonging to his principal in security for a debt due by himself before the date of the pledge, the pledgee does not acquire a good title to the goods as against the true owner, the principal.   It is only where the pledge is given for an advance made to the agent at the time, or to be made to him thereafter, that the statutory rule applies.   Corresponding provisions are contained in the Sale of Goods Act, 1893.[93]

93 s. 25.

CHAPTER 3

RIGHTS IN SECURITY OVER MOVEABLES

1. NATURE OF RIGHTS IN SECURITY

THE term " right in security " may be defined to mean any right which a creditor may possess for the recovery of his debt in the event of non-payment, and which, in the event of the bankruptcy of his debtor, is distinct from and in addition to the right which he possesses in common with other creditors of claiming a ranking in the sequestration. Hence bankruptcy (or, in the case of a company, liquidation) is the ultimate test whether a security has been created.[1]

A security may consist of either (a) a nexus over some particular property, or (b) the corroborative obligation of some third party, *e.g.*, a cautionary obligation.[2] There is a nexus when the creditor has a real right over the subjects of security. A real right implies either possession by or delivery to the creditor (or on his behalf) of the subjects of security. It is thus a general principle in the law of Scotland that without such possession, or delivery, neither contract nor implication of law can create an effectual right in security.[3] There are certain exceptions called hypothecs which are effectual securities without possession or delivery. A further exception is the case of securities over incorporeal moveables.

2. HYPOTHECS

The term " hypothecs " is used to denote securities without possession. They are either conventional, *i.e.*, created by express contract, or legal, *i.e.*, implied by law.

The only conventional hypothecs recognised in the law of Scotland are bonds of bottomry and bonds of respondentia.[4]

Among the recognised legal hypothecs are certain maritime hypothecs or liens. These give certain creditors a right in security over a ship without possession and with the power of enforcing the right by a sale under order of the court. Such securities have priority over all other securities created over the ship, such as mortgages.[5] Thus,

---

[1] See Gloag and Henderson's *Introduction to the Law of Scotland*, 6th ed., p. 185.
[2] See Chap. 9, *infra*.
[3] *Scottish Transit Trust Ltd.* v. *Scottish Land Cultivators Ltd.*, 1955 S.L.T. 417; *Clark* v. *West Calder Oil Co.* (1882) 9 R. 1017; Bell's Prin., § 1385.
[4] See Shipping Law, Chap. 7, *infra*.
[5] *Harmer* v. *Bell* (1851) 7 Moore P.C. 267; *Currie* v. *McKnight* (1896) 24 R.(H.L.) 1.

seamen have a maritime lien for wages,[6] the master of a ship for his wages and disbursements,[7] a salvor for any sum due for salvage [8]; and a maritime lien exists for repairs executed or necessaries supplied to a ship in a foreign port, but not in a home port.[9] There is also a maritime lien for damages suffered in a collision between ships over the ship which was to blame.

3. SECURITIES CONSTITUTED BY EXPRESS CONTRACT

Securities may be created by express contract between the parties or may be implied by law.

(1) Forms and effect.—When the security is constituted by express contract it may take one or other of two forms with different effects. It may take the form of a transfer to the creditor of a right in the subject expressly as a security, *e.g.*, a pledge in the case of moveable property. Possession of the subject is given but the right of property is not transferred.[10] Its effect is limited in two ways. First, an *ex facie* express security such as pledge covers only the debt for which it was granted and not debts subsequently contracted.[11] Second, transfer of possession has not the effect of giving a pledgee an implied power to sell the subjects. He must either have an express power of sale or obtain that power by application to the court.[12]

On the other hand, the security may take the form of a transfer of the right of property in the subjects by an *ex facie* absolute conveyance, subject to a separate obligation, in the form of a backletter or other agreement, to reconvey them on repayment of the debt. An example in the case of moveables is where a document of title to goods, *e.g.*, a bill of lading, is transferred, although only with the intention to give a security. The result is to vest in the security-holder a right of property in the goods thereby represented and not merely a right of pledge.[13] The effect is twofold. First, the creditor has a "right of retention," *i.e.*, the security will cover any debt contracted by the debtor in the future.[14] This right of retention may be limited by express contract [15] or by notice to the holder of the security that the

---

[6] M.S.A., 1894, s. 156. *Inter-Islands Exporters Ltd.* v. *Berna Shipping Co. Ltd.* 1960 S.L.T. 21.
[7] *Ibid.* s. 167.
[8] *Harmer* v. *Bell, cit. sup.*
[9] *Clydesdale Bank* v. *Walker & Bain*, 1926 S.C. 72.
[10] Bell's Comm., 7th ed., i, 278.
[11] *National Bank* v. *Forbes* (1858) 21 D. 29; contrast *Hamilton* v. *Western Bank of Scotland* (1856) 19 D. 152.
[12] Bell's Prin., § 207.
[13] *Hamilton* v. *Western Bank of Scotland, supra; Hayman* v. *McLintock*, 1907 S.C. 936.
[14] *Hamilton* v. *Western Bank, supra; National Bank* v. *Union Bank* (1886) 14 R.(H.L.) 1.
[15] *Anderson's Tr.* v. *Somerville* (1899) 36 S.L.R. 833.

reversion has been assigned by the granter of the security.[16]   Second, the creditor is invested with a power of sale.   The power is absolute, hence he may give a good title to a purchaser notwithstanding a separate agreement with the debtor not to do so.[17]

The form of the security differs also according as the subject of security is corporeal or incorporeal in its character.   A security over corporeal moveables is known as a pledge.   Pawn is a form of pledge.

(2) Securities over corporeal moveables.—(a) Pledge.—The general rule is that in order effectually to create a security over corporeal moveables actual possession must be given to the creditor.   Some moveables, however, require a written conveyance to create a security over them.   This is so either on account of the titles by which they are in law transferable, e.g., ships,[18] or on account of their situation at the time the security is constituted, e.g., consignments of goods at a distance or goods at sea, or goods in another's custody.[19]

Pledge is the contract whereby in the ordinary case corporeal moveables are transferred in security.   Pledge is a real contract, by which one places in the hands of his creditor a moveable subject, to remain with him in security of a debt or engagement, to be redelivered on payment or satisfaction; and an implied mandate, on failure to fulfil the engagement at the stipulated time or on demand, to have the pledge sold by judicial authority.[20]

The person who gives the moveables in security is the pledger. The person who gets them in security of the obligation owing to him is the pledgee.   Pledge is constituted by the delivery of the subject pledged, on terms or conditions.[21]   A mere agreement to pledge not followed by actual delivery is not a right of security effectual in a question with the general creditors of the debtor.[22]   *Traditionibus non nudis pactis dominia rerum transferuntur.*

Delivery.[19]—Delivery must be actual or at least the best which the circumstances will allow.   It may be actual, symbolical, or constructive.

Actual delivery.—Actual delivery takes place (1) when goods are physically transferred from one party to another, (2) if goods are in any confined space and the complete command of that space is transferred to the pledgee, e.g., where the key of a yard enclosed by a fence containing barrels is given to the pledgee of the barrels.[23]

---

16   *National Bank* v. *Union Bank, supra.*
17   *Duncan* v. *Mitchell & Co.* (1893) 21 R. 37.
18   Chap. 7, *infra.*
19   Bell's Comm., 7th ed., ii, 11.
20   Bell's Prin., § 203.   21   *Ibid.,* § 204.
22   *Robertson & Baxter* v. *Inglis* (1897) 24 R. 758.
23   Gloag and Henderson's *Introduction to the Law of Scotland* 6th ed., p. 192; *West Lothian Oil Co.* v. *Mair* (1892) 20 R. 64.

Symbolical delivery.—The main instance of symbolical delivery is the case where it is desired to give goods which are at sea in pledge and for which a bill of lading has been taken. The bill is recognised as a symbol for the goods, and if it is transferred in pursuance of a pledge of the goods it has the same legal effect as the delivery of the goods.[24] It carries the real right in the goods without intimation to the captain of the ship in which they are situated.[25]

Constructive delivery.—Constructive delivery is the term applied when the goods assigned in security are in a store and delivery of them is attempted by a delivery order addressed by the pledger to the storekeeper or by endorsation to the pledgee of the storekeeper's warrant. Such delivery is effectual to transfer a real as distinguished from a mere personal right in the goods if intimation of the assignation is made to the keeper of the store. On intimation being made, the custodier of the goods becomes custodier for the transferee in place of the transferor.[26] But the keeper of the store must be a person independent of the pledger, *e.g.*, not a mere excise official having a key of the store of which the pledger is tenant.[27] And the goods transferred must be ascertained, *i.e.*, identified, so that they are distinguishable from the general mass of goods kept by the transferor in the particular store. So where a flour merchant sold to purchasers a certain number of sacks of flour, part of a large number of sacks in a neutral store, and not separated, marked, or identified in any way or separated from the other sacks of flour in the store, and gave to the purchaser delivery orders which were intimated to the storekeeper, it was held that constructive delivery had not been effected.[28] Goods, however, which are brought into separate existence after the intimation of the delivery order are constructively delivered as they come into separate existence.[29]

(b) Pawn.—Pawn is a form of pledge regulated by statute, *viz.*, the Pawnbrokers Acts, 1872 and 1960, and the Moneylenders Act, 1927. The term pawnbroker is defined as including every person who carries on the business of taking goods and chattels in pawn.[30] Such a person is further defined as " every person who keeps a shop for the purchase or sale of goods or chattels, or for taking in goods or chattels

---

[24] Bell's Prin., § 417; Gloag and Henderson's *Introduction to the Law of Scotland,* 6th ed., p. 192.
[25] See *Hayman* v. *McLintock,* 1907 S.C. 936, *per* Lord McLaren at p. 952 as to unascertained goods, and contrast Sale of Goods Act, 1893, s. 16, *infra* p. 109.
[26] *Rhind's Tr.* v. *Robertson & Baxter* (1891) 18 R. 623.
[27] *Anderson* v. *McCall* (1866) 4 M. 765.
[28] *Hayman* v. *McLintock supra;* contrast *Price & Pierce* v. *Bank of Scotland,* 1912 S.C.(H.L.) 19.
[29] *Black* v. *Incorporation of Bakers* (1867) 6 M. 136.
[30] Act of 1872, s. 5.

by way of security for money advanced thereon, and who purchases or receives or takes in goods or chattels, and pays or advances or lends thereon any sum of money not exceeding fifty pounds, with or under an agreement or understanding, expressed or implied, or to be from the nature or character of the dealing reasonably inferred, that these goods or chattels may be afterwards redeemed or repurchased on any terms." [31]

The leading provisions of the Acts are as follows: A pawnbroker must hold a licence, and his name with the word " Pawnbroker " must be exhibited over his door. For every advance he must give a ticket in statutory form indicating the terms of the contract and the amount (regulated by statute) which he is entitled to charge.[32] A loan on special terms is legal if it exceeds five pounds,[33] but the transaction may be reopened by the court in any proceedings for the recovery of the money lent or the enforcement of the agreement or of any security.[34] In cases to which the Acts apply all goods [35] pledged remain redeemable for six months and seven days. Thereafter, if the amount advanced does not exceed forty shillings, the article becomes the absolute property of the pawnbroker; if more than forty shillings, it remains redeemable until sold by the pawnbroker.[36] If a pledge pawned for above forty shillings is sold a record of the price must be kept, and the pawnbroker is liable to account to the holder of the pawn-ticket within three years for the surplus over the amount advanced and the statutory charges.[37] Any sale must be by public auction and the pawnbroker is entitled to bid.[38] So long as the goods remain redeemable a pawnbroker is liable for loss of or injury to them by fire. The value of the goods so destroyed is estimated at the amount of the loan and charges, plus 25 per cent. of the amount of the loan.[39] It is a criminal offence for a pawnbroker knowingly to take in pledge any clothing, unfinished goods, or material entrusted to the pawner to clean, mend, or finish,[40] or to take any thing from a person apparently under the age of fourteen.[41]

Under the Moneylenders Act, 1927, s. 14, a pawnbroker must deliver or send to the pawner within seven days a note or memorandum containing all the terms of the contract with interest not over 20 per

[31] *Ibid.* s. 6, as amended by 1960 Act, s. 1.
[32] 1872 Act, s. 14, Sched. 3.
[33] 1872 Act, s. 24, Sched. 3, as amended 1960 Act, s. 1.
[34] Moneylenders Act, 1900, s. 1, as applied by the Moneylenders Act, 1927, ss. 10 (3).
[35] 1872 Act, s. 16, as amended 1960 Act, s. 2.
[36] *Ibid.* ss. 17–18, as amended 1960 Act, s. 3.
[37] *Ibid.* s. 22, amended by 1960 Act, s. 3.
[38] *Ibid.* s. 19, amended by 1960 Act, s. 3.
[39] *Ibid.* s. 27.
[40] s. 35, as amended by S.I. 1952 No. 1334.
[41] Children and Young Persons (Scotland) Act, 1937, s. 19.

cent. and limited charges.   If he does not send such a memorandum
he may be, like the moneylender, not entitled to enforce his contract
or make charges.

A pawnbroker obtains no title to stolen goods but has been held
entitled to hold, until his advances are repaid, goods pawned by a
party in a position to give a good title to a purchaser and with no
right to pawn.[42]

(3) Securities over incorporeal property.—Debts cannot like simple
moveables or cash be corporeally delivered; but being mere rights to
demand payment of a sum of money at a stipulated time the act by
which they are to be transferred is such only as can convert the obligation to pay to the cedent into a debt to the assignee.   This is accomplished by a mandate empowering the assignee to demand payment,
accompanied by intimation to the debtor that henceforward he is to
hold the money for behoof of the assignee.[43]   Mere possession of the
document of debt, e.g., a policy of insurance, without any assignation
confers no right to any claim arising in respect of it.   Without intimation no effectual security is created in Scotland except in the case of
a negotiable instrument.[44]   For example, an assignation of the uncalled capital of a company is ineffectual as a security unless it is
completed by intimation to each shareholder of the company.[45]

Shares in a company are frequently used as a security.   The mere
deposit of share certificates with the creditor cannot in Scotland create
a security over them, nor is the deposit of a duly signed transfer and
the share certificate with the creditor effectual to create a security.
The creditor is, however, in the latter case placed in a position to
complete his security by having himself registered in the books of the
company as owner.   Until he is so registered the security is liable to
be defeated by diligence used upon the shares by another creditor or
by a subsequent and fraudulent transfer of them by the debtor.[46]   In
Scotland, though not in England, transfers signed by the granter, but
blank in the name of the creditor, may be void under the Act, 1696,
c. 25.[47]   Such a security is therefore of doubtful effect.

4. SECURITIES IMPLIED BY LAW FROM POSSESSION—LIEN AND RETENTION

Lien is a right implied by law to retain property until some debt or
other obligation is satisfied.   It is a right founded on mere possession.

---

[42] *Bryce* v. *Ehrmann* (1904) 7 F. 5; *Robertson* v. *Burns*, 1943 S.C.(J.) 1.
[43] Bell's Comm., 7th ed., ii, 15.   [44] *Wylie's Exrx.* v. *M'Jannet* (1901) 4 F. 195.
[45] *Liqrs. of Union Club* v. *Edinburgh Life Assurance Co.* (1906) 8 F. 1143; *Clark* v.
West Calder Oil Co. (1882) 9 R. 1017.
[46] *Rainford* v. *Keith* [1905] 1 Ch. 296.
[47] See *Shaw* v. *Caledonian Ry.* (1890) 17 R. 466 at p. 478.

For example, a seller of goods who has not parted with the goods which he has sold to a buyer has a lien over the goods for the unpaid price.[48]   Right of retention, on the other hand, is the right of a party, whose title is one of ownership subject to an obligation to convey, to refuse implement until some counter-obligation due by the party entitled to a conveyance is fulfilled.   The law of Scotland does not recognise any right in a mere possessor to continue in possession until all debts due to him by the owner are paid.[49]

Special and general lien.—Liens are either special or general, and are in all cases limited rights.   A special lien is a right implied by law to retain an article until payment of some debt arising out of the contract under which possession of the article was obtained, e.g., the lien of a carrier,[50] or a salvor.[51]   A general lien is a right to retain an article until some general balance, e.g., arising out of a course of employment, is discharged.

General lien.—A general lien is recognised by custom of certain professions and trades.   Its extent depends on the usage of the particular trade.   For example, a law agent has a general lien on his client's titles covering all debts due by his client from prior employment.[52]   The extent of a general lien in any particular trade must be proved by evidence showing that the dealings of parties were on the footing of a lien of the extent claimed.[53]   Examples of general lien are those of a law agent, a factor or mercantile agent, including an auctioneer,[54] and of a banker.[55]

Limits of rights under lien.—No lien can be asserted if it is inconsistent with the terms, express or implied, of the contract under which possession was obtained.   The plea of lien is barred by the specific appropriation.   Thus if a bill is sent to a banker for discount and he refuses to discount it, he cannot retain it under a general lien.[56]   Further, lien is a right over which the court may exercise an equitable control.   For example, a ship may be released from a lien for repairs on terms to be fixed by the court.[57]

Extinction of lien.—Being founded on possession, lien is lost if possession is relinquished.   But where lien covers a number of articles

---

[48] Sale of Goods Act, 1893, s. 39 (1).   [49] *Anderson's Tr.* v. *Fleming* (1871) 9 M. 718.
[50] *Infra*, p. 129.
[51] *Infra*, p. 149.
[52] *Garden, Haig-Scott & Wallace* v. *Stevenson's Trs.*, 1962 S.C. 51.
[53] *Anderson's Tr.* v. *Fleming, supra.*
[54] *Mackenzie* v. *Cormack*, 1950 S.C. 183.
[55] See as to bankers and factors, Law of Agency, p. 83.
[56] *Borthwick* v. *Bremner* (1833) 12 S. 121; see also *Middlemas* v. *Gibson*, 1910 S.C. 577.
[57] *Ferguson & Stewart* v. *Grant* (1856) 18 D. 536; *Garscadden* v. *Ardrossan Dry Dock Co.*, 1910 S.C. 178, *per* Lord Ardwall.

some may be restored to the owner without affecting the lien over the rest.[58]

5. OBLIGATIONS OF A SECURITY HOLDER

The right of property in the subject of security remains with the debtor. The creditor's obligation is to restore the subject of security on payment of the debt, bestowing ordinary care in the custody of the subject while in his possession.[59] Hence a creditor is not liable for the accidental loss or destruction of the security subjects before payment of the debt is tendered, nor is his right of recovering his debt affected thereby.[60] If, however, the creditor is unable to return the subjects by reason of his own fault he cannot demand payment of his debt.[61] On payment of the debt it is the duty of the creditor to restore the exact subjects given in security. He is liable in damages if he fail, even where his security is merely over the reversion of the security-subjects, e.g., shares, and the failure to restore is due to action by the holder of a prior security over them which the postponed creditor ought to have prevented.[62] Hence it was held that a bank to whom numbered shares of a company had been transferred in security were only justified in tendering in return equivalent shares of the same company because it was in accordance with their usual practice to do so, and this practice was known to and approved by the debtor.[63]

---

[58] Gray v. Wardrop's Trs. (1855) 2 Macq. 435.
[59] Bell's Prin., 10th ed., § 206; Coggs v. Bernard, 1 Smith's L.C. 177, 191.
[60] Syred v. Carruthers (1858) E.B. & E. 469; Fraser v. Smith (1899) 1 F. 487.
[61] Ellis & Co's Tr. v. Dixon-Johnston [1925] A.C. 489.
[62] Nelson v. National Bank of Scotland, 1936 S.L.T. 396.
[63] Crerar v. Bank of Scotland, 1921 S.C. 736; 1922 S.C.(H.L.) 137.

CHAPTER 4

THE LAW OF SALE OF GOODS

The Sale of Goods Act, 1893.—The law of sale in the United Kingdom is now governed principally by the Sale of Goods Act, 1893. That statute codified the law existing prior to its passing and assimilated the laws of England and Scotland. In the assimilating process certain distinctive characteristics of the law of Scotland have been retained and apply still only to Scotland, while certain principles of the law of England have been extended to and made applicable to Scotland. Two examples may be given. In Scotland prior to the Act the property in the article sold did not pass to the purchaser until delivery. Now the property in the goods may pass, irrespective of delivery, when the parties intend it to pass. Again the *actio quanti minoris, i.e.,* a claim of damages in diminution or extinction of the price of goods bought by a buyer who retains the goods although the seller has failed to perform a material part of the contract,[1] is now recognised to an extent which, before the Act, was unknown in Scotland.[2]

Parties to a contract of sale, as to all legal contracts, are free to make their own terms, and effect will be given to the bargain thus made. Recourse to the statute is only justified where no specific contract has been made or the intention not clearly defined. In construing questions arising under the statute the language of the Act must receive its natural meaning uninfluenced by what may have been the interpretation of the law prior to its coming into operation. But the rules of the common law save in so far as inconsistent with the statute continue to apply.[3]

The Sale of Goods Act is applicable only to the United Kingdom, and sales in a foreign country are in general regulated by the law of the country where the sale takes place. If the law of a foreign country regulates the contract, but an action on the contract takes place in the United Kingdom, effect will be given to the foreign law if it be proved to be different from the law as codified in the Sale of Goods Act.[4]

---

[1] Act, s. 11 (2).

[2] As to law of Scotland before the Act, see *M'Cormick & Co.* v. *Rittmeyer & Co.* (1869) 7 M. 854, *per* Lord President Inglis at p. 858; *Pearce Bros.* v. *Irons* (1869) 7 M. 571.

[3] Act, s. 61 (2). The provisions of the Act relating to contracts of sale do not apply to any transaction in the form of a contract of sale which is intended to operate by way of security: s. 61 (4). *G. & C. Finance Corporation Ltd.* v. *Brown,* 1961 S.L.T. 408 (hire-purchase agreement).

[4] *The Parchim* [1918] A.C. 157, *per* Lord Parker at pp. 160, 161.

1. THE CONTRACT OF SALE

(a) Sale and agreement to sell.—A contract of sale of goods is a contract whereby the seller transfers or agrees to transfer the property in goods to the buyer for a money consideration, called the price.

Where under the contract of sale the property in the goods is transferred from the seller to the buyer the contract is called a sale. The contract is called an agreement to sell where the transfer of the property in the goods is to take place at a future time or subject to some condition thereafter to be fulfilled. But an agreement to sell becomes a sale when the time elapses or the conditions are fulfilled subject to which the property in the goods is to be transferred.[5]

It should be noted, however, that there may be an unfulfilled condition and yet be a sale. Conditions in Scotland are either suspensive or resolutive. A suspensive condition holds the sale in suspense until the condition is fulfilled. Until the condition is so fulfilled the contract between the parties is merely an agreement to sell. A resolutive condition, however, implies that a sale has taken place, but that in a certain event the contract will be resolved or dissolved and each party restored as nearly as possible to his former position. The rights of parties are affected differently by the two kinds of conditions. Where there is an unfulfilled suspensive condition the property in the goods has not passed to the buyer, and the seller may accordingly maintain his right to the property as against other parties whose only right is derived from the buyer, even though the buyer has obtained possession of the goods. A resolutive condition, on the other hand, does not affect the passing of the property from seller to buyer, and accordingly does not prevent the buyer from giving a title to others which will prevent the seller from reclaiming the property on the occurrence of the event which constitutes the condition. Thus, where goods are sold by weight or measure, the weighing and measuring, and, if sent on approval, the buyer's approval, constitute suspensive conditions.[6] But if goods be sold by auction with a condition that they may be resold if not paid for within a stated time, the condition is resolutive.

By an agreement to sell a *jus in personam*, *i.e.*, a claim against the seller is created; by a sale a *jus in re, i.e.*, a right of property in the goods themselves is transferred. Where an agreement to sell is broken by the buyer the seller's remedy is only an action of damages; but where goods have been sold and the buyer makes default in paying the contract price the seller may sue for it.

(b) How the contract of sale is constituted and proved.—A contract of sale may be made in writing or by word of mouth, or partly in

---

[5] Act, s. 1; *Mischeff* v. *Springett* [1942] 2 K.B. 331.
[6] *Ibid.* s. 18, Rule 4.

writing and partly by word of mouth, or may be implied from the conduct of the parties. Writing is not necessary, even for the sale of a ship, although writing is essential to enable the purchaser to become the registered owner of the vessel.[7]

Being a mutual or consensual contract the sale of goods may be proved either by writing or parole testimony. If, however, the parties stipulate for writing the contract is not complete without it.[8] A verbal contract of sale falls under the quinquennial prescription introduced by the Act of 1669, c. 9, and if action is not brought within five years can only be proved by writ or oath.[9]

(c) Subject-matter.—What the contract includes.—The Act applies to the sale of goods. Goods include in Scotland all corporeal moveables except money, e.g., machinery, parts of machinery, horses, cattle, articles of vertu, etc.[10] It embraces industrial growing crops, and things attached to or forming part of the land which are agreed to be severed before sale or under the contract of sale, e.g., standing trees [11] and ships.[12] It does not apply to incorporeal moveable property such as stocks and shares. It necessarily excludes money because in sale the goods and the price are contrasted.

The goods which form the subject of a contract of sale may be either existing goods owned or possessed by the seller, or future goods, i.e., goods to be manufactured or acquired by the seller after the making of the contract of sale.[13] Existing goods may be either (a) specific, i.e., identified and agreed on at the time the contract of sale is made; or (b) generic or unascertained, e.g., a portion of a larger quantity of goods lying in a store or forming the cargo of a ship.[14]

Specific goods may be the subject either of a sale or of an agreement to sell. In the case of a sale, however, if at the time the contract was made the goods, without the knowledge of the seller, have perished, the sale is void.[15] Thus where a cargo of corn at sea was sold and it was afterwards discovered that the cargo, having got heated, had been sold at a foreign port before the date of the contract, the contract was held void.[16] Similarly, where there is merely an agreement to sell

---

[7] M'Connachie v. Geddes, 1918 S.C. 391; Merchant Shipping Act, 1894, ss. 24, 26, as extended by M.S. Act, 1921, s. 1.

[8] See Contract, supra, p. 4.

[9] See Prescription, supra, p. 53.

[10] A contract to paint a picture is not a sale of goods. The passing of the property in the paint and canvas is only ancillary to the contract—Robinson v. Graves [1935] 1 K.B. 579.

[11] Morison v. Lockhart, 1912 S.C. 1017; Munro v. Liquidator of Balnagown Estates Co., 1949 S.C. 49; see 1962 S.L.T.(News) 13.

[12] Behnke v. Bede Shipping Co. [1927] 1 K.B. 649.

[13] Act, s. 5 (1).

[14] See Hayman v. M'Lintock, 1907 S.C. 936.

[15] Act, s. 6.   [16] Couturier v. Hastie (1856) 5 H.L.C. 673.

specific goods, as where goods though specific are not in a deliverable state or the price is not ascertained,[17] or the parties have agreed to postpone the passing of the property in the goods,[18] the contract is void if at the time it was made the goods, without the knowledge of the seller, have perished, or if subsequently and before the agreement to sell becomes a sale the goods, without any fault on the part of seller or buyer, perish.[19] The contract is in each case void because of impossibility of performance.

Both these cases of impossibility are peculiar to the law of sale, but there are, of course, cases common to the whole field of contract where performance of a contract of sale is excused on that ground. Thus a declaration of war by this country operates as an Act of Parliament prohibiting all intercourse with the enemy. If a contract of sale made before war involves intercourse with the enemy for its due performance, the contract is dissolved.[20]

Where, however, the contract is for the sale of generic or un-ascertained goods the seller fulfils his contract by delivering any goods which answer to the description in the contract.[21]

Future goods may form the subject of an agreement to sell, as where the seller has still to acquire the goods he presently contracts to sell,[22] but not of a sale so as to pass the property.

(d) The price.—This must consist of money, else the contract is one of exchange or barter, not sale.[23] If required by the seller payment must be made in legal tender.

The price may be ascertained in three different ways: (1) fixed by the contract; (2) fixed in manner specified in the contract; (3) determined by the course of dealing between the parties.[24] Failing these, the buyer must pay a reasonable price.[25] A reasonable price may or may not be the market price according to circumstances. The course of dealing between the parties has no necessary connection with the usages of trade. Trade usage, however, may be implied so as to fix the price or mode of payment.[26] Thus in some trades a large proportion of the price, e.g., 20 or 30 per cent., is allowed as discount if

---

[17] Act, s. 18, Rules 2 and 3.
[18] Sibson & Kerr v. Ship "Barcraig" Co. Ltd. (1896) 24 R. 91.
[19] Act, s. 7.
[20] Ertel Bieber v. Rio Tinto Co. [1918] A.C. 260; Claddagh Steamship Co. Ltd. v. Steven & Co., 1919 1 S.L.T. 31; 1919 2 S.L.T. 170; see Impossibility of Performance, supra, p. 57.
[21] Blackburn Bobbin Co. v. Allen [1918] 2 K.B. 467.
[22] Act, s. 5 (3).
[23] Act, s. 1 (1).
[24] Ibid. s. 8 (1).
[25] Ibid. s. 8 (2).
[26] Athya v. Rowell (1856) 18 D. 1299. Cf. Duthie & Co. v. Merson and Gerry, 1947 S.C. 43.

the price is punctually paid when due. Again, sometimes part of the price is prepaid by way of security when the contract is entered into. This money is called a deposit. Unless otherwise agreed, if the sale goes off through the buyer's fault the deposit is forfeited.[27]

Proof of payment of the price.—Proof of payment of the price differs in Scotland and England. In England parole evidence is allowed, but in Scotland written evidence only is permitted, except in ready money transactions, or where the amount is under £8 6s. 8d. The receipt must, if the sum be £2 or over, be stamped with a 2d. stamp. It does not require to be witnessed, nor to be holograph.

(e) Conditions and warranties.—A contract of sale may be conditional.[28] The Act [29] states the effect in a contract for the sale of goods of failure to comply with a condition, lays down the law as to conditions or stipulations as to time, and provides that certain conditions as to title, description, and quality or fitness are to be held as implied.

Condition and warranty.—A condition is a stipulation which goes to the root of the contract, and breach of which on the part of the seller entitles the buyer to reject the goods and treat the contract as void. A distinction between a condition and a warranty is made in the Act. It is really one of English law, and hardly exists in the Scottish law of sale, for in Scotland a breach of warranty, which is defined [30] as a failure to perform a material part of the contract, entitles the buyer [31] to reject the goods, although he may retain them and claim damages.[32]

Stipulations as to time.—The Act expressly says that stipulations as to time of payment are not deemed to be of the essence of the contract.[33] The contract may, however, expressly make them so. As to other stipulations as to time, they may or may not be of the essence of the contract, but time is usually of the essence of the contract in mercantile transactions.[34]

Implied undertaking as to title.—Unless the contract shows a contrary intention the seller impliedly undertakes that in the case of

---

[27] *Commercial Bank of Scotland* v. *Beal* (1890) 18 R. 80; *Roberts and Cooper* v. *Salvesen & Co.*, 1918 S.C. 794.
[28] Act, s. 1 (2).
[29] *Ibid.* ss. 10, 11 (2) (3), 12–14, 62.
[30] *Ibid.* s. 62 (1).
[31] Act, s. 11 (2).
[32] As to English law, see the Act, s. 11 (1); *Wallis* v. *Pratt* [1911] A.C. 394; *Baldry* v. *Marshall* [1925] 1 K.B. 260; *Nicholson & Venn* v. *Smith Marriott & Anor.* (1947) 177 L.T. 189; *Couchman* v. *Hill* (1947) 63 T.L.R. 81.
[33] Act, s. 10 (1).
[34] *Hartley* v. *Hymans* [1920] 3 K.B. 475.

sale he has the right to sell the goods, and in the case of an agreement to sell that he will have a right to sell the goods at the time when the property is to pass, that the buyer will have and enjoy quiet possession, and that the goods are free from any charge or incumbrance unknown to the buyer when the contract is made.[35] Thus where a horse was sold by mistake and the purchaser was afterwards, though on the same day, informed of the mistake, he was held entitled to damages for loss of the bargain.[36]

Sale of goods by description.—There is an implied condition that the goods shall conform with the description [37]; but in sales by description it is to be noted that there is no implied warranty of quality or fitness, except in purchases from a seller who deals in the goods that they shall be of merchantable quality.[38] The two things—description and quality—are distinct. Description means that the buyer has not seen the goods,[39] or is buying something displayed before him on the counter, so long as it is sold not merely as the specific thing but as a thing corresponding to the description, *e.g.*, woollen garments.[40] A description may consist of a single word, *e.g.*, an adjective, as " flax "-yarn or " oxalic " acid, or " ship," which includes all necessary sailing gear.[41] If, of course, the name of the article indicates its purpose it must also be fit for the purpose.[42] The buyer is not bound to take an article which does not correspond with the description, even where the sale is by sample as well as by description and the bulk of the goods correspond to the sample.[43]

Quality or fitness.—There is no implied condition as to quality or fitness of the goods for any particular purpose, except (1) where the buyer expressly or by implication makes known to the seller the particular purpose for which the goods are required, so as to show that the buyer relies on the seller's skill or judgment, and the goods are of a description which it is in the course of the seller's business to supply (whether he be the manufacturer or not), when there is an implied condition that the goods shall be reasonably fit for such purpose; provided that in the case of a contract for the sale of a specified article under its patent or other trade name there is no implied condition as

---

[35] Act, s. 12; *e.g.*, *McDonald* v. *Provan* (*of Scotland Street*) *Ltd*, 1960 S.L.T. 231.
[36] *Anderson* v. *Croall & Sons Ltd.* (1903) 6 F. 153.
[37] *Nicholson & Venn* v. *Smith Marriott & Anor.*, *cit. sup.*
[38] Act, s. 14 (2).
[39] *Varley* v. *Whipp* [1900] 1 Q.B. 513.
[40] *Grant* v. *Australian Knitting Mills Ltd.* [1936] A.C. 85 at p. 100.
[41] *Armstrong & Co.* v. *M'Gregor & Co.* (1875) 2 R. 339.
[42] *Vide* Quality or Fitness, next paragraph; *Van Offen* v. *Arbuckle* (1855) 18 D. 113.
[43] *Bowes* v. *Shand* (1877) 2 App.Cas. 455 at p. 480. Act, s. 13. A seller may, of course, by express notice given to the buyer, exclude any warranty as to the actual species of an article sold by description: *Rutherford & Son* v. *Miln & Co.*, 1941 S.C. 125.

to its fitness for any particular purpose [44]; (2) where goods are bought by description from a seller who deals in goods of that description (whether he be the manufacturer or not), when there is an implied condition that the goods shall be of merchantable quality; provided that if the buyer has examined the goods, there shall be no implied condition as regards defects which such examination ought to have revealed.[45]

These are exceptions to the general rule of *caveat emptor,* which means that the buyer must take care when he purchases a specific thing that it is of good quality or fitness, *e.g.,* a picture or a horse. The real question which distinguishes the rule from the statutory exceptions is whose judgment was relied on in making the purchase. Knowledge of the seller of the purpose for which the goods are required may be gathered by implication from any circumstances tending to show his knowledge. Thus the known occupation or trade of the buyer may be important, as where flour is sold to a baker. And where the goods sold can only be used for one purpose, that purpose is a particular purpose in the sense of the Act according to decisions in England and by the Judicial Committee of the Privy Council, and is sufficiently made known to the seller simply by asking for it. Thus milk must be fit for consumption as food.[46] On the other hand where an article sold is capable of general use for many purposes, it is necessary to show that in the particular case it was sold with reference to a particular purpose.[47]

Merchantable quality.—The implied condition as to merchantable quality is present only when the sale is a sale by description. The fact that goods are sold under a patent or other trade name does not exclude the implied warranty of merchantable quality.[48] Of merchantable quality means something saleable in the market as goods of the description [49] when the tender of the article is made by the seller, not something which can be made so by the expenditure of labour upon it; and, if the article is only meant for one particular use in ordinary course, covers fitness for that use, and freedom from defects unfitting

---

[44] *M'Callum* v. *Mason,* 1956 S.C. 50.
[45] Act, s. 14. An implied term as to quality or fitness for a particular purpose may be annexed by usage of trade: *ibid.* s. 14 (3).
[46] *Frost* v. *The Aylesbury Dairy Co. Ltd.* [1905] 1 K.B. 608; *cf. Preist* v. *Last* [1903] 2 K.B. 148 (hot water bottle); *Knutzen* v. *Mauritsen,* 1918, 1 S.L.T. 85 (ship's mutton); *Grant* v. *Australian Knitting Mills Ltd.* [1936] A.C. (J.C.) 85.
[47] *Preist* v. *Last, supra, per* Collins M.R. at 153; see also *Cammell Laird & Co.* v. *Manganese Bronze and Brass Co.* [1934] A.C. 402 (as to area within which reliance required).
[48] *M'Millan* v. *Dick & Co.* (1903) 11 S.L.T. 210; *Bristol Tramways Co.* v. *Fiat Motors Ltd.* [1910] 2 K.B. 831 (C.A.); *Pommer* v. *Mowat* (1906) 14 S.L.T. 373.
[49] *Sumner, Permain & Co.* v. *Webb & Co.* [1922] 1 K.B. 55.

it for that use not reasonably discoverable to the buyer on such examination as he made or could make.[50]

Damages.—The measure of damages for breach of warranty is the estimated loss directly and naturally resulting in the ordinary course of events from the breach of warranty.[51]

(f) Sale by sample.—A sale is said to be a sale by sample where there is a term in the contract, express or implied, to that effect.[52] The exhibition of a sample does not necessarily make it a term of the contract.[53] It is of no consequence that samples have been shown at entering into the bargain, and have induced it, unless the sale has been made distinctly in reference to them.[54]

A sample has been defined as a description wanting words. In one respect, however, there is a marked difference between description and sample. In a sale by description the buyer (except as above where he buys from a dealer in goods of a particular description) takes the risk of defects in quality or fitness of the goods. Sample, however, involves quality. The Act assumes that the bulk of the goods corresponds in description with the sample.

In a sale by sample there is an implied condition (a) that the bulk shall correspond with the sample in quality; (b) that the buyer shall have a reasonable opportunity of comparing the bulk with the sample; (c) that the goods shall be free from any defect, rendering them unmerchantable, which would not be apparent on reasonable examination of the sample.[55] If the sale be also by description, the bulk must correspond not only with the sample but also with the description.[56]

2. EFFECTS OF THE CONTRACT

Two questions fall to be considered: first, when do the goods which form the subject-matter of the contract cease to be the property of the seller and become the property of the buyer; and what are the considerations which, in various circumstances, determine the time at which the property passes? In most cases the risk of loss of the goods passes with the property,[57] and accordingly the question may be otherwise put thus, when does the risk of the loss or destruction of the

---

[50] *Jackson* v. *Rotax Motor and Cycle Co.* [1910] 2 K.B. 937, *per* Kennedy L.J. at p. 950; *Grant* v. *Australian Knitting Mills Ltd.* [1936] A.C. (J.C.) 85 at p. 100.
[51] Act, s. 53 (2).
[52] *Ibid.* s. 15 (1).
[53] *White & Co. Ltd.* v. *Dougherty* (1891) 18 R. 972.
[54] Bell's Comm., i, 470; *Magistrates of Glasgow* v. *Ireland & Son* (1895) 22 R. 818.
[55] Act, s. 15 (2); *Joseph Travers & Sons Ltd.* v. *Longel Ltd.* (1948) 64 T.L.R. 150; *Champanhac & Co. Ltd.* v. *Waller & Co. Ltd.* [1948] 2 All E.R. 724.
[56] Act, s. 13.
[57] *Ibid.* s. 25.

goods pass from the seller to the buyer? Secondly, when a seller who
is not the true owner of goods transfers the property in them to a
buyer, what is the effect of the contract on the right of the buyer to
the goods?—*i.e.*, is there a transfer of title?

(a) **Transfer of property as between seller and buyer.**—The kind of
property here referred to is the general property, not merely, in the
phraseology of English law, a special property. An example of a
special property is the right of a pledgee, which is an interest rather
than a property, *viz.*, a security interest. Again, property must be
distinguished from a mere right to present possession, an example of
which is a lien or right of retention. A carrier or warehouseman who
is in possession of goods has a right to retain them till his charges are
paid, but has no right of property in them.

Formerly the property could only pass by means of delivery; now
by the Act it may pass independently of delivery. The passing is now
merely a question of intention.[58] The parties may by express agreement regulate the passing of the property.[59] The Act is concerned
with determining when in the absence of express agreement such an
intention is to be inferred. To ascertain such intention regard is had
to the terms of the contract, the conduct of the parties, and the circumstances of the case.[60] The time at which the property, and
therefore in the general case the risk, passes is the time when both
parties, expressly or impliedly, consent that it passes. A statutory
exception to the rule that the risk passes when the property passes is
where there has been delay in delivery. There the party, buyer or
seller, who is in fault takes the risk.[61]

Different rules apply as to the time the property passes when the
goods are specific, *i.e.*, identified and agreed upon at the time the
contract was made, from the case where the goods were not at the time
the contract was made ascertained. There can be no transfer of the
property until the goods are ascertained.[62]

The times when the property is held to pass are as follows[63]:

(1) When the contract is for the sale of specific or ascertained
goods.[64]

(a) If the contract is unconditional and the goods are in a
deliverable state the property passes at the time the contract is
made. A contract is unconditional when it is not subject to a

---

[58] Act, s. 17 (1).
[59] *Ibid.* s. 20.
[60] *Ibid.* s. 17 (4); *e.g.*, *Eldon (Lord)* v. *Hedley Brothers* [1935] 2 K.B. 1.
[61] *Ibid.* s. 20.
[62] *Ibid.* s. 16.
[63] *Ibid.* s. 18, Rules 1, 2, 3, 5.
[64] *Ibid.* s. 17.

suspensive or a resolutive condition. Deliverable state means a state in which the buyer is bound to accept the goods.[65] When the goods are not in a deliverable state the property passes only when the seller has put them in a deliverable state and the buyer has notice thereof. Thus, where a farmer sold his growing crop of potatoes, they were held to be in a deliverable state when pitted.[66] Where growing timber was sold, the property therein was held to pass, in the absence of anything in the contracts to indicate a contrary intention, on severance from the ground.[67] The same holds good when the seller has, in order to ascertain the price, to do something with reference to the goods, such as to weigh, measure, or test them. (b) When specific goods are delivered to the buyer on approval or on sale or return or other similar terms, the property passes when the buyer signifies his approval or acceptance to the seller, or does any other act adopting the transaction. If he wishes to reject the goods he must do so within the time for doing so if there is a time stated, or within a reasonable time, otherwise he may be held to have accepted them at such times.[68]

(2) When the contract is for the sale of unascertained or future goods by description.

If goods of a particular description and in a deliverable state have been unconditionally appropriated to the contract by either party with the consent of the other, the property is transferred at the time of such appropriation.[69] It is not sufficient to pass the property that the goods are sufficiently described to be identified by the seller on acquisition. Until appropriation a second purchaser from the seller might obtain the legal property in the goods first.[70]

The commonest mode of appropriating goods to the contract is by delivering them to a carrier or other custodier, and then, if so delivered in pursuance of the contract and the seller does not reserve the right of disposal, the moment the goods which have been selected in pursuance of the contract have been delivered to the carrier he becomes the agent of the buyer, and such a delivery amounts to delivery to the buyer.[71]

(3) When the seller reserves a right of disposal.

[65] Act, s. 62.
[66] Gowans v. Bowe & Sons, 1910 2 S.L.T. 17.
[67] Munro v. Liquidator of Balnagown Estates Co., 1949 S.C. 49; Morison v. Lockhart, 1912 S.C. 1017.
[68] Act, s. 18, Rule 4.
[69] Ibid. s. 18, Rule 5; Langton v. Higgins (1859) 28 L.J.Ex. 252 (a sale of future crop).
[70] Joseph v. Lyons (1884) 15 Q.B.D. 280 (C.A.).
[71] Act, Rule 5 (2).

The seller may, whether in the case of specific goods, or goods appropriated to the contract, reserve, in the contract or at the time of appropriating, the right of disposal until certain conditions are fulfilled. In such case there is transfer of the property only when such conditions are fulfilled.[72]

When goods are shipped and the seller in the bill of lading makes the goods deliverable to the order of himself or his agent, he is prima facie deemed to reserve the right of disposal.

When the seller of goods draws on the buyer for the price, and transmits the bill of exchange and bill of lading to the buyer together to secure acceptance or payment of the bill of exchange, the buyer is bound to return the bill of lading if he does not honour the bill of exchange, and if he wrongfully retains the bill of lading the property in the goods does not pass to him.[73]

(b) Transfer of title.—A seller impliedly warrants to the buyer that he can give him a good title and quiet possession.[74] No title can, however, pass from the true owner of goods without his consent, express or implied. In certain circumstances the consent of the true owner to a sale by an apparent owner is implied.

There are three cases. The first case is where the true owner by his conduct bars himself from denying the seller's authority to sell.[75] Thus A, a timber merchant, instructed the dock company with whom his timber was warehoused to accept delivery orders signed by his clerk. The clerk had a limited authority to sell to known customers. The clerk in an assumed name sold some of the timber to B, who knew nothing of A, or of the clerk under his real name. The clerk carried out the fraud by giving the dock company delivery orders to his assumed name, and then in that name giving delivery orders to B. It was held that A could recover the value of the timber from B.[76] If, however, the facts had been that A had represented his clerk to be invested with disposing power, and B, supposing the clerk to be invested with the power, had bought from him, A would have been barred from denying that the clerk had authority to sell to him.

The second case is that while a seller without any title (e.g., the clerk in the example given) cannot confer on a third party any higher right than his own,[77] a seller with a voidable title can give a good title to a third party who takes the goods in good faith. Thus a contract of sale induced by the buyer's fraud is voidable (i.e., good until set

---

[72] Act, s. 19 (1).
[73] Ibid. s. 19.
[74] Ibid. s. 12.
[75] Ibid. s. 21 (1).
[76] Farquharson Bros. v. King & Co. [1902] A.C. 325.
[77] Act, s. 21 (1).

aside), not void, and accordingly until set aside the buyer can give a good title to a purchaser from him.[78] Where, however, the buyer's fraud has not only induced the contract, but has also led to certain kinds of error, *viz.*, error *in substantialibus*,[79] on the part of the seller, the contract is void, and the buyer, having no title, cannot give a title even to a third party who takes in good faith. Thus in *Morrisson*, T pretended to the seller that he was the son of W, and had authority from him to buy two cows. W was known to the seller to be of good credit, and he accordingly sold to T. T resold them to a third party, who took them in good faith. It was held that the seller could reclaim the cows from the third party, T's title being void on the ground that the seller was under essential error as to the party with whom he was contracting.[80] When the true owner has recovered the goods from a bona fide third-party purchaser, the latter would be entitled to recover their value from the person from whom he bought them, under the rule, already stated, that a seller warrants his title to sell.

The third case embodies a species of reputed ownership.[81] It applies in two instances: (a) A seller who, having sold goods continues in possession of the goods or a document of title to the goods, can give a good and indefeasible title without the authority of the true owner to a purchaser from him in good faith. A document of title means a document used in the ordinary course of business as proof of the possession or control of the goods, or authorising the possessor of the document to transfer it or the goods or receive the goods, *e.g.*, a bill of lading, warehouse-keeper's certificate, dock warrant or order for the delivery of goods.[82] (b) A buyer or person who has agreed to buy goods which are still subject to a lien or other right of the original seller over the goods, and who, with the consent of the seller, is in possession of the goods or of the documents of title to them, and who transfers them or the documents of title to a purchaser who has no notice of the lien or other right of the original seller, is, as regards purchasers from him, in the same position as a mercantile agent in possession of the goods or documents of title with consent of the owner. Instances of mercantile agents are factors and auctioneers. A sale by such an agent, when acting in the ordinary course of his business as such an agent, is as valid as if he were expressly authorised by the owner to make the same, provided that the person to whom he has sold acts in good faith and has no notice that the agent has not

---

[78] *Cundy* v. *Lindsay* (1878) 3 App.Cas. 459; *Henderson & Co.* v. *Williams* [1895] 1 Q.B. 521; *Robin & Rambler Coaches Ltd.* v. *Turner* [1947] 2 All E.R. 284. Act, s. 23.
[79] See Contract, *supra*, p. 18 *et seq.*
[80] *Morrisson* v. *Robertson*, 1908 S.C. 332.
[81] Act, s. 25.
[82] Factors Act, 1889, s. 1 (4), and Factors (Scotland) Act, 1890, s. 1.

authority to sell.[83] This case is well illustrated by a hire-purchase agreement, or any agreement to sell as distinguished from a complete sale. A person who obtains goods on sale or return is not in possession of the goods under an agreement to buy them within the meaning of the above rules.

Sale in market overt.—A specialty of the law of England may be referred to, *viz.*, sale in market overt. The general rule is that a man cannot make a valid sale of goods that do not belong to him. But where goods are sold in market overt (*i.e.*, in the country at the particular spot of ground set apart by custom for the sale of particular goods, not including shops, and in London every shop in which goods such as the owner openly professes to trade in are exposed publicly for sale), according to the usage of the market, the buyer acquires a good title to the goods, provided he buys them in good faith and without notice of any defect or want of title on the part of the seller.[84] This does not apply to the sale of horses, to which special rules are applicable owing to the peculiar facility with which these animals when stolen can be removed from the neighbourhood of the owner and disposed of in markets and fairs.[85] And a sale by sample is not a sale in market overt.

3. PERFORMANCE OF THE CONTRACT

It is the duty of the seller to deliver the goods and of the buyer to accept and pay for them in accordance with the terms of the contract.[86] These are concurrent conditions, unless otherwise agreed; that is, to paraphrase the words of the Act, the seller is liable to deliver the goods whenever they are demanded upon payment of the price, but the buyer has no right to have possession of the goods until he pays the price. Where these conditions are not concurrent, as in sale on credit, the buyer is entitled to immediate delivery, though the right is liable to be defeated if he becomes insolvent before he obtains possession.[87]

(a) **Seller's duty to deliver.**—The contract may or may not regulate the manner, place and time in or at which delivery is to be given and taken. If delivery of the goods is not given in accordance with the terms of the contract, express or implied, the buyer is not under obligation to accept them. On the other hand, where delivery is properly offered, the buyer must take delivery.

---

[83] Factors Acts, 1889, s. 2 (1); 1890, s. 1; and *vide* Mercantile Agents, *supra*, p. 83.

[84] Act, s. 22 (1); *Bishopsgate Motor Finance Corporation Ltd.* v. *Transport Brakes Ltd.* [1949] 1 K.B. 322.

[85] *Ibid.* s. 22 (2).

[86] *Ibid.* s. 27.

[87] *Vide* Rights of Unpaid Seller against the Goods, *infra*, p. 109 *et seq.*

Manner of delivery.—The delivery may be actual or constructive. "Where goods are ponderous and incapable of being handed over from one to another there need not be an actual delivery; but it may be done by that which is tantamount, such as the delivery of the keys of a warehouse in which the goods are lodged, or by delivery of other *indicia* of property." [88] Thus delivery may be made by transfer of a document of title, *e.g.*, a bill of lading. The transfer of a bill of lading operates as a delivery of the goods themselves, because while goods are at sea they cannot be otherwise dealt with. But the transfer of, for example, a delivery order or dock warrant operates only as a token of authority over the goods or possession until intimation of the transfer to the storekeeper or other custodier of the goods, when it operates as a transfer of possession. [89]

When it is arranged that the seller is to send the goods to the buyer, the delivery of the goods to a carrier, whether named by the buyer or not, is prima facie deemed to be a delivery of the goods to the buyer. [90] The carrier is the agent of the buyer to receive goods. (He is not his agent to accept them as in conformity with the contract.) But it is the seller's duty to exercise due care and diligence in making the contract with the carrier, otherwise the buyer, if the goods are lost or damaged in transit, may decline to treat the delivery to the carrier as a delivery to himself, or may hold the seller responsible in damages. [91] Where the goods are sent by sea or rail, under circumstances in which it is usual to insure, the seller must give such notice to the buyer as may enable him to insure them during their sea transit. Otherwise the goods are at the seller's risk during the sea transit. [92] This does not apply where the contract between seller and buyer is either c.i.f. (*i.e.*, at a price to cover cost, insurance, and freight [93]) or ex-ship (*i.e.*, delivery to be from a ship at the port of delivery), for the seller is then the insurer. Where, however, the contract is f.o.b. (free on board) or f.o.r. (free on rail), it does apply, for after the seller has delivered the goods on board ship the goods are at the buyer's risk, and the seller must give him notice if he has not already sufficient information to enable him to insure. Where the seller is at fault in omitting to give

---

[88] *Per* Lord Ellenborough in *Chaplin* v. *Rogers* (1801) 1 East 192.
[89] *Blackburn on Sale*, 3rd ed., pp. 447, 451; *Hayman* v. *M'Lintock,* 1907 S.C. 936; *Price & Pierce Ltd.* v. *Bank of Scotland,* 1910 S.C. 1095.
[90] Act, s. 32 (1).
[91] *Buckman* v. *Levi* (1813) 3 Camp. 414.
[92] Act, s. 32 (3).
[93] A contract c.i.f. has been described as "a contract for the sale of insured goods, lost or not lost, to be implemented by the transfer of proper documents."—Chalmers, *Sale of Goods Act, 1893*, commentary to s. 32 (3). When the buyer has agreed to open a confirmed credit with his banker in favour of the seller, the buyer must do so before he can require the seller to tender the documents: *Pavia & Co.* v. *Thurmann-Nielsen* [1951] 2 T.L.R. 802.

notice the buyer may refuse to pay for the goods, the concurrent condition of delivery not having been fully satisfied.

Unless otherwise agreed the buyer of goods is not bound to accept delivery thereof by instalments.[94]

Place of delivery.—Unless otherwise stipulated in the contract, the place of delivery is the seller's place of business, or if he has none, his residence, or if the parties when making the contract know the goods in the case of specific goods [95] to be in some other place, that place.[96] Where the seller of goods agrees to deliver them at his own risk at a place other than where they are when sold, the buyer must, nevertheless, take any risk of deterioration in the goods necessarily incident to the course of transit.[97] The seller would have to stand the risk of any extraordinary or unusual deterioration, and in the case of perishable goods, such as fish, flesh, and the like, they must, when sent off by the seller, be in such condition as to continue saleable for a reasonable time.

Time of delivery.—When the seller is bound to send the goods to the buyer and the time for delivery is not fixed he must do so within a reasonable time,[98] and both demand and tender of delivery may be treated as ineffectual unless made at a reasonable hour. Where the goods at the time of sale are in the possession of a third party there is no delivery by the seller to the buyer unless and until such third party acknowledges to the buyer that he holds the goods on his behalf. This is a case of constructive delivery. The section saves the effect of the issue or transfer of any document of title to goods, *e.g.*, a bill of lading or a delivery order.

(b) **Buyer's duty to accept.**—It is the duty of the buyer to accept goods of which delivery in accordance with the contract has been tendered. If he neglect or refuse to take delivery of goods of which he is bound to take delivery he is liable for loss occasioned to the seller thereby.[99]

When goods are delivered to the buyer which he has not previously examined he is not deemed to have accepted them unless and until he has had a reasonable opportunity of examining them for the purpose of ascertaining whether they are in conformity with the contract. If he has not such opportunity he is entitled to demand it.[1] On the other hand, the buyer is deemed to have accepted the goods (a) when he intimates to the seller that he has accepted them (unless of course

---

[94] Act, s. 31 (1).
[95] *Ibid.* s. 62 (1).
[96] *Ibid.* s. 29 (1): *e.g., Paterson* v. *Aird*, 1937 S.C.(J.) 128.
[97] *Ibid.* s. 33.
[98] *Ibid.* s. 29 (2).
[99] Act, s. 37.
[1] *Castle* v. *Sworder* (1860) 29 L.J.Ex. 25 at p. 238.   Act, s. 34.

he accepts them conditionally) [2]; (b) when the goods have been delivered to him and he does any act in relation to them which is inconsistent with the ownership of the seller, as, for example, where feed tanks were purchased by shipbuilders to fit into a tug they were building, subject to their being passed by the Admiralty, and they were fitted in without being so passed and were subsequently condemned [3]; or (c) when, after the lapse of a reasonable time, he retains the goods without intimation to the seller that he has rejected them.

The question of acceptance is material where there is a right to reject. In Scotland a buyer may in certain circumstances reject goods which he has accepted if he do so timeously.[4]

4. RIGHTS OF UNPAID SELLER AGAINST THE GOODS

An unpaid seller is one to whom the whole price has not been paid or tendered, or who has been conditionally paid by means of a negotiable instrument, such as a bill of exchange or cheque, which has been subsequently dishonoured.[5] Seller includes any person in the position of a seller, e.g., an agent for the seller to whom the bill of lading has been indorsed.[6]

The unpaid seller of goods has means of securing himself against the buyer's failure to pay the price until the goods are actually or constructively in the possession of the buyer, even though the property in the goods has passed to the buyer. And even when the goods are constructively in the possession of the buyer if they are in course of transit to the buyer the seller has a special remedy should the buyer be insolvent, i.e., has ceased to be able to pay his debts in the ordinary course of business, or cannot pay his debts as they become due.[7] These are remedies against the goods, as distinct from remedies by action against the buyer, and exist only so long as the seller is unpaid.

The unpaid seller's rights against the goods are (1) a lien or right of retention for the price, (2) stoppage in transitu, (3) a limited right of resale, and (4) attachment of the goods by arrestment or poinding.

Lien or right of retention and stoppage in transitu are analogous rights, but are to be kept distinct, for they are in certain respects governed by different considerations. The seller's lien attaches when the buyer is in default in payment of the price, whether he is solvent or insolvent. The right of stoppage in transitu arises only where the buyer is insolvent. Moreover, it does not arise until the seller's lien

---

[2] *Heilbutt* v. *Hickson* (1872) L.R. 7 C.P. 438.
[3] *Mechan & Sons Ltd.* v. *Bow, M'Lachlan & Co. Ltd.*, 1910 S.C. 758; *cf. Woodburn* v. *Andrew Motherwell Ltd.*, 1917 S.C. 533.
[4] *Vide* Rejection, *infra*, p. 116 *et seq.*   [5] Act, s. 38 (1).
[6] *Feise* v. *Wray* (1802) 3 East 93; *Gunn* v. *Bolckow, Vaughan & Co.* (1875) L.R. 10 Ch.App. 491. Act, s. 38 (2).   [7] Act, s. 62 (3).

is gone, for it presupposes that the seller has parted with the possession as well as the property in the goods.[8]

The unpaid seller's rights apply where the property in the goods has passed to the buyer. Where the property has not passed the unpaid seller has, in addition to his other remedies, a right of withholding delivery similar to, and co-extensive with, his rights of lien and stoppage *in transitu* where the property has passed.[9] He is still the owner, and cannot, properly speaking, have a lien over his own goods. Moreover, he has the more extensive rights of an owner, and in Scotland an owner's right of retention entitles him to retain the things sold not only for the price, but for any debt or general balance owing to him by the buyer.[10] Where, however, the property passes before delivery the seller is no longer owner, but on the other hand he acquires the inferior right of a lien for the price.

Unpaid seller's lien.—This remedy is available to the seller only where he has possession of the goods, but irrespective of whether the property has passed or not. The unpaid seller is entitled to retain possession of the goods until payment or tender of the price (1) where the goods have been sold without any stipulation as to credit; (2) where the goods have been sold on credit, but the term of credit has expired; and (3) where the buyer becomes insolvent; and all these even where he is in possession of the goods as agent or custodier of the buyer. The lien is more than an interference with the buyer's right of possession. It also interferes with his right of property.[11] While it does not amount to treating the contract as rescinded, it does enable the seller, should he resell or pledge the goods, to confer a title on a third party.[12] The lien is a lien for the price only, and not for charges for keeping the goods.[13] A sale on credit excludes the lien during the currency of the credit, but not in instalment contracts if the price of instalments already delivered is due and unpaid.[14] Where an unpaid seller has made part delivery he may exercise his right of lien on the remainder in his hands.[15] Where the buyer has been sequestrated his trustee in bankruptcy may affirm the contract and obtain the goods by tendering the price within a reasonable time.[16]

The unpaid seller's lien comes to an end (a) when he delivers the goods to a carrier or other custodier for the purpose of transmission

---

[8] Chalmers, *Sale of Goods Act, 1893*, 14th ed., p. 127.
[9] Act, s. 39 (2).
[10] *Black* v. *Incorporation of Bakers, Glasgow, etc.* (1867) 6 M. 136.
[11] *Blackburn on Sale*, 3rd ed., p. 482.
[12] Act, s. 48 (2).
[13] *Field* v. *Lelean* (1861) 30 L.J.Ex. 168.
[14] *Ex p. Chalmers* (1873) L.R. 8 Ch.App. 289.
[15] Act, s. 42.
[16] *Ex p. Stapleton* (1879) 10 Ch.D. 586 (C.A.).

to the buyer without reserving the right of disposal; (b) where the buyer or his agent lawfully obtains possession of the goods; and (c) by waiver. Waiver may be express or by implication. Thus the seller may assent to a sub-sale by the buyer, or part with the documents of title so as to exclude his lien if the documents get into the hands of a holder for value taking them in good faith.[17] The mere obtaining of a decree for payment of the price against the buyer does not terminate the lien, unless and until the buyer pays the price.[18]

Stoppage in transitu.—Where the buyer is insolvent the unpaid seller, though he has lost his lien by parting with the possession of the goods, has a right of resuming possession of them so long as they remain in transit, and retaining them until payment.[19] Transit embraces not only the carriage of the goods to the place where delivery is to be made, but also delivery of the goods there according to the terms of the contract of carriage.[20]

The following rules [21] as to duration of transit show that the right of stoppage ceases after the goods have been delivered into the actual or constructive custody of the buyer, or his agent other than a carrier conveying the goods to the buyer, or in terms of the contract: (1) Goods are deemed to be in course of transit from the time when they are delivered to a carrier by land or water, or other bailee or custodier for the purpose of transmission to the buyer, until the buyer, or his agent in that behalf, takes delivery of them from such carrier or other bailee or custodier. This applies even where the contract makes the goods deliverable at the port of loading.[22] (2) If the buyer or his agent in that behalf obtains delivery of the goods before their arrival at the appointed destination the transit is at an end. (3) If, after the arrival of the goods at the appointed destination the carrier or other bailee or custodier acknowledges to the buyer, or his agent, that he holds the goods on his behalf and continues in possession of them as bailee or custodier for the buyer, or his agent, the transit is at an end, and it is immaterial that a further destination for the goods may have been indicated by the buyer.[23] (4) If the goods are rejected by the buyer, and the carrier or other bailee or custodier continues in possession of them, the transit is not deemed to be at an end, even if the seller has refused to receive them back. (5) When goods are delivered to a ship chartered by the buyer it is a question depending on the circumstances

---

[17] Act, s. 47.
[18] *Ibid.* s. 43 (2).
[19] *Ibid.* s. 44.
[20] *Kemp* v. *Falk* (1882) 7 App.Cas. 573.
[21] Act, s. 45.
[22] *M'Dowall & Neilson's Trs.* v. *Snowball Co.* (1904) 7 F. 35.
[23] *e.g., Muir* v. *Rankin* (1905) 13 S.L.T. 60.

of the particular case whether they are in the possession of the master as a carrier or as agent of the buyer. (6) Where the carrier or other bailee or custodier wrongfully refuses to deliver the goods to the buyer, or his agent in that behalf, the transit is deemed to be at an end. (7) Where part delivery of the goods has been made to the buyer, or his agent in that behalf, the remainder of the goods may be stopped *in transitu*, unless such part delivery has been made under such circumstances as to show an agreement to give up possession of the whole of the goods.[24]

Stoppage *in transitu* is effected in the following manner [25]: (1) The unpaid seller may exercise his right of stoppage *in transitu* either by taking actual possession of the goods, or by giving notice of his claim to the carrier or other bailee or custodier in whose possession the goods are. Such notice may be given either to the person in actual possession of the goods or to his principal. In the latter case, the notice, to be effectual, must be given at such time and under such circumstances that the principal, by the exercise of reasonable diligence, may communicate it to his servant or agent in time to prevent a delivery to the buyer. (2) When notice of stoppage *in transitu* is given by the seller to the carrier or other bailee or custodier in possession of the goods he must redeliver the goods to, or according to the directions of, the seller. The expenses of such redelivery must be borne by the seller.

Resale.—The seller may expressly reserve the right to resell should the buyer be in default, and in such case should the seller resell to another the contract is rescinded.[26] And where the goods are of a perishable nature, or where the unpaid seller gives notice to the buyer of his intention to resell, and the buyer does not within a reasonable time pay or tender the price, the unpaid seller may resell the goods.[27] In all these cases the unpaid seller may recover from the original buyer damages for any loss occasioned by his breach of contract.[28] And should the seller exercise his right of lien or stoppage *in transitu* and resell, the buyer acquires a good title to the goods as against the original buyer.[29] The exercise by the seller of his right of lien or stoppage *in transitu* does not rescind the contract.[30] Hence the seller, if the property has passed to the buyer, exercises his right of resale as a pledgee, and is accountable to the buyer for any balance resulting from the resale.

---

[24] *Mechan* v. *North-Eastern Ry.*, 1911 S.C. 1348.
[25] Act, s. 46.
[26] *Ibid.* s. 48 (4).
[27] *Ibid.* s. 48 (2) and (3).
[28] Brown, *Sale of Goods Act, 1893*, 2nd ed., p. 360. Act, s. 48 (3).
[29] *Milgate* v. *Kebble* (1841) 3 Man. & Gr. 100.
[30] Act, s. 48 (1).

Defeat of unpaid seller's rights.—The buyer can defeat the seller's unexercised rights of stoppage *in transitu*, lien, and resale where the buyer transfers the documents of title to a third party who has taken the documents in good faith and for valuable consideration.[31]   Thus, to take an instance of stoppage *in transitu*: A sells certain coffee to B, forwarding bill of lading indorsed in blank, and bill of exchange for acceptance.   B, who is insolvent, does not accept the bill of exchange. It is his duty to return the bill of lading to A,[32] but he does not.   Instead he transfers it to X in fulfilment of a contract to supply him with coffee.   X in good faith pays the price.   A cannot stop the coffee *in transitu*.[33]   Further, where a document of title has been transferred by a buyer to a person who takes the document in good faith and for valuable consideration by way of pledge or other disposition for value, such as one intended to operate as a security, the unpaid seller's right of lien or stoppage *in transitu* can only be exercised subject to the rights of the transferee.

Arrestment or poinding.—The Act provides (s. 40): " In Scotland the seller of goods may attach the same while in his own hands by arrestment or poinding; and such arrestment or poinding shall have the same effect in a competition or otherwise as an arrestment or poinding by a third party."   Arrestment is the appropriate diligence.[34]

5. ACTIONS FOR BREACH OF CONTRACT

(a) Actions by the seller against the buyer.—The seller has two forms of remedy against the buyer for breach of the contract, namely, (1) an action for the price, and (2) an action for damages for non-acceptance of the goods.   These are remedies, not against the goods as in the case of lien and stoppage *in transitu* and resale, but against the buyer by action.

If the property in the goods has passed to the buyer the seller may, if the buyer makes default in payment, bring an action for the price,[35] or, if the buyer neglects or refuses to accept, he may bring an action for damages for not accepting the goods.[36]   On the other hand, if the property in the goods has not passed, as where it is to pass on delivery, the action is usually one for damages for not accepting.   But

---

[31] Act, s. 47.
[32] *Ibid.* s. 19 (3).
[33] *Cahn & Mayer* v. *Pockett's Bristol Channel Steam Packet Co. Ltd.* [1899] 1 Q.B. 643.
[34] *Wyper* v. *Harvey* (1861) 23 D. 606.
[35] Act, s. 49 (1).   Where the buyer's banker gives the seller a confirmed credit, *i.e.*, undertakes to pay for the goods against presentation of the invoice, the banker is liable if he refuses to pay on presentation of the invoice, even though directed by the buyer to refuse payment—*Urquhart, Lindsay & Co.* v. *Eastern Bank* [1922] 1 K.B. 318, 323.
[36] *Ibid.* s. 50 (1).

where the price is payable on a day certain, irrespective of delivery, and the buyer wrongfully neglects or refuses to pay the price, the seller may maintain an action for the price, although the property in the goods has not passed, and the goods have not been appropriated to the contract.[37] Where the contract is to deliver by stated instalments, refusal by the buyer to accept or to pay for one or more instalments may entitle the seller to treat the contract as wholly repudiated, or it may give a right to sue only for damages arising from the particular default.[38] A similar principle would probably apply where the instalments were not specific.[39]

Action for the price.—In Scotland the seller can, as a rule, sue for the price and interest from the date when the money should have been paid. " I think it is a rule of law that interest is only due where there is either a contract to pay interest, or a duty to invest, or in respect of a *morata solutio*." [40] The only damages for delay in payment of money is the interest.[41]

Damages for non-acceptance.—The damages for non-acceptance may be general or special.[42] General damages are measured as the estimated loss directly and naturally resulting, in the ordinary course of events, from the buyer's breach of contract.[43] The object is to put the injured party, so far as money can do it, in the same position as if the contract had not been broken.[44] Thus where there is an available market for the goods in question the measure of damages is prima facie to be ascertained by the difference between the contract price and the market or current price at the time when the goods ought to have been accepted.[45] Special damages means the particular damages beyond the general damage which result from the particular circumstances of the case.[46] Should the contract provide for liquidate damages, *i.e.*, a pre-estimate of the loss which a breach of contract is likely to involve, that is the measure of damages.[47]

Damages for delay in taking delivery.—The seller has also a remedy for delay in taking delivery. When the seller is ready to deliver the

[37] *Stein, Forbes & Co.* v. *County Tailoring Co.* (1916) 115 L.T. 215; Act, s. 49 (2).
[38] Act, s. 31 (2).
[39] *Jackson* v. *Rotax Motor and Cycle Co.* [1910] 2 K.B. 937 (C.A.).
[40] Lord M'Laren in *Ross* v. *Ross* (1896) 23 R. 802 at p. 805.
[41] *Roissard* v. *Scott's Trs.* (1897) 24 R. 861.
[42] Act, s. 54.
[43] *Re Vic Mill Ltd.* [1913] 1 Ch. 465; *ibid.* s. 50 (2).
[44] *British Westinghouse Electric Co.* v. *Underground Railways of London Ltd.* [1912] A.C. 673; *Gunter & Co.* v. *Lauritzen* (1894) 1 S.L.T. 435; 31 S.L.R. 359.
[45] Act, s. 50 (3); *W. L. Thompson Ltd.* v. *R. Robinson (Gunmakers) Ltd.* [1955] 1 All E.R. 154 (as to available market).
[46] *Agius* v. *Great Western Colliery Co.* [1899] 1 Q.B. 413; *Hammond & Co.* v. *Bussey* (1887) 20 Q.B.D. 79; *Hadley* v. *Baxendale* (1854) 9 Ex. 341.
[47] *Diestal* v. *Stevenson* [1906] 2 K.B. 345.

goods, and requests the buyer to take delivery, and the buyer does not within a reasonable time after such request take the goods, he is liable to the seller for any loss occasioned by his neglect or refusal to take delivery, and also for a reasonable charge for the care and custody of the goods.[48]

(b) Actions by the buyer against the seller.—The buyer has the following remedies when the seller fails to perform his duty to deliver the goods according to the contract: (1) An action of damages for non-delivery [49]; (2) an action for specific performance [50]; (3) the right where the seller fails to perform any material part of the contract (a) to reject the goods within a reasonable time after delivery and treat the contract as repudiated, or (b) to retain the goods and claim damages.[51]

Damages for non-delivery.—Where the seller wrongfully neglects or refuses to deliver the goods to the buyer he may sue the seller for damages for non-delivery.[52] This remedy is always open to the buyer. It would lie when goods are tendered and rejected as not in conformity with the contract.[53] If the agreement was to deliver by stated instalments, to be separately paid for, and the seller fails to deliver one or more instalments, it is in each case a question depending on the terms of the contract whether the buyer is entitled to treat the contract as repudiated, or has merely a right of damages.[54] The measure of damages is the same as in the case of non-acceptance,[55] and where there is a claim for delay in delivery damages are estimated at the loss occasioned by the delay.

Where there is an anticipatory breach, *i.e.*, where the seller intimates in advance a refusal to deliver, the buyer may bring an action at once without waiting until the time fixed for delivery.

Specific performance.—In case of non-delivery of specific or ascertained goods the buyer can sue for, and in Scotland demand as of right wherever it is practicable, the delivery of the goods in terms of the contract. The goods must, however, be specific or ascertained. In England the granting of specific implement is entirely in the discretion of the court.[56]

---

[48] Act, s. 37.
[49] *Ibid.* s. 51.
[50] *Ibid.* s. 52.
[51] *Ibid.* ss. 11 (2), 53.
[52] *Ibid.* s. 51 (1).
[53] Chalmers, *Sale of Goods Act, 1893*, 14th ed., p. 154.
[54] *Ibid.* s. 31 (2).
[55] *Ibid.* s. 51 (2), (3); *Leavey & Co.* v. *Hirst & Co.* [1943] 2 All E.R. 581; *Brading* v. *F. M'Neill & Co. Ltd.* [1946] Ch. 145; *Household Machines Ltd.* v. *Cosmos Exporters Ltd.* (1946) 62 T.L.R. 757 (no available market).
[56] *Stewart* v. *Kennedy* (1890) 17 R.(H.L.) 1 at pp. 10 and 11.

Rejection on repudiation, or retention and damages.—The buyer may, where the seller fails to perform a material part of the contract, either (1) within a reasonable time after delivery reject the goods and treat the contract as repudiated [57]; or (2) retain the goods and claim damages.[58] Examples of a material failure are delivery of a short quantity, of a quantity larger than ordered, or of goods ordered mixed with goods of a different description. Where the defect is not material the buyer's remedy is a claim of damages.[59] A remediable defect in machinery has been held not to justify rejection. The buyer's remedy then is to have the defect cured at the expense of the seller.[60] Where there is a contract for the sale of goods to be delivered by stated instalments, which are to be separately paid for, and the seller makes defective deliveries in respect of one or more instalments, it is a question in each case, depending on the terms of the contract and the circumstances of the case, whether the breach of contract is a repudiation of the whole contract or whether it is a severable breach giving rise to a claim for compensation but not to a right to treat the whole contract as repudiated.[61]

REJECTION.—The right to reject the goods and treat the contract as repudiated may be exercised although the property in the goods has passed to the purchaser.[62] If the buyer rejects he must do so within a reasonable time, otherwise he may be held to have accepted the goods. If the breach is patent, *i.e.*, apparent on inspection of the goods, he must do so on delivery; if latent, *i.e.*, not discoverable by mere inspection, on discovery of the defect. The subject-matter of the contract has an important bearing on timeous or non-timeous rejection. Thus, in the case of seeds, the defect cannot generally be ascertained before the crop appears above ground,[63] or in the case of machinery, before it is tried, perhaps for some time.[64] The buyer is not bound to return the goods in order to reject them. He may reject them by returning them, or offering to return them on stating that they are not according to contract and are at the seller's risk. It is sufficient if he do any unequivocal act showing that he rejects them.

---

[57] *Aird & Coghill* v. *Pullan & Adams* (1904) 7 F. 258; *Nelson* v. *William Chalmers & Co.* 1913 S.C. 441 (yacht).

[58] Act, s. 11 (2).

[59] *Webster & Co.* v. *Cramond Iron Co.* (1875) 2 R. 752. *Cf. Wilkinson* v. *Barclay* (1946) 62 T.L.R. 581 (estimated quantity).

[60] *Morrison & Mason Ltd.* v. *Clarkson Bros.* (1898) 25 R. 427, *per* Lord M'Laren at p. 437.

[61] Act, s. 31 (2).

[62] *Nelson* v. *William Chalmers & Co., supra.*

[63] Express exclusion of warranty as to description will bar a claim of damages where the defect is of species—*Rutherford & Son* v. *Miln & Co.,* 1941 S.C. 125.

[64] *Morrison & Mason Ltd., supra,* at p. 434; *Aird & Coghill, supra.*

Where part of a consignment of goods is in conformity with the contract and the rest of inferior quality the buyer may reject the whole, but may not keep the part and reject the rest.[65]   On the other hand, where goods ordered are sent mixed with goods of a different description the buyer may accept the goods which are in accordance with the contract and pay the contract price for those he has retained, or he may reject the whole.[66]   So also if a larger quantity is delivered than ordered.[67]

The right to reject will be barred when the buyer accepts the goods as being in fulfilment of the contract,[68] and if he does any act in relation to the goods inconsistent with the seller's right of ownership he is held to have accepted them.[69]   A buyer who has ineffectively elected to reject the goods and treat the contract as repudiated may subsequently fall back upon the alternative remedy of retaining the goods and claiming damages.[70]   A buyer who rejects goods may also have a claim for damages for consequential loss,[71] but is not entitled to retain the goods in respect of damages and expenses.[72]   He may, after due notice to the seller, retain in security of repayment of the price.[73]

RETENTION AND DAMAGES.—The buyer, where the seller fails to perform a material part of the contract, has, alternatively to his right to reject the goods, the right to retain them and treat the breach as giving rise to a claim of damages in diminution or extinction of the price.[74]   In England he has no such option.[75]   This remedy, the *actio quanti minoris*, is to some extent new.   Prior to the Act it was confined in its application to defects of title or quality discovered when matters were no longer entire; unless restoration was impossible, the buyer had to restore the goods to the seller immediately on discovery of the defect, or be held to have waived the breach and be liable to pay the full contract price.[76]

---

[65] *Aitken, Campbell & Co.* v. *Boullen & Gatenby*, 1908 S.C. 490.
[66] Act, s. 30 (3).
[67] *Ibid.* s. 30 (2).
[68] *Long* v. *Lloyd* [1958] 2 All E.R. 402.
[69] *Mechan & Sons Ltd.* v. *Bow, M'Lachlan & Co. Ltd.*, 1910 S.C. 758; *Strachan & Co.* v. *Marshall & Co.*, 1910, 2 S.L.T. 108; *Woodburn* v. *Motherwell*, 1917 S.C. 533; *Hardy* v. *Hillerns & Fowler* [1923] 2 K.B. 490 (resale).   Act, s. 35; *Mechans Ltd.* v. *Highland Marine Charters Ltd.*, 1964 S.L.T. 27.   As to a custom barring the right to reject, see *Goddard* v. *Raahe & Co.* (1935) 53 Ll.L.Rep. 208.
[70] *Pollock & Co.* v. *Macrae*, 1922 S.C.(H.L.) 192, disapproving *Electric Construction Co.* v. *Hurry & Young* (1897) 24 R. 312.
[71] See p. 65.
[72] *Lupton* v. *Schulze* (1900) 2 F. 1118.
[73] *Laing* v. *Westren* (1858) 20 D. 519.
[74] Act, ss. 11 (2), 53.
[75] *Ibid*, ss. 11 (1), 53.
[76] *Louttit's Trs.* v. *Highland Ry.* (1892) 19 R. 791, *per* Lord M'Laren.

The buyer's claim for damages does not depend on his having given the seller notice of his claim before acceptance of the goods, even if he knew of the defects before taking delivery and paying the price, although he might be barred from rejecting them. He must, however, inspect the goods within a reasonable time, otherwise he may be barred from claiming damages. Thus if he resells and exports the goods before inspecting them he will be barred.[77]

In Scotland, where a buyer has elected to accept goods which he might have rejected and to treat a breach of contract as only giving rise to a claim of damages, he may, in an action by the seller for the price, be required by the court to consign or pay into court the price of the goods, or part thereof, or to give other reasonable security for the due payment thereof.[78] This acts as a check upon frivolous complaints and claims by the buyer.

Where a buyer has set up a breach in diminution or extinction of the price he is not thereby prevented from suing on the same breach if he has suffered further damage.[79]

6. SALES BY AUCTION

The law of Scotland as to sales of goods by auction has by the Sale of Goods Act been made to differ to some extent from the common law still applicable to sales of incorporeal moveables and heritage, so as to bring it into conformity with the law of England.

Where goods are put up for sale by auction in lots each lot is prima facie deemed to be the subject of a separate contract of sale.[80]

A sale by auction is complete when the auctioneer announces its completion by the fall of the hammer, or in other customary manner.[81] Until such announcement is made any bidder may retract his bid,[82] and the seller can likewise withdraw the article from sale.[83] Prior to the Act the rule in Scotland was that a subject exposed for sale by public auction and for which even a single bid had been made could not be withdrawn from the sale, nor could the bidder withdraw his offer.[84]

---

[77] Strachan & Co. v. Marshall & Co., 1910 2 S.L.T. 108; Dick v. Cochrane & Fleming, 1935 S.L.T. 432.

[78] Act, s. 59; see comments on consignation at common law by Lord Kilbrandon in George Cohen, Sons & Co. Ltd. v. Jamieson & Paterson 1963 S.L.T. 35.

[79] Bostock v. Nicholson [1904] 1 K.B. 725 (C.A.). Act, s. 53 (4).

[80] Act, s. 58 (1); Couston v. Chapman (1872) 10 M.(H.L.) 74; contrast Aitken, Campbell & Co. v. Boullen & Gatenby, 1908 S.C. 490 (part of goods of defective quality).

[81] Dennant v. Skinner & Collom [1948] 2 K.B. 164.   [82] Act, s. 58 (2).

[83] Cree v. Durie, Dec. 1, 1810, F.C.; Lord Trayner in Fenwick v. Macdonald, Fraser & Co. Ltd. (1904) 6 F. 850 at p. 854. Stipulations contained in the catalogue and in the conditions of sale may be varied by verbal warranty given before the fall of the hammer: Couchman v. Hill (1947) 63 T.L.R. 81.

[84] Lord Young in Fenwick, supra.

Where a sale by auction is not notified to be subject to a right to bid on behalf of the seller, the seller may not bid himself or employ any person to bid at such sale, and the auctioneer may not knowingly take any bid from the seller or any such person. Any sale contravening this rule may be treated as fraudulent, and so reducible by the buyer.[85] A person employed by a seller to bid so as to raise the price is known as a " puffer " in England and a " white-bonnet " in Scotland. The right of a seller to bid by express reservation is a novelty in Scotland. The court will take care that knowledge of the reservation is clearly made known to all intending offerers.

Bidders are under an obligation to the exposer that they will not use unfair means to prevent free competition at the roup.[86] It is a criminal offence under the Auctions (Bidding Agreements) Act, 1927, for a dealer at sales by auction to agree to give or for any person to agree to take from a dealer any reward for abstaining from bidding. And if conviction follows upon a prosecution under the Act the vendor may treat the sale as induced by fraud, as against a purchaser who was a party to the agreement for reward.[87]

A sale by auction may be notified to be subject to a reserved or upset price. In the case of a reserved price, common in English practice, it is in writing, sealed up, and its amount unknown even to the auctioneer until the hammer has fallen on the last bid and the writing opened. The practice in Scotland is to have an upset price, which is made known to intending offerers before the sale has begun.

An auctioneer, being a mercantile agent with a general lien for his charges and commission, has, notwithstanding that he acts for a disclosed principal, the right to sue a successful bidder for payment of the price of goods sold.[88]

7. HIRE-PURCHASE AGREEMENT

The idea of a hire-purchase agreement is that instead of the price for, for example, furniture which is supplied being paid in one sum, that price should be paid by instalments, in respect of those instalments the intending purchaser having the use of the furniture in the meantime, and the matter being so calculated that, when the last instalment is paid, the furniture should then become his property. The instalments will be so calculated as to provide for interest on so much of the principal as is not paid.[89] The advantage of an agreement of this sort is that it more readily enables sellers to obtain a sale of their goods,

[85] Act, s. 58 (3).   [86] *Murray* v. *Mackwhan* (1783) Mor. 9567.
[87] The Mock Auctions Act, 1961, makes it an offence knowingly to participate in a " mock action," as therein defined.
[88] *Mackenzie* v. *Cormack*, 1950 S.C. 183.
[89] Lord Dunedin in *Taylor* v. *Wylie & Lochhead Ltd.*, 1912 S.C. 978.

and at the same time to get security for their debts. The agreement usually reserves to the seller the right to resume possession of the property in the event of any default in the payment of the price or hire.

Questions frequently arise on the terms of such agreements whether they are ordinary sales where the price is payable by instalments, in which the hirer contracts to buy the goods, or whether they are merely hires until the full price is paid. The difference becomes of importance when the buyer who has the possession and is the apparent owner sells to a third party or a creditor poinds the goods. The question then arises whether the third party or the creditor gets a good title to the goods as against the original seller.[90] A contract of hire purchase has been held to be a sale to which the Sale of Goods Act, 1893,[91] applies, whereby, where a person having bought or agreed to buy goods obtains, with the consent of the seller, possession of the goods or the documents of title to the goods, the delivery or transfer by that person, or a mercantile agent acting for him, of the goods or documents of title under any sale, pledge, or other disposition, to any person receiving the same in good faith and without notice of any right of the original seller in respect of the goods shall have the same effect as if the person making the delivery or transfer were a mercantile agent in possession of the goods with the consent of the owner, and so having authority to sell them. But this provision and its legal effects may be evaded by, for example, the insertion in the agreement of an option to the purchaser to return the article without further penalty than payment of the proportion to date of the current instalment and forfeiture of the instalments already paid. Thus in one case the owner of a piano agreed to let it on hire, the hirer to pay a rent by monthly instalments, on the the terms that the hirer might terminate the hiring by delivering up the piano to the owner and remaining liable for all arrears of hire; also that if the hirer should punctually pay all the monthly instalments, the piano should become his sole and absolute property, and that until such payment the piano should continue the sole property of the owner. The hirer received the piano, paid a few of the instalments, and pledged it with a pawnbroker as security for an advance. It was held he was under no legal obligation to buy, and that the owner was entitled to recover the piano from the pawnbroker.[92] Where the purchaser has merely an option, he may assign his right to the effect of entitling the assignee to acquire the article by completing the instalments.[93] Articles the subject of a hire-purchase agreement fall under the landlord's hypothec.[94]

[90] *George Hopkinson Ltd.* v. *Napier & Son,* 1953 S.C. 139.   [91] Act, s. 25 (2).
[92] *Helby* v. *Matthews* [1895] A.C. 471.
[93] *Whiteley* v. *Hilt* [1918] 2 K.B. 808.   [94] *Rudman* v. *Jay,* 1908 S.C. 552.

The Hire-Purchase (Scotland) Acts, 1938 to 1964, apply to all hire-purchase agreements under which the total sum payable by the hirer does not exceed £2,000, except those made by or on behalf of a body corporate as the hirer. A hire-purchase agreement is defined as any contract whereby goods are taken on hire by one person from another person in consideration of periodical payments to be made by the hirer to the owner, with an option to the hirer to become the buyer of the goods. Where the Acts apply, the agreement must be in writing signed by the hirer and by or on behalf of the other parties. The written agreement must contain specified information relating to the transaction and a copy of it must be sent to the hirer within seven days of its execution. If the hirer signs the agreement at a place other than the dealer's business premises, the hirer may cancel the contract by sending a notice of cancellation to the owner at any time before the end of the period of four days after the day on which he receives the copy of the agreement. Certain stipulations as to the owner's title to the goods and as to the quality of the goods are implied in the agreement notwithstanding any contractual provision to the contrary. At any time before the final payment is due, the hirer may terminate the contract by giving written notice and making payment of the arrears of instalments to the date of termination together with the amount, if any, by which one-half of the total hire-purchase price exceeds the amount paid or due before the date of termination. After one-third of the hire-purchase price has been paid, the owner's right to recover possession of the goods on default is restricted.

Part III of the Hire-Purchase Act, 1964, provides that where the hirer of a motor-vehicle under a hire-purchase agreement disposes of the vehicle to a private purchaser who purchases in good faith and without notice of the hire-purchase agreement, the disposition has effect as if the owner's title to the vehicle had been vested in the hirer immediately before the disposition.

CHAPTER 5

TRADE MARKS AND NAMES

1. NATURE OF TRADE MARKS

A TRADE mark has been defined as "the mark under which a particular individual trades, and which indicates goods to be his goods—either goods manufactured by him, or goods selected by him, or goods which in some way or other pass through his hands in the course of trade." "It is a mode of designating goods as being the goods which have been in some way or other dealt with by the person who owns the trade mark." [1] Such a person obtains a property in the mark which he so affixes to his goods, and he is protected by the law in his right of property.

When the owner of a trade mark is asserting exclusive rights, "monopoly is not the thing for which the one party struggles and which the other resists. On the contrary, fair trading is all for which the protection of the law is invoked, and the public, as well as the manufacturer or merchant, are concerned that infringement of trade marks and trade designations should be prevented. For there is a double wrong: the public are or may be deceived, and the trader whose trade mark or trade designation is infringed is or may be injured." [2]

2. REGISTRATION OF TRADE MARKS

At common law there is a right of action for interdict and damages against any person who "passes off" goods as those of another person by, for instance, adopting or imitating the trade mark by which the other person identifies his goods. [3] Since the year 1875, however, when the Trade Marks Registration Act was passed, a person has been able, by registering a mark, to obtain the exclusive right to the use of the trade mark (subject to certain qualifications in respect of bona fide concurrent user by another person), [4] and may protect his right by action for infringement by way of interdict and damages. [5] The

---

[1] Kay J., *Re Australian Wine Importers Ltd.* (1889) 41 Ch.D. 278; and see Trade Marks Act, 1905, s. 3, now 1938, ss. 4, 5, and *Champagne Heidsieck et Cie Monopole Société Anonyme* v. *Buxton* [1930] 1 Ch. 330. The authorities are reviewed by Lord Hill Watson in *Haig & Co.* v. *Forth Blending Co.*, 1954 S.C. 35.

[2] *Per* Lord Craighill in *Dunnachie* v. *Young & Sons* (1883) 10 R. 874.

[3] *e.g.*, J. *Bollinger & others* v. *Costa Brava Wine Co. Ltd.* (No. 2) [1961] 1 All E.R. 561.

[4] T.M.A., 1938, s. 12.

[5] Such an action is now maintainable against the Crown—Crown Proceedings Act, 1947, s.3

present statutory law as to trade marks is contained in the Trade Marks Acts, 1905 to 1937, now consolidated by the Trade Marks Act, 1938.

Register of trade marks.—The Act of 1938 provides for the keeping of a register of trade marks under the control and management of the Comptroller-General of Patents, Designs, and Trade Marks, who is known as the Registrar. Special registers are kept by the Cutlers' Company at Sheffield in respect of metal goods, and by a Manchester Branch of the Trade Marks Registry at Manchester in respect of cotton goods. The registers are open to the inspection of the public, and certified copies of any entry may be obtained.[6]

By an Act of 1919 the register was divided into two parts, A and B, the former comprising trade marks registered or registrable under the Act of 1905, the latter comprising certain trade marks not so registrable. By the Act of 1938 the division into two parts is continued, registrability in one or other part depending on the distinctiveness of the mark.

What marks registrable.—A trade mark is registrable only in respect of particular goods or classes of goods.[7] But associations of persons who undertake to certify the origin, material, mode of manufacture, etc., of goods by marking the goods (called certification trade marks) may with leave of the Board of Trade register their marks.[8] A mark (other than a certification trade mark) to be registrable in Part A of the register must contain or consist of at least one of the following essential particulars: (1) The name of the company, individual or firm represented in a special or particular manner; (2) the signature of the applicant for registration or some predecessor in his business; (3) an invented word or words[9]; (4) a word or words having no direct reference to the character or quality of the goods and not being according to its ordinary signification a geographical name or a surname; (5) any other distinctive mark, but not a name, signature, or word or words other than as above except upon evidence of its distinctiveness, and in this connection " distinctive " means adapted to distinguish[10] the goods of the proprietor of the trade mark from those of other persons, e.g., by extent of user.[11] That is, distinctiveness is requisite for registration in Part A.

[6] T.M.A., 1938, ss. 1, 38, 39, 57 (2) and 2nd Sched.
[7] Ibid. s. 3.
[8] Ibid. s. 37 and 1st Sched.
[9] Re Eastman Photographic Materials Co. Ltd. [1898] A.C. 571.
[10] See George Banham & Co. v. F. Reddaway & Co. [1927] A.C. 406.
[11] T.M.A., 1938, s. 9; Yorkshire Copper Works Ltd. v. Registrar of Trade Marks [1954] 1 W.L.R. 554 (geographical name); Re Crosfield (1909) 26 R.P.C. 837.

To be registrable in Part B of the register a mark must be capable of distinguishing goods with which the proprietor of the trade mark is connected in the course of trade from goods in the case of which no such connection subsists. That is, capability of distinguishing is requisite for registration in Part B. A mark may be registered in Part B notwithstanding its registration in Part A.[12]

Application for registration.—In order to obtain registration of a trade mark application in the prescribed manner must be made to the Registrar. He may refuse the application, or accept it absolutely, or subject to amendments, modifications, conditions, or limitations,[13] or to disclaimer of right to the exclusive use of any part not separately registered or of matter common to the trade or otherwise of a non-distinctive character.[14] In case of refusal, or conditional acceptance, the applicant may appeal to the Board of Trade or court.[15] If an application is accepted (or before acceptance in the case of a distinctive mark under section 9 (i) (e) or in exceptional circumstances), advertisement is made by the Registrar, and any person may give notice to the Registrar of opposition to the registration. The Registrar decides the matter after hearing the parties, subject to appeal to the court.[16] If registration is permitted, it dates from the date of application, and a certificate by the Registrar is issued to the applicant.[17] The registration endures for seven years and may be renewed for further periods of fourteen years.[18]

Effect of registration.—No person is entitled to institute any proceeding to prevent, or to recover damages for, the infringement of an unregistered trade mark.[19] The effect of a valid registration of a person in Part A of the register as proprietor of a trade mark under the Act of 1938 is to give such person the exclusive right to the use of such trade mark in relation to the goods in respect of which it is registered [20] (subject, as already mentioned, to certain qualifications in respect of bona fide concurrent user by another person [21]). This right is deemed to be infringed by any person who, not being the proprietor of the trade mark, or a registered user thereof, uses a mark identical with it or so nearly resembling it as to be likely to deceive or cause confusion in the course of trade in relation to these goods, and in such a manner as to

---

12 T.M.A., 1938, s. 10.
13 *Ibid.* s. 17.
14 *Ibid.* s. 14.
15 *Ibid.* ss. 17 (4), 66.
16 *Ibid.* s. 18.
17 *Ibid.* s. 19.
18 *Ibid.* s. 20.
19 *Ibid.* s. 2. This does not exclude an action for " passing off."
20 *Ibid.* s. 4 (1).
21 *Ibid.* s. 12; *Bass Ratcliffe and Gretton Ltd.* v. *Nicholson & Sons Ltd.* [1932] A.C. 130.

render the use of the mark likely to be taken either as being use as a trade mark, or as importing a reference to the proprietor or registered user or to his goods.[22]   Registration is prima facie evidence of the validity of the original registration and all subsequent assignments and transmissions,[23] and registration for seven years is conclusive evidence of validity unless the original registration was obtained by fraud, or the mark is such that its use would, by reason of its being likely to deceive or cause confusion [24] or otherwise, be disentitled to protection in a court of justice, or contrary to law or morality or of a scandalous design.[25]

Registration of a person in Part B of the register as proprietor of a trade mark in respect of goods is prima facie evidence of the validity of the original registration and all subsequent assignments and transmissions,[23] and gives that person the like right in relation to those goods as if the registration had been in Part A of the register, except that an alleged infringer may resist an application by the registered owner for interdict against him by showing that his user of the mark is not likely to deceive, or cause confusion, or to be taken as indicating a connection in the course of trade between the goods and some person having the right either as proprietor or as registered user to use the trade mark.[26]   The provision that registration for seven years is conclusive evidence of validity does not apply to registration in Part B.[27]

Correction and rectification of register.—The Act of 1938 [28] provides for the correction of the register, and the alteration of registered trade marks, at the instance of the proprietor, with right of appeal from the Registrar to the Board of Trade or to the court; and also on application to the court, or the Registrar, at the instance of persons aggrieved by an entry, for rectification of the register,[29] or for expunging or varying an entry for breach of a condition,[30] or for removal from the register of a trade mark on the ground that the proprietor never intended to use and has made no bona fide use of the mark in connection with the goods or has in fact made no bona fide use of it during the preceding

---

[22] T.M.A., 1938, s. 4 (1).   This extension of the right originally conferred by the 1905 Act, s. 39, was first made by the 1937 Act, s. 15.   The change thereby made in the law is discussed in *Bismag Ltd.* v. *Amblins (Chemists) Ltd.* [1940] Ch. 667.

[23] *Ibid.* s. 46.

[24] See *M'Dowell* v. *Standard Oil Co. (New Jersey)* [1927] A.C. 632.

[25] T.M.A., 1938, s. 11.

[26] *Ibid.* s. 5.

[27] *Ibid.* s. 13.

[28] *Ibid.* ss. 34, 35.

[29] *Ibid.* s. 32.

[30] *Ibid.* s. 33.

five years. In this last case the Tribunal may, instead of removing the trade mark from the register, impose limitations on its use.[31]

Defensive registration of well-known registered trade marks consisting of an invented word or words may be obtained under the Act by the registered proprietor to prevent their use in relation to other goods of the proprietor in respect of which he does not use or propose to use the mark.[32]

3. Transfer of Rights in Trade Mark—Transfer of Property

A trade mark, when registered, can be assigned and transmitted either in connection with the goodwill of a business or not; but only subject to the conditions laid down in the Act can a trade mark be assigned or transmitted so as to give to more than one of the persons concerned exclusive right to the use of the mark in relation to the same goods or description of goods.[33]

Registered users.—Where a person becomes entitled by assignment or transmission to a registered trade mark, he must apply to the Registrar to register his title.[34] A person other than the proprietor of a trade mark may be registered as a registered user thereof on the application of the proprietor and the proposed registered user in the prescribed manner. The Registrar, if satisfied that the use would not be contrary to the public interest, may grant the application, or he may refuse it, and he may vary or cancel a registration which has been granted, his decision being subject to appeal to the court.[35]

4. International and Colonial Arrangements

The protection of trade marks is included in the arrangements made for the protection of patents and designs.

5. Trade Name

Apart from registration a right which at least resembles a right of property may be acquired in a trade name with which a particular business has come to be identified,[36] even though not registrable as a trade mark. Thus, it may be the name of an hotel, when it is regarded as attaching particularly to the premises.[37] Again, Bass's Ale is an

---

[31] Act, s. 26. See *Re Ducker* [1929] 1 Ch. 113.
[32] *Ibid.* s. 27. See *Re Ferodo's Application* (1945) 61 T.L.R. 478, where the court indicates the evidence required in support of an application for such registration.
[33] T.M.A., 1938, s. 22.   [34] *Ibid.* s. 25.
[35] *Ibid.* s. 28.
[36] *e.g.*, *Singer Manufacturing Co.* v. *Loog* (1882) 2 App.Cas. 15; *Argyllshire Weavers Ltd.* v. *A. Macaulay (Tweeds) Ltd.*, 1965 S.L.T. 21, the *Harris Tweed* case, was a case of slander of title.
[37] *Great North of Scotland Ry.* v. *Mann* (1892) 19 R. 1035.

instance of a name which could not be safely used by another Bass without clearly distinguishing his goods from the well-known goods of that name.

6. MERCHANDISE MARKS ACTS

The Criminal Law in relation to trade marks is contained in the Merchandise Marks Acts, 1887 to 1953.

The Merchandise Marks Act, 1887, makes it an offence against the Act, subject to imprisonment, fine and forfeiture of the goods, (1) to forge any trade mark; (2) falsely to apply to goods any trade mark or any mark so nearly resembling a trade mark as to be calculated to deceive; (3) to make an instrument for the purpose of forging a trade mark; (4) to dispose of or possess such an instrument; (5) to apply any false trade description to goods [38]; or (6) to cause any of these things to be done.[39] It is likewise an offence for a person to sell, expose for sale or be in possession of for purposes of trade or manufacture goods under a forged mark or false description, unless such person proves that he has acted innocently.[40] Persons whose ordinary business is to make dies or to apply marks or descriptions to goods on behalf of other persons are protected from prosecution.[41] A trade mark to which the Act applies is a trade mark registered under the Trade Marks Acts, and a " trade description " means any description or statement as to quantity, standard of quality, fitness for purpose, place of production, manner of making, material of which the goods are made, or existing patent or copyright protecting the goods.[42] The customs entry relating to imported goods is deemed to be a trade description applied to the goods.[43] Special provision is made for distinguishing the place of making watches and watch cases, and having the watch case stamped at an assay office.[44] The Board of Trade are empowered to undertake prosecutions in cases appearing to affect the general interests of the country.[45] Similar powers in certain cases are given to the Board of Agriculture.[46]

With a view to preventing the importation of goods liable to forfeiture, all such goods, and all goods of foreign manufacture bearing

---

[38] *Henderson and Turnbull* v. *Adair,* 1939 J.C. 83. See M.M.A., 1953, s. 2.

[39] M.M.A., 1887, s. 2 (1), as amended by M.M.A., 1953, s. 2; *Kat* v. *Diment* [1951] 1 K.B. 34.

[40] M.M.A., 1887, s. 2 (2), as amended by M.M.A., 1953, s. 4; *Stoodley* v. *H. D. Thomas & Sons Ltd. and Anor.* [1945] 1 K.B. 413; *Kat* v. *Diment, cit. sup.*

[41] *Ibid.* s. 6.

[42] *Ibid.* s. 3, as amended by M.M.A., 1953, s. 1 (1). *Cf. Henderson and Turnbull* v. *Adair, cit. sup.*

[43] *Ibid.*, 1891, s. 1.

[44] *Ibid.*, 1887, ss. 7 and 8.

[45] *Ibid.*, 1891, s. 2.

[46] Merchandise Marks (Prosecutions) Act, 1894, s. 1; Agricultural Produce (Grading and Marking) Act, 1928.

any name or trade mark purporting to be that of a trader within the United Kingdom, or a certification trade mark registered in the name of a person in the United Kingdom, unless there is a clear indication that they have been manufactured abroad, are prohibited to be imported.[47]   Further, it is an offence under the Act of 1926 to sell imported goods bearing a name or trade mark of a British manufacturer or trader, or a certification trade mark registered in the name of a person in the United Kingdom, unless accompanied by an indication of origin,[48] *e.g.*, " foreign " or " Empire," or a definite indication of the country where they were manufactured or produced.   Distribution in the United Kingdom of imported goods by way of advertising goods of some other kind is also prohibited.   And power is given to the Commissioners of Customs and Excise to require information from importers of goods bearing fraudulent marks as to the name and address of the person by whom the goods were consigned and of the person to whom the goods were sent.   Information so obtained may be communicated to the person whose name or trade mark, including a " certification trade mark," is alleged to have been used or infringed.[49]

A person who falsely represents that any goods are made by a person holding a Royal Warrant, or for the service of the Queen or Royal Family or for a government department, is liable to a penalty of £20 [50]; and a person using, without the authority of the Queen, or of a member of the Royal Family, any device, emblem or title in such manner as to be calculated to lead to the belief that he is employed by, or supplies goods to, the Queen or such member of the Royal Family may be restrained by interdict at the instance of any person authorised to use such device, emblem or title, or authorised by the Lord Chamberlain to take proceedings in that behalf.[51]

---

[47] M.M.A., 1887, s. 16, extended by M.M.A., 1953, s. 3.
[48] M.M.A., 1926, s. 1, amended by M.M.A., 1953, ss. 3 and 5.
[49] M.M.A., 1911, s. 1, amended by M.M.A., 1953, s. 3 (1).
[50] M.M.A., 1887, s. 20.
[51] T.M.A., 1938, ss. 61, 68 (3).

CHAPTER 6

THE LAW OF CARRIAGE OF GOODS

1. NATURE OF THE CONTRACT

The contract for the carriage of goods (*locatio operis mercium vehendarum*) is a species of the consensual contract of hiring. A carrier is one who undertakes to convey for hire goods, animals or passengers from a place within the realm to a place within or without the realm. The contract for the carriage of goods is for the safe carriage of commodities and their delivery in good condition in consideration of a hire. The carriage may be gratuitous. The contract may be express, when the carrier's rights and obligations depend upon the terms of the agreement, or implied from his receipt of goods.

The general law is as follows.

2. RIGHTS OF A CARRIER

The rights of a carrier are to have the goods to be carried delivered to him and his remuneration paid. He has a lien over every parcel of goods carried by him for the price of the carriage of it, but he has no lien over a parcel for the price of the carriage of a previous parcel, *i.e.*, his lien is a special not a general lien.[1]

3. OBLIGATIONS OF A CARRIER

If a carrier carries gratuitously he is only liable for gross negligence. If he carries for hire his obligations are determined (a) under the contract, or (b) in the case of common carriers, under certain rules of public policy.

(a) **Obligations under the contract.**—The responsibility of a carrier commences when he is charged with the goods by their complete delivery to him to be forwarded. In the absence of agreement to the contrary the carrier is held to undertake (1) that the vehicle shall be sufficient for safely carrying the goods.[2] This extends also to the accessories. Thus in land carriage the tackle, harness, horses, drivers, etc., and in railway carriage the permanent ways, signals, signalmen, etc., must be sufficient; and in sea carriage not only must the vessel be tight, staunch and strong for the voyage, but it must be properly manned and navigated and provided with all stores and documents

---

[1] *Stevenson* v. *Likly* (1824) 3 S. 291.
[2] *e.g.*, *Elliot* v. *Young's Bus Service*, 1945 S.C. 445.

129

necessary for the voyage. The carrier is not, however, liable for latent defects, *i.e.*, such as the eye cannot discover. The carrier is held to undertake (2) that the goods shall be properly packed and placed in the vehicle so as to withstand the necessary movement and concussion of the journey. The consignor may himself undertake the responsibility, in which case only ordinary diligence to notice and correct any defect is required of the carrier. In the case of dangerous goods the sender's duty is to specify their nature. The carrier is held to undertake (3) that ordinary care and the regular course of the journey shall be observed in the transit. The carrier is not bound to take precautions involving any unusual expenditure, nor is he responsible for damage arising from wholly unusual and unexpected causes. Should he deviate from the route he professes to carry or his usual route unnecessarily and the goods be lost, even by inevitable accident, he is liable.[3] If he receives goods to be conveyed to a place beyond his terminus he is responsible for their safe carriage during the whole of their transit, even though during part of the way they should be carried by another carrier, the latter being regarded as the agent of the original carrier.[4] The carrier is held to undertake (4) that he will forward the goods in due course, *i.e.*, with reasonable speed, especially in the case of perishable goods. He is justified in delay if delay be necessary for safe carriage. But if he has knowledge of any unusual cause of delay he is bound to advise the sender on receiving the goods.[5]

The carrier's responsibility ceases with the delivery of the goods according to the undertaking. His undertaking must be exactly fulfilled. Thus the goods must be delivered to the person indicated in the contract or according to the address, unless the address be defective.[6] Their delivery on board a wrong vessel subjects the carrier to liability.[7] Should the carrier be unable to find the consignee, or the latter refuse delivery, the carrier is liable for the safe custody of the goods while waiting the consignor's orders and for their redelivery according to his orders.[8] If before the carrier has parted with the goods to the consignee the consignor orders him to retain the goods or deliver them elsewhere he is bound to do so. The obligation to deliver under his contract is discharged by the destruction or loss of the goods from a cause for which he is not responsible, or even where by his own act he is compelled to sacrifice them by manifest necessity, *e.g.*, to save life.

---

[3] *Polwarth* v. *North-Western Ry.*, 1908 S.C. 1275.

[4] *Caledonian Ry.* v. *Hunter* (1858) 20 D. 1097; *Metzenburg* v. *Highland Ry.* (1869) 7 M. 919.

[5] *M'Connachie* v. *Great North of Scotland Ry.* (1875) 3 R. 79.

[6] *Caledonian Ry., supra.*

[7] *Gilmour* v. *Clark* (1853) 15 D. 478.   [8] *Metzenburg, supra.*

(b) Obligations of a common carrier.—A common carrier is one who undertakes for hire to convey the goods or money of all who think fit to employ him in the business which he professes to ply, *i.e.*, a public carrier. He need not profess to carry all kinds of goods but may limit his business to the carriage of any particular class of goods. A common carrier is subject to the Edict Nautae, Caupones, etc., adopted in Scotland from the Roman law, whereby he is held to insure the safe delivery of goods committed to his charge, and is responsible for any loss or damage, though no neglect on his part be proved, if such loss do not arise from natural and inevitable accident, the act of God or of the Queen's enemies. The larger responsibility of the common carrier is due to the supposed dangers of collusion and carelessness in his case.

As an insurer of the goods a common carrier is, at common law and apart from special agreement, liable for all injury to them whatever except, in addition to the exceptions under the Edict, (1) where due to neglect of the owner without negligence on the part of the carrier; (2) where due to an inherent vice in or natural deterioration of the goods, *e.g.*, a restive horse becoming alarmed and hurting itself during the journey [9]; and (3) injury due to the nature of the goods requiring special care of which he was ignorant through not being informed. [10] He is thus liable for loss due to robbery or theft, to accidental fire, [11] and to the fraud or negligence of his servants. The liability for loss through fire is different in sea carriage. [12]

The common carrier may by special agreement exclude his liability as such, as where he delivers a ticket or other notice to the person from whom he receives the goods specifying the terms upon which he agrees to carry. [13] But the evidence of the sender's knowledge of the notice must be clear. [14]

While carriers of persons are not common carriers, the obligations under a contract upon a carrier of passengers with respect to their luggage are the same as those of a common carrier during the transit, [15] but to the full extent only when the luggage has been delivered to the carrier's servants for carriage under his exclusive custody and control. He is not liable where the passenger takes his luggage with him in the

---

[9] *Ralston* v. *Caledonian Ry.* (1878) 5 R. 671.
[10] *Baldwin* v. *London, Chatham and Dover Ry.* (1882) 9 Q.B.D. 582.
[11] Mercantile Law Amendment Act, 1856, s. 17.
[12] *Vide infra*, p. 134.
[13] *Wood* v. *J. & J. Burns* (1893) 20 R. 602.
[14] *Macrae* v. *Hutchison* (1886) 14 R. 4, and *vide Henderson* v. *Stevenson* (1875) 2 R.(H.L.) 71; *Watkins* v. *Rymill* (1883) 10 Q.B.D. 178; *Richardson & Co.* v. *Rowntree* [1894] A.C. 217; *Hood* v. *Anchor Line* [1918] A.C. 837; *cf. McCutcheon* v. *David MacBrayne Ltd.*, 1964 S.L.T. 66.
[15] *Campbell* v. *Caledonian Ry.* (1852) 14 D. 806.

carriage and loss is due to the passenger's negligence. The luggage must be the passenger's own and must be personal luggage. Personal luggage means such as is ordinarily and usually carried by passengers as their luggage, the taking of which has arisen from the fact of their journeying [16]—e.g., clothes, the fishing apparatus of the sportsman, the books of the student, but not what is carried for the purpose of business or household goods. The carrier is bound to receive and take charge of the usual amount of luggage allowed to a passenger, and he has a lien upon the luggage both for the passenger's fare and the charge for luggage.

4. MEASURE OF LIABILITY

The consignor of goods is entitled to fair compensation from the carrier for loss of the goods. The general rule as to the measure of damages is the market price of the goods at the place of delivery. The facts of each case must be looked to.[17]

Valuable goods.—Carriers Act, 1830.—In the case of valuable goods the severity of the responsibility put upon common carriers led to the passing of the Carriers Act, 1830.

By that Act [18] no common carrier by land for hire is liable for loss or injury to certain articles when the value exceeds £10,[19] unless when they are received the value is declared and an increased charge accepted by, or agreed to be paid to, the carrier. The articles include gold or silver coin, precious stones, jewellery, watches, bills, bank notes, title-deeds, paintings, glass, china, silks, lace and furs, and others.

The increased rate of charge must be notified by the carrier to the public by a notice conspicuously affixed in every place where such articles are received,[20] and the carrier must give a receipt for such increased charge or lose the benefit of the Act.[21] Other than as provided for by the Act no public notice can limit or affect the liability of a common carrier.[22] The carrier can still enter into special contracts limiting his responsibility, but these will not deprive the carrier of the protection of the Act, unless their terms are inconsistent with the goods having been received by him in his capacity of common carrier.[23] A sender entitled to damages may in addition to the value of the parcel

---

[16] *Hudston* v. *Midland Ry.* (1869) 4 Q.B. 366.
[17] *Ciceri* v. *Sutton* (1889) 16 R. 814; *Keddie, Gordon & Co.* v. *N.B. Ry.* (1886) 14 R. 233.
[18] Act, s. 1.
[19] £25 in carriage by rail.
[20] Act, s. 2.
[21] *Ibid.* s. 3.
[22] *Ibid.* s. 4.
[23] *Baxendale* v. *Great Eastern Ry.* (1869) L.R. 4 Q.B. 244. Act, s. 6; *Great Northern Ry.* v. *L.E.P. Ltd.* [1922] 2 K.B. 742.

receive the increased charges.[24]   The carrier is not relieved by the Act
of liability for the felonious acts of his servants.[25]

While statutory carriers and carriers by sea are at common law
subject to the rules affecting the liability of common carriers, their
liability is in some respects determined by rules more special to themselves, statutory and other.

5. STATUTORY CARRIERS

(a) **Carriage by rail.**—The Transport Act, 1962, abolished the
Transport Commission set up by the Transport Act, 1947, whereby
the railways were nationalised.   The Act of 1962 set up four public
authorities or Boards, one of them a Railways Board, divided into six
regions.   The Board has power to carry goods and passengers by rail
within Great Britain.   The Board has power to demand, take and
receive such charges for their services and facilities and subject to such
terms and conditions as they think fit.[26]   The Board is thus now a
private carrier to which the Common Carriers Act, 1930, does not
apply.

(b) **Carriage by road.**—British Road Services Limited and B.R.S.
(Parcels) Limited and other companies through which the Transport
Commission provided carriage by road became under the 1962 Act
subsidiaries of a new Transport Holding Company.   They operate
under comprehensive Conditions of Carriage which are incorporated
expressly or by reference in each contract of carriage.

(c) **Postal services.**—The rights and liabilities of the Postmaster
General as a carrier of postal packets are regulated by statute.[27]

6. CARRIAGE BY SEA
(a) **Common law**

A shipowner is deemed to be a common carrier only in respect of
such ships as are employed as general ships, *i.e.*, ships intended on a
particular voyage for a miscellaneous cargo composed of goods of any
person that chooses to ship.   When goods are shipped a special
contract (contract of affreightment) is almost always made, and this
may vary the liability of the carrier to any extent.   The responsibility
of the shipowner has, however, been limited in some respects by statute.

(b) **Liability under the Merchant Shipping Acts, etc.**

By the Merchant Shipping Acts, 1894 to 1964,[28] the owner of a
British ship is not liable for any loss or damage happening without his

[24] Act, s. 7.   [25] *Campbell* v. *N.B. Ry.* (1875) 2 R. 433.
[26] s. 43 (3).
[27] Post Office Act, 1953; Crown Proceedings Act, 1947, s. 9; *Triefus & Co. Ltd.* v. *Post
     Office* [1957] 2 Q.B. 352.   [28] Act of 1894, s. 502.

actual fault or privity (1) where any goods are lost or damaged by reason of fire on board the ship; (2) where any gold, silver, diamonds, watches, jewels or precious stones, the true nature and value of which have not at the time of shipment been declared by the owner or shipper to the owner or master of the ship in writing, are lost or damaged by reason of any robbery, embezzlement, making away with or secreting thereof. In contracts of carriage falling within the provisions of the Carriage of Goods by Sea Act, 1924,[29] a limit of £100 per package or unit is imposed unless the nature and value of such goods has been declared by the shipper before shipment and inserted in the bill of lading.[30] By agreement another maximum may be fixed provided that it is not less than the figure above mentioned.

By the 1894 Act [31] the owner of a British or foreign ship is not liable without his actual fault or privity [32] beyond certain limited amounts, (1) for loss of life or personal injury to anyone being carried on the ship [33]; (2) for damage to or loss of goods on board; (3) for loss of life or personal injury caused by improper navigation of the ship to any person not carried in the ship ; (4) for loss or damage to any property by improper navigation of the ship.[34]

By the Pilotage Act, 1913,[35] the owner of a ship compulsorily in charge of a pilot is answerable for loss or damage in the same manner as he would if pilotage were not compulsory.

By the Carriage of Goods by Sea Act, 1924, the responsibilities and liabilities, and the rights and immunities, of carriers by sea under bills of lading are defined.[36]

(c) The contract of affreightment

This contract is for the carriage of goods in vessels for a price or freight. There is no general rule of law which requires it to be in writing, but it usually is. Contracts of carriage embodied in charter-parties are occasionally entered into verbally,[37] and this as a general rule would appear to be permissible in contracts normally embodied in bills of lading. The Carriage of Goods by Sea Act, 1924,[38] however,

29 14 & 15 Geo. 5, c. 22. *Infra*, p. 145.
30 *Pendle & Rivet Ltd.* v. *Ellerman Lines Ltd.* (1927) 33 Com.Cas. 70.
31 Act, s. 503, as amended by the Merchant Shipping (Liability of Shipowners and others) Act, 1958, s. 2.
32 *The Empire Jamaica* [1957] A.C. 386,
33 " Person carried in the ship " includes a member of the crew: *Innes* v. *Ross*, 1956 S.C. 468.
34 These provisions now apply also to ships owned by the Crown—Crown Proceedings Act, 1947, s. 5.
35 Act, s. 15.
36 See Carriage of Goods by Sea Act, 1924, *infra*, p. 145.
37 *Rederi Aktiebolaget Nordstjernan* v. *Salvesen* (1903) 6 F. 64 at p. 75.
38 14 & 15 Geo. 5, c. 22.

appears to require contracts falling within its scope to be embodied in writing.[39]

(i) Forms of the contract

The contract of affreightment has two forms: (1) charterparty; (2) bill of lading.

(1) *Charterparty*.—Affreightment by charterparty is a contract whereby an entire ship, or some principal part thereof, is let by the owner for the specified purposes of the merchant or charterer who hires it during a specified term (time charter) [40] or for a specified voyage (voyage charter), in consideration of a certain sum of money, called freight, per ton, or per month, or for the whole period of the adventure described.

A charterparty may operate in two ways: (1) It may confer on the charterer simply the right to have his goods carried by a particular vessel. In this case the possession and control of the ship are not transferred to the charterer. The master and crew are the shipowner's servants. The shipowner is responsible for the goods shipped and has a lien over the goods for freight. (2) It may amount to a " demise " or lease of the ship. The possession and control of the ship in this case are in the charterer. The master and crew are his servants and the master is the agent of the charterer. Demise is not very common and need not be further dealt with.[41]

(2) *Bill of lading*.—A bill of lading is a receipt for goods shipped, signed by the person who contracts to carry them, or his agent, and stating the terms on which the goods were delivered to and received by the ship. It is not a contract, for that has been made before the bill of lading was signed, but it is excellent evidence of the terms of the contract.[42]

The charterer may himself supply the cargo, or he or the shipowner where the ship is not chartered may advertise the ship for a specified voyage to carry for any persons who wish to send goods to places mentioned. In the latter case the ship is said to be employed as a general ship and the contract with the shippers of goods is embodied in a bill of lading given to each shipper when the goods are put on board. Where the charterer himself supplies the cargo he usually obtains bills of lading signed by the master as evidence that the goods have been shipped. In such case the bill of lading is generally merely a receipt

---

[39] Act, Art. III, Rules 3, 7; Art. VI. *infra*, p. 145.
[40] The nature of a time charter is discussed in *Sea and Land Securities Ltd.* v. *William Dickinson & Co. Ltd.* [1942] 2 K.B. 65.
[41] Charter by demise is described in *Sea and Land Securities Ltd.* v. *William Dickinson & Co. Ltd., cit. sup.*, as " now obsolete."
[42] *Scrutton on Charterparties*, 17th ed., p. 9; *Sewell* v. *Burdick* (1884) 10 App.Cas. 74 at p. 105.

for the goods shipped, and the rights of shipowner and charterer will be governed by the charterparty. Where the shipper is not the charterer the rights of the shipper will not be subject to the terms of the charterparty unless there is a clear stipulation in the bill of lading to that effect,[43]—e.g., " freight and all other conditions as per charterparty," and, under such a clause, only in so far as the stipulations in the charterparty affect the delivery of the goods.[44]   It has been stated that such a clause will not import into the bill of lading a clause in the charterparty exempting the carrier from the consequences of his negligence,[45] but this rule has been questioned.[46] If, in consequence of discrepancies between the terms of the charterparty and the bill of lading, the shipowner incurs liability in excess of that which he would have incurred had the charterer incorporated into the bill of lading the clauses which he was bound to insert, the charterer will be liable to relieve the shipowner.[47]

A bill of lading differs from a charterparty in being a receipt and a document of title.[48]   They resemble each other in embodying the terms of the contract, although, while the charterparty is the contract, the bill of lading is merely evidence of its terms.   Where, however, the shipper, whether he be charterer or another, assigns the bill of lading, with the intention to pass the property in the goods, the bill of lading is the contract as between the assignee and the shipowner.[49]

When a ship is put up and advertised as a general ship for a particular voyage the person who wishes to send goods communicates with the master or shipowner's agents and with him or them fixes the quantity of goods to be sent for carriage and the rate of freight.   The goods are delivered at the quay or in lighters alongside the ship to the custody of the person in charge of the ship in exchange for a receipt called the mate's receipt.   The bills of lading are then filled up by the shipper stating the quantity of goods sent for shipment and describing their identification marks.   The goods are then put on board and checked with the figures in the bill of lading by the master, who then signs the bill and returns it to the shipper in exchange for the mate's receipt.

Usually the bill is signed in triplicate, " bills in a set."   One copy is retained by the master, the shipper takes the other two—one to retain as a protection against fraud on the part of the master, and the

43 *Pearson* v. *Goschen* (1864) 33 L.J.C.P. 265.
44 *e.g. Hill Steam Shipping Co.* v. *Hugo Stinnes Ltd.* 1941 S.C. 324.
45 *Delaurier* v. *Wyllie* (1889) 17 R. 167; *Rodocanachi* v. *Milburn Bros.* (1886) 18 Q.B.D. 67.
46 Scrutton, *op. cit.,* p. 56 *et seq.*
47 *Kruger* v. *Moel Tryvan Ship Co.* [1907] A.C. 272.
48 *Vide infra,* p. 150.
49 *Leduc* v. *Ward* (1888) 57 L.J.Q.B. 379.

other to transmit to the consignee. For, the bill of lading being a document of title to the goods mentioned in it, the master will deliver the goods only to a person who presents a proper bill of lading. He is entitled to deliver the goods to the person who first presents one of the bills to him on payment of freight, unless he has notice that there is another party holding a bill and claiming the goods, in which case he must not deliver until the true owner is ascertained.

The master is presumed to be the servant of the registered owner of the ship, but if he signs bills of lading or a charterparty without words showing he is merely acting as agent for the owner, the other party may treat either him or the owner as the person liable on the contract, and the master likewise may himself sue on the contract.

(ii) Construction of the contract.—Implied undertakings by shipowner

In all contracts for the carriage of goods by sea, the shipowner impliedly undertakes (1) that the vessel is seaworthy; (2) that the ship shall proceed with reasonable dispatch; and (3) that it shall not unjustifiably deviate. Under the laws of the United Kingdom the above undertakings may be excluded or varied to any extent by express contract. It is otherwise in the United States and most Continental countries, and in contracts to which the Carriage of Goods by Sea Act, 1924,[50] and similar Acts apply. The Water Carriage of Goods Act, 1936 (Canada); Sea-carriage of Goods Act, 1924 (Australia); and the Indian Carriage of Goods by Sea Act, 1925 (India and Pakistan) are examples of similar Acts within the British Commonwealth. This becomes of importance where the contract is to be construed with reference to the law of another country. For instance, by the Carriage of Goods by Sea Act, 1936, of the United States,[51] a clause in the contract exempting the shipowner from liability for the negligence of himself and his servants, or a clause exempting him from liability to provide a seaworthy ship, would be void as enabling the shipowner to escape his liability to exercise due diligence under his otherwise implied undertaking.

(1) *Seaworthiness.*—This means seaworthy for the particular voyage and for the cargo carried. It is an absolute undertaking, but relates merely to the ordinary perils likely to be encountered on such a voyage with the cargo agreed on.[52] The ship must be in a fit state as to repairs, equipment, crew, and in all other respects.[53] The implied

---

[50] *Infra*, p. 145 *et seq.*

[51] Superseding, for most practical purposes, the Harter Act, 1893. See *Scrutton on Charterparties*, 17th ed., p. 478.

[52] *Kopitoff* v. *Wilson* (1876) 34 L.T. 677; *Paterson Steamships Ltd.* v. *Canadian Co-operative Wheat Producers Ltd.* [1934] A.C. 538.

[53] *Dixon* v. *Sadler* (1891) 5 M. & W. 405 at p. 414; *The " Gunford " Ship Co. Ltd.*, 1911 S.C.(H.L.) 84; *Rio Tinto Co.* v. *Seed Shipping Co.* (1925) 42 T.L.R. 381.

warranty of seaworthiness relates to the time of sailing from the port of loading. It is a condition precedent.[54] Accordingly if the charterer prior to the commencement of the voyage discovers that the ship is unseaworthy and the defect cannot be remedied within a reasonable time he may rescind the contract. After the voyage has begun he cannot rescind, but can claim damages for loss. On the other hand, a clause in a charterparty that the ship is to be " tight, staunch and strong, and in every way fitted for the voyage," refers to the time the contract is made or to the time of sailing for the port of loading, and so may relate to the preliminary voyage to the port of loading. The clause, therefore, does not displace the implied undertaking.[55] While a breach of the implied warranty of seaworthiness entitles the charterer to refuse to load, a breach of the express warranty, relating as it does to the time the contract was made, does not, unless it is such as to frustrate the object of the charterer.[56] Accordingly an unseaworthiness existing when the contract was made, but cured before arrival at the port of loading, would not suffice to entitle the shipper to refuse to load. The burden of proving unseaworthiness is on those who allege it. Where, as under the Carriage of Goods by Sea Act, 1936, of the United States, or the Carriage of Goods by Sea Act, 1924, of the United Kingdom, and similar Acts, the obligation is to use reasonable diligence to provide a seaworthy ship, this does not displace the common law warranty but gives immunity in certain cases if it is shown that due diligence has been used to make the vessel seaworthy.[57]

(2) *Undertaking of reasonable dispatch.*—The shipowner impliedly undertakes that the ship shall proceed on the voyage with reasonable dispatch.[58] Failure may entitle the charterer to repudiate the contract if such as to frustrate the venture as a commercial enterprise, otherwise he has merely a claim for damages. On the other hand, a clause in the contract expressly exempting the shipowner from liability for or loss due to a peril of the sea is a good defence to a claim of damages for delay due to such a peril. Thus in *Jackson* v. *Union Marine Insurance Co.*,[59] a ship was chartered in November, 1871, to proceed to Newport and there load iron rails for San Francisco. She sailed for Newport on January 2, 1872, but was stranded on the way and could not be repaired for some months. On February 15 the charterers

---

[54] *Stanton* v. *Richardson* (1874) 45 L.J.C.P. 78.
[55] *Lindsay* v. *Klein* [1911] A.C. at p. 205.
[56] *Tarrabochia* v. *Hickie* (1856) 26 L.J.Ex. 26.
[57] *McFadden* v. *Blue Star Line* [1905] 1 K.B. 697; *Northumbrian Shipping Co. Ltd.* v. *E. Timm & Son Ltd.* [1939] A.C. 397 (insufficient coal in bunkers at commencement of stage of voyage); *The Makedonia* [1962] P. 190.
[58] *Suzuki & Co.* v. *Benyon & Co.* (1926) 42 T.L.R. 269.
[59] (1873) L.R. 8 C.P. 572; *cf. W. J. Tatem Ltd.* v. *Gamboa* [1939] 1 K.B. 132 (ship detained by hostile power).

repudiated the contract. It was held that they had a right to do so; but as the delay arose from the perils of the sea, which were excepted by the charterparty, the shipowner was not liable in damages for failure to perform his contract.

(3) *Deviation.*—The shipowner undertakes that the ship shall proceed on the voyage without unnecessary deviation, *i.e.,* he must follow the prescribed route, or, if none be prescribed, the ordinary route. The general presumption is that the route to be followed will be the shortest geographical sea track between the two points, but that presumption may be displaced by the existence of alternative routes or of a customary route.[60] The contract may of course give liberty to call at ports out of the ordinary course. But a general permission will not permit a vessel to call at ports off the course altogether.[61] And liberty to deviate will not be sanctioned so as to defeat the object of the contract.[62] Apart from express contract, deviation is justifiable (1) for purposes necessary to the prosecution of the voyage or to the safety of the adventure, *e.g.,* to put into the nearest port for necessary repairs, even though this involves deviation [63]; (2) to save life, but not property.[64] The implied undertaking not to deviate is regarded as a vital term of the contract. Breach of it sweeps aside the whole of the special contract in the charterparty or bill of lading. If the ship deviates the shipowner is liable for any loss, whether it arose out of the deviation or not, and whether it occurred before of after the deviation, subject only to the common law exceptions, *i.e.,* the shipowner's liability becomes in effect that of a common carrier.[65]

(iii) Charterparty.—Form

The following is a simplified form of charterparty:

" It is this day mutually agreed between the
Steamship Company Limited, owners of the good steamship
      of   tons net register or thereabouts, *now lying* in the
Port of London, and   Merchant: That the said *ship being tight, staunch and strong, and in every way fitted for the voyage,*

60 *Frenkel* v. *MacAndrews & Co. Ltd.* (1929) 45 T.L.R. 311, *per* Lord Dunedin at p. 314; *Tsakiroglou & Co. Ltd.* v. *Noblee Thorl G.m.b.* [1962] A.C. 93 (closing of Suez Canal).
61 *United States Shipping Board* v. *Bunge y Born Ltd.* (1926) 42 T.L.R. 174.
62 *Glynn* v. *Margetson* [1893] A.C. 351; *cf. G. H. Renton & Co. Ltd.* v. *Palmyra Trading Corpn. Ltd., of Panama* [1957] A.C. 149. Liberty to deviate will not relieve the shipowner of liability for deviation rendered necessary by delay resulting from initial unseaworthiness: *A/B Karlshamns Oljefabriker* v. *Monarch Steamship Co.,* 1949 S.C.(H.L.) 1.
63 *Phelps* v. *Hill* (1891) 1 Q.B. 605.
64 *Scaramanga* v. *Stamp* (1880) 5 C.P.D. 295.
65 *Thorley* v. *Orchis Steamship Co.* [1907] 1 K.B. 660; *International Guano Co.* v. *McAndrew* [1909] 2 K.B. 360; *Cunard Steamship Co.* v. *Buerger* (1925) 42 T.L.R. 653; *Compagnie Primera de Navagaziona Panama* v. *Compania Arrendataria de Monopolia de Petroleos S.A.: The Yolanda* [1940] 1 K.B. 362 (charterparty for more than one voyage).

shall *with all reasonable dispatch proceed to* and *there load a full and complete cargo of* and/or *other lawful merchandise*, and, being so loaded, *shall proceed to* , *or so near thereto as she may safely get, and deliver the same*, on being paid freight at the rate of per bale of 100 lb., with liberty to call at any port or ports on the way (*the Act of God, the Queen's enemies, restraints of princes, fire and all and every other peril of the sea always mutually excepted*).

" Ten days to be allowed for loading and discharge and five days on *demurrage* over and above the said *lay days* at £10 per working day."

Terms common in charterparties.—Some usual terms of a charterparty may be explained:

" Now lying at." The shipowner agrees to provide a ship. The position of the ship at the time of the contract is made is generally a material part of the contract. If the position is falsely represented the charterer can rescind, for on the whereabouts of the ship depends the time it will be available at the port of loading. Thus a charter was made on a certain date for a ship described as " now in the port of Amsterdam " to proceed with all possible dispatch to Newport and there load a cargo. She did not in fact arrive at Amsterdam till four days later. The charterer was held justified in refusing to load.[66]

" And there load a full and complete cargo of and/or other lawful merchandise." The charterer is under obligation to provide a full cargo, corresponding to the shipowner's duty to provide a ship and to receive it. The shipowner must give notice to the charterer that the ship is ready to load. The charterer must thereafter provide the cargo before the expiry of the lay days, *i.e.*, the time agreed to be allowed for loading, by bringing it to the place where the ship is lying. If there is a custom at the port of loading it will bind the parties unless inconsistent with the written contract. Thus it may be customary at the port of loading to ship coal cargo direct from the colliery.[67] The fact that it has become impossible to provide a cargo does not as a rule excuse the charterer, but he is excused where events have rendered performance of the contract illegal,[68] or the shipowner has broken a condition precedent, *e.g.*, to provide a seaworthy ship, or there are express provisions in the contract relieving him in certain circumstances. Thus in one case a cargo of wheat was to be loaded at Odessa. Before the ship arrived there war broke out between Britain and Russia. The charterer was relieved from liability to load a cargo.[69]

66 *Behn* v. *Burness* (1863) 32 L.J.Q.B. 204.
67 *Ardan Steamship Co.* v. *Weir* [1905] A.C. 501.
68 *Esposito* v. *Bowden* (1857) 27 L.J.Q.B. 17.   69 *Esposito, supra.*

If a full cargo is not provided the charterer must pay not only freight on the goods shipped but also damages, known as " dead freight," at the same rate for the unoccupied space.[70] " Other lawful merchandise " means goods of a similar kind ordinarily shipped from the port of loading.[71] The shipowner becomes responsible for the goods directly they are handed over to the person authorised to receive them, e.g., the mate.[72]

" Shall proceed to   or so near thereto as she may safely get." In the case of a general ship the port of discharge is stated in the bill of lading. Where the ship is chartered by one merchant the port may be agreed on or named in the charterparty, in which case the obligation to go to the named port is absolute. If not named in the charterparty the charterer must name a safe port, i.e., safe enough to enable ships to load and unload there by taking reasonable precautions. " Or as near thereto as she may safely get " refers to obstacles which are regarded as permanent, not temporary obstacles such as an unfavourable state of the tide. Thus in one case delivery was to be made at Taganrog, in the Sea of Azov. In December when the vessel arrived the Sea of Azov was closed by ice and would not be open for five months. It was held that the shipowner was not entitled to freight by delivering as near as he could get.[73] The question really is what may be regarded as contemplated incidents of the voyage.[74]

" And deliver the same." It is the duty of the holders of the bills of lading to look out for the arrival of the ship. The reason is that the master may not know who is entitled to the goods, for the bills of lading may have been assigned during the voyage. But a reasonable time must be allowed for claiming the goods, and until that time has elapsed the shipowner's liability as a carrier continues. The custom of the port may, in place of personal delivery, recognise another method, e.g., delivery to a dock company.[75] In questions of discharge weight is given to the custom of the port in interpreting the various terms used in the contract.[76] The shipowner may limit his liability for safe custody of the goods to that of an ordinary custodier by notice, accepted by the consignee, that he has warehoused the goods. The shipowner's liability is ended by refusal of the consignee to take delivery within a reasonable time, or under the Merchant Shipping

---

[70] *Mikkelsen* v. *Arcos Ltd*. (1925) 42 T.L.R. 3. *Infra*, p. 152.
[71] *Vanderspar* v. *Duncan* (1891) 8 T.L.R. 30.
[72] As to responsibility for proper stowage, see *Canadian Transport Co.* v. *Court Line Ltd*. [1940] A.C. 934.
[73] *Metcalfe* v. *Britannia Ironworks Co.* (1877) 46 L.J.Q.B. 443.
[74] *Cf. Matheos (Owners of)* v. *Dreyfus Co.* [1925] A.C. 654.
[75] *Grange* v. *Taylor* (1904) 20 T.L.R. 386.
[76] *The Turid* [1922] A.C. 397; *Hillas & Co.* v. *Rederi Aktiebolaget Acolus* (1926) 43 T.L.R. 67; *Smith, Hogg & Co.* v. *Louis Bamberger & Sons* [1929] 1 K.B. 150.

Act, 1894,[77] in the case of imported goods, if the owner fails to make entry of the goods at the Customs House or having made entry fails to take delivery, by warehousing the goods at any time after that fixed for delivery in the bill of lading or charterparty, or, if none is fixed, after the expiration of three working days from the time when the master reports the ship at the Customs House.

" The act of God, the Queen's enemies, restraints of princes, fire, and all and every other peril of the sea mutually excepted." These are the " excepted perils." They apply to the preliminary voyage to the port of loading, to the loading, to the voyage itself and to the unloading; but not, unless expressly, to any detention of the ship beyond the agreed period for loading and unloading. The effect of the excepted perils clause is to relieve the shipowner from liability for delay or loss of or damage to the goods while on the agreed voyage,[78] but not for failing to perform an obligation he is bound to perform, e.g., to deliver the goods at the port of destination. Therefore no freight is payable if the ship is prevented from completing the voyage even by excepted perils. If loss to the shipper arises from an excepted cause, the shipowner will not be protected if that cause operates owing to his negligence.[79] Since the decision in the *Xantho*,[80] it has been the law that a collision due to the negligence of the other vessel is a peril of the sea. If, however, the carrying ship is alone to blame, the shipper can sue the ship on the contract, and if both ships were to blame, the shipper can recover damages from each in proportion to the degree of blame attributable to each.[81]

" Lay days " and " demurrage." The earning power of a ship depends upon her continuous employment with as little delay as possible beyond the time occupied by the voyage. The charterparty generally specifies a certain number of days, called " lay days," within which the ship is to be loaded and discharged. Lay days are presumed to mean running days, i.e., all days whatsoever, but by the contract they may be only working days, e.g., excluding Sundays and Customs House holidays. Lay days begin to run when the ship is actually ready to receive or to discharge the cargo, and the charterer has notice from the shipowner that the ship is ready to load.[82] When no provision is made for lay days a reasonable time is allowed for loading and unloading. When the ship is detained beyond the lay days or a

---

[77] Act, s. 493.
[78] *Harrowing S.S. Company* v. *Thomas* [1913] 2 K.B. 171.
[79] *Paterson Steamships Ltd.* v. *Canadian Co-operative Wheat Producers Ltd.* [1934] A.C. 538 at pp. 544–545, *per* Lord Wright.
[80] (1887) 12 App.Cas. 503.
[81] Maritime Conventions Act, 1911, s. 1.
[82] *United States Shipping Board* v. *Strick & Co.* [1926] A.C. 545.

reasonable time the shipowner may have a claim of damages for detention of the ship. The contract may stipulate for a sum, usually *per diem* for so many days, called " demurrage," as damages for detention beyond the lay days. Where no provision is made in the contract the shipowner has a claim of unliquidated damages.[83]

Where no period of lay days is fixed the circumstances of the case are taken into consideration in determining whether there has been an unreasonable detention of the ship. For example, where a strike of dock-labourers caused delay, the shipowner was held to have no claim.[84] Prima facie the measure of damages is the rate, if any, agreed on as demurrage, but either party may show this is not a correct measure of the damage sustained.[85]

When lay days are specified there is an absolute obligation on the charterer to complete the loading or unloading within the specified time. A strike of dock-labourers causing detention beyond the lay days would not in this case excuse the charterers.[86] On the other hand, if delay is caused by the default of the shipowner, whose servants usually load and unload the cargo, as by failing to supply sufficient labour, the charterer will not be liable.[87]

Shippers or consignees who are not parties to the charterparty may be made liable for charterparty demurrage by a stipulation in the bill of lading, usually " freight and all other conditions as per charterparty." [88]

(iv) Bill of lading

(1) *Form.*—The following is a simplified form of a bill of lading:

" Shipped in good order and condition by   in and upon the good ship called the   , whereof   is the master for this present voyage, now riding at anchor in the port of   and bound for   [*here specify goods*] marked and numbered as in the margin, and are to be delivered in the like good order and condition at   aforesaid (the act of God, the Queen's enemies, fire, and all and every other dangers and accidents of the seas, rivers, and navigation of whatever nature and kind soever excepted) unto   or to his assigns, he or they paying freight for the same at the rate of   with primage and average accustomed. In witness whereof the master or agent of the

---

[83] *Aktieselskabet-Reidar* v. *Arcos Ltd.* (1927) 42 T.L.R. 737.

[84] *Hick* v. *Raymond* [1893] A.C. 22.

[85] *Moorsom* v. *Bell* (1811) 2 Camp. 616.

[86] *Budgett* v. *Binnington* [1819] 1 Q.B. 35; *Dampskibsselskabet Svendborg* v. *Love & Stewart,* 1915 S.C. 543.

[87] *Hansen* v. *Donaldson* (1874) 1 R. 1066; *cf. Houlder* v. *Weir* [1905] 2 K.B. 267, and *Thiis* v. *Byers* (1876) 1 Q.B.D. 244.

[88] *Gardner* v. *Trechmann* (1885) 15 Q.B.D. 154.

said ship hath affirmed to   bills of lading all of this tenor
or date, the one of which bills being accomplished the others to stand
void.

" Dated at   the   day of

" [*Signature*]."

(2) *Admissions in the bill of lading.*—The bill of lading usually
contains an admission as to the quantity, quality, and condition of
goods shipped. The shipowner undertakes to deliver all the goods
put on board " in like good order and condition," provided freight is
paid as agreed and he is not prevented by any of the excepted perils.
When the goods are not in good order when shipped a note should be
made to that effect in the margin of the bill. A bill without such a
note is known as a clean bill of lading. Broadly such admissions are
evidence against the shipowner, for the master is his agent to make all
admissions ordinarily made in the bill of lading,[89] but are not conclusive.[90] The master's signature only admits the receipt of a certain
number of packages, and that the goods or packages were externally
in good condition. Accordingly the onus of proving that goods mentioned in the bill of lading were not shipped is on the shipowner.[91]
He may escape liability by proving that the master had exceeded his
authority by signing for goods not actually shipped,[92] or that the
master incorrectly stated the quality marks in the bill of lading,[93] or
that defects in the condition of the goods were not apparent on reasonable inspection,[94] or if the bill of lading contains a qualification such
as " weight, quality, and contents unknown." [95] And where the
consignee is also shipper he must show that damage was due to fault
on the part of the shipowner or else that the goods were in fact shipped
in good condition.[96] Where the bill of lading has got into the hands
of a consignee or endorsee for value the bill is conclusive evidence as
against the person signing it that the goods represented to have been
shipped have been actually shipped, unless the holder of the bill knew
when he took it that the goods had not been shipped or the person
signing can show that the misrepresentation was due to the fraud of
the shipper, holder of the bill of lading, or someone under whom the
holder claims.[97]

---

[89] *Evans* v. *Webster & Bros. Ltd.* (1929) 45 T.L.R. 136.
[90] *Canada and Dominion Sugar Co. Ltd.* v. *Canadian National (West Indies) Steamships
Ltd.* (1946) 62 T.L.R. 666.
[91] *Smith* v. *Bedouin S.N. Co.* [1896] A.C. 70; *Mantoura & Sons* v. *David* (1926) 32
Com.Cas. 4.
[92] *Grant* v. *Norway* (1851) 20 L.J.C.P. 93.   [93] *Cox* v. *Bruce* (1886) 56 L.J.Q.B. 121.
[94] *Martineaux Ltd.* v. *R.M.S. Packet Co.* (1912) 28 T.L.R. 364.
[95] *Craig Line Steamship Co. Ltd.* v. *North British Storage and Transit Co.*, 1921 S.C. 114.
[96] *The Ida* (1875) 32 L.T. 541.
[97] Bills of Lading Act, 1855, s. 3; *Parsons* v. *New Zealand Shipping Co.* [1901] 1 Q.B. 548.

(3) *The Carriage of Goods by Sea Act*, 1924.—(i) GENERAL.—The Act gives the force of law to the " Rules relating to Bills of Lading " set out in articles in the schedule to the Act.[98] The object in view was to secure uniformity so that shippers and consignees might know the exact extent of the obligations and liabilities of shipowners carrying their goods. Acts in similar terms have been passed in other parts of the British Commonwealth.[99] The general intention of the Act is that the carrier of goods is to be subject to the responsibilities and liabilities set forth in Article III of the schedule, while at the same time he is to be entitled to the rights and immunities contained in Article IV. The responsibilities and liabilities imposed on the carrier are *minimum* responsibilities which he may not reduce, while the rights and immunities represent a *maximum* which he cannot enlarge.

(ii) THE SCOPE OF THE ACT.—The Act deals only with " Carriers under Bills of Lading." [1] It does not affect carriers under a charterparty beyond requiring them if they issue bills of lading to issue them in conformity with the requirements of the Act.[2] By section 1 of the Act it is provided that the Rules shall have effect in relation to and in connection with the carriage of goods by sea in ships carrying goods from any port in Great Britain or Northern Ireland to any other port. The Rules apply only to outward bills of lading. They do not, however, apply to contracts of carriage either of live animals or of deck cargoes which are in fact carried on deck. The Rules have a modified effect in relation to the coasting trade and shipments of particular goods made otherwise than in the ordinary course of trade.[3] Every bill of lading or similar document of title, including " Received for Shipment Bills of Lading," [4] issued in Great Britain or Northern Ireland, which contains or is evidence of any contract to which the Rules apply, must contain an express statement that it is to have effect subject to the provisions of the Rules as applied by the Act.[5]

The following definitions are contained in the Act:

Carrier includes the owner or the charterer who enters into a contract of carriage with a shipper.

---

[98] These rules, originally formulated as an international convention, are known as The Hague Rules.
[99] Australia (Sea-Carriage of Goods Act, 1924); India and Pakistan (Carriage of Goods by Sea Act, 1925); Canada (Water Carriage of Goods Act, 1936); and New Zealand (Sea Carriage of Goods Act, 1940). Also in the United States of America, Holland, Belgium, France, Denmark, Norway, Italy, Japan and several other countries. See *Scrutton on Charterparties*, 17th ed., pp. 490–494.
[1] See *Harland & Wolff* v. *Burns and Laird Lines*, 1931 S.C. 722.
[2] Art. V.
[3] *Infra.*
[4] See *infra*, p. 151.
[5] s. 3.

Ship means any vessel used for the carriage of goods by sea.

Carriage of goods covers the period from the time when the goods are loaded on board to the time when they are discharged from the ship. It is accordingly advisable that shippers should make provision to cover the periods before shipment and after discharge if the goods are to be in the hands of the carrier during these times.

Contract of carriage is defined as " contracts of carriage covered by a bill of lading or similar document of title in so far as such document relates to the carriage of goods by sea, including any bill of lading or similar document as aforesaid issued under or pursuant to a charterparty from the moment at which such bill of lading or similar document of title regulates the relations between a carrier and a holder of the same." It is not quite certain if these words mean contracts of carriage which are in fact embodied in a bill of lading or contracts of carriage which are usually and normally so embodied. From the general intention of the Act the latter would appear to be the correct meaning, and this view has judicial support.[6]

Particular goods.—The carrier is permitted to enter into a special agreement with the shipper in regard to any particular goods in certain circumstances.[7] This agreement may be upon any terms as to the responsibility and liability of the carrier for such goods, and his rights and immunities in respect of them, or his obligation as to seaworthiness, or the care or diligence of his servants or agents. The special circumstances in which such agreements may be entered into requires that the shipments shall be other than ordinary commercial shipments made in the ordinary course of trade and that they be shipments where the character or condition of the property, or the circumstances, terms, and conditions of carriage are such as to justify a special agreement. These special agreements are subject to three conditions:

(1) No bill of lading may be issued.
(2) The terms of the agreement shall be embodied in a receipt.
(3) This receipt is to be marked " Non-negotiable."

The term " particular goods " is not defined in the Act, but it is thought to be intended to cover new types of cargo or shipments involving a risk the extent of which cannot be accurately foretold.

Coasting trade.—Carriers and shippers in the coasting trade are at liberty to enter into special agreements covering the shipment of goods of any class or description. The coasting trade is defined as trade

---

[6] *Harland & Wolff* v. *Burns and Laird Lines,* 1931 S.C. 722.
[7] Art. VI; as to the effect of this article see the opinion of L.P. Clyde in *Harland & Wolff* v. *Burns and Laird Lines, supra.*

from any port in Great Britain or Northern Ireland to any port within the same limits or to a port in the Irish Free State [8] (now Republic of Ireland).

(iii) THE EFFECT OF THE RULES.—(a) GENERAL.—The responsibilities and liabilities of the carrier set out in the Act [9] cannot be reduced in any way whatsoever.[10] His responsibilities cover the loading, handling, stowage, carriage, custody, care, and discharge of the goods.[11] His liabilities are, however, subject to the provisions giving to him certain rights and immunities.[12] He may surrender any or all of these rights and immunities.[13]

(b) RESPONSIBILITIES AND LIABILITIES OF CARRIER.—*Seaworthiness.*— The Act makes a change of great importance in regard to the warranty of seaworthiness. The common law warranty that the vessel is seaworthy at the beginning of the voyage or stage of a voyage is abolished in any case to which the Rules apply,[14] and it is replaced by the less onerous obligation to exercise due diligence before and at the beginning of the voyage to make the vessel seaworthy, properly man, equip, and supply the ship and make the holds, refrigerating and cool chambers, and all other parts of the ship in which the goods are carried, fit and safe for their reception, carriage, and preservation. Neither the carrier nor the ship will be liable for loss or damage arising from unseaworthiness, unless caused by want of due diligence in these respects on the part of the carrier.[15] This obligation upon the carrier, while less onerous than that imposed by common law, applies to a period before the voyage commences as well as to the commencement of the voyage. The onus of proving that he has in fact used due diligence is laid upon the carrier.[16]

Loading and discharge.—The common law rule, that the carrier took over the goods and the liability for them at the ship's rail upon loading and was relieved from liability whenever he delivered at the ship's rail, was frequently altered by private agreement so as to place upon the shipper the duty of stowing on board or of unloading from the hold. The Act [17] requires the carrier properly and carefully to load, handle, stow, carry, keep, care for, and discharge the goods carried.[18] This would appear to strike at agreements under which the

[8] Act, s. 4.
[10] Rule 8 of Art. III.
[12] Art. IV.
[13] Art. V.
[14] Act, s. 2.
[15] Art. IV, Rule 1; *Angliss & Co. (Australia) Proprietary* v. *P. & O. S.N. Co.* [1927] 2 K.B. 456.
[16] *e.g., Parkyns & Peters* v. *Coppack Bros. Ltd.* (1934) 50 Ll.L.R. 17.
[17] Art. III, Rule 2.
[18] *Cf. Gosse Millerd Ltd.* v. *Canadian Government Merchant Marine Ltd.* [1929] A.C. 223.

[9] Art. III.
[11] Art. II.

responsibility for loading and discharging goods on board is placed upon the shoulders of the shipper. The carrier obtains some measure of protection under the Act.[19]

The bill of lading.—The carrier must,[20] on demand of the shipper, issue to the shipper a bill of lading. This bill of lading must show three things: (1) The leading marks necessary for the identification of the goods as the same are furnished in writing by the shipper before loading. (2) Either the number of packages or the quantity of goods or the weight, according to the method of measurement employed to record the quantum of goods. The particulars are to be as furnished by the shipper in writing. (3) The apparent order and condition of the goods.

The carrier is not bound to state or show in the bill of lading any marks, number, quantity or weight which he has reasonable grounds for suspecting not accurately to represent the goods actually received or which he has no means of checking.

The bill of lading is prima facie evidence of the receipt of the goods.[21] The shipper is deemed to have guaranteed to the carrier the accuracy of the marks, number, quantity, and weight as furnished by him and is liable to indemnify him against loss resulting from inaccuracies therein.[22] It should be noted that the apparent order and condition of the goods is not one of the particulars to be furnished by the shipper. By the terms of the Bills of Lading Act, 1855, a consignee under a bill of lading acquires the same rights and liabilities as the shipper. Where a shipowner issues a bill of lading acknowledging the receipt of the goods in " apparent good order and condition " he cannot afterwards prove, as against a holder or indorsee of the bill of lading, that the goods were damaged before shipment, if such damage would have been apparent on reasonable inspection.[23]

Notice of damage must be given in writing to the carrier or his agent at the port of discharge before or at the time of the removal of the goods or, if the loss and damage be not apparent, within three days. Failing such notice, removal of the goods is deemed to be prima facie evidence of delivery by the carrier of the goods as described in the bill of lading. The carrier and the ship are discharged unless suit is brought within one year after delivery of the goods or the date when the goods should have been delivered.[24]

[19] Art. IV, Rule 2. As to the position of stevedores see *Scruttons Ltd.* v. *Midland Silicones Ltd.* [1962] A.C. 446.
[20] Art. III, Rule 3.   [21] Art. III, Rule 4.
[22] *Ibid.* Rule 5.
[23] *Silver* v. *Ocean Steamship Co.* (1929) 46 T.L.R. 78; see also *White & Son (Hull) Ltd.* v. *Hobsons Bay (Owners)*, 47 Ll.L.R. 207.
[24] Art. III, Rule 6.

(c) RIGHTS AND IMMUNITIES OF CARRIER.—GENERAL.—Nothing in the rules is to prevent a carrier or shipper from entering into any agreement as to liability for loss and damage to or in connection with the custody, care, and handling of goods prior to the loading on and subsequent to the discharge from the ship on which the goods are carried.[25]

The provisions in the Rules are not to affect the rights and obligations of the carrier under any statute for the time being in force relating to the limitation of the liability of owners of seagoing vessels.[26]

Particular immunities.—In addition to the provisions dealing with Seaworthiness,[27] Deviation,[28] Limitation of Liability,[29] and Dangerous Goods,[30] the Act provides [31] that neither the carrier nor the ship shall be responsible for loss and damage arising or resulting from certain enumerated causes. These are: (1) Act, neglect or default of the master, mariner, pilot, or the servants of the carrier in the navigation or in the management of the ship.[32] Failure to prevent theft is not an act of management.[33] (2) Fire, unless caused by the actual fault or privity of the carrier. (3) Perils, dangers, and accidents of the sea or other navigable waters. (4) Act of God. (5) Act of war. (6) Act of public enemies. (7) Restraint or arrest of princes, rulers or people, or seizure under legal process. (8) Quarantine restrictions. (9) Act or omission of the shipper or owner of the goods, his agent or representative. (10) Strikes or lockouts or stoppage or restraint of labour from whatever cause, whether partial or general. (11) Riots and civil commotions. (12) Saving or attempting to save life or property at sea. (13) Wastage in bulk or weight or any other loss or damage arising from inherent defect, quality, or vice of the goods. (14) Insufficiency of packing. (15) Insufficiency or inadequacy of marks. (16) Latent defects not discoverable by due diligence.[34] (17) Any other cause arising without actual fault or privity of the carrier or without the fault or neglect of the agents or servants of the carrier.[35] The burden of proof is on the person claiming the benefit of this exception to show that neither the actual fault or privity of the carrier nor the fault or neglect of the agents or servants of the carrier

---

[25] Art. VII.
[26] Art. VIII.
[27] *Supra*, p. 147.
[28] *Infra*, p. 150.
[29] *Infra*, p. 150.
[30] *Infra*, p. 150.
[31] Art. IV.
[32] *Gosse Millerd* v. *Canadian Government Merchant Marine* [1929] A.C. 223; *Goodwin Ferreira & Co.* v. *Lamport & Holt* (1929) 45 T.L.R. 521.
[33] *The Touraine* [1928] P. 58; *The Glenochil* [1896] P. 10; *Foreman & Ellams* v. *Federal Steam Navigation Co.* (1928) 44 T.L.R. 250; " *City of Baroda* " (Owners) v. *Hall Line Ltd.* (1925) 42 T.L.R. 717.
[34] *The Dimitrios Rallias* (1923) 128 L.T. 491.
[35] *Broun & Co.* v. *Harrison* (1926) 43 T.L.R. 633.

contributed to the loss or damage. Stevedores are agents or servants of the carrier within the meaning of this section.[36]

The shipper is not to be responsible for loss or damage sustained by the carrier or the ship arising or resulting from any cause without the act, fault or neglect of the shipper, his agents or his servants. The effect of this provision would appear to be far reaching and there might be cases in which it would exempt an assignee from payment of a demurrage claim.

Deviation.—Deviation in saving or attempting to save life and property at sea, or any other reasonable deviation, is not to be deemed to be an infringement or breach of the Rules or of the contract of carriage, and the carrier is not to be liable for any loss or damage resulting therefrom.[37]

Limitation of liability.—Neither the carrier nor the ship is, in any event, to be liable for loss or damage in an amount exceeding £100 per package or unit unless the nature and value of the goods shall have been declared by the shipper before shipment and inserted in the bill of lading. By agreement this figure may be increased.[38]

Dangerous goods.—Goods of an inflammable, explosive, or dangerous nature, to the shipment whereof the carrier has not consented with knowledge of their nature and character, may be landed at any time or place and destroyed or rendered innocuous by the carrier without compensation.[39] The shipper of such goods is liable for all damages and expenses directly or indirectly resulting from such shipment.

If such goods are shipped with the knowledge and consent of the carrier and they become a danger to the ship or cargo they may be likewise landed, destroyed, or rendered innocuous by the carrier without liability on the part of the carrier except to general average,[40] if any. These powers in regard to dangerous goods are in addition to the powers conferred upon him by the Merchant Shipping Act, 1894.[41]

(4) *The bill of lading as a document of title.*—By the custom of merchants the bill of lading operates to pass the property in the goods when indorsed and delivered with that intention to a bona fide indorsee for value,[42] and the indorsee has all the rights of action which

[36] *Heyn* v. *Ocean Steamship Co.* (1926) 43 T.L.R. 358.
[37] Art. IV, Rule 4; *Foreman & Ellams* v. *Federal Steam Navigation Co.* [1928] K.B. 424; *Stag Line* v. *Foscolo Mango & Co.* [1932] A.C. 328.
[38] *Ibid.* Rule 5.
[39] *Ibid.* Rule 6.
[40] For Average, see p. 153.
[41] ss. 446–450.
[42] *Lickbarrow* v. *Mason* (1793) 6 East 19; *Sewell* v. *Burdick* (1884) 10 App.Cas. 74; *Hayman* v. *McLintock*, 1907 S.C. 936.

the consignee had as if the contract contained in the bill of lading had been made with himself.[43] If the bill is drawn " to order or assigns," the person to whom the bill is made out may transfer his rights under it by indorsing and delivering it to the assignee. He may merely indorse it in blank (*i.e.,* without specifying any indorsee) in which case his rights are transferred by mere delivery, the holder being entitled to fill up the blank as he chooses. If made out to a specified person without the addition of the words " to order or assigns," it is not negotiable to any extent. A bill of lading is not a negotiable instrument in the full sense like a bill of exchange,[44] for a bona fide indorsee for value of a bill of lading cannot get a good title from a transferor whose title is defective. The transfer of a bill of lading to a bona fide indorsee for value does, however, defeat the right of stoppage *in transitu* of an unpaid vendor.[45]

In recent times a form of bill of lading, known as a " Received for Shipment Bill of Lading," has come into general use. It is in the same form as an ordinary bill of lading, but instead of acknowledging receipt of goods on board it merely acknowledges that the goods have been received for shipment either by a named ship or by any ship of a particular description.[46] It is not clear if such a document is the same as a true bill of lading or is more of the nature of a storekeeper's warrant. The Carriage of Goods by Sea Act, 1924, seems to assume that it is a true bill of lading, and this is in accordance with the view taken in *The Marlborough Hill.*[47] Whether such a bill of lading is a good tender under a contract of sale on c.i.f. terms depends on custom of trade, or a course of dealing.[48]

(v) *Freight*

Freight is the consideration paid to the shipowner for the carriage of goods in his ship. Payment of freight and delivery of the goods are, unless otherwise agreed, concurrent conditions. Unless non-delivery is caused by the fault of the shipper alone, freight is payable only on delivery of the goods in terms of the contract of affreightment. The excepted perils may excuse the shipowner from liability for non-delivery, but will not entitle him, generally speaking, to earn freight, as where the master has to abandon the voyage. He must still forward the goods in order to earn freight.

---

[43] Bills of Lading Act, 1855, s. 1. *A/B Karlshamns Oljefabriker* v. *Monarch Steamship Co.,* 1949 S.C.(H.L.) 1.
[44] *Vide* Bills of Exchange, *infra,* pp. 163, 164.
[45] *Vide* Sale of Goods, *supra,* p. 112; also p. 42, note 4.
[46] *Weiss & Co.* v. *Produce Brokers Co.* (1921) 7 Ll.L.R. 211.
[47] [1921] 1 A.C. 444.
[48] *Diamond Co.* v. *Bourgeois* [1921] 3 K.B. 443. *Cf. Weiss* v. *Produce Brokers Co.* (1921) 7 Ll.L.R. 211; see *Scrutton on Charterparties,* 17th ed., p. 175, note (*u*).

Advance freight.—Freight may be payable in advance, *e.g.*, on shipment, or at a definite time thereafter. In that case, in England, payment does not depend on delivery and is due though the ship is lost or the voyage abandoned and the cargo never delivered. In Scotland an advance of freight is recoverable if the consideration fails.[49] Sometimes the charterer agrees to make payments in advance to meet the current expenses of the ship and to be deducted from the freight when it becomes payable. Such advances are merely a loan and can be recovered if delivery is not made.

Pro rata freight.—The parties may agree, or it may be implied, that delivery at an intermediate port is to be accepted as part-performance of the contract. In that case freight is payable *pro rata, i.e.*, in proportion to the part of the voyage completed. To raise an implication that *pro rata* freight is due the shipowner must have been able and willing to carry the cargo to its final destination. Mere acceptance by the merchant of delivery of the goods at an intermediate port where the master insisted on leaving them will not imply an obligation to pay *pro rata* freight. The merchant must have had a real option to have the goods conveyed to their destination.[50]

Lump sum freight.—Sometimes the charterer agrees to pay " lump sum freight " for the use of the ship, payable on delivery of the cargo. The full sum is payable when the shipowner has delivered or is ready to deliver the full cargo, or such part of it as has not been lost by reason of excepted perils,[51] but probably subject to deduction where part of the cargo has been lost through the negligence of the master. As already stated, the excepted perils do not, generally speaking, affect the shipowner's rights as to freight, whether payable on delivery, in advance, or lump sum.[52]

Dead freight.—Where a merchant undertakes to supply a given quantity or weight of goods and fails to supply the specified quantity, the shipowner is entitled under a claim for dead freight to receive freight in respect of the goods not supplied. It is the shipmaster's duty to try to obtain additional cargo and so lessen the claim to be borne by the charterer.[53]

Cesser clause.—A charterer is primarily liable for freight, and the fact that he has sub-let the services of the ship to persons who have put

---

[49] *Watson & Co.* v. *Shankland* (1871) 10 M. 142; *Cantiere San Rocco* v. *Clyde Shipbuilding and Engineering Co.*, 1923 S.C.(H.L.) 105.
[50] *Metcalfe* v. *Britannia Iron Works Co.* (1887) 46 L.J.Q.B. 443.
[51] *Harrowing Steamship Co.* v. *Thomas* [1913] 2 K.B. 171; affd. [1915] A.C. 58.
[52] *Supra*, p. 151. As to *quantum meruit* freight, see *Hain Steamship Co. Ltd.* v. *Tate & Lyle Ltd.* (1936) 41 Com.Cas. 350, *per* Lord Wright at 368, 369; *Aktieselskabet Olivebank* v. *Dansk Fabrik* [1919] 2 K.B. 162.
[53] *Wallems Rederi A/S* v. *Muller & Co., Batavia* [1927] 2 K.B. 99.

the goods on board under bills of lading reserving the same freight does not release him. Sometimes the charterer is merely an agent or · broker to fill the ship with the goods of other persons. A clause is then inserted in the charterparty called a " Cesser Clause," making his liability to the shipowner for freight to cease when the goods are supplied,[54] and giving the shipowner a lien on the cargo for freight and other claims, e.g., demurrage, under the charterparty. The clause may run, " charterer's liability to cease when the ship is loaded, the captain having a lien on the cargo for freight, dead freight, and demurrage." There is a general presumption that the extent of the shipowner's lien is the measure of the charterer's exemption.[55]

Lien for freight.—The shipowner has at common law a lien over goods shipped for the freight. This is a possessory lien, and so can only be enforced by retaining the goods. It arises only when freight is payable on delivery. Therefore, if freight is payable in advance or after delivery, there is no lien at common law. The lien is presumed not to extend to or be enforceable against persons not parties to the charterparty. Accordingly in their case, apart from clear indication in the bill of lading, the lien will be enforceable only as regards freight specified in the bill of lading.

If the goods on delivery are damaged or deteriorated the merchant cannot deduct from the freight. He may sue for the amount of the damage.

(vi) *Average* [56]

If in the course of the voyage it is necessary to sacrifice the ship or cargo the loss will generally fall on the owner of what is sacrificed. But where, to avert a common danger, the ship or part of the cargo is intentionally sacrificed, or extra expenditure is incurred to avert the danger, the loss or expenditure will be apportioned among the various interests in proportion to their saved values. This is called a " general average " sacrifice or expenditure. An interest sacrificed and claiming contribution will not, however, be entitled to it if the danger has arisen from the fault of that interest. Thus the shipowner cannot recover in respect of extra expenditure to further the adventure where such expenditure was due to the ship's own unseaworthiness.[57] If, however, the fault is excepted in the contract of carriage, contribution may be claimed. Thus in one case the charterparty excepted negligence of the shipowner's servants. By reason of negligence on the part of the ship's engineers water got into the ship and the shipowner claimed

[54] e.g., Hill Steam Shipping Co. v. Hugo Stinnes Ltd., 1941 S.C. 324.
[55] Jennenson, Taylor & Co. v. Secretary of State for India [1916] 2 K.B. 702.
[56] Vide also Marine Insurance, infra.
[57] Schloss v. Heriot (1863) 32 L.J.C.P. 211.

against the cargo-owner in respect of expenditure necessary to remove it and was held entitled to contribution.[58]   The sacrifice or expenditure must have effected the preservation of the ship or cargo or part thereof, otherwise there is no case for general average contribution.[59]

Common instances of general average sacrifices are jettison of the cargo in order to lighten the vessel, sacrifice of the ship or its tackle, stranding of the ship to avoid its sinking, and deviation to put into a port of refuge to save the ship and cargo.

The shipowner has a lien on the cargo for general average contributions, and must retain the goods until contributions due in respect of them to other persons are paid.[60]

7. CARRIAGE BY AIR

Contracts for the carriage of goods by air are ordinary commercial contracts.   The general law of contract as applied to the construction of commercial contracts applies to them.[61]

The conditions under which an aircraft can be used for the carriage of goods, the licensing of air transport and commercial flying and the registration of British aircraft, are the subject of regulation by Orders in Council under the Civil Aviation Acts, 1949 and 1960.

The international carriage of goods by air is regulated by the Carriage by Air Act, 1961.[62]   What is " international carriage " is elaborately discussed in *Grein* v. *Imperial Airways Ltd.*,[63] and in *Philippson* v. *Imperial Airways Ltd.*[64]   The Act gives effect to an international convention set out *in extenso* in the First Schedule to the Act.   The Convention, which has the force of law in the United Kingdom, applies to all international carriage of persons, luggage or goods, performed by aircraft for reward, and to gratuitous carriage by aircraft performed by an air transport undertaking, and regulates, *inter alia*, the documents of carriage, the liability of the carrier, and " combined carriage," *i.e.*, carriage performed partly by air and partly by any other mode of carriage.   Conditions based on the Convention

58 *The Carron Park* (1890) 59 L.J.Adm. 74.
59 As to liability for contribution by holders of bills of lading where loss occurs during wrongful deviation, see *Hain Steamship Co. Ltd.* v. *Tate & Lyle Ltd.* (1936) 41 Com.Cas. 350.
60 *Strang* v. *Scott* (1889) 14 App.Cas. at p. 606. As to liability for such contributions, see *The Cheldale* [1945] P. 10 and *Hain Steamship Co. Ltd.* v. *Tate & Lyle Ltd.* (1936) 41 Com.Cas. 350, *per* Lord Atkin at p. 356.
61 *Aslan* v. *Imperial Airways Ltd.* (1933) 49 T.L.R. 415. See also *M'Kay* v. *Scottish Airways Ltd.*, 1948 S.C. 254 (carriage of passengers).
62 This Act applies the Warsaw Convention also to non-international carriage by air. A Convention supplementary to the Warsaw Convention is given effect to in the Carriage by Air (Supplementary Provisions) Act, 1962.
63 (1936) 52 T.L.R. 681.
64 [1939] A.C. 332.

may be included in the documents of carriage (passenger ticket, luggage ticket and air consignment note for goods).[65] Statutory provision has been made regarding the insurance of goods,[66] and salvage.[67] A right to damages is extinguished if an action is not brought within two years.[68]

By the Air Corporations Act, 1949, there have been established two corporations, the British Overseas Airways Corporation, and the British European Airways Corporation, with a power to provide air transport services.[69] These corporations carry passengers, passengers' luggage and goods under General Conditions, which are incorporated in the documents. Actions for *inter alia* breach of contract may be brought against them within three years.[70] By the Civil Aviation (Licensing) Act, 1960, other air operators may provide similar services under licence from the Air Transport Licensing Board established under the Act.

---

[65] *e.g., Philippson* v. *Imperial Airways Ltd., cit. sup.*
[66] Civil Aviation Act, 1949, ss. 43–45; War Risks Insurance Act, 1939; Marine & Aviation Insurance (War Risks) Act, 1952.
[67] Crown Proceedings Act, 1947, s. 8; Civil Aviation Act, 1949, s. 51.
[68] Act of 1961, s. 5.
[69] Act, ss. 1, 2 and 15.
[70] Air Corporations Act, 1953, s. 3.

CHAPTER 7

THE LAW OF MERCHANT SHIPPING

THE law maritime as administered in Scotland is in substance that of
the United Kingdom. To a great extent it is codified in the Merchant
Shipping Acts, 1894 to 1964, the principal Act being the Act of 1894.
The principal amending Acts are the Act of 1906, the Maritime
Conventions Act, 1911, and the Pilotage Act, 1913. The Act of 1911
largely altered the law of liability in cases of collision.[1]

1. BRITISH SHIP

A British ship is a vessel that belongs wholly to (1) natural-born
British subjects, unless they have become citizens or subjects of a
foreign State; (2) naturalised British subjects or denizens who, while
they are owners, continue resident within Her Majesty's dominions or
are partners in a firm actually carrying on business within Her Majesty's
dominions, and have, since naturalisation or denization, taken the
oath of allegiance; and (3) bodies corporate established under the
laws and having their principal place of business in these dominions,
even though there be alien shareholders on the register.[2]

With unimportant exceptions every British ship must be registered.[3]
Registers of shipping are provided at ports in the United Kingdom
and colonies and, in certain cases, foreign ports.[4] Preparatory to
registration the ships have to be surveyed, measured, tonnage ascertained, a certificate of survey produced identifying the ship,[5] and, in
the case of the first registration, a builder's certificate produced giving
particulars as to the build and tonnage and of the sale to the person
desiring to be registered as owner.[6] The name of the vessel must be
marked on the bows and her name and the name of the port of registry
on the stern, the official number and tonnage cut on her main beam,
and her draught painted on the stern or sternpost.[7]

The applicant for registration must make a declaration of his

[1] ss. 1, 2 and 3 of this Act, which relate to the apportionment of damage or loss caused
be vessels, now apply in the case of vessels belonging to the Crown—Crown Proceedings Act, 1947, s. 6.

[2] *R.* v. *Arnaud* (1846) 9 Q.B. 806.

[3] M.S.A., 1894, s. 3; 1921, s. 1.

[4] M.S.A., 1894, s. 87.

[5] *Ibid.* s. 6.

[6] *Ibid.* s. 10.

[7] *Ibid.* s. 7.

qualification to own a British ship, the time and place of building and the name of the master.[8]

An entry of the above particulars is then made in the register by the principal officer of customs of the port of registry and a certificate of registry given containing similar particulars.[9]

If the ship is lost or ceases to be a British ship the certificate of registry must be given up.[10] If the ownership changes hands or there is a change of master an endorsement to that effect must be placed on the certificate at the port of registry.[11]

2. PROPERTY IN A BRITISH SHIP

The property in a British ship is divided into sixty-four shares and no more.[12] No person is entitled to be registered as owner of a fractional part of a share. But a share may be held by joint owners, not exceeding five in number, who will be considered as constituting one person. And any number of persons may have a beneficial title in a single share, the registered individual representing them. A corporation may be registered as owner by its corporate name. No notice of any trust may be entered in the register book, or received by the registrar, and the registered owner of a ship or share has accordingly absolute power to deal with his interest in the manner provided by the Act.

All deeds relating to the ownership of ships must be on printed forms, which can be obtained at the Customs House of a port of registry.

3. ACQUISITION OF OWNERSHIP

While a contract for the sale of a ship may be made verbally,[13] ships or shares of ships must be transferred by bills of sale in the form prescribed by the Act.[14] These have to be entered on the register by the registrar. If two bills of sale are granted by a registered owner, *i.e.*, to two different transferees, the first one produced to the registrar, even though second in date, takes preference, assuming bona fides on the part of the transferee.[15] The transferee is not entitled to be registered without making a declaration of transfer stating his qualification to own a British ship and that no unqualified persons have any legal or beneficial interest in the ship or any share.[16] A statement of the entry in the register is endorsed on the bill of sale itself.[15]

[8] *Ibid.* s. 9.
[9] *Ibid.* s. 14.
[10] *Ibid.* s. 21, am. 1906, s. 52.
[11] *Ibid.* s. 20.
[12] *Ibid.* s. 5.
[13] *McConnachie* v. *Geddes*, 1918 S.C. 391
[14] M.S.A., 1894, s. 24 *et seq.*
[15] *Ibid.* s. 26.
[16] *Ibid.* s. 25.

Where the property in a registered ship or share therein is transmitted on the marriage, death or bankruptcy of a registered owner or otherwise by means other than bill of sale, a declaration of transmission must be made containing statements as in a declaration of transfer, and a statement, accompanied by the appropriate evidence, of the manner in which and the person to whom the property has been transmitted.[17] When the person to whom a ship or share is so transmitted is a person not qualified to own a British ship, the court may, on application by the unqualified person within four weeks (or one year if extension allowed) of the transmission, order a sale of the property so transmitted, the proceeds to be paid to the person entitled. In ordering a sale the court names a person in whom it vests the right to transfer the ship or share.[18]   If no application is made or no order for sale is pronounced the ship or share so transmitted is subject to forfeiture.[19]

4. MORTGAGES

A registered ship or share therein may be the subject of a security for debt. The security instrument is called a mortgage. The mortgage must be in the statutory form prescribed by the Act and must be entered in the register to have effect.[20]   Mortgages enter the register in the order of time in which they are produced to the registrar, irrespective of their date. The registrar notes on the mortgage the fact, the time and the date of registration.[21]   Similarly, the discharge of a mortgage must be entered on the register.[22]

The mortgage confers on the mortgagee a power of sale of the ship on non-payment of the debt.[23]   If there are several recorded mortgages, a subsequent mortgagee cannot, without the order of the court, sell the ship or share without the concurrence of every prior mortgagee.[24]

The Act [25] also contains provision for the issue by the registrar of certificates of sale and mortgage whereby the ship may be sold or mortgaged while out of the country or colony where the ship is registered.

The mortgagor remains the owner of the ship,[26] and can continue to use the ship in a reasonable and ordinary way. But he cannot do

17 *Ibid.* s. 27.
18 *Ibid.* s. 29.
19 *Ibid.* s. 28.
20 *Ibid.* s. 24.
21 *Ibid.* s. 31.
22 *Ibid.* s. 32.
23 *Clydesdale Bank* v. *Walker & Bain*, 1926 S.C. 72.
24 M.S.A., 1894, s. 35.
25 *Ibid.* ss. 39–46.
26 *Ibid.* s. 34.

unusual acts whereby the security is impaired.[27]   Should he do so, or should he be in default in payment, the mortgagee may take possession of the ship in order to enforce his security, as by placing someone on board to represent him, such as a new captain.   He is then entitled to any freight which is in course of being earned.   The mortgagee of a majority of shares in the ship, but not the mortgagee of a minority, may enter into possession.

5. THE MASTER

The master is presumed to be the servant of the registered owner of the ship.   He has authority to do all acts usual and necessary for the employment of the ship, unless persons dealing with him have notice to the contrary.   He is also in certain circumstances the agent of the cargo-owner to take special measures to preserve the cargo or minimise loss in cases of necessity—this as part of his general authority as servant of the shipowner.   Thus he may, when in a foreign port and unable to communicate with the owners, make contracts for the hire of the ship, or enter into agreements to carry goods for freight.   He may sign bills of lading for goods shipped, sell the cargo at an intermediate port in order to prevent loss to the cargo-owner when it has become unfit to be carried farther, make a general average sacrifice of ship, freight or cargo, or hypothecate the ship or cargo in security of money borrowed by him in foreign ports for necessary expenses.   On the other hand, he cannot cancel or alter contracts already made by the owners.

6. BOTTOMRY AND RESPONDENTIA

When it is necessary for purposes essential to the prosecution of the voyage to raise money the master has power to do so by hypothecating the ship, freight and cargo in security for the loan, *e.g.*, to pay for repairs.   When ship, freight and cargo are given in security the contract of loan is embodied in a " bottomry bond."   When only the cargo is hypothecated a " respondentia bond " is given.   The master cannot hypothecate the cargo unless the interests of the cargo-owner require it and the ship and freight are an insufficient security for the sum required.[28]

The purpose of a bottomry bond being to enable the ship to complete the voyage and of a respondentia bond to secure the safe arrival of the cargo, if the ship does not arrive at her destination the lender loses his money.   Where several bonds have been given at different times on the same voyage, the later bond, being given at a time of

---

[27] *The Heather Bell* [1901] P. 272; *Law Guarantee Trust Society* v. *Russian Bank of Foreign Trade* [1905] 1 K.B. 815.
[28] *The Onward* (1873) 42 L.J.Adm. 61.

necessity when the earlier hypothecation would otherwise fail of its purpose, is entitled to be satisfied before the bond of earlier date.

A bottomry bond confers on the creditor a maritime hypothec on the ship, freight and cargo. It therefore attaches to the property even if that has passed into other hands, and ranks above all claims other than any given priority over it by statute. The court will if necessary sell the property charged to satisfy the bond. The cargo cannot be resorted to unless the ship and freight are insufficient to satisfy the charge.

Resort to borrowing by hypothecation is rarely necessary nowadays owing to the facilities for communicating with the owners by telephone, telegraph, or wireless. It should only be resorted to when no better way can be adopted of obtaining the money required.

7. SALVAGE

The term " salvage " is used to mean either salvage services or the reward for such services. There are two kinds of salvage, civil and military. The latter, which consists in the rescue of property from the enemy in time of war and may found a claim for reward before a Prize Court, is regulated by prize law, which applies to aircraft and goods carried therein, as well as to ships and cargoes.[29] Only civil salvage is considered here.[30]

A salvor is " a person who, without any particular relation to a ship in distress, proffers useful service and gives it as a volunteer without any pre-existing covenant that connected him with the duty of employing himself for the preservation of that ship." [31] All claims by the Admiralty in respect of salvage services, including claims for the use of the Queen's ships as salving instruments, were formerly excluded.[32] This is, however, no longer the law, and the Crown is now entitled to claim salvage in respect of services rendered by or with the aid of any ship, aircraft or other property belonging to the Crown and has the same rights and remedies as any other salvor. Salvage claims against the Crown are also now competent.[33]

The subjects of salvage are a ship, its apparel and cargo, including such when in the form of jetsam, flotsam or lagan,[34] or life.[35] Salvage

---

[29] Prize Acts, 1864 to 1939. See also *The Alwaki* [1940] P. 215.
[30] The law of salvage now applies to aircraft—Civil Aviation Act, 1949, s. 51.
[31] Lord Stowell in *The Neptune* (1824) 1 Hagg.Adm. 227 at p. 236. For a discussion of what are salvage services, see *The Troilus* v. *The Glenogle* [1951] A.C. 820; *Lord Advocate* v. *Owners of Graziella*, 1962 S.L.T. (Notes) 4.
[32] M.S.A., 1894, s. 557; *Admiralty Commissioners* v. *"Valverda" (Owners)* [1938] A.C. 173.
[33] Crown Proceedings Act, 1947, ss. 8, 9 (6).
[34] *The Gas Float Whitton No.* 2 [1896] P. 42; affd. H.L. [1897] A.C. 337
[35] M.S.A., 1894, s. 544.

is payable by ship, cargo and freight " at risk," *i.e.*, if it has not been paid in advance and its payment is dependent on delivery; but not the personal effects of master and crew or the wearing apparel of passengers.

In order that services may be rewarded as salvage they must be voluntary. Thus the crew cannot be salvors, unless and until the ship has been abandoned with the authority of the master or person in command.[36] The services must also have been successful.[37] Salvors are not entitled to reward for saving property which they have, by their own wrongful acts, contributed to place in jeopardy.[38] But a ship which has rendered salvage services is not prevented from obtaining a salvage reward merely because she belongs to the person who also owns the vessel which caused the necessity for the salvage services.[39]

In estimating the amount of salvage reward the following elements are taken into account: (1) the enterprise of the salvors and the risk they run; (2) the degree of peril encountered by the salved ship; (3) the degree of labour and skill which the salvors incur and display, and the time occupied; (4) the value of the ship salved.[40]

The right to salvage reward, while it arises independently of contract, may be the subject of contract.[41] An agreement between those in charge of a ship and the salvors as to the amount of the salvage award will in general be upheld by the court.[42] It may, however, be disregarded if, in the opinion of the court, it would be inequitable to enforce it. An agreement to pay an exorbitant sum made where the master was acting under stress of circumstances will be regarded as inequitable.[43]

The salvage reward is apportioned amongst the owners, master, pilot and crew, and any other persons taking part, and, where the services are from a foreign vessel, in accordance with the law of the country to which the vessel belongs.[44]

The salvor has two forms of action to recover his salvage reward. He has a personal action against the shipowner and each cargo-owner. In addition he can proceed against the ship and cargo themselves, *i.e.*,

[36] *The Warrior* (1862) Lush. 376.
[37] *Melanie* v. *San Onofre* [1925] A.C. 246.
[38] *Cargo ex "Capella"* (1867) L.R. 1 A. & E. 356.
[39] *The Beaverford* v. *The Kafiristan* [1938] A.C. 136, applied in *The Susan V. Luckenbach* [1951] P. 197.
[40] *Owners of the "Vulcan"* v. *Owners of the "Berlin"* (1882) 9 R. 1057, *per* Lord Deas at p. 1062; *Lord Advocate* v. *Owners of Graziella*, 1962 S.L.T. (Notes) 4.
[41] *Nicholson* v. *Leith Salvage and Towage Co.*, 1923 S.C. 409.
[42] *The Arthur* (1862) 6 L.T.(N.S.) 556.
[43] *The Port Caledonia and The Anna* [1903] P. 184.
[44] Maritime Conventions Act, 1911, s. 7.

in rem.[45]   If the property salved is in the salvor's possession he has a
lien over it until he is paid what is due him.   If not in his possession
he has a maritime lien [46] (hypothec) over it which he can enforce no
matter in whose hands the property is.[47]

[45] Bell's Comm., i, 592; ii, 103.
[46] *Supra*, pp. 91–2.
[47] *Currie* v. *McKnight* (1896) 24 R.(H.L.) 1; *The Goulandris* [1927] P. 182.   See also
supra, pp. 86, 87.

CHAPTER 8

BILLS OF EXCHANGE, CHEQUES AND PROMISSORY NOTES

NEGOTIABLE INSTRUMENTS

WHERE a document involving a personal obligation to pay money is assigned, the general rule is, as we have seen,[1] that the assignation must be completed by intimation to the debtor, and that, notwithstanding such completion, the title of the assignee remains subject to any defect which affected the title of the cedent. The necessities of commerce, however, in course of time obtained for certain documents used by merchants recognition by the courts as being exempt from this rule, and as being, in effect, equivalent to money. These documents are known as negotiable instruments, and any document which evidences a debt, and (1) is transferable by simple delivery, and (2) confers on a bona fide holder for value a valid right to the obligation which it embodies, is a negotiable instrument. Both of these features must be present, otherwise the document, although it may be a valid document of debt, is not a negotiable instrument.[2]

What documents are negotiable instruments.—The only documents which are negotiable are those which are made so by statute, or by mercantile custom recognised by the courts. Private persons cannot by stipulation confer this character on a document. Such a stipulation binds only those who are parties to it, but cannot bind any subsequent holder of the document.[3]

Examples of negotiable instruments are bank notes, bills of exchange, cheques, promissory notes, dividend warrants, and debenture bonds and share warrants payable to bearer. The class is not, however, closed; other documents may be made, or come to be recognised as, negotiable instruments.[4] Examples of instruments which are not negotiable are Post Office money orders and postal orders,[5] deposit receipts,[6] and I O U's. A bill of lading, though transferable by

---

[1] *Supra*, pp. 38–42.
[2] *London Joint Stock Bank* v. *Simmons* [1891] 1 Ch. 270, *per* Bowen L.J. at 294; [1892] A.C. 201.
[3] *Crouch* v. *Credit Foncier of England* (1873) L.R. 8 Q.B. 374, *per* Lord Blackburn at 381; *Dixon* v. *Bovill* (1856) 3 Macq. 1, *per* Lord Cranworth L.C. at 16.
[4] *e.g., Goodwin* v. *Robarts* (1875) L.R. 10 Ex. 337, 1 App.Cas. 476; *Bechuanaland Exploration Co.* v. *London Trading Bank* [1898] 2 Q.B. 658.
[5] *Fine Art Society* v. *Union Bank of London* (1886) 17 Q.B.D. 705.
[6] *Barstow* v. *Inglis* (1857) 20 D. 230; *Wood* v. *Clydesdale Bank Ltd.*, 1914 S.C. 397. As to the nature of a deposit receipt, see *Dickson* v. *National Bank of Scotland*, 1917 S.C.(H.L.) 50.

delivery without intimation, does not confer on the transferee a better title than the transferor had, and is therefore not, strictly speaking, a negotiable instrument.[7] Documents of title under the Factors Acts [8] are also not fully negotiable, inasmuch as the effect given to them by the Acts rests on personal bar, and the unauthorised transfer by an agent is effectual only because he has been allowed by the owner to be in possession of the document.[9]

BILLS OF EXCHANGE

1. Origin

The origin of bills of exchange is involved in obscurity. They appear to have originated from the necessities of foreign trade and the difficulty of transmitting coin from one country to another, and to have been extended only later to inland trade. They were brought into use by the Florentines in the twelfth century, and by the Venetians in the thirteenth century, and were subsequently used in France and Britain. In England, mention is made of them in a statute of Richard II in 1379, but they first appear in the law reports only in 1603. In Scotland, it is clear, from the provisions of an Act of 1681, that bills of exchange must have been in use prior to that time, for in that year an Act of the third Parliament of Charles II was passed, providing for summary diligence upon foreign bills. This provision was, in 1696, extended by the first Parliament of King William to inland bills. Gradually, as trade prospered, the use of such instruments increased, and in course of time they became a great constituent in commercial credit and currency; and, though now replaced in many transactions by cheques and bank drafts, they have still many important functions.[10]

2. Function

A claim by a creditor to be paid a sum of money by his debtor being an incorporeal right cannot, according to the general law,[11] be effectively assigned by the creditor to a third party unless intimation of the assignation be given to the debtor; and the effect of the assignation is only to give the third party such right as the creditor had. Commercial men, however, having discovered the great convenience of a written assignation as a means of liquidating a trading debt, agreed that the necessity for intimation be waived, and that an assignee, if he took in good faith and gave value, should get an absolute title to the

---

[7] *Scrutton on Charterparties and Bills of Lading*, 17th ed., pp. 169–170; British Shipping Laws, Vol. 3, §§ 1045–1087. *Supra*, p. 150.

[8] *Supra*, pp. 83, 84.

[9] *Supra*, Sale of Goods, p. 111.

[10] For a statement of the history of bills of exchange and other negotiable instruments, see opinion of Cockburn C.J. in *Goodwin* v. *Robarts, cit. sup.*

[11] *Supra*, pp. 38–42.

debt: and the law, following the custom of merchants in these matters, gave to any document in a certain form the privileges of transferability by delivery without intimation, and, on certain conditions, of giving to the transferee an absolute right to the obligations contained in it. Documents in this form thus became negotiable instruments under the name of bills of exchange.

3. Examples

Bills of exchange came to fulfil various functions, of which three illustrations may be given. (a) Their primary function was, and still is, to settle debts between merchants in different countries. For example, A, a London merchant, buys goods from B, a Paris merchant, at the price of £100. B agrees to accept from A, in place of payment in cash, his obligation expressed in a bill of exchange for £100 drawn payable by A's bankers in London. B owes £100 to C, a Glasgow firm. Instead of collecting the bill, *i.e.*, getting payment from A's bankers in London, and having the proceeds remitted to Paris, and then sent back to Glasgow, B may transfer his right against A to C by transferring his right in the bill to them. They can then, through their bankers in Glasgow, collect the £100 from A's bankers in London, and the whole transaction is thus settled without any movement of actual money. (b) Bills of exchange play an important part also in shipping transactions. For example, a Glasgow firm buys a cargo of wheat from a Canadian firm. The goods are duly shipped from Canada, and the Canadian seller gets a bill of lading for the cargo from the master of the ship. The only way in which the Glasgow buyer can get delivery of the cargo at Glasgow is by presenting the bill of lading to the captain on the arrival of the vessel. The seller wants to make sure that the buyer, before getting the cargo, will pay, or at least admit his indebtedness for the amount of, the purchase price. He therefore draws a bill of exchange for the amount on the buyer, *i.e.*, writes out an order addressed to the buyer directing him to pay the amount specified in the order, attaches this bill to the bill of lading, and sends both bills through his bankers in Canada to their banking correspondents in Glasgow, with instructions only to deliver the bill of lading to the buyer against payment of the price or acceptance of the bill of exchange, *i.e.*, against the buyer's writing on the bill of exchange an admission of indebtedness for the amount. (c) A bill may be used, also, in order to get immediate payment of a debt due at some future date. Thus, one merchant sells goods to another, the bargain being a three months' credit. The seller draws a bill upon the buyer for the amount of the price, payable at three months' date, and this bill the buyer accepts, *i.e.*, undertakes to pay. The seller has at once an acknowledgment for the amount due to him payable three months later, and the means of obtaining cash at once by taking that bill to his bankers and having it discounted, *i.e.*, obtaining from them payment of the bill less a sum of discount the amount of which depends on, amongst other things, the time when the bill is payable. The banker may discount the bill before its acceptance by the drawee, if he thinks that, in the event of the drawee's failing to accept or pay, the drawer can be relied on to repay the amount of the bill when payment is due three months later.

4. Leading characteristics

A bill of exchange has various characteristics, the principal of which are the following:

(1) **Fixes a debt.**—A bill is evidence of an obligation to pay money. The drawer, by signing, warrants that the drawee is due him the sum in the bill and will pay it when due.   The drawee, by signing it as acceptor, acknowledges that he is indebted to the drawer in the sum stated, and that, at maturity, he will pay the amount.   An indorser, by signing it as such, guarantees that the bill will, if not already accepted, be accepted and will be paid, and that, if it is dishonoured by non-acceptance, or non-payment, he will compensate the holder or a subsequent indorser who is compelled to pay it.

(2) **Is negotiable.**—This characteristic is imposed on the bill by mercantile usage, with the following results, namely: (a) unless it be expressly declared to be not negotiable, it will, by mere delivery without intimation, pass the right to the obligation contained in it to the transferee; it may, however, require indorsation in order to be in a state in which transfer by delivery can be accomplished; and (b) the transferee by delivery will, if certain conditions are satisfied,[12] get a complete and absolute title to it, even though the transferor's title to it was defective.   In the event of any of the conditions not being satisfied, a person taking it, even for value, gets no better title to it than the person had from whom he took it.

(3) **Operates as assignation.**—A bill, when negotiated, operates as an intimated assignation of the debt of which it is evidence and, in Scotland, when presented to the drawee, operates as an assignation of funds then in his hand, provided that certain conditions are fulfilled.[13]

5. The code

The law relating to bills of exchange, as also to cheques and promissory notes, is now mainly governed by the Bills of Exchange Act, 1882, which codified and, to some extent, modified the law existing

---

[12] *Infra*, p. 188.
[13] *Infra*, p. 184.

prior to its passing. It does not deal with the stamp law, or bills in bankruptcy, or prescription, and enacts that the rules of common law, save in so far as they are inconsistent with the express provisions of the Act, shall continue to apply.[14] It has been amended by three one-clause Acts, namely, the Bills of Exchange (Crossed Cheques) Act, 1906, the Bills of Exchange (Time of Noting) Act, 1917, the Bills of Exchange Act (1882) Amendment Act, 1932, and the Cheques Act, 1957.

6. Form

Bills are privileged documents inasmuch as they are freed from all ordinary formalities by which instruments of value require to be authenticated. So long as they comply with the provisions of the Act, they are, however expressed, entitled to the benefits pertaining to a bill. They prove their own dates without witnesses, and the designation, *i.e.*, occupation and address, of drawer, acceptor or indorser is not essential. The Act distinguishes between inland and foreign bills,[15] but the distinction is important only as regards the necessity for protest [16] and stamping.[17]

Forms which bills in daily use may take may be indicated thus:

£50   Glasgow,
                            August 1, 1945.

At sight   James White or order
On demand   pay to { me
Three months after { date   bearer
                      { sight

within the Head Office of the Bank of Scotland, Edinburgh, the sum of Fifty pounds. Value received.

                                       JOHN SMITH.

To PETER BROWN
    141 High Street,
       Edinburgh.

7. Terms

(1) *Drawer* is the person who draws the bill, *i.e.*, gives the order (John Smith). (2) *Drawee* is the person on whom the bill is drawn, *i.e.*, to whom the order is given (Peter Brown). (3) *Acceptor* is the drawee when he has acknowledged his liability to the drawer by signing his name, with or without the word " accepted." (Peter Brown, after he has accepted the bill.) [18] (4) *Payee* may be the drawer (me) or

[14] s. 97 (2).
[15] s. 4.
[16] *Infra*, pp. 190, 191.
[17] *Infra*, p. 174.   [18] Act, s. 17 (1).

someone else mentioned in the bill (James White) or bearer. (5) *Bearer* is the person in possession of a bill or note payable to bearer.[19] (6) *Indorser* is the holder of a bill payable to order who indorses it, *i.e.*, writes on the back of it his signature, with or without the name of a transferee, in order to put it in a proper state for transfer by delivery. The term includes also anyone who signs a bill otherwise than as a drawer or acceptor in order to make himself liable on the bill to a subsequent holder in due course, *e.g.*, to a bearer.   (7) *Indorsee* is the person to whom the bill is specifically assigned by name written on the back of the bill by the holder, who is then the indorser; *e.g.*, James White writes on the back of the bill, " Pay to Thomas Gray or his order.   James White."   Thomas Gray is the indorsee.   (8) *Issue* means the first delivery of a bill or note, complete in form, to a person who takes it as a holder,[20] *e.g.*, delivery by John Smith to James White, or retention by John Smith as being himself payee, or delivery by him to bearer.   (9) *Negotiation* means the transfer of a bill from one person to another in such a manner as to constitute the transferee the holder of the bill,[21] *e.g.*, indorsement by James White to Thomas Gray. (10) *Holder* means the payee or indorsee of a bill or note who is in possession of it, or the bearer,[22] *e.g.*, James White, or Thomas Gray, or a bearer.   (11) *Holder in due course* is included in the term holder and means a holder who gets an absolute title to the bill, because certain conditions are satisfied.[23]   (12) *Maturity* is the time at which payment of the bill may be demanded by the holder, *e.g.*, at sight, on demand, or three months after date or sight.   After maturity it is overdue, and loses its negotiable character.   It can still be transferred, but not so as to give an absolute title to the transferee.   (13) *Dishonour by non-acceptance* is the refusal of the drawee (Peter Brown) to accept the bill on presentment to him for acceptance prior to maturity.[24] (14) *Dishonour by non-payment* is the refusal or failure of the drawee or acceptor (Peter Brown), to pay the bill at maturity on due presentment when presentment is necessary, or his failure to pay when presentment is not necessary, and not made and the bill is overdue.[25]

8. Definition of a bill

The statutory definition of a bill of exchange is: A bill of exchange is an unconditional order in writing, addressed by one person to another, signed by the person giving it, requiring the person to whom

---

[19] s. 2.
[20] s. 2.
[21] s. 31 (1).
[22] s. 2. *Infra*, pp. 188–189.
[23] s. 29. *Infra*, p. 188.
[24] s. 43. *Infra*, p. 184.
[25] s. 47 (1). *Infra*, p. 186.

it is addressed to pay on demand or at a fixed or determinable future time a sum certain in money to or to the order of a specified person, or to bearer. An instrument which does not comply with these conditions, or which orders any act to be done in addition to the payment of money, is not a bill of exchange.[26]

9. Essentials

The essentials of a bill, as indicated in the statutory definition, are as follows:

(a) **The order to pay must be unconditional.**[27]—The reason is that it would perplex commercial transactions if bills were issued encumbered with conditions and contingencies, and if the persons to whom they were offered in negotiation were obliged to enquire when these uncertain events would probably be reduced to a certainty.[28] No one would rely on such instruments, and their negotiability would thus be destroyed. For example, an order to pay out of a particular fund in the hands of the drawee is conditional, for such a fund may, for all a transferee might know, not exist, and the debt is accordingly not certainly fixed. But an unqualified order to pay, coupled with an indication of a particular fund out of which the drawee is to reimburse himself, e.g., " out of funds in your hands belonging to me "; or with an indication of a particular account to be debited with the amount, e.g., " debit the same to my overseas account "; or a statement of the transaction which gives rise to the bill, e.g., " being the price of goods sold and delivered by me to you," does not affect its validity.[29] An instrument expressed as a conditional order is not a bill of exchange, but it may, if transferred to a third party, be used by him as a proof of debt.[30]

(b) **The order must be an order in writing** [31] **signed by the person giving it, that is, the drawer.**—It need not be holograph of the drawer, nor need his signature be attested by witnesses. The writing may be signed by procuration,[32] or, if the drawer cannot write, it may be signed on his behalf by a notary public and two witnesses. The drawer's signature may even be adhibited by some person duly authorised to do so.[33] A bill signed by initials or a mark may be sustained as a ground of action on proof that the party alleged to be the subscriber

[26] s. 3 (1) (2).
[27] s. 3 (3).
[28] Lord Kenyon C.J. in *Carlos* v. *Fancourt* (1794) 5 T.R. 482, at 485; *Story on Bills,* para. 46.
[29] Act, s. 3 (3).
[30] See *Lawson's Exrs.* v. *Watson* (1907) S.C. 1353.
[31] Writing includes print—s. 2.
[32] *Supra,* p. 71.
[33] s. 91 (1).

usually signed by initials or mark, and did so sign the bill in question,[34] but it does not warrant summary diligence.[35]

(c) **The order must be addressed to another person,** *i.e.,* the drawee must be named or otherwise indicated in the bill with reasonable certainty.[36] If this were not so, a holder would not know to whom to present it for acceptance, if such presentment were necessary, and a person to whom it was presented would not know whether he would be justified in accepting or paying it.

(d) **Time of payment.**—The order to pay must be on demand or at a fixed or determinable future time. This is of prime importance, for it fixes the date when the bill may be presented for payment, and enforced by action, and when also it ceases to be a negotiable instrument, *i.e.,* when a transfer can give a transferee no better title than his cedent.[37]

(i) *On demand.*—A bill is payable on demand which is expressed to be payable on demand or at sight or on presentation, or in which no time for payment is expressed.[38] If a demand bill is post-dated, *i.e.,* is issued prior to the date it bears, payment cannot be demanded until on or after the date stated therein.[39]

(ii) *Fixed or determinable future time.*—A fixed future time would be, " Three months after date pay to me or my order the sum of £50." A determinable future time would be, " Three months after sight . . ." *i.e.,* after the bill is presented to the drawee for acceptance; when so presented, the fact of presentment and the date are noted on the bill: or on, or at a fixed period after, the occurrence of a specified event which is certain to happen, though the time of happening may be uncertain, *e.g.,* " Three months after the death of A . . . . " An order for payment on a contingent event, however, *e.g.,* " Three months after the arrival of the ship *Dunedin* at Glasgow . . .," might be a valid document of debt, but would not be a bill of exchange, for the vessel might never arrive.[40] A demand bill may become payable at a fixed or determinable future time, *e.g.,* if post-dated.[41]

(iii) *Undated bills.*—A bill is not invalid by reason only that it is not dated,[42] *i.e.,* bears no date of issue. In such a case, the date is the date of issue. The convenience of dating a bill is, however,

34 Bell's Prin., § 323.
35 *Infra,* pp. 191–193. For the drawing of a bill on behalf of a company, see *infra,* p. 181.
36 s. 6.
37 s. 36 (2).
38 s. 10.
39 s. 13.
40 s. 11.
41 *Robinson* v. *Benkel* (1933) 29 T.L.R. 475.
42 s. 3 (4).

obvious, as this fixes the date of maturity, and also because a dated bill proves its own date, and the onus of proof of a different date is on the party alleging it.[43] A bill may be ante-dated, or post-dated, or bear date on a Sunday.[44] Where a bill payable at a fixed period after date is issued undated or where the acceptance of a bill payable at a fixed period after sight is undated, any holder may insert therein the true date of issue or acceptance, and the bill is payable accordingly. But where a wrong date is inserted, and the bill subsequently comes into the hands of a holder in due course, the bill is payable as if the date so inserted had been the true date, *i.e.*, the later holder, if in due course, is entitled to take the statement in the bill as accurate. If a wrong date is fraudulently inserted, and the bill never comes into the hands of a holder in due course, the bill, it would appear, would be void.[45]

(iv) *Due date of bill.—Days of grace.—Usance.—*When a bill is drawn payable at a certain specified period after date or after sight, three days, called days of grace, are, in every case where the bill itself does not otherwise provide, added to the time of payment as fixed by the bill, and the bill is due and payable on the last day of grace.[46] A bill provides otherwise if it is drawn payable " *ex grace*," " fixed," or the like. No days of grace are allowed on bills payable on demand. In most countries days of grace have been abolished but are still recognised in the United Kingdom and parts of the Empire, and some states in the United States of America. In reckoning the days of grace, if the month, which means calendar month,[47] in which the bill falls due has no day corresponding to the day of issue or acceptance, the last day of the month in which it falls due is the day from which the days of grace are reckoned. Thus a bill drawn on January 28, 29, 30 or 31, and payable one month after date, is normally due on March 3, because February normally has only twenty-eight days. If, however, a bill be drawn on January 28 in a leap year, payable one month after date, it will fall due on March 2. The importance of the due date and days of grace is that the holder has no right of action against any party to the bill until the expiry of the last day of grace.[48]

Foreign bills were at one time occasionally drawn at one or more usances, or at double, treble, or half usance. By usance was meant the customary time at which bills were made payable in a particular country or town, *e.g.*, France, thirty days; Hamburg, one calendar

[43] s. 13 (1).
[44] s. 13 (2).
[45] s. 12.
[46] s. 14 (1).
[47] s. 14 (4).
[48] *Kennedy* v. *Thomas* [1894] 2 Q.B. 759.

month; Leghorn, three calendar months. This practice is now obsolete, but the term is still used with reference to the time customary in a particular trade.[49]

(e) **A sum certain in money.—Interest.**—The bill must state, as the amount to be paid, a sum certain in money. The amount is certain although it is required to be paid with interest, or by stated instalments, or by stated instalments with a provision that upon default in payment of any instalment the whole shall become due, or according to an indicated rate of exchange.[50]   If the sum payable is expressed in words and also in figures, and there is a discrepancy between the two, the sum denoted by the words is the amount payable.[51]

Where a bill is expressed to be payable with interest, then, unless the instrument otherwise provides, interest runs from the date of the bill, and, if the bill is undated, from the issue thereof.[52]   If the bill has been issued either ante-dated or post-dated, interest runs from the date it bears.[53]   If there is no stipulation as to the rate of interest on an interest-bearing bill, interest is payable at five per cent. from the date of the bill.   Whether or not the bill is expressly interest-bearing, interest is due as liquidate damages on an overdue bill from date when payment was due.

(f) **The bill is to be paid to, or to the order of, a specified person or to bearer.**[54]—Where a bill is not payable to bearer, the payee must be named or otherwise indicated therein with reasonable certainty.[55]

(i) *Payable to order.*—In bills payable to order, *i.e.*, " Order Bills," the usual phraseology is " Pay to me or my order . . ." or " Pay to James White or order . . . "   In these cases the payee is " me " or " James White," and the bill is payable either to the payee or to someone to whom he orders payment to be made.[56]   A bill may be payable to two or more payees jointly, or in the alternative to one of two, or one or some of several payees, or to the holder of an office for the time being.[57]   It must not contain words prohibiting transfer.[58]

(ii) *Payable to bearer.*   A bill payable to bearer may take one of several forms.   It may be expressly so drawn, *e.g.*, " Three months after date pay to bearer. . . ."   An order bill, if indorsed by the payee " in blank " (*i.e.*, by simple signature, without specifying a

49 *Chalmers on Bills,* 13th ed., p. 37.
50 s. 9 (1).
51 s. 9 (2).
52 s. 9 (3)
53 s. 13.
54 s. 3.
55 s. 7.
56 *Infra,* pp. 174, 175.
57 s. 7 (2).   58 s. 8 (4).

particular indorsee) becomes payable to bearer.[59] The blank indorsement may, however, be converted by any holder into a " special indorsement " (*i.e.*, an indorsement specifying the person to whom, or to whose order, the bill is to be payable) by his writing above the indorser's signature a direction to pay to or to the order of the holder himself or some other person.[60] The bill then ceases to be negotiable until indorsed by the holder or such other person. A bill may be treated as payable to bearer also when the payee is a fictitious or non-existent person, *i.e.*, when a genuine indorsement by the payee cannot be obtained.[61] This includes not only the case where the payee is actually non-existent, but also the case where the name of an existing person is inserted by the drawer without any intention that that person should receive the money or have any connection with the bill.[62] On the other hand, a bill is not treated as payable to bearer where the drawer intended the payee, an existing person, to receive the money, though the drawer may have been induced to form that intention by fraud, and the payee may be unaware that his name has been used.[63] The authorities show that, if the bill may be treated as payable to bearer, anyone who takes it with the name of the payee indorsed upon it, though a forgery, may enforce it at maturity against prior parties, but if the bill cannot be so treated, no one can acquire a valid title except on a genuine signature by the nominal payee.

10. Non-essentials

A bill is not invalid by reason only that it is not dated, *i.e.*, no date of issue [64]; that it does not specify the value given, or that any value has been given for it; or that it does not specify the place where it is drawn or the place where it is payable.[65] The expression "value received " is thus superfluous. The insertion of the place of drawing, however, helps to fix the bill as an inland or foreign bill,[66] and it is usual and advisable that a place of payment be stated, either in the body of the bill or in the acceptance. The use of figures in the top left-hand corner of the bill to indicate the amount is merely for the convenience of bankers, brokers and others who handle bills in bulk.

11. Issue.—Stamping

Issue means the first delivery of a bill or note, complete in form, to a person who takes it as holder,[67] *e.g.*, the payee, " James White,"

[59] ss. 8 (3), 34 (1).
[60] s. 34 (2) (4).
[61] s. 7 (3).
[62] *Bank of England* v. *Vagliano* [1891] A.C. 107; *Clutton* v. *Attenborough* [1897] A.C. 90.
[63] *North and South Wales Bank* v. *Macbeth* [1908] A.C. 137.
[64] *Supra*, pp. 170, 171.
[65] s. 3 (4).
[66] *Infra*, p. 174.
[67] s. 2.

or " me," or " bearer." It then becomes a document of debt. It should also bear a twopenny stamp, impressed or adhesive, in payment of revenue duty,[68] for every person who issues, indorses, transfers, negotiates, presents for payment, or pays any bill of exchange liable to duty and not being duly stamped, incurs a fine of £10, and the person who takes or receives it is not entitled to recover on it, or to make it available for any purpose whatever.[69] The person to whom an unstamped bill is presented for payment may affix and cancel an adhesive stamp of twopence, and the bill is then, so far as respects the duty, deemed valid.[70]

Inland and foreign bills.—An inland bill is one which is, or on the face of it purports to be (a) both drawn and payable within the British Islands, or (b) drawn within the British Islands upon some person resident therein.[71]

A foreign bill is a bill which is not an inland bill.[72] It also must be stamped with an adhesive twopenny stamp. The first party in the United Kingdom into whose hands the bill comes unstamped must, before he uses the bill in any way, affix to it a proper adhesive stamp and cancel the stamp [74] by writing over it his name or initials and the date of his doing so. A bill, if presented for acceptance, or accepted or payable, outside the United Kingdom, i.e., a foreign bill, if unstamped or improperly stamped, may be received in evidence on payment of the proper duty and certain penalties.[75] This obviates the incongruous result of the bill being an enforceable document of debt against persons abroad, but not against those in this country.

12. Negotiation of bills.—Meaning

A bill is negotiated when it is transferred from one person to another in such a manner as to constitute the transferee the holder of the bill.[76] Holder means the payee or indorsee of a bill who is in possession of it, or the bearer thereof.[77]

When negotiable.—A bill, to be negotiable at all must be negotiable in its origin. If it contains words clearly prohibiting transfer, e.g., " Pay James White only . . . " or indicating an intention that it should not be transferable, e.g., " Not negotiable," [78] it is valid as

---

[68] Finance Act, 1961, s. 33. An unappropriated stamp, i.e., a postage stamp, is now permitted—s. 33 (5).
[69] Stamp Act, 1891, s. 38 (1).
[70] Ibid. s. 38 (2), as amended by Finance Act, 1961, s. 33.
[71] B. of E. Act, 1882, s. 4.
[72] B. of E. Act, 1882, s. 4.
[74] Stamp Act, 1891, s. 35 (1).
[75] Finance Act, 1933, s. 42.
[76] B. of E. Act, 1882, s. 31 (1).
[77] s. 2; Dickson v. Clydesdale Bank Ltd., 1937 S.L.T. 585.
[78] Contrast the meaning of "not negotiable" in the case of a cheque, infra, p. 214.

between the parties thereto but it is not negotiable.[79] If it is negotiable in origin, it may be negotiated at any time after issue, and even before acceptance, and it continues to be negotiable until it is restrictively indorsed or is discharged.[80] A bill can be negotiated even after it is overdue, but only subject to any defect of title affecting it at its maturity.[81] A bill payable on demand is, for this purpose, deemed to be overdue when it appears on the face of it to have been in circulation for an unreasonable length of time.[82]

Method of negotiation.—A bill payable to bearer is negotiated by delivery. A bill payable to order is negotiated by the indorsement of the holder, completed by delivery.[83]

Indorsement.—An indorsement, in order to operate as a negotiation, must be written on the bill itself and be signed by the indorser. If there is no room on the bill for further indorsement, an indorsement may be written on an *allonge*, or slip of paper, attached to the bill; and it may be written on a " copy " of the bill issued or negotiated in a country where " copies " are recognised.[84] It may be made in blank, or special, or contain terms making it restrictive. It may also be conditional. Indorsement in blank and special indorsement have already been considered.[85]

Restrictive indorsement.—An indorsement is restrictive which either prohibits further negotiation, *e.g.*, " Pay D only," or expresses that it is a mere authority to deal with the bill as directed by the indorsement, and not a transfer of the ownership of the bill, *e.g.*, " Pay D for the account of X." Such an indorsement gives the indorsee the right to receive payment of the bill and to sue any party thereon whom the indorser could have sued, but no power to transfer his rights otherwise than as expressed in the indorsement. Where a restrictive indorsement authorises further transfer, *e.g.*, " Pay D or order for my use," all subsequent indorsees take the bill with the same rights and subject to the same liabilities as the first indorsee under the restrictive indorsement.[86] A bill which is restrictively indorsed thus ceases to be fully negotiable.

Conditional indorsement.—A conditional indorsement, *e.g.*, " Pay D on arrival of the ship *Dunedin* at Glasgow," affects only the conditional indorser and indorsee. It does not affect the complete

[79] s. 8 (1). *Hibernian Bank Ltd.* v. *Gysin & Hanson* [1939] 1 K.B. 483.
[80] s. 36 (1).
[81] s. 36 (2).
[82] s. 36 (3).
[83] s. 31 (2) (3).
[84] s. 32 (1).
[85] *Supra*, pp. 172, 173.
[86] s. 35; *Lloyd* v. *Sigourney*, 5 Bing. 525.

negotiability of the bill, the payer may disregard the condition, and payment to the indorsee is valid, whether the condition has been fulfilled or not.[87]

Sale of bill.—When the holder of a bill payable to his order transfers it for value without indorsing it, this is not negotiation, but what is known legally as " sale of the bill." The transferee gets such title only as the transferor had in the bill, and, in addition, acquires the right to have the indorsement of the transferor for the purpose of enforcing the latter's right. On the other hand, the transferor is not liable on the bill until he indorses it.[88]

Effect of negotiation.—This will appear from the following consideration of the liability of parties and the rights and powers of the holder.

13. Liability on bills

(1) **General.**—The function of a bill is, in the normal case, to fix, or evidence, a debt. We now consider who are the parties who may be called on to pay the debt to the holder of the bill when it becomes payable. The general principle is that all the parties whose signatures are on the bill, *i.e.*, the acceptor, drawer and indorsers, are all liable, jointly and severally, to pay to a holder in due course. Amongst themselves, however, one of these parties is primarily liable, the others are only subsidiarily liable, in a certain order.

(2) **Order of liability.**—The only parties liable are those whose signatures are on the bill. A person who transfers a bill payable to bearer and does not indorse it, and the drawee of a bill who does not accept it, incur no liability thereon. The party primarily, or finally, liable may be the drawee who has accepted the bill, or the drawer. If it is accepted, the acceptor is primarily liable to pay it. If it is not accepted, the drawer is primary liable. The parties subsidiarily liable are then the indorsers.

(A) PRIMARY LIABILITY

(i) *Acceptor*

Acceptance is the signification by the drawee of his assent to the order of the drawer,[89] *i.e.*, it is the acknowledgment by the drawee of his liability to the drawer for the amount stated in the bill. The bill may be accepted before issue, or issued and negotiated before it is accepted. It may even go through the hands of a series of holders before it is presented to the drawee for acceptance.

[87] s. 33.
[88] ss. 31 (4), 23.
[89] s. 17 (1).

In order that a person may be liable as acceptor, the following three conditions must, in the ordinary case, be fulfilled. First he must appear in the bill as drawee and must be named or otherwise indicated with reasonable certainty,[90] *i.e.*, in the bill itself, and without extraneous evidence, there must be sufficient identification of the person who is to become the principal debtor. Secondly, he must have signed the bill.[91] This he usually does on the face of it, but he may do so on the back. Thirdly, he must have parted with the bill to the drawer or to the holder who presents it for acceptance, or have given notice to the presenter that he has accepted it. If he keeps possession of the bill and does not notify acceptance, any acceptance he may have given is revocable and he is not liable on the bill.[92] In the special case where a man has drawn a bill on himself, a holder may, in his option, treat it as a bill requiring acceptance, or as a promissory note, which does not require acceptance. A bill drawn on a person who is fictitious, or who has no capacity to contract, may also be so treated.[93]

General and qualified acceptances.[94]—An acceptance may be either general or qualified. A general acceptance assents without qualification to the order of the drawer, *e.g.*, " Accepted." A qualified acceptance varies the effect of the bill as drawn by incorporating restrictions of some nature. It may do so in almost any way, but it must not promise performance by any means other than the payment of money. Examples of a qualified acceptance are a conditional acceptance, that is, one which makes payment by the acceptor dependent on the fulfilment of a condition therein stated, *e.g.*, " on delivery of a bill of lading "; or an acceptance qualified as to time, *e.g.*, six months instead of three. The necessity for so qualifying an acceptance may arise, for example, from the drawee's not having, at the time the bill is presented to him, any funds of the drawer, but expecting to have them on the arrival of a ship with a consignment of goods, or by a sale of goods in his hands. In such a case, he may be willing to engage, and may validly qualify his acceptance by a condition of arrival, or of sale.[95] Other examples of qualified acceptance are a partial acceptance, that is, for part only of the amount for which the bill is drawn; the acceptance of some one or more of the drawees, but not of all; and a local acceptance, that is, an acceptance to pay only at a particular specified place, and not elsewhere.[96] An acceptance simply to pay at a particular

---

90 s. 6 (1).
92 ss. 2, 21 (1).
93 s. 5 (2).
94 s. 19.
95 Bell's Prin., § 317.
96 s. 19 (2); *Bank Polski* v. *K. J. Mulder & Co.* [1942] 1 K.B. 497.

91 s. 17 (2).

place is a general acceptance so far as the acceptor's liability is concerned, but to preserve recourse against the drawer and indorsers, presentment for payment must be made at that place. To this extent only is an acceptance in these terms a qualified acceptance.

Effect of qualified acceptance.—A holder who presents a bill for acceptance may refuse to take a qualified acceptance, and, if he does not obtain an unqualified acceptance, may treat the bill as dishonoured by non-acceptance.[97]   If a qualified acceptance is taken, the qualification is operative in a question with the parties who held the bill subsequent to acceptance. Parties to the bill prior to acceptance, *i.e.*, the drawer, and any indorser by whom the bill has been validly negotiated, are discharged of liability on the bill unless they have been given notice of the qualified acceptance and have concurred in its being taken. Where, however, the acceptance is merely partial, such parties are not discharged, if they have been given notice.[98]   Their concurrence is, in this case, not required.

The acceptor's contract.—The acceptor of a bill, by accepting it, engages that he will pay it according to the tenor of his acceptance. He is also precluded from denying to a holder in due course the existence of the drawer, the genuiness of his signature, and his capacity and authority to draw the bill; in the case of a bill payable to drawer's order, the then capacity of the drawer to indorse, but not the genuineness or validity of his indorsement; and, in the case of a bill payable to the order of a third person, the existence of the payee and his then capacity to indorse, but not the genuineness or validity of his indorsement.[99]   The effect of these provisions is that the acceptor is barred from pleading non-liability on the ground that the bill as originally issued was invalid in some respect; that is, he warrants that the bill was, at the time of his acceptance, in every respect a genuine and valid bill. He may, however, still refuse to pay to a person who acquired a title to the bill through a forged indorsement. He has no duty to take precautions against fraudulent alterations in the bill after acceptance.[1]

Referee in case of need.—*Acceptor for honour.*—These are two special cases where a person who is not the drawee may incur liability as acceptor. A referee in case of need is a person whose name has been inserted by the drawer or an indorser as one to whom the holder may apply in case of need, that is, in case the bill is dishonoured by

---

[97] s. 44 (1); p. 184, *infra.*
[98] s. 44 (2).
[99] s. 54.
[1] *Scholfield* v. *Earl of Londesborough* [1896] A.C. 514. Contrast the duty of the drawer of a cheque, *infra,* pp. 206–207.

non-acceptance or non-payment. It is in the option of the holder to apply to a referee in case of need or not.[2] Before, however, the bill can be presented to the referee in case of need, it must have been presented to the drawee for acceptance, and the fact of non-acceptance recorded by a method called " protesting." [3]

An acceptor for honour is a person who, with the consent of the holder, intervenes and accepts a bill which has been protested for dishonour by non-acceptance and is not overdue. This may be done by anyone not already liable as a party to the bill and for the honour of any party liable thereon. Where such acceptance does not expressly state for whose honour it is made, it is presumed to be made for the honour of the drawer. The acceptor for honour thereby incurs liability on the bill to the holder and to all parties subsequent to the party for whose honour he has accepted.[4]

(ii) *Drawer*

If the drawee has not accepted liability, or, having accepted, does not pay at maturity, the drawer is the person primarily liable. He may, however, exclude this liability by appropriate terms,[5] the usual phrase being " without recourse," and if he does so, he cannot be sued upon the bill in the event of dishonour by non-acceptance or non-payment.

The drawer's contract.—The drawer of a bill, by drawing it, engages that, on due presentment, it shall be accepted and paid according to its tenor, and that, if it be dishonoured, he will compensate the holder or any indorser who is compelled to pay it, provided that the requisite, proceedings on dishonour be duly taken; and he is precluded from denying to a holder in due course the existence of the payee and his then capacity to indorse.[6] The drawer is thus practically a guarantor for the drawee, and, if the bill is dishonoured by non-acceptance, and he gets due notice thereof, he will be primarily liable on the bill.

(B) SECONDARY LIABILITY

Indorsers.—If the party primarily liable is called on to pay, after payment becomes due, and pays, to the holder, his liability and the liability of all other parties also is at an end. If, however, the party primarily liable does not pay after payment is due, the other parties, *i.e.*, the indorsers, may be called on to pay to the holder, and any party so paying has then a right to call on all parties whose signatures were

---

[2] s. 15.
[3] *Infra*, pp. 190–191.
[4] ss. 65–66.
[5] s. 16.
[6] s. 55 (1).

prior to his to pay to him.   The parties other than the party primarily liable are thus subsidiarily liable as indorsers.

The indorser's contract.—The indorser of a bill, by indorsing it, engages that on due presentment it shall be accepted and paid according to its tenor, and that if it be dishonoured, he will compensate the holder or a subsequent indorser who is compelled to pay it, provided that the requisite proceedings on dishonour be duly taken; and he is precluded from denying to a holder in due course the genuineness and regularity in all respects of the drawer's signature and all previous indorsements, and from denying to his immediate or a subsequent indorsee that the bill was at the time of his indorsement a valid and subsisting bill, and that he had then a good title thereto.[7]   That is, the indorser is by his indorsement barred from pleading certain defects in the bill as it was at the time he indorsed it, and is thus, in a question with the holder, in the position of a drawer of a fresh bill and is liable as such.   He has also, in many respects, the position of a cautioner to later parties and to the holder for those who are already parties to, and liable on, the bill at the time of his indorsement, but, if forced to pay, he is entitled to recover the whole, and not merely a contribution, from anyone who, in the order of liability on the bill, ranks before him. That order is, in the absence of proof to the contrary, the order in which they appear in the bill.[8]

(3) Proof as to order of liability.—Accommodation parties.—These rules as to the order of liability on a bill hold only in the absence of proof to the contrary.   It may be proved that it is not the acceptor, but the drawer, or an indorser, who is the principal debtor.   Such cases generally occur when a bill is used, not for its original purpose of transferring a debt, but as a means whereby money is borrowed by one party, the drawer or an indorser, and its repayment is guaranteed by another party, the acceptor.   These are known as accommodation bills.[9]   A party to an ordinary trade bill, whether drawer, acceptor or indorser, may prove also that he signed it as an accommodation party without receiving value therefor, and for the purpose of lending his name to some other person.[10]   It is only in questions between such parties that their rights are regulated by the true relations between them; an accommodation party is liable on the bill to a holder for value.[11]

(4) Quasi-indorser.—Transferor by delivery.—There are to be mentioned two cases in which persons who are not parties to a bill incur

[7] s. 55 (2).
[8] s. 32 (5).
[9] *Infra*, p. 194.
[10] s. 28 (1).

[11] s. 28 (2).

a certain liability. The first is the case of the quasi-indorser, *i.e.*, a stranger who signs the bill otherwise than as drawer or acceptor. He is said thus to " back " the bill. He is not an indorser, but he incurs the liabilities of an indorser to a holder in due course.[12] The second is the case of the transferor by delivery, *i.e.*, where the holder of a bill, payable to bearer, negotiates it by delivery without indorsing it. He is not thereby liable on the bill, but, by negotiating it, he warrants to his immediate transferee, being a holder for value, that the bill is what it purports to be, that he has a right to transfer it, and that, at the time of the transfer, he is not aware of any fact which renders it valueless.[13]

(5) **Conditions of liability.**—The liability of parties to a bill depends on the fulfilment of the following four conditions:

(i) *Signature*

Signature is essential to liability. No person, including a body of persons, whether incorporated or not,[14] is liable as drawer, indorser, or acceptor of a bill who has not signed it as such. Where a person signs a bill in a trade or assumed name, he is liable thereon as if he had signed it in his own name. The signature of the name of a firm is equivalent to the signature by the person so signing of the names of all persons liable as partners in that firm.[15] With regard to companies, a bill or note shall be deemed to have been made, accepted or indorsed on behalf of a company if made, accepted, or indorsed in the name of, or by or on behalf or on account of, the company by any person acting under its authority.[16] Where a person adds to his signature words indicating that he signs for and on behalf of a principal, or in a representative character, he is not personally liable on the bill; but the mere addition of words describing him as an agent or as filling a representative character, does not exempt him from personal liability.[17] Signature by procuration has already been considered.[18]

Forged or unauthorised signature.—Subject to the provisions of the Act, a forged or unauthorised signature is wholly inoperative, and no right to retain the bill, to discharge it, or to enforce payment of it, can be acquired through or under the signature.[19] This means that the true owner, *i.e.*, the person with the right to the bill, cannot be deprived of his rights thereunder by his name being forged or affixed

[12] s. 56.
[13] s. 58.
[14] s. 2.
[15] s. 23. See further as to signature, p. 169, *supra*.
[16] Companies Act, 1948, s. 33.
[17] s. 26 (1).
[18] *Supra*, p. 71.
[19] s. 24.

without his authority. This general principle has two consequences.
First, no one can be a holder in due course, with a consequent right
to retain or enforce the bill, who derives his title through a forged or
unauthorised signature, and it does not matter that the holder has no
notice of the forgery or want of authority. This applies to every
holder subsequent to the forgery. Secondly, if the holder derives his
title through a forged or unauthorised signature, payment to him in
due course by the acceptor does not discharge the bill. The acceptor
remains liable to pay over again to the true owner, *i.e.*, to the party
whose signature was forged.

This general principle is, however, subject to certain qualifications.
The Act provides that the party against whom it is sought to retain or
enforce payment of the bill may be precluded from setting up the
forgery or want of authority,[20] *i.e.*, from saying he is the owner and
not liable to subsequent parties. This may be on one or other of
several grounds, namely—

(a) *Ratification.*—A signature which is merely unauthorised, and
not forged, may be subsequently ratified so as to preclude the person
so ratifying it from pleading the want of authority.[21]

(b) *Adoption.*—A forged signature cannot be ratified, but may be
expressly or implicitly adopted, *e.g.*, the person whose signature has
been forged may write to the holder saying, " I accept the signature
as mine."

(c) *Bar.*—A person may, without actually ratifying or adopting his
unauthorised or forged signature, be personally barred from disputing
its validity if his conduct has caused loss to the holder, *e.g.*, by his
delaying to give notice to the holder on discovering the forgery, and
so prejudicing the latter's right of recourse against the forger.[22]

(d) *Other provisions of the Act.*—The general principle is subject
also to other provisions of the Act.[23] These provisions are four in
number, namely (1) the clauses safeguarding a banker who, in good
faith and in the ordinary course of business, pays, on a forged or
unauthorised indorsement, a demand bill drawn on him, or pays a
crossed cheque in accordance with the crossing [24]; (2) the right to
treat as payable to bearer a bill the payee in which is a fictitious person,
including a real person not intended to receive payment, or a non-
existing person—anyone who takes it with the name of the payee
indorsed on it, though a forgery, may enforce it against prior parties

---

20 s. 24.
21 s. 24. *Mackenzie* v. *British Linen Co.* (1881) 8 R.(H.L.) 8.
22 *Imperial Bank of Canada* v. *Bank of Hamilton* [1903] A.C. 49.
23 s. 24.
24 ss. 60, 80. *Infra*, pp. 212–214.

as if it were a bearer bill [25]; (3) the rule that, in a question with a holder in due course, the acceptor is precluded from denying the genuineness of the signature of the drawer,[26] and an indorser from denying the genuineness of the signatures of the drawer and prior indorsers,[27] *i.e* if the holder has had to give up the bill to the true owner, and sues an indorser subsequent to the forgery for repayment, it is no defence for the indorser to say that the holder, because of the forgery has no right to the bill; and (4) the provision that a principal is only bound by a signature by procuration if the agent in so signing was acting within the actual limits of his authority.[28]

(ii) *Presentment for acceptance*

The second condition of liability on a bill is presentment of the bill by the holder to the drawee for acceptance. The object of such presentment is twofold, being, first, to satisfy the holder as to whether he is to rely on payment by the drawee; and, secondly, if the drawee should not accept,[29] to preserve a right of recourse against the drawer and indorsers, these parties having dealt with the bill on the assumption that the drawee would be asked to accept, and that they would get notice of his not having done so. If a bill is not presented for acceptance, where such presentment is necessary, there is no right of recourse until the bill has been presented for payment and dishonoured.

When necessary.—Presentment for acceptance is necessary in only three cases, *viz.*: where a bill is payable after sight, in order to fix its maturity; where a bill expressly stipulates that it shall be presented for acceptance; and where a bill is drawn payable elsewhere than at the residence or place of business of the drawee. In no other case is presentment for acceptance necessary in order to render liable any party to the bill.[30] When a bill payable after sight is negotiated, the holder must either present it for acceptance or negotiate it within a reasonable time, and if he does not do so, the drawer and all indorsers prior to that holder are discharged.[31]

When excused.—Presentment, where required, is excused, and the bill may be treated as dishonoured by non-acceptance, in certain cases, *viz.*: Where the drawee is dead or bankrupt, or is a fictitious person or a person not having capacity to contract by bill; where after the exercise of reasonable diligence, such presentment cannot be effected; and where, although the presentment has been irregular, acceptance has

[25] s. 7 (3). *Bank of England* v. *Vagliano* [1891] 1 A.C. 109.
[26] s. 54 (2) (*b*).
[27] s. 55 (2) (*b*).
[28] s. 25.
[29] Bell's Prin., § 336.
[30] s. 39.
[31] s. 40.

been refused on some other ground. The fact that the holder has reason to believe that the bill, on presentment, will be dishonoured, does not excuse presentment.[32] A holder has always the right to present for acceptance, and is wise to do so, if he conveniently can, for acceptance adds another party to the bill, and gives it additional credit; and presentment has, in Scotland, the legal effect now to be mentioned.

Effect.—The laws of Scotland and England differ in regard to the effect of presentment.[33] In Scotland, where the drawee of a bill has in his hands funds available for the payment thereof, the bill operates as an assignment of the sum for which it is drawn in favour of the holder, from the time when the bill is presented to the drawee.[34] As, however, a drawee is not liable on a bill until he has signed it, it is necessary, in order to obtain the funds attached, to sue for the debt due by the drawee to the drawer, and to found on the bill as an assignation of the debt. The date of presentment to the drawee decides the precedence bills have, both amongst themselves and also in questions with other competing assignations.[35] In England a bill, of itself, does not operate as an assignment of funds in the hands of the drawee available for payment thereof.[36]

Dishonour by non-acceptance.—A bill is dishonoured by non-acceptance when it is duly presented for acceptance, and acceptance is refused or cannot be obtained, or when presentment for acceptance is excused, and the bill is not accepted. An immediate right of recourse for payment against the drawer and indorsers thereupon accrues to the holder, and no presentment for payment is necessary.[37] When a bill is duly presented for acceptance and is not accepted within the customary time, usually twenty-four hours, the person presenting it must treat it as dishonoured by non-acceptance, or lose his right of recourse.[38] In order to preserve a right of recourse, notice of dishonour must be given by the holder to the drawer and each indorser, and, in certain cases, the bill must be protested.[39]

Acceptance for honour.—This has already been considered.[40]

(iii) *Presentment for payment*

The third condition of liability on a bill is due presentment for payment. If the bill is not so presented the drawer and indorsers are

[32] s. 41 (2) (3).
[33] This applies both to presentment for acceptance and presentment for payment.
[34] s. 53 (2).
[35] *Supra*, pp. 38, 39.   *Watt's Trs.* v. *Pinkney* (1853) 16 D. 279.
[36] s. 53 (1).
[37] s. 43.
[38] s. 42.
[39] *Infra*, pp. 190–191.
[40] *Supra*, pp. 178, 179.

discharged.[41] Due presentment is presentment in accordance with the following rules. Where the bill is not payable on demand, presentment must be made on the day it falls due, or, at latest, on the last day of grace. A bill payable on demand must be presented for payment within a reasonable time after its issue in order to render the drawer liable, and within a reasonable time after its indorsement, in order to render the indorser liable. Presentment must be made by the holder, or by some person authorised to receive payment on his behalf, at a reasonable hour on a business day, at the proper place, usually the address of the drawee as given in the bill, or the place where the bill is accepted payable, and to the proper person, that is, to the person designated by the bill as payer, *i.e.,* the drawee or acceptor, or some person authorised to pay or refuse payment on his behalf, if with the exercise of reasonable diligence such person can be found. If there are two or more drawees or acceptors, presentment must be made to all, unless one has authority to accept for the rest; if the drawee or acceptor is dead, to his personal representative; if bankrupt, to him or his trustee; if authorised by agreement or usage, through the Post Office.[42]

When necessary.—Presentment for payment is not necessary in order to make liable an acceptor who has accepted generally. He is liable to pay in terms of his contract. In order to preserve recourse against the other parties, however, the bill must be duly presented to the acceptor for payment, and notice of dishonour, if such be the case, given to each. If it be not so presented, and notice given, the drawer and indorsers, even though they have suffered no loss by the omission, are discharged.

When delay excused.—Delay in presentment is excused when it is caused by circumstances beyond the control of the holder, and not imputable to his default, misconduct, or negligence, as, for example, by his sudden illness or death. When the cause of delay ceases to operate, presentment must be made with reasonable diligence.[43] Delay is excused also when caused, in certain special circumstances, by delay in presentment for acceptance.[44]

When presentment dispensed with.—Presentment for payment is dispensed with where, after the exercise of reasonable diligence, it cannot be effected; where the drawee is a fictitious person; as regards the drawer, where the drawee or acceptor is not bound, as between himself and the drawer, to accept or pay the bill and the drawer has

---

[41] s. 45.
[42] s. 45, Rules 1–8.
[43] s. 46 (1).
[44] s. 39 (4).

no reason to believe that the bill would be paid if presented; as regards an indorser, where the bill is accepted or made for his accommodation and he has no reason to expect that the bill would be paid if presented; and where presentment is waived, expressly or by implication. The fact that the holder has reason to believe that the bill will, on present-ment, be dishonoured, e.g., where acceptor is bankrupt, does not dispense with the necessity for presentment.[45]

Dishonour by non-payment.—A bill is dishonoured by non-payment when it is duly presented for payment and payment is refused or cannot be obtained, or when presentment is excused and the bill is overdue and unpaid.[46] An immediate right of recourse against the drawer and indorsers then accrues to the holder,[47] but, in order to preserve this right, notice of dishonour must be given to each, and, in certain circumstances, the bill must be protested.[48]

Payment for honour.—Where a bill has been protested for non-payment, any person may intervene and pay it *supra* protest for the honour of any party liable thereon. Such payment must be attested by a notarial act of honour. When a bill has been so paid, all parties subsequent to the party for whose honour it is paid are discharged, but the payer for honour is subrogated for, and succeeds to both the rights and duties of, the holder as regards the party for whose honour he pays, and all parties liable to that party.[49]

(iv) *Consideration*

Holder for Value.—On this topic of consideration or value, the fourth condition of liability on a bill, the Act provides that valuable consideration for a bill may be constituted by any consideration suffi-cient to support a simple contract; or by an antecedent debt or liability, such being deemed valuable consideration whether the bill is payable on demand or at a future time.[50] On what is consideration sufficient to support a simple contract, there is a material difference between the laws of Scotland and England. In England, it is essential that a person sued on a bill should have received value for it.[51] In Scotland, a contractual obligation may be gratuitous, and accordingly a bill does not require to be granted for value, adequate or inadequate; it may be granted from goodwill or in fulfilment of some moral obligation.

---

45 s. 46 (2).   46 s. 47 (1).
47 s. 47 (2).
48 *Infra*, pp. 190–191.
49 s. 68.
50 s. 27 (1).
51 Real consideration has been defined in England to mean "Some right, interest, profit, or benefit accruing to one party, or some forbearance, detriment, loss or responsibility given, suffered or undertaken by the other "; *Currie* v. *Misa* (1856) L.R. 10 Ex. 153, at 162, discussed in *Oliver* v. *Davis* [1949] 2 K.B. 727.

Want of value, or non-onerosity, is therefore, as a general rule, not of itself a sufficient defence to a claim on a bill. It may, however, be pleaded when the bill is challenged on a ground other than initial invalidity, so as to preclude a holder who has not given value for it from enforcing it. Thus, an indorser who has not received value from his indorsee may plead against him that the bill was indorsed by him without the intention of granting an obligation; that it was obtained from him by fraud, force, or fear; that it was given under an agreement which had failed [52]; that it is an accommodation bill, or that it was granted for a consideration which the law does not recognise, *e.g.,* for a gambling debt, or for concurring in or obtaining an illegal preference in bankruptcy. It is, however, only as between parties who have, *inter se,* given and received no value for the bill that a defence on the above lines would be sustained. If the person in possession of the bill has given value for it to the indorser to him, he is, even in such cases, entitled to enforce the bill against all parties without exception, unless he has himself been a party to the transaction founded on in defence.

Where value has at any time been given for a bill, the holder is deemed to be a holder for value as regards the acceptor, and all parties to the bill who became parties prior to such time [53]; and every party whose signature appears on a bill is prima facie deemed to have become a party thereto for value.[54]

(6) **Proof of liability.**—The Bills of Exchange Act, 1882, provides in section 100 that in any judicial proceedings in Scotland any fact relating to a bill of exchange, bank cheque, or promissory note, which is relevant to any question of liability thereon, may be proved by parole evidence.[55] Such proof has been held to be admissible in Scotland to show that what purports, *ex facie* of the bill, to be a complete contract has never come into operative existence, *e.g.,* for want of delivery; and to show value was not given for the bill.[56]

The provision does not make competent parole proof of payment of the bill, proof of payment of a written obligation being limited to the writ or oath of the creditor.[57]

14. The holder.—Rights and powers

The holder is the payee or indorsee of a bill or note who is in possession of it, or the bearer thereof.[58] He may sue on the bill, in

---

[52] *e.g., Pert* v. *Bruce,* 1937 S.L.T. 475.
[53] s. 27 (2).
[54] s. 30 (1); *Churchill & Sim* v. *Goddard* [1937] 1 K.B. 92.
[55] s. 100.
[56] See Bell's Prin., § 333 B; *Pert* v. *Bruce, cit. sup.*
[57] *Robertson* v. *Thomson* (1900) 3 F. 5, approved in *Nicol's Trs.* v. *Sutherland,* 1951 S.C.(H.L.) 21.
[58] s. 2.

his own name,[59] any or all of the parties liable on it unless it can be shown that he holds the bill adversely to the interests of the true owner. If, however, a bill be payable to a specified person or persons, any action on the bill must be raised in the name of such person or persons. A holder who might have sued a party to a bill is entitled to claim against such party's estate in bankruptcy. On the death of a holder his rights pass to his executors, and, on his bankruptcy, if he be the beneficial owner of the bill, or if the bill be payable to him for his own account, his rights pass to his trustee. If he is a holder in due course, his rights and powers are more extensive.

Holder in due course.—Every holder is prima facie deemed to be a holder in due course. By this is meant a holder who has taken a bill, complete and regular on the face of it, under the following conditions, namely, (i) that he became the holder of it before it was overdue, and (ii) without notice that it had been previously dishonoured, if such was the fact; (iii) that he took the bill in good faith, and (iv) for value; and (v) that at the time the bill was negotiated to him he had no notice of any defect in the title of the person who negotiated it.[60] Such a holder holds the bill free from any defect of title of prior parties, as well as from mere personal defences available to prior parties among themselves, e.g., compensation, and has a right of recourse, and may enforce payment, against all parties liable on the bill[61]; and he can give a valid discharge to any person from whom he obtains payment of the bill. A holder in due course can also confer on any subsequent holder, whether for value or not, who derives his title through him and who is not himself a party to any fraud or illegality affecting it, all his rights as holder in due course as regards the acceptor and all parties to the bill prior to himself.[62]

Holder not in due course.—Such a holder is one who takes the bill when it is overdue or dishonoured[63]; when it is not complete and regular on the face of it; or with notice or good reason to suppose that the title of the party from whom he takes it is defective.[64] Even though he has given value for the bill, he takes no higher right than that of the person indorsing it to him. He may thus have only a voidable title to the bill. Further, he is subject to all equities affecting the indorser to him, e.g., compensation, and accordingly may not be entitled to enforce payment against all parties to the bill. He can, however, if he negotiates the bill to a holder in due course, confer

---

[59] s. 38 (1); *Churchill & Sim* v. *Goddard* [1937] 1 K.B. 92.
[60] s. 29 (1).
[61] s. 38 (2).
[62] s. 29 (3).
[63] *Semple* v. *Kyle* (1902) 4 F. 421.
[64] *Jones* v. *Gordon* (1877) 2 App.Cas. 616.

upon that holder a good and complete title to the bill; if he obtains payment of the bill, the person who pays him in due course [65] gets a valid discharge for the bill,[66] and if, as mentioned, he derives his title to a bill through a holder in due course, and is not himself a party to any fraud or illegality affecting it, he has all the rights of that holder in due course as regards the acceptor and all parties prior to that holder.[67]

15. Right of recourse

If the drawee of a bill should refuse to accept, or refuse to pay, the holder has a right of recourse against the drawer and indorsers, but must take certain proceedings in order to preserve this right. These proceedings are giving notice of dishonour, and protest.

Notice of dishonour.—Notice of dishonour by non-acceptance or by non-payment must be given to the drawer and each indorser, for it is implied in the contract of these parties that they should have such notice.[68] It need not be given to the acceptor.[69] The object of giving notice is to inform the person receiving it not only that the bill has been dishonoured, but also that the person giving notice looks to him for payment, and to enable each in his order of liability to take precautions for his safety and indemnification, that is, to put himself in funds to meet the bill, and, in the case of an indorser, by notice of dishonour, if not already given, to parties prior to himself, to preserve his own right of recourse against them. The notice may be given in writing or by personal communication, and may be in any terms which sufficiently identify the bill. Return of a dishonoured bill to the drawer or an indorser is, in point of form, deemed sufficient notice.[70] The notice may be given as soon as the bill is dishonoured, and must be given within a reasonable time thereafter.[71] The effect of the holder's giving notice is that it preserves not only his own right of recourse, but enures for the benefit of, *i.e.*, preserves the right of recourse of, all subsequent holders and all prior indorsers who have a right of recourse against the party to whom it is given.[72] Notice may also be given by an indorser who is himself liable on the bill, and, if given, enures for the benefit of the holder and all indorsers subsequent to the party to whom notice is given.[73]

[65] See p. 197, *infra*.
[66] s. 38 (3).
[67] s. 29 (3).
[68] *Supra*, pp. 183, 184.
[69] s. 52 (3); *e.g.*, where accepted payable at a bank and on presentation for payment it is dishonoured.
[70] s. 49, Rules (5) and (6); *Re Fenwick, Stobart & Co. Ltd.* [1902] 1 Ch. 507.
[71] *Ibid*. Rule (12).
[72] *Ibid*. Rule (3).   [73] s. 49, Rule (4).

Any drawer or indorser to whom notice is not given is discharged, but the rights of a holder in due course subsequent to an omission to give notice of dishonour by non-acceptance are not prejudiced by the omission. Where a bill is dishonoured by non-acceptance and due notice of dishonour is given, it is not necessary to give notice of a subsequent dishonour by non-payment unless the bill has in the meantime been accepted.[74] Delay in giving notice is excused on the same grounds as delay in presenting for payment, and notice is dispensed with in certain circumstances specified in the Act.[75]

Protest.—Besides giving notice of dishonour, the holder of a bill which, on the face of it, bears to be a foreign bill must, in order to preserve recourse against the drawer and indorsers, protest it in the case of dishonour by either non-acceptance or non-payment. If it is not so protested, the drawer and indorsers are discharged.[76] This proceeding is supplementary to giving notice of dishonour, and its purpose is to provide authentic proof of due presentment and dishonour to any tribunal at home or abroad. In the case of an inland bill protest is not necessary merely to preserve recourse against the drawer or an indorser,[77] but it is useful as showing due presentment, and it is necessary if it is desired to enforce the bill by summary diligence.[78]

Protest is a formal act, and is usually preceded by an informal proceeding known as noting. This is effected by a Notary Public or his clerk presenting the bill for acceptance or payment to the drawee and noting thereon the date of dishonour, the fact of non-acceptance or non-payment (P.N.P. or P.N.A.C.), his initials, and the letters N.P. When no notary can be found at the place where the bill is presented,[79] any householder of the place may, in the presence of two witnesses, give a certificate signed by the witnesses, attesting the dishonour of the bill.[80] It is doubtful whether a householder's certificate will form a warrant for summary diligence.[81] A bill may be noted for protest on the day of its dishonour, and must be noted not later than the next succeeding business day.[82] This applies to all parties except the acceptor, against whom, as primary obligant, a bill may be noted even after its due date, and need not be noted or protested at all,[83] unless it

---

[74] s. 48.
[75] s. 50.
[76] s. 51 (2).
[77] s. 51 (2).
[78] s. 98. *Infra*, p. 191.
[79] *Sommerville* v. *Aaronson* (1898) 25 R. 524.
[80] s. 94. A form of certificate is given in the First Sched. to the Act.
[81] Hamilton, *Bills of Exchange*, p. 210.
[82] Bills of Exchange (Time of Noting) Act, 1917, s. 1.
[83] s. 52 (3).

is desired to proceed with summary diligence against him. Delay in noting is excused on the same grounds as delay in presenting for payment or giving notice of dishonour.[84]

Upon the noting is based the protest or formal notarial certificate attesting the dishonour of the bill. It may be extended, or written out at length, as of the date of the noting,[85] but only within six months after the due date of the bill. It must contain a copy of the bill, and be signed by the notary making it, and specify the person at whose request the bill is protested, the place and date of protest, the cause or reason for protesting the bill (i.e., non-acceptance or non-payment), the demand made and the answer given, if any, or the fact that the drawee or acceptor could not be found.[86] A certificate given by a householder operates in all respects as if it were a formal protest of the bill.[87] Protest is dispensed with by any circumstance which would dispense with notice of dishonour, and delay in protesting is excused on the same grounds as delay in noting.[88] When notice of dishonour has been duly given, and the bill, when necessary, protested, and not accepted or paid for honour, the holder may proceed to enforce payment by any party against whom a right of recourse has been preserved.

Enforcement.—Summary diligence.—Enforcement may be by an ordinary action for payment founded on the bill as the document of debt. It may also be by summary diligence, a remedy which is available only in Scotland.[89] This procedure enables the creditor, without raising an action, to get a warrant which is equivalent to a decree of the court against the debtor for the amount of the bill with interest and expenses. Damages can only be recovered by ordinary action.[90] It is a privilege of statutory creation, and was first introduced in 1681. The requisites in the case of a bill payable at a currency are that it be: (1) duly presented for payment, (2) noted as of the day of its dishonour, or not later than the next succeeding business day, and (3) the protest extended and registered in the Books of Council and Session, which are kept in Edinburgh, or in the books of the Sheriff Court of the county within which the person sought to be charged resides, within six months after the date of the bill in the case of non-acceptance, and within six months after the falling-due thereof in the case of non-payment. Protests of bills payable on demand, or at sight, or on

---

[84] s. 51 (9).
[85] s. 51 (4).
[86] s. 51 (7).
[87] s. 94.
[88] s. 51 (9).
[89] s. 98.
[90] Erskine, III, 2.36.

presentation, are registrable within six months from the date of presentation for payment, and not from the date of the bill. When the protest is registered, an extract, *i.e.*, a certified copy, thereof is obtained containing a warrant to charge the party liable on the bill to pay the sum due, with interest and expenses, within six days if he resides in Scotland, and within fourteen days if he is in Orkney or Shetland or furth of Scotland. By a charge is meant a written call upon the debtor to pay within the time specified. It is handed to him by a messenger-at-arms or sheriff officer. If the debtor fails to pay, proceedings for sequestration may be instituted. In addition to charging, the creditor may at once arrest in the hands of third persons any money or goods belonging to the debtor. The process cannot be used against a party who is not subject to the jurisdiction of the Scottish courts, even although the bill may be payable in Scotland.[91] The warrant contained in the extract may be enforced at any time before the sexennial prescription has run on the bill.[92]

This diligence is competent when a bill is dishonoured by non-acceptance or non-payment, and may proceed at the instance of any person to whom or to whose order the bill is made payable, *i.e.*, to the holder whether payee, indorsee, or bearer; but his title must be clear on the face of the bill, and every link of the chain connecting the creditor with the debtor must be complete. When a bill has not been accepted, diligence may be used against the drawer and prior indorsers, but not against the drawee, though he has funds in his hands sufficient to meet the bill. If he has accepted the bill, diligence may be used against him as the party primarily liable thereon. If the bill is accepted payable in England, although there is no equivalent in English law to our process of summary diligence, the protest may be extended by an English notary, and thereafter summary diligence may proceed in Scotland against any of the parties resident in Scotland.

The debtor in the bill may, if he thinks fit, take proceedings in the Court of Session to have the diligence suspended, but he will, as a condition of being allowed to do so, have to find caution or consign the sum in the bill unless it appears on the face of it that it has been vitiated by a material alteration, or that the signatures have been forged, or where there has been any incompetency in the protest or charge.

Summary diligence, when competent, is so on conditions. (1) It is generally only competent when the liability of the party against whom it is used to the person using it appears on the face of the bill without extrinsic evidence, and, accordingly, no document which requires proof,

---

[91] *Charteris* v. *Clydesdale Bank* (1882) 19 S.L.R. 602; *Davis* v. *Cadman* (1897) 24 R. 297.
[92] Bell's Prin., § 596.

especially parole proof, to support it can be used to found summary diligence. Thus, it is not competent against an acceptor who has accepted conditionally [93]; against a party who has signed by mark, whether in the presence of witnesses or not, or by initials; or against a party who has accepted or indorsed by procuration, except where the procuration is notorious. Where, however, the bill is drawn by procuration, the acceptor cannot object to diligence raised in the name of the principal, inasmuch as his act of acceptance infers a recognition of the principal's right to the debt. Summary diligence is competent on a bill subscribed for a granter who cannot write by a notary public or justice of the peace before two witnesses; against a firm carrying on business under a descriptive name on a bill signed by all the partners [94]; against a person who has signed a bill in a trade or assumed name; and against any member of a firm on a bill signed in the firm-name, by another partner, notwithstanding that the name of such member does not appear on the bill.[95] (2) Again, to warrant summary diligence, the bill must be without alteration or vitiation in essential parts. Thus, it has been decided that an obvious change in the date from October 1 to 8, and the superinduction of a five in the date December 25, it being uncertain whether there had been erasure, made summary diligence incompetent; and, in another case, it was decided that a bill torn in three pieces and pasted together again was not a document entitled to the privilege of summary diligence, unless these alterations or vitiations were approved by the initials of the parties.[96] (3) Summary diligence may be excluded also by express enactment, e.g., bills granted to or in favour of or held by a moneylender.[97]

16. Special forms of bill—Blank or inchoate bill [98]

Where a blank stamped paper with a simple signature is delivered by the signer in order that it may be converted into a bill, it operates as a prima facie authority to fill it up as a complete bill for any amount the stamp will cover,[99] using the signature for that of the drawer, or the acceptor, or an indorser. In like manner, when a bill is wanting in any material particular, the person in possession of it has a prima facie authority to fill up the omission in any way he thinks fit.[1] In

---

[93] *Summers* v. *Marianski* (1843) 6 D. 286.
[94] *Rosslund Cycle Co.* v. *M'Creadie*, 1907 S.C. 1208.
[95] s. 23.
[96] *Thomson* v. *Bell* (1850) 12 D. 1184. See also *Dominion Bank* v. *Bank of Scotland* (1889) 16 R. 1081, affd. (1891) 18 R.(H.L.) 21.
[97] Moneylenders Act, 1927, s. 18 (*h*).
[98] s. 20.
[99] *Garrard* v. *Lewis* (1882) 10 Q.B.D. 30.
[1] *Russell* v. *Banknock Coal Co.* (1897) 24 R. 1009; *Lawson's Exr.* v. *Watson*, 1907 S.C. 1353; *Macdonald* v. *Nash* [1920] A.C. 625.

order that any such instrument when completed may be enforceable against any person who became a party thereto prior to its completion, it must be filled up within a reasonable time, and strictly in accordance with the authority given.[2]   Reasonable time for this purpose is a question of fact.   The onus of proof that the bill has not been filled up in accordance with the authority given rests on the party who signed and delivered it.[3]   If any such instrument after completion is negotiated to a holder in due course, it is valid and effecutal for all purposes in his hands, and he may enforce it as if it had been filled up within a reasonable time and strictly in accordance with the authority given.[4]   These instruments are usually given for accommodation, *i.e.*, for a loan of money.

Accommodation bill.—Accommodation party.—An accommodation bill is a bill whereof the acceptor is in substance a mere surety for some other person who may or may not be a party thereto.[5]   An accommodation party to a bill is a person who has signed a bill as a drawer, acceptor, or indorser, without receiving value therefor, and for the purpose of lending his name to some other person.[6]   An accommodation bill, or wind bill, as it is sometimes called, differs in no respect in form from an ordinary bill, but it is different in its effect as regards the parties to it.   As between accommodation parties it does not represent a real debt, and their rights are regulated by the true relations between them, which may be proved by parole evidence.[7]   In a question with a third party, however, an accommodation bill is in the same position as any other bill issued in the ordinary course of business, the legal presumption being that it is a bill drawn and issued for value, and a holder for value [8] is entitled to call upon all prior parties to the bill to make payment to him, notwithstanding the fact that at the time such holder took the bill he knew that it was an accommodation bill, or that a party whom he seeks to make liable was an accommodation party.[9]   Accommodation bills, at one time an important feature in commercial transactions, have now been largely superseded by bonds of cash credit and guarantees.[10]

Bill in a set.—A bill in a set is one bill drawn in duplicate or triplicate or in more numerous " parts," with the intention that any one part should represent the others, and that payment of one part

[2] *M'Mechin* v. *Russell* (1891) 18 R. 567.
[3] *Anderson* v. *Somerville* (1898) 1 F. 90.
[4] *Ex p. Hayward* (1871) L.R. 6 Ch. 546; *M'Mechin* v. *Russell, cit. sup.*
[5] *Chalmers on Bills,* 13th ed., p. 92.
[6] s. 28.
[7] s. 100.   *Macdonald* v. *Whitfield* (1883) 8 App.Cas. 733.
[8] *Supra,* pp. 186, 187; *Hood* v. *Stewart* (1890) 17 R. 749.
[9] s. 28 (2).
[10] *Infra,* Chap. 9.

should discharge the set.[11]   The object of so drawing a bill is to meet any risk of loss.   Each part can be sent separately and by different mails so as to ensure, as far as possible, that at least one part reaches its destination.   Inland bills are seldom drawn in a set, but foreign bills frequently are.

17. Lost bills

Where a bill has been lost before it is overdue, the person who was the holder of it may apply to the drawer to give him another bill of the same tenor, and, if he refuses, may compel him to do so.   As a condition of getting such a duplicate bill, however, the person so applying must, if required, give security to the drawer to indemnify him against all persons whatever in case the bill alleged to have been lost should be found again.[12]   The reason for this provision is that the acceptor, or, if the drawee did not accept, the drawer, might be called on to pay the bill twice.   For example, if a bearer bill were acquired from the finder by a holder for value, the latter, as well as the rightful owner of the bill, would be entitled to enforce it; or if a bill, payable to order of the drawer, had the drawer's indorsement, the finder could get it discounted by someone who would thereupon be entitled as well as the rightful owner to enforce it.

Special provision is made for the enforcement of lost bills, the Act providing that, in an action or proceeding upon a lost bill, the court may order that the loss of the instrument shall not be set up, provided that an indemnity be given against the claims of any other person upon the instrument in question.[13]   Protest of a lost bill may be made upon a copy or written particulars thereof.[14]

18. Discharge of bill—Discharge of party—Effect

A bill is discharged when all rights of action thereon as a bill are extinguished.   It then ceases to be negotiable, and if it subsequently comes into the hands of a holder in due course he acquires no right of action on the instrument as a bill.   Although this is so, however, a party to the bill, or the holder, may still have a right of action arising out of the bill transaction, and wholly independent of the instrument. Rights of action on the bill pass to the transferee when it is negotiated to him, but rights of action arising out of the bill transaction do not pass.   Hence rights of action on the bill are discharged when the bill is discharged, but rights of action on the bill transaction may or may not be.   For example, if one of three joint acceptors pays a bill, it is

[11] s. 71.
[12] s. 69.
[13] s. 70.
[14] s. 51 (8).

discharged, but he personally retains his right of contribution from his co-acceptors.

A party to a bill may be discharged without the bill being discharged; *e.g.*, a particular indorser, by not receiving notice of dishonour, or in other ways to be noted, may be discharged, but the bill may nevertheless remain enforceable against the drawer and other indorsers.

Methods of discharge.—The Act contains five methods of discharge, to which falls to be added a sixth, namely prescription. These methods are as follows:

(1) *Payment in due course.*—A bill is discharged by payment in due course by or on behalf of the drawee or acceptor. " Payment in due course " means payment made at or after the maturity of the bill to the holder thereof in good faith and without notice that his title to the bill is defective.[15] The following points are to be noted regarding this method of discharge, *viz.*: (a) Payment does not necessarily mean payment in cash. As in contract generally, it may be by the equivalents, *i.e.*, novation, delegation, confusion, or compensation.[16] (b) Payment must be at or after maturity. If paid by the drawee, or acceptor, before maturity, a bill is not discharged; and if he so pays it and it is either stolen from him and transferred to a holder in due course, or reissued by himself, he may have to pay over again.[17] (c) Payment must be made to the holder, *i.e.*, to the payee or indorsee of the bill who is in possession of it, or the bearer thereof.[18]   (d) Payment must be made by the drawee, or acceptor, in good faith, and (e) without notice of any defect in the holder's title.   (f) Payment must be made by or on behalf of the drawee or acceptor, he being the party ultimately liable on the bill. The only case in which payment by another party will serve to discharge the bill and relieve all other parties from liability is where an accommodation bill is paid in due course by the party accommodated, he being in this case the original debtor.[19]

Special provision is made for cases of payment by the drawer or an indorser, that is, by some party other than the original debtor. The bill is not discharged by such payment, but where it is payable to, or to the order of, a third party, and is paid by the drawer, the drawer may enforce payment thereof against the acceptor, but may not reissue the bill.[20]   In this case, the drawer is not an indorser, and the bill is dead, the drawer merely retaining his right of recourse against the acceptor. Where, on the other hand, it is paid by an indorser, or

---

[15] s. 59 (1).
[16] *Supra*, p. 42 *et seq.*
[17] *Burbridge* v. *Manners* (1812) 3 Camp. 193, *per* Lord Ellenborough at p. 194.
[18] s. 2.
[19] s. 59 (3).
[20] s. 59 (2) (*a*).

where a bill payable to drawer's order is paid by the drawer, *i.e.*, the drawer is also an indorser, the party paying it is remitted to his former rights as regards the acceptor or antecedent parties, *i.e.*, becomes holder as if he had never negotiated the bill, and he may, if he thinks fit, strike out his own and subsequent indorsements, and again negotiate the bill.[21]

(2) *Acceptor becomes holder.*—When the acceptor of a bill is or becomes the holder of it at or after its maturity, in his own right, the bill is discharged.[22]

(3) *Renunciation or waiver.*—This may discharge the whole bill, or it may discharge only a party thereto. When the holder of a bill, at or after its maturity, absolutely and unconditionally renounces his rights against the acceptor, the bill is discharged. The renunciation must, however, be in writing, or the bill delivered up to the acceptor. The liabilities of any party to a bill may in like manner be renounced by the holder. When the holder renounces his rights against any party other than the acceptor, that party, and other parties subsequent to him, are discharged. This the holder can do before, at, or after maturity of the bill, *i.e.*, at any time. The rights of a holder in due course, taking the bill subsequent to the renunciation and without notice of it, are not, however, affected, and he can enforce the bill against any of the parties.[23]

(4) *Cancellation.*—This also may amount to a discharge of the bill, or merely a discharge of a party to it. Where the bill is intentionally cancelled by the holder or his agent, and the cancellation is apparent thereon, the bill is discharged.[24] Where the signature of any party liable on a bill is intentionally cancelled by the holder or his agent, the party whose signature is cancelled is discharged, and so also is any indorser who would have had a right of recourse against him.[25] A subsequent holder in due course takes with notice of the cancellation of the signatures, and accordingly cannot enforce the bill against those who have been thus discharged. In all cases, a cancellation which is made unintentionally, or under a mistake, or without the authority of the holder, is inoperative, but the onus of proof that the cancellation was so made is on the party alleging it.[26]

(5) *Material alteration.*—An alteration to a bill or acceptance is material if it alters its business effect for business purposes, *e.g.*, an

---

[21] s. 59 (2) (*b*).
[22] s. 61.
[23] s. 62.
[24] s. 63 (1).
[25] s. 63 (2).
[26] s. 63; *Dominion Bank* v. *Anderson* (1888) 15 R. 408.

alteration of the date, the sum payable, the time of payment, the place of payment, and, where a bill has been accepted generally, the addition of a place of payment without the acceptor's assent.[27] If such an alteration is made without the assent of all parties to the bill, and is apparent, the bill is avoided except as against a party who has himself made, authorised, or assented to the alteration, and subsequent indorsers. If, however, the alteration is not apparent, and the bill is in the hands of a holder in due course, he may enforce payment of it according to its original tenor.[28] An acceptor is not bound, when he accepts, to take precautions against fraudulent alterations in the bill after acceptance.[29] He owes no duty to a holder in due course.

(6) *Sexennial prescription.*[30]—No bill of exchange or promissory note is of force or effectual to found any diligence or action in Scotland unless such diligence be executed or action commenced within six years from and after the term at which the sum in the bill or note becomes exigible.

CHEQUES

1. Origin and history

The instrument now known as a cheque originated when the banker, instead of issuing notes in return for money which the customer deposited with him, began to place the deposits to the credit of an account in the name of the customer and allow the customer to draw upon him, to bearer or order, by means of a form of bill of exchange.[31] This practice became general in the latter part of the eighteenth century, custom recognised by the courts gave these instruments special incidents of their own, and the law relating to them was developed, and ultimately codified in the Bills of Exchange Act, 1882.

2. Definition

A cheque is a bill of exchange drawn on a banker payable on demand.[32] Part III of the Act makes special provision for cheques in respect of presentment for payment, revocation of the banker's authority, and crossing, but except as otherwise provided in that Part, the provisions of the Act applicable to a bill of exchange payable on demand apply to a cheque.[33]

---

27 s. 64 (2); *Koch* v. *Dicks* (1933) 49 T.L.R. 241; [1933] 1 K.B. 307.
28 s. 64 (1).
29 *Scholfield* v. *Earl of Londesborough* [1896] A.C. 514. Contrast the duty of the drawer of a cheque, *infra*, p. 206.
30 See *ante*, p. 53.
31 Cockburn C.J. in *Goodwin* v. *Robarts* (1875) L.R. 10 Ex. 337 at p. 351.
32 B. of E. Act, 1882, s. 73.
33 B. of E. Act, 1882, s. 73.

3. Form—Stamping

The Act does not prescribe any particular form, but only an instrument which complies with the statutory definition is a cheque within the meaning of the Act. For example, an order to pay money in the form of an ordinary cheque, with a proviso that a receipt form attached should be filled up, has been held not to be a cheque.[34] Like ordinary bills, cheques do not require to be written on paper specially appropriated to their use. Notepaper or any other material upon which writing is legible is sufficient.

The stamp required is that required for a bill of exchange, *i.e.*, 2d.,[35] and may be impressed or adhesive,[36] or paid by the banker by composition with the Commissioners of Inland Revenue.[37] If a stamp is not impressed or paid by composition, it is essential that the drawer affix a 2d. postage stamp and cancel it by writing his name, and the date, across it.[36] If it is presented for payment unstamped, the banker may affix the proper adhesive stamp, and charge the drawer, *i.e.*, the customer, with the amount.[38] Only the drawer and the banker to whom the cheque is presented for payment may affix and cancel a stamp.[38]

4. Specialities of a cheque

(1) Date.—A cheque need not be dated, and is not invalid by reason only that it is post-dated or ante-dated, or that it bears date on a Sunday.[39] If it is post-dated, *i.e.*, dated at a day after issue, it may, like a bill of exchange, be validly negotiated for value prior to the date on which it bears to be drawn.[40] A banker is not, however, entitled to pay a cheque prior to the date on which it purports to be drawn, and he does so at his own risk, for it is contrary to the drawer's order.

(2) Signature of Drawer.—The signature must be that of the person in whose name the bank account is kept, or of someone authorised by him to sign that name, or the signature of a person who has authority, as agreed between banker and customer, to operate on the account. Any number of persons can sign as drawers of a cheque so long as the bank account is in their joint names.

Signature, as in the case of a bill, does not necessarily mean subscription. It is sufficient if adequate means of the customer's

---

34 *Bavins* v. *London and South-Western Bank* (1899) 5 Com. Cas.1.
35 Stamp Act, 1891, s. 2 and First Sched.
36 Finance Act, 1961, s. 33 (2).
37 Finance Act, 1956, s. 39.
38 Stamp Act, 1891, s. 38 (2).
39 B. of E. Act, 1882, ss. 3 (4), 13 (2).
40 *Royal Bank of Scotland* v. *Tottenham* [1894] 2 Q.B. 715.

identification be afforded to the banker, and, accordingly, a cheque which is holograph of the drawer, and contains his name, is sufficient authority to the banker to honour the cheque. A cheque is valid if initialled by the drawer, if initialling be his usual mode of signature; or it may be signed on behalf of any person, drawer or indorser, who is unable to write, by a notary public or justice of the peace. If, however, a customer's signature differs from that with which the banker is familiar, the banker is under no obligation to pay the cheque; and if the drawer's signature has been forged or adhibited without his authority and the banker pays the cheque, he cannot debit the customer's account with the amount, but must bear the loss, for he is presumed to be familiar with his customer's signature.[41] Where a cheque is returned because the signature differs from the customer's usual or specimen signature, this reason should be stated, and the cheque not merely marked " Refer to drawer."

(3) **Sum certain in money.**—The sum payable may be expressed in words or figures or both, and where there is a discrepancy between the two the sum denoted by the words is the sum payable. Where, however, the amount is expressed in foreign currency, or in that of some British possession, the amount is payable in British currency at the customary rate of exchange.

(4) **Drawn on banker.**—It is of the essence of a cheque that it is drawn on a banker, that is, addressed by name to a person, or body of persons, whether incorporated or not, who carry on the business of banking.[42] This speciality has three consequences. (a) A cheque does not require to be accepted by the drawee, *i.e.*, the banker, and, being payable on demand, and intended for immediate payment and not for circulation, it is not normally accepted. It has been held that acceptance might be made, but only in very unusual and special circumstances, and that its certification by the banker on whom it is drawn is not acceptance.[43] (b) Although it is, like a bill of exchange, strictly speaking, an order by a creditor, *i.e.*, the customer, upon a debtor, *i.e.*, the banker, to pay to a third person the whole or part of a debt, *i.e.*, of the banker's debt to the customer, it is not, in ordinary understanding, so considered. It is more like an appropriation by the customer, *i.e.*, the drawer, to the payee of what is treated as ready money of the customer in the hands of the banker, as his agent. Hence the drawer, in giving the order to the banker to appropriate to a creditor of the drawer, must be considered as the person primarily liable to pay;

---

[41] *e.g. Dickson* v. *Clydesdale Bank Ltd.,* 1937 S.L.T. 585. See p. 206, *infra.*

[42] B. of E. Act, 1882, s. 2.

[43] *Bank of Baroda Ltd.* v. *Punjab National Bank Ltd.* [1944] A.C. 176. As to certified cheques, see, *infra,* p. 215.

that is, as drawer of the cheque, he is in reality the acceptor of it as a bill of exchange. (c) Further, he is in the position of an acceptor who qualifies his acceptance by making the bill payable at a particular place, *i.e.*, where his bank account is, and, being an acceptor, has no right to insist, as a condition of his liability to any holder, on immediate presentment at that place by a holder, although the cheque is a bill payable on demand.

(5) **Liability where more than one drawer.**—In a question with a bank which has paid a cheque drawn upon an account in joint names the drawers' liability to the bank is *pro rata* in the absence of agreement with the bank for their joint and several liability. The several drawers are, however, liable jointly and severally to a holder in due course of the cheque. The drawers' bank does not by paying the cheque become a holder in due course of it.[44]

(6) **Payable on demand.**—An instrument, in order to be a cheque, must be payable on demand.

(7) **Presentment for payment.**—As between the holder of a cheque and the banker on whom it is drawn, presentment must be made within bank hours, on a business day, and at the banker's place of business, by the holder or some person authorised by him to receive payment on his behalf. A cheque payable at a branch office must be presented there, and not at the head office.

As between the holder and the drawer of a cheque, there is, in respect of the time within which presentment must be made, an important difference between a cheque and an ordinary bill of exchange payable on demand. This is due to the fact that a cheque is not meant for circulation. An ordinary bill payable on demand, including a cheque used as such a bill, must, as has been seen, be presented within a reasonable time after its issue in order to render the drawer liable, and within a reasonable time after its indorsement in order to render the indorser liable.[45] In the case of a cheque, on the other hand, although a holder delays unreasonably to present it, the drawer continues to be liable on it until the expiry of the period of the sexennial prescription,[46] unless he suffers damage by the delay.[47] This he can do only if the banker fails in the interval. On this matter, the Act provides that where a cheque is not presented for payment within a reasonable time of its issue, and the drawer, or the person on whose account it is drawn, had, at the time of such presentment, the right as

[44] *Coats* v. *Union Bank of Scotland Ltd.*, 1929 S.C.(H.L.) 114.
[45] s. 45, Rule 2. *Supra*, p. 185.
[46] s. 45, Rule 2, does not apply to cheques used as such, these being regulated by the common law as modified by s. 74.
[47] *Lawes* v. *Rand* (1857) 27 L.J.C.P. 76.

between him and the banker to have the cheque paid, *i.e.*, had a sufficient balance at his credit, and suffers actual damage through the delay, he is discharged to the extent of such damage, that is to say, to the extent to which such drawer or person is a creditor of such banker to a larger amount than he would have been had such cheque been paid.[48] The holder of the cheque as to which such drawer or person is discharged is a creditor, in lieu of such drawer or person, of the banker to the extent of the discharge, and entitled to recover the amount from him.[49]

While the liability of the drawer continues for six years, it is the practice of bankers to mark a cheque which has been outstanding for more than six months " Out of date—requires drawer's confirmation," and to refer to the drawer before cashing it. This is, however, simply a precaution.

Reasonable time.—The question whether the time that has elapsed between issue and presentment of a cheque is reasonable arises only where the drawer has been prejudiced by delay in presentment, and, in determining it, regard is to be had to the nature of the instrument, the usage of trade and of bankers, and the facts of the particular case.[50] It has been held in England, in a question between payee and drawer, that the payee of a cheque received during banking hours has till the end of banking hours on the day next after receiving the cheque to present it; if received after banking hours, he has an additional day; and if the place of payment is at a distance, the payee must send it off to his correspondent by post on the day he receives it, or the first post of the following morning, and his correspondent has till the close of banking hours on the day after he received it to present it. When a banker is entrusted by the payee or holder with a cheque for presentment and collection, he has, as between himself and his customer, the day after receipt of the cheque to present it, unless circumstances exist from which a contract or duty on the part of the banker to present earlier or to defer presentment to a later date can be inferred. If the banker employ an agent to present the cheque on his behalf, he will have the day after receipt to post it to such agent, and the agent similarly will have the day after his receipt of the cheque to present it to the banker upon whom it is drawn. Delay in presentment may be excused and presentment dispensed with in certain circumstances.[51]

Where a cheque is used as a bill of exchange, what is a reasonable time is computed as for a bill, regard being had to the nature of the

48 s. 74 (1).
49 s. 74 (3).
50 s. 74 (2).
51 s. 46.

bill, the usage of trade with regard to similar bills, and the facts of the particular case.[52]

Stale cheques.—A cheque is stale or overdue when it appears on the face of it to have been in circulation for an unreasonable length of time. An unreasonable length of time means such length of time as ought to have excited suspicion in the mind of an ordinary careful holder. One who takes such a cheque by indorsement cannot acquire or give a better title than his indorser had.

Special effect in Scotland of presentment.—In Scotland, but not in England, a cheque when presented for payment operates as an intimated assignation in favour of the payee or other holder of any funds of the drawer in the banker's hands available to meet it.[53] This is of particular importance in certain circumstances in which the banker's authority to pay has been determined.[54]

(8) **Summary diligence.**—To protest and do summary diligence upon an unpaid bank cheque has been held to be incompetent.[55]

5. Relation of banker and customer

(a) **General principle.**—A person is a customer where the bank accepts his money on deposit or current account, and undertakes to honour his cheques up to the amount standing at his credit.[56] The customer has right to a sum equivalent to that which he has paid to the banker, and the relationship is therefore, strictly speaking, that of creditor and debtor. It is subject to the general law of contract,[57] and agency,[58] and also to particular rules governing special rights and duties on both sides.

(b) **Banker's duty to honour customer's cheques.**—(i) *General duty.* A banker is, under his contract with his customer, impliedly bound to honour his customer's cheques if these be presented to him for payment within banking hours, and he has funds belonging to his customer sufficient to meet them. He must do so within a reasonable time, but only after he is in receipt of the customer's money, and he is therefore under no obligation to allow an overdraft, *i.e.*, to cash a cheque for more than the sum at the customer's credit. Should he fail in this duty without adequate grounds, he will, as a general rule, be liable in

---

[52] s. 45, Rule 2.
[53] s. 53 (2), *British Linen Co. Bank* v. *Carruthers and Fergusson* (1883) 10 R. 923. See also p. 199, *supra*.
[54] *Infra*, p. 221.
[55] *Glickman* v. *Linda*, 1950 S.C. 18.
[56] *G. W. Ry.* v. *London and County Bank* [1901] A.C. 414, at p. 420; *Comrs. of Taxation* v. *English, Scottish and Australian Bank* [1920] A.C. 683, at p. 687. As to what constitutes a person a customer of a banker, see also p. 213, *infra*.
[57] *Supra*, pp. 43–45, *et passim*.
[58] *Supra*, p. 83.

damages to his customer for breach of contract should the customer
suffer loss or damage through such failure or refusal, or even without
proof that the customer has sustained measurable loss.[59]   The usual
measure of damage is loss of credit through such wrongful dishonour,
and it has been held that in such circumstances a trader is entitled to
recover substantial damages without pleading and proving actual
damage, but a person who is not a trader is only entitled to recover
nominal damages unless he pleads and proves special damage.[60]

A customer, whether his account is debtor or creditor, may wish to
pay in certain sums to meet cheques which he has issued and which
are about to fall due.   The position of the banker with regard to such
a request is that he may refuse to enter into a special bargain of this
nature; but if he accepts the money, he is bound to pay the cheques
when presented, notwithstanding what may then be the position of the
customer's account.

(ii) *Where customer has several accounts.*—Where a customer keeps
current accounts at several branches of the bank, some accounts being
in credit and some overdrawn, the banker is entitled, on giving reasonable notice to the customer, to transfer all the accounts at the various
branches to one account, and so diminish, or extinguish, any debtor
balance that may be due to him, and he is thereafter bound to honour
cheques only if there be sufficient at the credit of the combined account
to meet them.[61]   So also where a customer has several accounts of a
different nature, *e.g.*, a current and a loan account—it may be at the
same branch of the bank—the banker is entitled, but only after notice
to the customer, to mass the accounts together and refuse to honour a
cheque, payment of which would result in a debit balance on the massed
accounts.[62]   The customer has not the corresponding right to combine
accounts kept at different branches so as to draw cheques indiscrimi-
nately, but he has, as a general rule, the right to transfer a creditor
balance from one account to another account.[63]   Where, however,
there is a liquid, *i.e.*, an ascertained and immediately enforceable, debt
due to the banker under any obligation of his customer other than a
debit balance on his other accounts, for example, where the customer
is indorser of a bill of which the banker is the holder, the banker is
entitled to hold a creditor balance on a particular account against that
debt.   If, on the other hand, the debt is illiquid, *i.e.*, if it cannot be
immediately ascertained and enforced, or if there is only a presumption
of liability, the banker has no right to withhold the creditor balance,

59   *King* v. *British Linen Co.* (1899) 1 F. 928.
60   *Gibbons* v. *Westminster Bank Ltd.* [1939] 2 K.B. 882.
61   *Farnett* v. *M'Kewan* (1872) L.R. 8 Ex. 10.
62   *Kirkwood* v. *Clydesdale Bank*, 1908 S.C. 20, at p. 25.
63   See, however, *Gibb* v. *Lombank Scotland Ltd.*, 1962 S.L.T. 288.

and must honour the customer's cheques, at least up to the amount at the credit of the massed accounts.

(iii) *Where banker's authority is determined.*—A banker's authority may be " determined," *i.e.*, terminated, by countermand of payment; by closing the account; by notice of the customer's death; and by analogous events.

A person who issues a cheque is entitled to countermand payment thereof before it is paid by the banker upon whom it is drawn.[64] The countermand may be made verbally, by letter, or by telegram. Where a cheque is drawn by two or more persons, any one of them can countermand it, and when it is drawn by a partner in the firm name, any partner can countermand it, and that notwithstanding the fact that he may not be the partner who signed the cheque. When a cheque, payment of which has been countermanded, is presented for payment to the banker upon whom it is drawn, the banker cannot pay the cheque, but he must, in Scotland, although not in England, retain sufficient money to meet the cheque, if there is enough in the customer's account, since a cheque, duly presented, is, as has been seen, equivalent to an intimated assignation in favour of the payee of any funds of the customer in the banker's hands available to meet it.[65] Countermand of payment does not affect the liability of the drawer to an indorsee of the cheque who is in the position of a holder in due course, *e.g.*, to a collecting bank which has given the payee credit for the amount of the cheque.[66] Such a holder can sue the drawer on the cheque as a bill of exchange.

A banker's contract with his customer may be determined at any time by either party giving notice to the other to close the account. Where the banker gives such notice, he must pay cheques drawn and issued before the notice was received by the customer, provided he has funds in the account to meet them.[67] The customer is entitled to payment of any balance at the credit of the account when it is closed.

Notice of the customer's death also determines the duty and authority of a banker to pay a cheque.[68] Until, therefore, the banker has actual notice, or has knowledge otherwise, of the death of the customer, he is entitled, and bound, if he has funds of the customer, to honour his cheques. If he has such notice or knowledge, he must not pay the cheque, but must retain its amount, due presentment of the cheque operating in this case also as intimation of an assignation in favour of

64 Act, s. 75 (1).
65 Act, s. 53 (2). *Supra*, p. 203.
66 *M'Lean* v. *Clydesdale Bank* (1883) 11 R. (H.L.) 1.
67 *King* v. *British Linen Bank* (1899) 1 F. 928.
68 Act, s. 75 (2).

the payee.[69]   In determining whether any funds are available, the balance on all accounts kept by the customer must be considered.[70]

Analogous events which also determine the banker's authority to pay a cheque are notice of the customer's sequestration,[71] or of the appointment of a *curator bonis* on his estate,[72] or arrestment,[73] *i.e.*, a creditor's judicially attaching the customer's funds in the hands of the banker in security of his debt.   Arrestment, if justifiable, prevents the subsequent presentment of a cheque from operating as intimation of an assignation of funds arrested.

It is doubtful whether a banker is entitled to refuse to honour a cheque on the ground that he has notice that the drawer is acting fraudulently or in breach of trust in drawing it.[74]   He is, moreover, under no obligation to inquire into the motives of the payee, *e.g.*, as to what use he will make of the money.

(c) **Customer's duty to banker.**—The customer, in drawing a cheque, owes a duty to the banker to take reasonable and ordinary precautions against forgery, and if, as the natural and direct result of the neglect of those precautions, the amount of the cheque is increased by forgery, the customer must bear the loss as between himself and the banker, *e.g.*, if a cheque be drawn with spaces left in it so that the amount may be altered in a way which cannot be detected, and the banker pays the amount so altered, he may debit the drawer's account with such amount.[76]   The drawer has, however, no duty to fill up blanks after the name of the payee, so that the payee's name may not be altered, as this is not a usual and reasonable precaution against forgery.[77]

If a customer's cheque, *ex facie* valid, is presented for payment, the banker is bound to pay it, the responsibility for what has happened to it between the dates of signature and presentation resting, not upon him, but upon the customer.[78]   If, however, a cheque bears obvious marks of alteration, and the banker is so negligent as to pay it, he cannot debit the customer's account with the amount so paid.[79]   The question whether there was negligence as between banker and customer is a question of fact in each particular case, and can be decided only

---

[69] s. 53 (2).   *Supra*, p. 203.
[70] *Kirkwood* v. *Clydesdale Bank*, 1908 S.C. 20.
[71] Bankruptcy Act, 1913, s. 107.
[72] *Mitchell and Baxter* v. *Cheyne* (1891) 19 R. 324.
[73] *Graham* v. *Macfarlane* (1869) 7 M. 640.
[74] *Byles on Bills*, 21st ed., p. 17.
[75] *Dickson* v. *National Bank*, 1917 S.C. (H.L.) 50.
[76] *London Joint-Stock Bank Ltd.* v. *Macmillan and Arthur* [1918] A.C. 777.   Contrast absence of such duty in case of acceptor of bill of exchange, *supra*, pp. 187, 209.
[77] *Slingsby* v. *District Bank Ltd.* [1932] 1 K.B. 544.
[78] *London Joint-Stock Bank Ltd.* v. *Macmillan and Arthur*, *cit. sup.*, *per* Lord Shaw of Dunfermline at pp. 824, 825.
[79] *Bank of Ireland* v. *Evans' Charities* (1855) 5 H.L.C. 389.

on a view of the cheque as issued by the drawer, with the help of any evidence available as to the course of dealings between the parties or otherwise.[80] If the banker presents and receives payment of a cheque for a customer who has no title to it, the onus of proving absence of negligence is on the banker.[81]

6. Relation of banker and third parties.—Negotiation of cheques

A cheque may, like any other bill of exchange payable on demand, be indorsed so as to entitle the indorsee or any subsequent holder to sue prior indorsers thereon, and the ordinary rules applicable to indorsers of such bills apply to cheques. They are negotiable instruments. The ordinary indorsation of a cheque to a banker, *i.e.*, where it is indorsed and handed over to the banker and the proceeds are paid to the indorser or credited to his account, does not, however, subject the indorser to liability to the banker or to a prior holder, such indorsation being really of the nature of an acknowledgment of receipt of payment. It is also evidence to the drawer that the banker has paid the cheque, and is therefore entitled to debit his account with the amount.

A cheque drawn payable to bearer, *e.g.*, " Pay AB or bearer," is negotiated by delivery without indorsation, and may be passed from hand to hand like an ordinary bank note, and, when presented to a banker for payment, requires no indorsation. Such a cheque, so long as it purports to be payable to bearer, cannot be restrictively indorsed by the payee or any subsequent holder so as to be payable to the order of the indorser, but the payee of such a cheque is entitled to substitute the word " order " for the word " bearer " in the body of the cheque, and thus change the cheque from one payable to bearer to one payable to order. A cheque payable to order, *e.g.*, " Pay AB or order," is negotiated by the indorsation of the payee, *i.e.*, AB, and delivery to the indorsee. Any person fulfilling the necessary conditions [82] may be a holder in due course of a cheque as of a bill. The original payee has, however, been held not to be a holder in due course within the meaning of the Act.[83]

An indorsement may be general, *i.e.*, consist simply of the signature of the indorser. A cheque which is thus " blank indorsed " is then payable to bearer. Or an indorsement may be special, *i.e.*, it specifies the person to whom or to whose order the cheque is to be

---

[80] *London Joint Stock Bank Ltd.* v. *Macmillan and Arthur, cit. sup., per* Lord Finlay L.C. at p. 810; *Slingsby* v. *District Bank Ltd.* [1931] 2 K.B. 588, 601.

[81] *Midland Bank* v. *Reckitt* [1933] A.C. 1. *Cf. Bute (Marquess)* v. *Barclays Bank Ltd.* [1955] 1 Q.B. 202.

[82] *Supra*, p. 188.

[83] *R. E. Jones Ltd.* v. *Waring & Gillow Ltd.* [1926] A.C. 670.

payable; or restrictive, *i.e.*, it prohibits the further negotiation of the cheque, for example, " Pay D. only," or expresses that it is a mere authority to deal with the cheque as thereby directed and is not a transfer of ownership, as, for example, " Pay D for the account of X." Where a person is under obligation to indorse a cheque in a representative capacity, *e.g.*, as agent, director, trustee, or executor, he may indorse it in such terms as to negative personal liability by the addition of words indicating that he signs merely as an agent or in a representative capacity, or words such as " without recourse."

A banker is bound to pay an indorsed and uncrossed cheque, drawn on him, which purports to be indorsed by the person to whom it is drawn, or indorsed, payable, and so long as the indorsement is regular the banker is under no obligation to see that it is bona fide. If, however, he suspects on reasonable grounds that an indorsation has been forged, he is justified in taking time to inquire into its genuineness. He may also pay an uncrossed cheque payable to bearer to a finder or a thief, as he is not under any obligation to see that the person who presents the cheque for payment is the person who is entitled to it. In the case of a crossed cheque, this freedom from liability depends on his obeying the direction conveyed by the crossing.

7. Protection of banker

The Act provides for the protection of a banker who (a) pays a cheque whereon the indorsement has been forged or made without authority, or (b) pays, or collects payment of, a crossed cheque in accordance with the direction contained in the crossing. The Cheques Act, 1957, further provides for the protection of a banker paying an unindorsed or irregularly indorsed cheque. A banker who pays a cheque drawn on himself is the " paying banker." The banker who collects payment on behalf of the holder from the " paying banker " is the " collecting banker."

(a) **Forged or unauthorised indorsement.**—A banker is not, as we have seen, protected if he pays a cheque on which the drawer's, *i.e.*, his customer's, signature has been forged or made without his authority.[84] If, however, a cheque payable to order is drawn on him, and he pays it in good faith and in the ordinary course of business, it is not incumbent on him to show that the indorsement of the payee, or any subsequent indorsement, was made by or under the authority of the person whose indorsement it purports to be, and the banker is

---

[84] *Dickson* v. *Clydesdale Bank Ltd.*, 1937 S.L.T. 585.

deemed to have paid the cheque in due course, although such indorsement has been forged or made without authority.[85]

This protection is not, however, available where the paying banker is also the collecting banker [86]; where the indorsement is obviously not regular [87]; where the cheque has been altered in a material particular [88]; or where the cheque is crossed and the banker pays in disregard of the crossing.

(b) Unindorsed or irregularly indorsed cheques.—A banker who in good faith and in the ordinary course of business pays a cheque drawn on him which is not indorsed or is irregularly indorsed does not, in doing so, incur any liability by reason only of the absence of, or irregularity in, indorsement, and he is deemed to have paid it in due course.[89]

A banker who gives value for, or has a lien on, a cheque payable to order which the holder delivers to him for collection without indorsing it, has such (if any) rights as he would have had if, upon delivery, the holder had indorsed it in blank.[90]

(c) Crossed cheques.[91]—(1) Origin and purpose.—The introduction of the crossing of cheques is of comparatively recent date. It is an example of a mercantile practice becoming part of the statutory law. The practice owes its inception to certain private bankers in London, who in 1775 instituted the London Clearing House as a means of economising their capital as well as of saving much unnecessary trouble in the collection of cheques. Cheques paid into a bank were taken to the Clearing House in the afternoon of the following day, and, in order to facilitate business there and also to preserve a record of the channel through which the cheque came, the clerks of the several bankers were in the habit at first of writing, and afterwards of stamping, the names of their principals across the documents presented by them for payment. The object of this crossing was to secure that, in the event of the cheque being dishonoured, it should be at once returned to the banker who presented it, so that the payee could be informed that payment had not been obtained. Also, the crossing afforded a means

---

[85] s. 60.

[86] *Carpenters' Co. of London* v. *British Mutual Banking Co.* [1938] 1 K.B. 511, 529.

[87] e.g., *Godfrey Phillips Ltd.* v. *Italian Bank Ltd.,* 1933 S.N. 101.

[88] *Slingsby* v. *District Bank* [1932] 1 K.B. 544.

[89] Cheques Act, 1957. As to ordinary course of business in this connection, see *Chalmers on Bills of Exchange,* 13th ed. p. 302.

[90] *Ibid.,* s. 2. See Chalmers at p. 307. The person for whom the cheque is collected need not be the holder; *Westminster Bank Ltd.* v. *Zang* [1964] 3 W.L.R. 1105.

[91] The Cheques Act, 1957, applies the provisions of the Act of 1882 as to crossed cheques to other instruments which are not bills of exchange.

of tracing the person by whom the cheque had been paid in, if a question afterwards arose as to the true ownership of it.

The convenience of the system led to other private bankers in London being admitted to the Clearing House, and merchants then found that they did not require to provide for payment of such of their cheques as were presented through a bank until the afternoon of the day on which they were drawn; and, in order to secure that all their cheques should be so presented, the practice grew up of writing the name of a banker across the cheque. Afterwards, it became common for a drawer, instead of writing the name of a banker, to cross the cheque with the words " and Company " or " & Co.," usually between parallel lines, and sometimes merely by drawing two parallel lines, across the face of the document. Where the name of the banker was written, the crossing was termed a special crossing. The other forms were termed general crossings. Drawers' bankers paid attention to these crossings, and generally refused payment of cheques so crossed unless presented to them through a banker, if crossed generally, or through the banker to whom they were specially crossed.

It was then seen that crossing afforded great protection against the risk attending the loss or theft of a cheque, inasmuch as a banker to whom a crossed cheque was presented would not cash it unless he knew the person and signature of the payee or indorsee, and it was with a view to attaining this protection that the practice became common. It in effect compels a person who seeks to cash a crossed cheque to have an account with a bank or to negotiate it to someone who has. A crossing may also be such as to leave a cheque transferable, but prevent a transferee from becoming a holder in due course.[91a]

Several Acts of Parliament were passed dealing with crossed cheques, but these were repealed by the Act of 1882, which, with the Cheques Act, 1957, contains the statutory enactments on the subject.[92]

(2) *General statutory effect.*—When a cheque is crossed, a direction is thereby conveyed to the banker upon whom it is drawn that payment can only be made in a particular way, *i.e.*, through a banker, and to the holder of the cheque that he can only receive payment in that way. The effect of crossing accordingly is to secure as far as possible that the cheque shall only be paid to the person intended by the drawer to receive payment, or a person deriving right through him.

(3) *Lawful crossings.*—Only two kinds of crossing are authorised by the Act, namely (a) a general crossing, and (b) a special crossing. These may be illustrated thus:

[91a] *Infra*, p. 214.
[92] 1882 Act, ss. 76–81 1957 Act.

(a) General.[93]

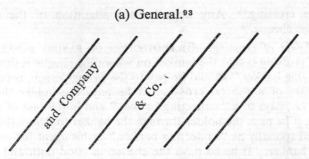

The words " not negotiable " may be added to any one of these.

(b) Special.[94]

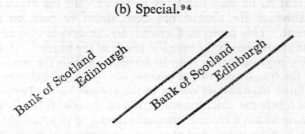

The words " not negotiable " may be added to either of these.

(4) *Who may cross and how.*[95]—A cheque may be crossed generally or specially by the drawer. If it is uncrossed, the holder may cross it generally or specially. Where a cheque is crossed generally, the holder may cross it specially. If it is crossed generally or specially, the holder may add the words " not negotiable." [96] Where a cheque is crossed specially, the banker to whom it is crossed may again cross it specially to another banker for collection. The drawer's banker, or paying banker, can then pay only to the collecting banker. This is the only case in which a cheque may be crossed specially to more than one banker.[97] Where an uncrossed cheque or a cheque crossed generally is sent to the banker for collection, he may cross it specially to himself.

These are the only crossings authorised by the Act. Any such crossing is a material part of the cheque, and it is not lawful for any person to obliterate, or, except in the above respects, to add to or

[93] s. 76 (1).
[94] s. 76 (2).
[95] s. 77.
[96] *Infra*, p. 214.
[97] s. 79 (1).

alter the crossing.[98] Any unauthorised alteration of the crossing avoids the cheque.[99]

(5) *Effect of crossing.*—(i) PROTECTION OF PAYING BANKER.—The effect of crossing is that the banker on whom the cheque is drawn, *i.e.*, the " paying banker," should he pay to the wrong person, is protected, in the case of a general crossing, if he pays the holder through a banker, *i.e.*, pays to a " collecting banker," and in the case of a special crossing, if he pays the holder through the banker to whom the cheque is crossed specially as " collecting banker," or his agent for collection, being a banker. If he so pays the cheque in good faith and without negligence, he is entitled to the same rights and is placed in the same position as if payment of the cheque had been made to the true owner thereof, that is, he may debit his customer with the amount of the cheque although the cheque has been stolen or paid on a forged indorsement. This protection extends to the drawer also in the case where the cheque has come into the hands of the payee.[1] If, however, the banker pays otherwise than in accordance with the crossing, he is liable to the true owner of the cheque, *i.e.*, payee or indorsee, for any loss the latter may sustain owing to the cheque having been so paid.[2]

While this is the strict interpretation of the law, it is not illegal for a banker on whom a crossed cheque is drawn to pay that cheque over the counter if he is satisfied that the person by whom the cheque is presented and indorsed is the person to whom it is payable. In the case of such a payment it is preferable, although not necessary, that the words " Pay in cash " be added to the indorsement; and if they are added, no stamp is required. No crossed cheque should, however, be paid over the counter to an employee of the person or company in whose favour the cheque is drawn. The risk of departing from this rule is thus illustrated. A commercial traveller had authority to collect cheques payable to his company but he had no authority to cash such cheques. He presented certain crossed cheques, drawn in favour of his employers and indorsed by him in their name with his own name added but without any indication of his relation to the company or his authority, to the office of the bank on which the cheques were drawn, received payment and appropriated it. In an action by the employers against the bank for the amount of the cheques so paid, it

---

[98] s. 78. As to the effect of the drawer "opening a crossing" by a mandate on the face of the cheque to his banker to pay cash, see Wallace & M'Neil, *Banking Law*, 8th ed., 223; *Byles on Bills*, 21st ed., 35; *Chalmers on Bills*, 13th ed., p. 265; *Scottish Bankers' Magazine*, Vol. 43, p. 231.

[99] *Cf.* unauthorised alteration of material part of a bill, *supra*, p. 197.

[1] s. 80. If the cheque be payable to order, and the indorsation is forged, the drawer or the payee, as the case may be, has the right of repayment from the person who received payment of the cheque, *Chalmers on Bills*, 13th ed., p. 268.

[2] s. 79 (2).

was held that the bank was liable in respect that the crossed cheques should have been paid only through a bank and not over the counter.[3] The only safe course for a banker in such circumstances is to credit the account of the person in whose favour the crossed cheque is drawn and allow the money to be withdrawn in a manner authorised by him.

The liability imposed by the Act on a banker who pays a crossed cheque otherwise than in accordance with the crossing is qualified by a provision that where the crossing has been obliterated or altered, but this is not apparent on the face of the cheque, a banker who pays in good faith and without negligence does not incur any liability, and may debit his customer with the amount paid.[4]

(ii) PROTECTION OF COLLECTING BANKER.—A banker who, in good faith and without negligence (a) receives payment of a cheque for a customer, or (b) having credited a customer's account with the amount thereof, receives payment thereof for himself, and the customer has no title, or a defective title thereto, the banker does not incur any liability to the true owner of the cheque by reason only of having received payment thereof.[5] This protection applies to the collection of all cheques, whether crossed or uncrossed.[6]

To bring a case within the statutory protection, the following facts must co-exist:

(1) The person for whom the cheque is collected, i.e., the holder, must be a customer of the collecting bank, i.e., there must be some sort of an account between them, either a current or a deposit account, or some similar relation.[7] Other dealings may not be sufficient. For example, it has been held that a bank's cashing of a cheque for a stranger did not constitute him their customer.[8] A bank, in receiving payment for another bank, receives payment for a customer within the meaning of the statute, and is entitled to the statutory protection.[9]

(2) The cheque must be collected in good faith and without negligence, that is, without want of reasonable care in reference to the interests of the true owner. Thus in a case decided in 1900,[10] a cheque was drawn payable to Hannan's Lake View Central Ltd., and crossed

---

[3] *Phillips* v. *Italian Bank Ltd.*, 1934 S.L.T. 78.
[4] s. 79 (2).
[5] Cheques Act, 1957, s. 4 (1). The Act applies this provision to other instruments which are not cheques—s. 4 (2).
[6] Chalmers, *Bills of Exchange*, 13th ed., p. 310.
[7] *Great Western Ry.* v. *London and County Bank* [1901] A.C. 414, *per* Lord Davey at pp. 420, 421.
[8] *Matthews* v. *Williams, Brown & Co.* (1894) 63 L.J.Q.B. 494.
[9] *Importers Co.* v. *Westminster Bank* [1927] 2 K.B. 297.
[10] *Hannan's Lake View Central Ltd.* v. *Armstrong & Co.* (1899) 16 T.L.R. 236. *Cf. Carpenters' Co.* v. *British Mutual Banking Co. Ltd.* [1938] 1 K.B. 511; *Bute (Marquess)* v. *Barclays Bank Ltd.* [1955] 1 Q.B. 202; *Baker* v. *Barclays Bank Ltd.* [1955] 2 All E.R. 571.

generally. The secretary of that company indorsed the cheque in name of his company, subscribing his own name as secretary. He then paid it in to the credit of a private account which he had with the company's bankers, and drew out the amount as he required it. It was decided that, though the bankers had acted in good faith, they were liable to the company in the amount of the cheque. The ground of the decision was that it was apparent on the face of the transaction that the secretary was using for himself a valuable document, which, on the face of it, bore evidence of having been granted for the benefit of his employers, and was their property; that the whole course of ordinary business was opposed to the idea that the secretary of a company was likely to have been paid money due to him as salary or otherwise by the authorisation of the indorsement by himself to himself of a cheque payable to the order of the company; and that, in accepting such a cheque so indorsed for his private account, the bank were guilty of negligence, and thus lost the protection of the statute.

" **Account payee.**"—These words, which are frequently added to the crossing of a cheque, are neither part of the crossing, nor an unlawful addition thereto. They are simply a direction to the collecting banker that the proceeds are to be credited only to the payee specified in the cheque.[11] They do not make a cheque not negotiable,[12] and they do not deprive a banker, collecting payment for a customer whom he reasonably but wrongly believes to be the payee, of his statutory protection.[13]

" **Not negotiable.**"—Where a cheque is crossed generally or specially, the holder may add the words " not negotiable."[14] The effect of these words is that a person taking the cheque does not have, and is not capable of giving, a better title to it than that which the person from whom he took it had,[15] i.e., the cheque can be transferred from one person to another, but no transferee can be a holder in due course.[16] This applies where the person taking the cheque is himself the payee as well as in the case of any other person.[17] It is probably the law that no other words on a cheque can make it not negotiable in this sense.[18]

[11] *Akrokerri Mines* v. *Economic Bank* [1904] 2 K.B. 465 at p. 472.
[12] *National Bank* v. *Silke* [1891] 1 Q.B. 435.
[13] *Importers Co.* v. *Westminster Bank* [1927] 2 K.B. 297.
[14] s. 77 (4).
[15] 1882 Act, s. 81.
[16] Contrast the meaning of " not negotiable " in the case of a bill of exchange, *supra*, p. 174.
[17] *Wilson and Meeson* v. *Pickering* (1945) 62 T.L.R. 223.
[18] *National Bank* v. *Silke, supra; Glen* v. *Semple* (1901) 3 F. 1134.

8. Certified cheques

When a banker certifies a cheque, he undertakes that the customer has, at the time when the cheque is certified, funds sufficient to meet it.[19] Certification is not acceptance [20]; and whether it would amount to a representation that funds were available to meet it has not yet been decided. Its only effect is therefore to give the cheque additional currency by showing on the face of it that it is drawn in good faith on funds sufficient to meet its payment, and, by adding to the credit of the drawer the credit of the banker on whom it is drawn, to raise an expectation that the cheque will be met.[21] Certified cheques are now largely superseded in this country by bankers' drafts.

9. To whom does a cheque which has been paid belong?

When a cheque is paid, the holder is bound forthwith to deliver it up to the paying banker, in whose hands it is evidence of payment of the amount. It then becomes the property of the drawer, but the banker is entitled to keep it until his account with the drawer is settled or is docqueted by the latter as correct.

10. Bankers' drafts

A banker's draft is an instrument issued in the form of a cheque drawn by a banker on himself. It is issued usually at the request of a customer and in favour of a payee specified by him, the amount being debited to the customer's account. It is a convenient method of paying large sums in circumstances in which a cheque would not be acceptable.[22] These drafts were at one time not recognised as cheques, and were therefore not entitled to the statutory privileges of cheques, but by the Cheques Act, 1957, such drafts are in the same position under the provisions of that Act as cheques as regards protection of the collecting banker, the effect of crossings, and the lack or irregularity of an indorsement. In this connection the expression " banker's draft " means any draft payable on demand drawn by a banker upon himself, whether payable at the head office or some other office of his bank.

PROMISSORY NOTES

1. Origin and history

Promissory notes were not in use until long after bills of exchange, and were not at first entitled to the special privileges of bills. They had their origin in " goldsmiths' notes," an invention of the goldsmiths in Lombard Street. These were not, as bills might be, drawn on

---

19 *Gaden* v. *Newfoundland Bank* [1899] A.C. 281.
20 *Bank of Baroda Ltd.* v. *Punjab National Bank Ltd.* [1944] A.C. 176.
21 *Chalmers on Bills*, 13th ed., pp. 249–250.
22 See Jacobs, *Bills of Exchange*, 4th ed., p. 253 *et seq.*

another person, but contained a simple promise by the maker to pay the sum specified therein and rested on his credit alone. They were at first payable to bearer, but soon the practice in bills of exchange was followed, and they also could be made payable to order and so transferred by indorsation. This practice was first recognised by the courts in England in 1680, and, in 1704, their negotiability was recognised by statute.[23] By two Acts of Parliament passed in the reign of George III,[24] it was enacted that the same diligence and execution should be competent and should proceed upon promissory notes, whether holograph or not, as was provided to pass upon bills of exchange and inland bills by the law of Scotland; that promissory notes should bear interest as bills and should pass by indorsation; and that indorsees of promissory notes should have the same privileges as indorsees of bills in all points. The existing statutory provisions as to promissory notes are contained in the Bills of Exchange Act,1882. Part IV of the Act contains special provisions relating to notes, but since these, although distinct in form, are in their essentials bills of exchange, most of the provisions of the Act relating to bills apply, with the necessary modifications, and subject to the provisions contained in Part IV as to notes.[25] The provisions relating to bills which do not apply are those relating to presentment for acceptance, acceptance, acceptance *supra* protest, and bills in a set. A further difference is that where a foreign note is dishonoured, protest is unnecessary.[26]

2. Definition—Inland and foreign notes

A promissory note is an unconditional promise in writing made by one person to another, signed by the maker, engaging to pay, on demand or at a fixed or determinable future time, a sum certain in money to, or to the order of, a specified person or to bearer.[27] A note which is, or on the face of it purports to be, both made and payable within the British Islands is an inland note. Any other note is a foreign note.[28]

3. Essentials

The above definition indicates the essentials, of which the following may be mentioned:

(1) *Promise.*—The instrument must contain a promise, *i.e.*, some phrase expressing engagement to pay, although the word " promise "

---

[23] 3 & 4 Anne, c. 9.
[24] 12 Geo. 3, c. 72; 23 Geo. 3, c. 18.
[25] s. 89 (1).
[26] s. 89 (3) (4).
[27] s. 83 (1).
[28] s. 83 (4).

itself need not be used; otherwise the document is merely evidence of a debt between the original parties, like an IOU.

(2) *Payee.*—The obligation to pay must be addressed to some person, or to bearer. A document which contains a mere obligation to pay is not a promissory note, and a person to whom it is given cannot fill in his own name as payee.[29]

(3) *Stamp duty.*—The instrument must be stamped with the appropriate stamp duty.[30] The rate is the same as for bill, *i.e.*, twopence.[31] An unstamped note cannot be afterstamped and founded on in support of a claim by the holder against the maker of the note.[32]

To the essentials contained in the statutory definition there has to be added another, namely:

(4) *Delivery.*—An instrument which conforms to the above requirements must, in order to become a promissory note, be delivered to the payee or bearer. Until delivery, it is inchoate and incomplete.[33]

4. Form

As with bills, there is no statutory form, and it is immaterial how the instrument is framed or expressed, so long as it contains the essentials of a promissory note. A usual form is " On demand (or, " Three months after date) I promise to pay to A.B., or order, the sum of £50. Value received." This is the simplest form, but other provisions may be added without depriving an instrument of its validity as a note. It is expressly enacted that a note is not invalid by reason only that it contains also a pledge of collateral security with authority to sell or dispose thereof,[34] and an instrument in the following terms has been held to be a promissory note, *viz.*, " We beg to acknowledge receipt of yours of date . . . covering cheque for £100 sterling, which we hereby agree to pay to you in two years and six months from date, with interest at the rate of 6 per cent. per annum, interest payable half-yearly. In security, we now enclose policies on the Life Association of Scotland on the lives of A.B. and C.D., No. . . . , value £200, and No. . . . , value £300 sterling, which are thus to be considered as assigned to you until the payment of the loan is made." Again, a note may contain provisions safeguarding the holder in the

---

[29] *Duncan's Trs.* v. *Shand* (1872) 10 M. 984.

[30] As to whether a particular instrument is, for the purposes of stamp duty, a promissory note, see *M'Taggart* v. *MacEachern's Judicial Factor,* 1949 S.C. 503; *Henderson* v. *Dawson* (1895) 22 R. 895; *Todd* v. *Wood* (1897) 24 R. 1104; *Lamberton* v. *Aitken;* (1899) 2 F. 189.

[31] The Statutory provisions concerning issue, transfer and payment of unstamped bills apply also to notes. *Supra,* p. 174.

[32] Stamp Act, 1891, ss. 38 (1), 14 (4); *M'Taggart* v. *MacEachern's Judicial Factor, cit. sup.; Thomson* v. *Black,* 1936 S.N. 78.

[33] s. 84.
[34] s. 83 (3).

event of time being given to one or other of the parties jointly liable thereon.[35]

The mere fact also that a promissory note contains a statement of facts not necessary to its validity as such does not make it any the less a promissory note. For example, a document in the following terms, *viz.*: " I hereby promise to give my sister Elizabeth . . . the sum of £300 . . . immediately I receive the money left to me by my sister Helen . . . , " was held to be a promissory note.[36] If, however, a document contains something more than has been referred to, it may not be valid as a promissory note although it may still be valid as an expression of an obligation.

An instrument in the form of a note payable to the order of the maker is not a note within the meaning of the statutory definition unless and until it is indorsed by him [37]; and a bill in which drawer and drawee are the same person, or where the drawee is a fictitious person or a person not having capacity to contract, may be treated by the holder, at his option, either as a bill of exchange, or as a promissory note.[38]

5. Parties

The drawer of the note is known as the maker. The only other parties to it are the indorsers. In applying the provisions of the Act relating to bills of exchange, the maker of a note is deemed to correspond with the acceptor of a bill, and the first indorser of a note is deemed to correspond with the drawer of an accepted bill payable to drawer's order.[39] The maker is therefore the party primarily liable, the indorsers being liable only subsidiarily.

6. Liability

The maker of a note, by making it, engages that he will pay it according to its tenor. Further, he is precluded from denying to a holder in due course the existence of the payee and his then capacity to indorse,[40] *i.e.*, he is barred from pleading, if called upon to pay, that the note is invalid in respect of the matters which it contained when he issued it.

A promissory note may be made by two or more makers, and they may be liable thereon jointly, or jointly and severally, according to its tenor.[41] Where a note runs, " I promise to pay," and is signed

[35] *Kirkwood* v. *Carroll* [1903] 1 K.B. 531.
[36] *Thomson* v. *Black,* 1936 S.N. 78.
[37] s. 83 (2).
[38] s. 5 (2).
[39] s. 89 (2).
[40] s. 88.
[41] s. 85 (1).

by two or more persons, it is deemed to be their joint and several note,[42] with the result that the holder can select any one from amongst the persons who have signed it and ask him to pay the full sum due. Where a note runs, " We promise to pay," and is signed by two or more persons, liability is, in Scotland, joint and several.[43] In all such cases, the proper course is to see that the promissory note reads thus: " We jointly and severally promise to pay."

An indorser, by indorsing a note, incurs a liability corresponding to that undertaken by an indorser of a bill of exchange.[44]

7. Presentment for payment

(1) *When a condition of liability of maker.*—The maker being always liable in his obligation, presentment to him of the note for payment is not necessary in order to render him liable, except in one case, namely, where the note is, in the body of it, made payable at a particular place. It must then be presented to him for payment at that place.[45] It need not, however, be presented on the day when payment is due, presentment on a subsequent day being sufficient.[46]

(2) *When a condition of liability of indorser.*—In order to render the indorser of a note liable presentment to the maker for payment is necessary.[47] Where the note is in the body of it made payable at a particular place, presentment must be made at that place; but where a place of payment is indicated by way of memorandum only, presentment at that place is sufficient, but presentment to the maker elsewhere also suffices.[48] Where the note is one payable on demand, it must be presented for payment within a reasonable time of the indorsement, and if it is not so presented, the indorser is discharged. In determining what is a reasonable time regard is to be had to the nature of the instrument, the usage of trade, and the facts of the particular case.[49]

(3) *Where a note payable on demand is negotiated.*—The Act makes special provision regarding the effect of delay in presenting for payment a note payable on demand which has been negotiated. Such a note is not deemed to be overdue, for the purpose of affecting the holder with defects of title of which he had no notice, by reason that it appears that a reasonable time for presenting it for payment has elapsed since

---

[42] s. 85 (2).
[43] Bell's Prin., 10th ed., § 81; Act, s. 97 (2). This is contrary to the general rule that a joint obligation is *pro rata.* See *Coats* v. *Union Bank of Scotland,* 1929 S.C.(H.L.) 114.
[44] s. 55 (2). *Supra,* pp. 179, 180.
[45] s. 87 (1).
[46] *Gordon* v. *Kerr* (1898) 25 R. 570.
[47] s. 87 (2).
[48] s. 87 (3).
[49] s. 86 (1) (2).

its issue.[50]   A promissory note payable on demand thus differs from a bill of exchange payable on demand, and a cheque.[51]   These are intended to be presented and paid immediately, whereas a promissory note often is made or indorsed with the intention that it be a continuing security.

(4) *Due presentment.*—The rules regulating due presentment, excuses for non-presentment and delay, and protest, are, with the exception above-mentioned,[52] the same as those applicable to bills.

8. Summary diligence

Payment of a note, as of a bill, may be enforced by summary diligence.[53]

9. Sexennial prescription

The sexennial prescription applies to promissory notes.[54]

I O Us

I O Us are frequently granted in acknowledgment of loans or other like indebtedness.

Such writings are usually in the following terms: "I O U fifty pounds," and are signed by the granter.   The writing requires no stamp.   It need not be addressed to any person, but the writing must be holograph of the granter.   An I O U cannot be transferred by indorsement, but it may be assigned by a formal deed which must be intimated to the granter.

An I O U is not a promissory note, but is an acknowledgment of debt of a stated amount due by the granter to the grantee, and implying an obligation to repay on demand.   It may be open to the granter in defence to prove a collateral agreement as to the date at which payment is to be made, and if both parties are at one in admitting that the document is not a true record of the transaction between them, the circumstances of the transaction will fall to be investigated as if the I O U had not been granted.[55]

Interest, if not expressly stipulated for in the I O U, is exigible only from the date of citation in an action for payment of the principal sum.[56]

Opinions are conflicting as to the prescription of such documents. In the latest case on the subject it was held that the vicennial prescription applied.[57]

[50] s. 86 (3).   [51] s. 36 (2) (3).
[52] *i.e.,* that a foreign note which is dishonoured need not be protested; *supra,* p. 246.
[53] *Supra,* p. 207.   [54] *Supra,* p. 53.
[55] *Bishop* v. *Bryce,* 1910 S.C. 426; *Black* v. *Gibb,* 1940 S.C. 24.
[56] *Winestone* v. *Wolifson,* 1954 S.C. 77.
[57] *Dick* v. *Thomson's Trs.,* 1929 S.L.T. 637.   *Supra,* p. 53.

CHAPTER 9

CAUTIONARY OBLIGATIONS

1. DEFINITION AND NATURE

A CAUTIONARY obligation is "an accessory engagement, as security for another, that the principal obligant will pay the debt or perform the act for which he has engaged, otherwise the cautioner shall pay the debt or fulfil the obligation." [1] The person undertaking the accessory obligation is called a cautioner or, mostly in mercantile business, a guarantor or in England a surety.[2] The party to whose obligation the accessory obligation is accessory is called the principal debtor.

It is of the essence of a cautionary obligation that it is an accessory obligation, collateral to another. There must therefore be a principal obligation constituted or at least contemplated by the principal debtor to the creditor in the obligation at the time the accessory obligation is undertaken, and the continuance of the principal is necessary to the continuance of the accessory obligation. Accordingly, there can be no accessory obligation and no contract of cautionry if the principal obligation is in law a nullity, e.g., undertaken by a person unable to contract, or void from illegality [3]: the obligation of the cautioner as such never comes into existence. He is either not liable at all, or is liable as an independent obligant, with different consequences. So also, if when the cautionary engagement is undertaken, the principal obligation is merely contemplated and never in fact comes into existence. And if the principal obligation comes to an end, e.g., by prescription or novation, before the cautionary obligation is exacted against the cautioner, it falls with the principal obligation.[4]

If, on the other hand, the principal obligation is not null, but merely unenforceable, the cautionary obligation can be enforced as such though the principal obligation cannot. The ground is that the principal debtor has come under a natural, though not legally enforceable, obligation, to which the cautioner's obligation is accessory.

---

[1] Bell's *Principles of the Law of Scotland*, § 245.

[2] As to the value of English decisions in dealing with questions of cautionry under the law of Scotland, see *Aitken's Trs.* v. *Bank of Scotland*, 1944 S.C. 270, *per* Lord Justice-Clerk Cooper at 279; 1945 S.L.T. 84.

[3] *Swan* v. *Bank of Scotland* (1836) 10 Bligh(N.S.) 627; *Coutts & Co.* v. *Browne-Lecky* [1947] 1 K.B. 104.

[4] *Aitken's Trs.* v. *Bank of Scotland*, 1944 S.C. 270; 1945 S.L.T. 84.

Thus, if a deed constituting the principal obligation is invalid owing to some informality of execution, the informal or natural obligation of the principal may suffice to sustain the accessory liability of the cautioner, at least if he knew of the informality.[5]

2. ANALOGOUS OBLIGATIONS

A comparison of the cautionary obligation with certain analogous obligations which are independent obligations assists towards a more exact understanding of the distinctive characteristics of the cautionary obligation. To distinguish it from them may be of importance because in a true contract of cautionry the obligation is *in dubio* to be construed favourably to the cautioner,[6] and because in cautionry the creditor may readily lose his rights against the cautioner.[7]

As the cautionary obligation is essentially accessory in nature, it is necessary that the obligation of a principal debtor, if not in existence when the cautionary obligation is undertaken, should at least be clearly contemplated. If not, it is an independent obligation and it is not sufficient to make it accessory that a third party obligation in fact comes into existence later. And the mere fact that the promise of the supposed cautioner is for the benefit of a third party will not make it a cautionary obligation: it must be shown that the intention was that a third party be primarily liable. The test of whether an obligation is accessory or primary is on whose credit did the creditor rely—that of both or only that of the alleged cautioner.

Cautionry being the acceptance by the creditor of an additional debtor, it is essential that a new debtor by undertaking the same obligation does not exonerate the principal debtor nor extinguish the principal debt. If he does there is *delegation* of the obligation and no cautionry.[8] The presumption is that he is additional.

It being essential to a cautionary undertaking that it be granted to and in favour of the creditor in a primary obligation and also be dependent on the default of a principal debtor, a promise made, not to the creditor but to the debtor under a contract which involves him in possible liability, to keep him indemnified against that liability, is not a cautionary obligation, but a contract of *indemnity*.

---

[5] *Nimmo* v. *Brown* (1700) Mor. 2076 and other cases therein collected; *Stevenson* v. *Adair* (1872) 10 M. 919. In England a person who, in the knowledge that the obligation of the principal is invalid, undertakes as surety its fulfilment is held to his obligation on the ground of personal bar or that the surety obligation means that if the principal does not in fact perform, the surety will; *e.g.*, *Yorkshire Railway Wagon Co.* v. *Maclure* (1881) 19 Ch.D. 478.

[6] *Aitken's Trs.* v. *Bank of Scotland*, 1944 S.C. 270; 1945 S.L.T. 84.

[7] See *infra*.

[8] See *Jackson* v. *MacDiarmid* (1892) 19 R. 528.

Contracts of insurance known as guarantee policies, though very like cautionry, are contracts of indemnity.[9] Thereby the insurer agrees to pay any loss incurred by the assured through the default of a debtor in an obligation to the assured.[10] This is a contract on the basis of indemnity, for the obligation undertaken by the insurer may be to pay a sum different from that which the defaulting person becomes liable to pay, and, further, may depend upon contingencies of time and event which had no place in the debtor's obligation. In the ordinary case it is undertaken upon the application not of any debtor but of the assured person, that is, of a prospective creditor, and upon statements or other representations made by him affecting the nature and extent of the risk. One consequence of its being a contract of insurance, and so *uberrimae fidei*, is that the creditor, *i.e.*, the assured, is bound to disclose all material facts affecting the risk, in contrast, in general,[11] to cautionry.

It is inconsistent with the character of accessory obligant that an obligant should himself have an interest in the granting of the principal obligation. For example, if he is one of several parties to a *cash credit bond* in security of bank advances and the object is to apply the moneys for his sole behoof, *e.g.*, to pay off his debts, the others may be cautioners, but he cannot be.

Representation as to credit.—This is a representation made by one person to another as to the solvency, credit or trustworthiness of a third party which induces the person to whom the representation is made to contract with the third party. It may give rise to liability by the person making the representation for loss which that other suffers by having acted on the representation. It may thus in the result have much the same effect as a guarantee. That will be so in only two cases, however. These are: (1) if the representation is falsely and fraudulently made,[12] in which case the maker, though not liable in contract, is liable *ex delicto* as for a wrong[13]; and (2) where

---

[9] The matter is decided mainly on the effects of the contract. A contract may have the attributes of a contract of insurance as regards the relationship of the parties and at the same time the attributes of a contract of guarantee in a question as to the rights of third parties: *Shaw* v. *Royce Ltd.* [1911] 1 Ch. 138 (insurance); *Denton's Estate, Re Licences Insurance Corporation and Guarantee Fund Ltd.* v. *Denton* [1904] 2 Ch. 178 (guarantee).

[10] It is a positive contract that, for example, if the debtor does not pay a certain amount on a fixed day the insurance company will pay that amount; *Dane* v. *Mortgage Insurance Corporation* [1894] 1 Q.B. 54 at 61. The specified default of the debtor is the occasion, not necessarily the measure, of the insurer's liability; *e.g.*, *Laird* v. *Securities Insurance Co. Ltd.* (1895) 22 R. 452.

[11] *Cooper* v. *National Provincial Bank Ltd.* [1946] K.B. 1; he may in the circumstances have such a duty.

[12] And is in a signed writing, p. 226, *infra*.

[13] *Clydesdale Bank* v. *Paton* (1896) 23 R.(H.L.) 22.

innocently and negligently made and a fiduciary relation exists between the person making and the person receiving the representation, with a consequent and corresponding duty on the maker to take care in making his statements that they are true.[14]

3. FORMS OF THE CAUTIONARY RELATIONSHIP

The relation of creditor, principal debtor and cautioner may subsist where the creditor is a party to the contract of cautionry; or where the relation arises in equity though the creditor is not a party to the cautionry agreement; or, by implication of law, where without any contract of cautionry there exists a primary and a secondary liability on the part of two or more persons for the same debt.

Creditor a party to the contract of cautionry.—In this case the contract may take either of two forms. In the one, known as proper cautionry, the cautioners are bound to the creditor expressly as cautioners for the principal debtor. Each cautioner, where there are several, is impliedly liable to the creditor only for his *pro rata* share of the debt. It is also implied that if one of the cautioners be insolvent, and cannot pay his *pro rata* share in whole or in part, the others are liable *pro rata* for the deficiency. In the other form, known as improper cautionry, the cautioners are bound to the creditor as co-principals and full debtors jointly and severally with the principal debtor and one another, each being thus liable *in solidum* to the creditor. That is so expressly where certain of the co-principals are described as cautioners and co-principals. It is so impliedly where a bond of cautionry expressly confers against one of the co-principals a right on the others of repayment from him if they have to pay to the creditor, known as a clause of relief. It is so also in the case of the cash credit bond, where all are liable for a sum advanced by a bank on loan account and one alone draws on the account.[15] And it may be so also in other cases. For, notwithstanding the joint and several liability to the creditor of the co-obligants in improper cautionry, in all cases where it clearly appears that certain of the obligants, though co-principals as regards the creditor, are *inter se* principal debtor and cautioner, the cautioners are entitled from the date of the contract to the special rights of cautioners in a question with the creditor or the principal debtor.[16]

Creditor not a party to the contract of cautionry.—Where on the other hand the relation of principal debtor and cautioner is constituted

---

[14] *Nocton* v. *Lord Ashburton* [1914] A.C. 932: a verbal representation is in this case enough. See p. 24.
[15] For the heritable security of such a bond, see Debts Securities (Scotland) Act, 1856, s. 7.
[16] See *Rights and Privileges of Cautioners, infra.*

by a separate agreement to which the creditor is not a party, the relation between the creditor and all the debtors is that of creditor and principal debtor simply. The creditor is not subject by virtue of his contract alone to the duties of a creditor towards cautioners. But if the true mutual relation of the debtors *inter se* is brought to his knowledge, then from that moment, whether at constitution of the debt or later, while retaining right to enforce payment against all the debtors, he is liable in all the duties of a creditor in a cautionary obligation towards the cautioners. This liability arises in equity solely from the creditor's knowledge.

Joint and several liability for the same debt arising by implication of law.—In this form the relations of the parties are in great measure regulated by the principles which govern cautionary contracts. That is so where their relation is that between the successive parties to a bill of exchange and where their relation is that of partners in a firm. In a bill accepted and indorsed for value, the acceptor is in a position similar to that of a principal debtor, the drawer and indorsers being cautioners liable to the holder on the acceptor's default in payment, and each subsequent party to the bill is liable as cautioner to the holder for all prior parties. An accommodation party to a bill is in every respect in the position of a cautioner for the person accommodated.[17] A contract of partnership implies a guarantee by each partner to third parties of all engagements legally undertaken in the firm name.[18]

4. CONSTITUTION AND FORM

The constitution of a cautionary obligation is governed both by the common law and by statute. At common law the obligation may arise it may be said, in two ways. It may arise from an offer, addressed by an intending cautioner to a particular creditor, offering to guarantee the debt or the actings of a third party. In this case it is a question of intention and construction whether an express acceptance by the creditor is required to complete the contract or whether the cautioner's liability is created only when credit is actually given by the creditor to the party whose actings or dealings are guaranteed. Or the obligation may arise from an undertaking to guarantee a debt or the dealings of another, not addressed to any particular creditor, but with the intent on it should be shown by the intending debtor to particular persons or a class of persons [19] or, it may be, to any persons, to induce them, for example, to advance money to the intending debtor. In this case the

[17] *Oriental Financial Corporation* v. *Overend, Gurney & Co.* (1874) L.R. 7 (H.L.) 348.
[18] See Chapter on " Partnership."
[19] *Fortune* v. *Young*, 1918 S.C. 1; 1917, 2 S.L.T. 150.

person who has given credit on the faith of the guarantee is entitled to enforce it against the cautioner.

As regards form, the Mercantile Law Amendment (Scotland) Act, 1856, requires that the obligation be in writing and signed by or on behalf of the granter.[20] But while subscription of a writing is a *sine qua non*, it may not of itself be sufficient as regards form. It is undecided whether a formal probative writing is at all required.[21] Though not in a formal deed, it is valid at all events if actings have taken place in reliance on the signed writing [22] or if it is *in re mercatoria*. If not formal the granter may in all cases resile before the guarantee has been acted upon.[23] If not attested it is advisable in ordinary mercantile transactions that the document should be holograph of the granter or adopted by him as such.[24]

It may further be noticed that the Act also requires a subscribed writing in the case of " representations as to credit." These are " representations and assurances as to the character, conduct, credit, ability (*i.e.*, ability to pay [25]), trade or dealings of any person, made or granted to the effect or for the purpose of enabling such person to obtain credit, money, goods or postponement of payment of debt or of any other obligation demandable from him." Hence in general no claim in an action can be founded on any verbal statement of the character referred to, even if fraudulent.[26]

If, however, the relations of the maker of the representations and the person he addresses are of such a fiduciary character as to involve a duty to take reasonable care in making statements, *e.g.*, the relation of agent to client,[27] action may lie though the representation was merely verbal, and though not fraudulent but merely negligently made.[28]

---

[20] s. 6. A written undertaking to give a guarantee satisfies the Act. See *Wallace* v. *Gibson* (1895) 22 R.(H.L.) 56. At common law cautionry is a consensual contract to the constitution of which writing is not essential, but if gratuitous it requires proof by writ or oath of the cautioner. See Gloag and Irvine, *Law of Rights in Security,* 684.

[21] See *Snaddon* v. *London, Edinburgh and Glasgow Assurance Co.* (1902) 5 F. 182; 10 S.L.T. 410.

[22] *National Bank of Scotland* v. *Campbell* (1892) 19 R. 885.

[23] See Lord Eldon in *Grant* v. *Campbell* (1818) 6 Dow 239. Accordingly the undecided question can arise only where a guarantee is of an obligation already attaching to the principal debtor, and is not in a formal deed.

[24] In England it has been held that the requirement of the Act of a signed writing does not apply to agency *del credere*—*Sutton & Co.* v. *Grey* [1894] 1 Q.B. 285.

[25] *Irving* v. *Burns*, 1915 S.C. 260; 1915, 1 S.L.T. 2.

[26] If the statement is in writing the person making the representation, though not liable in contract, may be liable *ex delicto*, *i.e.*, as for a wrong, *e.g.*, if his statements are fraudulent—*Clydesdale Bank* v. *Paton* (1896) 23 R.(H.L.) 22.

[27] *Nocton* v. *Lord Ashburton* [1914] A.C. 932; *Banbury* v. *Bank of Montreal* [1918] A.C. 626.

[28] *Banbury, cit. sup.*

5. MATTERS AFFECTING THE VALIDITY OF THE CONTRACT

(1) Capacity and authority to incur a cautionary obligation.—In cautionry the rules as to capacity or authority to enter into personal obligations apply but in general with greater strictness.[29]

There is a strong presumption of law that a minor who has no curators or who acts with consent of his curators in undertaking a cautionary obligation has suffered lesion so as to make the obligation reducible within the *quadriennium utile*.[30]

As to authority to act as agent in undertaking a cautionary obligation, express authority is usually required. Thus a partner of a firm, though he has impliedly a general authority to bind the firm, has not as a general rule implied authority to bind the firm in guaranteeing the obligation of a third party. Authority to do so will be implied only if the granting of guarantees is necessary for carrying on the business of the firm in the ordinary way, *e.g.*, in a guarantee association, or if it was the usage of the firm to do so or the general custom of firms in the same kind of business.[31] Accordingly in the general case a partner who signs the firm name to a guarantee obligation outwith the scope of the business of the firm binds himself only.[32] The directors of a company may bind it in a guarantee in general only if a power to do so clearly appears from its constituting documents. An ordinary commercial agent or manager, however general his authority in conducting the business of his principal, has no implied authority to bind him in a guarantee of the credit of a third party.[33] The local agent of a bank has no implied authority to bind the bank by granting guarantees or making representations as to the credit of its customers amounting to a guarantee, for example, of payment of the customer's cheque or draft.[34]

(2) Obligations by several cautioners.—Where a cautionary obligation is to be undertaken by more than one cautioner it is implied that any one cautioner undertakes liability on condition that the others do so also.[35] It is then as a general rule the duty of the creditor, after obtaining the obligation of one cautioner, to secure that all become bound. The reason is that the cautioner who signed would have no right of relief against those who did not sign if he paid more than his

---

[29] Gloag and Irvine, *Law of Rights in Security,* p. 686.

[30] Bell's Prin., 10th ed., § 2100.

[31] *Brettel* v. *Williams* (1849) 4 W.H. & G. Ex.Rep. 623.

[32] Partnership Act, 1890, s. 7; *Fortune* v. *Young,* 1918 S.C. 1, *per* Lord Justice-Clerk Scott-Dickson at 6; 1917, 2 S.L.T. 150.

[33] *Hamilton* v. *Dixon* (1873) 1 R. 72.

[34] *Hockey* v. *Clydesdale Bank Ltd.* (1898) 1 F. 119; 6 S.L.T. 210 As to certifying cheques see chapter on Bills of Exchange.

[35] *Paterson* v. *Bonar* (1844) 6 D. 987.

share. This rule holds even though the form of the obligation of all
the obligants whether principal or accessory, is joint and several,
provided, in this case, the creditor was aware that some of the obligants
were really cautioners.[36] Judicial cautionry is an exception, the bond
being a condition of the court making an order at the instance of the
debtor, e.g., of suspension.[37]

(3) Effect of fraud or concealment.—The effect differs according as
the guarantee is of a money debt or is a fidelity guarantee.

Where the principal obligation is a money debt a creditor who
requires a cautioner is in no way bound to make any representation to
a proposed cautioner or give him any warning or information as to the
extent of the risk he is undertaking.[38] But if the creditor makes a
statement the duty of full and fair disclosure is very strict, otherwise
the cautioner is entitled to be freed of his obligation. If therefore the
creditor, whether spontaneously or in reply to questions, makes a
statement which is untrue or is partial and fragmentary as to the
nature of the undertaking, the cautioner will be liberated.[39] It is also
sufficient to liberate the cautioner if the creditor knowingly allows the
cautioner to undertake the obligation in an erroneous belief as to
material facts.[40] But subsequent knowledge by the creditor of matters
materially affecting the cautioner and increasing the risk of his undertaking need not be communicated if the guarantee was valid at its
inception.[41]

In a fidelity guarantee the position is in many respects different.[42]
The ground of distinction from the case of a money debt is that a
fidelity guarantee is in substance one of insurance against dishonesty
and therefore, as in insurance contracts, all matters of material fact
must be disclosed by the creditor to the guarantor.[43] The fact of
employment imports a representation that the servant is trustworthy

---

36 e.g., Scottish Provincial Assurance Co. v. Pringle (1858) 20 D. 465; see also Ellesmere
   Brewery Co. v. Cooper [1896] 1 Q.B. 75.
37 Simpson v. Fleming (1860) 22 D. 679.
38 Young v. Clydesdale Bank (1889) 17 R. 231. If asked, the agent of a creditor bank
   is bound to give the information—per Lord Shand at 244, or he may refuse to answer—
   per Lord McLaren in Wallace's Factor v. M'Kissock (1898) 25 R. at 653.
39 Falconer v. North of Scotland Bank (1863) 1 M. 704, at 712, per Lord President Inglis.
40 Royal Bank of Scotland v. Greenshields, 1914 S.C. 259, at 272, per Lord Mackenzie;
   1914, 1 S.L.T. 74.
41 The cautioner's liability for subsequent advances might be affected—Bank of Scotland
   v. Morrison, 1911 S.C. 593, per Lord Salvesen at 605–606; 1911, 1 S.L.T. 153.
42 The reason is that in the relation between creditor and principal obligant there may
   exist some material fact which the cautioner might reasonably expect not to exist.
   This might of course be so also in the case of the guarantee of a money debt, but
   exceptionally. See note 41, supra and text. Hamilton v. Watson (1845) 4 Bell's
   App. 67; Falconer v. North of Scotland Bank, supra.
43 Wallace's Factor v. M'Kissock (1898) 25 R. 642, per Lord McLaren at 653; 5 S.L.T.
   343.

so far as the employer knows. For an employer is entitled to inquire into his antecedents when engaging him, and has opportunities not available to the cautioner of knowing the character and conduct of the servant. Hence non-disclosure of a fact known to the employer and not to the cautioner, and materially affecting the trustworthiness of the servant, avoids the obligation of the cautioner; and if during the currency of the guarantee the servant commits an act of dishonesty the employer should inform the guarantor so that he may decide as to continuing the guarantee.[44]

6. CONSTRUCTION OF THE CONTRACT

(1) Extent of the cautioner's liability to the creditor.—It is a general rule that the cautioner's undertaking is to be construed in the narrowest sense which the words used will reasonably bear, that is, *contra proferentem*, where the document is a formal bond.[45] The cautioner can never be liable for a greater sum than that due by the principal debtor,[46] the outside measure of the cautioner's liability being the total actual loss sustained by the creditor from the principal debtor's failure to perform his obligation,[47] including interest and expenses reasonably incurred in enforcing the principal debt.[48] The obligation of the cautioner may be limited to a certain amount, less than the principal's obligation,[49] or in respect of duration or otherwise.

In proper cautionry the liability of several cautioners to the creditor is *pro rata* among those who are solvent.[50] In improper cautionry it is joint and several with the principal debtor.

Where a cautionary obligation contains no limit of time of its subsistence, but does contain a limit of the amount for which the cautioner undertakes liability, it is a question of construction whether it is to be construed as a continuing guarantee for that amount, so that the cautioner is liable for the balance due by the principal debtor when the obligation is ultimately enforced, up to the full amount of the liability undertaken by the cautioner; or whether the cautioner's obligation crystallises when its amount is reached in the debtor's obligation, so that payments made by the debtor thereafter go to

---

[44] *Snaddon* v. *London, Edinburgh and Glasgow Assurance Co., Ltd.* (1902) 5 F. 182; 10 S.L.T. 410.
[45] *Harmer & Co.* v. *Gibb*, 1911 S.C. 1341; 1911, 2 S.L.T. 211; *cf. Veitch* v. *National Bank of Scotland*, 1907 S.C. 554; 14 S.L.T. 800; Bell's Prin., § 256.
[46] *Jackson* v. *M'Iver* (1875) 2 R. 882.
[47] *Anderson* v. *Mackinnon* (1876) 3 R. 608.
[48] *Struthers* v. *Dykes* (1847) 9 D. 1437.
[49] See *Gloag on Contract*, 2nd ed., 211; *Harvie's Trs.* v. *Bank of Scotland* (1885) 12 R. 1141.
[50] Practical insolvency is meant; *Buchanan* v. *Main* (1900) 3 F. 215; 8 S.L.T. 297. This is also the measure of the right of relief—*ibid.*

diminish the cautioner's liability and he is not liable for advances subsequently made.[51] In both cases, the cautioner's obligation not being for any definite period, he may safeguard himself against additional liability by notice to the creditor that his guarantee is withdrawn.

The parties may so contract that the cautioner remains liable for the creditor's loss after he has ranked for the whole amount of the debt in the bankruptcy of the principal debtor up to the limit of the cautioner's obligation,[52] *e.g.*, by an " ultimate loss clause," common in guarantees to banks.

(2) **Rights and privileges of cautioners.**—*Benefit of discussion.*— Prior to the Mercantile Law Amendment (Scotland) Act, 1856,[53] it was essential for the creditor in a proper cautionary obligation, before calling upon a cautioner to make good his undertaking, to " discuss " the principal debtor. The creditor had, if necessary, to proceed with an action and exhaust his remedies against the estate of the principal debtor before calling upon the cautioner. Since the Act the creditor may, if discussion is not stipulated for in the contract, proceed directly against the cautioner without taking any proceedings against the principal debtor, as soon as there has been default by him, *e.g.*, on demand made for a debt payable on demand, or expiry of the date for payment, without payment.[54] Or the creditor may proceed against both cautioner and principal debtor in one action. The Act does not apply when the principal debtor's obligation is *ad factum praestandum*, *i.e.*, to perform an act within his power alone to perform. Only on proof of his failure does the cautioner's liability emerge.[55]

Right of relief.—A cautioner who has paid has a right of repayment from the principal debtor, and from his co-cautioners in as far as he has paid more than his share of the debt.[56]

Relief against principal debtor.[57]—The cautioner, upon implementing his obligation or any portion thereof, is entitled to total relief from the principal debtor, including any necessary expenses he may have incurred.[58] When all the obligants are *ex facie* of the deed principals and it regulates only the relation between the creditor and the obligants, and not the relation of the obligants *inter se*, proof, which may

---

[51] *e.g., Scott* v. *Mitchell* (1866) 4 M. 551.

[52] *Harvie's Trustees* v. *Bank of Scotland* (1885) 12 R. 1141.

[53] s. 8.

[54] *Johannesburg Municipal Council* v. *Stewart & Co. Ltd.,* 1909 S.C.(H.L.) 53; 1909, 2 S.L.T. 313.

[55] *Wright* v. *O'Henley* (1827) 5 S. 311.

[56] The effectiveness of the right is qualified by the rule against double ranking in bankruptcy. See Bankruptcy.

[57] Bell's Prin., § 255.

[58] The right may be restricted by agreement: *Williamson* v. *Foulds,* 1927 S.N. 164.

be by parole evidence, is competent in order to establish the cautioner's right of relief against the principal debtor.[59] In relation to the principal debtor the principle is that the cautioner is his implied mandatory to pay the debt; as soon, therefore, as any definite sum has become due to the creditor by the principal debtor the cautioner has the right to have the sum paid and his own liability ended. He may therefore himself pay it and sue the principal debtor for repayment. Further, if the principal debtor is *vergens ad inopiam*, the cautioner, even though the term of payment has not arrived, may take precautionary measures to secure his right of relief, as by attaching goods belonging to the principal debtor or retaining funds belonging to him.[60]

In relation to the creditor the cautioner's right of relief against the principal debtor rests upon the principle of the *beneficium cedendarum actionum*. Thereby the cautioner on paying the debt is entitled, if he has paid in full, to require the creditor to communicate to him the full benefit of the creditor's contract with the debtor, and to be put for all purposes in the place of the creditor as regards both the principal debtor and other cautioners in order to enforce his relief against them. He may sue the principal debtor for relief and for that purpose is entitled to an assignation of the debt from the creditor and of any available diligence or remedy, *e.g.*, arrestment, and of all securities held by the creditor over the estate of the debtor.[61]

Relief against co-cautioners.—In a question between cautioners, unless otherwise agreed, each is liable only for his rateable proportion of the obligation undertaken by them, and one who has paid more, the debt being actually due to the creditor, is entitled to a rateable relief from his co-cautioners,[62] and to charge interest against them from the date of his payment of their share. He must of course communicate to his co-cautioners any deduction the creditor may make from his claim. Further, a cautioner who is threatened with diligence for more than his share of the debt may bring an action against his co-cautioners to have them ordained to pay their proportions. In determining the amount of relief he can claim from each cautioners who are insolvent are not counted.[63] These rules apply only where the cautioners are bound jointly and severally, or substantially so, and though in separate documents.[64]

Right to benefit of securities.—The cautioner is entitled, upon his payment of the debt, to have transferred to him any securities or other

[59] *Hamilton & Co.* v. *Freeth* (1889) 16 R. 1022.
[60] *M'Pherson* v. *Wright* (1885) 12 R. 942.
[61] Bell's Prin., § 255.
[62] *Marshall & Co.* v. *Pennycook*, 1908 S.C. 276; 15 S.L.T. 581.
[63] *Buchanan* v. *Main* (1900) 3 F. 215; 8 S.L.T. 297.
[64] *Morgan* v. *Smart* (1872) 10 M. 610.

remedies the creditor may hold for the performance of the obligation, so as to enable the cautioner to enforce his right of relief. The *ratio*, that is, the reason and measure, of this right is that it is a convenient means of enforcing a right of relief.[65] Hence it cannot enlarge it.[66] Hence also a cautioner has the right only to securities over the estate of the debtor, not to those granted to the creditor by a third party.[67] It is a condition of the right to securities granted to the creditor that the debt has been paid to the creditor in full. Accordingly, if a cautioner is bankrupt and the creditor ranks on his estate for the whole debt unpaid, obtaining less than twenty shillings in the pound, the trustee of the bankrupt estate is not entitled to an assignation of collateral securities.[68] Further, even when the debt is paid in full, the matter being one of equity, the creditor may refuse an assignation of securities if it would conflict with some legitimate interest of his own [69]; and in any event he may qualify his assignation with a clause that it shall not be used in competition with some prior right of his own.[70]

In relief between cautioners, a cautioner is entitled to share in the benefit of any securities which any of his co-cautioners may have obtained over the estate of the principal debtor.[71] The theory is that the estate of the principal debtor is to be regarded as a fund in which all the cautioners have an equal right to share. The right does not therefore extend to securities obtained by one cautioner from a third party.[72] Also it matters not that the cautioner claiming the right to share had engaged without any security or before the other obtained the security.[73] It may of course be expressly agreed otherwise among the cautioners, and any such agreement may be proved by parole evidence.[74]

7. TERMINATION OF THE CONTRACT

The obligation of the cautioner may be terminated either by the extinction of the principal debtor's obligation, or independently of its extinction or by prescription.

(a) **Extinction of the principal obligation.**—In general, extinction of the obligation of the primary obligant, the principal debtor, extinguishes the obligation of the accessory obligant, the cautioner. This may take place by discharge of the principal debtor or by payment

---

[65] *Sligo* v. *Menzies* (1840) 2 D. 1478.
[66] *Thow's Tr.* v. *Young*, 1910 S.C. 588; 1910, 1 S.L.T. 134.
[67] *Thow's Tr.* v. *Young, supra, per* Lord Dunedin at 596.
[68] *Ewart* v. *Latta* (1865) 3 M.(H.L.) 36.
[69] Bell's Prin., § 557.
[70] See *Gloag on Contract*, 2nd ed., 213.
[71] Bell's Prin., § 270.
[72] *Scott* v. *Young*, 1909, 1 S.L.T. 47.
[73] *Steel* v. *Dixon* (1881) 17 Ch.D. 825.
[74] *Hamilton* v. *Freeth* (1889) 16 R. 1022.

by him or its equivalents, such as novation, compensation or operation of the rule in *Clayton's* case.[75]

By discharge of the principal debtor.[76]—If the principal debtor be discharged by the creditor without the cautioner's assent or without so qualifying the discharge as not to injure the cautioner's right of relief, he is freed of his obligation.[76] There is an exception under the Bankruptcy (Scotland) Act, 1913,[77] namely, the case of the discharge of a principal debtor who is bankrupt and whose estate is sequestrated. The creditor who has ranked and obtained less than twenty shillings in the pound, though theoretically his claim against the principal debtor is exhausted, retains his claim against the cautioner for the balance of his debt. Where the discharge is not by operation of law but by the voluntary act of the creditor, *e.g.*, under a private trust deed for creditors, and is absolute, the cautioner is discharged. He is not discharged if his right of relief is expressly reserved in the discharge, and as a result the principal debtor's discharge is not absolute.[78]

Discharge of the principal debtor must accordingly be distinguished from a *pactum de non petendo*, whereby the creditor gives up his right to sue the principal debtor and reserves his claim against the cautioner. The latter does not involve any interference with the cautioner's right of relief against the principal debtor, and does not release the cautioner. The cautioner, therefore, on paying the debt, may demand an assignation of it from the creditor and sue the debtor and use other available remedies.[79]

By novation.—In order to extinguish the obligation of the cautioner a new obligation by the debtor must discharge the old.[80]

By compensation.—On a claim being made against a cautioner he is entitled to plead compensation of the debt he owes as cautioner against any then compensatable debt due by the creditor to the principal debtor.[81]

By operation of the rule in Clayton's case.—By this rule, where it applies,[82] payments on the credit side of an account current are held to extinguish the items on the debit side in the order of their date.[83]

---

[75] Assignation by the creditor of his right to the debt does not extinguish the obligation of the cautioner: *Bradford Old Bank* v. *Sutcliffe* [1918] 2 K.B. 833.

[76] See Bell's Prin., 10th ed., § 260.

[77] s. 52.

[78] See *Muir* v. *Crawford* (1875) 2 R.(H.L.) 148.

[79] *Ibid.*

[80] *Hay & Kyd* v. *Powrie* (1886) 13 R. 777.

[81] *Bechervaise* v. *Lewis* (1872) L.R. 7 C.P. 372.

[82] See Contract, *supra*. The cautioner is entitled to appropriation of payments to the guaranteed debt only by contract express or implied: *Gloag and Irvine on Rights in Security*, 852; *Scott's Trustees* v. *Alexander* (1884) 11 R. 407, *per* Lord Young.

[83] *Christie* v. *Royal Bank of Scotland* (1839) 1 D. 745; 2 Robin. 118.

When a guarantee is non-continuing, all payments made by the debtor after the date when the guarantee crystallises go to reduce the debt for which the cautioner may be held liable, and when the sums so paid in make up the amount of the cautioner's debt it is extinguished. If the guarantee is continuing, the rule operates only when an event occurs which fixes the cautioner's liability as at a particular date, *e.g.*, his sequestration, or dissolution if a firm.[84]

By prescription of the principal debt.—The principle, as in the case of compensation, is that any defence against payment competent to the principal debtor is open to the cautioner.[85]

(b) Independently of extinction of the principal obligation.—*By direct discharge of cautioner by creditor.*—This of course discharges the cautioner, even although the principal debtor remains liable.[86]

By expiry of the period of the cautioner's liability.—Where the cautioner's undertaking covers only liabilities of the principal debtor contracted within a limited time, the expiry of the period without there having occurred any default on the part of the principal debtor extinguishes the liability of the cautioner. A creditor should therefore, if he may, demand payment from the debtor at or before that date if he wishes to keep the cautioner undischarged.

By revocation by the cautioner.—The right to revoke depends in each case upon the contract.[87]

Where a debt is guaranteed and the cautioner's obligation is for a fixed period, he cannot withdraw before its expiry without " taking the debtor into his own hand," that is, paying the creditor, and himself becoming creditor.[88] Where, however, the guarantee of a debt is for an indefinite period until recalled in writing, the cautioner is entitled, after notice in writing to the principal debtor to relieve him of his already incurred obligation, to bring an action of relief against him, if necessary, for what is due to the creditor. The principal debtor must, within a reasonable time after the notice, obtain from the creditor a discharge of the cautioner and pay what is then due under the guarantee.[89] And, the period being unlimited, the cautioner may at any time stop further dealings and advances on his responsibility by giving notice to the creditor that he will not be liable for future dealings or advances.[90] The liability of the cautioner for past advances remains.

---

[84] *Cuthill* v. *Strachan* (1894) 21 R. 549; *Christie* v. *Royal Bank of Scotland, supra.*
[85] Ersk. iii, 3,66.
[86] Bell's Prin., § 257.
[87] *Roughead* v. *White*, 1913 S.C. 162, at 169; 1913, 1 S.L.T. 23.
[88] Bell's Prin., § 266; *Spence* v. *Brownlee* (1834) 13 S. 199. Where a cautioner's offer is not embodied in a formal acceptance, he may of course resile at any time as to future advances: see *supra*, Constitution and form.
[89] *Doig* v. *Lawrie* (1903) 5 F. 295; 10 S.L.T. 523.   [90] Bell's Prin., § 266.

In the case of fidelity guarantees it is a general principle that where the person whose conduct is guaranteed is guilty of misconduct, the cautioner may at once revoke the guarantee *quoad* the future. And on the like principle it has been held that, if an employer fails to intimate to the cautioner timeously misconduct of the nature of embezzlement or forgery by the servant, the employer forfeits all right under the guarantee, if thereby he prevents the cautioner from taking immediate measures to protect himself against loss.[91]

Where the employment, faithful performance of which is guaranteed, is for a fixed period, the cautioner, in the absence of misconduct by the servant entitling the employer to dismiss him, cannot revoke the guarantee.[92] Where the duration of the employment is indefinite, depending on the pleasure of employer and employed, the cautioner may give reasonable notice terminating his liability to the creditor, taking care to have his bond cancelled or given up.[93] The reasonableness of the period of notice depends *inter alia* on the time which would be necessary in the kind of service to determine the engagement as between employer and employed.

By death.—Of an accessory.—Where a guarantee is one which the cautioner himself might have revoked at any time, *e.g.*, a continuing guarantee, then, unless and until notice of the cautioner's death is given to the creditor, the cautioner's representatives are liable not only for existing but also for future incurred indebtedness of the principal debtor.[94] As, however, the representatives may not know of the guarantee, the creditor, on learning of the death, should inform the representatives, for otherwise he may in equity, depending on the circumstances, be refused enforcement by the court.[95]

Where the guarantee is one which the cautioner himself could not by notice terminate, as where it is for a definite period, notice of his death will not operate a revocation.[96]

Of a principal.—Unless the contract otherwise intends or the nature of the contract so requires,[97] the cautioner's obligation ceases to run.[98]

---

[91] *Snaddon* v. *London, Edinburgh and Glasgow Assurance Co.* (1902) 5 F. 182; 10 S.L.T 410.

[92] *Smith* v. *Bank of Scotland* (1813) 1 Dow's App. 272; *Leith Bank* v. *Bell* (1830) 8 S. 721, affd. (1831) 5 W. & S. 703.

[93] Bell's Prin., § 266; *Kinloch* v. *McIntosh* (1822) 1 S. 491.

[94] Bell's Comm., 1, 385, 387. Notice of the death of one of several cautioners bound jointly and severally does not of itself end the guarantee: *Beckett* v. *Addyman* (1882) 9 Q.B.D. 783.

[95] Bell's Comm., 1, 387; *Caledonian Banking Co.* v. *Kennedy's Trs.* (1870) 8 M. 862, at 868.

[96] *Re Crace* [1902] 1 Ch. 733.

[97] *Wilson* v. *Ewing* (1836) 14 S. 262.

[98] *Reddie* v. *Williamson* (1863) 1 M. 228.

By change in firm.—In the analogous case of a change in the personnel of a firm, whether by introduction of a new [99] or death or retiral of an existing partner, a continuing obligation in which the firm is either creditor or principal debtor is revoked as to future transactions, apart from agreement express or implied to the contrary.[1]

By conduct of creditor.—Any positive act of the creditor, without the consent of the cautioner, in particular if affecting his right of relief, discharges the cautioner. Hence, if the creditor " gives time " to the principal debtor, or releases a co-cautioner, or gives up securities held for the debt, or otherwise acts prejudicially to the interests of the cautioner, he is freed from his obligation.

(1) BY GIVING TIME.—By giving time is meant any act amounting to a positive contract by which the creditor deprives himself of the right to sue the debtor for immediate payment, the debt being due. This is not a *pactum de non petendo*, in which the creditor gives up his right against the principal debtor and reserves his right against the cautioner and so preserves the cautioner's relief against the principal debtor. A creditor may give time by express agreement or, for example, by taking a bill payable at a future date [2] for an existing debt, or by an arrangement for payment by instalments.[3] The ground of the cautioner's discharge is that his right of relief against the principal debtor is interfered with, the time at which the right of relief operates being postponed. It is a variation of the original contract. It is an exception by usage of trade that where the obligation guaranteed is payment for goods to be supplied to the debtor in the future, the creditor may allow any ordinary period of credit to, or take a bill at a currency for the price from, the debtor without giving time so as to release the cautioner.[4]

It must be noticed, first, that the rule as to giving time applies whether the cautioner is actually prejudiced by it or not, it being a variation of the original contract.[5] Secondly, the cautioner is not released if the creditor in giving time to the principal debtor expressly reserves the creditor's rights against the cautioner; the cautioner's remedy of relief against the principal debtor is unaltered [6]; the due date in a question with the cautioner is still the original due date and

[99] *Bowie* v. *Watson, McNight & Co.* (1840) 2 D. 1061.
[1] Partnership Act, 1890, s. 18. It may be readily so implied where the firm is creditor and its members are numerous and frequently changing: Bell's Comm., 1, 387.
[2] *C. & A. Johnstone* v. *Duthie* (1892) 19 R. 624; *Goldfarb* v. *Bartlett and Kremer* [1920] 1 K.B. 639.
[3] *Wilson* v. *Lloyd* (1873) L.R. 16 Eq. 60.
[4] *Calder & Co.* v. *Cruikshank's Tr.* (1889) 17 R. 74.
[5] *Johnstone* v. *Duthie, supra.*
[6] *Muir* v. *Crawford* (1875) 2 R.(H.L.) 148.

the cautioner may take immediate measures for his own relief. Thirdly, after decree against the debtor the creditor may give time to pay without prejudice to the cautioner as his right of relief already operates.[7]

(2) BY RELEASE OF CO-CAUTIONER.—The voluntary act of a creditor in releasing a co-cautioner, without the consent of the other co-cautioners, where the cautioners are jointly and severally liable, discharges the others.[8] For it is an essential part of the contract of each that all shall be and remain bound, so that discharge of one is an alteration of the contract of all. If, however, the discharge of a co-obligant is qualified by a reservation of the creditor's right against the other cautioners it is a mere *pactum de non petendo* and the right of relief of the others against the discharged co-obligant is not affected.[9]

(3) BY GIVING UP SECURITIES.—The release of securities, if a voluntary act on the part of the creditor and without the consent of the cautioner, may operate a release of the cautioner.[10] That is so also where the creditor, without giving up a security, fails to make it effectual, as where the creditor under a bond and disposition in security over heritable property of the debtor failed to complete his title by registering it in the Register of Sasines, with the result that the trustee in the debtor's sequestration acquired a preferable right to the subjects by registering his title first.[11] In a release of securities by the creditor the cautioner is released as a rule only in so far as he is prejudiced, that is, to the extent of the value of the security given up.[12] It is matter of equity. If, however, there is an express agreement that the creditor shall avail himself of a particular security before calling upon the cautioner, its release operates an absolute discharge of the cautioner.[13] It is matter of contract.

(4) BY ALTERATION OF THE PRINCIPAL CONTRACT.—A cautioner is discharged if his position is affected by an alteration of the contract between the creditor and the principal debtor, *e.g.*, if the risk which the cautioner has incurred is increased without his knowledge or consent.[14] This is already exemplified in " giving time," but is well

---

[7] *Aikman* v. *Fisher* (1835) 14 S. 56.

[8] Mercantile Law Amendment Act, 1856, s. 9; *Morgan* v. *Smart* (1872) 10 M. 610. This does not extend to the case of a cautioner consenting to the discharge of a co-cautioner who may have become bankrupt: s. 9.

[9] *Muir* v. *Crawford* (1873) 1 R. 91, affd. 2 R.(H.L.) 148; *Morton's Trs.* v. *Robertson's J.F.* (1892) 20 R. 72; contrast *Smith* v. *Harding* (1877) 5 R. 147.

[10] *Sligo* v. *Menzies* (1840) 2 D. 1478.

[11] *Fleming* v. *Thomson* (1826) 2 W. & S. 277.

[12] *Sligo* v. *Menzies, supra.*

[13] *Drummond* v. *Rannie* (1836) 14 S. 437.

[14] *W. G. Napier Ltd.* v. *Crosbie & Anor.*, 1964 S.L.T. 185.

illustrated by a fidelity guarantee. A change in the duties to be performed by the servant guaranteed will release the cautioner if the terms
of the servant's appointment were made known to the cautioner at the
time he undertook his obligation. That is so even when the change
is not in the circumstances material, that is, has no bearing on the
loss for which the cautioner is sued.[15] If, on the other hand, the
terms of the servant's appointment were not known to the cautioner,
he must prove materiality of the change in order to be released.[16]

(c) Termination by prescription.—Cautionary obligations fall under
the septennial limitation or prescription introduced by the Act, 1695,
c. 5. The Act does not apply to all forms of the obligation nor in all
circumstances. The purpose is to limit the burden of such obligations
and to extinguish the cautioner's obligation if not enforced against
him within seven years.

Generally stated, the Act applies to two classes of cautionary
obligants only, namely, those who engage for or with another in a bond
or contract expressly as cautioners, and those who, though cautioners
as between the obligants, are principals as regards the creditor; provided, in the latter case, there be a clause in the bond itself which gives
the creditor notice of an obligant's accessory character or a separate
bond of relief between the obligants of which the creditor has personal
notice in writing at the time of receiving the principal bond.[17]

The Act does not apply where the obligation guaranteed is not
payment of a sum of money, but is, for example, *ad factum praestandum*,[18] or faithful discharge of an office,[19] or in judicial cautionry.[20]
Further, the criterion of whether the Act applies is the liability of the
cautioner, and not that of the principal debtor; and it must be prestable
against the cautioner within the term of seven years from the date of
the principal bond. Hence the Act does not apply if the obligation
of the principal debtor is not fully exigible against the cautioner during
the septennium, so that the creditor could, had he chosen, have
enforced it by diligence against the cautioner—such as an obligation
to see paid a sum of money already lent [21]; or where the debt is not
liquid.[22] In such cases the Act would not apply. Further, the Act
does not apply where the term of payment is or may be beyond the

---

15 *Bonar* v. *McDonald* (1850) 7 Bell's App. 379.
16 *Nicolsons* v. *Burt* (1882) 10 R. 121.
17 *Drysdale* v. *Johnstone* (1839) 1 D. 409.
18 *Stewart* v. *Campbell* (1726) Mor. 11010.
19 *Strang* v. *Fleet* (1707) Mor. 11005.
20 *Kerr* v. *Bremner* (1843) 1 Bell's App. 280. This includes a composition contract in
   bankruptcy: *Cuthbertson* v. *Lyon* (1823) 2 S. 330.
21 *Howison* v. *Howison* (1784) Mor. 11030.
22 *Anderson* v. *Wood* (1821) 1 S. 31.

seven years, as in marriage contracts,[23] nor where a new obligation arises each year such as an annuity or interest on a loan [24] or, it seems, a cash credit bond.[25] Further, it does not apply where the obligation of the cautioner is in the form of acceptance as cautioner of a bill of exchange, as this can have no effect as against a holder of the bill.[26] Further, it can have no application to bonds of corroboration [27] or of relief between cautioners,[28] as these are separate contracts from the debt transaction.

The operation of the Act can be elided only by proof of a renewal or corroboration in writing of the original cautionary obligation,[29] or by diligence done or decree obtained against the cautioner within the seven years.[30] Accordingly, otherwise, a cautioner who pays the principal sum after the expiry of the septennium is entitled to get it back.[31] The effect of such diligence is to preserve recourse against the cautioner for any debt incurred by the principal debtor to the creditor in the septennium, but not for any incurred later.[32]

---

[23] *Monteith* v. *Paterson* (1841) 4 D. 161, *per* Lord Moncreiff at 167.
[24] *Balvaird* v. *Watson* (1709) Mor. 11005; *Molleson* v. *Hutchison* (1892) 19 R. 581.
[25] *Alexander* v. *Badenach* (1843) 6 D. 322.
[26] See *Gloag and Irvine on Rights in Security*, pp. 681–683.
[27] *Scott* v. *Rutherford* (1715) Mor. 11012.
[28] *Forbes* v. *Dunbar* (1726) Mor. 11014.
[29] *M'Gregor's Exrs.* v. *Anderson's Trs.* (1893) 21 R. 7; *Stocks* v. *M'Lagan* (1890) 17 R. 1122.
[30] Query as to action raised. A plea of personal bar might (Lord Kinnear in *M'Gregor's Exrs.*), and a renunciation of the right to plead the statute in a deed subsequent to the original deed would, suffice to elide the operation of the Act: *Wallace* v. *Campbell* (1749) Mor. 11026.
[31] *Carrick* v. *Carse* (1778) Mor. 2931. The ground is *condictio indebiti*, *i.e.*, payment *sine causa; cf. Stocks* v. *M'Lagan, supra.*
[32] Bell's Prin., § 603.

CHAPTER 10

PARTNERSHIP

1. GENERAL.—THE SOCIETY

PARTNERSHIP involves the concept of association or society. An association of persons may have legal relations with other persons, and so rights and obligations, as if, *mutatis mutandis*, it were an individual. That will be so when in the eye of the law the association is a person, that is, a legal entity, distinct from the persons individually and collectively who compose it. If that be not so, the association is regarded in the common law as simply an aggregation of the individual persons who are in association, and not a legal entity. In Scotland, though not in England, at common law a business partnership has such separate personality. That case apart, formal incorporation is in general required to give an association a *persona* in law.

While in Scotland at common law and also under the Partnership Act, 1890,[1] a business partnership is in law a person, by statute, if the members exceed a certain number, incorporation is necessary, both to the legality of the association and to its recognition in law as a person distinct from the persons who compose it,[2] and the law of partnership[3] does not apply to it.

The characteristic of legal personality at common law attaches only where the association conforms with the definition of partnership in the Partnership Act, 1890,[4] that is, is a business partnership. An association which is not a business partnership has not at common law legal personality, and does not require incorporation to give it legality where its members are numerous. An example is a club.

The common law partnership and the incorporated partnership or company have in some respects different attributes. In the common law partnership, notwithstanding its separate legal *persona* and consequent ability to contract and own property, the members are liable for its debts (more as guarantors than as principals)[5] and their liability is unlimited. In an incorporation the extent of the liability of the members individually for the debts of the incorporation depends on

---

[1] s. 4 (2).
[2] This may be achieved by registration under the Companies Act.
[3] Whether at common law or as contained in the Partnership Act, 1890, s. 1.
[4] The Act codified the law and, so far as inconsistent with the common law, superseded it: s. 46.
[5] See *infra*.

the incorporating authority and the terms of the incorporating documents.[6] The large partnership or company may accordingly be incorporated with limited liability of the members for its debts.

Again the common law partnership will for most purposes lose its identity on a change occurring in the membership. An incorporation, however, retains its identity notwithstanding such change.

Again, in an ordinary common law partnership each partner is *praepositus negotiis societatis*, and so has a general implied authority to act for and bind the firm and the other partners.[7] In an incorporation the individual member as such has no power to deal with the public on behalf of the association, the administration being vested in certain officers or directors made known to the public by advertisement and other methods of publication.

Principles and sources of the law of partnership.[8]—The principles mainly applicable are those operative in the law of agency and the law of cautionry. The principles of the law of agency are definitive of the authority of a partner to bind the firm; of the fiduciary relation in which the partners stand to the firm and to one another as agents for the firm; of the *delectus personae* and mutual confidence involved in the partnership relation and, arising thereout, of the continuance of the relationship and of the assignability by a partner of his interest under the partnership contract. As regards cautionry, the partners are cautioners for, as well as co-principal debtors with, the firm and one another. The rules of improper cautionry in general apply to them.

The main source of the present law is the Partnership Act, 1890. It codified the law, and saves the effect of the common law except so far as inconsistent with the Act.[9] It does not deal with the bankruptcy of a firm: that is regulated by the common law and the bankruptcy statutes.[10] It does not deal with the subject of goodwill as an asset of the firm: that is regulated by the equitable considerations of the common law. The Act has been supplemented by two later Acts, namely, the Limited Partnerships Act, 1907, which regulates the position of the " sleeping partner," and the Registration of Business Names Act, 1916,[11] which provides for the public identification of the

---

[6] In incorporation by Royal Charter limited liability of the members is implied and unlimited liability requires express provision. See the Chartered Companies Act, 1837. Vice versa in other cases.

[7] In a limited partnership the " sleeping partner " has no such authority—see *infra*, Limited Partnerships Act, 1907.

[8] For a historical sketch, see *Clark on Partnership*, Vol. 1, pp. 1–3. The earliest reported case under " Society " is *Inglis* v. *Austine* (1624) Mor. 14562. See also *The Juridical Review*, Vol. 8, p. 239 *et seq.*, and Green's *Encyclopaedia of the Laws of Scotland*, 3rd ed., Vol. 11, pp. 1–7.

[9] s. 46.

[10] As to the effect of bankruptcy of a firm, see chapter on Bankruptcy.

[11] Amended by the Companies Act, 1947, ss. 116 and 123 (3).

members of the partnership for the benefit of third parties having
business relations with the firm.

2. NATURE OF PARTNERSHIP [12]

The Partnership Act, 1890, in section 1 defines partnership, in section 2
sets out certain rules for determining whether a partnership does or
does not exist, and in section 4 defines the meaning of a firm.

(a) **Definition.**[13]—Partnership is the relation which subsists between
persons carrying on a business [14] in common with a view of profit.
By section 1 (2) the generality of this definition is curtailed. It excludes
the relation between members of a company or association registered
under the Companies Acts or formed or incorporated under any other
Act of Parliament, Letters Patent or Royal Charter. The effect of the
Companies Act, 1948,[15] is to require registration and so incorporation
of such an association where the number of its members exceeds ten
in the case of the business of banking, and twenty in the case of any
other business.[16] The Partnership Act has thus no application to
associations which are or should be incorporated. An unincorporated
association of the nature of a partnership, the number of whose
members at formation or later exceeds the prescribed limits, is an
illegal association. It cannot sue and each member is severally
responsible for all its debts.[17]

It is obvious that there must be at least two persons in voluntary
association to form a partnership. A single trader may, however,
trade in a name which suggests that the business is that of a firm. He
does not thereby create or sustain a firm *persona* separate from his own.

As the relation of partnership is constituted by agreement express
or implied to be associated in the carrying on of a business with a view
to profit, this involves a contribution by the partners of stipulated
shares of money or other property or of skill and industry, the stock
or property being held by the partners *pro indiviso* for the purposes of
the business and in trust for the creditors [18] in the first place, and thereafter division among the partners at the close of the partnership
relation. The right to a share in profits is an indispensable element
in partnership.[19]

---

[12] See Mitchell, *History of the Law Merchant*, as to the Société en Commandite.
[13] s. 1 (1). *Cf.* Indian Contract Act, 1872, s. 239, " Partnership is the relation which
subsists between persons who have agreed to share the profits of a business carried
on by all or any of them on behalf of all of them."
[14] Business includes any trade, occupation or profession: s. 45.   [15] ss. 1, 424, 434.
[16] Incorporation under the Companies Act is permissible with a lesser number, s. 1 (1).
Registration was first required by the Companies Act, 1862.
[17] *e.g.*, *Greenberg* v. *Cooperstein* [1926] 1 Ch. 657.   [18] Bell's Prin., §§ 351–352.
[19] It may yet devote its whole profits to charity. *Cf. Commissioners of Inland Revenue* v.
Falkirk Temperance Café Trust, 1927 S.C. 261; 1927 S.L.T. 87.

(b) The separate persona of the firm.[20]—Persons who have entered into partnership are for the purposes of the Act called collectively a firm, and the name in which the business of the firm is carried on is called the firm name.[21] In Scotland, the firm being a legal person distinct from its members, it may maintain contractual relations with third parties in the firm name, the partners being, individually or collectively, its agents in so doing. In undertaking obligations to third parties the partners are cautioners for the firm, but bound with it as co-principals jointly and severally.[22] The firm may incur liability for civil wrongs; that is, it may be a principal, the partners being its agents in committing the wrong.[23] The separate *persona* of the firm is given effect to in actions by or against the firm, in doing diligence, in ranking in bankruptcy, and in compensation between debts of the firm and debts of the partners.[24] Further, the members in a question with the firm or, subject to the partnership agreement, *inter se*, are cautioners for the firm.

3. CONSTITUTION OF PARTNERSHIP

(a) General.—The contract of partnership is consensual and so writing is not required for its constitution. The consent to enter into it may thus be express or may be inferred from appropriate facts and circumstances. In general, when two or more persons are found carrying on business together with a view to profit, it will be presumed that they have agreed to do so as partners. The question whether a partnership has been constituted may however arise in two ways involving in some respects different considerations, namely, where the question is between alleged partners, and where the question is between alleged partners and a third party alleging their partnership.

In a question between the alleged partners, it is a question purely of their mutual intention.

In questions with third parties as to liability for the debts of a business, a person may, though he may not have regarded himself as a partner or even may have expressly disclaimed that position, be held to be a partner and as such liable for the debts of the business. That may be so if he is adjudged to have intended to assume a position in

---

[20] See Bell's Comm., ii, 507.

[21] s. 4 (1); as to the exclusive right to a firm name, see *Smith* v. *McBride & Smith* (1888) 16 R. 36.

[22] See *Clark on Partnership*, 285.

[23] s. 10; see also p. 81.

[24] A partnership cannot claim from a third party damages for loss sustained through personal injury caused to a partner by the third party: *Gibson & Co.* v. *Glasgow Corporation*, 1963 S.L.T.(Notes) 16.

relation to the business from which the law will infer partnership.[25] So a partnership may be held to have been created when the question is with creditors although, on the same facts, it would be held there is no partnership, because no such intention, between the alleged partners themselves.[26]

In a question as to the constitution of the partnership contract arising between the alleged partners to it, this may be affected by the general rules of the common law, *e.g.*, capacity to contract in general or to enter into a particular contract, illegality, etc. In a question with third parties these considerations do not necessarily affect the joint and several liability of the supposed partners to third parties bona fide contracting with them as such partners.[27]

(b) Analogous relations.—Rules for determining existence of partnership.—The Act provides [28] certain rules which afford guides to the determination of whether in certain cases or circumstances the relation under consideration is partnership or not. The rules apply both where the question is between alleged partners and where with a third party subject to their respective standpoints. The relation to which the rules primarily refer is that between alleged partners. That case apart, it would seem that in relation to third parties partnership may be assumed to exist where in effect the alleged partners have held themselves out to be in partnership. The Rules are now considered.[29]

(i) *Joint or common property or tenancy or part ownership* [30]

None of these relations of itself creates a partnership as to anything so held or owned, whether the owners do or do not share any profits made by the use thereof.[31] But the addition of control over a business in which the property is used may imply partnership.[32]

(ii) *Sharing of gross returns* [33]

Gross returns means gross profits.[34] The sharing of gross returns does not of itself create a partnership.[35] It is not necessarily enough

---

[25] *McCosh* v. *Brown & Co.'s Trustee* (1899) 1 F.(H.L.) 86; 7 S.L.T. 253; *Adams* v. *Newbigging* (1888) 13 App.Cas. 308—opinion of Lord Halsbury; *Charlton & Bagshaw* v. *Highet*, 1923 S.L.T. 493.

[26] Bell's Comm., i, 511; *Clippens Shale Oil Co.* v. *Scott* (1876) 3 R. 651; *Stewart* v. *Buchanan* (1903) 6 F. 15, at p. 22, *per* Lord Moncrieff; 11 S.L.T. 347 at p. 350.

[27] *Blackwood* v. *Thorburn* (1868) 7 M. 318; as to supervening illegality, see p. 259, note 44.

[28] s. 2.

[29] See *per* Lord McLaren in *Laing Bros. & Co.'s Tr.* v. *Low* (1896) 23 R. at 1115.

[30] s. 2 (1).

[31] In *French* v. *Styring* (1857) 2 C.B.(N.S.) 357, there was held no partnership though joint ownership of a racehorse, but partnership as to profits and losses on the racing there might be.

[32] *Stewart* v. *Buchanan* (1903) 6 F. 15; 11 S.L.T. 347.   [33] s. 2 (2).

[34] As to the meaning of net profits see *Watson* v. *Haggitt* [1928] A.C. 127.

[35] The law before the Act was the same: *Cox* v. *Hickman* (1860) 8 H.L.Cas. 268; *Eaglesham & Co.* v. *Grant* (1875) 2 R. 960.

to infer partnership that the persons sharing gross returns have in addition a joint or common right or interest in any property from which or from the use of which the returns are derived. Cases of difficulty are where those sharing gross returns are not all interested in the property or concern from which they are derived.[36]

(iii) *Sharing of profits*

In this context profits means net profits. The receipt by a person of a share of the net profits of a business is prima facie evidence that he is a partner in the business. But the receipt of such a share or of a payment contingent on or varying with the profits of a business " does not of itself " [37] make him a partner in the business. Otherwise put, the matter turns upon the inference to be drawn from the whole circumstances. But if there is nothing else bearing upon the matter the sharing of profits is proof of partnership [38]; otherwise, there must be something from which, looking at the whole circumstances, it can be said that the relation of principal and agent has been created between the alleged partner and those in whose profits he shares.[39] Thus creditors appointing a manager to carry on a debtor's business under an agreement whereby the profits are to meet the debts are not partners in the business,[40] and persons registered as owners of shares in a ship,[41] or employed on board and remunerated by a share of the earnings, such as share fishermen, are not merely from their ownership or method of remuneration to be deemed partners.[42] It seems clear that an agreement to share in the profits and the losses necessarily involves partnership.[43] It has been held that a right to share in profits and in addition a right, absolute or conditional, to receive or dispose of partnership assets involves partnership.[44]

Illustrative of the general rule are set out in the Act certain specific cases where the sharing of profits does not of itself involve an inference of partnership. These are: (1) the receipt by a person of a debt or

---

[36] The possibility that sharing of gross returns is, along with other circumstances, consistent with partnership, would seem to negative the view (expressed, *e.g.,* in *Underhill on Partnership,* 7th ed., 6) that the " relations of persons with a view to profit means net profits necessarily." As to meaning of "profits" see Fletcher Moulton L.J. in *Re Spanish Prospecting Co. Ltd.* [1911] 1 Ch. 92 at 98.

[37] This represents a change in the law. Formerly receipt of a share of profits was conclusive evidence of partnership: *Waugh* v. *Carver* (1793) 3 Ross L.C. 426. This was altered by *Cox* v. *Hickman* (1860) 8 H.L.Cas. 268.

[38] See *per* Lindley L.J. in *Badeley* v. *Consolidated Bank* (1888) 38 Ch.D. at 238.

[39] *Cox* v. *Hickman, supra; Laing Bros. & Co's Tr.* v. *Low* (1896) 23 R. 1105 at 1113.

[40] *Cox, supra; Stott* v. *Fender & Crombie* (1878) 5 R. 1104.

[41] *Sharpe* v. *Carswell,* 1910 S.C. 391; 1910, 1 S.L.T. 80.

[42] *Clark* v. *Jamieson,* 1909 S.C. 132, 16 S.L.T. 450.

[43] Lindley, 12th ed., p. 53.

[44] *McCosh* v. *Brown & Co.'s Tr.* (1899) 1 F (H.L.) 86; 7 S.L.T. 253; *Charlton & Bagshaw* v. *Highet,* 1923 S.L.T. 493.

other liquidated amount by instalments or otherwise out of the accruing profits of a business [45]; (2) a contract for the remuneration of a servant or agent of a person engaged in a business by a share of the profits of the business.[46] Here the element of control of the business affairs by the servant or agent may be important [47] in relation to the question whether the alleged partner is agent for himself along with others or for others alone [48]; (3) an annuity out of profits to the widow or child of a deceased partner [49]; (4) a loan to the business in return for a share in or sum payable out of profits [50]; the question here is whether the lender and borrower are truly in the relation of creditor and debtor involving a personal liability to repay, the creditor neither being limited to repayment out of the business nor having an interest in the capital, as such, of the business [51]; but in this case, if the enactment is to have effect, so like is the relation to partnership, the contract must be in writing signed by or on behalf of all the parties thereto [52]; (5) where one has sold the goodwill of a business and has stipulated for payment by a share of future profits by way of annuity or otherwise.[53] He is in much the same position as a lender to a person or firm carrying on a business who is to be repaid by a share of the profits of the business. But there is no requirement of a signed writing. The seller of the goodwill is not by reason only of such receipt a partner in the business or liable as such. But if the buyer of the goodwill is bankrupt or dies insolvent the seller may not compete in respect of the share of profits contracted for with the other creditors of the buyer, whether creditors in the business or creditors otherwise, if for valuable consideration in money or money's worth.[54]

[45] s. 2 (3) (a)

[46] s. 2 (3) (b).

[47] Cf. Walker v. Reith (1906) 8 F. 381; 13 S.L.T. 660.

[48] Cf. Gatherer (1893) 1 S.L.T. 401; Stewart v. Buchanan (1903) 6 F. 15; 11 S.L.T. 347.

[49] s. 2 (3) (c).

[50] s. 2 (3) (d).

[51] Stewart v. Buchanan, supra. See also McCosh v. Brown's Tr. (1899) 1 F.(H.L.) 86, 7 S.L.T. 253; Charlton & Bagshaw v. Highet, 1923 S.L.T. 493; Stott v. Fender & Crombie (1878) 5 R. 1104; Laing Bros. & Co.'s Trs., supra; Meason or Thomson v. Bell (1894) 1 S.L.T. 433. Contrast an advance by way of capital repayable out of the profits of the business.

[52] Laing Bros. & Co.'s Trs., supra. Limited Partnerships Act, 1907, provides a means of avoiding such questions.

It would appear that in the absence of a signed writing the transaction can infer only partnership where there is nothing else to rebut the inference of partnership from sharing of profits. The Act relegates such lenders to the position of postponed creditors in the bankruptcy, whether judicial or extra judicial, of the borrower, s. 3. The lender may, however, retain and realise any security he may have obtained for the loan: Badeley v. Consolidated Bank Ltd. (1888) 38 Ch.D. 238. S. 2 does not apply to a person who has advanced money merely on the condition that some third person shall receive a share of profits: Re Pinto Leite & Nephews [1929] 1 Ch. 221.

[53] s. 2 (3) (e).

[54] s. 3.

4. Relation of Partners to Persons Dealing with Them

Two general matters arise for consideration. The first is the question of when a person is liable as for a firm debt on an obligation arising ostensibly between a firm and a third person. The second is the effect of a change in the membership of a firm on existing contracts if executory or of a continuing character. The former question involves consideration of the liability of partners for firm debts; the authority of partners to bind the firm; the liability of a person for debts of the business incurred subsequent or prior to his membership of a firm; and liability by holding out.

(a) Liability for firm debt

(1) **Liability of partner for firm debt.**—(a) *General.*—Every partner in a firm is liable jointly and severally for all debts and obligations of the firm incurred while he is a partner; and after his death his estate is severally liable, in a due course of administration, for such debts and obligations, so far as they remain unsatisfied.[55]

This enactment would seem to express the common law. As stated by Bell,[56] the partners are liable *singuli in solidum* and more as guarantors than as principals. As long as the firm remains solvent, the partners are not called upon to pay firm debts. But they are not, as cautioners formerly were, entitled to the benefit of discussion. The non-payment on the part of the firm at once raises their responsibility. Like other mercantile guarantors, they are conditional debtors if the debt is not paid at the day. The debt must first therefore be constituted against the firm, whereupon the joint and several liability of the partners at once arises. If not so constituted prior to dissolution of the firm, all the partners within the jurisdiction of the court must, in any action to enforce the debt against one of them, be convened as defenders.[57]

A firm, and so the partners, may incur liability for wrongs done by a partner. The general rule is that where, by any wrongful act or omission of any partner acting in the ordinary course of the business of the firm or with the authority of his co-partners, loss or injury is incurred, the firm is liable therefor to the same extent as the partner so acting or omitting to act.[58] In particular this applies where one partner acting within the scope of his apparent authority receives the money or property of a third person and misapplies it; and where a firm in the course of its business receives money or property of a third

---

[55] s. 9.
[56] Comm., ii, 507, 508.
[57] *Muir* v. *Collett* (1862) 24 D. 1119; *M'Naught* v. *Milligan* (1885) 13 R. 366.
[58] s. 10. This applies only where the person wronged is a third party, not where he is a partner: *Mair* v. *Wood*, 1948 S.C. 83; 1948 S.L.T. 326.

person and the money or property is misapplied by one or more of the partners while it is in the custody of the firm.[59] The liability of the partners under the general rule and these cases is joint and several, but the test and measure of their liability is the liability of the firm. Accordingly the liability must first be constituted against the firm.[60] The partner guilty of the wrong is of course personally liable in any event.

Liability of the firm does not attach to improper use of trust property in the business or on account of the partnership, but only liability of the partner in breach of trust or a partner having notice of the breach; and trust money may be followed and recovered from the firm if still in its possession and control.[61]

(b) *Authority of partners.*—Whether a firm, and therefore the whole partners under their joint and several liability, are bound by the particular act of a partner depends on whether he has authority, real or ostensible, to bind the firm in that particular.

In matters of contract by a firm the authority of a partner to bind the firm in particular matters, in a question between the partners themselves, may be regulated by the partnership agreement. In questions with third parties every partner is an agent of the firm and of the other partners.[62] He is *praepositus negotiis societatis* and so has an implied mandate to act for the firm. More specially the rule is that his acts in carrying on for the firm in the usual way business of the kind carried on by the firm bind the firm. This is so unless he has in fact no authority and the person with whom he deals either knows this or does not know or believe him to be a partner.[63] If so, the obligation, though in the firm's name, is binding only on the partner as an individual.[64]

The limitation of the implied mandate of each partner to acts in carrying on in the usual way business of the kind carried on by the firm would appear to be referable to the test of the way businesses of the like kind are carried on.[65] Thus as a general rule a partner has not implied authority and therefore requires specific authority to borrow money for the business on the firm's credit. But a partner of a trading firm has such implied authority.[66] Matters outside this test

---

[59] s. 11.

[60] s. 12.

[61] s. 13.

[62] s. 5: the " limited partner " is an exception.

[63] s. 5. This was the common law rule in Scotland, *e.g., Nisbet* v. *Neil's Tr.* (1869) 7 M. 1097.

[64] *Fortune* v. *Young,* 1918 S.C. 1; 1917, 2 S.L.T. 150.

[65] *Lindley on Partnership,* 12th ed., 167.

[66] *Clark on Partnership,* Vol. 1, pp. 215–216.

but within the scope and objects of the particular partnership are of course not affected by the limitation.

As regards the limitation on the general rule of undertakings in the the firm name known to the other party to be granted in the private interests of the partner acting, it is only where the partner's authority is in fact so limited as not to cover the undertaking that this knowledge may be material.[67]   For the basis of liability of the firm being agency of the partner, if in fact agency is present, its efficacy to bind the principal cannot be affected by any want of knowledge of, or absence of reliance on, the fact of the person dealt with being a partner.[68]

The principle of agency of partners applies also to admissions and representations by a partner and to notices given to or by a partner. An admission or representation by any partner concerning the partnership affairs and in the ordinary course of its business is evidence, not necessarily conclusive, against the firm,[69] except where the representation is as to the extent of the partner's authority.[70]   Notice given by a third party to any partner who habitually acts in the firm's business, of any matter relating to partnership affairs, operates as notice to the firm, except in the case of a fraud on the firm committed by or with the consent of the partner receiving the notice.[71] [72]

(c) *Liability of retired partner for debts and obligations of the firm incurred during membership of the firm.*—The partners being co-cautioners for the firm, a partner who has retired does not thereby cease to be liable for all debts or obligations incurred while he was a partner.[73]   No arrangement between him and the remaining partners alone is of any avail against the creditors.   He may avoid liability by an arrangement between himself and the firm, as newly constituted without him, and the creditors of the old firm.   Such an arrangement may be express or inferred from a course of dealing between the firm as newly constituted and the creditors.[74]   The inference is usually not easy.   The agreement, in order to infer discharge of the former partner, must amount to delegation.   Thus the mere fact of acceptance by the creditors from the new firm of partial payment and a bill for the balance was held, on the bill not being met, not to free the retiring partner, as he had not been discharged of liability, the new firm in granting the bill being merely a cautioner for the old.[75]   On the

---

[67] *Cf.* s. 6: *Crum & Co.* v. *McLean* (1858) 20 D. 751.
[68] *Cf.* Agent for undisclosed principal.
[69] s. 15.
[70] See *Pollock on Partnership*, 15th ed., 56.
[71] s. 16.
[72] As to execution of deeds, see s. 6.
[73] s. 17 (2).
[74] s. 17 (3).
[75] *Pollock & Co.* v. *Murray & Spence* (1863) 2 M. 14.

other hand, the retiring partner being a cautioner for the debt, actings of the creditor, such as giving time,[76] when in knowledge of the retirement, may give rise to equitable defences in the hands of the retired partner.[77]

(d) *Liability of a retired partner for debts and obligations incurred by a firm subsequent to his retirement.*—A partner who has retired from a firm may or may not be liable on obligations incurred by the firm susbsequent to his retirement.

WHEN LIABILITY.—The liability of a retired partner for a new debt of the firm rests upon the principle of personal bar by holding out. Where a person deals with a firm after a change in its constitution, he is entitled to treat all apparent members of the firm as being still members of the firm until he has notice of the change.[78]

Where the, to the creditor, apparent debtor is the old firm and the true debtor is the new, the creditor may hold the new firm and the retired partner jointly and severally liable for the debt.[79]

WHEN NO LIABILITY.—A partner who has become bankrupt and so ceased to be a partner, or the representative of one who has died, is not in any event liable for obligations subsequently incurred by the firm, death and bankruptcy being public facts.[80] The estates cannot therefore be subjected to liability by holding out. Apart from these cases a *Gazette* advertisement giving notice of the retirement is sufficient to exempt the retiring partner from liability for future debts of the firm incurred to persons who had no prior dealings with the firm.[81] In the case of persons who have had dealings with the old firm prior to the retirement a *Gazette* or newspaper advertisement is not as such sufficient. Intimation to them expressly, or by an equivalent such as an obvious change in the firm name, is required.[82] But knowledge of the retirement of a partner, or ignorance of his being a partner (if such were the case), at the time the new debt was contracted, if established against a particular such creditor, exempts the retired partner from liability to him.[83] Otherwise put, any customer who has had such notice that he knew or ought to have known of the retirement, or who

76 See *supra*, p. 236.
77 *Goldfarb* v. *Bartlett & Kremer* [1920] 1 K.B. 639, *Rouse* v. *Bradford Banking Co.* [1894] A.C. 586.
78 s. 36 (1); see also s. 37.
79 *Blacks* v. *Girdwood* (1885) 13 R. 243. The retired partner has a claim of relief against the new firm: *Mann* v. *Sinclair* (1879) 6 R. 1078. In England the creditor has right of action against the retired partner on the principle of holding out or against the new firm. He must elect between them: *Scarf* v. *Jardine* (1882) 7 App.Cas. 345.
80 s. 36 (3).
81 s. 36 (2).
82 Bell's Prin., § 382.
83 s. 36 (3); *Tower Cabinet Co. Ltd.* v. *Ingram* [1949] 2 K.B. 397.

was ignorant of a retired partner's membership, is barred from claiming against the old firm or persons secondarily liable for its debts.[84]

(e) *Liability of new partner for pre-existing debts of firm.*—There is a presumption against the liability of a new partner for existing debts of the firm.[85] The presumption may be displaced by facts and circumstances.[86] In a question with a creditor of the old firm the liability may arise from agreement between him and the new firm or it may be determined to arise on equitable considerations raising a presumption that the new firm has taken over the liabilities of the old; for example, if it has taken over the whole assets.[87] This would appear to be enough to entitle the creditor to sue the new firm, on the principle apparently of *jus quaesitum tertio*, especially if the new partner is admitted without contributing any capital.[87] Unless delegation has taken place, however, the creditor has only his right of action against the original debtor and, if it be a firm, its partners as guarantors of its debts.[88]

Person liable by holding out.—A person who is not in fact a partner may be barred by his conduct from denying that he is a partner and may therefore properly be held liable as such. The holding out must be by him or with his consent, express or implied.[89] The liability attaches only where the creditor has relied upon the truth of the representation of membership.[90] The person so holding himself out or being held out is liable to all who, relying on his being a partner, have given credit to the firm.[91]

What is sufficient to constitute liability by holding out is a question of circumstances. It is specially important in relation to liability of a partner for debts incurred by the firm after his retirement.

[84] *Mann* v. *Sinclair* (1879) 6 R. 1078.   [85] s. 17 (1).

[86] e.g., *Nelmes* v. *Montgomery & Co. and Loudon* (1883) 10 R. 974; *Heddle's Exrx.* v. *Marwick & Hourston's Tr.* (1888) 15 R. 698; *Stephen's Tr.* v. *Macdougall & Co.'s Trs.* (1889) 16 R. 779.

[87] *Cf. Thomson & Balfour* v. *Boag*, 1936 S.C. 2; 1936 S.L.T. 2.

[88] *Miller* v. *Thorburn* (1861) 23 D. 359; see, on the whole matter, *Clark on Partnership*, Bk. ii, 297 *et seq.*

[89] (a) This, according to Lindley (*The Law of Partnership*, 12th ed., 90), includes the case where his consent was obtained by fraud. Where the members of the firm know of the holding out, query whether the person held out has thereby indemnity against the others. It is thought he has, for they are *ad hoc* partners by agreement: *Mann* v. *Sinclair, supra.*

    (b) The case of a firm holding out to be a partner a person who is not a partner, and so becoming bound by his acts in line with the firm's business, is covered only by the common law: see *Moyes* v. *Cook* (1829) 7 S. 793. The person held out, unless aware of the fact, will, it seems clear, be under no liability: *Tower Cabinet Co.* v. *Ingram* [1949] 2 K.B. 397.

[90] The liability in this case cannot be enforced by charging the person under a decree obtained against the other: *Bremer* v. *Rutherford* (1901) 4 F. 62; 9 S.L.T. 256.

[91] s. 14 (1). The question can only arise with third parties, not, that is, between partners: *Clippens Oil & Shale Co.* v. *Scott* (1876) 3 R. 651.

(b) Effect of change in firm on contracts

The Partnership Act, 1890, does not define whether a change in the membership of a firm has any effect on continuing contracts except in the case of cautionry. There is at common law no general rule that such a change necessarily affects continuing contracts. But wherever the nature of the contract or the consideration for it is founded in any material degree upon the confidence of the one party in the integrity, ability and judgment of the other (the firm), it must be assumed that the contract was intended to be limited to the firm as originally constituted.[92] It is matter of decision that contracts of personal service (*locatio operarum*) with a firm are not dissolved by a mere change in the constitution of the firm of employers.[93] The conversion of a partnership into a limited company, however, does release all servants of the partnership from their engagements.[93]

Cautionary obligations.—A continuing guarantee or cautionary obligation given either to a firm, or to a third person in respect of the transactions of a firm, is, in the absence of agreement to the contrary, revoked as to future transactions by any change in the constitution of the firm to which, or of the firm in respect of the transactions of which, the guarantee or obligation was given.[94]

5. RELATION OF PARTNERS TO ONE ANOTHER AND TO THE FIRM

(a) The partnership agreement.—If there is a partnership agreement with express, and it may be implied, terms, each partner must abide by it. In so far as there is no agreement as to terms, the rules provided in the Act apply.[95] This is by force of the statute an implied term of every contract of partnership, but the rules may be varied or excluded by the terms of the partnership agreement. In every case no subsequent variation of the rights and duties of the partners is permissible without the consent of all the partners. Such consent may be express or inferred from a course of dealing.[96]

(b) Delectus personae.—The partnership relation is a highly personal one, and one of mutual confidence. Hence no person can be

---

[92] *Alexander* v. *Lowson's Trs.* (1890) 17 R. 571, *per* Lord Kinnear at 575.
[93] *Campbell* v. *Baird* (1827) 5 S. 335; *Berlitz Schools* v. *Duchêne* (1903) 6 F. 181; 11 S.L.T. 491, opinion of Lord McLaren.
[94] s. 18. This repeals and substantially re-enacts s. 7 of the Mercantile Law Amendment (Scotland) Act, 1856, which, however, also applied to the case of a single person trading under the name of a firm. That case must now be decided on common law principles, where the trader is principal debtor, in respect that such a single person is not a firm in the sense of the Partnership Act, 1890: see s. 4.
[95] s. 24. These have their origin in the law merchant.
[96] s. 19. Such variations do not usually affect the relation of the firm to third parties. But see s. 5. The test is the apparent rather than the actual authority of the partners or partner acting in the matter.

introduced as a partner without the consent of all existing partners.[97] Hence, also, apart from agreement to the contrary, a partnership can be dissolved if confidence can no longer be placed in a partner by the others.[98] Hence, also, where no fixed term for the duration of a partnership is agreed expressly or by inference, any partner can determine the partnership by giving notice of his intention to do so to the other partners.[99] Hence, also, no assignation of the interest of a partner has the effect of making the assignee a partner in his room without the consent of the other partners.[1]

Assignation of interest.—Short of making the assignee a partner, the interest of a partner is assignable absolutely or in security. The cedent retains his position as a partner. The assignee, not being a partner, has no right to interfere in the administration of the firm, or to require accounts, or to inspect the partnership books, or otherwise exercise the rights of a partner *inter socios*.[2] He is entitled while the firm is a going concern to the share of profits to which the cedent had right, and must accept the account of profits to which the partners, including the cedent, have agreed.[3] On dissolution of the firm he is entitled to receive the share of the partnership assets to which the cedent is entitled as between himself and the other partners, and to that end to an account as from the date of dissolution.[4]

(c) **Fiduciary element in partnership.**—Partnership is a contract *uberrimae fidei*. Hence both at entering into the partnership and during its currency each partner must make full disclosure of all things affecting the partnership to any partner or his legal representatives.[5] Thus he must render full accounts, and this the court can be invoked to enforce.[6]

Further, every partner must account to the firm for any benefit derived by him, without the consent of the other partners, from any transaction concerning the partnership, or from the use by him of the

---

[97] s. 24 (7). Testamentary nomination to a partnership can receive effect only if authorised by the contract of co-partnery and made expressly in the testament: *Thomson* v. *Thomson*, 1962 S.C.(H.L.) 28.

[98] *Cf. Loch* v. *J. Blackwood, Ltd.* [1924] A.C. 783, *per* Lord Shaw.

[99] See *Scott* v. *Dick*, 1909 2 S.L.T. 118.

[1] s. 31; except under the provisions of the Limited Partnerships Act, 1907, s. 7—*i e.*, unless the assignee becomes a " sleeping partner."

[2] *Re Garwood's Trusts* [1903] 1 Ch. 236.

[3] s. 31 (1).

[4] s. 31 (2); *cf. Cassels* v. *Stewart* (1881) 8 R.(H.L.) 1; *Trimble* v. *Goldberg* [1906] A.C. 494 at 512.

[5] s. 28.

[6] *Ibid. Lawson* v. *Lawson's Trs.* (1872) 11 M. 168. This is subject to agreement to the contrary: *Pollok, Gilmour & Co.* v. *Ritchie* (1850) 13 D. 640.

partnership property, name or business connections.[7] That is to say, a partner cannot receive any private profit when acting on behalf of the firm, and is liable to repay to the firm any commission earned by him while really acting on its behalf or in the line of the business connection.[8] Hence also a partner must account for and pay to the firm all profits made by him in any business of the same nature as and competing with that of the firm, which without the consent of the other partners he carries on.[9] This applies even if he is merely a member of another firm so competing. Otherwise he may, in general, carry on an independent trade not within the scope of the partnership business.[10]

(d) Partnership property.—Definition and nature.—In Scotland a firm, being a legal person distinct from the partners of whom it is composed, may own property. Such property is known as partnership property and must be held and applied by the partners exclusively for the purposes of the partnership and in accordance with the partnership agreement.[11] It means and includes all property and rights and interests in property originally brought into the partnership stock or since acquired, whether by purchase or otherwise, on account of the firm or for the purposes of and in the course of the partnership business.[12] Hence a firm has as against a partner the right of possession of partnership property and the title to transfer it.[13] The right of the firm may be proved *prout de jure.*[14]

The interest of each partner is a right to a *pro indiviso* share of the firm's assets on dissolution of the firm. It is thus an incorporeal moveable right and can be assigned or attached[15] only as such, and is moveable in succession.[16]

---

[7] s. 29 (1). This applies even after the death of a partner before the affairs of the partnership have been completely wound up: s. 29 (2). See *McNiven* v. *Peffers* (1868) 7 M. 181; Bell's Comm., ii, 522.

[8] *Scottish Pacific Coast Mining Co.* v. *Falkner, Bell & Co.* (1888) 15 R. 290. The purchase by a partner of another partner's interest in the firm is an exception: *Cassels* v. *Stewart* (1881) 8 R.(H.L.) 1.

[9] s. 30; *e.g., Stewart* v. *North* (1893) 20 R. 260; *Pillans Bros.* v. *Pillans* (1908) 16 S.L.T. 611.

[10] See *Aas* v. *Benham* [1891] 2 Ch. 244.   [11] s. 20 (1).

[12] s. 20 (1). For cases of difficulty as to what are assets of the firm, see *Miles* v. *Clarke* [1953] 1 W.L.R. 537; *Munro* v. *Stein,* 1961 S.C. 362; *Adam* v. *Adam,* 1962 S.L.T. 332.

[13] *Forrester* v. *Robson's Trs.* (1875) 2 R. 755; *Galloway* v. *Galloway,* 1929 S.C. 160; 1929 S.L.T. 131. The special case of co-owners of an interest in land who are partners as to profits made by its use is dealt with in s. 20 (3).

[14] The Blank Bonds and Trusts Act, 1696, which requires proof of trust by writ or oath of the alleged trustee, does not apply to agents or partners: *Forrester, supra; Galloway, supra.* If, however, the property is held in name of a partner in absolute terms by written title a declarator of trust for the firm is required under the Act of 1696: *Laird & Co.* v. *Laird & Rutherford* (1884) 12 R. 294.

[15] The proper diligence is arrestment: *cf. Parnell* v. *Walter* (1889) 16 R. 917 .

[16] s. 22.

As to the title, that is, the formal as distinct from the beneficial right to partnership property, the partnership contract has the effect only of conveying the *jus ad rem* and so is effective only *inter socios*. In a question with a third party the right of the firm to property which, *inter socios*, is partnership property depends in general on proper completion of the firm's title to the property according to the nature of the property. Thus, if corporeal moveable property be in question, it is enough in order to vest its ownership in the firm in a question with a third party that in fact it is partnership property and is in the possession of a partner as such. If, however, partnership corporeal moveables be in the hands of a third party, it depends on the character in which he holds them. Thus, if held on behalf of a partner as such by a person as his agent, delivery to, or to someone on behalf of the firm is not required to give the firm a title to it. If, however, held for example by a seller to the firm or to a contributing partner, delivery to or for behoof of the firm or that partner will be required; and if necessary to affect the seller with knowledge of the firm's right, intimation should be made to the seller on behalf of the firm that the property has passed to the firm.

If the property contributed by a partner or otherwise acquired by a firm is incorporeal moveables, the firm's title depends on its conveyance to the firm and completion by intimation of the assignation to the debtor in the obligation.

In the case of feudal property contributed by a partner, it is necessary, in order to exclude the diligence of private creditors of that partner, that he convey the property to the partners or other persons in trust for the firm.[17]

(e) Partners as debtors or creditors of the firm.—Subject to any agreement, express or implied, between the partners, the rules which govern their financial interest in the firm while a going concern are [18]:

(1) All the partners are entitled to share equally in the capital and profits of the business and must contribute equally towards the losses, whether of capital or otherwise, sustained by the firm.

Both the capital and the profits aspects of this rule apply though one partner has contributed more capital than another. A partner who contributes less capital may contribute more in skill and industry. Hence at dissolution of the firm, apart from agreement express or implied,[19] it would be implied from the fact that A had contributed all the capital, if the capital were lost, that B, who had contributed

---

[17] In a question with a partner's heir-in-law, such a conveyance is not required: *Munro v. Stein*, 1961 S.C. 362. As to leases, see *Clarke on Partnership*, 170; *Rankine on Leases*, 3rd ed., 86 *et seq.*
[18] s. 24.
[19] s. 44 (a).

none, would owe half to A. So also, if there were surplus assets, the partners would share equally.

(2) The firm must indemnify any partner in respect of payments made and personal liabilities incurred by him either in the ordinary and proper conduct of the business of the firm, or in or about anything necessarily done for the preservation of the business or property of the firm.

This rule is based upon the agency, and implied mandate, of the partners.

(3) A partner making for the purposes of the partnership any actual payment or advance, beyond the amount of capital he had agreed to subscribe, is entitled to interest at five per centum per annum from the date of payment or advance—that is, he is creditor in a loan.

(4) A partner is not entitled, before the ascertainment of profits, to interest on the capital subscribed by him.[20]

It follows from the above rules that in so far as a partner has failed to pay his stipulated share of capital he is a debtor to the partnership, and in so far as he has paid more he is a creditor. Also, he is debtor to the firm if he draws more from profits than he is entitled to, and creditor if he allows to remain undrawn profits he is entitled to. But though a creditor of the firm in respect of such capital or profits, he is a postponed creditor in a question with the general creditors, e.g., in a winding up. He is also as such creditor a creditor of the other partners for the amount due him, and may, in the event of the bankruptcy or dissolution of the firm, demand from each, as a co-cautioner for the debts of the firm, his proportional share of the debt. He has no claim *in solidum* against his co-partners as such.[21]

(f) **Management.**[22]—Subject to any agreement, express or implied, between the partners, every partner may take part in the partnership business. The partners may agree to delegate management exclusively to one of their number or to employ a manager. No partner is entitled to remuneration for acting in the partnership business.[23] Any difference arising as to ordinary matters connected with the partnership business may be decided by a majority of the partners, but no change may be made in the nature of the partnership business without the consent of all existing partners. In matters not requiring the consent of all, a minority of partners is entitled to notice and discussion of the

---

20 In most partnership agreements interest on capital subscribed is provided for before dividing profits.
21 Bell's Comm., ii, 536.
22 s. 24 (6)—(9).
23 Bell's Prin., § 370. It is an open question whether a partner can enter into a contract for service with his firm: *Fife C.C.* v. *Ministry of National Insurance*, 1947 S.C. 629; 1948 S.L.T. 63.

matter.   Default in this does not, in the absence of knowledge, affect the rights of third parties dealing with a partner as such.

6. TERMINATION OF PARTNERSHIP

The relation of partnership comes to an end by the operation of the conditions attached to its endurance by agreement or in its absence by operation of law.   It may be void *ab initio* as being illegal or be terminated by force of law as for supervening illegality or voidable if induced by misrepresentation.   As it is a contract *uberrimae fidei* it is readily reducible on the ground of misrepresentation inducing the contract.   The Act provides special remedies over and above the common law remedies where the contract is rescinded on this ground.

(1) **Rescission for misrepresentation.**—As partnership is a contract *uberrimae fidei*, misrepresentation inducing the contract, *e.g.*, as to the profits of a business to be taken over by the firm from one of the partners,[24] though not fraudulent,[25] or concealment of material facts, will justify rescission.   If the misrepresentation be fraudulent it will, in addition to rescission, found a claim of damages.   In addition a party entitled to rescind has certain rights.[26]   He has a lien on the surplus of the partnership assets over its liabilities for any sum of money paid by the party rescinding for the purchase of a share in the partnership, and for any capital he has contributed.   This so-called lien is a right as against the other partners to have a specific portion of the assets surplus to liabilities applied in satisfaction of these particular claims.[27]   He has further the right to stand in the place of the creditors of the firm for any payments made by him in respect of the partnership liabilities.   And he has a right to be indemnified by the one of the parties guilty of the fraud or making the misrepresentation against all the debts and liabilities of the firm.[28]

(2) **Dissolution of partnership.**—Dissolution means that the partnership relation is ended except so far as necessary for winding up the partnership affairs.   Winding up accordingly is necessarily preceded by dissolution.

A partnership may be dissolved in ordinary course by agreement; or apart from agreement, by virtue of the *delectus personae* involved, by notice or by death or bankruptcy; or by illegality; or in certain

---

[24] *Adam* v. *Newbigging*, 13 App.Cas. 308.

[25] *Ferguson* v. *Wilson* (1904) 6 F. 779; 12 S.L.T. 117.

[26] s. 41.

[27] See *Modern Law Review*, Vol. 12 (1949) 432, " The so-called Lien of a Partner," by Walter Rayburn Q.C.

[28] The section is supposed to be founded mainly on *Adam* v. *Newbigging* (1888) 13 App.Cas. 308, as decided by the Court of Appeal, 34 Ch.D.582.

circumstances at the discretion of the court in the exercise of its equitable jurisdiction.

(3) Grounds of dissolution.—(a) *By agreement—Expiration of the term.*—If the partnership be entered into, expressly or by inference,[29] for a fixed term, it is automatically dissolved on expiry of the term.[30] It may, however, be continued after the term has expired without any express agreement by the partners or such of them as habitually acted therein during the term and without any settlement or liquidation of the partnership affairs.[31] It then becomes a partnership at will and is dissoluble as such.[32] The rights and duties of the partners remain the same as they were at expiration of the term so far as consistent with the incidents of a partnership at will.[33]

(b) *By termination of a single adventure or undertaking.*—This is a joint adventure and indistinguishable from an ordinary partnership in that it establishes the relation of persons carrying on business in common with a view to profit.[34]

(c) *Dissolution by notice—Partnership at will.*—If a partnership has been entered into for an undefined term it may, because of the *delectus personae* involved, be dissolved by any partner giving notice to the other or others of his intention to dissolve the partnership. It is then dissolved as from the date mentioned in the notice as the date of dissolution, or, if no other date is mentioned, as from the date of communication of the notice.[35] Where originally constituted by deed, a notice in writing is required and if signed by the partner giving it will be sufficient for the purpose.[36] After the notice operates the partnership relation subsists, *inter socios*, only for the purpose of winding up the affairs of the firm.[37] Though the remaining partners agree to carry on the business as a new firm the retiring partner is nevertheless entitled to have his interest dealt with as if upon a dissolution, and he will upon publication of the dissolution cease to be affected by the acts done by his former partners thereafter.

(d) *Death or bankruptcy.*[38]—Death of a partner has the same effect *inter socios* as notice to dissolve. It *ipso facto* operates dissolution.

[29] s. 32 (a).
[30] See *Gracie* v. *Prentice* (1904) 12 S.L.T. 15; *Scott* v. *Dick*, 1909, 2 S.L.T. 118.
[31] s. 27.
[32] s. 26.
[33] s. 27 (1). See *McGown* v. *Henderson*, 1914 S.C. 839; 1914, 2 S.L.T. 66. This would in general not include provisions as to notice. *Neilson* v. *Mossend Iron Co. &c.* (1886) 13 R.(H.L.) 50.
[34] s. 32 (b); *Mair* v. *Wood*, 1948 S.C. 83; 1948 S.L.T. 326; *Parker* v. *Walker & Ors.*, 1961 S.L.T. 252.
[35] s. 32 (c).
[36] s. 26 (2).
[37] *Cf. Wallace* v. *Wallace's Trs.* (1906) 8 F. 558; 13 S.L.T. 844.   [38] s. 33.

Also, death being a public fact, no notice is required to free the representatives from liability for debts incurred in name of the firm after the date of death.[39] Winding up of the business may be obviated in this event by, for example, a provision in the partnership agreement for the interest of a deceasing partner being paid out to his representatives.

The situation is the same in the case of bankruptcy as in that of death of a partner.[40] His estate cannot thereafter be made liable for the acts of his solvent co-partners.[41] But the principle of holding out may render the other partners liable for the acts of the bankrupt partner after his bankruptcy.[42] In this context bankruptcy means sequestration.[43]

(e) *By illegality.*—A contract of partnership, though not tainted with illegality at its constitution, may become illegal and so void as regards the future. The supervening illegality operates from the date it occurs. A partnership is in every case dissolved by the happening of any event which makes it unlawful for the business of the firm to be carried on or for the members of the firm to carry it on in partnership.[44]

Inter socios the normal consequences of dissolution, namely sale and distribution of the assets, may be affected by the nature of the illegality. Thus, a partnership between an English company and an alien company was dissolved on the outbreak of war with the country of the alien. On the resumption of peace the alien partner was held entitled, there having been no winding up, to an account of profits made since dissolution.[45] This appears to be based upon the fiduciary relation between partners.

(f) *Dissolution by the court.*[46]—The grounds upon which the court may be asked to decree a dissolution are grounds which neither necessarily operate a dissolution nor entitle a partner as a matter of right to a dissolution. The court has an equitable discretion to end the relationship upon the specific grounds set out in the Act. These grounds are not necessarily exhaustive, as the court's jurisdiction is based upon the rules of the common law [47] and so extends to any case

---

[39] *Oswald's Trs.* v. *City of Glasgow Bank in Liqn.* (1879) 6 R. 461.
[40] s. 33.
[41] s. 36 (3).
[42] s. 38.
[43] s. 47 (1).
[44] s. 34. See *Cartonnagen-Industrie* v. *Stevenson* [1918] A.C. 239. Such dissolution in a question between the firm and a third party will not affect his position unless his relation with the firm involves him in the illegality or was entered into by him in knowledge of it. See *Lindley on Partnership,* 12th ed., 151–152.
[45] *Cartonnagen-Industrie* v. *Stevenson, supra.* In effect, s. 34, in the cases to which it applies, does not abrogate s. 42.
[46] s. 35.
[47] s. 46.

where in the opinion of the court it has become just and equitable to
end the partnership relation.[48]

The specific grounds are the insanity of a partner; his permanent
incapacity to perform his part under the partnership [49]; misconduct
calculated to affect prejudicially the carrying on of the business [50];
wilful and persistent breach of the partnership agreement or such
conduct in relation to the business that it is not reasonably practicable
to carry on in partnership with him; and when the business of the
partnership can only be carried on at a loss.[51]

(4) Effects of dissolution.[52]—As regards the partners, the effect of
dissolution is to terminate the general authority of the partners to
bind the firm. But each partner thereafter, unless he is bankrupt,[53]
retains a limited authority to bind the firm in so far as may be necessary
to wind up the affairs of the partnership, and to complete unfinished
transactions.[54] It is, however, a question of circumstances whether in
any particular case an obligation of a continuing kind undertaken by
the firm continues to be binding on the firm after its dissolution.[55]

On dissolution, the winding up of the partnership affairs is primarily with the surviving partner or partners. But any partner or his
representatives may apply to the court to wind up the business and
affairs of the firm for the purpose of having its assets applied in
payment of its debts and the surplus distributed among the partners.[56]
But the court will not readily, or merely upon averments that differences have arisen among the partners, accede to the application of one
partner for the appointment of a judicial factor.[57]

If a premium has been paid for entering into a partnership for a
fixed term,[58] and the partnership has been dissolved before the expiration of that term otherwise than by the death of a partner, e.g., by

[48] s. 35. The circumstances need not be *ejusdem generis* of the specific grounds: *cf.*
Loch v. *John Blackwood* [1924] A.C. 783, *per* Lord Shaw; *Baird* v. *Lees*, 1924 S.C.
83; 1923 S.L.T. 749.
[49] In this case the terms of the partnership contract may affect the result; *e.g.*, if under
the contract the partner in question is not bound to give personal services: *Eadie*
v. *MacBean's Curator* (1885) 12 R. 660.
[50] *e.g.*, *Hill* v. *Clifford* [1907] 2 Ch. 236 (a doctor).
[51] *e.g.*, *Miller* v. *Walker* (1875) 3 R. 242.   [52] ss. 38–40.
[53] The principle of holding out may render the other partners liable for the acts of the
bankrupt partner: s. 38.
[54] s. 38; *e.g.*, *Dickson* v. *National Bank of Scotland*, 1917 S.C.(H.L.) 50; 1917, 1 S.L.T.
318.
[55] *Cf. Menzies' Trs.* v. *Black's Trs.*, 1909 S.C. 239; 16 S.L.T. 580. See *ante*, Effect of
Change in Firm on Contracts.
[56] s. 39.
[57] *Gow* v. *Schulze* (1877) 4 R. 928; *cf. Elliott* v. *Cassils & Co.* (1907) 15 S.L.T. 190
Dickie v. *Mitchell* (1874) 1 R. 1030. The partners can agree to exclude the power
of the court to intervene under s. 39: *McKersie* v. *Mitchell* (1872) 10 M. 861 at 864;
Carabine v. *Carabine*, 1949 S.C. 521; 1949 S.L.T. 429.
[58] There is no return if the partnership be at will unless perhaps in the case of fraud.

supervening illegality, the court may order repayment of the whole or part of the premium. This provision for return does not apply where the dissolution is due wholly or chiefly to the misconduct of the partner who paid the premium, or where the firm is dissolved by agreement containing no provision for the return of the premium.[59]

(5) Carrying on business after dissolution without winding up.[60]—It may be that after dissolution of the partnership by the ceasing to be a partner of any of the partners the remaining partners carry on the business in partnership and there is no winding up. If they carry on the business with its capital or assets without any final settlement of accounts as between the firm and the outgoing partner or, if deceased, his estate, then the outgoing partner or his estate has the option of claiming such share of the profits made after dissolution as the court may find to be attributable to the use of his share of the partnership assets or to interest at the rate of five per cent. per annum on the amount of his share of the partnership assets.[61] These alternative remedies are excluded where by the partnership contract an option is given to surviving or continuing partners to purchase the interest of a deceased or outgoing partner and that option is duly exercised and strictly in accordance with the terms of the option.[62]

(6) Winding up.—The process of winding up has as its purpose the ascertainment, ingathering and realisation of the assets of the firm and the distribution of the proceeds in accordance with, first, the rights of the creditors and, thereafter, the respective rights and interests of the partners.

Assets which are claims of the firm against its debtors include claims against a partner. These may be claims in respect of any benefit derived by a partner without the consent of the other partners from any transaction concerning the partnership or from the use by him of the partnership property, name or business connection [63] or

---

[59] s. 40.

[60] s. 42.

[61] The case where there remains only one partner carrying on after dissolution is not apparently covered by the Act, but the common law is substantially to the same effect as to the right to a share of profits: see *Clark on Partnership*, 669; Cairns L.C. in *Vyse* v. *Foster* (1874) L.R. 7 H.L. 318 at 329. The alternative option in the Act to take interest appears not to be derived from any precedent of the common law. But the amount due being a debt accruing at dissolution—section 43—would on general principles bear interest: *Gloag on Contract*, 2nd ed., 681. In *Vyse* v. *Foster* (*supra*) at pp. 335–336 Cairns L.C. suggested the proper claim to be an account of profits with interest as an alternative remedy if the former is not available. *Cf. Smith* v. *Barclay*, 1962 S.C. 1. The partners may contract otherwise—section 43: *Ewing & Co.* v. *Ewing* (1882) 10 R. (H.L.) 1.

[62] s. 42 (2).

[63] s. 29; *e.g., Scottish Pacific Coast Mining Co. Ltd.* v. *Falkner, Bell & Co.* (1888) 15 R. 290 (commissions).

from a competing business.[64] The assets may include the goodwill of the business so far as marketable or otherwise to be dealt with under the partnership agreement.

Goodwill.—Goodwill has been defined as the connection formed, together with circumstances, whether of habit or otherwise, which tend to make it permanent.[65] With it are involved the right to use the trade name of the business, and, if acquired, the right to trade marks.[66] Its value is what can be got for the chance of being able to keep the connection and improve it. The presence or absence of competition by a former partner may affect the value of the goodwill.[67] Partnership deeds usually provide for the disposal of the goodwill of the firm's business and for the method by which its amount may be estimated. Provisions in the partnership deed affecting the goodwill may pass to a purchaser of the business.[68]

Settling accounts between partners.—In settling accounts between the partners after a dissolution the following rules apply, subject to agreement otherwise [69]: (a) Losses, including losses and deficiencies of capital, are to be paid first out of profits, next out of capital and lastly, if necessary, by the partners individually in the proportion in which they were entitled to share profits; (b) The assets of the firm, including the sums, if any, contributed by the partners to make up losses and deficiencies of capital, are to be applied as follows and in the order stated, *viz.* (i) in paying the debts and liabilities of the firm to persons who are not partners therein; (ii) in paying to each partner rateably what is due from the firm to him for advances as distinguished from capital [70]; (iii) in paying to each partner rateably what is due from the firm to him in respect of capital [70]; (iv) the ultimate residue, if any, is to be divided among the partners in the proportion in which profits are divisible.

7. THE LIMITED PARTNERSHIP

General.—The Limited Partnerships Act, 1907, makes provision for partnership with limited liability. Little advantage has been taken of

---

[64] s. 30. [65] Herschell L.C. in *Trego* v. *Hunt* [1896] A.C. 7 at 17.
[66] These can be disposed of as a separate asset.—Trade Marks Act, 1938, s. 22.
[67] If sold, a former partner may engage in competing business, but may not represent the new concern to be the successor of the old, as by using the former name or trade marks; nor may he solicit the customers, so long as they remain such, to transfer their custom to him: *Dumbarton Steamboat Co.* v. *MacFarlane* (1899) 1 F. 993; 7 S.L.T. 75.
[68] *Townsend* v. *Jarman* [1900] 2 Ch. 698.
[69] s. 44.
[70] *e.g.,* where the assets, after paying debts to non-partners, are less in value than the amount due by the firm to individual partners in respect of advances or capital, the partners must contribute equally to make up the deficiency—*Nowell* v. *Nowell* (1867) 7 Eq. 538; *Garner* v. *Murray* [1904] 1 Ch. 57—unless otherwise agreed.

it as its object can be better secured by incorporation as a private company. A limited partnership requires the existence of one or more partners, called general partners, responsible for all its debts, and one or more limited partners [71] who are liable only to the extent of the amount they have contributed at the time of entering into the partnership.[72] To secure this limitation of liability registration of the firm with the Registrar of Joint Stock Companies is essential, and an *ad valorem* duty on the amount contributed by the limited partners must be paid.[73] The limitation in the number of partners in ordinary partnerships applies.[74] An application for registration must state various particulars for the information of the public who may deal with the firm. These include the firm name, the general nature of the business and the principal place of business, the full name of each partner, the terms of the partnership agreement, if any, the date of commencement of the partnership, a statement that the partnership is limited, and which are the limited partners, and the sum contributed by each limited partner and whether paid in cash or how otherwise.[75] Changes in certain of these particulars during the continuance of the limited partnership must, under penalties for default exigible against the general partners, also be registered.[76]

Modifications of the general law.—Subject to the provisions of the Act of 1907, the law as to private partnerships applies with certain modifications.[77] During the currency of the partnership the limited partner may not take part in the management of the business and has not power to bind the firm; if he does take part he becomes liable for all the debts and obligations of the firm incurred while he so took part, as if he were a general partner. He may, however, inspect the books and advise with the general partners on the state and prospects of the business. The limited partner may assign his share and rights as a limited partner with the consent of the general partners.[78] A person may be introduced as a partner without the consent of the existing limited partners.[79]

As regards dissolution of the partnership, the limited partner may not dissolve the partnership by notice [80]; his death or bankruptcy does

---

[71] A limited partner may be a corporate body: s. 4 (4).
[72] s. 4 (2). The limited partner has no right to withdraw capital and if he does he is liable for the debts and obligations of the firm up to the amount as drawn out: s. 4 (3).
[73] ss. 5, 11.
[74] s. 4.
[75] s. 8.
[76] s. 9.
[77] s. 7.
[78] ss. 6, 10: notice in the *Gazette* is required.
[79] s. 6 (5) (*d*).
[80] s. 6 (5) (*e*).

not dissolve the firm; and his lunacy is not a ground for application to the court for dissolution unless his share cannot be otherwise ascertained and realised.[81] The winding up on a dissolution can be carried through only by the general partners, unless the court otherwise orders.[82] Application may however be made to the court to wind up either under the provisions of the Companies Act, 1948, unless the members are fewer than eight, or by appointment of a judicial factor.[83]

8. REGISTRATION OF BUSINESS NAMES

Before the passing of the Registration of Business Names Act, 1916,[84] there was no provision, except in the case of limited partnerships, for any public disclosure of the names of persons who carried on business either alone or in partnership. In relation to firms and individuals the Act provides for the registration with the Registrar of Companies of persons carrying on a business, including a profession, either alone or in partnership, and for the publication of their names on their business documents and correspondence, with certain exceptions. Neither registration nor publication is required when the business name consists of the name or names of the individual or individuals solely concerned, or with an addition to such names merely indicating that the business is carried on in succession to a former owner.[85] In other cases the particulars requiring to be registered are, as regards a firm, the business name, the general nature of the business, the principal place of business; and as regards the partners, the Christian name and surname, any former names, nationality, usual residence and any other business occupation; and the date of commencement of the business.[86]

Default in registration, without reasonable excuse, involves pecuniary penalties.[87] It also involves disability to enforce any contract, either in the business name or otherwise,[88] unless the court, on application by the defaulters, and after such service and public notice of the application as the court may order, grants relief. The court cannot grant relief in respect of any contract if any party to the contract proves to the satisfaction of the court that, if the Act had been complied with, he would not have entered into the contract. Relief may

---

[81] s. 6 (2).
[82] s. 6 (3).
[83] Companies Act, 1948, s. 398; *Muirhead* v. *Borland*, 1925 S.C. 474; 1925 S.L.T. 289.
[84] This Act as amended by the Companies Act, 1947, ss. 58 and 116, applies to individuals, firms and companies.
[85] s. 1.
[86] s. 3.
[87] s. 7.
[88] *e.g., Daniel* v. *Rogers* [1918] 2 K.B. 228. The Act refers only to claims made by the firm against third parties, and not claims *inter socios: Sterios Thomopulos* v. *John Mandilas* [1948] A.C. 12.

be granted on the ground that the failure was accidental or inadvertent or that on other grounds it is just and equitable to grant relief.[89] Ignorance of the Act has been accepted as a ground of relief.[90] The rights of other parties in respect of any such contract are not prejudiced by the failure to register and the defaulter, if sued, may plead set-off or counter-claim.[91]

---

[89] s. 8.
[90] *Clydesdale Motor Transport Co.,* 1922 S.C. 18; 1921, 2 S.L.T. 245.
[91] s. 8 (1) (c).

CHAPTER 11

LAW OF BANKRUPTCY

1. HISTORY OF THE LAW [1]

IN the earlier history of the Law of Scotland there was no provision whereby a person who had become insolvent might obtain a discharge from his debts unless by full payment or the favour of his creditors. He was liable to imprisonment and could escape it only by taking refuge in the Abbey of Holyrood. Where a debtor was imprisoned release was obtainable by the process of *cessio bonorum*, whereby the debtor, on giving up all his property, was released and could not be afterwards imprisoned for pre-existing debts. He did not, however, obtain a discharge, and any property he might afterwards acquire could be attached by his creditors for even pre-existing debts by appropriate diligence. Further, there were no general means for putting unsecured or general creditors on an equal footing. Creditors as a body might be ranked on the heritable estate of the debtor by the process of ranking and sale, but the moveable estate was open to the diligence of the individual creditor. That is to say, he could attach particular assets and use them to pay his debt in priority to or to the exclusion of others—there was a race of diligences, the earlier having priority over the later. But in 1772 sequestration, a process under which the bankrupt's estate is transferred to a trustee and which supersedes and stops diligence by individual creditors in the case of living debtors engaged in trade, was introduced. By subsequent Acts, and in particular the Bankruptcy (Scotland) Act, 1856, the process of sequestration was extended to all debtors, and to the estates of the deceased. The law now depends upon the Bankruptcy (Scotland) Act, 1913, and certain earlier statutes relating to the effect of insolvency on the actings of the bankrupt and his creditors. The process of *cessio bonorum* was preserved in name until it was abolished by the Act of 1913, though it had already been transformed into a species of sequestration adapted to small estates. Under the Act of 1913 such estates are to be dealt with by a process termed summary sequestration.

2. MEANING AND OBJECTS OF BANKRUPTCY

Meaning.[2]—The term bankruptcy, as used in the law of Scotland, has no specific technical meaning. It is a generic term covering

---

[1] See *Goudy on Bankruptcy,* 4th ed., Introduction.
[2] See *Goudy on Bankruptcy,* 4th ed., p. 15 *et seq.*

several species of insolvency. It may be used to denote simple insolvency, the condition of inability of a debtor to meet his obligations. It may also be used to denote " notour bankruptcy," a state of insolvency which has attained publicity.[3] Or it may be used to mean bankruptcy in the sense of divestiture of the insolvent of his estate and concourse of the creditors as in sequestration.[4] Insolvency is an element common to all conditions to which the term bankruptcy may be applied.

Objects of the law.—Whenever the state of insolvency emerges the debtor must thereafter act as if he were a trustee of his estate for the benefit of his creditors, and is no longer free to dispose of it as he thinks best.[5] The law of bankruptcy has for its aim the regulation of the actions of an insolvent person or of his creditors with a view to (1) the protection of the estate of the insolvent against his actings to the prejudice of those to whom he is indebted, *e.g.*, by making reducible gratuitous alienations by him of his estate; (2) the protection of the insolvent's estate in the interest of his creditors as a whole against the favouring of particular creditors, *e.g.*, by the reduction of fraudulent preferences; (3) an equitable distribution of the estate among the creditors, *e.g.*, by the equalisation of diligences; and (4) the setting of the bankrupt free from the claims of his creditors so that he may start afresh, *e.g.*, by sequestration and discharge.

3. INSOLVENCY AND ITS EFFECTS

(1) General.—Insolvency may be absolute or practical. A person is absolutely insolvent when his liabilities are greater than his assets. He is practically insolvent though his assets—it may be—are no less in value than the amount of his liabilities if assets are not immediately available in a sufficiency to meet his liabilities: that is a mere present inability to meet present debts.[6] This is treated as insolvency because what a creditor is primarily concerned with and entitled to, particularly in commercial dealings, is to get fulfilment of his claims as they fall due. Thus, under the Sale of Goods Act, 1893,[7] in a question as to the right of an unpaid seller of goods to stop them while in transit to an insolvent buyer, the latter is deemed to be insolvent when either he has ceased to pay his debts in the ordinary course of business or

---

[3] Originally, notour bankruptcy designated the condition of a man who, to avoid imprisonment for debt, had entered the sanctuary, the Abbey of Holyrood. It is now evidenced by definite statutory *indicia:* see *infra*, Notour Bankruptcy.

[4] *e.g.*, in Partnership Act, 1890, s. 47.

[5] See Bell's Comm., ii, 192.

[6] *Teenan's Tr.* v. *Teenan* (1886) 13 R. 833.

[7] s. 62 (3).

cannot pay his debts as they fall due. As an ingredient in the constitution of notour bankruptcy under the Bankruptcy (Scotland) Act, 1913, only practical insolvency is required. But, particularly in questions with creditors as a body or between creditors arising from insolvency of the debtor, insolvency in the absolute sense may be required, *e.g.*, for the purpose of reduction of gratuitous alienations or fraudulent preferences at common law.[8]

(2) Reduction of gratuitous alienations.—With a view to the protection of an insolvent's estate against his actings to the prejudice of his creditors, gratuitous alienations of his estate by the insolvent may be reduced either at common law or under the Bankruptcy Act, 1621.

At common law.—A gratuitous alienation in this connection means any alienation by an insolvent of his property without receiving valuable consideration therefor.[9] It may take the form, for example, of a gift,[10] or of a conveyance by a third party to a relative of the insolvent, the insolvent paying the price, or of the voluntary discharge of a debt due to the insolvent[11] or creation of a *spes successionis*[12]; but not, for example, of an alienation for money or money's worth,[13] or in implement of an obligation undertaken as the counterpart of another, as in a marriage contract,[14] or in settlement of a natural obligation, such as that of a husband or parent to aliment wife or children, or, generally, in implement of a legal obligation existing at the time of the alienation.[15]

An alienation may be challenged as being gratuitous either if made during insolvency or if insolvency is its result,[16] at the instance of any onerous creditor, whether he became such prior or subsequent to the alienation,[17] or by a trustee in the debtor's sequestration.[18]

---

[8] Where notour bankruptcy is the ground of the reduction practical insolvency is all that is required, see notes 38, 61, *infra*. Under the Companies Act, 1948, insolvency has a special meaning: s. 223.

[9] *Abram Steamship Co. Ltd.* (*in Liqn.*), 1925 S.L.T. 243.

[10] *Dobie* v. *Mitchell* (1854) 17 D. 97.   [11] *Obers* v. *Paton's Trs.* (1897) 24 R. 719.

[12] *Thomson* v. *Spence & anor.* 1961 S.L.T. 395.

[13] *Renton & Gray's Tr.* v. *Dickison* (1880) 7 R. 951.

[14] Bell's Comm., ii, 176. This applies both to antenuptial provisions by a husband for wife and children and by parents of intending spouses for behoof of them or the children of the marriage. But proof that the wife was aware of the insolvency may vitiate the transaction as fraudulent, and if grossly excessive it may be reduced *quoad* the excess: *M'Lay* v. *M'Queen* (1899) 1 F. 804; 6 S.L.T. 391. As to postnuptial settlement during insolvency, see Goudy, 4th ed., 29–31.

[15] *Taylor's Trs.* v. *Jones* (1888) 15 R. 328; *Pringle's Tr.* v. *Wright* (1903) 5 F. 522; 10 S.L.T. 716.

[16] *Abram S.S. Co.*, 1925 S.L.T. 243.

[17] *M'Cowan* v. *Wright* (1852) 14 D. 901; *Edmond* v. *Grant* (1853) 15 D. 703; *Wink* v. *Speirs* (1867) 6 M. 77, *per* Lord Justice-Clerk Patton.

[18] Bankruptcy (Scotland) Act, 1913, s. 9. It cannot, however, be challenged by a judicial factor appointed under s. 163 of the 1913 Act—*Reid's J. F.* v. *Reid*, 1959 S.L.T. 120.

The challenger, to succeed, must prove the non-onerosity of the alienation and absolute insolvency of the debtor both at the date of making the alienation and of the challenge, and that the alienation was made to the prejudice of lawful creditors. Proof of fraudulent intent is not required [19]; there is breach of trust on the part of the insolvent inferred from proof of the other circumstances; and in consequence it does not matter whether the alienee knew of the debtor's insolvency or not.[20]

Under the Bankruptcy Act, 1621.[21]—The purpose and effect of this Act as construed in the courts was to facilitate the challenge of gratuitous alienations if made in writing [22] in prejudice of creditors of an insolvent by raising a presumption [23] of insolvency at the date of the alienation—at least in a question with prior creditors [24]—and of non-onerosity in a question with both prior and posterior creditors [25] where the alienation was to a conjunct or confident person.

The challenger must prove that the receiver of the property was conjunct or confident, that the debtor was absolutely insolvent at the raising of the action and that the creditor was an onerous creditor [26] prior to the alienation. Thereafter it is presumed that the alienation was made "without true just and necessary causes," and that the debtor was insolvent at the time of granting the alienation.[27] The onus of rebutting these presumptions is on the debtor.

Conjunct persons are those nearly related to the debtor by blood or affinity.[28] Confident persons are those standing in a confidential relation with the debtor, such as partners in business, servants and the like.[28]

(3) Reduction of fraudulent preferences.—*At common law.*—With a view to the protection of the estate of an insolvent debtor against his action in favour of particular creditors to the prejudice of his other creditors, preferences so acquired and having that effect may be reduced

---

[19] Fraud here is constructive fraud.

[20] Bell's Comm., ii, 170.

[21] The Act also provided for reduction of voluntary alienations after diligence begun but not completed by any creditor. It did not prevent voluntary preference to particular creditors; hence the Bankruptcy Act, 1696. Preferences by diligence were not dealt with until 1772, by general sequestration of assets.

[22] See Goudy, 4th ed., 44. There is no such limitation at common law.

[23] *Presumptio juris*, and rebuttable.

[24] The Act of 1913, s. 9, adds the trustee on a sequestrated estate whether representing prior creditors or not. The trustee is entitled to the benefit of any presumption competent to any creditor: *Goudy on Bankruptcy*, 4th ed., 52; *Neil's Tr.* v. *British Linen Co.* (1898) 6 S.L.T. 227; 36 S.L.R. 139.

[25] See comment in Goudy, 4th ed., 51–52.

[26] See note 23, *supra*.

[27] *Bolden* v. *Ferguson* (1863) 1 M. 522; *Dawson* v. *Thorburn* (1888) 15 R. 891.

[28] *Edmond* v. *Grant* (1853) 15 D. 703; *Bank of Scotland* v. *Gardiner* (1907) 15 S.L.T. 229. Not insurer and insured: *Todd* v. *Anglian Insurance Co. Ltd.*, 1933 S.L.T. 274.

as "fraudulent." For this purpose the rights of creditors *inter se* are held to be fixed at the date of the insolvency.[29] In general every kind of transaction by which a benefit is given by the debtor voluntarily, that is, not under legal compulsion,[30] while insolvent and in knowledge by the debtor [31] of his insolvency, to one creditor in preference to others, whether directly or indirectly,[32] is presumed fraudulent on the part of the debtor,[33] and so challengeable if the debtor is absolutely insolvent at the date of challenge. Certain such transactions however, though voluntary on the part of the debtor, are not reducible as fraudulent in the absence of fraudulent contrivance between the debtor and the creditor. These are cash payments, transactions in course of trade, and *nova debita*.[34] An example of a challengeable transaction is the giving of a security for an unsecured debt.[35] The effect of reduction is to lay the subject of the preference open to the diligence of creditors according to their respective priorities or preferences.[36]

Under the Bankruptcy Act, 1696.[37]—The statute facilitates a successful challenge by a prejudiced creditor. This it does by providing for the declaring of an insolvent [38] person notour bankrupt upon certain requisites concurring,[39] and by declaring null all deeds embodying transactions of the kinds struck at by the common law, that is, in satisfaction or further security of prior debts if granted at or after or within sixty days [40] before notour bankruptcy. Proof of insolvency at the date of challenge, if within this period,[40] is not required.

The persons entitled to make the challenge are a prior creditor,[41] that is, a creditor prior to the transaction challenged, a trustee in the debtor's sequestration, whether he represents prior creditors or not,[42]

---

[29] *M'Ewen* v. *Doig* (1828) 6. S 889, *per* Lord Corehouse.

[30] *M'Cowan* v. *Wright* (1852) 14 D. 968.

[31] As to need for knowledge of the creditor: see Goudy, 38.

[32] *Smart & Co.* v. *Stewart*, 1911 S.C. 668; 1911, 1 S.L.T. 275.

[33] *M'Cowan* v. *Wright* (1853) 15 D. 494. It is a breach of trust.

[34] See under Bankruptcy Act, 1696, *infra*. For an illuminating exposition of the ambit of these three exceptions, see Gow, 620 *et seq.*

[35] *M'Cowan* v. *Wright* (1853) 15 D. 494.

[36] *Cook* v. *Sinclair & Co.* (1896) 23 R. 925; 4 S.L.T. 70, *per* Lord M'Laren.

[37] Bell's Comm., ii, 192 *et seq.*

[38] Practical insolvency is enough; *Teenan's Tr.* v. *Teenan* (1886) 13 R. 833.

[39] These are now as provided in the Bankruptcy (Scotland) Act, 1913, ss. 5 and 6; see Notour Bankruptcy, note 61, *infra*.

[40] The period is now six months in a question with a company: Companies Act, 1948, s. 320; *e.g., Barclay* v. *Cuthill* 1961 S.L.T.(Notes) 62. The assumption has been made that the six months' period applies in bankruptcy. The statement in Gow, at pp. 265–266, seems to embody a doubt. A strong case against this assumption can be stated.

[41] Under the statute this includes, where the transaction challenged is a trust deed for creditors, a non-acceding creditor: *Mackenzie* v. *Calder* (1868) 6 M. 833. Such a deed is not challengeable at common law: Bell's Comm., ii, 387–388.

[42] Bankruptcy (Scotland) Act, 1913, s. 9.

a liquidator of a public company, provided he represents prior creditors.[43] A title to challenge may be acquired by a trustee under a private trust deed for creditors by assignation if the trust deed confers power to challenge and creditors having a title to challenge accede thereto [44]; by the bankrupt where he is reinvested on composition [45]; and by the purchaser of a sequestrated estate under a deed of arrangement.[44] In addition, a third party who has obtained a prior title to the subject, whether fully completed or not, has a title to challenge.[46] In all cases an interest as well as a title is required,[47] and the transaction challenged will be set aside only in so far as the interest of the challenger extends.[48] The subject cannot be vindicated from a third party who has acquired it onerously and in good faith from the preferred creditor.[49] As at common law, cash payment [50] of debts actually due, transactions in the ordinary course of trade [51] and *nova dehita* are not reducible as fraudulent preferences except on proof of fraudulent contrivance between debtor and creditor. Thus cash payment of a debt actually due is not " satisfaction or further security " of the debt, but simply fulfilment of an obligation of the debtor according to its terms.[52] Nor is delivery of goods in implement of an ordinary trade contract such as sale.[53] Nor is a transference of property, though during insolvency, for a consideration given at the time the debt was contracted [54]; it is *novum debitum*. Thus, if at the date of a loan to a person there be granted by him a security or an obligation to grant a specified security forthwith which is in fact granted only after a lapse of time and when the debtor is insolvent, it is nevertheless effectual. It is consideration upon which the loan was given. Or again, if the security granted at the time is over heritable property, but is not then completed by registration, it is nevertheless effectual as its completion, though later and during insolvency, does not depend on any voluntary act of the debtor.

On the other hand, anticipatory payments or deliveries of goods, *i.e.*, made before exigible, are not payments in cash or in ordinary

---

[43] *Clark* v. *West Calder Oil Co.* (1882) 9 R. 1017.
[44] *Smith & Co.* v. *Smyth* (1889) 16 R. 392.
[45] Bankruptcy (Scotland) Act, 1913, s. 137; *Drummond* v. *Watson* (1850) 12 D. 604.
[46] *Wright* v. *Walker* (1839) 1 D. 641.
[47] *Brown & Co.* v. *M'Callum* (1890) 18 R. 311.
[48] *Ker* v. *Graham* (1830) 8 S. 408.
[49] *Drummond* v. *Watson, supra; Adamson, Howie & Co.* v. *Guild* (1868) 6 M. 347.
[50] This includes payment by the debtor's cheque: *Carter* v. *Johnstone* (1886) 13 R. 698
[51] Even though a preference is thereby conferred on a prior creditor, *e.g.*, an auctioneer's lien: *Crockart's Tr.* v. *Hay & Co. Ltd.*, 1913 S.C. 509; 1913, 1 S.L.T 102.
[52] *Carter* v. *Johnstone, supra.*
[53] *Taylor* v. *Farrie* (1855) 17 D. 639.
[54] *Whatmough's Tr.* v. *British Linen Bank*, 1932 S.C. 525; 1932 S.L.T. 386; 1934 S.C.(H.L.) 51; 1934 S.L.T. 392.

course of trade [55]; nor is transfer of a debt due to the insolvent.[56] And whereas endorsation and payment by the debtor into his bank account of a third party's cheque in his favour in reduction of an overdraft is payment in cash as being the ordinary method of making payment into a bank and also a transaction in the ordinary course of business between banker and customer,[57] on the other hand payment by debtor to creditor by the endorsation and delivery of a bill or cheque granted by a third party is not in the general case payment in cash.[58] And an obligation undertaken at the time to grant a specified security at some indeterminate time or to grant an unspecified security, if implemented during insolvency, is not *novum debitum*.

If, however, there be proof of fraudulent contrivance between debtor and creditor, these exceptions will not hold. Thus, where an insolvent debtor sells goods to his creditor to enable the creditor to set off a debt due to him by the insolvent and so obtains satisfaction of his debt to the extent of the value of the goods, this, though a transaction in the ordinary course of trade, is challengeable as a fraudulent preference.[59]

(4) Equalisation of diligences.—Notour bankruptcy, originally defined by statute in the Bankruptcy Act, 1696, was redefined in the sequestration statutes,[60] the latest of which is the Bankruptcy (Scotland) Act, 1913; and, apart from its effect in relation to the reduction of preferences given voluntarily by debtors to particular creditors under the Statute of 1696, notour bankruptcy is given the effect of equalising preferences obtained by creditors by doing diligence upon assets of the estate of an insolvent. This will now be considered, noticing in the first place how notour bankruptcy may now be constituted, and in the second place its effect by way of the equalisation of diligences.

Constitution of notour bankruptcy.[61]—It is now constituted (1) by sequestration or by the issuing of an adjudication of bankruptcy or the granting of a receiving order in England or Ireland; or (2) by insolvency [62] concurring (a) (i) with a duly executed charge [63] for

---

55 *Angus's Tr.* v. *Angus* (1901) 4 F. 181; 9 S.L.T. 166.
56 *Newton & Sons' Tr.* v. *Finlayson & Co.,* 1928 S.C. 637; 1928 S.L.T. 468.
57 *Whatmough's Tr.* v. *British Linen Bank,* 1932 S.C. 525; 1932 S.L.T. 386; 1934 S.C. (H.L.) 51; 1934 S.L.T. 392.
58 *Carter* v. *Johnstone* (1886) 13 R. 698. Usage in a particular trade may make it so, see *Whatmough's Tr.* v. *British Linen Bank, cit. sup., per* Lord President Clyde at p. 754.
59 *e.g., Stewart* v. *Scott* (1832) 11 S. 171.
60 The earliest was in 1772.
61 s. 5. As to persons liable to notour bankruptcy, see Goudy, 4th ed., 68.
62 Practical insolvency is meant: *Teenan's Tr.* v. *Teenan* (1886) 13 R. 833. It includes wilful refusal to pay a debt though solvent: *Scottish Milk Marketing Board* v. *Wood,* 1936 S.C. 604; 1936 S.L.T. 470.
63 *Inland Revenue* v. *Gibb,* 1963 S.L.T.(Notes) 66.

payment, where a charge is necessary, followed by expiry of the days of charge without payment; (ii) where a charge is not necessary, with the lapse without payment of the days which must elapse before poinding or imprisonment can follow on a decree or warrant for payment of a sum of money; (iii) with a poinding or seizure of any of the debtor's moveables for non-payment of rates or taxes; (iv) with a decree of adjudication of any part of his heritable estate for payment or in security: or (b) with sale of any effects belonging to the debtor under sequestration for rent. Insolvency is presumed if the other requisites are present, but the presumption is rebuttable.[64]

Notour bankruptcy of a company, including a partnership, may be constituted in any of the foregoing ways or by any of the partners being rendered notour bankrupt for a firm debt.[65]

Effects in equalising diligences.—Arrestments and poindings used within sixty days prior to the constitution of notour bankruptcy or within four months thereafter are ranked *pari passu* as if they had all been used of the same date.[66] This of course relates to diligences of either kind or of both, used against the same subject. The diligences are not by this provision annulled, but merely made to rank *pari passu* and retain their preference as against later diligences of other creditors, while diligences executed before the sixty days rank before the diligences equalised and in the order of their dates. If, however, sequestration has been obtained within the four months, as it is equivalent[67] to a completed diligence of both these kinds over the whole moveable assets, it prevents any such preference being effectually created after the beginning of the sixty days.[68] Any creditor judicially producing in a process relative to the subject of such arrestment or poinding[69] liquid grounds of debt is entitled to rank as if he had executed an arrestment or a poinding.

Apart from its effect in the annulling of preferences and the equalisation of diligence, notour bankruptcy enables creditors to take proceedings for the sequestration of the estates of a debtor.

---

[64] Rebuttal by the debtor by proof of solvency may be made in any proceedings based upon notour bankruptcy: *Fleming* v. *Yeaman* (1884) 9 App.Cas. 966; 21 S.L.R. 722; *Teenan's Tr.* v. *Teenan* (1886) 13 R. 833; *Michie* v. *Young,* 1962 S.L.T.(Notes) 70.

[65] s. 6. A member of an incorporation is of course not liable to diligence for a debt of the incorporation.

[66] Bankruptcy (Scotland) Act, 1913, s. 10. The landlord's hypothec is not affected: s. 115. The *pari passu* ranking of adjudications of the heritable estate was provided for by the Act, 1661, c. 62, and the Judicial Procedure Act, 1856, and is independent of notour bankruptcy: see Goudy, 4th ed., 531.

[67] It is not itself a diligence, but an action or congeries of actions.

[68] This has been held to be the combined effect of ss. 10 and 104: *Stewart* v. *Jarvie,* 1938 S.C. 309; 1938 S.L.T. 383.

[69] This refers to the action of furthcoming in the case of arrestment and to the action of poinding and sale in the case of poinding.

4. SEQUESTRATION

(1) Definition.—Sequestration in bankruptcy is a judicial process for rendering litigious the whole estate of the bankrupt in order that no part of it may be carried away by a single creditor for his own benefit, but that the whole may be vested in a trustee, to be administered by him and distributed among the creditors according to certain fixed rules for distribution.[70] It is applicable to a partnership or an incorporation, but not to a company under the Companies Acts, nor to an unincorporated association,[71] as it cannot be made notour bankrupt. Being a judicial process, it requires an award of a court.[72] The requisites of an award differ according as the debtor is alive or is dead or is a firm.

(2) Requisites of an award.—*In the case of a living debtor.*—The petition to the court for an award of sequestration may be at the instance of the debtor or of a duly qualified creditor or creditors. In either case the debtor must be subject to the jurisdiction of the Supreme Courts of Scotland [73] at the date of presentation of the petition. If on the debtor's petition, it must be with the concurrence of a duly qualified creditor or creditors, and the debtor need not be notour bankrupt or even insolvent. If on the petition of a duly qualified creditor or creditors, the debtor must be notour bankrupt and, if without the debtor's concurrence, it is competent only within four months of, that is, after, his notour bankruptcy, whether the first or any subsequent constitution thereof.[74] In addition the debtor must within a year before the presentation of the petition have resided or had a dwelling-house or place of business within Scotland.[75]

In the case of a deceased debtor.—He must at death have been subject to the jurisdiction of the Supreme Courts of Scotland, and the award may be made without concurrence of creditors on the petition of a mandatory to whom the debtor had granted a mandate to apply for sequestration or on the petition of a duly qualified creditor or creditors.[75] If on the petition of creditors, no sequestration may be awarded until the expiration of six months from the debtor's death,[76] unless the debtor was at the time of his death notour bankrupt or his

---

[70] *Sinclair* v. *Edinburgh Parish Council,* 1909 S.C. 1353, *per* Lord Kinnear at 1359; 1909, 2 S.L.T. 189.

[71] *Pitreavie Golf Club* v. *Penman,* 1934 S.L.T. 247.

[72] This may be the Court of Session or a sheriff. See ss. 16–19.

[73] This means the Court of Session: see Goudy, 4th ed., 115.

[74] ss. 13, 7.

[75] s. 11.

[76] If ultimately awarded, it dates back to the date of the first deliverance in the application for sequestration and takes effect as at that date: s. 41.

successors concur in the petition or renounce the succession, in which cases the award may be made forthwith.[77]

In the case of a firm.—The requisites are that the firm be notour bankrupt and either have within the year carried on business in and a partner have resided or carried on business in Scotland; or the firm have had a place of business in Scotland.[78]

Qualification of creditors.—The debt or debts of the petitioning or concurring creditor or creditors must together amount to not less than fifty pounds and may be liquid or illiquid, provided they are not contingent.[79] The creditor must lodge with the petition [80] an oath in which he swears to the verity of the debt and specifies *inter alia* any securities he holds for the debt and any other obligants who may be liable along with the debtor.[81] He must also produce vouchers affording prima facie evidence of the debt.[82] Where the debtor is not a party to the petition, the creditor must produce evidence of the debtor's notour bankruptcy or apply for a diligence for recovery of such evidence.[83]

(3) Procedure in application for an award.—*First deliverance.*— Where the petition is presented by the debtor or by creditors with his concurrence, or, if he is deceased, with concurrence of his successors [84] or by his mandatory,[85] the court must award sequestration forthwith.[86] Where the petition is by creditors alone, the first deliverance of the court is an order for intimation and service of the petition on the debtor, ordering him within so many days (called the *induciae*), if he is to oppose the application, to appear and show cause why sequestration cannot competently be awarded. If the debtor does not oppose or pay the debt in respect of which he was made notour bankrupt and the debt of the petitioning creditor and of any other creditors appearing and concurring, sequestration must be awarded.[87] The deliverance declares the debtor's estates to belong to the creditors for the purposes of the Act.[88]

---

[77] s. 13.
[78] s. 11. 1st (B).
[79] s. 12.
[80] ss. 20 and 21.
[81] He does not deduct the value of the securities he holds.
[82] *Scott* v. *Scott* (1847) 9 D. 1347; *Simpson* v. *Myles* (1881) 9 R. 104.
[83] s. 25; *Drummond* v. *Clunas Tiles and Mosaics Ltd.,* 1909 S.C. 1049; 1909, 1 S.L.T. 508.
[84] Renunciation of the succession has the same effect.
[85] This is not provided in the Act. But see Goudy, 4th ed., 133.
[86] s. 28. A creditor may oppose: *Tennent* v. *Crawford* (1878) 5 R. 433. He usually lodges a *caveat* so that he may be heard. The award is subject to possible recall later: ss. 30 and 31.
[87] s. 29. A creditor may also oppose: Bell's Comm., ii, 293. In all questions where the date of sequestration is material, *e.g.,* cutting down of diligences, it is to be taken as that of the first deliverance, though the award be later.
[88] s. 28.

Publication of award.[89]—In order to make the award fully effectual it must be published and recorded. The party applying for sequestration is bound, within two days of the first deliverance, to present for recording an abbreviate of the petition and first deliverance to the Keeper of the Register of Inhibitions and Adjudications and to insert a notice of the award in the *London* and *Edinburgh Gazettes.* The recording has the effect of an inhibition by rendering the debtor incapable of granting voluntarily any deed or incurring any debt that may affect his heritable estate to the prejudice of his creditors,[90] and has the effect of a citation in an adjudication in rendering his heritable estate litigious and incapable of attachment by one creditor to the prejudice of any other.[91] If it is not recorded within two days, or if there is an error in the recording, creditors may acquire preferences they are in course of perfecting, until a proper recording, which only the court can authorise, but the sequestration proceedings are otherwise effectual. A party applying for an award does the recording as acting for all creditors: hence he may be liable for any loss caused to them from his failure to comply.[92]

(4) Effects of award.—*Vesting in trustee.*—The effect of an award is to vest in the trustee under the sequestration, when appointed, the whole property of the debtor.[93] The order of the court confirming the election of a trustee by the creditors, known as the Act and Warrant, forms the title of the trustee to the estate and so to recover any property belonging or debt due to the bankrupt and to maintain actions for recovery of it.[94] Until then the personal title, *i.e.,* the right of property in the estate and the right of action, remains with the bankrupt.

The general right of the trustee is to the estate of the bankrupt *tantum et tale, i.e.,* the same extent and quality of right as the bankrupt had at the date of the award,[95] including heritable estate situated in England or Ireland or the British Dominions. His right accordingly vests in him all rights in moveable or heritable estate belonging beneficially to the bankrupt and legally attachable for debt, whether the right be present, future or contingent, but subject to any valid preferable securities over it at the date of sequestration.[96]

In particular the trustee's right includes non-vested contingent rights of succession or interests in property, *e.g.,* a *spes successionis*

[89] s. 44.
[90] Bell's Comm., ii, 134.
[91] Bell's Comm., ii, 144–146: *Jarvie* v. *Robertson* (1865) 4 M. 79.
[92] *Gray* v. *Cockburn* (1844) 6 D. 569.
[93] *White* v. *Stevenson,* 1956 S.C. 84.
[94] s. 70.
[95] See Goudy, 4th ed., 248–249.
[96] ss. 2, 97.

under a will, under a marriage contract or a deed of an irrevocable character; alimentary provisions in favour of the bankrupt in so far as in excess of an aliment suitable in his existing circumstances [97]; a portion of any salary, pension or other emoluments enjoyed by the bankrupt [98]; *acquirenda*, *i.e.*, all property acquired by the bankrupt after sequestration and prior to his discharge [99]; rights of action which the bankrupt has, *e.g.*, for personal injury [1]—the trustee may raise action or sist himself if success in the action would preserve or enlarge the estate [2]; and the right to adopt any contracts to which the bankrupt is a party if *delectus personae* is not present to prevent him [3]; a copyright, on the terms as to royalties to the author binding on the bankrupt. [4]

On the other hand the trustee's title will not suffice to vest in him property held by the bankrupt in trust and to which the bankrupt has no beneficial right [5]; necessary wearing apparel of the bankrupt, his wife and family, and working tools or implements of the bankrupt necessary to enable him to earn a living, these not being attachable for debt [6]; and property fraudulently in possession of the bankrupt. [7]

Interruption of prescription.—Presentation by a creditor of or concurrence in a petition for sequestration interrupts prescription of the debt of the creditor and so does lodging of a claim. The interruption is effectual though sequestration should later be recalled. [8]

---

[97] s. 98.

[98] *Caldwell* v. *Hamilton*, 1919 S.C.(H.L.) 100; 1919, 2 S.L.T. 154; *Macdonald's Tr.* v. *Macdonald*, 1938 S.C. 536; 1938 S.L.T. 443.

[99] s. 98. The bankrupt must notify the trustee or he will forfeit the benefits of the Act, *e.g.*, the privilege of discharge. The trustee must apply for and obtain a vesting order; otherwise, meanwhile, creditors subsequent to the award may do diligence against the acquired property: *Grant* v. *Green's Tr.* (1901) 3 F. 1016; 9 S.L.T. 139.

[1] But not those affecting his personal character like defamation, or his feelings like seduction: *Thom* v. *Bridges* (1857) 19 D. 721, or solatium: *Muir's Trs.* v. *Braidwood*, 1958 S.C. 169.

[2] The trustee incurs risk of personal liability for expenses: *Cowie* v. *Muirden* (1893) 20 R. (H.L.) 81; 1 S.L.T. 176. If the trustee does not so act the bankrupt retains his title and interest to sue in virtue of his radical right in reversion if there is any prospect of a reversion: *Whyte* v. *Forbes* (1890) 17 R. 895; and if the bankrupt is defender in an action already raised, the pursuer, if successful, may rank as a creditor: *Dow* v. *Pennell's Tr.*, 1929 S.L.T. 674.

[3] Goudy, 4th ed., 284.

[4] s. 102.

[5] *Heritable Reversionary Co. Ltd.* v. *Millar* (1892) 19 R. (H.L.) 43. See also *Newton's Extrix.* v. *Meiklejohn's J.F.*, 1959 S.L.T. 71. It is an exception where the bankrupt's wife is the beneficiary. She cannot claim property she has lent or entrusted to her husband or allowed to be immixed with his funds. She is a postponed creditor in the sequestration for its value: Married Women's Property Act, 1881, s. 1 (4).

[6] *Pennell* v. *Elgin*, 1926 S.C. 9; 1925 S.L.T. 620.

[7] *e.g.*, *Watt* v. *Findlay* (1846) 8 D. 529; *Gamage Ltd.* v. *Charlesworth's Tr.*, 1910 S.C. 257; 1910, 1 S.L.T. 11.

[8] s. 105. This refers to the negative prescription. As to effect on the sexennial prescription, see *Crawford's Trs.* v. *Haig* (1827) 5 S. 658; and on the quinquennial prescription see *Cochrane* v. *Fergusson* (1831) 9 S. 501.

Concourse of debit and credit.—Concourse of debit and credit between the bankrupt and his creditors takes place at the date of the first deliverance. Hence the sequestration stops the running of interest on unsecured claims, and from claims for debts payable after the date of sequestration interest accruing thereafter is deducted.[9] Where, however, the creditor holds a security for his debt, he is entitled to hold it for payment of his full debt and interest to the date of payment.

Effect on diligence.—Diligence being a way of obtaining a security for a debt, if completed it gives a preference over the subjects affected. Where the subject is heritable, sequestration is equivalent to a decree of adjudication in favour of the trustee to the effect that adjudications made effectual less than a year and a day prior to the first deliverance are cut down and confer no preference. If the sequestration be posterior to year and day, the adjudication will have a preference, unless the trustee have, in the case of feudal subjects, first completed his title by infeftment.[10]

As regards moveable estate, sequestration, as from the date of the first deliverance, is equivalent to an arrestment in execution of a decree and decree of furthcoming, and to an executed and completed poinding. This gives sequestration, when obtained within four months of notour bankruptcy, equality of ranking with all arrestments and poindings executed not earlier than sixty days before notour bankruptcy and thus prevents any preferences being created thereby.[11]

Effect on personal rights.—A party who has an incomplete and merely personal right to any property falling under the sequestration cannot as a general rule complete his right after the date of the first deliverance, *e.g.*, by intimation of an assignation by the bankrupt to him of an incorporeal moveable right. The right of the trustee is an impediment.[12] But if a party's title to property acquired from the bankrupt requires only entry in a register to complete it—*e.g.*, registration of a transfer of share [13] or recording of a disposition of land in the Register of Sasines [14]—if he completes title before the trustee, the property does not fall within the sequestration.

(5) Procedure in sequestration proceedings.—(i) *Jurisdiction.*[15]— Sequestration may be awarded by the Court of Session or by the sheriff of the county in which the debtor, if alive, has resided or carried on

---

[9] s. 48. Full interest is payable out of any residue after all claims are ranked.
[10] *i.e.*, by recording in the Register of Sasines: s. 103.
[11] *Per* Lord Deas in *Wyper* v. *Harveys* (1861) 23 D. 606.
[12] *e.g.*, assignee of a lease who has not entered into possession: *Clark* v. *West Calder Oil Co.* (1882) 9 R. 1017.
[13] *Morrison* v. *Harrison* (1876) 3 R. 406.
[14] *Cormack* v. *Anderson* (1829) 7 S. 868.
[15] ss. 16–19.

business for the year preceding the date of the petition, and, if deceased, the year preceding his death. If sequestration is awarded by the Court of Session the subsequent proceedings are in the Sheriff Court, and if awarded in more than one court are usually remitted to the court of the sequestration first in date.

Interim preservation of the estate.[16]—The court may take measures for preserving the estate at any time between the presentation of the petition and the confirmation of the trustee.[17] This is done usually by the appointment of a judicial factor who holds office until a trustee is elected by the creditors. The court has power, after presentation of a petition and before election of a trustee by the creditors, to grant warrant to put under safe custody any bank notes, money, bills, cheques or other moveable property, and also, after an award, to cause to be sealed up and put under safe custody the books and papers of the bankrupt and to lock up his shop, warehouse or other repositories.

(ii) *First meeting of creditors*

Election of trustee.—In the deliverance awarding sequestration the court appoints a meeting of creditors to be held to elect a trustee. At this meeting a trustee and commissioners are appointed and the bankrupt submits a state of his affairs.

Persons ineligible to be trustee are the bankrupt, any conjunct or confident person, any person who holds an interest opposed to the general body of creditors,[18] any person whose residence is not within the jurisdiction of the Court of Session,[19] and a minor.[20] Further, circumstances may render a person ineligible, such as collusive transactions entered into by him to secure his election.[21] There must be a majority in value of the creditors, *i.e.*, more than half the value of the debts, supporting the election. The judgment of the sheriff declaring the person elected to be trustee is final.[22] A person once appointed may be removed by the creditors or the court.[23]

Title of creditors to vote.—In order to certiorate the voting value of the claim of a creditor voting he or a mandatory on his behalf must attend the meeting and produce an affidavit and claim duly sworn to as to the verity of the debt and produce vouchers.[24] He may have to

---

[16] ss. 14 and 15.
[17] *Partridge* v. *Baillie* (1873) 1 R. 253.
[18] *Philip Woolfson Ltd., Petrs.*, 1962 S.L.T. 252.
[19] s. 64.
[20] *Threshie*, May 30, 1815, F.C.
[21] *Mann* v. *Dickson* (1857) 19 D. 942.
[22] s. 67. *Grierson* v. *Ogilvy's Tr.*, 1908 S.C. 959; 16 S.L.T. 161.
[23] s. 47.
[24] Prima facie evidence of the debt is all that is required. Contrast claims for ranking, see *infra*.

make deductions. Where he holds a security over any part of the debtor's estate he must in his claim put a specified value on his security, deduct it from his claim and vote only in respect of the balance.[25] He must also value and deduct the obligation of any co-obligant of the bankrupt bound to the creditor with but liable in relief to the bankrupt, e.g., where the bankrupt is cautioner.[26] Thus, on a claim on the estate of a bankrupt firm it is not necessary to value and deduct the claim on the estates of the individual partners, they not being liable in relief to the firm; but in a claim on the estate of a bankrupt partner for a firm debt it is necessary to value and deduct the partner's claim on the estate of the firm and the other partners who are liable in relief to him.[27]

The creditors at the meeting for election of the trustee fix the amount of caution he must find before entering upon his office for due performance of it.

Election of commissioners.—At the meeting for election of the trustee the creditors present or their mandatories elect three commissioners who must be either creditors or mandatories of creditors.[28] Their duties are: to superintend the proceedings of the trustee [29]; to give him their advice and assistance relative to the management of the estate [29]; to concur with him in making compromises, transactions and references to arbitration [30]; to decide as to paying a dividend [31]; to assemble at any time to ascertain the situation of the bankrupt estate [32]; to fix the commission or fee payable to the trustee.[33] Any commissioner may make such report as he thinks proper to a general meeting of creditors.[32] He is precluded from purchasing any part of the estate which is publicly sold.[34]

Bankrupt's state of affairs and position.—At the meeting to elect a trustee the bankrupt must produce a state of his affairs showing his property, the debts due to or by him, the names of his creditors and

---

[25] s. 55; *Clydesdale Bank* v. *Allan,* 1926 S.C. 235; 1926 S.L.T. 204. Provisions to secure correct valuation in voting are contained in s. 58. In questions as to the disposal or management of the subject of the security the creditor votes at the full amount of his debt without deduction. See s. 2 as to meaning of " security."

[26] s. 56.

[27] s. 57. Debts depending on a contingency or annuities due by the bankrupt must be valued by the sheriff: ss. 48–50.

[28] The rules as to these elections correspond to those for election of a trustee, but caution is not required from them: ss. 72, 73.

[29] s. 81.

[30] s. 172; *Hamilton's Exr.* v. *Bank of Scotland,* 1913 S.C. 743; 1913 1 S.L.T. 296; *e.g.,* fixing an upset price for the sale of heritable property under ss. 110, 111.

[31] ss. 81, 121, 127, 131.

[32] s. 81.

[33] ss. 121, 122.

[34] s. 116.

debtors and the rental of the heritable property.[35] He must, under
penalty of imprisonment and forfeiture of the benefit of the Act, give
the trustee every assistance necessary to enable him to execute his duty.
As the bankrupt is deprived of his estate no act or deed of his is
effectual without the consent of the trustee.[36] For failure in duty or
intent to defraud in various ways he is liable to punishment by the
court.[37] Four-fifths in value of the creditors present may give him a
weekly allowance up to three guineas a week if he has complied with
the Act.[38] An undischarged bankrupt cannot get credit for more than
£10 unless he discloses he is an undischarged bankrupt.[39]

(iii) *Duties of the trustee*

These begin with the issue to him of the Act and Warrant of the
court confirming his election as trustee. His appointment is recorded
in a register of sequestrations kept by the Accountant of Court, who
has the duty of supervision of all bankruptcies.[40] To him the trustee
must make, through the sheriff clerk, an annual return of specified
particulars.[41]

(A) EXAMINATION OF THE BANKRUPT.[42]—Within eight days of the
issue of the Act and Warrant the trustee must petition the sheriff for
examination of the bankrupt with a view to ascertaining what his
estate consists of, where it is and what he has done with it or to affect
it.[43] And the sheriff may at any time on the application of the trustee
order examination of the bankrupt's wife and family, clerks, servants,
factors, law agents and others who can give information relative to
his estate on oath.[44]

(B) TAKING POSSESSION AND REALISATION OF THE ESTATE.—The
trustee must as soon as possible take possession of the bankrupt's
estate and the documents relating thereto, make an inventory and
valuation, and transmit these to the Accountant.[45] He must then
convert the estate into money according to the directions of the

---

[35] s. 77.
[36] A person who in ignorance of the bankruptcy has purchased and received goods of
the bankrupt, if ready to pay the price, is not bound to restore them, and a debtor
to the estate who, in ignorance of the bankruptcy, has paid a debt *in bona fide* to the
bankrupt is not bound to pay again to the trustee:—s. 107.
[37] ss. 178 and 182.
[38] s. 74.
[39] s. 182: *Kaye* v. *H.M. Advocate*, 1957 J.C. 55.
[40] ss. 70, 158.
[41] s. 137; Sch. H.
[42] ss. 83–89.
[43] *Delvoitte & Co.* v. *Baillie's Trs.* (1877) 5 R. 143.
[44] s. 86.
[45] ss. 76 and 78.   *Garden, Haig-Scott & Wallace* v. *Stevenson's Tr.*, 1962 S.C. 51
(title deeds).

creditors at a meeting or, if none are given, the advice of the commissioners.[46] Realisation of the heritable estate is usually made by public sale, and any creditor, but not a commissioner, may purchase.[47] A sale by private bargain requires the concurrence of a majority of the creditors in number and value, of the bondholders, if any, and of the Accountant of Court.[48] The trustee must try to recover book debts in full within a year of the award and only thereafter may they be sold.[49] The trustee must lodge all money in bank in his official character; failure may involve him in liability for interest, dismissal from office, and loss of remuneration.[50]

(C) DIVISION OF THE ESTATE.—The whole estate of a bankrupt to which he is beneficially entitled,[51] when reduced into money, and after paying all necessary charges and a commission to the trustee, is divided among those who were creditors of the bankrupt at the date of sequestration, ranked according to their several rights and interests.[52] The vesting of the trustee does not affect such preferable securities as existed at the date of the sequestration and are not null or reducible.[53] Where the security creates a nexus over property in the bankrupt's possession, such as attachments by arrestment, the trustee takes the subject attached, giving effect to the creditor's preference in the ranking.[54] Where the security confers a real right of possession on the creditor, such as lien or pledge, the trustee can recover the security subject only on paying the debt.

Payment of dividends.—There usually are several dividends according as funds are available. The date of payment of the first dividend may not be earlier than four months from the date of the deliverance awarding sequestration.[55] The normal period is six months [56] but a dividend may be accelerated; or it may be postponed.[57] Later dividends may be paid at stated intervals.[58]

Right to dividend.—This is constituted by a ranking. A claim must be made to entitle a creditor to a ranking. To participate in a first dividend a claim for ranking must be lodged within four months

---

[46] s. 78.
[47] The trustee, his law agent or his partners may not purchase: s. 116.
[48] s. 111.
[49] *Stewart* v. *Crookston,* 1910 S.C. 609; 1910, 1 S.L.T. 340; s. 123.
[50] ss. 78 and 79.
[51] *Heritable Reversionary Co. Ltd.* v. *Millar* (1892) 19 R.(H.L.) 43.
[52] s. 117. This applies " unless otherwise provided in the Act."
[53] s. 97 (2); *Littlejohn* v. *Black* (1855) 18 D. 207, *per* Lord President M'Neill.
[54] *Gibson* v. *Greig* (1853) 16 D. 233.
[55] s. 130.
[56] s. 126.
[57] ss. 130, 131.
[58] ss. 128, 129.

of the deliverance awarding sequestration, and creditors must be prepared to prove their claims by appropriate evidence.[59] The trustee then examines and allows or disallows claims and his deliverance is subject to appeal to the court. Finally the trustee makes up a scheme of division of the sum to be divided apportioned among the creditors whose claims have been sustained. A creditor entitled to a ranking who has not claimed to be ranked for a first dividend may do so for a later and is entitled to an equalising dividend if funds are available.[60]

Proof of claims for ranking.—The creditor must produce an affidavit and claim and the vouchers necessary to prove it[61]; and if he claims a preference for the whole or part of the debt, he must expressly make and vouch this claim in his oath.[62] He must specify what securities he holds over the estate and must value and deduct[63] such as affect subjects which would go to increase the general estate for distribution.[64] The trustee, with consent of the commissioners, may demand a conveyance to him of securities deducted for ranking at the expense of the estate on his paying the specified value; or he may reserve to the creditor the full benefit of his security.[65] The creditor ranks only for the balance in either case. Where the creditor holds the obligation of an obligant other than the bankrupt for his debt or a collateral security, while he must specify them, he does not require to make any valuation or deduction therefor for the purpose of ranking.[66] Where the bankrupt is a firm, the rules are special in view of the separate *persona* of a firm and the liability, joint and several, of the partners as co-obligants for the debts of the firm.

Ranking on estates of a firm and partners.—Creditors of a bankrupt firm rank on the firm's estate for the full amount of their debts to the exclusion of the separate creditors of the partners. The firm's creditors

---

[59] Not by reference to the oath of the bankrupt: *Adam* v. *Maclachlan* (1847) 9 D. 560. The trustee may, however, refer to the oath of the claimant: *Jackson* v. *McIver* (1875) 2 R. 882.

[60] s. 119.

[61] ss. 20, 45. The trustee must investigate the claim even though insufficiently vouched: ss. 123, 124.

[62] *Brown* v. *Blaikie* (1849) 11 D. 474.

[63] This does not apply where the creditor claims a preference: *Goudy on Bankruptcy*, 4th ed., 320.

[64] *Royal Bank of Scotland* v. *Millar's Tr.* (1882) 9 R. 679; *University of Glasgow* v. *Yuill's Tr.* (1882) 9 R. 643, *per* Lord President Inglis.

[65] s. 61. If it is not taken over, the creditor may but need not realise it: *Wood* v. *McKay's Trs.*, 1936 S.C. 93; 1936 S.L.T. 71. If his dividend plus proceeds of realisation results in a surplus over his debt, he must account to the trustee, or, if the trustee is discharged, to the bankrupt: *Kinmond, Luke & Co.* v. *Finlay & Co.* (1904) 6 F. 564; 11 S.L.T. 458, who cannot refuse a reconveyance: *Clydesdale Bank* v. *McIntyre*, 1909 S.C. 1405; 1909, 2 S.L.T. 217.

[66] *University of Glasgow* v. *Yuill's Tr., supra.* For the purpose of voting all these are valued and deducted.

are entitled to rank on the separate estates of the partners for the balance unpaid, after exhausting the funds of the company, *pari passu* with the separate creditors of the partners.[67] In ranking on the firm's estate no deduction is made in respect of the creditor's claim against the separate estates of the partners.[68] In ranking on a partner's estate for a firm debt the creditor is entitled to be ranked only for the balance after deducting his claim against the firm.[69]

Rule against double ranking.—It is a consequence of the principle that the bankrupt's estate in sequestration is handed over to the creditors according to the amount of their several debts at the moment of divestiture that when there are several obligants for the same debt, a ranking on the estate of one of them, and for the balance unpaid a ranking on the estate of another, does not permit of a ranking by the latter on the estate of the former by way of relief. To do so would give the latter as creditor a preference over the other creditors.[70] There would be double ranking for the same debt in whole or part. The rule applies in cautionry and bills of exchange. It applies only where there is divestiture of the debtor of his estate and therefore not where the debtor compounds with his creditors.[71] A co-obligant, where there is divestiture, can rank in relief only by paying the debt and claiming in the creditor's place.[72] Wherever there is divestiture of a bankrupt debtor, payment of a dividend is equivalent to payment of the debt [73] only so as to discharge the estate, and the bankrupt remains liable for any deficiency until he is discharged judicially or by his creditors extrajudicially.[74] Where the creditor ranks on the estate of all the co-obligants for his full debt, he may do so to the effect of drawing twenty shillings in the pound and no more, and there is no recourse by one of the estates against the others.[75]

Preferential debts.—Some creditors, though unsecured, are entitled to payment in priority to other creditors. There are paid in priority to all other debts the remuneration of the trustee and the law agent's

---

[67] In England it is only if there is a surplus after paying 20s. in the pound out of the firm's estate to firm creditors or out of a partner's estate to his private creditors that the creditors of the one can claim against the estate of the other: *Nicol* v. *Christie* (1827) 5 S. 882.

[68] s. 57. This assumes the creditor is a third party. Where the firm is creditor of the partners, the trustee of the firm will rank *pari passu* with the separate creditors of the partners.

[69] *Ibid.* The valuation and deduction are made by the trustee on the partner's estate: s. 62.

[70] *Anderson* v. *MacKinnon* (1876) 3 R. 608; *Mackinnon* v. *Monkhouse* (1881) 9 R. 393.

[71] *Mackinnon* v. *Monkhouse, supra.* It is a rule of the common law and applies wherever there is divestiture in bankruptcy.

[72] *Ewart* v. *Latta* (1865) 3 M.(H.L.) 36; *Harvie's Trs.* v. *Bank of Scotland* (1885) 12 R. 1141.

[73] *McMillan* v. *Smyth* (1879) 6 R. 601.

[74] *Per* Lord President Inglis in *Mackinnon* v. *Monkhouse, supra.*

[75] Bell's Comm., ii, 416.

account, and death-bed and funeral expenses in the case of a deceased debtor's estate.[76] Thereafter there rank *pari passu inter se* various claims including claims for rates, taxes, wages, national insurance payments and others.[77] Thereafter the general creditors rank *pari passu inter se*.[78] Postponed creditors, entitled to be ranked after all other creditors have been paid in full, are the bankrupt's wife claiming in respect of property she has lent or entrusted to her husband or allowed to become immixed with his funds,[79] and parties who have lent money to a firm or sold to it the goodwill of a business on terms which involve the receipt of a share in the profits of the firm's business or interest at a rate varying with the profits.[80]

(6) Deeds of arrangement and composition contracts.—The normal course of sequestration proceedings may be superseded at the instance of the bankrupt and of his creditors or particular majorities of them in two ways, both of them sanctioned and regulated by the Act of 1913. In both cases specified majorities of the creditors are empowered to bind a minority and the approval of the court is required. These ways are winding up by deed of arrangement, and the composition contract.

(i) *Deed of arrangement* [81]

A deed of arrangement is a deed embodying an arrangement between a sequestrated bankrupt and his creditors having the effect of annulling the sequestration process. The bankrupt and the creditors arrange the terms of the deed as they choose. The arrangement may provide for the realising and distributing of the estate by the creditors themselves or by handing it over to a trustee for realisation or to the debtor himself on his undertaking to pay a composition.[82] It must, however, be approved by the court as reasonable, that is, one which may fairly be enforced on a dissentient minority of the creditors.[83] If approved by the court after hearing parties having an interest to object, it is thereafter binding on all the creditors as if they had acceded to it. The sequestration is declared at an end, but receives full effect so far as necessary for the purpose of preventing, challenging or setting

[76] s. 118.
[77] s. 118.
[78] Contingent creditors have their debts valued and a dividend is set aside until the right to it emerges.
[79] Married Women's Property Act, 1881, s. 1 (4).
[80] Partnership Act, 1890, s. 3.
[81] ss. 34–39.
[82] s. 34.
[83] An offer of less than 5s. in the pound is said to be an additional reason for inquiring into the reasonableness of the composition offered: *Stone* v. *Woodhouse, Hambly & Co.* 1937 S.C. 824; 1937 S.L.T. 626.

aside preferences over the estate.[84]   The deed need not provide for
the discharge of the bankrupt, for the arrangement may be to hand
over the estate to the bankrupt, he undertaking to pay so much in the
pound of each creditor's debt and without caution, so that his failure
to pay the composition revives the original debt and for it the creditor
may sue him. [85]

At the meeting for the election of a trustee or at any subsequent
meeting called for the purpose a majority in number and three-fourths
in value of the creditors present or represented at such meeting may
resolve that the estate be wound up by deed of arrangement and that
an application be made to the court to sist procedure in the sequestration for a period not exceeding two months.   If such a resolution is
carried at the first meeting, it is not necessary to elect a trustee.   The
bankrupt or any person appointed by the meeting then reports the
resolution to the court within four days and applies for a sist of proceedings.   The application is usually granted.   If within the period of
sist the creditors produce to the court a deed of arrangement subscribed
by or by authority of a majority in number and three-fourths in value
of the creditors, the court, after hearing parties, may approve thereof
and declare the sequestration at an end.

(ii) *Composition contract* [86]

The essence of a judicial composition contract is that the bankrupt
buys from his creditors the estate which would fall to be divided among
all the creditors while intact in the hands of the trustee and the consideration is the value, in the opinion of the parties to the contract,
of what the creditors would have drawn in the shape of dividends.
It is also a contract between the bankrupt and each creditor to purchase
the value of his dividend, that is, its value in the sequestration and,
therefore, its value after deduction of securities.[87]   In general, the
advantage of its adoption is that the estate can more readily and
cheaply be realised by the bankrupt himself and he can therefore afford
to make the highest bid for it.   Also the creditors avoid the risk of
taking over the bankrupt's contracts.   The creditors are secured by
caution and may require other security.   If the composition is not
paid, the original claim of a creditor does not revive: he is only a

---

[84] s. 37. This is a provision in favour of the creditors and would not apply if the estate
were made over by the creditors to the bankrupt or a purchaser unless the right to
challenge was expressly assigned by the creditors to the bankrupt or purchaser.
Smith & Co. v. *Smyth* (1889) 16 R. 392.

[85] *Alexander and Austin* v. *Yuille* (1873) 1 R. 185.

[86] ss. 134–142.

[87] See *Macbride* v. *Stevenson* (1884) 11 R. 702, opinion of Lord President Inglis. As a
contract it and the discharge of the debtor may be reduced for breach of the regulations
in the Act, or for collusion to obtain discharge, or, if induced by fraud, either as a
whole by the whole body of creditors or by an individual creditor as regards himself.

creditor of the bankrupt and his cautioner for the amount of the agreed-on composition. As the offer must apply to the debts of all creditors, the bankrupt is entitled to be discharged upon the contract being approved by the court.[88] He is reinvested in his estate as it was in the hands of the trustee.[88]

The offer of composition must be made either at the meeting to elect a trustee or at any subsequent meeting called for the purpose by the trustee with consent of the commissioners. If a majority in number and three-fourths in value of the creditors present decide that the offer be entertained for consideration, another meeting is held, after examination of the bankrupt and due advertisement, to decide as to acceptance of the offer of composition and security; and if acceptance be resolved upon by a majority in number and three-fourths in value of creditors present, the trustee reports the resolution to the court, which, after hearing objections and being otherwise satisfied, may approve of the offer or refuse to sustain it.[89]

When claims for payment of the composition are made, neither the bankrupt nor the cautioner can object to the claim of any creditor for a debt which the bankrupt has given up in the state of his affairs as due by him or which has been admitted without question to be reckoned in the acceptance of the offer of composition; nor can they object to the security held by any creditor, unless such debt or security was stated in the offer of composition as objected to and notice in writing of the objection given to the creditor.[90] In the case of other debts, if illiquid, they must be constituted before diligence to enforce the composition can be done. Further, no person who has not produced an oath as creditor can claim against the cautioner after the lapse of two years from the date of the deliverance approving the composition, but the claim against the bankrupt is not affected.[91]

(7) Discharge of the bankrupt.—At common law an insolvent debtor could obtain protection for his person by *cessio*, but future acquired property was not protected from the diligence of creditors whether prior or posterior. The main feature of sequestration is the discharge of the bankrupt after surrender of his estate. It is a privilege, not a right. The power to determine whether it shall be granted or refused rests generally with the creditors as a body, and it requires the sanction of the court.[92]

---

[88] See *infra, Discharge of the Bankrupt.* He may disentitle himself. *Cf.* note 87, *supra.*

[89] ss. 134–136. A subsequent offer may be made: s. 142.

[90] s. 140.

[91] s. 141.

[92] s. 143 sets out the times and majorities necessary for a competent application for discharge. Where the statutory procedure is not available, application may be made to the *nobile officium—Laings, Petrs.,* 1962 S.C. 168.

There are certain statutory conditions which must be observed.[92]
Application must be made to the court by the bankrupt for his discharge, and it must be proved to the court that a dividend or composition of not less that five shillings in the pound has been paid out
of the bankrupt estate or security for payment thereof found to the
satisfaction of the creditors; or, if not so paid or secured, that failure
to pay has arisen from circumstances for which the bankrupt cannot
justly be held responsible.[93]

The court must further be satisfied that the conduct of the bankrupt
warrants discharge. A report by the trustee on the bankrupt's conduct
must be produced along with the petition for discharge. It should
state whether he has made a fair discovery and surrender of his estate;
whether he has attended the diets of examination; whether he has been
guilty of any collusion; and whether his bankruptcy has arisen from
innocent misfortune or from culpable or undue conduct.[94] Further,
the bankrupt must make oath, if required by the trustee or any creditor,
that he has made a full and fair surrender, and has not granted or
promised any preference or security, nor made or promised any payment, nor entered into any secret or collusive transactions to obtain
the concurrence of any creditor to his discharge.[95] Further, it may
be made a condition of discharge that a portion of an alimentary fund
enjoyed by the bankrupt be given up to creditors.[96]

Effects of discharge.—Although the bankrupt be discharged the
sequestration may go on until the whole assets falling under it have
been realised and divided. But after discharge no claim can be made
against the bankrupt in respect of any debt that might have been
ranked for in the sequestration.[97] The bankrupt is not released from
any obligation incurred by him subsequent to the date of sequestration
or from obligations depending on contingencies too remote to admit
of their valuation, e.g., the obligation to aliment relatives in the event
of their becoming indigent.[98] Nor does the discharge relieve the

---

[93] s. 146. A discharge should not be refused on the ground of mere improvident trading:
Phillips (1885) 13 R. 91; *Gemmell* (1902) 4 F. 441. Discharge will be refused if the
expenses of the sequestration are not paid out of the estate: *M'Carter* v. *Aikman*
(1893) 20 R. 1090.

[94] s. 143. Where the trustee has not been confirmed, the court may, in the exercise
of its *nobile officium*, grant a discharge to the bankrupt—*Black, Petr*. 1964 S.L.T. 308.

[95] s. 144. The penalties on both the bankrupt and the creditor are severe. The bankrupt
forfeits all right to discharge and the benefits of the Act, and discharge may be annulled:
ss. 150–151; *Pendreigh's Tr*. v. *M'Laren & Co*. (1871) 9 M.(H.L.) 49 (creditor). As
to the effect at common law of such a *pactum illicitum*, see *Farmer's Mart Co*. v.
Milne, 1914 S.C. 129; 1913, 2 S.L.T. 410; *Macfarlane* v. *Nicoll* (1864) 3 M. 237.

[96] *Hamilton* v. *Caldwell*, 1916 S.C. 809; 1916, 2 S.L.T. 50. As to Government pay or
pension, see s. 148.

[97] s. 144.

[98] *Downs* v. *Wilson's Tr*. (1886) 13 R. 1101.

bankrupt of any debt due to the Crown.[99] The discharge does not
release co-obligants of the bankrupt who were such at the date of
sequestration, even though the creditor had assented to the discharge
of the bankrupt.[1] In a discharge without composition the bankrupt
is not reinvested in his estate. It remains with the trustee and, after
his discharge, with the creditors, who may claim right to property later
recovered by petition to the Court of Session to appoint a new trustee.[2]
The bankrupt, after the discharge of himself and of the trustee, has a
title to sue on a claim which the trustee has not chosen to pursue.[3]

(8) Discharge of the trustee.[4]—After a final division of the funds
the trustee summons creditors who have produced an oath in the
sequestration to consider as to his application for discharge, and
thereafter he may apply to the court, who may, after hearing any
creditor who appears in order to object, pronounce or refuse decree
of exoneration.[5]

Unclaimed dividends.[6]—Before his discharge the trustee must deposit
in bank any unclaimed dividends and any unapplied balances, and the
deposit receipt is transmitted to the Accountant of Court.   Thereafter
any person producing evidence of his right may apply to the Accountant for authority to receive any such dividend which has been so
deposited within the seven years preceding the application.   Seven
years after the date of deposit the deposit receipt is handed over to the
Queen's Lord Treasurer's Remembrancer, who obtains payment of it.
But creditors have the same right to claim payment against the
Remembrancer as they had against the Accountant.[7]

Any surplus in the sequestration is paid to the bankrupt in virtue
of his radical right to the estate.[8]

(9) Recall of the sequestration.[9]—The deliverance awarding sequestration is not subject to review by appeal, but it is competent to present
a petition to a judge of the Court of Session for its recall at the instance
of particular persons on particular grounds and within particular times.

[99] s. 147.
[1] s. 52.
[2] *Whyte* v. *Northern Heritable Securities Investment Co.* (1891) 18 R.(H.L.) 37.
[3] *Cooper* v. *Frame & Co.* (1893) 20 R. 920; 1 S.L.T. 125.
[4] ss. 152–155.
[5] s. 152. A creditor may object on the ground, *inter alia*, that there are assets still to be
recovered: *Hamilton's Tr.* v. *Caldwell*, 1918 S.C. 190; 1917 2 S.L.T. 159.
[6] s. 153.
[7] See *Scott* v. *King's and Lord Treasurer's Remembrancer*, 1920 S.C. 555; 1920 2 S.L.T.
141.
[8] For observations on the nature of the bankrupt's radical right, see *White* v. *Stevenson*,
1956 S.C. 84.
[9] ss. 30–32 and 43.

A petition for recall of a sequestration is competent within forty days of its award at the instance of any debtor whose estate has been sequestrated without his consent, or at the instance of the successors of a deceased debtor whose estate has been sequestrated without their consent, the award not having been made on the application of a mandatory of the deceased, or at the instance of any creditor.[10]   The onus is on the petitioner to show cause why it should be recalled.

The grounds for recall are such as would have been grounds for opposing the award at the time it was made, whether then stated [11] or not,[12] or which have since emerged.[13]   Where the ground is an *ex facie* defect in the sequestration proceedings, the court must recall. But where nullity of the proceedings can be made out only on investigation, that is, where the defect is latent, the court has a discretion as to recall, even where nullity is made out.[14]   Such defect may be, for example, that notour bankruptcy has not been properly constituted,[15] or the creditors applying or concurring were not duly qualified.

Apart from these cases, a petition for recall is competent on similar grounds where the debtor was deceased and his successor was cited edictally [16] in the application for an award, at the instance of the successor and any person having interest, if made before advertisement of payment of the first dividend.[17]   A petition for recall is also competent at any time at the instance of nine-tenths in number and value of the creditors ranked on the estate.   The onus in this case is on persons opposing recall to show cause why it should not be granted.[18] Recall is also competent within three months of the award, at the instance of the Accountant of Court or any creditor or other person having interest, on the ground that a majority of the creditors in number and value reside in England or Ireland and that from the situation of the property of the bankrupt or other causes his estate and effects ought to be distributed among the creditors under the bankruptcy or insolvency laws of England or Ireland.   The court has a discretion whether or not to grant recall on this ground.   It is a question of *forum conveniens*, that is, of the balance of convenience.[19]

---

[10] s. 30.
[11] *Elder* v. *Thomson, Elder & Burn* (1850) 12 D. 994.
[12] *Campbell* v. *Myles* (1853) 16 D. 685.
[13] *Muir* v. *Stevenson* (1850) 12 D. 512.
[14] *Ballantyne* v. *Barr* (1867) 5 M. 330.
[15] *Michie* v. *Young*, 1962 S.L.T.(Notes) 70.
[16] This is a formal citation where the person to be cited is out of Scotland or cannot be found in Scotland.
[17] s. 30.
[18] s. 31.
[19] s. 43. Formerly forty days' residence of a debtor in Scotland entitled him to sequestration in Scotland.

Effect of recall.—The effect of a recall is to reinvest the bankrupt in his estate subject to all legal or voluntary preferences which were, but for sequestration, unobjectionable.[20] But pending any petition for recall and until sequestration be finally recalled, the proceedings in the sequestration go on as if no such petition had been presented,[21] and therefore transactions which have been bona fide carried through under it, *e.g.*, sales, discharges for debt, etc., are left intact.

(10) Summary sequestration.[22]—The Bankruptcy (Scotland) Act, 1913, abolished [23] the old process of *cessio bonorum*, and introduced a new process known as summary sequestration, applicable to estates where the debtor's assets of every description do not exceed in the aggregate £300 in value. It is not applicable to the estates of deceased debtors or of a firm. Subject to certain exceptions [24] and except so far as they are not consistent with the special provisions for summary sequestration, the whole provisions of the Act regulating ordinary sequestrations apply to summary sequestrations.[25]

The main differences are as follows. The court has a discretion either to entertain an application or order the sequestration to proceed as an ordinary sequestration. The debtor may apply without the concurrence of creditors. The debts of creditors applying need amount only to £10. A state of affairs is produced at the outset to enable the court to say whether to proceed as a summary sequestration. An award may be refused where in ordinary sequestration the court has no discretion, *e.g.*, where the bankrupt applies. The second meeting of creditors is held at no fixed time after examination of the bankrupt, for the statute contemplates that normally the estate will be realised and ready for distribution by the second meeting and a dividend announced. The dividend is declared, not by the creditors, but by the trustee and commissioners. After a final division of the funds the trustee applies to the Accountant of Court for a certificate that he is entitled to discharge, and reports to the sheriff, who orders advertisement in the *Edinburgh Gazette* of a diet for hearing any objections. If there are no funds for dividend the sheriff may in writing dispense with further procedure and the bankrupt may forthwith apply for discharge without consent of creditors.

5. EXTRA-JUDICIAL SETTLEMENTS WITH CREDITORS

These are usually in the form of either a trust deed granted by the debtor or an offer of composition by him.

---

20 Goudy, 4th ed., 146.   21 s. 37.
22 ss. 174–177. See Goudy, pp. 447 *et seq.*
23 s. 191, Sched. 1.
24 s. 176.
25 This includes deeds of arrangement and composition settlements.

(1) The trust deed.—Nature and characteristics.—This is often more economical and speedy than sequestration. There is no statutory form. The deed is one granted by the debtor in which he conveys to a named trustee his whole estate for realisation and division among his creditors according to their rights and preferences, with a provision for restitution of any reversion to the debtor.[26] As however no creditor is bound to accede to a trust deed, one recalcitrant creditor may stultify this proposed arrangement. For, in the first place, such a deed is reducible under the Act, 1696, c. 5, if granted after the constitution of notour bankruptcy or within sixty days prior thereto, at the instance of a non-acceding creditor, as a fraudulent preference.[27] In the second place a non-acceding creditor may have the deed superseded by sequestration under the Bankruptcy Act.[28] But apart from the effect of these statutes a voluntary trust deed granted by a party insolvent but not notour bankrupt, for behoof of all his creditors equally, and containing no extraordinary clauses,[29] is irrevocable by the granter, and good and available to bind non-acceding as well as acceding creditors, if the estate be reduced into possession of the trustee and the debtor be not rendered bankrupt within sixty days thereafter. As, however, such a trustee has no statutory title he must complete his right to the various subjects conveyed to him by appropriate methods. Should he fail to do so, the subjects left in the debtor's possession may be attached by diligence at the instance of non-acceding creditors or of creditors to whom the debtor may have become indebted subsequent to the granting of the deed. When the trustee has completed his title to the subjects forming the estate the result is that nothing is left with the debtor which can be attached by diligence. For the trustee in such case does not represent the debtor, but the creditors in their just proportions, they having the radical *jus crediti*, and all preferences by arrestment are excluded.[30] As regards illegal preferences already granted by the debtor, the trustee has no title to challenge these, unless the trust deed confers such power and a creditor entitled to challenge has acceded to the trust, and has assigned his title to sue to the trustee.[31]

---

[26] Bell's Comm., ii, 385.

[27] *Mackenzie* v. *Calder* (1868) 6 M. 833. It is not so reducible at common law. It is also reducible under the Act, 1621, c. 18, if it defeats lawful diligence already begun: *ibid.*

[28] See *infra.*

[29] Such as would be inconsistent with equitable distribution: *Nicolson* v. *Johnstone & Wright* (1872) 11 M. 179, *per* Lord Deas.

[30] *Nicolson* v. *Johnstone & Wright, supra.* The debtor retains a radical right in the estate, and the reversion, if any, remains open to arrestment: *Globe Insurance Co.* v. *Scott's Trs.* (1849) 11 D. 618.

[31] *Fleming's Trs.* v. *M'Hardy* (1892) 19 R. 542.

Ranking of claims of creditors.—It is now usually stipulated in the trust deed that the rankings of creditors are to be the same as under the Bankruptcy Act. This means that a secured creditor requires to value his security and rank only on the difference. If there is no such stipulation a secured creditor would be entitled to rank for the full amount of the debt without deducting his security and then make what he can of his security to the effect of receiving full payment of his debt.[32]

In dividing the estate the trustee is bound to provide for all claims intimated to him, including those of non-acceding creditors.[33]

Supersession by sequestration.—This is not always possible, for if all the creditors accede the deed becomes a mutual contract and excludes the right of creditors to challenge the deed on the ground of insolvency or notour bankruptcy of the debtor or to resort to sequestration.[34] If, however, not all the creditors consent to the deed the trust may at any time be superseded by sequestration at the instance of either a non-acceding creditor,[35] or of the debtor with concurrence of a non-acceding creditor, or of a creditor who has acceded, in the event of non-acceding creditors taking proceedings which might result in giving them preferential rights.[36]

The effect of sequestration is that the estate is vested in the trustee in the sequestration, and the trust deed falls without any process of reduction, and any rights acquired under the private trust deed must be asserted in the bankruptcy proceedings.[37]

(2) The extra-judicial composition contract.[38]—This is more suitable than a trust deed where the debtor is engaged in business and it is intended that he carry on rather than that it be realised.

Nature and characteristics.—A composition contract is an agreement between a debtor and his creditors whereby the creditors agree to accept a portion of their debts in full discharge thereof. It may be with some only of the creditors, a " special composition," or with all, a " general composition."

It may be carried out in a variety of ways. The most common is for the debtor to offer a composition of so much per pound with or

---

[32] *Kirkcaldy* v. *Middleton* (1841) 4 D. 202.
[33] *Ogilvie* v. *Taylor* (1887) 14 R. 399.
[34] *Campbell* v. *Macfarlane* (1862) 24 D. 1097. A creditor's consent may be proved in writing or by oath or in some cases by parole evidence: Bell's Comm., ii, 393 *et seq.*
[35] *Kyd* v. *Waterston* (1880) 7 R. 884.
[36] *Jopp* v. *Hay* (1844) 7 D. 260.
[37] *Salaman* v. *Rosslyn's Trs.* (1900) 3 F. 298; 8 S.L.T. 26. The private trustee has a lien over assets in his possession for any expenses he may have incurred and may obtain a preferential ranking therefor: *Thomson* v. *Tough's Tr.* (1880) 7 R. 1035. Contrast *Mess* v. *Sime's Tr.* (1899) 1 F.(H.L.) 22; 6 S.L.T. 207.
[38] See *Goudy on Bankruptcy*, 4th ed., pp. 489 *et seq.*

without security, and grant bills payable in instalments for that amount. This confers on each creditor in the event of failure in payment a liquid debt on which diligence may at once proceed.

The effect is that the debtor remains in possession of his estate and usually carries on his business. The arrangement differs from composition in sequestration in that it does not imply divestiture of the debtor; it binds no creditor who has not acceded, so that the estate remains open to his diligence; the creditor does not, unless the contract so requires, deduct securities; and if the composition is not paid, the original debt revives.

Unless otherwise specially agreed, in a contract with general creditors, it is implied that all the creditors will be treated with equality, and that they all concur in the arrangement. Usually a time limit for concurrence is stated. If this or any of the express conditions of the contract, such as giving security, or obtaining a cautioner, is not implemented, no creditor is bound by his acceptance of the offer. Any misrepresentation by the debtor as to his estate renders the whole contract voidable. Secret preferences, given in order to obtain a creditor's consent to the composition, are voidable at common law as being *pactum illicitum*.

CHAPTER 12

THE LAW OF COMPANIES

I. DEFINITION

A DEFINITION which brings out the chief distinctive features of a
company is—" A company is an association of persons formed for
the purpose of carrying on some business or undertaking in the name
of the association, each member having the right, subject to the regulations governing the administration of the association, to transfer his
interest therein to any other person." These features are thus (a) it
is a legal person different from the individuals who compose its membership, therein resembling a partnership; (b) its identity is not affected
by change in its membership, i.e., the members may change from time
to time without the necessity either of consent between the members
or of novation as regards the creditors,[1] therein differing from a
partnership: an apparent but not a real exception is that there must be
in the constitution of a private company a provision for the consent
of the members through the directors to a change in the membership;
(c) it enters into relations with third parties through its officers.

II. CLASSIFICATION

Companies may be classified according to the authority under which
they have been constituted: (a) under the common law, (b) under
Royal Charter granted by the Crown, (c) under the Companies Clauses
Acts, (d) under the Companies Acts. Only with the first and last of
these is this chapter concerned.

Common law companies.—Some still exist, but they cannot now be
created. These Joint Stock Companies are unincorporated companies
or large partnerships with transferable shares. They were recognised
in Scotland prior to the Companies Acts. Their leading features are [2]
the separate *persona* of the company, the right to sue and be sued in
the company's name with the names of the directors added, the
transferability of the stock, and the management of the company's
affairs by directors and officials, not by the shareholders. Other
characteristics are as follows. As in the case of partnerships proper,

---

[1] *Smith* v. *Anderson* (1880) 15 Ch.D. 247, *per* James L.J. at 273.
[2] *Insurance Company of Scotland* v. *Gairn* (1827) 5 S. 348. Lord President Inglis in
Muir v. *City of Glasgow Bank* (1878) 6 R. 392 at 399; (1879) 6 R. (H.L.) 21.

the liability of the members is unlimited; debts must first be constituted against the company before any shareholder can be called upon to pay; and the company cannot hold land in the corporate name; it must be held in name of trustees for the company.

Companies registered under the companies acts.—The first Act dealing with the incorporation, regulation and winding up of joint stock companies, limited and unlimited, including those established in Scotland, was that of 1856, amended in 1857 and 1858. These allowed but did not compel incorporation with limited or unlimited liability. These are the " Joint Stock Companies Acts." They were repealed by the Companies Act, 1862, which compelled incorporation of large partnerships. The act provided [3] that no company or partnership consisting of more than twenty (or in the case of a banking company, ten) members could after November 2, 1862, be formed unless registered under the Act. That is, new companies formed after that date must be registered under the Act, and thus incorporated. The Act permitted existing companies formed and registered under the Joint Stock Companies Acts, and companies registered but not formed under these Acts and others already formed but un-registered, to register, if consisting of seven or more members. Provision was further made for unregistered companies being wound up by the court compulsorily. The Act of 1862 was amended by several Acts and in 1908, 1929 and 1948 codifying Acts were passed which had an application similar to the Act of 1862.

The Act of 1948 provides [4] accordingly that no company, association, or partnership consisting of more than twenty persons (ten in a banking business) shall be formed for the purpose of carrying on any business that has for its object the acquisition of gain by the company, association, or partnership, or by the individual members thereof, unless it is registered as a company under the Act, or is formed in pursuance of some other Act of Parliament, or of letters patent. Any such companies not so registering are illegal associations. The statute means to deal with people who are associated together for the purpose of *carrying on a business* having for its object the acquisition of gain.[5] This provision does not apply to Trade Unions,[6] or to oversea companies, except to regulate the conditions under which such companies may have a place of business in Great Britain and may offer their shares for sale in Great Britain.

---

[3] s. 4.
[4] ss. 434, 429.
[5] *Smith* v. *Anderson* (1880) 15 Ch.D. 247 at 278; *Greenberg* v. *Cooperstein* [1926] 1 Ch. 657.
[6] Trade Union Act, 1871, s. 5, Companies Act, 1948, s. 459 (9) (*b*).

III. FORMATION OF A COMPANY UNDER THE COMPANIES ACT, 1948

1. Registration and its effects [7]

It is essential to the formation of a company under the Companies Acts that it be registered. The Act of 1948 (repeating the provision of the earlier Acts) provides for the establishment of offices for that purpose under the control of the Board of Trade with officers called " Registrars " appointed by the Board. The company is registered under its chosen name. In order to obtain registration, certain documents, including in particular a memorandum of association, containing the constitution, require to be lodged, and fees, proportioned to the amount of the company's nominal capital,[8] paid. If the documents are in order and the fees paid the registrar issues a certificate of incorporation under the Act.

The certificate is conclusive evidence of the registration and therefore of the incorporation of the company under the Act.[9] The company is thereafter a legal entity distinct from the members.[10] Once registered, it must comply with the provisions of the Act with regard to making returns of various kinds to the registrar, and if these are not complied with it may lose the benefits of the Act by being ordered to be wound up [11] or in some other way. As the registers are public and may be inspected by any person who pays the necessary fee, the documents so filed and returns made are public documents, and accordingly anyone, whether shareholder or outsider, who has dealings with the company must be taken to have notice thereof, and of their terms.

2. Forms in which a company is registrable

A company may be registered, in terms of liability of the members for its debts, in various forms, namely, with unlimited liability of members, with liability limited by guarantee, with liability limited by shares, with liability limited as to the shareholders but unlimited as to the directors, or as an association not formed for profit.[12]

In an unlimited company, each shareholder is liable for all the debts of the company. In a company limited by guarantee the members of the company undertake to contribute, in the event of the company being wound up, a certain sum to pay its debts.[13] In a

---

[7] s. 424.
[8] Sched. 12.
[9] s. 15.
[10] s. 13 (2); *Salomon* v. *Salomon & Co. Ltd.* [1897] A.C. 22; *Lee* v. *Lee's Air Farming Ltd.* [1961] A.C. 12.
[11] s. 222.
[12] ss. 1, 19, 202, 212.
[13] *Robertson* v. *British Linen Bank* (1874) 18 R. 1225.

company limited by shares each member is liable only for the amount of the shares which he has agreed to take.

A company may also be registered either as a public company, in which case the minimum number of members is seven and the maximum unlimited, or as a private company, in which case the minimum number is two and the maximum limited.[14]

3. The company's constitution if limited by shares

(1) **How effected.**—Any seven or more persons (two if a private company, as after defined), associated for any lawful purpose, may, by subscribing their names to a memorandum of association, and otherwise complying with the requirements of the Act in respect of registration, form an incorporated company with limited liability.[15] The effect of the corresponding section of the Act of 1862 was considered by the House of Lords in the case of *Salomon* v. *Salomon & Co. Ltd.* [1897] A.C. 22, the so-called " one-man company " case, the most important case in company law, in which it was held that the true meaning of the legislature must be taken to be that, when the formalities prescribed by the Act have been complied with, and there is a memorandum subscribed by seven persons for one share each, the company, however small, when duly registered, comes into existence as a real independent legal entity or *persona* and cannot be treated as a sham or an *alias* for the promoter merely because six of the seven shareholders are his nominees or even trustees—mere dummies—nor does it signify what were the motives or schemes of the promoter.

(2) **The constituting documents.**—The principal document is the memorandum of association. The purpose of the memorandum is to define (1) the name of the company, (2) the situation of the registered office, (3) the objects, *i.e.*, business objects, of the company, (4) that the liability of the members is limited, and (5) the capital of the company. These are known as the statutory conditions of the memorandum. It may contain other conditions, but need not, and rarely does. Another document, the articles of association, may be registered also. The object of the articles is to regulate the rights and duties of the members among themselves (*inter se*). They contain the rules for the " internal management " of the company. These are the " constituting documents " of the company, and their effect is subject to the provisions of the Companies Act.

(3) **General legal effect of memorandum and articles as constituting documents.**—(*a*) *Relation of memorandum to articles.*—The memorandum of association is the dominant instrument. The articles of the

---

14 *Infra*, p. 329.
15 s. 1 (1).

company are subordinate to and controlled by the memorandum. " The memorandum of association is, as it were, the area beyond which the action of the company cannot go; inside that area the share holders may make such regulations for thier own government as they think fit." [16]   Accordingly, in so far as the articles purport to confer on the company powers beyond the company's sphere of action, they are invalid and ineffectual.   If, however, there be an ambiguity in the memorandum, in respect of a matter which need not be but is contained in the memorandum, the articles, as a contemporaneous document, may, it is said, be used to explain it.[17]

(b) Implied covenant between company and members

The effect of the memorandum and articles upon incorporation of the company is, as between the company and its members, to bind the company and the members, including future members, thereof as if these documents had respectively been signed and sealed by each member, whether original or subsequent, and contained covenants on the part of each member to observe all the provisions of the memorandum and articles, subject to the provisions of the Act.[18]   As the " implied covenant " is between the members and the company, the company is entitled, as a general rule, i.e., unless in exceptional cases, to sue its members for the enforcement of its articles, and to restrain a breach by them.   Likewise the company may be sued by a member qua member for breach of the articles by the company.[19]

(c) Articles a contract between members

The articles, in addition to constituting a contract between the company and its members, regulate the rights of the members inter se. It is quite true that there is in terms no such contract between the individual members of the company; but the articles do not any the less regulate their rights inter se.[20]

(d) Articles as affecting third parties

The articles do not constitute a contract with a third party, e.g., a promoter, even though also a shareholder.   But as the articles are public documents a third party is fixed with notice of the directors' powers and the limitations thereon.[21]   On the other hand, such a

---

[16] Per Lord Cairns L.C. in Ashbury Railway Carriage & Iron Co. v. Riche, L.R. 7 H.L. 653, 671.
[17] Per Buckley J. in Southern Brazilian Rio Grande Do Sul Ry. [1905] 2 Ch. 78, at p. 84; Marshall Fleming & Co., 1938 S.L.T. 527.
[18] s. 20.
[19] Lord Herschell in Welton v. Saffrey [1897] A.C. 299; Burland v. Earle [1902] A.C. 83; Browne v. La Trinidad, 37 Ch.D. 1; Oakbank Oil Co. v. Crum (1882) 10 R. (H.L.) 11.
[20] Lord Herschell in Welton v. Saffrey, cit. sup., at 315.
[21] Notwithstanding the rule, there may be a question whether an agent of the company who has no authority has an ostensible authority, see Houghton & Co. v. Nothard, Lowe & Wills Ltd. [1927] 1 K.B. 246.

third person need not inquire into the regularity of the company's internal proceedings, *i.e.*, whether the regulations have in fact been observed in a particular case. The rule *omnia rite acta praesumuntur* applies to protect him.[22] The rule is based upon the principle of convenience otherwise business could not be carried on.[23] But a person dealing with the company who has notice of an irregularity cannot found upon the rule.[24]

(e) Alterability of memorandum and articles

The memorandum is unalterable except in certain limited respects defined in the Act,[25] short of winding up and reforming the company. Hence if it contains anything not required by the Act and not capable of inclusion in the articles, this *may* be unalterable, unless alteration is specially provided for in the memorandum itself.[26] The articles are always alterable by the company and no article can validly be declared unalterable. The court, where oppression is complained of by a minority of members, may alter or add to the memorandum or articles, and any further alteration or addition inconsistent therewith may require the leave of the court.[27]

(4) The memorandum of association.—*(a) Form.*[28]—The memorandum must bear the same stamp as if it were a deed, and must be signed by each subscriber in presence of, and the signatures be attested by, at least one witness.[29] There must be not less than seven subscribers, and in the case of a private company not less than two.[30]

Above the signatures and below the "conditions" is a clause which runs:

"We, the several persons whose names and addresses are subscribed, are desirous of being formed into a company in pursuance of this memorandum of association, and we respectively agree to take the number of shares in the capital of the company set opposite our respective names."

(b) The contents or "conditions" of the memorandum

1. *The name of the company.*—"The name of the Company is The   Company, Limited."

No company can be registered with a name which, in the opinion of the Board of Trade, is undesirable.[31] This is to prevent a company

---

22 *Heiton* v. *Waverley Hydropathic Co.* (1877) 4 R. 830.
23 *Biggerstaff* v. *Rowatt's Wharf Co.* [1896] 2 Ch. 93.
24 *Howard* v. *Patent Ivory Manufacturing Co.,* (1888) 38 Ch.D. 156.
25 ss. 5, 22, 395.
26 s. 23.
27 s. 210. *Meyer* v. *Scottish Coop. Wholesale Soc.* 1958 S.C. (H.L.) 40.
28 s. 11 and Sch. 1, Table B.
29 s. 3.
30 s. 1 (1).   31 s. 17.

by reason of its name getting the business of another company with a similar name. If a limited company, it must use the word " Limited " as the last word in the name.

Every limited company is required to paint or affix its name, including the word " Limited," outside every office or place where its business is carried on, to have its name engraven on its seal, and to have its name mentioned in all business letters of the company and in all its notices and official publications and business documents.[32]

The reason for the solicitude on the part of the legislature as to the publication of the company's name with the word " Limited " is that, while allowing limited liability, it desired by this means to make the company itself continually bring to the notice of those who dealt or might deal with it the fact that it was limited; and it has fortified its policy by pecuniary penalties.[33]

2. *Situation of registered office.*—" The Registered Office of the Company is situated in Scotland."

The place where the registered office is situated determines generally, but not necessarily,[34] the domicile of the company, and the country to whose law it is primarily subject, *e.g.*, in winding up. Hence, once the company is registered, the registered office, although its situation may be changed locally,[35] *i.e.*, within Scotland, cannot be transferred to another part of the United Kingdom. The Memorandum in regard to this is unalterable.

3. *The objects clause.—Its legal effect.—The rule of ultra vires.* The objects clause defines the purposes for which the company is incorporated, *e.g.*, bootmaking, engineering, investment, insurance. The company has therefore no power to do anything not in furtherance of these objects, *i.e.*, it cannot employ its funds for the purpose of any transactions which do not come within its objects as defined in the memorandum.[36] Further, all persons dealing with the company are entitled to rely on the capital remaining undiminished by any expenditure outside these limits. Hence any act of the directors outside these limits is said to be *ultra vires* of the company and is incapable of ratification by the company.[37]

Further, should the memorandum, in furtherance of its objects, contain power to do any things inconsistent with the Act, these also are *ultra vires* of the company, *e.g.*, power to the company to purchase

---

[32] s. 108.
[33] Palmer's *Company Law*, 26th ed., p. 60. Without the word the document may be a legal document: *Whittam* v. *W. J. Daniel & Co. Ltd.* [1961] 3 W.L.R 1123.
[34] *Calcutta Jute Co.* v. *Nicholson* (1876) 1 Ex. 428.
[35] *Ross* v. *Invergordon Distillers Ltd.,* 1961 S.C. 286.
[36] *Trevor* v. *Whitworth* (1887) 12 App.Cas. 409 at 414.
[37] *Ashbury* v. *Riche* (1875) L.R. 7 H.L. 653.

its own shares, as involving a reduction of the share capital in disregard of the prescribed conditions in the Act for such reduction [38] or to issue its shares at a discount, except as permitted in the Act under certain limited conditions.[39]

The doctrine of *ultra vires*, it has been said judicially, is to be reasonably understood and applied, and whatever may be fairly regarded as incident to or consequential upon those things which the legislature has authorised will not (unless expressly prohibited by the memorandum) be held *ultra vires*.[40] Hence the objects clause of most companies concludes with such general words as " and doing of all such other things as are incidental or conducive to the attainment of the above objects or any of them." Apart from such a clause it has been held that power to do such things as are ordinarily and reasonably done in such business as the company carries on may be implied though not referred to in the memorandum or articles, *e.g.*, power in an ordinary trading company to borrow money, as incidental to carrying on the business,[41] or to vote a gratuity to its officers.[42]

Alteration of the objects.—This can be done either (a) by a winding up or (b) without a winding up.

(A) BY WINDING UP.—Under the provisions of the Companies Act alteration of objects may be effected by voluntary winding up followed by reconstruction of the company,[43] *i.e.*, reconstituting it with wider objects, the new company taking over the assets and business of the old, or by exercise of a power of sale contained in the objects clause of the memorandum, *i.e.*, selling the assets to a newly formed company with wider objects after or before liquidation.

(B) WITHOUT WINDING UP.—The objects may be altered in certain limited respects by special resolution of the company unless cancelled by the court on an application to cancel by opponents of the alteration.[44] The reason is that the court must be satisfied that the alteration does not go beyond what the statute permits. The alterations permitted [45] are such as may be required to enable the company (a) to carry on its business more economically or more efficiently; (b) to attain its main purpose by new or improved means; (c) to enlarge or change the local area of its operations; (d) to carry on some business

---

[38] *Trevor* v. *Whitworth, supra.*
[39] *Klenck* v. *East India Co.* (1888) 16 R. 271; *Ooregum Gold Mining Co.* v. *Roper* [1892] A.C. 125.
[40] *Att.-Gen.* v. *Great Eastern Ry.* (1880) 5 App.Cas. at 478.
[41] *General Auction Estate Co. Ltd.* v. *Smith* [1891] 3 Ch. 432.
[42] *Mackison's Trs.* v. *Burgh of Dundee*, 1910 S.C.(H.L.) 27.
[43] ss. 206, 208, 287, 298.
[44] ss. 5, 395.
[45] s. 5.

which under existing circumstances may conveniently or advantageously be combined with the business of the company [46]; (e) to restrict
or abandon any of the objects specified in the memorandum; (f) to
sell or dispose of the whole or any part of the undertaking of the
company; (g) to amalgamate with any other company or body of
persons. The construction of these provisions, *i.e.*, without reconstituting by winding up, has been that they do not authorise the adoption
of any new and separate objects.

4. *Limitation of liability.*—" The liability of the members is
limited."

This means that each of the members of the company is liable to
contribute to the capital of the company only such sum as he has
agreed to contribute by taking and paying for so many shares of a
specified value, *e.g.*, 100 shares of £1 each. This privilege of limited
liability is lost if the membership is reduced below seven in the case of
a public, and two in the case of a private, company, and while the
number is so reduced it carries on business for more than six months.
If it does that, any person who is a member of the company during the
time it so carries on business after the six months and is aware of the
fact is severally liable for the whole debts of the company contracted
during that time.[47]

5. *Capital clause.*—" The share capital of the company is £
divided into   shares of £   each."

Contents of clause.—The clause originally states the amount of
the capital with which the company proposes to be registered, and its
division into shares of a fixed amount. This is called the nominal
capital or authorised capital, *i.e.*, the company cannot issue shares for
more, but may for less. Its amount usually has some relation to the
probable capital needs of the company. It is contrasted with loan
capital which the company borrows by the issue of debentures.

Alteration of capital clause.—It may be altered in certain respects
if power to do so be contained in the Articles and in other respects
without such power. If in the former case the articles do not contain
the power, they must first be altered by special resolution of the
company so as to confer the power. The respects in which the capital
clause may be altered are (a) to increase the nominal capital: the
company can in this way obtain more capital; (b) to consolidate and
divide share capital into shares of larger amount, *e.g.*, 10,000 shares of
£1 each into 100 shares of £100 each; the effect is to reduce the number

---

[46] *Hugh Baird & Sons Ltd.*, 1932 S.C. 455—fruit-growing company to add the canning
of fruit.
[47] s. 31.

of shares and the possible number of shareholders; (c) to convert fully paid shares into stock and *vice versa*: the unit involved in the share being of fixed amount is thus abolished: the shares must be fully paid before conversion; (d) to subdivide shares into shares of smaller amount: the effect is to increase the possible number of shares and shareholders and make the shares more marketable, *e.g.*, 100 shares of £1 each into 1,000 of 2s. each; (e) to cancel shares which have not been taken up, with resultant diminution of nominal capital [48]—these five operations can be carried out by a resolution passed at a general meeting of the company; (f) reduction of capital.[49] These six operations require power in the articles. Reduction involves reducing the amount of nominal capital apart from cancellation of unissued capital. It requires a special resolution of the company and also confirmation of the reduction by the court because the interests of creditors may be adversely affected and the incidence of the proposed reduction on the various shareholders may be inequitable. It is a common and important business operation and will be considered more fully later.[50] In all these cases publication of the alteration of the capital conditions must be made by notice given to the registrar,[51] and in the case of reduction it is given under order of the court.

Reorganisation of capital.—The only other permissible alteration of the capital conditions of the memorandum, namely, reorganisation, is provided for in the Act.[52] It does not require a power in the memorandum of articles. Authority to do it rests solely on the provisions of the Act. It includes (1) the consolidation into one class of different classes of shares having different rights attached to them, or (2) the division of shares of the same class into shares of different classes, *e.g.*, preference into ordinary and preference. Where reorganisation involves an alteration of the terms of the memorandum, through class rights being specified in the capital clause, it requires the holding of meetings under order of the court and approval by special majorities of the holders of each class of shares, and the sanction of the court to the scheme of reorganisation. If, however, no alteration of memorandum capital conditions is involved, it may be carried out as provided in the articles without an order of the court. Holders of 15 per cent. of the shares affected may apply to the court to have the variation cancelled, on the ground that the variation will unfairly prejudice the holders of shares of that class.[53]

---

48 s. 61. 49 ss. 66–71.
50 *Infra*, p. 305.
51 ss. 62, 63.
52 s. 206.
53 *Underwood* v. *London Music Hall* [1907] 2 Ch. 309. Variation includes abolition— *Frazer Brothers Ltd., Petrs.*, 1963 S.C. 139.

Reduction of capital.[54]—The general principle of the Act is that the capital of a company is not to be reduced without the sanction of the court in any case where the rights of creditors are or may be affected. The reason is that apart from the ordinary business risks of the diminution or loss of capital, persons dealing with the company are entitled to rely on the capital remaining undiminished either by any expenditure of it outside the limits of the business, or by the return of any part of it to the shareholders unless under the safeguard of the sanction of the court.[55]

The Act of 1948 confers a perfectly general power of reduction of capital.[56] This power is subject to the sanction of the court except in the following cases: (1) where the company has power in its articles to forfeit or accept surrender of shares on non-payment of calls, and issued shares with uncalled liability are so forfeited or surrendered; (2) the redemption of redeemable preference shares.

(A) WITHOUT CONFIRMATION BY THE COURT.—(1) *Forfeiture and surrender of shares.*—Forfeiture of shares is contemplated by the Act [57] on account of non-payment of calls, and it is a proceeding at the option of the company and *in invitum*, *i.e.*, independent of the consent of the shareholder. It puts the company in a position to place the shares in other hands and so obtain payment of the balance of capital outstanding. It is, however, until that is done, a reduction of capital, *i.e.*, there is no holder of the shares liable as such for the unpaid capital. Surrender of shares is not referred to in the Act, but it is admitted by the courts as having the same effect as forfeiture in the case of im-pecunious shareholders; the shareholders, however, in this case, being assenting parties.[58] Its validity without the sanction of the court, except as a substitute for forfeiture, is doubtful.[59] Power to forfeit or accept surrender of shares must be contained in the articles.[60]

(2) *Redemption of redeemable preference shares.*—As a rule a company cannot pay back to members the capital subscribed by them without the sanction of the court, but by the Act it can, if the articles so provide, issue preference shares on the terms that they may be redeemed out of profits or out of the proceeds of a fresh issue of shares.[61] Where it is done by a fresh issue of shares, that is really substituting new shares, possibly with different rights, for the old.

54 ss. 66–71.
55 *Trevor* v. *Whitworth* (1887) 12 App.Cas. 409.
56 See *British & American Trustee & Finance Co.* v. *Couper* [1894] A.C. 399; *Poole* v. *National Bank of China* [1907] A.C. 229; *Doloi Tea Co.* 1961 S.L.T. 168.
57 s. 124 (1), Sched. 6, Part I, 3, and Table A, Arts. 33–39.
58 *Gill* v. *Arizona Copper Co.* (1900) 2 F. 843.
59 *Rowell* v. *John Rowell & Sons Ltd.* [1912] 2 Ch. 609.
60 *Allen* v. *Gold Reefs of West Africa* [1900] 1 Ch. 656.
61 s. 58.

There is thus a reduction and an equivalent increase. Where, however, redemption is out of profits, the company must put an equivalent sum out of profits to a capital redemption reserve fund and can pay that to shareholders only with sanction of the court as in a reduction of capital. In either case, the redemption is not to be taken as reducing the amount of the company's authorised capital, and the capital redemption reserve fund may be applied in paying up unissued shares to be issued to members as fully paid bonus shares.[62] The reduction is in fact merely notional.[63]

(B) WITH CONFIRMATION BY THE COURT.—Subject to confirmation by the court, a company limited by shares, if so authorised by its articles,[64] may by special resolution reduce its share capital in any way, and may, if and so far as necessary, alter its memorandum by reducing the amount of its share capital and of its shares accordingly.[65]

In particular (without prejudice to the generality of the foregoing power) a company limited by shares may (a) extinguish or reduce the liability on any of its shares in respect of share capital not paid up, or (b) cancel any *paid-up* share capital which is lost or unrepresented by available assets, or (c) pay off any paid-up share capital which is in excess of the wants of the company. These ways may be combined.

There is, however, no limit to the ways in which a company may reduce its share capital,[66] however much against any provision in the memorandum or articles of the company's constitution it may be.[67] But (a) the statutory provisions must be complied with, *i.e.*, there must be power in the articles and a special resolution of the company; (b) the creditors, where their interests are affected, must be protected; and (c) the court is not to confirm, " unless it thinks that on the whole the new arrangement is a just and equitable arrangement," as between the shareholders.[68]

In the event of opposition by shareholders, the court decides whether the method of reduction proposed is fair and equitable as between the shareholders, *e.g.*, different classes treated differently and not in accordance with their rights. The Act in fact is silent as to the manner in which, in case of reduction, loss of capital is to be borne,

---

[62] s. 58 (3). Before the Act of 1948 such redemption was held to be a way of reducing capital. See *Re Serpell & Co. Ltd.* [1944] Ch. 233.

[63] There may be redemption of redeemable preference shares by repayment without resorting to s. 58. This requires the sanction of the court.

[64] See Table A, Art. 46.

[65] s. 66.

[66] *Westburn Sugar Refineries*, 1951 S.C.(H.L.) 57; *Stevenson Anderson & Co.*, 1951 S.C. 346 (on the footing that money returned may be called up again).

[67] *Ormiston Coal Co.*, 1949 S.C. 516.

[68] *Per* Lord President Dunedin in *Balmenach-Glenlivet Distillery Ltd.* v. *Croall* (1906) 8 F. 1135 at p. 1141.

or money to be returned as among the several shareholders, apart from special provision in the articles. The inference is that, if it be loss, it is to be borne among the shareholders in such manner as under the company's constitution loss in respect of capital on a winding up is to be borne; and, if it be money to be returned, it is to be returned in like manner as capital is returnable on a winding up; but these are only prima facie the equities.[69]

(C) GENERAL EFFECT OF REDUCTION.—The effect of reduction, if confirmed, is that no members of the company, past or present, can be made liable in respect of any share to any call exceeding its reduced amount,[70] e.g., if a reduction of £1 shares, 15s. paid, to 10s. shares is effected by repaying each holder of £1 shares 5s. in respect of each share, the uncalled liability of 5s. is wiped out. This exemption is subject to the proviso that any unpaid creditor, entitled to object to the reduction, who failed to object by ignorance of the proceedings for reduction or of their effect on his claim, is protected against non-payment of his debt through the insolvency of the company, i.e., every person who was a member of the company at the date of the reduction is liable to contribute to the payment of such creditor's debt as if the company had passed into liquidation on the day prior to such reduction. Any such creditor might, in the illustration given, apply to the court to enforce calls and orders on the persons then holding shares with the uncalled liability of 5s.

(5) The articles.—Form.—The regulations for the management of the affairs of a company are usually contained in articles of association registered along with the memorandum of association, i.e., agreed to by the original members. The Act of 1948 [71] provides that in the case of a company limited by shares, if articles are not registered, the regulations in Table A [72] shall, so far as applicable, be the regulations of the company as if they were contained in duly registered articles. In the case of companies previously registered under the Acts of 1862 or 1908 or 1929, Table A of these Acts respectively continues in force, as also does Table B of the Joint Stock Companies Act, 1856.[73]

It is usual to have special articles, but these may adopt Table A in whole or in part.[74] If articles are registered, they must be signed by the signatories to the memorandum and stamped as a formal contract.

[69] *Floating Dock Co. of St. Thomas Ltd.* [1895] 1 Ch. 691; Palmer's *Company Law,* 19th ed., p. 76.
[70] s. 70.
[71] s. 8.
[72] Act, 1st Sched.
[73] s. 459.
[74] s. 8.

The object of signature is to secure the adhesion of the only members of the company at that time to the regulations contained therein.[75]

Contents.—The contents of the articles are in the choice of the shareholders themselves. Subject to the terms of the memorandum of association, the company has full power to make and to alter such regulations for its own government as it may think fit.[76] The articles being, however, subordinate to and controlled by the memorandum, any article which goes beyond the company's area of action, as defined in the memorandum and the Act, is void and incapable of ratification.[77] The articles in Table A having received the sanction of the legislature cannot any of them be said to be *ultra vires.*

Alteration of articles.—A company's articles may be altered or added to by special resolution.[78] That again is subject to the limitations contained in its memorandum. Subject to this, any alteration or addition made is, in general, as valid as if originally contained in the articles and is likewise subject to alteration.[79] It is therefore not competent for the company to except any article from alteration,[80] as between the company and its shareholders, whether as regards the rights of members or mere administration.[81] A company cannot, however, alter articles so as to commit a breach of contract with an outsider,[82] *e.g.,* so as to take away the right of the outsider to nominate directors.

Accordingly, a company desirous of doing something not within the articles must first alter the articles so as to acquire the power. It may then exercise the power.[83] The alteration comes into force at the date of the resolution. Any condition contained in the memorandum which could lawfully have been contained in the articles may, where the memorandum does not itself regulate the matter of alteration, be altered by special resolution of the company.[84]

In questions with third parties, resolutions for the alteration of articles are presumed to have been validly passed as regards all preliminary formalities,[85] *e.g.,* requisite notice by proper notices. In a

---

[75] *Man On Insurance Co.* [1902] A.C. 232, Lord Davey at 236.
[76] *Per* Lord Cairns in *Ashbury Railway Carriage & Iron Co.* v. *Riche* (1875) L.R. 7 H.L. 653 at p. 671.
[77] *Guiness* v. *Land Corporation of Ireland* (1882) 22 Ch.D. 349 at p. 376; *Gill* v. *Arizona Copper Co.* (1900) 2 F. 843.
[78] s. 10.
[79] ss. 10, 380.
[80] *Malleson* v. *National Insurance & Guarantee Corporation* [1894] 1 Ch. 200.
[81] *Allen* v. *Gold Reefs of West Africa* [1900] 1 Ch. 656.
[82] *British Murac Rubber Syndicate* v. *Alperton Rubber Co.* [1915] 2 Ch. 186.
[83] *Imperial Hydropathic Hotel Co.* (*Blackpool*) v. *Hampson* (1882) 23 Ch.D. 1.
[84] s. 23.
[85] *Montreal & St. Lawrence Light & Power Co.* v. *Robert* [1906] A.C. 196; *Heiton* v. *Waverley Hydropathic Co.* (1877) 4 R. 830.

question, however, between members of the company and the directors who act upon the articles, an article may be open to exception on the ground of an irregularity in the passing of a resolution to alter.[86] Apart from irregularity in procedure an alteration may be bad though not *ultra vires*. The power to alter articles must be exercised fairly and for the benefit of the company as a whole,[87] *e.g.*, not so as to commit a fraud on a minority by taking power to expropriate them.[88] But an alteration is not invalid merely because it *may* affect prejudicially the rights under the original articles of a particular shareholder or class of shareholders.[89]   And in general it is no objection to the alteration of articles that the alteration has a retrospective effect.[90]

4. The company's constitution if limited by guarantee

Such, for example, are companies for mutual insurance, trade protection, testing patents, pooling and marketing produce, or supported by donations or subscriptions and not for profit.

A company limited by guarantee is defined by the Act as one having the liability of its members limited by the memorandum to such amount as the members may respectively thereby undertake to contribute to the assets of the company in the event of its being wound up.[91]

The memorandum resembles that of a company limited by shares. Its distinctive feature is, in the capital clause, an undertaking by each member to contribute to the assets of the company, in the event of its being wound up, for payment of the debts and liabilities of the company contracted before he ceases to be a member, and the costs of winding up, and for adjustment of the rights of the contributories *inter se*, such amount as may be required, not exceeding a specified amount.[92]   But the company may also have a share capital, and the Act contains forms of memorandum for the alternative cases.[93]   If it has a share capital it may reduce it as in the case of a company limited by shares.

Articles of association signed by the subscribers to the memorandum and prescribing regulations for the company must be registered with the memorandum.[94]   The reason is that after registration the memorandum must be stamped with a duty. If, as may be, there is

---

[86] *Per* Lord Watson in *Muirhead* v. *Forth & North Sea Steamboat Insurance Association* (1893) 20 R. 442; (1894) 21 R.(H.L.) 1 at p. 4.
[87] *Shuttleworth* v. *Cox Bros. & Co. (Maidenhead) Ltd.* (1926) 43 T.L.R. 83.
[88] *Brown* v. *British Abrasive Wheel Co. Ltd.* [1919] 1 Ch. 290.
[89] *Crookston* v. *Lindsay Crookston & Co.*, 1922 S.L.T. 62.
[90] *Allen* v. *Gold Reefs of West Africa* [1900] 1 Ch. 656 at p. 672.
[91] s. 1 (2).
[92] s. 2 (3).
[93] Tables C and D.
[94] ss. 6, 7, 8.

no capital divided into shares, the amount of duty is proportioned to the number of members. Hence the articles are required to state, if it has no share capital, the number of members with which the company proposes to be registered. If there is a share capital the duty is proportioned to its amount.

5. The company's constitution if unlimited

An unlimited company requires both a memorandum and articles of association. Its name will, of course, not include the word " Limited." The memorandum specifies only the name, the place of the registered office, and the objects. There is no liability clause, nor capital clause. It may have a joint stock capital divided into shares (with unlimited liability of course) or no such capital.

But if the company has a share capital, the articles state the amount of capital with which the company proposes to be registered, and each member requires to subscribe for one share at least. If the company has not a share capital, the articles must state the number of members with which the company proposes to be registered, for the purpose of enabling the registrar to determine the fees payable on registration. If it has a share capital, it may, the liability of members being unlimited, reduce it without the sanction of the court [95] if so authorised by its articles. Accordingly, articles may provide for a return of capital to members or for withdrawal of members from the company. The articles may also provide that a specified portion of uncalled capital shall not be called up except for purposes of winding up.

6. Limited company registered without the word " Limited " [96]

Where it is proved to the satisfaction of the Board of Trade that an association formed or about to be formed as a limited company is to be formed for promoting commerce, art, science, religion, charity or any other useful object, and intends to apply its profits, if any, or other income in promoting its objects, and to prohibit the payment of any dividend to its members,[97] the Board may by licence direct that the association may be registered as a company with limited liability, without the addition of the word " Limited " to its name, and the association may be registered accordingly. This provision is chiefly taken advantage of by companies limited by guarantee, e.g., Cyclists Touring Clubs. The advantage of incorporation is that it can own property and sue in its own name and limit its liability.

---

[95] ss. 10, 380.
[96] s. 19.
[97] *Inland Revenue Commissioners* v. *Forrest* (1890) 15 App.Cas. 334; *Income Tax Commissioners* v. *Pemsel* [1891] A.C. 531.

IV. PROMOTION OF A COMPANY

1. The promoters

The importance of this is that the persons who create companies, called promoters, stand in a fiduciary relation towards the as yet non-existent company and its members to be. The formation of a company is merely a means to an end, such as the carrying on by the company of some business, or the working of a mine or a patent or other enterprise. It is the person called a promoter who determines what this end shall be and who sets in motion the statutory machinery of formation. " Promotion " is accordingly a term not of law but of business, summing up a number of business operations familiar to the commercial world by which a company is generally brought into existence,[98] e.g., preparing or settling the terms of the prospectus, negotiating agreements between vendors and the intended company, or otherwise actively engaging either alone or in co-operation with others in the formation of a joint stock company. Therefore it is a question of fact in each case whether a person is or is not a promoter and is therefore in a fiduciary relation to the company. With reference to liability for misstatements in a prospectus, the expression " Promoter " means a promoter who was a party to the preparation of the prospectus or of the portion thereof containing the untrue statement, but does not include any person by reason of his acting in a professional capacity for persons engaged in procuring the formation of the company.[99]

Fiduciary relation of promoters to the company.—The control of the promoter over the inception of the company involves a correlative responsibility and out of this responsibility arises the doctrine of the fiduciary relation of the promoter towards the company he creates. It is an artificial doctrine, for the promoter is not, strictly speaking, an agent of or trustee for the company before incorporation, i.e., for the as yet non-existent company. But, as it is said, it is a salutary and necessary fiction of equity for the protection of the company which afterwards consciously and voluntarily adopts and becomes a party to the promoter's transaction. It is thus an extension of the doctrine of agency, a sort of agency by anticipation.

In virtue of this fiduciary relationship, the promoter (or even the firm of which he is a partner) is accountable to the company for all moneys secretly obtained by him from the promotion.[1] A promoter as such may not make a profit out of a company he promotes, unless

---

[98] Bowen L.J. in *Whaley Bridge Printing Co.* v. *Green* (1879) 5 Q.B.D. 109.
[99] s. 43 (5).
[1] *Mann* v. *Edinburgh Northern Tramways Co.* (1891) 18 R. 1140; (1892) 20 R.(H.L.) 7.

he makes full and fair disclosure to the shareholders of the company
of what he is getting and they assent to it.

In this connection, there are three sources from which a promoter
may get a profit legitimately, *i.e.*, provided he makes full and fair
disclosure.   He may get it (1) from the company; (2) from the vendor
to the company; or (3) where he is at once promoter and vendor.
(1) It is sufficient disclosure that the articles of the company provide
that a certain sum shall be paid by the company to its promoter for
his services.[2]   (2) The promoter may receive a commission from the
vendor in cash or fully paid shares of the company, provided it is
disclosed.   The Act provides for such disclosure in the prospectus.
(3) Where a promoter desires to sell his own property to the company,
i.e., gets the company formed for the purpose of purchasing from him
a business or property, he is bound to protect the company he has
created,[3] either (a) by furnishing the company with an independent
and competent board of directors, and by disclosing to the directors
his interest in the property sold, so that they can exercise an intelligent
judgment on the transaction of sale before assenting to his getting the
whole consideration for the sale, or (b) by making full disclosure to
those who are induced by him to join the company.[4]

Should a promoter fail to make such disclosure or obtain such
consent, he may be made to make over to the company the profit he
has made, and where there is a failure of disclosure by a promoter-
vendor the sale may be set aside at the instance of the company.   If
rescission is impossible, the company is entitled to damages, the
measure being the difference in value between the price paid by
the company and the actual value of the property at the date of the
purchase.[5]

2. The prospectus

A prospectus may be used to offer shares to the public at any
time before formation or afterwards.   Where promoters issue a prospectus before incorporation, that is not the company's prospectus
unless it adopts it after formation.   The prospectus holds out to the
public the advantage of taking shares in a proposed undertaking and
inviting them to take shares on the faith of the representations made
therein.   The relation between the parties, *i.e.*, the company and the
public, is *uberrimae fidei* and the fullest and fairest disclosure of all

[2] *Huntington Copper Co.* v. *Henderson* (1877) 4 R. at 302.
[3] *Erlanger* v. *New Sombrero Phosphate Co. Ltd.* (1887) 3 App.Cas. 1236, opinion of
Lord Cairns L.C.
[4] Opinion of Lindley M.R. in *Lagunas Nitrate Co.* v. *Lagunas Nitrate Syndicate* [1899]
2 Ch. 392, 422—a case where the promoters were also the original directors and the
only shareholders at the date of the sale of properties to the company.
[5] *Re Leeds & Hanley Theatres of Varieties Ltd.* [1902] 2 Ch. 809.

material facts is required, as in partnership. At common law the contract to take shares, if induced by misrepresentation, may therefore be voidable. This common law is now in large measure replaced by statute.[6] The general law as to liability for misrepresentation, however, is not abrogated.

Definition.—" Prospectus " is defined in the Act as meaning any prospectus, notice, circular, advertisement, or other invitation, offering to the public for subscription or purchase any shares or debentures of a company.[7]

A circular which states the prospects of the company, but does not offer shares to the public, is therefore not a prospectus within the definition. But to prevent evasion of the requirements as to disclosure in a prospectus by omitting the offer of shares from the prospectus, the Act provides that where the company allots or agrees to allot shares or debentures to persons with a view to these persons offering the shares or debentures for sale to the public, and these persons by any document make the offer to the public, such document is deemed to be a prospectus issued by the company. The statute goes on to provide that it is evidence of the allotment having been made to these persons with a view to an offer by them to the public if an offer to the public by them is in fact made within six months of the allotment to them of the shares, or if when the offer is made to the public the whole consideration for the allotment to these persons has not been received by the company from them,[8] *i.e.*, they are treated as agents of the company in making the offer if the allotment to them was made with a view to the offer to the public.

Registration of prospectus.[9]—The purpose of registration is (1) to preserve an authoritative record of the terms upon which the public are invited to subscribe, and (2) to secure that the directors of the company accept responsibility for the statements in the prospectus. Hence the Act provides that the prospectus (1) shall be signed by every person named therein as a director or proposed director and be delivered for registration before publication, (2) shall bear the date of publication, and (3) shall state that it has been delivered for registration. This must be done before any shares are allotted, and if no prospectus is issued a statement in lieu of prospectus must be filed, *i.e.*, when the issue of shares is to the public. This does not, of course, apply to a private company. Such a company does not issue shares to the public.

[6] s. 43.
[7] s. 455.
[8] s. 45.
[9] s. 41.

Issue.—The company usually broadcasts its prospectus through the post and encloses forms of application for shares. No form of application for shares may be issued to the public unless with a prospectus which complies with the requirements of the Act as to its contents. This does not apply if the form issued is in connection with an invitation to underwrite, *i.e.*, guarantee the taking up of shares or debentures, or the issue of the form is in relation to shares or debentures which were not offered to the public.[10]

Contents.—The prospectus must state the matters specified in the Fourth Schedule to the Act as material to be disclosed. In particular, there are to be stated the directors' and promoters' interests, the minimum cash required to be contributed to enable the company to commence business, and reports by accountants on previous profits of any business the company takes over.

Statement in lieu of prospectus.—A public company which does not issue a prospectus on or with reference to its formation, or which has issued such a prospectus but has not allotted any of the shares offered to the public for subscription, must not allot any of its shares or debentures unless, at least three days before the first allotment, there has been delivered to the registrar for registration a statement in lieu of prospectus, signed by every person who is named therein as a director or proposed director of the company or by his agent authorised in writing, in the form and containing the particulars set out in the Fifth Schedule to the Act.[11]

The matters requiring to be stated in a statement in lieu of prospectus are nearly co-extensive with the requirements for a prospectus. This requirement does not apply to a private company.[12]

3. Remedies of a person deceived by prospectus into taking shares

These are in substance two. A party who can prove that he has taken shares in reliance on a statement in the prospectus which is untrue may, while the company is a going concern, reduce the contract, and have the register of shareholders rectified by removing his name, whether the statement in question was fraudulent or not.[13] A mere failure to disclose a statutory requirement will not warrant rescission,[14] unless indeed on proof that but for its omission the member would not have taken the shares.[15] But rescission is not competent after

---

[10] s. 38 (3).
[11] s. 48.
[12] s. 48.
[13] *Mair* v. *Rio Grande Estates Co.*, 1913 S.C. 183; rev'd 1913 S.C.(H.L.) 74.
[14] *Re South of England Natural Gas and Petroleum Co.* [1911] 1 Ch. 573; but see *Lynde* v. *Nash* [1929] A.C. 158.
[15] *Macleay* v. *Tait* [1906] A.C. 24.

the company has stopped payment.[16] Insolvency fixes the membership, *i.e.*, the persons liable to contribute to payment of debts. A
shareholder, while he remains a member, cannot sue the company for
damages for fraud inducing his membership.[17] He would be suing
himself. But he may have a remedy against the directors or other
parties responsible for the prospectus. This matter has a history. In
Derry v. *Peek*,[18] it was held that while directors were liable in damages
for fraudulent statements in a prospectus they incurred no liability
for statements which were made honestly though without reasonable
care. The decision led to the passing of the Directors' Liability Act,
1890, which was repealed but is in substance reproduced in the Companies Act of 1948.[19] It provides that every director, promoter, or
other person responsible for the issue of a prospectus offering shares or
debentures is liable to pay compensation for any loss sustained by
reason of any untrue statement included therein unless he proves
certain things which are grounds for exculpating him from liability
for untrue statements.

V. THE CONTRACT OF MEMBERSHIP

1. Constitution

Membership of a company is constituted by two things together,
(a) agreement to become a member, and (b) the entry of the person's
name in the register of members.[20] A person cannot become a
member without a contract to do so.[21] Hence persons under disability
to contract cannot become members. Hence also the register is not
conclusive, but only prima facie evidence of membership,[22] and may
be rectified both before and after a winding up.[23]

(a) **Agreement to become a member.**—Unless where a company has
no share capital, the contract of membership is a contract with the
company to take shares of the company and to pay for them. The
agreement to become a member may be constituted in various ways.
A person may agree to become a member (1) by subscription of the
memorandum of association, (2) by application for shares and acceptance by the company, (3) by holding out, (4) by transfer of shares
from an existing member, or (5) by transmission of shares in succession
to a deceased or bankrupt member.

---

[16] *Addie* v. *Western Bank* (1867) 5 M.(H.L.) 80.
[17] *Houldsworth* v. *City of Glasgow Bank* (1880) 7 R.(H.L.) 53.
[18] (1889) 14 App.Cas. 337.
[19] s. 43.
[20] s. 26.
[21] *Hamley's Case* (1877) 5 Ch.D. 705.
[22] *Tufnell's Case* (1885) 29 Ch.D. 421.
[23] ss. 116, 257.

(1) *By subscription of the memorandum*

A subscriber of the memorandum is deemed to have agreed to become a member, and must be entered in the register of members.[24] He can only escape liability to pay for the shares by showing that all the shares have been allotted to others.[25]

(2) *By application and acceptance*

In ordinary circumstances, to constitute a binding contract to take shares in a company, there must be an application by the intending shareholder, and an acceptance by the company notified to the applicant.

The application need not be in writing.[26] It may be made by an agent having authority express or implied.[27] The rules of common law as to what amounts to an offer apply generally, *e.g.*, a mere expression of willingness to take shares is not necessarily an application,[28] and a person who has agreed to " place " shares, *i.e.*, to get other people to take them, does not thereby agree to take shares.[29] So also an application may be conditional. The condition may be suspensive,[30] or resolutive.[31] If suspensive, there is no contract unless the condition is purified. If resolutive, the contract is complete unless the resolutive condition operates before actual entry of the member on the register. But the condition cannot be one qualifying his liability.[32]

What constitutes a good acceptance.—Both common law and statute must be complied with.

Under common law.—Acceptance of an application is ordinarily evidenced by the act of allotment, that is, the appropriation to an applicant by a resolution of the directors of a certain number of shares in response to an application,[33] but it may be evidence in other ways, *e.g.*, a contract with the company.[34] Acceptance must be made within a reasonable time or the offer falls.[35] An acceptance must be unconditional. If it introduces a new term, it is a new offer.[36] Notice of the allotment to the applicant need not be formal; if brought home

24 s. 26.
25 *Evan's Case* (1867) L.R. 2 Ch. 427.
26 *City of Glasgow Bank* v. *Nelson Mitchell* (1879) 6 R. 420.
27 *Hindley's Case* [1896] 2 Ch. 121; *Re Henry Bentley & Co.* (1893) 69 L.T. 204.
28 *Mason* v. *Benhar Coal Co.* (1882) 9 R. 883.
29 *Gorrissen's Case* (1873) L.R. 8 Ch. 507.
30 *Waverley Hydropathic Co.* v. *Barrowman* (1895) 23 R. 136.
31 *Fisher's Case* (1885) 31 Ch.D. 125.
32 *Miln* v. *North British Fresh Fish Supply Co., Ltd.* (1887) 15 R. 21.
33 *Palmer's Company Law*, 20th ed., p. 183.
34 *Moore Brothers & Co. Ltd.* (1889) 1 Ch. 627.
35 *Crawley's Case* (1869) L.R. 4 Ch. 322.
36 *Pentelow's Case* (1869) L.R. 4 Ch. 178.

to him *aliunde*, it will bind him.[37] It would seem that the contract is not completed by the posting of a notice of allotment, if it never reaches the applicant.[38] This is in contrast to the general common law rule as to acceptance of an offer, unless, of course, there is an express agreement that acceptance of the application may be made by posting. Hence an application may be withdrawn at any time before notification of acceptance is received by the applicant, and may be withdrawn orally, the revocation operating from the date of its actual receipt, not of its posting.[39]

Under statute.—No allotment of share capital offered to the public for subscription may be made unless the minimum amount stated in the prospectus (referred to as the " minimum subscription ") has been subscribed, and the sum payable on application therefor has been paid to and received by the company.[40] If these conditions have not been complied with on the expiration of forty days after the first issue of the prospectus, the applicants' money is to be repaid to them without interest, and if not repaid within forty-eight days after the issue of the prospectus, the directors are jointly and severally liable to repay the money with 5 per cent. interest thereafter, unless default in repayment of the money was not due to any misconduct or negligence on their part.

Compliance with these requirements is of the essence of the contract to take shares.[41] They cannot be waived, but except as to the amount payable on application on each share (which must be not less than five per cent. of the nominal amount of the share), they apply only to the first allotment of shares offered to the public. Allotments in contravention of these provisions are voidable at the instance of the applicant for shares, but not at the instance of the company,[42] within one month of the holding of the statutory meeting, or if allotment be made later than the statutory meeting then within one month of allotment, notwithstanding that the company is then in course of being wound up.[43]

(3) *By holding out*

A person may also become a member by allowing his name to be on the register of members or otherwise holding himself out or allowing himself to be held out as a member. Thus, a person who, under the company's articles, is ineligible for membership, *e.g.*, as over age, but

---

[37] *Nelson* v. *Fraser* (1906) 14 S.L.T. 513.
[38] *Mason* v. *Benhar Coal Co.* (1882) 9 R. 883, *per* Lord Shand.
[39] *Henthorn* v. *Fraser* [1892] 2 Ch. 27.
[40] s. 47.
[41] *Finance & Issue Ltd.* v. *Canadian Produce Corporation Ltd.* [1905] 1 Ch. 37.
[42] *Burton* v. *Bevan* [1908] 2 Ch. 240.
[43] s. 49; *Re National Motor Co.* [1908] 2 Ch. 228.

has been admitted to and has accepted membership, cannot plead he is not a member.[44]

(b) Entry in the register of members.—The second requisite of membership is entry in the register. The register is prima facie evidence of matters recorded,[45] including the right and liability to be treated as a member and holder of particular shares of the company.

(1) *Contents of the register.*[46]—These are (1) name of the holder; (2) shares or stock held and identification numbers of the shares held and amount paid up; (3) date of entry; (4) date of ceasing to be a member; (5) the annual return. The dates of entry in the register and of ceasing to be a member are important as determining upon whom calls for unpaid capital may be made at a particular date or on liquidation, and who has the right to receive dividends at a particular date.

Special cases.—1. TRUSTEES.—It is provided in the Act [47] that no notice of any trust shall be entered on the register in the case of companies registered in England. This means persons can be members only as individuals, not in a representative capacity as trustees. Its objects are to relieve the company from taking notice of equitable interests in shares and to preclude persons claiming shares under equitable titles from converting the company into a trustee for them. In Scotland such an entry is allowed, but merely to mark the shares as the property of the particular trust for the benefit of the trust beneficiaries. That is to say, trustee holders are, in a question with the company, personally and jointly and severally liable for all the obligations and have personally all the rights of membership.[48] Their liability is not limited to the amount of the trust estate, but if they pay calls, they are entitled to be indemnified by the beneficiaries.

2. EXECUTORS.—Executors may have their title to the shares as executors recorded in the register without their names going on the register as members, and may execute transfers and receive dividends and in that state of matters they do not incur personal liability as shareholders. The executry estate and not the executor as an individual has the liabilities and the benefits of the deceased's membership. If an executor gives express or implied authority to place his name on the register, he becomes a member, but is entitled to be indemnified from the estate.

3. JUDICIAL FACTORS AND OTHERS.—A judicial factor, *e.g.*, a *curator bonis*, or a mandatary of a member, on intimating his title to the company, may receive dividends without going on the register.

---

[44] *Aberdeen Master Masons' Incorporation* v. *Smith*, 1908 S.C. 669.
[45] s. 118.   [46] s. 110.
[47] s. 117.   [48] *Cunninghame* v. *City of Glasgow Bank* (1879) 6 R. (H.L.) 98.

4. FIRM.—The right of a firm as such to go on the register has not been tested. The partners, therefore, must go on as individuals, that is, really in trust for the firm.[49]

Annual return.[50]—This is frequently contained in a separate part of the register. It is a list of all who, on the fourteenth day after the company's annual general meeting for the year, are members and of all who have ceased to be so since incorporation or the last return, *i.e.*, changes in membership during the year. It contains also many other things which are changes affecting the holding of the shares, liability on shares, directorate, mortgages, etc., during the year.[51] This must be sent to the registrar within forty-two days from the meeting. It is valuable information to an intending shareholder and to third parties.

(2) *Custody and inspection*

The Act [52] requires the register to be kept at the registered office or where the work of making it up is done, and allows members gratis and others for a small charge to inspect and make extracts from it. This right of inspection is part of the policy of the legislature, when conceding limited liability of members, to enable persons dealing with the company to know to whom and to what (*i.e.*, who are under a liability and for how much) they have to trust. No inspection is accordingly allowed after liquidation. The register may be closed for thirty days in each year. This is done at the time of the annual general meeting.

(3) *Rectification* [53]

Owing to the importance of having the register correct, a summary method is allowed of application to the court to rectify the register. Directors should never alter it at their own hand. The grounds are (1) name without sufficient cause entered or omitted, (2) default or unnecessary delay in entering the fact of a person having ceased to be a member. Rectification may be made after liquidation.[54]

2. Shares

(a) **Definition.**—A share in a company, like a share in a partnership, signifies a definite proportion of the joint estate after it has been turned into money and applied so far as necessary in payment of the

---

[49] *Gillespie & Paterson* v. *City of Glasgow Bank &c.* (1899) 6 R. (H.L.) 104.
[50] ss. 124, 126.
[51] 6th Sched.
[52] s. 110.
[53] s. 116.
[54] s. 257.

joint debts. Therefore, a shareholder has no right to any part of the property which belongs to the company as an undertaking. The business of the company is an entirety.[55] He can only sell his share. But it denotes also the various rights and liabilities which are incidental to the ownership of a share under the company's constitution. These rights usually include a right to receive dividends, *i.e.*, to share in the profits of the trading, a right to transfer the shares to another and a right to vote.[56]

(b) Shares as property.—A share is moveable or personal estate.[57] It may be held by several persons on the footing of a joint right and joint and several liability.[58]   It is incorporeal moveable property like a partnership interest.   It follows (1) that in Scotland it is arrestable in the hands of the company whether in security or in execution of a decree or to found jurisdiction, and whether a dividend has been declared or not, *i.e.*, the share itself and not merely the dividend on it is arrestable in the hands of the company [59]; (2) that security rights may be constituted over shares only by transfer to and registration in the name of the lender, *i.e.*, by completed assignation.

(c) Classes of shares.—The shares of a company may be of different amounts or denominations and be divided into different classes with different rights attached to them, as defined in the memorandum or articles of association.   The rights are properly defined in the articles, but may be included in the memorandum if it is desired to make them unalterable.   The commonest classes are ordinary, preference (redeemable and irredeemable) and founders' or deferred shares. Founders' or deferred shares are mostly of small amount held by vendors and promoters, often as a consideration for paying the expenses of forming and floating the company, hence called " founders' shares."   But they may be issued as a bonus to subscribers for other shares.   Often they are very valuable, being few in number and entitled as a class to valuable rights, usually defined in the memorandum, and not alterable by the company, and they have usually rights to dividend and capital postponed to the ordinary shares.   Hence they are often called " deferred " shares.   Preference shares may carry a right to a preferential dividend only or to a priority in the division of capital on winding up or to both.

(d) Calls.—The term " call " signifies the demand made by directors of a company upon shareholders or by a liquidator upon contributories,

55 *Zuccani* v. *Nacupai Gold Mining Co.* (1888) 60 L.T. 23.
56 *Lindley on Companies*, 6th ed., p. 628.
57 s. 73.
58 *Wishart & Dalziel* v. *City of Glasgow Bank* (1879) 6 R. 823.
59 *American Mortgage Co. of Scotland Ltd.* v. *Sidway*, 1908 S.C. 500.

to pay up in whole or in part the amount unpaid on shares held by them. A call can be made only in accordance with the regulations in the articles of association. A call is made by the directors passing a resolution, and a member is entitled to a notice stating when, where and to whom it is payable.[60]

The amount called is a debt due to the company as at the date mentioned in the notice of call. It is the duty of the directors to enforce payment of the debt so due. A call may be enforced in three ways (1) by action as for a debt; (2) by provision in the articles for forfeiture of the shares by resolution of the directors for failure to pay calls [61]; (3) by the exercise of a lien.

It is a relevant defence to an action by a company for a call (1) that it is not validly made, *i.e.*, in accordance with the articles,[62] (2) that the defender is not a member of the company—not having agreed to become one, or having been induced to become one by misrepresentations made by or on behalf of the company—and should not be on the register,[63] (3) that the power to make the call was not exercised by the directors for the general benefit of the company, as where directors who were subscribers of the memorandum made calls only on members to whom shares had been allotted, and so placed a greater burden on these other members.[64] It has been laid down that calls should be made *pari passu* on all shareholders unless on very special grounds.[65]

Power to forfeit is not inherent in a company, and is probably *ultra vires* and illegal except as regards forfeiture for non-payment of calls and other sums which by the terms of issue of shares become payable at a fixed time, *e.g.*, premiums on shares. The power must, therefore, be conferred in the articles and be exercised in accordance with the procedure prescribed therein. It is a fiduciary power and must be exercised for the benefit of the company as the directors in their discretion think expedient.[66]

The articles usually provide that forfeited shares may be sold on such terms as the directors think fit and that a purchaser of the forfeited shares from the company shall have an unchallengeable title. The position of the transferee of the forfeited shares is that he is free of liability for calls due prior to his purchase, unless his share certificate shows that the shares are only partly paid up, in which case he may to that extent be liable for calls made prior to the reissue of the shares

[60] *Re Cawley & Co.* (1889) 42 Ch.D. 209. [61] Table A. 33–39.
[62] *Ferguson* v. *Central Halls Coy. Ltd.* (1881) 8 R. 997.
[63] *City of Edinburgh Brewery Co.* v. *Gibson's Tr.* (1869) 7 M. 886.
[64] *Alexander* v. *Automatic Telephone Co.* [1900] 2 Ch. 56.
[65] *Odessa Tramways Ltd.* v. *Mendel* (1878) 8 Ch.D. 235 at 245.
[66] *Spackman* v. *Evans* (1868) L.R. 3 H.L. 171, at 187.

and unsatisfied. The articles usually provide that calls due at the date of forfeiture shall remain exigible against the owner with interest. Otherwise they could not be enforced against him. He is no longer a member, and is liable to the company for the calls as a mere debtor, and not as a member.

By the common law of Scotland a company has a lien over its shares for debts due by the holder to the company.[67] This entitles the company to refuse to register a transfer of shares from a holder who owes it a debt, and also to sell the shares in satisfaction of the debt, but the power to sell must probably be obtained from the court. Articles, however, commonly provide that the company shall have a lien upon shares for all debts of the holders thereof, and contain power to sell shares which are subject to a lien. Without a similar provision a company in England has no lien or charge.[68] The company's lien is, however, subject to any charge, e.g., arrestment or mortgage of the shareholder's interest, of which notice has been given to the company prior to the call.

Payment in advance of calls.—The articles may provide for the acceptance by the company of payment in advance of calls and for payment of interest on the sums so advanced by the company.[69] This power should only be exercised when in the opinion of the directors the moneys advanced can be advantageously employed for the purposes of the company.[70] Moneys so advanced are to be regarded as a loan to the company until a call is actually made, but the company cannot repay the loan unless with the assent of the shareholder or by way of reduction of capital.[71] Hence, being a loan, moneys so advanced rank for repayment in a winding up prima facie before capital not paid up in advance.[72]

(e) Certificate of shares—legal effect.—A share or stock certificate is a solemn affirmation, under the seal of the company, that a certain amount of shares or stock stands in the name of the individual named in the certificate.[73] It also states the amount paid up on the shares.

In a question between the grantee and the company, the certificate is prima facie evidence of the title of the grantee to the shares or stock. It does not constitute an absolute title. Hence, for example, the certificate would not give the holder a good title if he had obtained

---

[67] *Per* Lord President Inglis, in *Bell's Trs.* v. *Coatbridge Tinplate Co. Ltd.* (1886) 14 R. 246.
[68] *Dunlop* v. *Dunlop* (1882) 21 Ch.D. 583.
[69] *e.g.*, Table A, Art. 21.
[70] *Lock* v. *Queensland Investment and Land Mortgage Co.* [1896] 1 Ch. 397; [1896] A.C. 461.
[71] *London & Northern S.S. Co.* v. *Farmer* (1914) 111 L.T. 204.
[72] *Cf. Ex p. Maude* (1870) L.R. 6 Ch. 51.
[73] *Per* Lord Cairns in *Shropshire Union Rys. and Canal Co.* v. *The Queen* (1875) L.R. 7 H.L. 496, at p. 509.

the issue of the certificate by fraud, or if the certificate had been forged.[74] Further, certificates while they do not themselves give a title to the shares are the proper evidence or *indicia* of the title of a transferor. By giving a certificate the company arms the grantee with the power of holding himself out to all the world as the owner of the shares, and accordingly, a bona fide buyer from such grantee may, as the person whom the company is bound to treat as the real owner, maintain an action against the company.[75] Hence a transferee desiring to be registered as owner must produce to the company the transferor's certificate.[76] Such transferee must, however, in a question with the company, prove that he relied on the certificate as evidence of the transferor's right, and not, for example, on a forged transfer. Hence also if certificates are not forthcoming from the transferor, their non-production puts the transferee on inquiry and prevents him setting up a title as a buyer for value without notice of a defect in the seller's title.[77]

Further, a share certificate is evidence against the company of payment on the shares. The company is barred from disputing the terms of the certificate. If it bears that the shares are fully paid, an allottee, having adequate ground for believing the shares to be fully paid up, or a transferee acquiring shares in reliance on that representation in the transferor's certificate, cannot be made liable for calls.[78]

Share warrants to bearer.—A company limited by shares if authorised by its articles may, with respect to any fully paid up shares or stock, issue a warrant stating that the bearer is entitled to the shares or stock therein specified, and may provide by coupons or otherwise for payment of future dividends.

When a warrant is issued the name of the registered member is struck out of the register, and the fact and date of issue of the warrant noted. The bearer is, subject to the articles, entitled, on surrendering the warrant for cancellation, to have his name entered in the register of members and to receive a certificate. The shares or stock specified in the warrant may be transferred by delivery of the warrant. Share warrants to bearer are treated in mercantile practice as negotiable instruments.[79]

---

[74] *Ruben* v. *Great Fingal Consolidated* [1906] A.C. 439; *Clavering, Son & Co.* v. *Goodwins, Jardine & Co.* (1891) 18 R. 652.
[75] *Sheffield Corporation* v. *Barclay* [1905] A.C. 392.
[76] *Burkinshaw* v. *Nicolls* (1878) 3 App.Cas. 1004; *Simm* v. *Anglo-American Telegraph Co.* (1879) 5 Q.B.D. 188.
[77] *Société Générale de Paris* v. *Walker* (1885) 11 App.Cas. 20.
[78] *Penang Foundry Co. Ltd.* v. *Gardiner*, 1913 S.C. 1203; *Clavering, Son & Co.* v. *Goodwins, Jardine & Co.* (1891) 18 R. 652.
[79] *London & County Banking Co.* v. *London & River Plate Bank* (1887) 20 Q.B.D. 232; *Webb, Hale & Co.* v. *Alexandria Water Co.* (1905) 21 T.L.R. 572.

3. Termination of membership

This may result from forfeiture, surrender,[80] sale or transmission [81] of shares.

Sale.—(a) The right to sell.—The shares in a company are moveable estate transferable in manner provided by the articles of the company.[82] Every shareholder has prima facie a right to transfer his shares, and may do so up to the last moment prior to liquidation, even to a pauper, that is, a person unable to pay uncalled liability, and compel the registration of the transfer.[83] That is prima facie the member's right. But the power to transfer may be restricted by the articles, and the articles may also prescribe the mode of transfer.

(b) Effects of the contract of sale.—*The seller's obligations.*—The contract obliges the seller, on the one hand, to hand to the transferee a duly executed transfer and the certificate of his title, and that within a reasonable time after the contract is made, *i.e.*, to put the transferee in a position to seek registration as a member in place of the transferor.[84] The agreement for sale does not, however, impliedly bind the seller to secure registration of the transfer.[85] The effect of the contract in this matter is that until registration of the transfer the transferor is in the position of a trustee of the shares for the transferee,[86] *i.e.*, he is bound to receive the dividends and hand them over to the transferee, being trustee for him. The transferor may, however, be entitled to refuse to act as trustee for the buyer, for example, if the prospect of registering the transfer is remote owing to the directors having a right under the articles to refuse registration and being unlikely to register it. In that case, if the seller refuses to act as trustee, he is bound to repay the price on cancellation of the transfer.[87]

Where there is no agreement to the contrary, the seller is bound, although the transfer may not be completed, or the price paid, to pay to the buyer all dividends declared by the company after the date of the purchase, including any dividend declared for a period antecedent to his purchase.[88] It is in fact the universal custom of the Stock Exchange and also a term of the contract on the Exchange that, in a question between buyer and seller, the price includes accruing dividends.

Obligations of the buyer.—It is the duty of the transferee to get the transfer registered, and if he fails in this duty the transferor may apply

80 *Supra*, p. 306.   81 *Infra*, p. 325.
82 s. 73.
83 *Lindlar's Case* [1910] 1 Ch. 207 and 312.
84 *De Waal* v. *Alder* (1886) 12 App.Cas. 141.
85 *London Founders Association* v. *Clarke* (1888) 20 Q.B.D. 576.
86 *Hardoon* v. *Belilios* [1901] A.C. 118.
87 *Stevenson* v. *Wilson*, 1907 S.C. 445.
88 *Black* v. *Homersham* (1879) 4 Ex.D. 24.

to the company to register it.[89] Further, a buyer of shares impliedly agrees to indemnify the seller from any calls or liability which may arise in respect of the shares subsequently to the contract,[90] *e.g.*, before registration. It is not, however, clear that registration of the transfer divests the transferor of liability for calls in arrear to the company.[91] Damages for breach of the contract to transfer are measured by the difference between the contract price and the market price at the date of the breach.[92]

Transferees for onerous causes obtain a statutory title to the shares on registration.[93]

(c) Duty of directors to register transfers.—They cannot register a transfer unless a proper instrument of transfer has been delivered to the company.[94] Apart from that case, the articles may entitle them to refuse to register.[95] If the articles give the directors no discretion in accepting transferees, their function when a transfer is presented is merely ministerial. They are entitled to satisfy themselves that it is in order, *e.g.*, that it is properly stamped, and that the transferee is genuine, but they are bound to act honourably and according to the usual course of business, and not carelessly or purposely to delay.[96]

A power in the articles to the directors to veto transfers is a fiduciary power not to be arbitrarily or capriciously exercised,[97] for so exercised it means confiscation. The directors' duty is, keeping in view the terms in which their powers are expressed in the articles, fairly to consider the fitness of a proposed transferee at a board meeting.[98] If then the directors have fairly considered the question, the court will not interfere with their discretion.[99] But directors are not bound, in or out of court, to give their reasons for disapproving a transfer. The power to veto is only available when a company is a going one. If directors come to the conclusion that they cannot go on, and must wind up, they should pass a resolution to allow no more transfers.[1]

Transmission of shares.—On the death of a member of a company, his shares, as moveable estate,[2] vest in his executor or other personal

[89] s. 77; *Skinner* v. *City of London Marine Insurance Corporation* (1885) 14 Q.B.D. 882.
[90] *Spencer* v. *Ashworth Partington & Co.* [1925] 1 K.B. 589.
[91] *Re Hoylake Ry.* (1874) L.R. 9 Ch. 257.
[92] *Jamal* v. *Moolla Dawood & Co.* [1916] 1 A.C. 175.
[93] *Per* Lord Kinnear in *Edinburgh Northern Tramways Co.* v. *Mann* (1893) 20 R. (H.L.) 7.
[94] s. 75. A simplified form of transfer executed by the transferee only has been introduced by the Stock Transfer Act, 1963, p. 1, Sch. 1.
[95] *Lyle & Scott* v. *Scott's Trs.* 1959 S.C (H.L.) 64.
[96] *Nation's Case* (1886) L.R. 3 Eq. 77.
[97] *Hindle* v. *John Cotton Ltd.* (1919) 56 S.L.R. 625.
[98] *Re Ceylon Land and Produce Co. Ltd.* (1891) 7 T.L.R. 692.
[99] *Kennedy* v. *North British Wireless Schools Ltd.*, 1915 1 S.L.T. 196; 1916 1 S.L.T. 407.
[1] *Nation's Case* (1866) L.R. 3 Eq. 77; *Lowe's Case* (1869) L.R. 9 Eq. 589, at p. 595.
[2] s. 73.

representative. The personal representative does not *ipso facto* become a member of the company. The articles may disentitle him to become a member.[3] But in ordinary circumstances the presentation to the company of the confirmation or probate in favour of the executor entitles him to be registered, and if he authorises or afterwards adopts this step he becomes a shareholder to all effects.[4] If the executor wishes to transfer the shares, he is not bound to go upon the register, and may execute a transfer without doing so.[5]

It is no part of the duty of a trustee in bankruptcy to go upon the register, but his title may be noted and dividends drawn.[6] If he authorises the company to register the shares in his name, he is liable as a shareholder.[7] He can, without going on the register, execute a transfer of shares in favour of a purchaser, the bankrupt holder, as registered owner, being bound to concur.[8] The transmission of shares on the bankruptcy of a member is usually regulated by the articles.[9]

VI. REGULATION AND MANAGEMENT OF THE COMPANY

1. Directors

The company in general acts through its directors, who are, in the eye of the law, agents of the company for which they act, and the general principles of the law of principal and agent regulate in most respects the relationship of the company and its directors.[10] The authority of directors as agents of a company to act for it in a particular matter may be expressed through a resolution of the company in general meeting or by provision in the articles of association. The articles of a company, therefore, commonly provide that the directors may exercise all such powers of the company as are not by the Act or the articles required to be exercised by the company in general meeting.

Liability of a company for the acts of its agents.—A company is liable for the actings of its servants in the course of their employment, done in the interest and for the benefit of the company. That is so even if the actings are wrongful,[11] *e.g.*, negligent,[12] fraudulent, or in breach of duty.[13] A company is not liable for the acts of its agents, though acting with its authority, if the acts be *ultra vires* of the

---

[3] Table A, Arts. 29–32.
[4] *Buchan* v. *City of Glasgow Bank* (1879) 6 R. 567 (H.L.) 44. See also *supra*, p. 318.
[5] s. 76; *Trotter* v. *British Linen Bank* (1898) 6 S.L.T. 213.
[6] *Myles* v. *City of Glasgow Bank* (1879) 6 R. 718; *Lindsay* v. *Do., ibid.*, 671.
[7] *Lumsden* v. *Peddie* (1866) 5 M. 34.
[8] *Myles* v. *City of Glasgow Bank, cit. sup., per* Lord President Inglis at p. 726.
[9] *e.g.*, Table A, Art. 30.
[10] See Palmer's *Company Law*, 20th ed., pp. 513 *et seq.*
[11] *Lloyd* v. *Grace Smith & Co.* [1912] A.C. 716.
[12] *Scobie* v. *Steele & Wilson Ltd.*, 1963 S.L.T. (Notes) 45.
[13] *Royal British Bank* v. *Turquand* (1856) 6 E. & B. 327.

company. Such are void *ab initio* and cannot bind the company. If the agent acts ostensibly on behalf of but without the authority of the company, and the act done is *intra vires* of the company, it will be bound to a third party if he acted in ignorance of the agent's want of authority, on the principle that persons dealing with the company are not bound to enquire into the regularity of its internal proceedings.[14] This is known as the Rule in the *Royal British Bank* v. *Turquand*, or the rule *omnia rite acta praesumuntur*.[15] If the party dealing with the company has notice of the agent's want of authority, the company will not be liable to him, but he may have a claim upon the agent under his warranty of his own authority. If a contract *intra vires* of the company but made without authority is made with a member it is voidable.

Qualification of directors.—Directors are, under the Companies Act and the general law,[16] under no obligation to take qualification shares, but as a rule articles contain a qualification clause on the principle that a director should have a substantial stake in the company. The effect of such a clause is to create a duty to acquire the shares. It has not the effect of a contract to do so. Under the Act [17] every director who is required to hold a specified share qualification is bound to obtain his qualification within two months after his appointment, or such shorter time as may be fixed by the articles of the company; and the office must be vacated if within the time required the director has not qualified or if after the expiration of the time he ceases at any time to hold his qualification.

Liability of directors to the company.—This may arise from negligence, misfeasance or breach of trust.

Directors may incur personal liability for the company's loss due to their negligence in the conduct of the company's affairs. In the case of the City Equitable Fire Insurance Company, the duty of directors in their conduct of the company's affairs was closely examined, and the general principle laid down that they are bound to act honestly, and to use fair and reasonable diligence in the discharge of their duties, but they are not bound to do more.[18] They are not bound to exhibit greater skill in performance of their duties than can be expected from their knowledge and experience, and are not liable for mere errors of judgment. Directors must, however, exercise their judgment in the company's business.[19] In so doing, they are entitled

---

[14] *Gillies* v. *Craigton Garage Co.*, 1935 S.C. 423.
[15] *Supra*, p. 300.
[16] *De Ruvigne's Case* (1877) 5 Ch.D. 306.
[17] s. 182.
[18] *Re City Equitable Fire Insurance Co.* [1925] 1 Ch. 407.
[19] *Leeds Estate Building & Investment Co.* v. *Shepherd* (1887) 36 Ch.D. 787.

to rely upon information furnished to them by the proper officer of the company, and are not bound, in the absence of grounds for suspicion, to make personal investigation into its books and accounts.[20] Thus the rule of fair and reasonable diligence requires that each director see that the company's moneys are from time to time in a proper state of investment, except so far as the articles may justify him in delegating that duty to others.[21] The articles cannot exempt him from liability to the company for negligence. But if he has acted honestly and reasonably and ought fairly to be excused the court may relieve him of liability.[22]

If the directors apply the funds of the company to *ultra vires* purposes, e.g., in a line of trade not within the objects of the company, they are liable to replace them,[23] even although they have acted honestly, though mistakenly,[24] or in ignorance of the purposes for which the money was meant to be applied.[25] They may, however, be relieved of liability by the court. Thus, while directors are liable if they pay dividends out of capital, if they declare the dividend or a bonus in reliance on a balance sheet bona fide made out with proper assistance, the court will not, without strong reasons, declare the dividend improper, and make them recoup the company.[26] That is to say, they may employ accountants and actuaries to make up the accounts, but they must still exercise their judgment as business men upon the balance sheet and estimates submitted to them.[27]

A director is so far in the position of a trustee that like a promoter he cannot make any undisclosed or secret profit from his position as director.[28] Thus he may not accept a retaining fee, or a secret present, from a person with an interest adverse to the company, such as a vendor or promoter. To justify taking the profit, the transaction must be open and known to all the shareholders as capable of being ratified by them, and be actually ratified by them.[29] Non-disclosure is in fact a misfeasance.[30]

Meetings of directors.—The articles usually regulate the holding of meetings of directors. It is the duty of directors to keep minutes of their meetings.[31] Such minutes are prima facie proof of the matters

[20] *Dovey* v. *Cory* [1901] A.C. 477; *Lees* v. *Tod* (1882) 9 R. 807.
[21] *Re City Equitable Fire Insurance Co., supra.*
[22] s. 448.
[23] *Maxton* v. *Brown* (1839) 1 D. 367.
[24] *Re Liverpool Household Stores Association Ltd.* (1890) 59 L.J.Ch. 616.
[25] *Re National Funds Assurance Co.* (1878) 10 Ch.D. 118 at p. 128.
[26] *Rance's Case* (1870) L.R. 6 Ch. 104.
[27] *Leeds Estate Building & Investment Co.* v. *Shepherd* (1887) 36 Ch.D. 787.
[28] See *Parker* v. *M'Kenna* (1891) 10 Ch.App. 96 at 118.
[29] *Parker & Cooper Ltd.* v. *Reading* [1926] 1 Ch. 975.
[30] Lord Herschell in *Cape Breton Co.* (1887) 12 App.Cas. at 661.
[31] s. 145.

recorded.[32]   They are therefore not the only admissible evidence of the proceedings.   An unrecorded resolution may be proved *aliunde*.[33] No alteration of minutes should be made after they are signed by the chairman.[34]

2. Commencement of business

A private company may go to allotment immediately after the certificate of incorporation is obtained, and may commence business and exercise its borrowing powers forthwith.   But companies issuing a prospectus inviting the public to subscribe for shares may not commence any business or exercise any borrowing power unless, to state shortly the provisions of the Act of 1948, s. 109, (1) shares payable in cash have been allotted to the extent of the minimum subscription; (2) every director has paid on all shares payable in cash taken by him a proportion equal to the proportion payable on application and allotment on the shares offered for public subscription, and (3) the secretary or a director has delivered to the registrar for registration a statutory declaration that these conditions have been complied with. In the case of public companies not issuing a prospectus, there must have been filed with the registrar a statement in lieu of prospectus, and each director must have paid the amount payable on application and allotment on all shares payable in cash taken by him, and a statutory declaration that that amount has been paid filed.   In both cases, on the filing of the statutory declaration, the registrar must certify that the company is entitled to commence business, and his certificate is conclusive evidence of the fact.   The most important effect of this provision is that any contract, including a contract to take shares,[35] made by a company before the date at which it is entitled to commence business, is provisional only and is not binding on the company until that date.[36]

3. Meetings of the company

General meetings of a company comprise the statutory meeting, ordinary meetings and extraordinary meetings.

The statutory meeting.[37]—This meeting must be held from one to three months after the company is entitled to commence business. The provisions of the Act requiring it to be held apply only to

---

[32] *City of Glasgow Bank Liqrs.* (1880) 7 R. 1196.

[33] *Re Fireproof Doors Ltd.* [1916] 2 Ch. 142.

[34] *Re Cawley & Co.* (1889) 42 Ch.D. 209, *per* Esher M.R., at 226.

[35] See *Buckley on The Companies Acts,* 13th ed., 254.

[36] s. 109; *Re Otto Electrical Manufacturing Co.* [1906] 2 Ch. 390; *cf. Brown* v. *Stewart* (1898) 1 F. 316.

[37] s. 130.

companies limited by shares or by guarantee and having a share capital, other than private companies.

The purpose of the statutory meeting is to put the shareholders of the company as early as possible in possession of all the important facts relating to the new company, such as shares taken up, moneys received, contracts entered into, preliminary expenses and the names of officers and members of the company, and to discuss the management, methods and prospects of the company.[38] Fourteen days in advance of the meeting, a report, called the statutory report, certified by not less than two directors of the company and the auditors, stating various statutory particulars—shares allotted, cash received, directors, modification of contracts mentioned in the prospectus—relevant to the purpose of the meeting must be forwarded to the members. The directors must also cause a copy of the statutory report to be filed with the registrar forthwith after the sending thereof to the members. At the meeting, the directors must make available for reference by the members during the meeting a list of the members and the shares held by them. The members may discuss any matter relating to the formation of the company or arising out of the statutory report, but no resolution of which notice has not been given in accordance with the articles may be passed.

Ordinary general meetings.[39]—An ordinary general meeting of the company must be held once at least in every calendar year, and not more than fifteen months after the holding of the last preceding general meeting. If default is made in holding such a meeting, any member of the company may apply to the Board of Trade to call or direct the calling of a meeting. The articles usually regulate the holding of the annual meeting.

Extraordinary general meetings.[40]—Extraordinary general meetings are general meetings other than the statutory and the annual meeting. An appeal to a general meeting is the proper and only remedy of shareholders who complain of mismanagement.[41]

If for any reason it is impracticable to call or conduct a meeting of a company, the court may, of its own motion or on the application of any director or member, order a meeting to be called, held and conducted in such manner as it thinks fit, and such a meeting is for all purposes deemed to be a meeting of the company.[42]

---

[38] See Palmer's *Company Law*, 20th ed., pp. 455–456.
[39] s. 131.
[40] s. 132.
[41] *Isle of Wight Ry.* v. *Tahourdin* (1884) 25 Ch.D. 320.
[42] s. 135.

4. Resolutions

Resolutions may be ordinary, extraordinary or special.

Ordinary.—An ordinary resolution is a resolution passed by a majority of members, voting in person or by proxy, where the articles allow voting by proxy, at a general meeting. Where the articles provide that certain acts shall be done by the company in general meeting, an ordinary resolution is sufficient.[43]

Extraordinary.—An extraordinary resolution is one passed by a majority of not less than three-fourths of such members entitled to vote as vote in person or by proxy,[44] where proxies are allowed, at a general meeting of which notice specifying the intention to propose the resolution as an extraordinary resolution has been duly given.[45] An extraordinary resolution is sometimes prescribed by the articles in place of an ordinary resolution where the matter is of special importance, e.g., that it is advisable to wind up.[46]

Special.—A special resolution is one which has been passed in manner required for the passing of an extraordinary resolution at a general meeting of which not less than twenty-one days' notice, specifying the intention to propose the resolution as a special resolution, has been given. Certain acts may be done by a company only by special resolution, e.g., alteration of its objects or articles, reduction of its capital,[47] or to wind up voluntarily.[48]

A copy of every special and extraordinary resolution must, within fifteen days from the passing of the resolution, be forwarded to the Registrar of Companies to be recorded[49]; and where articles have been registered a copy of every special or extraordinary resolution for the time being in force must be embodied in or annexed to every copy of the articles issued after the passing of the resolution.

5. Accounts and audit.—Relation of auditor to company

The auditor is prima facie not an officer of the company. The mere performance of an auditor's services on a particular occasion will not make him an officer, but he may be held to be an officer of the company if appointed to the office of auditor of the company, either in the articles or at the annual general meeting.[50]

---

[43] *North West Transportation Co.* v. *Beatty* (1887) 12 App.Cas. 589, 593.
[44] *California Redwood Co.* (1885) 13 R. 335.
[45] s. 141.
[46] s. 278.
[47] *Supra*, pp. 306, 308
[48] s. 278.
[49] s. 143.
[50] *Western Counties Steam Bakeries & Milling Co.* [1897] 1 Ch. 617; contrast *Gibson* v *Barton* (1875) L.R. 10 Q.B. 329.

Every auditor has a right of access at all times to the books and accounts and vouchers of the company, and is entitled to require from the directors and other officers of the company such information and explanations as he thinks necessary for the performance of his duties.[51]

An auditor may be sued by the company for a breach of his duty, e.g., where the result is a misapplication of the company's funds by payment of dividends out of capital.[52] If he is an officer of the company he may, in the course of a winding up, be proceeded against for misfeasance.[53]

While auditors' reports and the balance sheets of a company are primarily addressed to the shareholders, they must be considered to be put into the hands of the public as well, and a member of the public is entitled to say in a question with the company that he purchased shares on the faith of their accuracy.[54]

Duties of auditors.—Auditors have a general duty to make themselves acquainted with their duties as laid down in the Companies Act,[55] and must conform to the terms of the articles imposing exceptional duties upon them unless there be a special contract defining their duties and liabilities.[56]

The main duty of the auditors of a company is to examine the company's accounts and the balance sheet to be laid before the company in general meeting, and to make a report to the shareholders, in short (1) whether they have obtained all the information and explanations which they required, and (2) whether, in their opinion, the balance sheet dealt with in the report is properly drawn up so as to exhibit a true and fair view of the state of the company's affairs to the best of their information and according to the explanations given to them, and as shown by the books of the company.[57] The duty so imposed on an auditor leaves abundant room for the exercise of his discretion as to what inquiries he must make. But the onus lies on him to make sufficient inquiry to ascertain and state the true financial position of the company at the time of the audit.[58] He must see that the books themselves, upon which the balance sheet is based, show the company's true position. But he is not bound to do more than exercise reasonable care and skill in making inquiries and investigations. He is not bound to be suspicious. But where there is something to excite his suspicion he must exercise more care. He may

---

[51] s. 162.
[52] *Leeds Estate Building and Investment Co.* v. *Shepherd* (1887) 36 Ch.D. 787.
[53] s. 333. *Re Kingston Cotton Mills (No. 2)* [1896] 2 Ch. 279.
[54] *Lees* v. *Tod* (1882) 9 R. 807.
[55] *Republic of Bolivia Exploration Syndicate* [1914] 1 Ch. 139.
[56] *Re City Equitable Fire Assurance Co.* [1925] 1 Ch. 407.
[57] s. 162, and 9th Sched.
[58] *Re City Equitable Fire Assurance Co.* [1925] 1 Ch. 407.

act upon the opinion of an expert where special knowledge is required, and he may rely upon the returns made by a competent and trusted expert relating to matters on which information from such a person is essential, *e.g.*, by a manager as to the values of stock-in-trade.[59]   An auditor is not justified in omitting to make personal inspection of securities that are in the custody of a person or company, *e.g.*, stock-brokers, with whom it is not proper that they should be left, whenever such personal inspection is practicable.   If he discovers that securities of the company are not in proper custody, it is his duty to require that the matter be put right at once, or if his requirement is not complied with, to report the fact to the shareholders, and this whether he can or cannot make a personal inspection.[60]   On the other hand, it is not part of the auditor's duty to give advice either to directors or share-holders as to what they ought to do.[61]   On completion of his inquiries the duty of the auditor is to convey information in his report to the shareholders and not merely so to express himself as to arouse inquiry on their part.[62]   The auditor's report must be attached to the balance sheet, and be read before the company in general meeting.   The auditors have the right to attend any general meeting of the company and to be heard on any part of the business which concerns them as auditors.[63]

A copy of the last balance sheet as audited and a copy of the auditor's report, certified by a director and the secretary as true copies, must be annexed to the annual return made by the company to the registrar.[64]

6. Dividends and profits

(a) **Source from which dividends payable.**—The Act of 1948, except in Table A, does not contain any express provision as to payment of dividends.   It is not, however, necessary to include payment of divi-dends among the objects in the memorandum.   The Act evidently treats the power to pay dividends as an object of every company and properly left to be dealt with and defined by the articles.   But payment of dividends out of capital, *i.e.*, out of moneys subscribed for shares, is *ultra vires* and contrary to the statute,[65] for the statute impliedly, if not expressly, provides that the paid-up capital shall, subject to its loss, of which creditors take the risk, be retained and kept up as a fund to

---

[59] *Kingston Cotton Mills Co. (No. 2)* [1896] 2 Ch. 279; *Re City Equitable Fire Assurance Co., supra.*
[60] *Re City Equitable Fire Assurance Co., supra.*
[61] *Per* Lindley L.J. *Re London and General Bank (No. 2)* [1895] 2 Ch. 673.
[62] *Re London and General Bank (No. 2) supra.*
[63] ss. 156, 162.
[64] s. 127.
[65] Palmer's *Company Law,* 20th ed., p. 635–636; Table A, Arts. 114–122; s. 59.

which creditors are entitled to look.[66]   Hence the elaborate regulation in the Act of reduction of capital.   The articles usually define the matter by providing that no dividend shall be paid otherwise than out of profits.[67]   A statutory exception [68] permits payment of interest out of capital on share capital issued to raise money to defray the cost of the construction of works or provision of plant which cannot be made profitable for a lengthened period.

(b) Profits available for dividend.[69]—There is nothing in the Act of 1948 or in the general law to prevent the distribution by way of dividend of profits of any description, whether arising from the business of the company or from other sources, e.g., a realised surplus on sale of a capital asset.[70]   Any increment of value whether by way of appreciation of the assets or by way of profit earned by employing them may be profit from which dividend can be paid.   But the House of Lords has declined to define in the abstract what is profit and what capital in dealing with questions of dividends; that is, each case depends on its own facts.[71]   The fact is that the law is much more accurately expressed by saying that dividends cannot be paid out of capital than by saying that they can only be paid out of profits.[72] The latter expression suggests that the capital issued must always be kept up and represented by assets, which, if sold, would produce it. This is more than the law requires.   For, in one and the same accounting period, capital may be sunk and lost, e.g., by the depreciation in value of buildings into which it has been put, and yet the excess of current receipts over current expenses may be divided.[73]

The matter may be specifically defined in the articles.   If not, the question arises whether a particular depreciation or loss of capital in an accounting period falls to be made up out of revenue before the profits arising on revenue account in that period are available for dividend.   Under the earlier decisions it was held that they must always be made up.   But as the law now stands it is as follows.   A distinction must first be appreciated, namely, between "fixed" and "circulating" capital.   Fixed capital means capital assets acquired for the purpose of being retained, e.g., buildings, works, ships. Circulating capital means capital assets acquired with a view to resale,

---

66 *Trevor* v. *Whitworth* (1887) L.R. 12 A.C. 409; *Ammonia Soda Co.* v. *Chamberlain* [1918] 1 Ch. 266, 292.
67 Table A, Art. 116.
68 s. 65.
69 *Buckley on The Companies Acts,* 13th ed., pp. 898–899.
70 *Lubbock* v. *British Bank of South America* [1892] 2 Ch. 198; Buckley, *op. cit.,* 751, *et seq.*
71 See *Dovey* v. *Cory* [1901] A.C. 486.
72 Buckley, *op. cit.,* p. 902.   *Verner* v. *General and Commercial Investment Trust* [1894] 2 Ch. 239, at p. 266.
73 *Lawrence* v. *West Somerset Mineral Ry.* [1918] 2 Ch. 250.

e.g., the goods of the merchant, or goods produced for sale at a profit. Accordingly, under more recent decisions, it is permissible to apply profits on revenue account to payment of dividend without keeping up fixed capital which has depreciated or been lost in the same accounting period. But where circulating capital, *i.e.*, capital which has been used in earning profits, has been lost in a particular accounting period, it must be restored out of profits earned in that period before profits so earned can be applied to dividend.[74] If, however, circulating capital on which no profits have been earned has been lost, and therefore the loss must necessarily have fallen on capital, it need not under these decisions be replaced out of profits earned in subsequent accounting periods.[75] These principles have been applied to the particular case of the wasting asset, *e.g.*, a coal mine purchased with capital under the objects clause. A wasting asset need not as a general rule be restored as it is consumed, that is, depreciation through wasting may be fixed capital depreciation and the regulations may so provide [76] unless in the circumstances of the case it is to be regarded as circulating capital.[77]

The result of the cases is that it is usually legal but not altogether safe to pay away profits as dividends without making any provision for making good loss of capital. In practice companies do not as a general rule distribute as dividend the whole profits they may be legally entitled to treat as such without making reasonable provision for meeting losses of capital; or if capital is lost, they take steps to reduce their nominal capital.[78]

(c) **Right to dividend.**—There is no principle which compels a company while a going concern to divide the whole of its divisible profits among the shareholders. The right to dividend arises only on a dividend being declared by the company.

The articles may regulate the manner in which a dividend may be declared.[79] Subject then to the articles, the company may pay the dividend to each shareholder in proportion to the number of shares held by him, and not in proportion to the amount of capital paid up on his shares.[80] But the articles may legitimately provide for paying dividend in proportion to capital paid up.[81] The persons entitled to

---

[74] *Verner* v. *General Commercial Trust* [1894] 2 Ch. 268.
[75] *Ammonia Soda Co.* v. *Chamberlain* [1918] 1 Ch. 266; *Stapley* v. *Read Bros.* [1924] 2 Ch. 1.
[76] *Lee* v. *Neuchatel Asphalte Co.* (1889) 41 Ch.D. 1.
[77] As in *Bond* v. *Barrow Haematite Co.* [1902] 1 Ch. 353.
[78] As to divisibility of an unrealised appreciation of fixed assets see *Westburn Sugar Refineries Ltd.* v. *Inland Revenue* 1960 S.L.T. 297. But see *Dimbula Valley (Ceylon) Tea* v. *Laurie* [1961] Ch. 353.   [79] Table A, Arts. 114–122.
[80] *Oakbank Oil Co.* v. *Crum* (1882) 8 App.Cas. 65; *cf. Re Bridgewater Navigation Co.* (1889) 14 App.Cas. 535.
[81] s. 59, Table A, Art. 118. *Cf. Andrews* v. *Gas Meter Co.* [1897] 1 Ch. 361; *Hoggan* v. *Tharsis Sulphur & Copper Co.* (1882) 9 R. 1191.

receive the dividend are the persons whose names appear on the register
of shareholders at the time of declaration, or if deceased prima facie
their legal personal representatives,[82] and unless the articles otherwise
provide they are entitled to be paid in cash, e.g., not in bonus shares.[83]
All shares with the same rights share equally. Where shares are
entitled to a preferential dividend at a specified fixed rate per cent., the
dividend is cumulative, that is, if profits are insufficient in one year,
the deficiency must, unless otherwise clearly indicated, be made up
out of profits of subsequent years,[84] before dividend is paid to the
ordinary shareholders. The declaration of a dividend creates a debt
from the company to each shareholder for which he is entitled to sue.[85]

(d) How profits may be dealt with apart from dividend.—If net
profits, after charges against revenue are deducted, are not applied to
pay dividend they may be left at credit of the profit and loss account
or put to a reserve account of some sort and so accumulated. Such
may be treated as accumulated profits or they may be capitalised, if the
constitution of the company so allows. This may be done by applying
reserve profits to making partly paid up shares further paid up, or the
profits may be capitalised by issuing bonus shares in satisfaction of a
bonus or dividend declared out of such profits, or even without
declaring a bonus.[86] This results in an increase in issued and paid-up
capital. The profits capitalised cease to be available for dividend.

7. Borrowing.—Power to borrow

Power to borrow is not inherent in all companies. It must be
found expressly or inferentially in the memorandum and may be
further regulated in the articles.[87] An implied power to borrow arises
when a power to borrow may fairly be regarded as incidental to the
company's objects. Thus, ordinary trading companies have an implied power to borrow for the purposes of the business.[88] But this
implied power may be expressly limited, e.g., to an amount equal to
the issued capital.[89]

If a company without power to borrow, or with a limit to borrowing
in its memorandum, borrows outwith its power, the act is *ultra vires*
of the company, even if it be a trading company, and in either case the

[82] *James* v. *Buena Ventura Nitrate Grounds Syndicate* [1896] 1 Ch. 456.
[83] *Wood* v. *Odessa Waterworks Co.* (1889) 42 Ch.D. 636.
[84] *Webb* v. *Earle* (1875) L.R. 20 Eq. 556.
[85] *Milne* v. *Arizona Copper Co.* (1899) 1 F. 935.
[86] Palmer's *Company Law*, 20th ed., p. 647; *Swan Brewery Co.* v. *The King* [1914] A.C.
231.
[87] *Baroness Wenlock* v. *River Dee Co.* (1885) 10 App.Cas. 354.
[88] *Cunliffe, Brooks & Co.* v. *Blackburn & District Benefit Building Society* (1884) 9
App.Cas. 857.
[89] *e.g.,* Table A, Art. 79.

loan is null and cannot be ratified.   But in England, and, it is thought, in Scotland also,[90] although the lender has no action against the company as for payment of a loan or debt,[91] he has a right to follow his money in the hands of the company before it is spent and to have the company interdicted from parting with it.   Thus, he may trace the money in the hands of the company by showing it was put into a particular investment.[92]   Or again, he may prove beneficial application of the loan to the company's purposes, for example, that it has been spent in paying off just debts of the company.   Then the lender may be entitled to stand in place of and be subrogated to the rights of the creditors so paid, and can rank in their place.   He is, however, not entitled to any preference in ranking which these creditors may have held.[93]

Another remedy is that a lender may have a right of action against the directors for breach of their implied warranty of authority.[94]

Power to grant security for money borrowed.—A company having power to borrow may, as incidental to the power to borrow, grant security over the company's property and rights.[95]   Express power to grant the security instruments is, however, usually contained in the memorandum or articles.

In the absence of special power in the memorandum and articles, the mortgage of uncalled capital is invalid as being an encroachment on the discretion of the directors in the future administration of the company [96]; the omission specifically to authorise such a charge in the memorandum may imply a prohibition.   The court in any event regards any such charge with disfavour.   Calls in arrear, on the other hand, being debts due to the company, may be the subject of security by assignment or arrestment, as also may calls made but payable at a future date, and, in England, calls determined on but not yet made.[97]

A security by way of floating charge was until the passing of the Companies (Floating Charges) (Scotland) Act, 1961, ineffectual by the law of Scotland.[98]   A floating charge is a security constituted in such a way as to give a creditor advancing money to a company the security of its whole assets generally, not only those in its possession at the

---

[90] See *Gloag on Contract,* 2nd ed., pp. 112 *et seq.*
[91] *Cunliffe, Brooks & Co., supra.*
[92] *Sinclair* v. *Brougham* [1914] A.C. 398.
[93] *Re Wrexham, etc., Ry.* [1899] 1 Ch. 440.
[94] *Chapleo* v. *Brunswick Permanent Building Society* (1887) 6 Q.B.D. 696.
[95] *Re Patent File Co.* (1870) L.R. 6 Ch. 83; *Paterson's Trs.* v. *Caledonian Heritable Security Co.* (1886) 13 R. 369.
[96] *Re Sankey Brook Coal Co. (No. 2)* (1870) L.R. 10 Eq. 381; *Newton* v. *Anglo-Australian Co.* [1895] A.C. 244.
[97] *Re Sankey Brook Coal Co.* (1870) 9 Eq. 721.
[98] *Ballachulish Slate Quarries* v. *Menzies* (1908) 45 S.L.R. 667; 16 S.L.T. 48; *Coppen* v. *Carse* 1951 S.C. 233.

date of the security, but all assets thereafter coming into its possession from day to day until the creditor steps in and makes specific subjects of his security assets the company had at the time. This he does by getting a receiver or factor appointed by the court to take them. In this way he may in England obtain a priority over them as against unsecured creditors. But in Scotland a security had to be over subjects specific and identified when the security is constituted. But the Act of 1961 has provided that such a charge may now be created by an instrument of charge, which requires registration with the Registrar of Companies in order to be effective against the liquidator or any creditor in a winding up of a company registered in Scotland, and extends to cover property[99] which includes heritable property in Scotland where the company is incorporated and not registered in Scotland or if the company has an established place of business in Scotland.[1] Until it is so completed, securities obtained by other creditors, and completed, will have priority over the floating charge creditors. A fixed security arising *ex lege, e.g.*, a repairer's lien, has priority over a floating charge. As between floating charges priority of registration rules, unless the instruments provide for ranking *pari passu* or the floating charges are received by the Registrar by the same post.[2] Whether a company registered in Scotland can by floating charge create an effectual security over its assets in England, having an established place of business there, seems a question of the law of England.[3]

How security effected.—Debentures.—When security is given, it is generally effected by a debenture containing an acknowledgment of indebtedness and a trust deed containing a conveyance by the company, in form appropriate to the subject of security, to trustees, to hold, and, when necessary, to administer and realise. In the trust deed for debenture holders it is generally provided that, notwithstanding the conveyance of the security subjects to trustees, the company shall continue in the management of its business and property, but may be suspended from doing so by the trustees on the occurrence of certain events, when the security shall become enforceable, *e.g.*, the failure of the company to pay interest or principal within a certain time, a winding-up resolution or order, or the breach of any of the covenants and conditions of the trust deed. Thereupon the trustees are authorised to enter into possession of the premises, and also of the stock and other moveable property thereon, with power either to sell and dispose

---

[99] The kinds of property affected are specified in the 2nd Schedule to the Act, s. 106A.
[1] *Ibid*, s, 106K.
[2] Act of 1961, s. 5.
[3] See Companies Act, 1948, s. 106.

thereof, or to carry on the business. The trustees' right to the subjects of security must be completed in the appropriate manner as before stated.[4]

VII. PRIVATE COMPANIES

The Act of 1948 [5] defines a private company as a company which by its articles (1) restricts the right to transfer its shares, (2) limits the number of its members to fifty, not including, *i.e.*, with in addition, present employees holding shares and past employees who held and still hold shares, and (3) prohibits any invitation to the public to subscribe for any shares or debentures of the company. These three requirements must be clearly provided for in the articles. As to restriction of the right to transfer, a power to the directors to refuse to pass any transfer, even of fully paid-up shares, will satisfy that requirement. If it alters its articles so as no longer to include the required restrictions, it becomes forthwith a public company, and liable to deliver to the registrar for registration a statement in lieu of prospectus in the form and containing the particulars set out in the Third Schedule to the Act.[6] Where, however, the company's articles contain the required restrictions, but these are not observed, the company remains a private company [7] but ceases to be entitled to certain of the privileges and exemptions of a private company. The court may grant relief if non-observance of the required provisions was due to inadvertence or other sufficient cause, or if it is just and equitable to do so.

A private company, like limited companies generally, is constituted by registration of a memorandum and articles of association. The application to register must be in a special form showing that the company does not issue an invitation to the public to subscribe. Upon the certificate of incorporation being issued, the company, unlike a public company, can commence business at once. " It attains its maturity at birth." [8]

Other distinctive features of a private company are as follows:— (1) It may consist of a minimum of two persons instead of seven [9]; (2) it does not require to file, prior to the first allotment of either shares or debentures, a statement in lieu of prospectus [10]; (3) a director may be appointed in the articles without first signing and filing with the registrar a consent in writing to act as such director, or, if the articles require a share qualification for the directors, without signing

---

[4] *Clark* v. *West Calder Oil Co.* (1882) 9 R. 1017.
[5] s. 28.
[6] s. 30.
[7] s. 29; *Park* v. *Royalties Syndicate* [1912] 1 K.B. 330.
[8] s. 109 (7) (*a*); Lord Macnaghten in *Salomon* v. *Salomon & Co.* [1897] A.C. 22.
[9] s. 1.
[10] s. 48 (3).

the memorandum or filing with the registrar a contract or undertaking to take qualification shares [11]; (4) it does not, but only if it is an " exempt private company," [12] require to annex to its annual return a certified copy of its balance sheet [13] and auditors' and directors' reports, but it must send in a special certificate that it has not issued any invitation to the public to subscribe for any shares or debentures, and that the number of members in excess of fifty consists of persons not to be included [14]; (5) it does not require to convene a statutory meeting [15]; and (6) it may have less than two directors.[16]

VIII. DISSOLUTION OF A COMPANY

Dissolution of a company may be brought about in one or other of two ways—1. Removal from the Register, and 2. Liquidation.

1. Removal from register [17]

Dissolution of the company may take place apart from liquidation in one case, *viz.*, under section 353 of the Act, where the company is defunct and is removed from the register. This can happen " when the registrar of companies has reasonable cause to believe that the company is not carrying on business or in operation." The section directs the registrar how to proceed to ascertain whether a company is defunct, and provides for the striking of its name off the register, and for the continuance of the liability of directors and members notwithstanding the dissolution. The property of the company is deemed to be *bona vacantia* and belongs to the Crown. The Act provides also for the restoration of the name of the company to the register by the court if satisfied that the company was at the time of striking off carrying on business or in operation, or otherwise that it is just that it be restored to the register; and the court may give directions for placing the company and all other persons in the same position as if the name of the company had not been struck off[18]

2. Liquidation or winding up.—Meaning

Liquidation is the process whereby the business relations into which a company has entered during its active life are brought to an end with due regard to the rights of the parties to the contracts into

---

[11] s. 181 (5).
[12] See s. 129.
[13] s. 129.
[14] s. 128.
[15] s. 130.
[16] s. 176.
[17] ss. 353–355.
[18] *Morris* v. *Harris* [1927] A.C. 252.

which it has entered, and the assets remaining are distributed among the members in terms of the contract between them.

Modes.—There are three modes of winding up (a) by the court, (b) voluntary, and (c) under supervision of the court. Of these, voluntary winding up is the most common. The policy of the Companies Act is that shareholders shall manage their own affairs, including the winding up of the company's affairs, but in certain circumstances the Act entitles creditors or contributories to its capital to invoke the intervention of the court and have the assets administered by it. In winding up by the court, the winding up is entirely in the hands of the court, through its appointed liquidator, who is subject to control by the court

(a) Winding up by the court.—1. *Grounds.*—A winding-up order is made on the application of the company, or a creditor or contributory, and may be made on one or more of certain specified grounds.[19] The court has a discretion to grant or refuse the order. As to the discretion, it is directed not to refuse it merely on the ground that the company has mortgaged all its assets, or has no assets, *i.e.*, that there is nothing for the general creditors.[20] The reason is public policy in regard to commercial morality, so that its affairs may be investigated by the court. The court will not readily refuse the application of a creditor.[21]

The specified grounds [22] are: (i) that the company has by special resolution resolved to be wound up by the court. This is purely a members' ground of application. The winding up may be for any cause whatever. (ii) that default has been made in filing the statutory report or in holding the statutory meeting. Only a shareholder can petition on this ground.[23] (iii) that the company has not commenced business within a year from its incorporation, or has suspended business for a year. The court will not, in its discretion, wind up unless there are indications that the company has no intention of continuing its business.[24] A company which has amalgamated with another company cannot be wound up on this ground. But the registrar may strike the company off the register as defunct. (iv) that the number of members is reduced below two if a private company, or seven if a public company. This ground is unusual. The company usually winds up voluntarily. (v) that the company is unable to pay its debts.

---

[19] s. 222.
[20] s. 225.
[21] *Gardner & Co.* v. *Link* (1894) 21 R. 967.
[22] s. 222.
[23] s. 224.
[24] *Capital Fire Insurance* (1882) 21 Ch.D. 209.

A company is deemed to be unable to pay its debts [25] when (a) a creditor to whom a debt exceeding fifty pounds is due has served on the company a demand to pay, and the company has for three weeks thereafter neglected to pay the sum or to secure or compound for it to the satisfaction of the creditor, or (b) the *induciae* of a charge for payment on an extract decree, or extract registered bond or protest, have expired without payment and though the debt is less than £50,[26] or (c) it is proved to the satisfaction of the court that the company is unable to pay its debts. The usual evidence of this is repeated application by the creditor for payment and non-payment, the debt not being disputed. But the court must take into account the contingent and prospective liabilities of the company. It is enough that it is practically though not absolutely insolvent and cannot possibly make a profit.[27] (vi) that the court is of opinion that it is just and equitable that the company be wound up.[28] The construction of the term " just and equitable " has been that it is not confined to cases *ejusdem generis* with the preceding grounds, but covers such cases as (a) loss of the substantial part of the company's business, *i.e.*, the *substratum* is gone, and it is therefore impossible to carry on the main or paramount object [29]; (b) persistent disregard by the directors of the provisions of the Act; (c) in a private company, a division between the directors which brings the affairs of the company to a deadlock [30]; (d) that the company was constituted to carry out a fraud [31]; (e) in order to defeat a reconstruction scheme predjudicial to the shareholders.[32]

2. *Who may petition*

Application is by petition presented either by the company or by any creditor or creditors, contributory or contributories, or by all or any of those parties, together or separately.

(1) The company may petition. This is unusual. It usually winds up voluntarily or under supervision.

(2) A contributory, *i.e.*, any person liable to contribute to the assets of the company on its being wound up,[33] may not petition unless either (a) the number of members has become less than seven, or two in the case of a private company, or (b) the shares in respect of which he is a contributory were originally allotted to him, or have been held

---

[25] s. 223.   [26] *Speirs* v. *Central Building Co.*, 1911 S.C. 330.
[27] *Suburban Hotel Co.* (1867) L.R. 2 Ch. 737.
[28] An alternative remedy to winding up in this case is provided in s. 210. See *Elder* v. *Elder & Watson*, 1952 S.C. 49.
[29] *The Bleriot Mfg. Aircraft Co.* (1916) 32 T.L.R. 253; *Levy* v. *Napier* 1962 S.C. 468, S.L.T. 264.
[30] *Baird* v. *Lees*, 1924 S.C. 83; *Symington* v. *Symington's Quarries* (1905) 8 F. 121.
[31] *Re T. E. Brinsmead & Sons Ltd.* [1897] 1 Ch. 45, 406.
[32] *Consolidated South Rand Mines Ltd.* [1909] 1 Ch. 491.
[33] s. 213. *Infra*, pp. 368, 369.

by him for at least six months during the eighteen months before the commencement of the winding up, or have devolved on him through the death of a former holder.[34] The object of this provision is to prevent a person buying shares in order to qualify himself to wreck the company. A voluntary liquidation is normally the appropriate method for contributories. A contributory, to obtain a compulsory order, must make out a special case, such as that the *substratum* of the company is gone.[35] The fact that a voluntary winding up is already in progress is prima facie a bar to an order, the shareholder being bound by the wishes of the majority of the members.[36] But a contributory may obtain an order if the court is satisfied that a voluntary winding up will prejudice the shareholders,[37] or that the shareholders may derive some real benefit from a compulsory order.[38]

(3) A creditor may petition. This includes a person to whom the company is indebted in a sum of money presently due, the assignee of a debt, a secured creditor, and a contingent or prospective creditor. A creditor who cannot get paid a sum presently payable has prima facie a right to an order.[39] But a prospective or contingent creditor requires to give security for costs and must make out a prima facia case for winding up before he will be heard. That prima facie right is qualified by another rule, *viz.*, that the court will regard the wishes of the majority in value of the creditors, and may refuse the order if for some good reason they object,[40] or if the order will benefit only the petitioning creditor and not the creditors generally.[41] Further, the exercise of the court's discretion does not depend solely on the wishes of the creditors. Under Part V of the Act (Winding Up), the court has a wide jurisdiction in the interests of commercial morality, and if the facts disclose a strong prima facie case for investigation into the formation or promotion of a company, or the issue of debentures by it, the court will make the order notwithstanding creditors' opposition.[42] The voluntary winding up of a company is not a bar to the right of a creditor to a compulsory winding up.[43]

3. *Effects of a winding-up order*

(i) It operates in favour of all creditors and contributories.[44] (ii) the winding up is deemed to commence at the date of presentation of

---

[34] s. 224.
[35] *Symington, supra; Pirie* v. *Stewart* (1904) 6 F. 847.
[36] *Imperial Bank of China* (1880) L.R. 1 Ch. 339.
[37] *Re National Co. for Distribution of Electricity* [1902] 2 Ch. 34.
[38] *Re Doré Gallery Co.* [1891] W.N. 98.
[39] *Amalgamated Properties of Rhodesia, Ltd.* [1917] 2 Ch. 115.
[40] *Chapel House Colliery Co.* (1883) 24 Ch.D. 259.
[41] *Re Greenwood* [1900] 1 Q.B. 306.
[42] *Re Bishop & Sons Ltd.* [1900] 2 Ch. 254.
[43] *Re The Gutta Percha Corporation* [1900] 2 Ch. 665. [44] s. 232.

the petition for winding up except for the purpose of calculating certain preferential payments like wages, when the date is the date of the order. If, however, the company is already in voluntary liquidation, the winding up is deemed to commence at the time of the passing of the resolution to wind up voluntarily.[45] (iii) No action or proceeding may be proceeded with or commenced against the company except by leave of the court and subject to such terms as the court may impose.[46] (iv) Any disposition of the property of the company, and any transfer of shares, or alteration in the status of members, made after the commencement of the winding up, is, unless the court otherwise orders, void.[47] Alteration of status refers to, for example, registering transfers of shares executed but not registered at the commencement of the winding up, forfeiture of shares, or making partly paid-up shares fully paid. (v) Current trading contracts are not affected. The liquidator may either perform the contract or repudiate it and allow the parties to sue for damages. But the order is equivalent to notice of discharge to all employees.[48] (vi) Fraudulent preferences are treated as in bankruptcy.[49] (vii) The effect of winding up on diligence is that it is, as from the date of its commencement, equivalent to an arrestment in execution and decree of furthcoming, and to an executed or completed poinding, and all arrestments or poindings executed on or after the sixtieth day prior to that date are cut down. It is also equivalent to a decree of adjudication of the heritable estates of the company for payment of its debts.[50]

4. *The liquidator's powers and duties*

Generally speaking, the liquidator requires the authority of the court for what he does. But certain powers he may exercise with the sanction either of the court or of a committee of creditors and, in certain cases, contributories, called a committee of inspection, which has similar powers to those of commissioners on a bankrupt estate.[51] Certain other powers he may exercise independently. But any creditor or contributory may ask the court to control him in his exercise of these powers.[52]

The chief duties of a liquidator consist in the collection of the assets and their application in discharge of liabilities, together with recovering moneys due by contributories, and assisting the court in adjusting

---

[45] ss. 229, 319 (8) (*d*).
[46] s. 231.
[47] s. 227.
[48] *Chapman's Case* (1866) L.R. 1 Eq. 346.
[49] s. 320. See Bankruptcy, *supra* at p. 270, note 40.
[50] s. 327.
[51] ss. 252–255.
[52] s. 245.

their rights *inter se* and in distributing any surplus among the parties entitled thereto.

Calling up uncalled capital.—It may be necessary to call up uncalled liability on shares to pay debts or adjust the rights of contributories *inter se*. Accordingly the court is directed by the Act, as soon as may be after a winding-up order is made, to settle a list of contributories, and if necessary rectify the register, so that the list and the register may conform.[53]

A contributory is a person who is liable to contribute to the assets of the company in the event of its being wound up.[54] In settling the list the court distinguishes between persons who are contributories in their own right and those who are representative, or liable for the debts, of others, *e.g.*, the personal representatives of a deceased member, and a trustee in bankruptcy. This is because special rules apply to their cases.[55]

There is liability for calls only for certain purposes and within certain limits. The purposes are payment of the debts, liabilities and winding-up expenses, and the adjustment of the rights of contributories among themselves.[56] In a company limited by shares there is a general limit that no contribution can be required from any past or present member exceeding the amount, if any, unpaid on the shares in respect of which he is liable at winding up. In a guarantee company no contribution can be required from any member exceeding the amount undertaken to be contributed by him to the assets of the company in the event of winding up, and, if it has a share capital, sums unpaid on the shares. Within the general limit the liability of a particular contributory depends on the class of contributory to which he belongs. There are two classes. Separate lists are made up of these. These are the A and B Lists.

The A List consists of present members. It includes members who are in right of fully paid shares,[57] for they may be entitled to a payment if there is a surplus to distribute after paying creditors. The A contributory is liable to the extent that his shares are not fully paid up.

The B List consists of past members who have ceased to be members within a year preceding the commencement of the winding up. The main purpose of the liability of the B contributory is to protect creditors against the transfer of shares in expectation of liquidation by solvent holders to insolvent holders. These past members are liable for calls made in the liquidation in respect of shares held by them

[53] s. 257.
[54] s. 213.
[55] ss. 215-216.
[56] s. 212.
[57] *Tannoch Chemical Co.* (1894) 2 S.L.T. 397.

during the year preceding the winding up. Successive transferors of the same shares within the year may be called on simultaneously, but each transferor who pays will be entitled to be indemnified by the transferee. The B contributory is not liable unless present members are unable to satisfy the contributions required of them under the Act, and debts remain unpaid after the assets of the company have been applied *pari passu* towards payment of all debts no matter when contracted. He is not liable beyond the amount still unpaid on the particular shares he held. He is not liable in respect of any debt or liability incurred after he ceased to be a member. The B contributions are not divided among the old creditors in respect of whose debts they are paid, but form part of the general assets of the company for payment of all the creditors.[58]

In addition to other defences to an action for a call before liquidation already noticed,[59] set-off, pleadable before liquidation, is also pleadable by a contributory. But until all the creditors are paid no contributory can set off any sum due to him in his character as a member, *e.g.*, dividends, profits, directors' fees, etc., against claims made against him by the company, *e.g.*, calls. He may set off later, after creditors are paid, when the rights of contributories among themselves are being adjusted.

Payment of debts.—The proof of debts and the ranking of claims is the same as in bankruptcy. Certain debts, of course, are preferential.[60]

Adjustment of rights of contributories and distribution of assets.— After the property of the company, including sums due by members for calls on shares, has been applied in satisfaction of its liabilities, then any surplus falls to be distributed among the persons entitled thereto in accordance with their rights and interests in the company.[61] Such surplus may be less than the paid-up capital or more. If less, the loss of capital is borne prima facie by the members in proportion to the nominal capital held by them respectively. The distribution may then require an adjustment, due to the share capital being fully paid on some shares and only partially as to other shares. This may necessitate calls in order to secure parity of treatment in the distribution of any surplus, that is to say, surplus assets, where there is a loss, means assets remaining after due equalisation of capital account. The contract between the members may alter this. Thus if the articles provide that losses are to be borne in proportion to capital paid up,

58 *Webb* v. *Whiffen* (1872) L.R. 5 H.L. 711.
59 *Supra*, p. 321.
60 ss. 318, 319.
61 s. 265.

no call can be made on shares not fully paid for the benefit of the fully paid shares.[62]

If there remains a surplus after repayment to each member of his capital, as such surplus forms part of the joint stock which at the winding up represented capital, then in the absence of provisions to the contrary it is divisible amongst members in proportion to the nominal amount of their shares. That applies even where there are shares of different classes with different rights in capital.[63]

(b) Voluntary winding up.—Voluntary liquidation is a step often taken where it is proposed to reconstitute the company with wider powers, or when two companies propose to amalgamate, or where for any reason it is desired to bring the company to an end. It is competent (1) by ordinary resolution when the period, if any, fixed for the duration of the company by the articles expires, or the event, if any, occurs on which the articles provide that the company is to be dissolved; (2) if the company resolves by special resolution that it be wound up voluntarily—any reason suffices; (3) if the company resolves by extraordinary resolution to the effect that it cannot, by reason of its liabilities, continue its business, and that it is advisable to wind up.[64] The extraordinary resolution is convenient, as requiring shorter notice and so being quicker than a special resolution, when the company is being pressed by creditors. The voluntary winding up dates from the passing of the resolution which authorises it.[65]

Effects of winding-up resolution.—(1) The company must cease to carry on business except so far as required for beneficial winding up.[66] (2) The corporate state and powers of the company continue until it is dissolved.[66] The company's property remains vested in it, not in the liquidator. (3) Transfers of shares after the resolution are void except with the sanction of the liquidator.[67] Debentures, however, may be transferred after the date of winding up.[68] (4) Alterations in the status of members are void. (5) Diligences are equalised and fraudulent preferences are cut down by reference to the date of commencement of winding up as in the case of winding up by the court.[69]

---

[62] *Re Kinatan (Borneo) Rubber Ltd.* [1923] 1 Ch. 124.

[63] A definition in articles of the preferential right to repayment of capital on winding up of holders of preference shares may exclude a right to share in such a surplus, unless that is given by the articles. *Wilsons and Clyde Coal Co.* v. *Scottish Insurance Corporation*, 1949 S.C.(H.L.) 90 (overruling expressly *William Metcalfe & Sons* [1933] 1 Ch. 142, and in effect also *Williamson-Buchanan Steamers, Liqrs.*, 1936 S.L.T. 106).

[64] s. 278.

[65] s. 280.

[66] s. 281.

[67] s. 282.

[68] *Buckley on The Companies Acts*, 13th ed., 579.

[69] ss. 320, 327. *Supra*, p. 344.

Proceedings in voluntary winding up.—There are are now two kinds of voluntary winding up, members' and creditors'. It is a members' winding up where a declaration of solvency has been made, otherwise it is a creditors' winding up.[70] In the case of a solvent company, a majority of the directors may make and deliver to the registrar a statutory declaration to the effect that in their opinion the company will be able to pay its debts in full within twelve months from the commencement of the winding up. This is called a " Declaration of Solvency." It is of no effect unless made within five weeks immediately preceding the passing of the resolution to wind up, and delivered to the registrar for registration, and embodies a statement of the company's assets and liabilities. The members appoint their own liquidator, who is accountable to them, and, if the debts are not paid within the twelve months, to the creditors.

Where a declaration of solvency is not made, the company must call a meeting of creditors for the same day or the day after the resolution for voluntary winding up is to be proposed. The meeting is advertised in the *Gazette* and the directors lay before it a statement of the position of the company and a list of creditors.

The creditors and the company at their respective meetings may each nominate a liquidator but the creditors' nomination will normally prevail. A committee of inspection, on which the members may have representation, is appointed by the creditors. The court may be applied to in both cases.

(c) Winding up under supervision of the court.[71]—When a company has passed a resolution to wind up voluntarily, the court may, on application, make an order that the voluntary winding up shall continue but subject to the supervision of the court. The court grants such a supervision order for two reasons mainly, (1) that the order stops actions,[72] and (2) that it subjects the costs to taxation.

---

[70] ss. 278–310.
[71] ss. 311 *et seq.*
[72] s. 312.

CHAPTER 13

THE LAW OF INSURANCE

I. GENERAL PRINCIPLES

Nature of the contract.—The aim of all insurance is to make provision against the dangers which beset human life and dealings. Those who seek it endeavour to avert disaster from themselves by shifting possible loss on to the shoulders of others, who are willing, for pecuniary consideration, to take the risk thereof; and in the case of life insurance they endeavour to assure to those dependent on them a certain provision in case of their death, or to provide a fund out of which creditors can be satisfied.[1]

Although risk is of the essence of the contract, insurance is not a gaming or wagering contract. In a pure wager the interest of the contracting parties in the event wagered on is created by the fact that they have contracted to pay each other certain sums in a certain event. In insurance the interest is in, and the risk is of loss of, something which exists already, and the owner pays, not merely risks, money in order to obtain security against the possible loss. As in a contract of suretyship the object is to shift the danger of loss, not to create an opportunity of gain.

The two leading principles of the law of insurance are the principle of indemnity and the principle that the contract is *uberrimae fidei*—*i.e.*, one requiring the utmost good faith on both sides.

The principle of indemnity

Indemnity is the controlling principle in insurance law.[2] Except in insurance on life [3] (and against accident) the insurer contracts to indemnify the assured for what he actually loses by the happening of the events upon which the insurer's liability is to arise, and under no circumstances is the assured in theory entitled to make a profit of his loss.[4] Were this not so the two parties to the contract would not have a common interest in the preservation of the thing insured, and the contract would create a desire on the part of the assured for the happening of the event insured against—temptation to crime, fraud, or such carelessness as to bring about the destruction of the thing insured being created.

---

[1] Bell's Comm., 7th ed., p. 645.
[2] *Castellain* v. *Preston* (1883) 11 Q.B.D. 380 at p. 386, *per* Brett L.J.
[3] See *infra*, p. 352.
[4] *Castellain* v. *Preston, supra*.

The consequences of the principle of indemnity are as follows: (1) Limitation of the claim.—The amount which the assured can claim is limited, not only by the amount insured for but also by the extent of the injury to the subject insured, and by the extent of the assured's interest in the subject. Only what has been actually lost need be made good, whether by payment or reinstatement of the thing damaged to its original condition, or construction of a new thing similar to it. If more than the amount of the loss is recovered the insurer can get the excess back again, if he paid unawares. (2) The insurer's right of contribution.—As the assured cannot recover more than the amount of his loss, if there are two or more insurances covering the same interest in the same property, the aggregate amount insured being greater than the loss, the insurers contribute rateably to the loss in the proportions of the total sums insured by the different policies. The several contracts are taken together as parts of one contract of indemnity. This is known as double insurance. If, however, separate interests in the same property are separately insured—e.g., by a carrier of goods and by the owner—the insurers, as regards their liability inter se, stand in the place of the parties they have insured, so that if one of the parties is primarily liable for the loss in a question with the other, his insurer must make good the whole loss. Thus, if a carrier or warehouseman, primarily liable for the safety of goods in his custody, insures to cover the risk by a policy on goods for which he is reponsible, and the owner also insures, there is no double insurance and no contribution.[5] (3) The assured's right of abandonment.—If the thing insured is not totally destroyed, but remains wholly or in part in a deteriorated or damaged condition, if the degree of damage is such that the identity of the property has been lost the assured may surrender it to the insurer and claim as for a total destruction of the thing insured.[6] This is known as the doctrine of abandonment. (4) The insurer's right of subrogation.—If the assured has any means open to him to repair his loss otherwise than at his own expense or at the cost of the insurer he must either exercise such means for the benefit of the insurer, or he must cede such means to the insurer on being paid the full amount of his loss. This is termed the insurer's right of subrogation. The assured cannot in such a case exonerate from liability to the detriment of the insurer third parties primarily responsible for the loss. The rule applies whether the liability of the third party rests upon contract or upon negligence or upon delict. The principle of subrogation would not apply in any case where the

---

[5] North British and Mercantile Co. v. London, Liverpool, and Globe Securities Insurance Co. (1876) 5 Ch.D. 569; Scottish Amicable Heritable Insurance Association Ltd. v. Northern Assurance Co. (1883) 11 R. 287.

[6] Castellain v. Preston (1883) 11 Q.B.D. 380.

assured would be the third party in law responsible if the property damaged were not his own. For example, if an insured ship were damaged by collision with another ship also belonging to the owner of the insured ship, there would be no right of subrogation, because the assured could have no right of action against himself, and because the insurers take the risk of the assured's negligence, if not wilful, as part of the risk against which they insure.[7]   On the other hand the liability of an insurer is a primary liability, not a secondary liability like a cautioner's and, consequently, he is not entitled to require the assured who has suffered a loss covered by the contract to exhaust his remedies against third parties for the loss before making a claim against the insurer.[8]   (5) Attachment of the risk is necessary.—The contract is contingent on the actual attaching of the risk.   Unless the property insured is for a time subject to the risk insured against, the contract of insurance, even if made, never operates, and the premium though paid, is recoverable.   The assured is not obliged to run the risk because of the contract.   It follows also that the contract no longer remains in force after the risk is determined one way or another, except in those special insurances where both parties, being equally ignorant of the position of the thing insured—e.g., a ship at sea—contract to insure it lost or not lost.

Insurance a contract uberrimae fidei.—From the fact that insurance is a contract to shift risk flows also the principle that the contract is *uberrimae fidei*, *i.e.*, one requiring the utmost good faith on both sides. This principle applies to every contract of insurance. The consequences are as follows: (1) There is a duty on the parties to make a complete disclosure to each other. The assured must disclose to the insurer every fact going to establish the character of the risk to be shifted by the contract which is within the knowledge of the assured, and which is not matter of common knowledge or speculation or mere opinion—that is, all material facts.[9] If the assured fails so to disclose, the contract is voidable,[10] and he will take nothing by the contract although in the absence of fraud on his part, or contrary stipulation, he will be entitled to retain or be repaid the premium. So also if the insurer grants a policy of insurance knowing he will never run any risk thereunder, whether because facts invalidate it or the risk is already determined in his favour, he will be equally subject to the rule of good faith. The rule of full disclosure applies also during the

---

[7] *Trinder, Anderson & Co.* v. *Thames and Mersey Marine Insurance Co.* [1898] 2 Q.B. 114.

[8] *Castellain* v. *Preston* (1883) 11 Q.B.D. 380.

[9] *Carter* v. *Boehm* (1766) 3 Burr. 1905 at 1910; " material " is defined in the Civil Aviation Act, 1949, s. 49.

[10] Bell's Prin., §§ 474, 522.

running of the contract,[11] and even after the risk has happened.[12] (2) There is a duty on the assured to avert the happening of the risk. Hence if he accelerates the happening of the risk, or when it has happened, fails to do what he can to lessen the consequent damage, he imperils his chance of recovering under the contract—for example, if he prevents others from endeavouring to save goods which would otherwise be destroyed, or wilfully neglects without reasonable excuse to save insured property, provided that he so acts with the fraudulent intention and purpose to throw the loss on the insurers. On the other hand, he is not bound to save the subject-matter insured at his own cost. The insurers are liable for such costs.

II. The Contract of Life Insurance

1. Definition

Life insurance is a contract by which the insurer, in consideration of a certain premium, either in a gross sum or by annual payments, undertakes to pay to the person for whose benefit the insurance is made a certain sum of money, or annuity, on the death of the person whose life is insured.[13] Where, as is common, the sum insured is payable on death or on the occurrence of a certain event, such as the attainment of a certain age, the principles applicable to the contract are the same.

2. Formation of the contract

A person desiring to insure against a contingency depending on the continuance of a life fills up a proposal containing questions as to age, health, habits, and medical attendance on the " life," and usually also signs a declaration that the answers are true and are to be the basis of the contract. Information is also usually obtained from friends of the " life," but as they are not regarded as agents of the applicant such information does not form the basis of the contract. As a rule also an insuring company has the life examined by its own medical officer. When an insuring company accepts a proposal for life assurance, the contract is embodied in a policy. The agreement to insure is not regarded as concluded until tender of the premium,[14] and where a company accepts a proposal the acceptance is usually subject to the condition that the insurance shall not begin until the premium is paid.

11 *Law Accident Insurance Society* v. *Boyd*, 1942 S.C. 384.
12 *Welch* v. *Royal Exchange Assurance* [1939] 1 K.B. 294.
13 Smith's *Mercantile Law*, 13th ed., p. 514; *Dalby* v. *The India and London Life Assurance Co.* (1854) 15 C.B. 365.
14 *Sickness and Accident Assurance Association* v. *General Accident Assurance Corporation Ltd.* (1892) 19 R. 977.

Any completed contract for the payment of a sum depending on a contingency connected with the duration of a life is a policy of life insurance under the description in the Policies of Assurance Act, 1867, and for the purposes of stamp duty.[15] It is provided by the Stamp Act, 1891,[16] that a policy must be made out and executed within one month of the receipt of or taking credit for a premium or consideration for any life insurance, under penalty.

3. Matters affecting the validity of the contract

(a) Void policies.—Insurable interest.—A policy of life insurance may be void if the assured has not the necessary interest to insure. The Life Assurance Act, 1774, provides that no insurance should be made by any person against the death of any person in whom he has not an interest, or made by way of gaming or wagering. Such a policy is declared void, but the insurance company may waive its defence on this ground.[17] The Act also requires the insertion in every policy of the names of the persons interested in the insurance.[18] Further, no person may recover more than the value of his interest.[19] Nevertheless, it has been held that a contract of life insurance is not a contract of indemnity. Where a man insures his own life he cannot be indemnified for the loss of it. It is usually a provision for relatives or creditors. Nor, it has been held, where the insurance is over the life of another, is it a contract of indemnity.[20] Such was not the earlier view, and seems open to objection.[21] Accordingly, life insurance not being a contract of indemnity, where an insurance is effected by one person over the life of another—for example, by a creditor over the life of his debtor—the insurer must pay on the death, even though the debt be already discharged, and the same interest may be insured with several insurers and all be liable, without right of contribution. It also follows that a life policy may be validly assigned to a person who has no interest in the life insured. There must, however, exist an interest at the time the insurance is effected, otherwise the contract is void. The interest required is a pecuniary interest. The pecuniary interest required may arise either out of contract or of relationship. Where the interest arises out of contract, the contract must establish the relation between the assured and the person whose life is insured of debtor and creditor, or cautioner and principal debtor, or otherwise

15 Stamp Act, 1891, s. 98.
16 Ibid. s. 100.
17 s. 1. Also known as the Gambling Act, 1774; see p. 30, supra.
18 Ibid. s. 2.
19 Ibid. s 3.
20 Dalby v. The India and London Life Assurance Co. (1854) 15 C.B. 365; Law v. London Indisputable Life Policy Co. (1855) 3 Eq.R. 338.
21 Preston and Colinvaux, Law of Insurance, 2nd ed., pp. 43 and 254.

create a reasonable expectation of advantage from the continuance of the life. The debt need not, however, be of ascertainable amount, nor immediately exigible at the time the policy is made. Where not so ascertainable, the value put upon the policy by the parties, except in so far as it exceeds the actual extent of the assured's interest at any time, is held to be the value of the interest.[22] Thus a master may validly insure the life of his servant or agent whose services may be a a source of profit, and vice versa.[23] But if the value of the interest is ascertainable at the time when the insurance is effected, the policy will be enforceable only for that amount.

Where the interest arises from relationship there is an insurable interest only where there is a legal obligation to support. Accordingly, while in England a parent has no insurable interest in the life of his child, having no direct claim for maintenance against it, in Scotland he probably has such a claim and insurable interest,[24] as have also husbands and wives in each other [25] and children in their parents.

(b) Voidable policies.—A policy of life insurance may be voidable at the instance of the insurer if induced by concealment or misrepresentation on the part of the assured, or if the assured is in breach of the conditions of the policy. In theory it is voidable also on these grounds at the instance of the assured, but any such question seldom, if ever, arises.

Disclosure and representations.—The general rule applicable to mercantile contracts that they are voidable on the ground of non-disclosure or misrepresentation of any material fact applies in contracts of life insurance.[26] The concealment or misrepresentation need not be fraudulent. It is sufficient if the party misled would not have entered into the contract at all, or would not have agreed to its essential terms if he had known the true state of the facts.[27] These general rules are modified in the case of life assurance policies by the terms of the proposal and declaration, or of the policy. The policy itself declares that the proposal and declaration shall be the basis of the contract, or incorporates them. The effect is to make the answers in the proposal warranties or terms of the contract, and so to exclude the question whether they are material.

Conditions.—Breach of a condition expressed in the policy also makes voidable the policy at the instance of the insurer. Conditions

---

22 *Barnes* v. *The London, Edinburgh and Glasgow Life Insurance Co.* [1892] 1 Q.B. 864.
23 *Turnbull & Co.* v. *Scottish Provident Institution* (1896) 34 S.L.R. 146; *Simcock* v. *Scottish Imperial Insurance Co.* (1902) 10 S.L.T. 286.
24 *Hadden* v. *Bryden* (1899) 1 F. 710; *Carmichael* v. *Carmichael's Exrx., per* Lord Dundas and Lord Guthrie, 1919 S.C 636; revd. 1920 S.C.(H.L.) 195.
25 *Wright* v. *Brown* (1849) 11 D. 459.   26 See Misrepresentation, *supra*, p. 20.
27 *London Assurance* v. *Mansel* (1879) 11 Ch.D. 363.

in policies usually are as to occupation, place of residence, travel, and suicide. If suicide takes place during insanity the condition is not strictly enforced, and suicide is not allowed to affect the interests of third parties, such as lenders on the security of the policy, intimated to the insurance company before death.[28] Policies usually provide that in case of suicide the policy shall not be paid in full, but treated as surrendered, and the surrender value paid to the deceased's personal representatives or other beneficiaries named in the policy.[29]

4. Construction of the contract

The language used in the policy being the language of the company insurer is, in the event of ambiguity, construed against the company and for the benefit of the assured.[30]

5. Assignation of the policy

The assignation of policies of life assurance is regulated by the Policies of Assurance Act, 1867. Assignees are given power to sue under the policy, and there is reserved to the insurance company any defence on equitable grounds which it would have had against the cedent, as in any other personal action.[31] The Act further provides for intimation of assignment being given to the company as a condition of a right of action by an assignee under a policy, for the specification in all policies of the company's place of business at which notices of assignment may be given, and for assignment being by indorsement on the policy or by separate assignment in accordance with a form given in the Act.

The right of an assignee to sue upon a policy depends on four conditions. The assignation must be in writing; the assignee must have a right to grant a discharge to the insurance company; the assignation must have been intimated to the company; and the assignation must be properly stamped.

6. Married Women's Policies of Assurance (Scotland) Act, 1880

A trust may be declared in a life policy by making it payable to a certain person as trustee for purposes set forth in the policy. Such a trust is not, at common law, effectual against creditors of the truster, unless the policy is delivered to the trustee [32] or intimated to the

---

28 *Ellinger* v. *Mutual Life of New York* [1905] 1 K.B. 31.
29 In England, when suicide was a crime, suicide while sane rendered the policy unenforceable: *Beresford* v. *Royal Insurance Co. Ltd.* [1938] A.C. 586. *Quaere* as to the effect in Scotland, where suicide is not a crime, and in England where suicide is no longer a crime. Suicide Act, 1961, s. 1.
30 *Life Association of Scotland* v. *Foster* (1873) 11 M. 351, 371.
31 Policies of Assurance Act, 1867, ss. 1 and 2.
32 *Jarvie's Tr.* v. *Jarvie's Trs.* (1887) 14 R. 411.

beneficiary.[33] Special provision is, however, made with regard to such policies by the Married Women's Policies of Assurance (Scotland) Act, 1880, where the policy is effected by a married man over his own life for the benefit of his wife or children or both. Such policies vest in him and his legal representatives in trust for the purposes so expressed, but are not otherwise subject to his control, part of his estate, revocable as a donation, subject to the diligence of his creditors, or reducible on any ground of excess or insolvency. The Act dispenses with delivery or intimation. But if it be proved that the policy was effected and the premiums paid to defraud creditors, or if the assured be made bankrupt within two years from the date of the policy, the creditors may claim repayment out of the proceeds of the policy of the premiums so paid. The interest of a married woman under such a policy cannot be assigned or charged by her.[34]

III. THE CONTRACT OF FIRE INSURANCE

1. Definition

Fire insurance is a contract of indemnity, by which the insurer undertakes, upon the terms and conditions in the policy, to indemnify the assured for loss or damage by fire.

2. Formation of the contract

A contract of insurance against fire may be constituted by writing or by parole.[35] But in order to constitute a valid insurance the essential elements of the contract—namely, the subject insured, the risk and the premium—must be determined.[36] A policy is the usual and proper form in which a contract for fire insurance is expressed.[37]

Covering notes.—Where an application is made for fire insurance, it is the practice of most companies to issue interim covering notes by which the property is protected until the company have determined whether to accept or decline the risk. The period of endurance of the covering note is usually limited to a month, and it is provided that on the termination of the insurance by the expiry of this period, or by refusal notified to the assured, the part of the premium unearned shall be returned. A covering note corresponds to a " slip " in marine insurance, but may constitute a valid contract, whereas a contract of marine insurance requires to be embodied in a marine policy.[38]

---

[33] *Carmichael* v. *Carmichael's Exrx.*, 1920 S.C.(H.L.) 195.
[34] *Pender* v. *Commercial Bank of Scotland Ltd.*, 1940 S.L.T. 306.
[35] *Christie* v. *North British Insurance Co.* (1825) 3 S. 519.
[36] *Ibid.*
[37] *M'Elroy* v. *London Assurance Corporation* (1897) 24 R. 287, *per* Lord M'Laren at p. 291.
[38] Marine Insurance Act, 1906, s. 22; *Thomson* v. *Adams* (1889) 23 Q.B.D. 361.

Agency.—An insurance entered into with an agent of a company is only valid when it is proved that the agent was authorised to bind the company.[39] The authority may be express or inferred from a course of practice acquiesced in by the company. It is not the practice of British companies to authorise their agents to issue policies or conclude a final contract of insurance.[40] But in most cases local agents have authority to conclude interim insurances by issuing covering notes which will bind the company until repudiated by either party.[41]

3. Matters affecting the validity of the contract

(a) **Void policies.—Insurable interest.**—Fire insurance being a contract of indemnity against loss, there can be no loss and no indemnity unless the assured has an interest in the property insured when the loss occurs, but not necessarily when the insurance is effected.[42] To constitute an insurable interest there must be an expectation of benefit or advantage from the preservation of the property insured, and this must be coupled with a legal right in the property. Accordingly, an interest which is merely contingent, such as that of an heir, is not insurable. On the other hand, an interest which exists, though it be defeasible as being subject to a resolutive condition,[43] is insurable. And any right which is incidental to ownership, such as a right to the rents of the property, or a right in security over the subjects, is insurable. A creditor has no insurable interest over the property of his debtor.[44] An insurer has an insurable interest in property insured by him, and may reinsure his risk in whole or part with another insurer with a view to distributing his loss.

(b) **Voidable policies.—Non-disclosure and misrepresentation.—Materiality.**—A contract of fire insurance is made upon the implied condition that all material facts have been disclosed. If there has been any misrepresentation or concealment of material facts known to either of the parties, although without fraudulent intention, the policy is voidable at the instance of the other.[45] The criterion of materiality of a fact is whether it is one which would usually be regarded in the business of insurance as material.[46] The following facts may be specially noted as having been held material facts, viz., those touching

---

[39] *M'Elroy* v. *London Assurance Corporation* (1897) 24 R. 287.
[40] *Linford* v. *Provincial Horse & Cattle Insurance Co.* (1864) 34 Beav. 291.
[41] *Mackie* (1869) 21 L.T. 102.
[42] *Williams* v. *Baltic Insurance Company of London* [1924] 2 K.B. 282.
[43] *Vide* Conditions, *supra*, p. 33.
[44] *Macaura* v. *Northern Assurance Co.* [1925] A.C. 619.
[45] *Law Accident Insurance Society* v. *Boyd*, 1942 S.C. 384 (renewed policy).
[46] *Ionides* v. *Pender* (1874) 9 Q.B. 531, *per* Blackburn J. at p. 537; *Bhugwandass* v. *Netherlands Insurance Co.* (1888) 14 App.Cas. 83; *Locker & Woolff Ltd.* v. *Western Australian Insurance Co.* [1936] 1 K.B. 408.

the terms upon which the insurers have undertaken the risk insured against, and overvaluation of the subject insured, if excessive. The question of the materiality of representations may be excluded by agreement of the parties. This is done by making the statements of the assured part of the contract, *i.e.*, making them warranties.[47]

The duty of disclosure is subject to certain limitations. Thus the assured is not bound to disclose (1) what the insurer knows or ought to know as part of his business; (2) what the insurer takes upon himself the knowledge of; (3) what he has waived information of; or (4) what is covered by warranty. Further, the assured need not generally state the nature of his interest or the fact that, prior to effecting the policy, he has contracted with third parties so as to deprive the insurer of a right of recourse in the event of a loss, unless, of course, the premium has been adjusted on the footing of a right of subrogation being kept open to the insurer.[48] If, since the policy was effected and before a loss, any material change of circumstances occurs, this must be communicated to the insurers.[49] The onus is on the insurers to prove a misrepresentation.

4. Construction of the contract

Where a proposal is accepted by a company upon the condition that the insurance shall not begin until the premium is paid, they are not bound to issue a policy or make good a loss if, before the premium is tendered, the risk has terminated or has materially altered.[50]

The policy.—The conditions upon which the policy is issued are set out in the body of the policy, and deal mainly with questions of misrepresentation, excepted risks, adjustment of loss, and contribution. The instrument being prepared by the company, if the conditions are ambiguous and admit of interpretation they are to be read in the sense most favourable to the assured. The policy is to be construed with reference to the principle of indemnity. Thus if two fires occur within the period of insurance, each causing a loss not exceeding the sum assured, but together exceeding it, the insurer is not liable beyond the amount assured.

Policies are usually for a year, terminal days being included in the period. In some cases fifteen days of grace are allowed for payment of the premium, but this does not, unless expressly so provided, mean that the insurance subsists during that period. It gives an option to the assured to continue the insurance, if he pays.

---

[47] *Dawson's Ltd.* v. *Bonnin*, 1922 S.L.T. 444.
[48] *Tate* v. *Hyslop* (1885) 15 Q.B.D. 368.
[49] *London Assurance* v. *Mansel* (1879) 11 Ch.D. 363.
[50] *Sickness and Accident Assurance Association* v. *The General Accident Assurance Corporation Ltd.* (1892) 19 R. 977.

The risk insured against.—Proximate cause.—The risk against which a fire policy provides is loss or damage by fire. There are usually exceptions to the general liability of the insurer expressed in the conditions of the policy. Usual exceptions are losses by lightning, explosion, incendiarism, riot, and by military or usurped power. In a question whether the loss or damage was caused by a peril insured against, the general rule is that where there are two or more causes forming a chain of events leading up to the loss, the cause nearest in point of time is to be regarded as the cause of the loss. Thus where a fire is caused by the negligence of the assured, or his servants, the proximate cause of damage being fire, the loss will be covered. And where loss results from a peril insured against, though not proximately the cause of it, yet as a material or necessary consequence of it, the loss is covered. Thus damage caused by water used to extinguish a fire or by the removal of goods will be covered. Where, on the other hand, the fire is a natural or reasonably to be expected result of an excepted risk—for example, lightning—the loss is not covered.

Reinstatement and measurement of the loss.—The amount required to reinstate the subjects injured is not necessarily the limit for which insurers are liable under a contract of indemnity.[51] That is not necessarily the measure of the loss. But the insuring company frequently makes it a condition of the policy that it may, if it think fit reinstate or replace property damaged or destroyed, instead of paying the amount of the loss or damage. If the insurer elects to reinstate, the contract becomes a building contract, and the pecuniary measure of the insurer's obligation has no necessary relation to the amount for which he would have been liable as under a contract of indemnity.

Rights of the insurer on payment.—Subrogation.—Contribution.—The contract being one of indemnity, the insurer has a right of subrogation,[52] and the principle of contribution in double insurances applies.[53]

5. Assignation of the policy

It is a consequence of the contract being one of indemnity that an assignation to a person who has no insurable interest has no validity. A policy of fire insurance issued to a person named cannot be assigned upon a transfer of the property without the insurer's consent.[54]

---

[51] *Westminster Fire Office* v. *The Glasgow Provident Investment Society* (1888) 13 App.Cas. 699.

[52] *Vide supra*, pp. 350, 357.

[53] *Supra*, p. 350.

[54] *Castellain* v. *Preston* (1883) 11 Q.B.D. 380.

IV. The Contract of Marine Insurance

1. History of the law

The law of marine insurance is contained in the Marine Insurance Act, 1906, a United Kingdom statute, which embodied and codified the law as developed and settled by the courts during a long period of years. The practice of marine insurance is inseparably connected with the name of Lloyd's, and the development of the law with that of Lord Mansfield, when Lord Chief Justice of England in the latter half of the eighteenth century. Traceable originally to the Lombards, many of whom settled in England in the thirteenth century, the first statute relating thereto is in 1601, now repealed, and it well describes the objects which " such insurance " is designed to further. " And whereas it has been time out of minde an usage amongst merchantes, bothe of these realms and of foreign nations, when they make anay great adventure (specially into remote parts), to give some consideration of money to other persons (which commonly are in no small number), to have from them assurance made of the goods, merchandises, ships, and things adventured, or some part thereof, at such rates and in such sort as the parties assurers and the parties assured can agree, which course of dealing is commonly termed a policy of assurance; by means of which policy of assurance it cometh to pass that upon the loss or perishing of any ship there followeth not the undoing of any man, but the loss lighteth rather easily upon many than heavily upon few, and rather upon them that adventure not than those that do adventure, whereby all merchantes, especially the younger sort, are allured to venture more willingly and more freely." The business of marine insurance received its first great impetus with the advent of the coffee houses in London after the Great Fire of 1666. There met there the merchants and business men, and Lloyd's Coffee House in Lombard Street in time assumed prominence as the meeting-place of the leading merchants. The society so formed was responsible for fixing the terms of the printed form of policy known as Lloyd's S.G. Policy, which is the basis of all contracts of marine insurance.[55]

2. Nature of the contract of marine insurance

A contract of marine insurance is a contract whereby the insurer undertakes to indemnify the assured, in manner and to the extent thereby agreed, against losses incident to marine adventure.[56] There is a marine adventure, in particular (a) where any ship, goods, or other moveables are exposed to maritime perils; (b) where the earning or acquisition of any freight, passage money, commission, profit or other

[55] See Lloyd's Act, 1871.
[56] M.I.A., 1906, s. 1.

pecuniary benefit, or the security for any advances, loan, or disbursements, is endangered by the exposure of insurable property to maritime perils; (c) where any liability to a third party may be incurred by the owner of or other person interested in or responsible for insurable property by means of maritime perils. Maritime perils means perils of the seas, fire, war perils, pirates, rovers, thieves, captures, seizures, restraints, and detainment of princes and peoples, jettisons, barratry, and any other perils, either of the like kind, or which may be designated by the policy.[57] The contract may be extended, expressly or by usage of trade, to protect the assured against losses on inland waters or on any land risk incidental to a sea voyage,[58] and where a ship in the course of building or the launch of a ship is covered by a marine policy the Act applies.

3. Constitution of the contract

The terms of the contract are usually noted on a " slip " or memorandum, which is initialled by the underwriters. But a contract of marine insurance cannot be enforced in a court of law unless it is embodied in a stamped marine policy in accordance with the Marine Insurance Act.[59] That is to say, the policy must specify (1) the name of the assured or of some person who effects the insurance on his behalf, usually an insurance broker; (2) the subject-matter insured, and that with reasonable certainty, and the risk insured against; (3) the voyage or period of time, or both, as the case may be, covered by the insurance; (4) the sum or sums insured; and (5) the name or names of the insurers.[61] The policy must be signed by or on behalf of the insurer, and in the case of a corporation may be sealed.[62] When the same policy is subscribed by two or more insurers, each subscription constitutes a distinct contract with the assured. The policy may be executed and issued either at the time when the contract was concluded or afterwards. The slip is useful evidence of the date at which the contract was concluded. It must be stamped with a 6d. stamp.[63]

In specifying the subject-matter insured it is not essential to specify the nature and extent of the assured's interest,[64] unless perhaps where the interest is that of a lender on bottomry or respondentia. Nor is it essential that the value of the subject-matter insured be stated. Where it is stated, the policy is a " valued " policy; where unstated,

[57] *Ibid.* 1906, s. 3.
[58] *Ibid.* s. 2 (1).
[59] *Ibid.* s. 22.
[61] *Ibid.* s. 23.
[62] *Ibid.* s. 24 (1).
[63] Finance Act, 1959 § 30 (5).
[64] *Ibid.* s. 26.

an " unvalued " policy. The value stated in the policy may exceed the actual value of the thing insured, and the stated value will be recoverable. The Act provides rules for ascertaining value in an unvalued policy in the case of ships, freight, and goods, and in the case of any other subject-matter states the value to be the amount at the risk of the assured when the policy attaches.[65] When cargo is insured, the name of the ship or ships in which it is to go need not be defined when the policy is signed, but may be so by subsequent declarations,[66] usually endorsed on the policy in the order of dispatch or shipment. This is called a " floating policy." In such policies, where a declaration of value is not made until after notice of loss or arrival, the goods in question are treated as unvalued. In every case the charges of the insurance are an item in the value. Nor is it necessary to specify in the policy the premium, which may be independently arranged. Unless otherwise agreed, however, the insurer need not complete the contract by delivering the policy except upon payment of the premium.

4. Matters affecting the validity of the contract

(a) Void policies.—Insurable interest.—The contract being one of indemnity, the assured must at the time of the loss, but not necessarily at the time the contract is effected,[67] have an interest at risk. Accordingly a contract of marine insurance is void if the assured has not an insurable interest as defined by the Act,[68] and the contract was entered into with no expectation of acquiring such an interest. He cannot acquire an interest after he is aware of a loss.[69] So also are void contracts which bind the insurer " interest or no interest,' or " without further proof of interest than the policy itself," or " without benefit of salvage to the insurer," unless there was no possibility of salvage.[70] Such policies are unenforceable as gaming or wagering contracts.[71] The taint of illegality is, however, not stretched to cover policies effected to insure interests which are merely defeasible or contingent.[72] In fact, such unenforceable policies are commonly entered into, the assured depending solely on the honour of the insurer. Such policies are known as " honour policies," and cover cases where there is doubt as to the assured having in law an interest. An exception to the rule that an interest must exist at the time the loss

---

[65] Ibid. s. 16.
[66] Ibid. s. 29.
[67] Ibid. s. 6 (1).
[68] Ibid. s. 5.
[69] Ibid. s. 6 (2).
[70] See Re London County Reinsurance Co. [1922] 2 Ch. 67.
[71] See Illegal and Immoral Contracts, supra, p. 25.
[72] M.I.A., 1906, s. 7 (1).

occurs is where the subject-matter is insured "lost or not lost." Such a contract is good even though the assured acquired his interest after the loss occurred, unless at the time of the insurance he was aware of the loss and the insurer was not. Such a contract is useful to cover the case of the insurance of a ship which is at sea.

Moreover, it is a criminal offence for a person to effect a marine insurance without having a bona fide interest or expectation of interest. So also is it a criminal offence for a person in the employment of the owner of a ship, other than a part owner, to effect an honour policy.[73] It is a matter of public policy that life and property at sea be protected against the unscrupulous, who, without having an interest, effect insurances in order to obtain the insurance moneys by contriving the loss of the subject-matter.

(b) Voidable policies.—Disclosure and representations.—Like other contracts of insurance, marine insurance is a contract *uberrimae fidei*, requiring the utmost good faith as between the parties to it in negotiating the contract. If the utmost good faith be not observed by either party the contract may be avoided by the other party.[74] In negotiating, the assured must disclose everything he knows—and he is assumed to know everything which, in the ordinary course of business, ought to be known to him—which would influence the judgment of a prudent insurer in fixing the premium or determining whether he will take the risk.[75] The measure of disclosure required from an agent of the assured in making the contract is the same, unless it be of a circumstance which has come to the assured's knowledge too late to communicate to the agent.[76] An agent having knowledge material to be disclosed, though unknown to his principal, must disclose it.[77] In the absence of inquiry by the insurer the assured need not disclose any circumstance which diminishes the risk, or is known, or presumed to be known, to the insurer, or as to which information is waived by the insurer.[78] Further, any material representation of fact which is made by the assured or his agent during negotiations must be true or substantially correct, and, if of belief, made in good faith. Non-disclosure and misrepresentation are to be tested when the contract is concluded, that is, when the proposal is accepted, whether the policy be then issued or not. A slip or covering note or other customary memorandum of the contract is usually made at the time the proposal is accepted, and is the usual evidence of acceptance.

[73] Marine Insurance (Gambling Policies) Act, 1909, s. 1(1) (*b*).
[74] M.I.A., 1906, s. 17.
[75] *Ibid.* s. 18 (2).
[76] *Ibid.* s. 19.
[77] *Blackburn* v. *Vigors* (1887) 12 App.Cas. 531.
[78] M.I.A., 1906, s. 18 (3).

5. Construction of the contract

(a) **Form of the policy.**—The Marine Insurance Act gives a form of policy,[79] namely, that known as a Lloyd's S.G. Policy. It is in the following terms:

LLOYD'S S.G. POLICY.—BE IT KNOWN THAT   as well in
          own name as for and in the name and names of all and
every other person or persons to whom the same doth, may, or
shall appertain, in part or in all doth make assurance and cause
          and them, and every of them, to be insured lost or not
lost, at and from
Upon any kind of goods and merchandises, and also upon the
body, tackle, apparel, ordnance, munition, artillery, boat, and
other furniture, of and in the good ship or vessel called the

whereof is master under God, for this present voyage,
or whosoever else shall go for master in the said ship, or by
whatsoever other name or names the said ship, or the master
thereof, is or shall be named or called; beginning the adventure
upon the said goods and merchandises from the loading thereof
aboard the said ship,

upon the said ship, &c.

and so shall continue and endure, during her abode there, upon
the said ship, &c. And further, until the said ship, with all her
ordnance, tackle, apparel, &c., and goods and merchandises whatsoever shall be arrived at

upon the said ship, &c., until she hath moored at anchor twenty-
four hours in good safety; and upon the goods and merchandises,
until the same be there discharged and safely landed. And it
shall be lawful for the said ship, etc., in this voyage, to proceed
and sail to and touch and stay at any ports or places whatsoever

without prejudice to this insurance. The said ship, &c., goods
and merchandises, &c., for so much as concerns the assured by
agreement between the assured and assurers in this policy, are and
shall be valued at
Touching the adventures and perils which we the assurers are
contented to bear and do take upon us in this voyage: they are
of the seas, men of war, fire, enemies, pirates, rovers, thieves,

---

[79] *Ibid.* 1st Sched.

jettisons, letters of mart and contermart, surprisals, takings at sea, arrests, restraints, and detainments of all kings, princes, and people, of what nation, condition, or quality soever, barratry of the master and mariners, and of all other perils, losses, and misfortunes, that have or shall come to the hurt, detriment, or damage of the said goods and merchandises, and ship, &c., or any part thereof. [*Sue and Labour Cause.*]—And in case of any loss or misfortune it shall be lawful to the assured, their factors, servants and assigns, to sue, labour, and travel for, in and about the defence, safeguards, and recovery of the said goods and merchandises, and ship, &c. or any part thereof, without prejudice to this insurance; to the charges whereof we, the assurers, will contribute each one according to the rate and quantity of his sum herein assured. [*Waiver Clause.*]—And it is especially declared and agreed that no acts of the insurer or insured in recovering, saving, or preserving the property insured shall be considered as a waiver, or acceptance of abandonment. And it is agreed by us, the insurers, that this writing or policy of assurance shall be of as much force and effect as the surest writing or policy of assurance heretofore made in Lombard Street, or in the Royal Exchange, or elsewhere in London. And so we, the assurers, are contented, and do hereby promise and bind ourselves, each one for his own part, our heirs, executors, and goods to the assured, their executors, administrators, and assigns, for the true performance of the premises, confessing ourselves paid the consideration due unto us for this assurance by the assured, at and after the rate of

IN WITNESS whereof we, the assurers, have subscribed our names and sums assured in London.

N.B.—[*Memorandum.*]—Corn, fish, salt, fruit, flour, and seed are warranted free from average, unless general, or the ship be stranded—sugar, tobacco, hemp, flax, hides and skins are warranted free from average under five pounds per cent., and all other goods, also the ship and freight, are warranted free from average under three pounds per cent., unless general, or the ship be stranded.

(b) Description of subject-matter.—The term " ship " includes the hull, materials and outfit, stores and provisions for officers and crew, the ordinary fittings requisite in a trader in a particular trade, and, in the case of a steamship, the machinery, boilers, and engine stores, if owned by the assured.[80]   Freight does not include passage money.[81]

---

[80] M.I.A., 1906, 1st Sched., Rule 15.   [81] *Ibid.* Rule 16.

Where the subject-matter insured is " goods," that means goods in
the nature of merchandise, and does not include personal effects or
provisions and stores for use on board, and in the absence of any
usage to the contrary deck cargo and living animals must be insured
specifically and not under the general denomination of goods.[82] If
the subject-matter is sufficiently designated in general terms, and a
question is raised what interest is covered, the interest intended by the
assured will, in the absence of other indication, be held that insured
against.[83]

The interest which an underwriter acquires in the safety of that
which he has insured is a good insurable interest. When he insures
that interest it is known as a reinsurance.[84]

(c) Implied warranties.—A warranty is a term or condition of the
contract. It may be an undertaking that some particular thing shall
or shall not be done, or that some condition shall be fulfilled, or the
affirmation or negativing of the existence of a particular state of facts.[85]
It must be exactly complied with, whether material to the risk or not.
If not so complied with, the insurer, unless otherwise agreed, is discharged from liability as from the date of the breach of warranty,
although it does not relieve him of any liability incurred by him
before the breach.[86] It is no defence for the assured to show that the
breach has been remedied and the warranty complied with before
loss.[87] Warranties may be express or implied. The Act lays down
that certain warranties are implied in every contract of marine insurance. The implied warranties are:

(1) Of seaworthiness of the ship;
(2) Of legality of the adventure; and
(3) Of neutrality.

(1) *Seaworthiness.*—Seaworthiness in a contract of marine insurance
means seaworthiness for the particular adventure insured.[88]
A ship is deemed to be seaworthy when she is reasonably fit
in all respects to encounter the ordinary perils of the seas of
the adventure insured,[89] including, if the ship is in port when the
policy attaches, the ordinary perils of the port.[90] Where
the policy relates to a voyage which is performed in different
stages during which the ship requires different kinds of or

82 *Ibid.* Rule 17.
83 *Ibid.* s. 26.
84 See Reinsurance, p. 377, *infra.*
85 M.I.A., 1906, s. 33 (1).
86 *Ibid.* s. 33 (3).
87 *Ibid.* s. 34 (2).
88 *Ibid.* s. 39 (1).
89 *Ibid.* s. 39 (4).
90 *Ibid.* s. 39 (3).

further preparation or equipment, there is an implied warranty that at the commencement of each stage the ship is seaworthy in respect of such preparation or equipment for the purposes of that stage. In a voyage policy on goods or other moveables there is a further implied warranty that the ship is reasonably fit to carry them to the destination contemplated by the policy,[91] but this warranty is rarely insisted on against the assured as the insurer in virtue of his right of subrogation [92] has a right to sue the shipowner. In a time policy there is no implied warranty that the ship shall be seaworthy at any stage of the adventure, but where, with the privity of the assured, the ship is sent to sea in an unseaworthy state, the insurer is not liable for any loss attributable to unseaworthiness.[93]

(2) *Legality.*—There is an implied warranty that the adventure insured is a lawful one, and that, so far as the assured can control the matter, the adventure shall be carried out in a lawful manner.[94]

(3) *Neutrality.*—Where insurable property, whether ship or goods, is expressly warranted neutral, there is an implied condition that the property shall have a neutral character at the commencement of the risk, and that, so far as the assured can control the matter, its neutral character shall be preserved during the risk, and in the case of a ship that she shall carry the necessary papers to establish her neutrality.[95]

There is no implied warranty as to the nationality of a ship, or that her nationality shall not be changed during the risk.[96]

(d) **The risk insured against.**—The insurer remains liable under the contract of insurance only in accordance with the risk undertaken. It is therefore important to define not only what is the subject-matter insured and the perils insured against, but also when the risk begins and when it ends.

Commencement of risk.—In the case of a time policy the risk commences at the date from which the policy runs. In the case of a voyage policy it is indicated in the policy, and is introduced by such words as " from," " at and from," " beginning the adventure of the said goods," and " from the loading thereof." Where the subject-matter is insured from a particular place the risk does not attach until

[91] *Ibid.* s. 40.
[92] *Supra,* p. 350; *infra* 376.
[93] M.I.A., 1906, s. 39 (5).
[94] *Ibid.* s. 41; *e.g. Regazzoni* v. *K. C. Sethia (1944) Ltd.* [1958] A.C. 301.
[95] *Ibid.* s. 36.
[96] *Ibid.* s. 37.

the ship starts on the voyage insured.[97] Where the ship or chartered freight [98] is insured at and from a particular place the risk attaches immediately the policy is concluded, or as soon thereafter as she arrives at that place, provided in both cases she is there in good safety. In the case of other freight, as where the ship is a general ship,[99] the risk attaches *pro rata*, as the goods and merchandise are shipped, or, if the cargo is in readiness, as the ship is ready to receive the cargo.[1] Where goods are insured " from the loading thereof " the risk does not attach until the goods are actually on board.[2]

Termination of the risk.—The contract in the policy is against the risk of loss until, in the case of the ship under a voyage policy, it has arrived at the port of destination and has moored at anchor twenty-four hours in good safety, and in the case of goods, they are discharged and safely landed in the customary manner and within a reasonable time after arrival at the port of discharge.[3] In the case of a time policy the natural termination of the risk undertaken is the expiry of the time. But the liability of the insurer in both cases may cease earlier. The underwriter only undertakes to indemnify the assured upon the implied condition that the risk shall remain precisely the same as it appears to be on the face of the policy as interpreted, it may be, by usage. Directly this risk is by the act of the assured or his agents in any degree varied, even though it be not increased, the underwriters' liability ceases by the breach of the condition on which alone he is engaged to be liable. The true position therefore is that every voluntary and unnecessitated departure from the prescribed course of the voyage, by which the risk in varied, is a deviation, whether the risk be thereby increased or not.[4] The real ground of the underwriters' discharge is change of risk. Any change of risk accordingly will be a good defence to an action by the assured if the underwriter can show it to have arisen from the fault or with the knowledge of the assured, but not otherwise. It is accordingly not every change of risk that releases the insurers.

The change of risk may take place at the very outset, so that the policy never attaches at all. That is so where the place of departure is specified by the policy, and the ship instead of sailing from that place sails from any other place.[5] Where the destination is specified,

97 *Ibid.* 1st Sched., Rule 2.
98 See Charterparty, *supra,* p. 135.
99 See Bill of Lading, *supra,* p. 135.
1 M.I.A., 1906, 1st Sched., Rule 3.
2 *Ibid.* Rule 4.
3 *Ibid.* Rule 5.
4 *Per* Lord Mansfield in *Hartley* v. *Buggin* (1781) 3 Doug. 39.
5 M.I.A., 1906, s. 43; *cf. Union Castle Mail S.S. Co.* v. *U.K. Mutual War Risks Assn.* [1958] 1 Q.B. 380.

and the ship sails instead for any other place after the commencement of the risk, *i.e.*, where there is a " change of voyage," the insurer is discharged from liability as from the time of change, that is, the time when the determination to change is manifested, whether the ship has or has not in fact left the course of voyage contemplated by the policy when the loss occurs.[5] Again, the change of risk may take place through the ship without lawful excuse deviating from the voyage contemplated by the policy, as from the time of deviation—that is, the departure from the course of voyage specifically contemplated by the policy, or the usual and customary course where not so designated. There must be a deviation in fact, and a mere intention to deviate is immaterial.[6] The ship is held to have deviated if, where several ports of discharge are specified in the policy, she does not go to them in the order designated by the policy, or in their geographical order if the policy is to ports of discharge not named but within a given area. A failure to prosecute the voyage with reasonable dispatch without lawful excuse likewise terminates the insurer's liability.[7]

Deviation or delay in prosecuting the voyage are excusable (1) where authorised by any special term of the policy; (2) where caused by circumstances beyond the control of the master and his employer; (3) when reasonably necessary in order to comply with an express or implied warranty; (4) where reasonably necessary for the safety of the ship or subject-matter insured; (5) for the purpose of saving human life, or aiding a ship in distress where human life may be in danger; (6) where reasonably necessary for obtaining medical or surgical aid for any person on board the ship; or (7) where caused by the barratrous conduct of the master or crew if barratry be one of the perils insured against. When, however, the cause excusing the deviation or delay ceases to operate, the ship must resume her course and prosecute her voyage with reasonable dispatch.[8]

Return of the premium.[9]—If the risk has never attached, the general rule is the insurer must return the premium if it has been paid, and cannot recover it if not. The assured is, moreover, under no obligation to run the risk so as to let the insurer earn the premium. Thus if a ship insured from a port never sails, the premium must be returned. If, however, the ship starts, but immediately after deviates, there is no return. Where part of the subject-matter insured has not been put at risk, there is a proportionate return of premium. So also if the policy is voided, as by a breach of the implied warranty of seaworthiness, or

[6] M.I.A., 1906, s. 46.
[7] *Ibid.* s. 48.
[8] *Ibid.* s. 49.
[9] *Ibid.* ss. 82–84.

void in respect that the insured has no insurable interest, there must be return. It does not prevent the assured claiming return that there has been concealment or misrepresentation. There will be no return where there has been either fraud or illegality on the part of the assured. In such cases the courts decline to interfere.[10]

(e) **The perils insured against.**—These depend on the will of the parties as expressed in the policy. Those referred to in the form of policy annexed to the Act are to be construed as set out in the Schedule to the Act.

(1) *Perils of the Seas.*—This refers only to fortuitous accidents or casualties of the seas and does not include the ordinary action of the wind and waves,[11] nor scuttling nor barratry.[12] It includes an ordinary storm, and measures taken to prevent the incursion of sea-water in such a storm.[13] A collision with another ship is within the words, but not a claim against the insured ship for damage by collision due to the negligence of those in charge of her. This is usually covered by a clause called a Collision or Running Down Clause. The words cover risks which may, not those which must happen, as where a steamer insured by a time policy sailed with insufficient bunker coal and in consequence had to accept aid from another ship and to pay her salvage.[14] They cover sums which the assured have to pay for the salvage of the subject-matter insured from perils insured against[15]; but not claims for salvage in respect of life.

(2) *Men-of-war, enemies, letters of mart and countermart, surprisals, takings at sea, arrests, restraints, and detainments of all kings, princes and peoples of what nation, condition, or quality soever.* —These are mainly war risks, *e.g.,* capture. Insurers will not be liable for loss by perils insured where the assured at the time of the insurance are alien enemies or become so after the insurance is effected. On the outbreak of war the contract becomes void. By arrests, restraints, and detainments are meant generally not acts of an enemy of the assured's country, but in connection, it may be, with hostilities against another

---

10 See Illegal and Immoral Contracts, *supra,* p. 25.
11 M.I.A., 1906, 1st Sched., Rule 7.
12 *Samuel* v. *Dumas* [1924] A.C. 431.
13 *Hamilton, Fraser & Co.* v. *Pandorf & Co.* (1887) 12 App.Cas. 518; *Mountain* v. *Whittle* [1921] 1 A.C. 615; *Canada Rice Mills Ltd.* v. *Union Marine and General Insurance Co. Ltd.* [1941] A.C. 55.
14 *Ballantyne* v. *Mackinnon* [1896] 2 Q.B. 455; *Park and Others* v. *Duncan & Sons* (1898) 35 S.L.R. 378.
15 *Aitchison* v. *Lohre* (1879) 4 App.Cas. 755.

country, such as an embargo by which a government interdicts ships from sailing from a particular port. The words refer to political or executive acts, and do not include a loss caused by riot or by ordinary judicial process.[16]

Fire.—This does not cover a fire caused by the inherent vice of the subject-matter insured, nor damage caused by the explosion of machinery.[17] It includes fire voluntarily caused to avoid capture by an enemy.

Pirates—Rovers.—Risks from pirates and rovers are covered by " perils of the sea." Risk from pirates includes mutiny of passengers and loss from rioters on shore,[18] but not loss due to the acts of persons against the property of a State for a political end.[19]

Thieves.—The term thieves covers only losses caused by persons not connected with the vessel who commit robbery with violence. It does not cover clandestine theft or a theft committed by any one of the ship's company, whether passengers or crew.

Jettison.—This is a peril of the sea.

Barratry of the master and mariners.—This includes every wrongful act wilfully committed by the master or crew to the prejudice of the owner or charterer. If the master was also owner or did the wrongful act with the privity of the owner to the loss of the charterer, that would not be barratry.[20]

All other perils.—These words cover, on the principle of *ejusdem generis*,[21] only perils similar in kind to the perils specifically mentioned in the policy,[22] for example, where dollars were thrown overboard to avoid capture by the enemy,[23] this was held *ejusdem generis* of jettison.

As already indicated, the parties may express the risks undertaken in such terms as they please. Thus they may desire expressly to cover the dangers and accidents incident to steam navigation, because of the judgment in the *Inchmaree* case,[22] or expressly to exclude the warranty of seaworthiness *quoad* latent defects, because of the judgment in the *Glenfruin* case,[24] or to cover risks to live stock where a question might

---

[16] M.I.A., 1906, 1st Sched., Rule 10; *Nobels Explosive Co.* v. *Jenkins & Co.* [1896] 2 Q.B. 326.

[17] *Thames and Mersey Marine Insurance Co.* v. *Hamilton* (1887) 12 App.Cas. 484.

[18] M.I.A., 1906, 1st Sched., Rule 8.

[19] *Republic of Bolivia* v. *Indemnity Mutual Marine Assurance Co. Ltd.* [1909] 1 K.B. 785.

[20] See *Hobbs* v. *Hannam* (1811) 3 Camp. 93.

[21] See Interpretation of Contracts, *supra*, p. 36.

[22] See *Thames and Mersey Marine Insurance Co.* v. *Hamilton, supra.*

[23] *Butler* v. *Wildman* (1820) 3 B. & Ald. 398. [24] (1885) 10 P.D. 103.

arise whether due to natural causes or to perils insured against,[25] or claims against a shipowner in respect of collision between his ship and another (Collision Clause), or to exclude loss due to capture or seizure known as the F.C. and S. (free of capture and seizure) Clause. Where a loss which would otherwise be covered is excluded the insurer has to prove the loss was due to the excluded risk,[26] and the insurer's liability will then cease, e.g., on capture of the vessel.[27]

(f) Losses due to perils insured.—Under this topic are considered the scope of the underwriter's liability, the rules applicable to total and partial losses, the meaning of the sue and labour clause, the rules as to successive losses and under-insurance, the rights of the insurer on payment and reinsurance.

(1) *Scope of the underwriter's liability.—Proximate cause*

An insurer is not liable for any loss which is not proximately caused by a peril insured against.[28] The principle of proximate cause is more rigorously applied in marine insurance cases than in the case of other liabilities. The term " proximate " cause does not necessarily mean the cause latest in time. In marine insurance law, where there is a succession of causes which must have existed in order to produce the result, the last efficient or dominant cause (which is not necessarily the last cause in point of time) only must be looked to and the others rejected, although the result would not have been produced without them.[29] To illustrate a question of proximate cause the case of *Montoya* v. *London Assurance Co.*[30] may be referred to. A vessel loaded with hides and tobacco shipped a quantity of sea-water, which rotted the hides but did not come directly into contact with the tobacco. The tobacco was, however, spoiled by the reek of the putrid hides. It was held that perils of the seas were the proximate cause of the loss of the tobacco. By this principle the underwriter's responsibility may be either limited or enlarged. Thus, where a voluntary act on the part of the assured to which the loss is more proximately due has intervened between the peril and the loss, as by abandonment with resulting loss of freight, the assured cannot recover.[31] On the other hand the insurer may be liable for losses proximately caused by a peril

---

25 See *Lawrence* v. *Aberdein* (1821) 5 B. & Ald. 107.
26 *Munro, Brice & Co.* v. *War Risks Association* [1918] 2 K.B. 78; *The Coxwold* [1941] 3 All E.R. 214; *J. Wharton (Shipping), Ltd.* v. *Mortleman* [1941] 2 K.B. 283.
27 *Anderson* v. *Marten* [1908] A.C. 334.
28 M.I.A., 1906, s. 55 (1).
29 *Leyland Shipping Co.* v. *Norwich Union Fire Insurance Society* [1918] 1 A.C. 350; see also *Britain S.S. Co.* v. *The King* [1921] 1 A.C. 99; *Canada Rice Mills Ltd.* v. *Union Marine and General Insurance Co. Ltd.* [1941] A.C. 55.
30 (1851) 6 Exch. 451.
31 *M'Carthy* v. *Abel* (1804) 5 East 388; *Scottish Marine Insurance Co.* v. *Turner* (1853) 1 Macq. 334; *Samuel* v. *Dumas* [1924] A.C. 431.

insured against, although remotely occasioned by the acts or negligence of the assured.[32] Loss attributable proximately to the wilful misconduct of the assured, to delay, although the delay be caused by a peril insured against, to ordinary wear and tear, ordinary leakage and breakage, inherent vice or nature of the subject-matter insured, or caused by rats or vermin, and injury to machinery not proximately caused by maritime perils, are by the Act expressly excluded, unless the policy otherwise provides, from the scope of the underwriter's liability.[33]

(2) *Total and partial losses*

The loss of the subject-matter insured owing to a peril insured against may be either (a) total, or (b) partial, with different effects in each case.

(a) TOTAL LOSS.—ACTUAL AND CONSTRUCTIVE TOTAL LOSS.—A total loss may be either actual or constructive,[34] and an insurance against total loss includes a constructive total loss, unless otherwise provided in the policy. There is an actual total loss where the subject-matter insured is destroyed, or so damaged as to cease to be a thing of the kind insured, or where the insured is irretrievably deprived thereof. Where no news is received of a missing ship for a reasonable time a total loss is presumed.[35] There is a constructive total loss where the subject-matter insured is reasonably abandoned on account of its actual loss appearing to be unavoidable, or because it could not be preserved from actual loss without an expenditure which would exceed its value,[36] so that a prudent uninsured owner would not prosecute the adventure to its termination. Where there is a constructive total loss the assured may either treat the loss as a partial loss, or abandon the subject-matter insured to the insurer and treat the loss as if it were an actual loss.[37] The phrase " constructive total loss " is inapplicable in determining whether there has been a total loss of freight. If there has not been an actual total loss, the test whether freight insurers are liable as on a total loss is analogous to that applicable to a ship policy in determining whether there has been a constructive total loss of ship.[38]

---

[32] *Busk* v. *Royal Exchange Assurance Co.* (1818) 2 B. & Ald. 72; M.I.A., 1906, s. 55 (2); *Trinder, Anderson & Co.* [1898] 2 Q.B. 114.

[33] M.I.A., 1906, s. 55 (2).

[34] *Ibid.* s. 56 (2).

[35] *Ibid.* s. 58.

[36] *Ibid.* s. 60 (1).

[37] *Ibid.* s. 61.

[38] *Carras* v. *London and Scottish Assurance Corporation* [1936] 1 K.B. 291.

Abandonment.—The effect of a valid abandonment is that the insurer is entitled to take over the interest of the assured in whatever may remain of the subject-matter insured, and all proprietary rights incidental thereto.[39] Consequently where the assured elects to abandon to the insurer he must give notice of abandonment. If he fails to do so the loss can only be treated as a partial loss.[40] He need not, however, give notice where, at the time when he receives information of the loss, there would be no possibility of benefit to the insurer if notice were given him.[41] The notice, which may be in writing or by word of mouth, must indicate the intention of the assured to abandon his insured interest in the subject-matter insured unconditionally to the insurer, and should be given with reasonable diligence after receipt of reliable information of the loss.[42] Upon the abandonment of a ship the insurer becomes entitled to any freight in course of being earned and which is earned by her subsequently to the casualty causing the loss.[43]

(b) PARTIAL LOSS.—GENERAL AND PARTICULAR AVERAGE.—A partial loss may be either a general average or a particular average loss. A general average loss is a loss caused by or directly consequential on a general average act, and includes a general average expenditure as well as a general average sacrifice; that is, where any extraordinary sacrifice or expenditure is voluntarily and reasonably made or incurred in time of peril for the purpose of preserving the property imperilled in the common adventure,[44] entitling the party on whom the loss falls to a rateable contribution from the other parties interested.[45] Every other loss is a particular average loss. A partial loss may be 100 per cent. of the sum insured or may even exceed it, although the insurer's liability is of course no more.[46] A sum payable for salvage proper, known as " salvage charges," is recoverable in the same way as a particular average loss.[47]

[39] M.I.A., 1906, s. 63 (1).
[40] *Ibid.* s. 63 (1).
[41] *Ibid.* s. 62 (7).
[42] *Ibid.* s. 62 (3).
[43] *Ibid.* s. 63 (2).
[44] *Ibid.* s. 66 (2).
[45] An international code of rules for the adjustment of general average, known as the York-Antwerp Rules (the latest formulation of which was made in 1950), is usually expressly incorporated by contract into policies of insurance, and also into charter-parties and bills of lading. See Average, *supra*, p. 153.
[46] *Aitchison* v. *Lohre* (1879) 4 App.Cas. 755.
[47] M.I.A., 1906 s. 65.

Particular average.—The insurer may in the contract expressly limit his liability. An example is the Memorandum Clause at the end of the form of policy given above, whereby certain perishable goods are warranted free from particular average, certain other goods free from average under 5 per cent., and all other goods, also ship and freight, free from average under 3 per cent., unless general, or the ship be stranded. The term " average unless general " means a partial loss of the subject-matter insured other than a general average loss, and does not include particular charges.[48] Where a ship is stranded, the insurer is liable for the excepted losses, although these be not attributable to the stranding,[49] provided, of course, that the risk has attached, and the goods, if goods be insured, are on board.[50] A ship is stranded which takes the ground out of the ordinary course and remains fast though only for a short time. It is usual to add to the memorandum the words " sunk or burnt [51] or in collision." The memorandum is designed to relieve the insurer from liability for partial loss due to the action of ordinary sea-water on these particular goods.

Apart from the memorandum the insurer may confine his liability to such loss due to the risks insured against as amounts to a total loss. This is done by a clause called an F.P.A. (free of particular average) Clause which reads usually, " warranted free from particular average unless the vessel or craft be stranded, sunk or burnt, each craft or lighter being deemed a separate insurance. Underwriters, notwithstanding this warranty, to pay for any damage or loss caused by collision with any other ship or craft, and any special charges for warehouse rent, reshipping or forwarding for which they would otherwise be liable. Also to pay the insured value of any package or packages which may be totally lost in trans-shipment. Grounding in the Suez Canal not to be deemed a strand, but underwriters to pay any damage or loss which may be proved to have directly resulted therefrom."

(3) *Sue and labour clause*

It is the duty of the assured and his agents in all cases to take reasonable measures for the purpose of averting or minimising a loss, and they cannot recover for damage in so far as aggravated by want of care in these respects.[52] The sue and labour clause (contained in the Lloyd's S.G. Policy) is deemed to be supplementary to the contract of insurance. Under it the assured may recover any expenses properly incurred, pursuant to the clause, notwithstanding that the insurer may

---

48 M.I.A., 1906, 1st Sched., Rule 13.
49 *The Alsace Lorraine* [1893] P. 209.
50 M.I.A., 1906, Sched. 1 Rule 14.
51 See *The Glenlivet* [1894] P. 48.
52 M.I.A., 1906, s. 78 (4); but see Gloag and Henderson's *Introduction to the Law of Scotland*, 6th ed., p. 329; British Shipping Laws, Vol. 10 § 788.

have paid as for a total loss or that the insurance may be warranted free from particular average either wholly or under a certain percentage. General average losses and contributions and salvage charges are not recoverable under the clause.[53]

(4) *Successive losses*

The insurer is liable for successive losses, unless the policy otherwise provides, even though the total amount of such losses exceeds the sum insured. But if, under the same policy, a partial loss which has not been repaired or otherwise made good is followed by a total loss, the assured can only recover in respect of the total loss.[54] If, however, the partial loss is claimable under one policy and the total loss under another, both can be recovered.[55]

(5) *Under insurance*

Where the assured is insured for an amount less than the insurable value, or, in the case of a valued policy, for an amount less than the policy valuation, he is deemed to be his own insurer in respect of the uninsured balance.[56]

(6) *Rights of insurer on payment.*[57]*—Subrogation*

Where one person has agreed to indemnify another, he will, on making good the indemnity, be entitled to succed to all the ways and means by which the person indemnified might have protected himself against, or reimbursed himself for the loss.[58] Thus, where the assured abandons to the insurer and is paid for a total loss, the property abandoned becomes the property of the insurer.[59] Likewise also, apart from a transfer of the property, on the principle of subrogation, if the assured has a right to recover from a third party, as in a case of loss by collision through the fault of another ship, and the insurer pays for a partial loss, the assured's rights and remedies pass to the insurer as from the time of the casualty causing the loss, but only in so far as the assured has been indemnified by such payment for the loss,[60] but not for any excess over the loss.[61] Thus, in the case of loss of goods, where there is a claim under the contract of carriage against the shipowner, the insurer can have this claim enforced in his interest. And the insurer of a mortgagee's interest in, say, a ship is

---

[53] See *Kidston* v. *Empire Marine Insurance Co.* (1866) L.R. 1 C.P. 535;](1867) L.R. 2 C.P. 357.

[54] M.I.A., 1906, s. 77.

[55] *Lidgett* v. *Secretan* (1871) L.R. 6 C.P. 616.

[56] M.I.A., 1906, s. 81.

[57] *Ibid.,* s. 79.

[58] *Per* Lord Chancellor Cairns in *Simpson* v. *Thomson* (1877) 3 App.Cas. at p. 284.

[59] See *supra,* pp. 350, 374.

[60] M.I.A., 1906, s. 79.

[61] *Yorkshire Insurance Co.* v. *Nisbet Shipping Co.* [1961] 2 All E.R. 487.

to the extent of any sum paid by him entitled to be subrogated to the mortgagee's personal claim on the shipowner for the debt secured on the ship. But the insurers, as they stand in the same position as the assured, may be met by any defence available against him.[62]

Contribution.—Where two or more policies are effected by or on behalf of the assured on the same adventure and interest, if the several insurances together make an over insurance the excess cannot be recovered by him. The assured can only recover what is sufficient to indemnify him. Accordingly if one of the insurers pays more than his rateable proportion of the indemnity he is entitled to recover the balance from the other insurers, or the assured if he has been overpaid.[63]

(7) Reinsurance

A reinsurance is quite independent of the original insurance, and the rights of the parties under each contract are distinct.[64] The reassured must prove his loss as if he were the original claimant. And the reinsurer may avail himself of all defences which were open to the original insurer.[65] In cases of constructive total loss, however, the reinsurer is not entitled to notice of abandonment.[66] The reinsurance may be limited to some only of the risks included in the original insurance.[67]

6. Assignation of the policy [68]

A marine policy is assignable by the assured unless it contains terms expressly prohibiting assignation. It may be assigned either before or after loss. But where the assured has parted with or lost his interest in the subject-matter insured before he has expressly or impliedly agreed to assign the policy, any subsequent assignment is inoperative. Where the policy has been effectually assigned, the assignee may sue on the policy in his own name, and all defences open to the insurer under the contract against the original assured are open to the insurer against the assignee.

---

[62] See *Société du Gaz* v. *Armateurs Français*, 1925 S.C. 332.
[63] M.I.A., 1906, ss. 32, 80.
[64] *Ibid.* s. 9 (2); *English Insurance Co.* v. *National Benefit Assurance Co.* [1929] A.C. 114; *Motor Union Insurance Co.* v. *Mannheimer Versicherungs Gesellschaft* [1933] 1 K.B. 812.
[65] Smith's *Mercantile Law*, 13th ed., p. 420.
[66] M.I.A., 1906, s. 62 (9).
[67] Under the Marine and Aviation Insurance (War Risks) Act, 1952, the Minister of Transport may undertake reinsurance of ships and cargoes against war and in certain circumstances other risks.
[68] *Ibid.* ss. 50, 51.

CHAPTER 14

ARBITRATION

1. DEFINITION

ARBITRATION is the voluntary and contractual submission by parties of any matter in dispute between them to the amicable and final decision of a person or persons in whom they repose confidence. By referring a disputed matter to arbitration the parties exclude themselves from the ordinary jurisdiction of the courts of law in regard to the merits of the dispute. There is practically no limitation to the nature or class of questions which may be referred, but questions of crime and questions of status cannot be made the subject-matter of an arbitration, and the existence of the contract to refer is a question for the court.[1] If the question submitted involves matters of public interest, *e.g.*, illegality, as well as private right, there can be no binding submission.[2] A question of status may be determined by an arbiter if incidental to the determination of the question referred.[3] Apart from these qualifications the scope of the submission depends on the terms agreed to by the parties, or, in the case of statutory arbitrations,[4] on the terms of the enactment. The decision of the arbiter is termed the award or decree arbitral.

2. CAPACITY TO ARBITRATE

The parties to all arbitrations must be capable of acting in regard to the questions to be arbitrated upon. Thus a minor cannot be a party to an arbitration, unless with the consent of his curator, except when engaged in trade and in regard to a trade question. A liquidator of a limited company in a compulsory liquidation can enter into an arbitration with the sanction of the Committee of Inspection.[5] On the other hand, the trustee on a sequestrated estate may, with consent of the commissioners, refer any questions that may arise in the course of the sequestration [6]; and trustees have, unless otherwise provided in the trust deed, power to submit and refer all claims connected with the trust estate.[7]

1 *Hoth* v. *Cowan*, 1926 S.C. 58, *per* Lord President Clyde at p. 65.
2 *Guild on Arbitration*, p. 18.
3 *Turnbull* v. *Wilsons and Clyde Coal Co.*, 1935 S.C. 580.
4 *Infra*, p. 384.
5 Companies Act, 1948, s. 245 (5); Bankruptcy (Scotland) Act, 1913, s. 172.
6 Bankruptcy (Scotland) Act, 1913, s. 172.
7 Trusts (Scotland) Act, 1921, s. 4.

3. THE ARBITER

An arbiter should be unbiased and should not have an interest in the subject-matter of the reference. Hence he may be disqualified to act if before the submission he has committed himself and insisted on a particular view, or if unknown to one of the parties he has an interest in the matter in dispute at the time of submission or if he has acquired a substantial interest during the course of the procedure.[8] The arbiter has no right at common law to remuneration. He may stipulate for a fee, and is in practice recognised to be entitled to one where acting in a professional capacity, for example, a lawyer in a dispute arising on the terms of a contract.[9]

Arbitrations may be classified as ordinary, ancillary, judicial references, and statutory.

4. ORDINARY ARBITRATIONS

The submission in Scotland may be agreed upon verbally, by informal writing or by formal deed, the general rules as to the constitution and proof of a contract and proof of its extinction being applicable to the contract of submission and the award following upon it.[10]

(a) **Verbal submissions.**—The verbal submission is common in mercantile affairs. Two business men having a difference may agree to accept the decision of a third, who may give his decision verbally. When the submission relates to a question of importance, if the fact of submission having been agreed on is disputed by one party, the court may not accept ordinary parole evidence, and may require proof by reference to the oath of the parties.[11] But verbal proof may be sufficient in such a case if there has been *rei interventus*.[12]

(b) **Informal written submissions.**—Informal written references are of common occurrence in the mercantile world. An informal reference is usually constituted by a joint letter to the arbiter requesting him to settle the points in dispute. Questions of law are frequently submitted to an advocate or solicitor in the form of a joint memorial. These are good references. A mere letter, written by the arbiter's clerk and signed by the arbiter, has been held to be a valid and sufficient award under a mercantile reference.[13]

(c) **Formal submissions.**—*Deed of submission.*—A submission constituted by formal writing is usually in the form of a deed of submission.

---

[8] *Tennant* v. *MacDonald* (1836) 14 S. 976; but see *Crawford Bros.* v. *Commissioners of Northern Lighthouses,* 1925 S.C.(H.L.) 22.
[9] *Macintyre Bros.* v. *Smith,* 1913 S.C. 129.
[10] *Vide* Contract, pp. 2 *et seq.*
[11] *Ferrie* v. *Mitchell and Ors.* (1824) 3 S. 75.
[12] *Otto and Ors.* v. *Weir* (1871) 9 M. 660; see p. 11, *supra.*
[13] *Dykes* v. *Roy* (1869) 7 M. 357.

The deed states the question being referred and the arbiter to whom the question is referred.

The deed should, in addition to stating accurately the question referred and nominating an arbiter, provide for the following matters, *viz.*, the arbiter's power to receive evidence, documentary, of witnesses or oath of parties; a time within which the decree arbitral is to be pronounced; a stipulated penalty on failure of either party to implement the award; the continuing of the submission in force, after the death of either party, against his heirs and representatives; the consent of parties to registration, for preservation and execution, of the deed itself and the decrees following upon it, so that they can be enforced against the parties by summary diligence, *i.e.*, without the intervention of any court. The deed may also provide for the appointment of a clerk to the arbitration, usually a solicitor, who guides the arbiter as to procedure and questions of law.

Sometimes each party nominates an arbiter. In such a case power is usually given to the arbiter to nominate an oversman, whose function it is decide the question in the event of the arbiters differing in opinion. The oversman may, however, be nominated in the deed. By the Arbitration (Scotland) Act, 1894, the arbiters have power to name an oversman though not empowered in the deed to do so, and in the event of their failing to agree in a nomination the court can make the nomination on the application of either party to the submission. The same Act provides that an agreement to refer to arbitration is not to be ineffectual by reason of the reference being to a person not named, or to be named by another person or to the holder of an office for the time being, and for the appointment of an arbiter by the court failing an appointment by the parties.

It should be noted that an arbiter has, by implication, a power to award expenses,[14] that he has no power to award damages unless expressly so empowered,[15] that where no time is stated within which the decree arbitral is to be pronounced it is limited to a year and a day, and that the arbiter cannot prorogate the submission, *i.e.*, extend the time, unless expressly empowered, or the parties consent.

The Decree arbitral.—The finding of the arbiter, called the award or decree arbitral, narrates the submission and the procedure which has followed on it, including, if such is the case, the difference of opinion between the arbiters and their devolution of the submission upon the oversman. Then the arbiter or oversman, as the case may be, states that being well and ripely advised, and having God and a good

---

[14] *Ferrier* v. *Alison* (1843) 5 D. 456; (1845) 5 Bell's App. 161; *Pollich* v. *Heatley*, 1910 S.C. 469.
[15] *Mackay & Son* v. *Leven Police Commissioners* (1893) 20 R. 1093.

conscience before his eyes, he gives forth his final sentence and decree in the terms stated and finds and decerns accordingly.

The arbiter may, if he chooses, issue an interim award, but interim awards are inherently subject to alteration or recall by the final award. A final award should, advisedly, reaffirm any interim award. In common practice the arbiter, before issuing his award to the parties, submits the draft award or proposed findings to the parties, and allows them to lodge, and be heard on, representations regarding these. When the final award has been issued and delivered to the parties, it is beyond recall, and is thereafter binding upon the parties, their heirs and successors.[16]

If the submission is formal and probative, the award also must be formal and probative.[17]

Reduction of decree arbitral.—By referring a disputed matter to arbitration the parties exclude themselves from the ordinary jurisdiction of the courts of law in regard to the merits of the dispute. The arbiter's decision on the merits is final, and in that matter he is beyond the control of the court.[18] " He may believe what nobody else believes, and he may disbelieve what all the world believes. He may overlook or flagrantly misapply the most ordinary principles of law, and there is no appeal for those who have chosen to submit themselves to his despotic power." [19] But the jurisdiction of the court is not wholly and to all effects ousted by a reference to arbitration. " It deprives the court of jurisdiction to inquire into and decide the merits of the case, while it leaves the court free to entertain the suit and to pronounce a decree in conformity with the award of the arbiter. Should the arbitration from any cause prove abortive the full jurisdiction of the court will revive, to the effect of enabling it to hear and determine the action upon its merits. When a binding reference is (successfully) pleaded *in limine,* the proper course for the court to take is either to refer the question in dispute to the arbiter named, or to stay procedure until it has been settled by arbitration." [20]

There are, however, certain exceptions to the rule that the arbiter's decision is final, even on the merits.

In 1695 there were passed, pursuant upon an Act of Parliament, Articles of Regulation, which provided " that for the cutting off of groundless and expensive pleas and processes in time coming," the court should not be entitled to reduce the decree of an arbiter except

16 *Bell on Arbitration,* 2nd ed., p. 262.
17 *M'Laren* v. *Aikman,* 1939 S.C. 222.
18 *e.g., Brown & Son* v. *Associated Fireclay Co.,* 1937 S.C.(H.L.) 42.
19 Lord Jeffrey in *Mitchell* v. *Cable* (1848) 10 D. 1297.
20 Lord Watson in *Hamlyn & Co.* v. *Talisker Distillery* (1894) 21 R.(H.L.) 21 at p. 25.

upon the grounds of "corruption, bribery, or falsehood to be alleged against the Judges Arbitrators." [21]

Apart from the Regulations the court will set aside an arbiter's award if it be shown that he has gone *ultra fines compromissi*,[22] *i.e.*, beyond the scope of the submission, or has violated any of the express conditions contained in the submission, or the essential principles of justice and even-handed dealing between the parties which the common law holds to be implied in every submission.[23] In the last-mentioned matter the arbiter as the judge chosen by the parties is entitled to a very wide measure of discretion as to the manner in which the proceedings are to be conducted, for example, as to the extent and mode of proof. Thus, where the question in dispute is a purely practical one, *e.g.*, the valuation of farm stock, and the arbiter has been chosen for his skill and knowledge of the matter in hand, he may even decide the matter without proof at all, if he takes proper means of informing his mind.[24] He may require and obtain the assistance of a man of skill, *e.g.*, an engineer, or consult counsel. On the other hand a refusal to receive proof where proof is necessary may amount to such misconduct of the case and want of fair dealing as will invalidate the award, and it is impossible an award should stand where the arbiter heard one party and refused to hear the other,[25] unless he decides wholly in favour of the latter.[26] Again, awards have been set aside where an arbiter refused to receive a claim tendered by one of the parties,[27] and where he had been misled by the improper and unfair proceedings of one of the parties.[28] And it has been held to amount to misconduct for an arbiter in a statutory arbitration, the opinion of the court having been taken on a question of law, to refuse to apply the law as laid down.[29] On the other hand, in purely mercantile arbitrations, even though procedure may have been irregular, the court will not set aside an award if it is substantially just.[30] An award which would restrain trade might be unenforceable.[31]

---

[21] *Adams* v. *Great North of Scotland Ry.* (1890) 18 R.(H.L.) 1.

[22] *Traill* v. *Coghill* (1885) 22 S.L.R. 616; *Miller & Son* v. *Oliver & Boyd* (1903) 6 F. 77.

[23] Lord Watson in *Adams, supra. David Taylor & Son Ltd.* v. *Barnett Trading Co.* [1953] 1 W.L.R. 562.

[24] *Paterson & Son Ltd.* v. *Corporation of Glasgow* (1901) 3 F.(H.L.) 34; *North British Ry.* v. *Wilson*, 1911 S.C. 730; *Henderson* v. *M'Gown*, 1915, 2 S.L.T. 316; *Cameron* v. *Nicol*, 1930 S.C. 1; *Mediterranean & Eastern Export Co. Ltd.* v. *Fortress Fabrics (Manchester) Ltd.* [1948] L.J.R. 1536.

[25] Lord Chancellor Eldon in *Sharpe* v. *Bickerdyke* (1815) 3 Dow 102 at p. 107; *Mitchell* v. *Cable* (1848) 10 D. 1297.

[26] *Black* v. *John Williams & Co.*, 1924 S.C.(H.L.) 22.

[27] *Drummond* v. *Martin & Ors.* (1906) 14 S.L.T. 365.

[28] *Calder* v. *Gordon* (1837) 15 S. 463.   [29] *Mitchell-Gill* v. *Buchan*, 1921, 1 S.L.T. 197.

[30] *Hope* v. *Crookston Bros.* (1890) 17 R. 868; *Guild on Arbitration*, p. 64.

[31] *Bellshill & Mossend Co-op. Society Ltd.* v. *Dalziel Co-op. Society Ltd.*, 1960 S.C.(H.L.) 64.

In an action of reduction, the arbiter cannot competently be examined unless to explain an ambiguity in his award, or to state whether, in making a valuation, he took into consideration any matters not included in the submission, and therefore not within his jurisdiction.[32]

An award may competently be reduced in part with a view to correcting what was incompetently done if that part can be severed from what the arbiter has competently awarded.[33] Otherwise, if not severable, the award as a whole must fall, for example, if the arbiter has to any extent proceeded *ultra fines compromissi*,[34] or has not exhausted the submission.[35]

Where there is a clause consenting to registration of the decree arbitral for execution, and summary diligence is done, any party having ground of objection to the award may state his objection by bringing a note of suspension. If there be no consent to registration for execution, the party wishing to enforce the award must bring an action in court for its implement, and in such a case a party having ground of objection to the award can state and maintain all objections thereto by the way of exception, *i.e.*, in defence, without the necessity of bringing a reduction thereof unless the court or Lord Ordinary shall consider that the matter can be more conveniently tried in a separate action of reduction.[36] If the action for implement is brought in an inferior court, objection by way of exception is not open, and a substantive action of reduction in the Court of Session is necessary.

5. ANCILLARY ARBITRATIONS

Ancillary arbitrations are those constituted by clauses of reference in deeds primarily regulating other matters. Thus in contracts of various sorts, *e.g.*, contracts of co-partnery or mercantile agreements, it is common to insert a clause referring to arbitration—frequently to the engineer, architect or other official of one of the contracting parties— the decision of claims or disputes arising in the execution of, or in connection with, the contract. The question frequently arises on the terms of such clauses whether they are confined to questions arising during the execution of the contract, or extend to questions arising out of it after its completion. The scope of the clause of reference is more strictly interpreted and defined by the court in the case of

---

[32] *Glasgow City and District Ry.* v. *Macgeorge, Cowan & Galloway* (1886) 13 R. 609; *Donald* v. *Shiell's Exrx.*, 1937 S.C. 52; *Dunlop* v. *Mundell*, 1943 S.L.T. 286.

[33] *Islay Estates* v. *M'Cormick*, 1937 S.N. 28.

[34] *Napier* v. *Wood* (1844) 7 D. 166.

[35] *Pollich* v. *Heatley*, 1910 S.C. 469, *per* Lord Dunedin at p. 481; *Donald* v. *Shiell's Exrx.*, 1937 S.C. 52; *Dunlop* v. *Mundell*, 1943 S.L.T. 286.

[36] Rules of Court of Session, 1965, Rule 174. For the procedure for enforcement in this country of foreign awards, see the Arbitration Act, 1950, ss. 34—41.

executorial references.[37]   Thus in an executorial reference as a general rule a claim of damages arising during the period of the contract's operation will not be covered by such a reference clause,[38] nor one arising after the completion of the contract.[39]   On the other hand, where liquidated damages were provided for in certain circumstances in the contract a reference as to the meaning of the contract entitled the arbiter, it was held, to dispose of a claim for liquidated damages.[40] Where there is doubt whether a dispute is covered by an ancillary reference it is usual to bring an action in court, and if the clause of reference is pleaded in defence and the court holds that the clause covers the dispute it will sist the action and remit to the arbiter to decide the question in dispute,[41] even where the party pleading the arbitration clause avers that the whole contract has been frustrated.[42] It may be noted that in English law the court is not compelled to give effect to an arbitration clause in a contract.[43]

In references *in re mercatoria*, which are usually very briefly expressed, the court will endeavour to give effect to them in so far as their terms will admit.   The court construes them liberally, but otherwise they are subject to the same rules as other ancillary submissions.[44]

6. JUDICIAL REFERENCES

A judicial reference is one entered into between parties to an action proceeding in court with regard to some matter in dispute between them arising in the action.   It may be entered into at any stage of the proceedings.   The submission is constituted by joint minute of the parties, to which the court interpones authority.   Once the court has remitted to a judicial referee it cannot recall his appointment.[45]   When the referee's award is issued it is lodged in process and the court interpones authority to it.

The proceedings under a judicial reference are conducted in the same way as in an ordinary arbitration.   Being a subscribed submission, the referee is the final judge both in questions of fact and law relating to the matters referred to him, and the award is protected by

---

[37] *Beattie* v. *Macgregor* (1883) 10 R. 1094; *Mackay & Son* v. *Leven Police Commissioners* (1893) 20 R. 1093; and see *R. & J. Scott* v. *Gerrard*, 1916, 2 S.L.T. 42.
[38] *Mackay & Son, supra.*
[39] *Aviemore Station Hotel Co. Ltd.* v. *Scott & Son* (1904) 12 S.L.T. 494.
[40] *Levy & Co.* v. *Thomsons* (1883) 10 R. 1134.
[41] *Cant* v. *Eagle Star & British Dominions Insurance Co. Ltd.*, 1937 S.L.T. 444; *Allied Airways (Gandar Dower), Ltd.* v. *Secretary of State for Air*, 1950 S.C. 249.
[42] *Mauritzen* v. *Baltic Shipping Co.*, 1948 S.C. 646.
[43] *Municipal Council of Johannesburg* v. *D. Stewart & Co.*, 1909 S.C.(H.L.) 53; *Hamlyn & Co.* v. *Talisker Distillery* (1894) 21 R.(H.L.) 21. See also *Heyman* v. *Darwins Ltd.* [1942] A.C. 356, applied in *Woolf* v. *Collis Removal Service* [1948] 1 K.B. 11.
[44] *Hope* v. *Crookston Bros.* (1890) 17 R. 868.
[45] *Walker* v. *Shaw Stewart* (1855) 2 Macq. 424.

the Articles of Regulation if the referee has exhausted the reference and the award is not *ultra fines compromissi*. The court has, however, some control over the proceedings. Any of the parties may apply to the court in regard to any alleged irregularities of procedure.[46] The court may in certain cases order rehearing,[47] and if the award is ambiguous the court may remit back to the referee for an explanation. The award is reducible only on the same grounds as in an ordinary arbitration.[48]

The judicial reference falls with the termination of the action under which it is made.[49] The referee and his clerk are entitled to remuneration and to decree for their fees against both parties to the reference jointly and severally,[50] and their fees are part of the judicia expenses of the action.[51]

7. STATUTORY ARBITRATIONS

A large number of Acts of Parliament provide for the settlement by arbiters of claims and disputes arising under their provisions. Perhaps the most important of these have been the arbitrations conducted under the machinery of the Lands Clauses Consolidation (Scotland) Act, 1845, under which provision was made for the compulsory acquisition of land for public purposes and for the payment of compensation to the owners. The machinery of the Act is incorporated into many other Acts both public and private. Another Act containing extensive machinery for arbitration is the Railway Clauses Consolidation (Scotland) Act, 1845, the provisions of which have also been incorporated in many other Acts. Where, however, the powers of compulsory purchase are exercised by any Government Department, or local or public authority, any question of disputed compensation is now referred to and determined by the arbitration of one of a panel of official arbiters appointed under the Land Compensation (Scotland) Act, 1963,[52] questions of law being referable to the court.[53] Another important class of statutory arbitrations is those under the provisions of the Agricultural Holdings (Scotland) Act of 1949 whereby compensation payable to outgoing tenants for improvements made by them during the tenancy and other questions arising out of the tenancy are determined. The Act provides that the arbiter may at any stage of

---

[46] *Welch* v. *Jackson* (1864) 3 M. 303.
[47] *Baxter* v. *M'Arthur* (1836) 14 S. 549.
[48] *Rogerson & Ors.* v. *Rogerson* (1885) 12 R. 583.
[49] *Gillon* v. *Simpson* (1859) 21 D. 243.
[50] *Beattie* (1873) 11 M. 954.
[51] *Carphin* v. *Sturrock*, 1913 2 S.L.T. 288.
[52] *e.g.*, Housing (Scotland) Act, 1950, s. 36.
[53] Act, s. 6.

the proceedings, and shall if so directed by the sheriff (which direction may be given on the application of either party), state in the form of a special case for the opinion of the sheriff any question of law arising in the course of the arbitration. Appeal from the Sheriff to the Court of Session is competent.[54] The arbiter is bound to apply the law as so laid down by the court.[55] Other important classes of statutory arbitrations which may be singled out for mention are those under the Finance Act, 1910, for the valuation of lands for increment duty [56]; and under the Acts regulating industrial and provident societies and friendly and building societies.

---

[54] Act, s. 74 and Sched. VI, Rules 19, 20. *Brodie* v. *Ker, M'Callum* v. *Macnair,* 1952 S.C. 216; *Chalmers Property Investment Co.* v. *MacCall,* 1951 S.C. 24.
[55] *Mitchell-Gill* v. *Buchan,* 1921 1 S.L.T. 197; *Johnstone* v. *Kennedy,* 1956 S.L.T. 73.
[56] The panel of referees appointed under Part I of this Act will be replaced by the Lands Tribunal to be appointed under the Lands Tribunal Act, 1949, when this Act is brought into operation in Scotland.

GLOSSARY

OF

LATIN WORDS AND PHRASES USED IN THE TEXT

[The literal translation has generally been given with a reference to the page or pages in the text where the term or maxim has been used, and the paraphrase generally from Trayner's *Latin Maxims*.]

Ab initio: From the beginning. 257, 327.

Acquirenda: Things to be acquired (in contrast to *acquisita*, things already acquired). 277.

Actio quanti minoris: Action for the amount by which the value [of goods] is less [than the price paid for them]. 94, 117.

Ad factum praestandum (plur. *ad facta praestanda*): [Obligation or decree] for the performance of an act (in contrast to one for payment of a sum of money). 35, 46, 60, 61, 230, 238.

Ad hoc: For this purpose. 251.

Ad valorem: According to value. 263.

Alias: [Name by which one is called] on other occasions. 298.

Aliunde: From another place, by another way. 317, 329.

Ante: Before, above.

Apocha trium annorum: Receipt or discharge for three years. 47.

Assignatus utitur jure auctoris: An assignee exercises the right of his cedent. 41.

Beneficium cedendarum actionum: The right to an assignation of rights of action. 231.

Bona fides: Good faith. *(In) bona fide:* In good faith.

Bona vacantia: Goods which are vacant, *i.e.*, without an owner. 340.

Caveat: literally, let him take heed that . . . A step in legal process by a third party requesting that he be heard before an order is made. 275.

Caveat emptor: Let the purchaser take heed, *i.e.*, satisfy himself as to the quality of the subject bought. 100.

Cessio bonorum: A surrender of goods or estate. 266, 287, 291.

Cf. (abbreviation of *confer*): Compare.

Chirographum apud debitorem repertum praesumitur solutum: A document of debt found in possession of the debtor is presumed to have been discharged. 47.

Cit. sup. (abbreviation of *citatum supra*): Cited above.

Concursus debiti et crediti: The concourse or concurrence of debt and credit. 50.

Condictio causa data causa non secuta: An action for restitution based on the failure of the consideration for which an obligation was granted or money paid. 58.

Condictio indebiti: An action for recovery of money paid under the mistaken belief that it was due. 239.

Confusio: Confusion, commingling, *e.g.*, where the same person becomes both debtor and creditor in an obligation. *Confusione*: By confusion. 49.

Consensus in idem: Agreement about the same thing. 1, 5, 11.

Contra proferentem: Against the person putting forward [a term or condition in a contract]. 35, 229.

387

Curator bonis: Literally, the guardian of goods or estate. An officer appointed by the court to manage an estate, the owner of which is unable to manage it. 15, 206, 318.

Delectus personae: Choice of a particular person [to the exclusion of others]. 40, 41, 241, 252, 257, 258, 277.

Delegatus non potest delegare: A person to whom a duty or power has been delegated cannot delegate it to another. 73.

E.g. (abbreviation of *exempli gratia*): For example.

Ejusdem generis: Of the same kind or class. 36, 260, 342, 371.

Error concomitans: Accompanying or collateral error. 18.

Error in substantialibus: Error as to matters which are of the substance of an agreement. 18, 105.

Et passim: And at various places.

Et seq. (abbreviation of *et sequentes paginae*): And the following pages.

Ex delicto: On the ground of, or arising from, delict. 223, 226.

Ex facie: On the face of [a document].

Ex lege: According to law.

Ex parte (abbreviation, *ex p.*): On behalf of. An application to the court by one party in the absence of the other.

Ex turpi causa non oritur actio: A right of action does not arise out of a disgraceful or immoral consideration. 31.

Expressio unius est exclusio alterius: The mention of the one is the exclusion of the other. 36.

Extra commercium: Outwith commerce. Said of things which cannot be bought or sold. 51, 56.

Forum conveniens: The court convenient for trying and deciding the question. 290.

Genus: Kind, class. 38.

Hinc inde: On this side and the other, reciprocally. 33.

Ib., Ibid. (abbreviation of *ibidem*): In the same place.

I.e. (abbreviation of *id est*): That is.

In bona fide: See *Bona fides*.

In dubio: In doubt or uncertainty; in a doubtful case.

In extenso: In extended form, in full.

In gremio: In the body [of a document].

In invitum: Irrespective of the will of [a person]. 305.

In limine: On the threshold, *i.e.*, at the outset.

In modum probationis: In the form or by way of proof. 4.

In pari delicto: In equal wrong, *i.e.*, equally blameworthy. 31.

In re, or *Re*: In the matter of.

In re mercatoria: In, or connected with, a mercantile transaction. 7, 9, 10, 36, 37, 226, 384.

In rem: Against the thing. Used of proceedings directed against a thing, in contrast to a claim against a person. 162.

In solidum: For the whole, *e.g.*, where each of several persons is bound for the whole of a divisible obligation. 34, 224, 256.

In transitu: In transit. 42, 72, 109 *et seq.*, 151.

In turpi causa melior est conditio possidentis: In a claim arising out of a disgraceful or immoral consideration the position of the possessor is the better. 25, 31.

Indicia: Things indicative of [a right or state]. 107, 267, 323.

Induciae: Literally, truce. Days of grace which intervene between the citation of the defender and the day ordained for his appearance in the cause. Sometimes used of the days of charge within which a debtor may pay a debt which he has been formally charged to pay. 275, 342.

Infra: Below

Inter alia: Amongst other things.

Inter se: Amongst themselves.

Inter socios: Amongst partners.

Intra vires: Within the powers. 327.

Ipso facto: By the very fact.

Jus ad rem: A right in respect of a thing. Used as alternative to *Jus in personam*, to denote a personal as distinct from a real right, or *jus in re*. 255.

Jus crediti: The right of a creditor. 292.

Jus in personam: A right against a person, a personal right. 95.

Jus in re: A right to a thing, a real right. 95.

Jus quaesitum tertio: A contractual right accruing to one who is not a party to the contract. 251.

Locatio operarum: The contract of hire of services. 252.

Locatio operis mercium vehendarum: Hire of the service of carrying merchandise. 129.

Locus poenitentiae: Room or opportunity for repentance or change of mind; right to resile. 4, 11.

Mala fides: Bad faith.

Morata solutio: Delayed payment. 114.

Mutatis mutandis: Things being changed which must be changed, *i.e.*, subject to inherent differences.

Nautae caupones stabulariique: Shipmasters, innkeepers and stablers. 131.

Nexus: Tie or hold [over property]. 86, 282.

Nobile officium: Supreme equitable jurisdiction of the Court of Session.

Nova debita (singular, *novum debitum*): New debts, *i.e.*, debts newly or recently contracted, as opposed to old or prior debts. 270, 271, 272.

Obligationes literis: Obligations for the constitution of which writing is required by law. 5.

Omnia rite acta praesumuntur: All things are presumed to have been done in proper form. 300, 327.

Op. cit. (abbreviation of *opus citatum*): Work, *i.e.*, book, cited.

Pactum de non petendo: See 233, 236-7.

Pactum illicitum (plur. *pacta illicita*): An illegal contract or agreement. 6, 25, 27 *et seq.*, 288, 294.

Pari passu: With equal step, equally. 273, 284, 285, 321, 338, 346.

Per: Through, by.

Per diem: Per day.

Persona: Personality. 240, 242, 243, 283, 295, 298.

Personali exceptione: By personal exception. When a party is, by his own act, incapacitated from maintaining a certain plea in an action or defence, he is said to be barred from maintaining that plea *personali exceptione*. 70.

Praeposita negotiis domesticis: Set over domestic affairs. 16.

Praepositus negotiis societatis: Set over the affairs of the partnership. 241, 248.

Presumptio juris: A presumption of fact fixed by law, but which may be redargued by contrary proof. 269.

Pretium affectionis: See 61.

Prima facie: At first sight.

Pro indiviso: Held undivided and in common. 242, 254.

Pro rata: Proportionally.

Pro tanto: By so much; to that extent.

Prout de jure: By any competent mode of proof.
Qua: As; as such only.
Quadriennium utile: The four-year period which may be used.   14, 15, 227.
Quaere: Literally, inquire.   Used to indicate doubt whether a question of law is
    rightly decided.
Quantum: How much, *i.e.*, amount.
Quantum meruit: As much as he has deserved.   76, 152.
Quoad: As regards.
Quoad ultra: As regards the rest.
Ratio: Reason, measure.
Re: See *In re*.
Rei interitus: The destruction of a thing.   57.
Rei interventus: Actings following on [an incomplete or improbative agreement].
    5, 11, 12, 38, 379.
Res judicata: Matter judicially determined.
Res merae facultatis: A matter entirely of a power [as distinct from an obligation],
    i.e., a right which may be exercised or not at pleasure.   51.
Sine causa: Without just cause.
Sine qua non: Indispensable condition.
Singuli in solidum: Each for the whole.   34, 247.
Spes successionis: The hope or expectancy of a succession, which may or may not
    materialise.   268, 276.
Sponsio ludicra (plur. *sponsiones ludicrae*): An obligation undertaken in sport.   30.
Substratum: Foundation.
Supra: Above.
Tantum et tale: Such in amount and kind.
Traditionibus non nudis pactis dominia rerum transferuntur: Rights of property in
    things are transferred by deliveries not by bare agreements.   88.
Uberrimae fidei: Of the greatest good faith.
Ultra fines compromissi: Beyond the limits of the submission.   382, 383, 385.
Ultra vires: Beyond the powers.   301, 302, 308, 309, 321, 326, 328, 333, 336.
V. (abbreviation of *versus*): Literally, turned towards; in citation of cases, against.
Vergens ad inopiam: Approaching insolvency.   231.
Vice versa: Conversely.
Vide: See.
Viz. (abbreviation of *videlicet*): Namely, to wit.

INDEX

404

INDEX